Dedication

Dedicated to the fine faculty at my alma mater, Northeast Missouri State University. In particular, I would like to thank Dr. Monica Barron, Dr. Dennis Leavens, Dr. Ed Tyler, and Dr. Cole Woodcox, whom I also have the pleasure of calling my friend. I would not be who I am as a writer, as a student, as a teacher, or as a person if it were not for the magnanimous, affecting, and brilliant instruction I received from these educators.

Special Thanks to:

My heartfelt thanks to everyone at Peachpit Press, as always.

My gratitude to the fine editor on this project, Mark Taber, for leading the way and putting up with too many delayed emails and chapters!

Thanks to David Van Ness and Elizabeth Welch for their hard work, helpful suggestions, and impressive attention to detail. Thanks to Scout Festa for ensuring the writing is "pixel perfect." Thanks also to Valerie Perry for indexing and Danielle Foster for laying out the book, and thanks to Timothy Boronczyk for his technical review.

Kudos to the good people working on PHP, MySQL, Apache, phpMyAdmin, MAMP, and XAMPP, among other great projects. And a hearty "cheers" to the denizens of the various newsgroups, mailing lists, support forums, etc., who offer assistance and advice to those in need.

Thanks, as always, to the readers, whose support gives my job relevance. An extra helping of thanks to those who provided the translations in Chapter 17, "Example—Message Board," and who offered up recommendations as to what they'd like to see in this edition.

Finally, I would not be able to get through a single book if it weren't for the love and support of my wife, Jessica. And a special shout-out to Zoe and Sam, who give me reasons to, and not to, write books!

Table of Contents

Introduction

Today's web users expect exciting pages that are updated frequently and provide a customized experience. For them, web sites are more like communities, to which they'll return time and again. At the same time, site administrators want pages that are easier to update and maintain, understanding that's the only reasonable way to keep up with visitors' expectations. For these reasons and more, PHP and MySQL have become the de facto standards for creating dynamic, database-driven web sites.

This book represents the culmination of my many years of web development experience coupled with the value of having written several previous books on the technologies discussed herein. The focus of this book is on covering the most important knowledge in the most efficient manner. It will teach you how to begin developing dynamic web sites and give you plenty of example code to get you started. All you need to provide is an eagerness to learn.

Well, that and a computer.

What Are Dynamic Web Sites?

Dynamic web sites are flexible and potent creatures, more accurately described as *applications* than merely sites. Dynamic web sites

- Respond to different parameters (for example, the time of day or the version of the visitor's browser)

- Have a "memory," allowing for user registration and login, e-commerce, and similar processes

- Almost always integrate HTML forms, allowing visitors to perform searches, provide feedback, and so forth

- Often have interfaces where administrators can manage the content

- Are easier to maintain, upgrade, and build upon than statically made sites

Many technologies are available for creating dynamic web sites. The most common are ASP.NET (Active Server Pages, a Microsoft construct), JSP (JavaServer Pages), ColdFusion, Ruby on Rails (a web development framework for the Ruby programming language), and PHP. Dynamic sites don't always rely on a database, but more and more of them do, particularly as excellent database applications like MySQL and MongoDB are available at little to no cost.

What Happened to PHP 6?

When I wrote a previous edition of this book, *PHP 6 and MySQL 5 for Dynamic Web Sites: Visual QuickPro Guide*, the next major release of PHP—PHP 6—was approximately 50 percent complete. Thinking that PHP 6 would therefore be released sometime after the book was published, I relied on a beta version of PHP 6 for a bit of that edition's material. And then... PHP 6 died.

One of the key features planned for PHP 6 was support for Unicode, meaning that PHP 6 would be able to work natively with any language. This would be a great addition to an already popular programming tool. Unfortunately, implementing Unicode support went from being complicated to quite difficult, and the developers behind the language tabled development of PHP 6. Not all was lost, however; some of the other features planned for PHP 6, such as support for *namespaces* (an object-oriented programming concept), were added to PHP 5.3.

When it was time to release the next major version of PHP, it was decided to name it PHP 7 to avoid confusion with the PHP 6 version that was started but never completed.

What is PHP?

PHP originally stood for "Personal Home Page" when it was created in 1994 by Rasmus Lerdorf to track the visitors to his online résumé. As its usefulness and capabilities grew (and as it started being used in more professional situations), it came to mean "PHP: Hypertext Preprocessor."

According to the official PHP web site, found at **www.php.net** 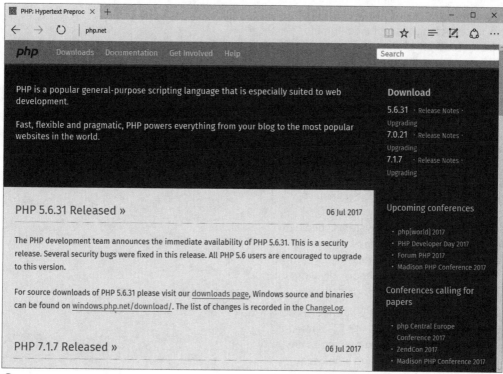, PHP is a "popular general-purpose scripting language that is especially suited to web development." It's a long but descriptive definition, whose meaning I'll explain.

continues on next page

Ⓐ The home page for PHP.

Starting at the end of that statement, to say that PHP *is especially suited to web development* means that although you can use PHP for non-web development purposes, it's best suited for that. The corollary is that although many other technologies can be used for web development, that may not be what they're best suited for. Simply put, if you're hoping to do web development, PHP is an excellent choice.

Also, PHP is a *scripting* language, as opposed to a *compiled* language: PHP was designed to write web scripts, not stand-alone applications (although, with some extra effort, you can create applications in PHP). PHP scripts run only after an event occurs—for example, when a user submits a form or goes to a URL (uniform resource locator, the technical term for a web site address).

I should add to this definition that PHP is a server-side, cross-platform technology, both descriptions being important. *Server-side* refers to the fact that everything PHP does occurs on the server. A web server application, like Apache or Microsoft's IIS (Internet Information Services), is required and all PHP scripts must be accessed through a URL (`http://something`). Its cross-platform nature means that PHP runs on most operating systems, including Windows, Unix (and its many variants), and Macintosh. More important, the PHP scripts written on one server will normally work on another with little or no modification.

At the time this book was written, PHP was at version 7.1.7. Although PHP 7 is a major release, the most important changes are in its core, with PHP 7 being significantly more performant than PHP 5.

For the most part, the examples in this book will work fine so long as you're using at least version 5.4. Some functions and

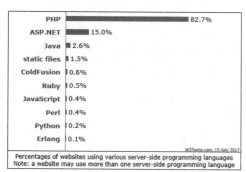

PHP	82.7%
ASP.NET	15.0%
Java	2.6%
static files	1.5%
ColdFusion	0.6%
Ruby	0.5%
JavaScript	0.4%
Perl	0.4%
Python	0.2%
Erlang	0.1%

W3Techs.com, 15 July 2017

Percentages of websites using various server-side programming languages
Note: a website may use more than one server-side programming language

B The Web Technology Surveys site provides this graphic regarding server-side technologies (**www.w3techs.com/technologies/overview/programming_language/all**).

features covered will require more specific or current versions, like PHP 5.6 or greater. In those cases, I will make it clear when the functionality was added to PHP, and provide alternative solutions if you have a slightly older version of the language.

More information about PHP can always be found at PHP.net.

Why use PHP?

Put simply, when it comes to developing dynamic web sites, PHP is better, faster, and easier to learn than the alternatives. What you get with PHP is excellent performance, a tight integration with nearly every database available, stability, portability, and a nearly limitless feature set due to its extendibility. All of this comes at no cost (PHP is open source) and with a very manageable learning curve. PHP is one of the best marriages I've ever seen between the ease with which beginning programmers can start using it and the ability for more advanced programmers to do everything they require.

Finally, the proof is in the pudding: PHP has seen an exponential growth in use since its inception, and is the server-side technology of choice on over 82 percent of all web sites **B**. In terms of all programming languages, PHP is the sixth most popular **C**.

continues on next page

Jul 2017	Jul 2016	Change	Programming Language	Ratings	Change
1	1		Java	13.774%	-6.03%
2	2		C	7.321%	-4.92%
3	3		C++	5.576%	-0.73%
4	4		Python	3.543%	-0.62%
5	5		C#	3.518%	-0.40%
6	6		PHP	3.093%	-0.18%

C The Tiobe Index (**https://www.tiobe.com/tiobe-index/**) uses a combination of factors to rank the popularity of programming languages.

Of course, you might assume that I, as the author of a book on PHP (several, actually), have a biased opinion. Although not nearly to the same extent as I have with PHP, I've also developed sites using JavaServer Pages (JSP), Ruby on Rails (RoR), Sinatra (another Ruby web framework), and ASP. NET. Each has its pluses and minuses, but PHP is the technology I always return to. You might hear that it doesn't perform or scale as well as other technologies, but Yahoo, Wikipedia, and Facebook all use PHP, and you can't find many sites more visited or demanding than those.

You might have heard that PHP is less secure. But *security isn't in the language*; it's in how that language is used. Rest assured that a complete and up-to-date discussion of all the relevant security concerns is provided by this book.

How PHP works

As previously stated, PHP is a server-side language. This means that the code you write in PHP sits on a host computer called a *server*. The server sends web pages to the requesting visitors (you, the client, with your browser).

When a visitor goes to a site written in PHP, the server reads the PHP code and then processes it according to its scripted directions. In the example shown in **D**, the PHP code tells the server to send the appropriate data—HTML code—to the browser, which treats the received code as it would a standard HTML page.

This differs from a static HTML site where, when a request is made, the server merely sends the HTML data to the browser and there is no server-side interpretation occurring **E**. Because no server-side action is required, you can run HTML pages in your browser without using a server at all.

continues on next page

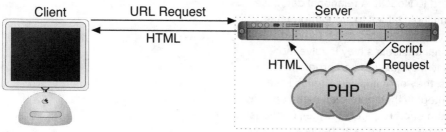

D How PHP fits into the client/server model when a user requests a page.

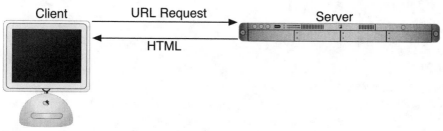

E The client/server process when a request for a static HTML page is made.

To the end user and the browser there is no perceptible difference between what **home.html** and **home.php** may look like, but how that page's content was created will be significantly different.

What is MySQL?

MySQL (**www.mysql.com**)  is the world's most popular open source database. In fact, today MySQL is a viable competitor to pricey goliaths such as Oracle and Microsoft's SQL Server (and, ironically, MySQL is owned by Oracle). Like PHP, MySQL offers excellent performance, portability, and reliability, with a moderate learning curve and little to no cost.

The home page for the MySQL database application.

MySQL is a database management system (DBMS) for relational databases (therefore, MySQL is an RDBMS). A database, in the simplest terms, is a collection of data, be it text, numbers, or binary files, stored and kept organized by the DBMS.

There are many types of databases, from the simple flat-file to relational to object-oriented to NoSQL. A relational database uses multiple tables to store information in its most discernible parts. Although relational databases may involve more thought in the design and programming stages, they offer improved reliability and data integrity that more than make up for the extra effort required. Further, relational databases are more searchable and allow for concurrent users.

By incorporating a database into a web application, some of the data generated by PHP can be retrieved from MySQL 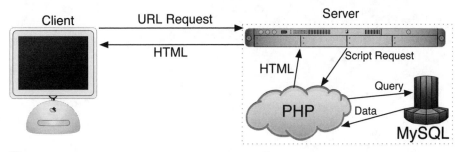. This further moves the site's content from a static (hard-coded) basis to a flexible one, flexibility being the key to a dynamic web site.

MySQL is an open source application, like PHP, meaning that it is free to use or even modify (the source code itself is downloadable). There are occasions when you should pay for a MySQL license, especially if you are making money from the sales or incorporation of the MySQL product. Check MySQL's licensing policy for more information on this.

The MySQL software consists of several pieces, including the MySQL server (*mysqld*, which runs and manages the databases), the MySQL client (*mysql*, which gives you an interface to the server), and numerous utilities for maintenance and other purposes. PHP has always had good support for MySQL, and that is even truer in the most recent versions of the language.

continues on next page

Client   URL Request   Server

HTML

Script Request

HTML

Query

PHP   Data

MySQL

G How most of the dynamic applications in this book will work, using both PHP and MySQL.

MySQL has been known to handle databases as large as 60,000 tables with more than several billion rows. MySQL can work with tables as large as thousands of terabytes on some operating systems, generally a healthy 4 GB otherwise. MySQL is used by NASA and the U.S. Census Bureau, among many others.

As of this writing, MySQL is on version 5.7.18. The version of MySQL you have affects what features you can use, so it's important that you know what you're working with. For this book, MySQL 5.7.14 was used, although you should be able to do everything in this book as long as you're using a version of MySQL greater than 5.0.

Pronunciation Guide

Trivial as it may be, I should clarify up front that MySQL is technically pronounced "My Ess Cue Ell," just as SQL should be said "Ess Cue Ell." This is a question many people have when first working with these technologies. Though not a critical issue, it's always best to pronounce acronyms correctly.

What You'll Need

To follow the examples in this book, you'll need the following tools:

- A web server application (for example, Apache, Nginx, or IIS)

- PHP

- MySQL

- A browser (Microsoft's Internet Explorer or Edge, Mozilla's Firefox, Apple's Safari, Google's Chrome, etc.)

- A text editor, PHP-capable WYSIWYG application (Adobe's Dreamweaver qualifies), or IDE (integrated development environment)

- An FTP application, if using a remote server

One of the great things about developing dynamic web sites with PHP and MySQL is that all of the requirements can be met at no cost whatsoever, regardless of your operating system! Apache, PHP, and MySQL are each free, browsers can be had without cost, and many good text editors are available for nothing.

The appendix discusses the installation process on the Windows and macOS operating systems. If you have a computer, you are only a couple of downloads away from being able to create dynamic web sites (in that case, your computer would represent both the client and the server in ⓓ and ⓔ). Conversely, you could purchase web hosting for only dollars per month that will provide you with a PHP- and MySQL-enabled environment already online.

About This Book

This book teaches you how to develop dynamic web sites with PHP and MySQL, covering the knowledge that most developers might require. In keeping with the format of the Visual QuickPro series, the information is discussed using a step-by-step approach with corresponding images. The focus has been kept on real-world, practical examples, avoiding "here's something you could do but never would" scenarios. As a practicing web developer myself, I wrote about the information that I use and avoided those topics immaterial to the task at hand. As a practicing writer, I made certain to include topics and techniques that I know readers are asking about.

The structure of the book is linear, and the intention is that you'll read it in order. It begins with three chapters covering the fundamentals of PHP (by the second chapter, you will have already developed your first dynamic web page). After that, there are four chapters on SQL (Structured Query Language, which is used to interact with all databases) and MySQL. Those chapters teach the basics of SQL, database design, and the MySQL application in particular. Then there's one chapter on debugging and error management, information everyone needs. This is followed by a chapter introducing how to use PHP and MySQL together, a remarkably easy thing to do.

The following five chapters teach more application techniques to round out your knowledge. Security, in particular, is repeatedly addressed in those pages. The next two chapters expand your newfound knowledge into subjects that, though not critical, are ones you'll want to pick up in time regardless. Finally, I've included two example chapters, in which the heart of different web applications are developed, with instructions.

Is this book for you?

This book was written for a wide range of people within the beginner-to-intermediate range. The book makes use of HTML5, so solid experience with HTML is a must. Although this book covers many things, it does not formally teach HTML or web design. Some CSS is sprinkled about these pages but also not taught.

Second, this book expects that you have one of the following:

- The drive and ability to learn without much hand holding, or...

- Familiarity with another programming language (even solid JavaScript skills would qualify), or...

- A cursory knowledge of PHP

Make no mistake: This book covers PHP and MySQL from A to Z, teaching everything you'll need to know to develop real-world web sites, but the early chapters in particular cover PHP at a quick pace. For this reason I recommend either some programming experience or a curious and independent spirit when it comes to learning new things. If you find that the material goes too quickly, you should probably start off with the latest edition of my book *PHP for the World Wide Web: Visual Quick-Start Guide*, which goes at a much more tempered pace.

No database experience is required, since SQL and MySQL are discussed starting at a more basic level.

What's new in this edition

The first four editions of this book have been very popular, and I've received a lot of positive feedback on them (thanks!). In writing this new edition, I focused on ensuring the material is accurate, up to date, and in keeping with today's standards and best practices. The changes in this edition include

- Updating all the code to use HTML5
- Use of more modern HTML design techniques, including multiple examples of the Twitter Bootstrap framework
- Updating everything for the latest versions of PHP and MySQL
- Additional PHP and MySQL examples, such as performing transactions from a PHP script
- Even more information and examples for improving the security of your scripts and sites
- Removal of outdated content (e.g., things used in older versions of PHP or no longer applicable)
- Return of the installation appendix to the printed book (in the fourth edition, the appendix was freely available online instead)

For those of you that also own a previous edition (thanks, thanks, thanks!), I hope you find this to be a fresh and sharp update to an already excellent resource.

How this book compares to my other books

This is my fourth PHP and/or MySQL title, after (in order)

- *PHP for the World Wide Web: Visual QuickStart Guide*
- *PHP Advanced and Object-Oriented Programming: Visual QuickPro Guide*
- *MySQL: Visual QuickStart Guide*

I hope this résumé implies a certain level of qualification to write this book, but how do you, as a reader standing in a bookstore, decide which title is for you? Of course, you are more than welcome to splurge and buy the whole set, earning my eternal gratitude, but...

The *PHP for the World Wide Web: Visual QuickStart Guide* book is very much a beginner's guide to PHP. This title overlaps it some, mostly in the first three chapters, but uses new examples so as not to be redundant. For novices, this book acts as a follow-up to that one. The advanced book is really a sequel to this one, as it assumes a fair amount of knowledge and builds on many things taught here. The MySQL book focuses almost exclusively on MySQL (there are but two chapters that use PHP).

continues on next page

With that in mind, read the section "Is this book for you?" and see if the requirements apply. If you have no programming experience at all and would prefer to be taught PHP more gingerly, my first book would be better. If you are already very comfortable with PHP and want to learn more of its advanced capabilities, pick up *PHP Advanced and Object-Oriented Programming: Visual QuickPro Guide*. If you are most interested in MySQL and are not concerned with learning much about PHP, check out *MySQL: Visual QuickStart Guide*.

That being said, if you want to learn everything you need to know to begin developing dynamic web sites with PHP and MySQL today, then this is the book for you! It references the most current versions of both technologies, uses techniques not previously discussed in other books, and contains its own unique examples.

And whatever book you do choose, make sure you're getting the most recent edition or, barring that, the edition that best matches the versions of the technologies you'll be using.

Companion Web Site

I have developed a companion web site specifically for this book, which you may reach at **LarryUllman.com**. There you will find every script from this book, a text file containing lengthy SQL commands, and a list of errata that occurred during publication. (If you have problems with a command or script, and you are following the book exactly, check the errata to ensure there is not a printing error before driving yourself absolutely mad.) At this web site you will also find a popular forum where readers can ask and answer each other's questions (I answer many of them myself), and more!

Questions, comments, or suggestions?

If you have any questions on PHP or MySQL, you can turn to one of the many web sites, mailing lists, newsgroups, and FAQ repositories already in existence. A quick search online will turn up virtually unlimited resources. For that matter, if you need an immediate answer, those sources or a quick online search will most assuredly serve your needs (in all likelihood, someone else has already seen and solved your exact problem).

You can also direct your questions, comments, and suggestions to me. You'll get the fastest reply using the book's corresponding forum (I always answer those questions first). If you'd rather email me, my contact information is available on my site. I do try to answer every email I receive, although I cannot guarantee a quick reply.

Accessing the free Web Edition

Your purchase of this book in any format includes access to the corresponding Web Edition, which provides several special online-only features:

- The complete text of the book, with all the figures and in full color
- Updates and corrections as they become available

The Web Edition can be viewed on all types of computers and mobile devices with any modern web browser that supports HTML5. To get access to the Web Edition of *PHP and MySQL for Dynamic Web Sites: Visual QuickPro Guide* all you need to do is register this book:

1. Go to `www.peachpit.com/register`.

2. Sign in or create a new account.

3. Enter ISBN: 9780134301846.

4. Answer the questions as proof of purchase.

The Web Edition will appear under the Digital Purchases tab on your Account page. Click the Launch link to access the product.

1

Introduction to PHP

Although this book focuses on using MySQL and PHP together, you'll do the majority of your legwork using PHP alone. In this and the following chapter, you'll learn PHP's basics, from syntax to variables, operators, and language constructs (conditionals, loops, and whatnot). As you are picking up these fundamentals, you'll also develop usable code that you'll integrate into larger applications later in the book.

This introductory chapter will cruise through most of the basics of the PHP language. You'll learn the syntax for coding PHP, how to send data to the browser, and how to use two kinds of variables—strings and numbers—plus constants. Some examples may seem inconsequential, but they'll demonstrate ideas you'll need to master in order to write more advanced scripts further down the line. The chapter concludes with some quick debugging tips...you know...just in case!

In This Chapter

Basic Syntax

As stated in the book's introduction, PHP is an *HTML-embedded* scripting language, meaning that you can intermingle PHP and HTML code within the same file. So to begin programming with PHP, start with a simple web page. **Script 1.1** is an example of a no-frills, no-content HTML5 document, which will be used as the foundation for most web pages in the book (this book does not formally discuss HTML5; see a resource dedicated to the topic for more information). Please also note that the template uses UTF-8 encoding, a topic discussed in the following sidebar.

To add PHP code to a page, place it within PHP tags:

```
<?php
?>
```

Script 1.1 A basic HTML5 page.

```
1    <!doctype html>
2    <html lang="en">
3    <head>
4       <meta charset="utf-8">
5       <title>Page Title</title>
6    </head>
7    <body>
8       <!-- Script 1.1 - template.html -->
9    </body>
10   </html>
```

Understanding Encoding

Encoding is a big subject, but what you most need to understand is this: *the encoding you use in a file dictates what characters can be represented* (and therefore, what languages can be used). To select an encoding, you must first confirm that your text editor or integrated development environment (IDE)—whatever application you're using to create the HTML and PHP scripts—can save documents using that encoding. Some applications let you set the encoding in the preferences or options area; others set the encoding when you save the file.

To indicate the encoding to the browser, there's the corresponding **meta** tag:

```
<meta charset="utf-8">
```

The *charset=utf-8* part says that UTF-8 encoding is being used, short for *8-bit Unicode Transformation Format*. Unicode is a way of reliably representing every symbol in every alphabet. Version 9.0.0 of Unicode—the current version as of this writing—supports over 128,000 characters!

If you want to create a multilingual web page, UTF-8 is the way to go, and I'll be using it in this book's examples. You don't have to, of course. But whatever encoding you do use, make sure that the encoding indicated by the HTML page matches the actual encoding set in your text editor or IDE. If you don't, you'll likely see odd characters when you view the page in a browser.

```
1   <!doctype html>
2   <html lang="en">
3   <head>
4      <meta charset="utf-8">
5      <title>Basic PHP Page</title>
6   </head>
7   <body>
8      <!-- Script 1.2 - first.php -->
9      <p>This is standard HTML.</p>
10  <?php
11  ?>
12  </body>
13  </html>
```

Anything written within these tags will be treated by the web server as PHP, meaning the PHP interpreter will process the code. Any text outside of the PHP tags is immediately sent to the browser as regular HTML. Because PHP is most often used to create content displayed in the browser, the PHP tags are normally put somewhere within the page's body.

Along with placing PHP code within PHP tags, your PHP files must have a proper *extension*. The extension tells the server to treat the script in a special way—namely, as a PHP page. Most web servers use **.html** for standard HTML pages and **.php** for PHP files.

Before getting into the steps, understand that *you must already have a working PHP installation*! This could be on a hosted site or your own computer, after following the instructions in Appendix A, "Installation."

To make a basic PHP script:

1. Create a new document in your text editor or IDE, to be named **first.php** (**Script 1.2**).

    It generally does not matter what application you use, be it Adobe Dreamweaver (a fancy IDE), Sublime Text (a great and popular plain-text editor), or vi (a plain-text Unix editor, lacking a graphical interface). Still, some text editors and IDEs make typing and debugging HTML and PHP easier (conversely, Notepad on Windows does some things that make coding harder: *don't use Notepad*!). If you don't already have an application you're attached to, search online or use the book's corresponding forum (**LarryUllman.com/forums/**) to find one.

    continues on next page

2. Create a basic HTML document:

```
<!doctype html>
<html lang="en">
<head>
   <meta charset="utf-8">
   <title>Basic PHP Page</title>
</head>
<body>
   <!-- Script 1.2 - first.php -->
   <p>This is standard HTML.</p>
</body>
</html>
```

This is a basic HTML5 page. One of the niceties of HTML5 is its minimal doc-type and syntax.

3. Before the closing **body** tag, insert the PHP tags:

```
<?php
?>
```

These are the *formal* PHP tags, also known as *XML-style* tags. Although PHP supports other tag types, I recommend that you use the formal type, and I will do so throughout this book.

4. Save the file as **first.php**.

Remember that if you don't save the file using an appropriate PHP extension, the script will not execute properly. (Just one of the reasons not to use Note-pad is that it will secretly add the **.txt** extension to PHP files, thereby causing many headaches.)

5. Place the file in the proper directory of your web server.

If you are running PHP on your own computer (presumably after following the installation directions in Appen-dix A), you just need to move, copy, or save the file to a specific folder on your computer. Check Appendix A or the documentation for your particular web server to identify the correct directory, if you don't already know what it is.

If you are running PHP on a hosted server (i.e., on a remote computer), you'll need to use a Secure File Transfer Protocol (SFTP) application to upload the file to the proper directory. Your hosting company will provide you with access and the other necessary information.

6. Run **first.php** in your browser .

Because PHP scripts need to be parsed by the server, you *absolutely must* access them via a URL (i.e., the address in the browser must begin with **http://** or **https://**). You cannot simply open them in your browser as you would a file in other applications (in which case the address would start with **file://** or **C:** or the like).

Ⓐ While it seems like any other (simple) HTML page, this is in fact a PHP script and the basis for the rest of the examples in the book.

If you are running PHP on your own computer, you'll need to use a URL like **http://localhost/first.php**, **http://127.0.0.1/first.php**, or **http://localhost/~<user>/first.php** (on macOS, using your actual username for **<user>**). If you are using a hosted site, you'll need to use **http://your-domain-name/first.php** (e. g., **http://www.example.com/first.php**).

7. If you don't see results like those in 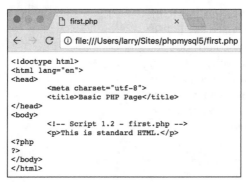, start debugging!

Part of learning any programming language is mastering debugging. It's a sometimes painful but absolutely necessary process. With this first example, if you don't see a simple, but perfectly valid, web page, follow these steps:

A. Confirm that you have a working PHP installation (see Appendix A for testing instructions).

B. Make sure that you are running the script through a URL. The address in the browser must begin with **http**. If it starts with **file://**, that's a problem **B**.

C. If you get a file not found (or similar) error, you've likely put the file in the wrong directory or mistyped the file's name (either when saving it or in your browser).

If you've gone through all this and you are still having problems, turn to the book's corresponding forum (**LarryUllman.com/forums/**).

TIP To find more information about HTML, check out Elizabeth Castro's excellent *HTML and CSS: Visual QuickStart Guide* (Peachpit, 2013), or search online.

TIP You can embed multiple sections of PHP code within a single HTML document (i.e., you can go in and out of the two languages). You'll see examples of this throughout the book.

TIP You can declare the encoding of an external CSS file by adding `@charset "utf-8";` as the first line in the file. If you're not using UTF-8, change the line accordingly.

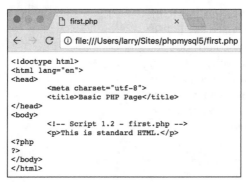

```
first.php                          ×
←  →  C   ⓘ file:///Users/larry/Sites/phpmysql5/first.php

<!doctype html>
<html lang="en">
<head>
        <meta charset="utf-8">
        <title>Basic PHP Page</title>
</head>
<body>
        <!-- Script 1.2 - first.php -->
        <p>This is standard HTML.</p>
<?php
?>
</body>
</html>
```

B PHP code will only be executed when run through http://.

Sending Data to the Browser

To create dynamic web sites with PHP, you must know how to send data to the browser. PHP has a number of built-in functions for this purpose; the most common are **echo** and **print**. I tend to favor **echo**:

```
echo 'Hello, world!';
echo "What's new?";
```

You could use **print** instead if you prefer (the name more obviously indicates what it does):

```
print 'Hello, world!';
print "What's new?";
```

As you can see from these examples, you can use either single or double quotation marks (but there is a distinction between the two types of quotation marks, which I'll make clear by this chapter's end). The first quotation mark after the function name indicates the start of the message to be printed. The next matching quotation mark (i.e., the next quotation mark of the same kind as the opening mark) indicates the end of the message to be printed.

Along with learning how to send data to the browser, you should also notice that in PHP all statements—a line of executed code, in layman's terms—must end with a semicolon. Also, PHP is *case-insensitive* when it comes to function names, so **ECHO**, **echo**, **eCHo**, and so forth will all work. The all-lowercase version is easiest to type, of course.

Needing an Escape

As you might discover, one of the complications with sending data to the browser involves printing single and double quotation marks. Either of the following will cause errors:

```
echo "She said, "How are you?"";
echo 'I'm just ducky.';
```

There are two solutions to this problem. First, use single quotation marks when printing a double quotation mark, and vice versa:

```
echo 'She said, "How are you?"';
echo "I'm just ducky.";
```

Or, you can *escape* the problematic character by preceding it with a backslash:

```
echo "She said, \"How are you?\"";
echo 'I\'m just ducky.';
```

An escaped quotation mark will merely be printed like any other character. Understanding how to use the backslash to escape a character is an important concept, and one that will be covered in more depth at the end of this chapter.

Script 1.3 Using **print** or **echo**, PHP can send data to the browser.

```
1   <!doctype html>
2   <html lang="en">
3   <head>
4      <meta charset="utf-8">
5      <title>Using Echo</title>
6   </head>
7   <body>
8      <!-- Script 1.3 - second.php -->
9      <p>This is standard HTML.</p>
10  <?php
11  echo 'This was generated using PHP!';
12  ?>
13  </body>
14  </html>
```

This is standard HTML.

This was generated using PHP!

A The results still aren't glamorous, but this page was in part dynamically generated by PHP.

To send data to the browser:

1. Open **first.php** (refer to Script 1.2) in your text editor or IDE.

2. Between the PHP tags (lines 10 and 11), add a simple message (**Script 1.3**):

   echo 'This was generated using
   ⇥ PHP!';

   It truly doesn't matter what message you type here, which function you use (**echo** or **print**), or which quotation marks, for that matter—just be careful if you are printing a single or double quotation mark as part of your message (see the sidebar "Needing an Escape").

3. If you want, change the page title to better describe this script (line 5):

   <title>Using Echo</title>

   This change affects only the browser window's title bar.

4. Save the file as **second.php**, place it in your web directory, and test it in your browser **A**.

   Remember that all PHP scripts must be run through a URL (**http://something**)!

   continues on next page

5. If necessary, debug the script.

If you see a parse error instead of your message , check that you have both opened and closed your quotation marks and escaped any problematic characters (see the sidebar). Also be certain to conclude each statement with a semicolon.

If you see an entirely blank page, this is probably for one of two reasons:

▶ There is a problem with your HTML. Test this by viewing the source of your page and looking for HTML problems there .

▶ An error occurred, but *display_errors* is turned off in your PHP configuration, so nothing is shown. In this case, see the section in Appendix A on how to configure PHP so that you can turn *display_errors* back on.

TIP Technically, echo and print are language constructs, not functions. That being said, don't be bothered as I continue to call them "functions" for convenience. Also, as you'll see later in the book, I include the parentheses when referring to functions—say, number_format(), not just number_format—to help distinguish them from variables and other parts of PHP. This is just my own little convention.

TIP You can, and often will, use echo and print to send HTML code to the browser, like so :

```
echo '<p>Hello,
→ <strong>world</strong>!</p>';
```

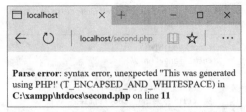

Parse error: syntax error, unexpected "This was generated using PHP!' (T_ENCAPSED_AND_WHITESPACE) in C:\xampp\htdocs\second.php on line 11

B This may be the first of many parse errors you see as a PHP programmer (this one is caused by the omission of the terminating quotation mark).

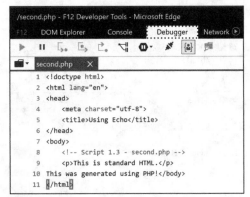

C One possible cause of a blank PHP page is a simple HTML error, like the closing **title** tag here (it's missing the slash).

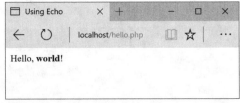

D PHP can send HTML code (like the formatting here) as well as simple text **A** to the browser.

E Printing text and HTML over multiple PHP lines will generate HTML source code that also extends over multiple lines. Note that extraneous white spacing in the HTML source will not affect the look of a page **F** but can make the source easier to review.

F The return in the HTML source **E** has no effect on the rendered result. The only way to alter the spacing of a displayed web page is to use HTML tags (like **
** and **<p></p>**).

TIP echo and print can both be used over multiple lines:

```
echo 'This sentence is
printed over two lines.';
```

What happens in this case is that the return (created by pressing Enter or Return) becomes part of the printed message and isn't terminated until the closing quotation mark. The net result will be the "printing" of the return in the HTML source code **E**. This will not have an effect on the generated page **F**. For more on this, see the sidebar "Understanding White Space."

Writing Comments

Creating executable PHP code is only a part of the programming process (admittedly, it's the most important part). A secondary but still crucial aspect to any programming endeavor is documenting your code.

In HTML you can add comments using special tags:

```
<!-- Comment goes here. -->
```

HTML comments are viewable in the source but do not appear in the rendered page (see **E** and **F** in the previous section).

PHP comments are different in that they aren't sent to the browser at all, meaning they won't be viewable to the end user, even when looking at the HTML source.

PHP supports three comment syntaxes. The first uses what's called the pound, hash, or number symbol (**#**):

```
# This is a comment.
```

The second uses two slashes:

```
// This is also a comment.
```

Both of these cause PHP to ignore everything that follows until the end of the line (when you press Return or Enter). Thus, these two comments are for single lines only. They are also often used to place a comment on the same line as some PHP code:

```
print 'Hello!'; // Say hello.
```

A third style allows comments to run over multiple lines:

```
/* This is a longer comment
that spans two lines. */
```

Understanding White Space

With PHP you send data—like HTML tags and text—to the browser, which will, in turn, render that data as the web page the end user sees. Thus, what you are often doing with PHP is creating the *HTML source* of a web page. With this in mind, there are three areas of notable *white space* (extra spaces, tabs, and blank lines): in your PHP scripts, in your HTML source, and in the rendered web page.

PHP is generally white space insensitive, meaning that you can space out your code however you want to make your scripts more legible. HTML is also generally white space insensitive. Specifically, the only white space in HTML that affects the rendered page is a single space (multiple spaces still get rendered as one). If your HTML source has text on multiple lines, that doesn't mean it'll appear on multiple lines in the rendered page (**E** and **F**).

To alter the spacing in a rendered web page, use the HTML tags **
** (line break) and **<p></p>** (paragraph). To alter the spacing of the HTML *source* created with PHP, you can

- Use **echo** or **print** over the course of several lines.

  or

- Print the newline character (**\n**) within double quotation marks, which is equivalent to Enter or Return.

Script 1.4 These basic comments demonstrate the three comment syntaxes you can use in PHP.

```
1    <!doctype html>
2    <html lang="en">
3    <head>
4        <meta charset="utf-8">
5        <title>Comments</title>
6    </head>
7    <body>
8    <?php
9
10   # Script 1.4 - comments.php
11   # Created March 16, 2011
12   # Created by Larry E. Ullman
13   # This script does nothing much.
14
15   echo '<p>This is a line of text.<br>This
     is another line of text.</p>';
16
17   /*
18   echo 'This line will not be
     executed.';
19   */
20
21   echo "<p>Now I'm done.</p>";
     // End of PHP code.
22
23   ?>
24   </body>
25   </html>
```

To comment your scripts:

1. Begin a new PHP document in your text editor or IDE, to be named **comments.php**, starting with the initial HTML (**Script 1.4**):

```
<!doctype html>
<html lang="en">
<head>
    <meta charset="utf-8">
    <title>Comments</title>
</head>
<body>
```

2. Add the initial PHP tag and write your first comments:

```
<?php
# Script 1.4 - comments.php
# Created April 23, 2017
# Created by Larry E. Ullman
# This script does nothing much.
```

One of the first comments each script should contain is an introductory block that lists creation date, modification date, creator, creator's contact information, purpose of the script, and so on. Some people suggest that the shell-style comments (**#**) stand out more in a script and are therefore best for this kind of notation.

3. Send some HTML to the browser:

```
echo '<p>This is a line of text.
→ <br>This is another line of
→ text.</p>';
```

It doesn't matter what you do here—just make something for the browser to display. For the sake of variety, the **echo** statement will print some HTML tags, including a line break (**
**) to add some spacing to the generated HTML page.

continues on next page

4. Use the multiline comments to comment out a second **echo** statement:

```php
/*
echo 'This line will not be
→ executed.';
*/
```

By surrounding any block of PHP code with **/*** and ***/**, you can render that code inert without having to delete it from your script. By later removing the comment tags, you can reactivate that section of PHP code.

5. Add a final comment after a third **echo** statement:

```php
echo "<p>Now I'm done.</p>";
→ // End of PHP code.
```

This last (superfluous) comment shows how to place a comment at the end of a line, a common practice. Note that double quotation marks surround this message, since single quotation marks would conflict with the apostrophe (see the "Needing an Escape" sidebar, earlier in the chapter).

6. Close the PHP section and complete the HTML page:

```php
?>
</body>
</html>
```

7. Save the file as **comments.php**, place it in your web directory, and test it in your browser **A**.

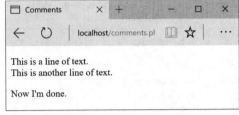

A The PHP comments in Script 1.4 don't appear in the web page or the HTML source **B**.

8. If you're the curious type, check the source code in your browser to confirm that the PHP comments do not appear there **B**.

TIP You shouldn't nest—place one inside another—multiline comments (/* */). Doing so will cause problems.

TIP Any of the PHP comments can be used at the end of a line (say, after a function call):

```
echo 'Howdy'; /* Say 'Howdy' */
```

Although this is allowed, it's far less common.

TIP In the interest of saving space, the scripts in this book will not be as well documented as I would suggest they should be.

TIP It's also important that you keep the comments up to date and accurate when you change a script. There's nothing more confusing than a comment that says one thing when the code really does something else.

TIP Some developers argue that it's unnecessary to comment individual bits of code because the code itself should make its purpose clear. In my experience, adding comments helps.

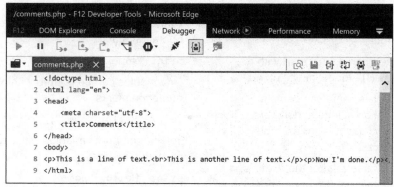

B The PHP comments from Script 1.4 are nowhere to be seen in the client's browser.

What Are Variables?

Variables are containers used to temporarily store values. These values can be numbers, text, or much more complex data. PHP supports eight types of variables. These include four scalar (single-valued) types—*Boolean* (TRUE or FALSE), *integer*, *floating point* (decimals), and *strings* (one or more characters); two nonscalar (multivalued)—*arrays* and *objects*; plus *resources* (which you'll see when interacting with databases) and *NULL* (which is a special type that has no value).

Regardless of what type you are creating, all variable names in PHP follow certain syntactical rules:

- A variable's name must start with a dollar sign (**$**)—for example, **$name**.
- The variable's name can contain a combination of letters, numbers, and the underscore—for example, **$my_report1**.
- The first character after the dollar sign must be either a letter or an underscore (it cannot be a number).
- *Variable names in PHP are case-sensitive!* This is a very important rule. It means that **$name** and **$Name** are different variables.

To begin working with variables, this next script will print out the value of three *predefined variables*. Whereas a standard variable is assigned a value during the execution of a script, a predefined variable will already have a value when the script begins its execution. Most of these predefined variables reflect properties of the server as a whole, such as the operating system in use.

Before getting into this script, there are two more things you should know. First, variables can be assigned values using the equals sign (**=**), also called the *assignment operator*. Second, to display the value of a variable, you can print the variable without quotation marks:

```
print $some_var;
```

Or variables can be printed within *double* quotation marks:

```
print "Hello, $name";
```

You cannot print variables within single quotation marks:

```
print 'Hello, $name';
→ // This won't work!
```

To use variables:

1. Begin a new PHP document in your text editor or IDE, to be named **predefined.php**, starting with the initial HTML (**Script 1.5**):

```
<!doctype html>
<html lang="en">
<head>
    <meta charset="utf-8">
    <title>Predefined Variables</title>
</head>
<body>
```

2. Add the opening PHP tag and the first comment:

<?php # Script 1.5 - predefined.php

From here on out, scripts will no longer comment on the creator, creation date, and so forth, although you should continue to document your scripts thoroughly. Scripts will, however, make a comment indicating the script's number and filename for ease of cross-referencing (both in the book and when you download them from the book's supporting web site, **LarryUllman.com**).

continues on next page

Script 1.5 This script prints three of PHP's many predefined variables.

```
1    <!doctype html>
2    <html lang="en">
3    <head>
4        <meta charset="utf-8">
5        <title>Predefined Variables</title>
6    </head>
7    <body>
8    <?php # Script 1.5 - predefined.php
9
10   // Create a shorthand version of the variable names:
11   $file = $_SERVER['SCRIPT_FILENAME'];
12   $user = $_SERVER['HTTP_USER_AGENT'];
13   $server = $_SERVER['SERVER_SOFTWARE'];
14
15   // Print the name of this script:
16   echo "<p>You are running the file:<br><strong>$file</strong>.</p>\n";
17
18   // Print the user's information:
19   echo "<p>You are viewing this page using:<br><strong>$user</strong></p>\n";
20
21   // Print the server's information:
22   echo "<p>This server is running:<br><strong>$server</strong>.</p>\n";
23
24   ?>
25   </body>
26   </html>
```

3. Create a shorthand version of the first variable to be used in this script:

```
$file = $_SERVER['SCRIPT_FILENAME'];
```

This script will use three variables, each of which comes from the larger predefined **$_SERVER** variable. **$_SERVER** refers to a mass of server-related information. The first variable the script uses is **$_SERVER['SCRIPT_FILENAME']**. This variable stores the full path and name of the script being run (for example, **C:\Program Files\Apache\htdocs \predefined.php**).

The value stored in **$_SERVER['SCRIPT _FILENAME']** will be assigned to the new variable **$file**. Creating new variables with shorter names and then assigning them values from **$_SERVER** will make it easier to refer to the variables when printing them. (It also gets around another issue you'll learn about in due time.)

4. Create a shorthand version of two more variables:

```
$user = $_SERVER
    → ['HTTP_USER_AGENT'];
$server = $_SERVER
    → ['SERVER_SOFTWARE'];
```

$_SERVER['HTTP_USER_AGENT'] represents the browser and operating system of the user accessing the script. This value is assigned to **$user**.

$_SERVER['SERVER_SOFTWARE'] represents the web application on the server that's running PHP (e.g., Apache, Abyss, Xitami, or IIS). This is the program that must be installed (see Appendix A) in order to run PHP scripts on that computer.

5. Print out the name of the script being run:

```
echo "<p>You are running the
    → file:<br /><strong>$file
    → </strong>.</p>\n";
```

The first variable to be printed is **$file**. Notice that this variable must be used within double quotation marks and that the statement also makes use of the PHP newline character (**\n**), which will add a line break in the generated HTML source. Some basic HTML tags—paragraph and strong—are added to give the generated page a bit of flair.

6. Print out the information of the user accessing the script:

```
echo "<p>You are viewing this page
    → using:<br><strong>$user</strong>
    → </p>\n";
```

This line prints the second variable, **$user**. To repeat what's said in the fourth step, **$user** correlates to **$_SERVER['HTTP_USER_AGENT']** and refers to the operating system, browser type, and browser version being used to access the web page.

7. Print out the server information:

```
echo "<p>This server is running:
    → <br><strong>$server</strong>.
    → </p>\n";
```

8. Complete the PHP block and the HTML page:

```
?>
</body>
</html>
```

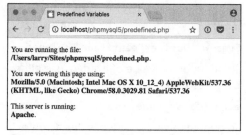

You are running the file:
/Users/larry/Sites/phpmysql5/predefined.php.

You are viewing this page using:
Mozilla/5.0 (Macintosh; Intel Mac OS X 10_12_4) AppleWebKit/537.36 (KHTML, like Gecko) Chrome/58.0.3029.81 Safari/537.36

This server is running:
Apache.

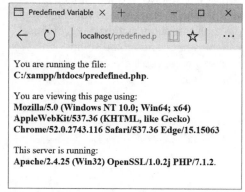

A The **predefined.php** script reports back to the viewer information about the script, the browser being used to view it, and the server itself.

You are running the file:
C:/xampp/htdocs/predefined.php.

You are viewing this page using:
Mozilla/5.0 (Windows NT 10.0; Win64; x64) AppleWebKit/537.36 (KHTML, like Gecko) Chrome/52.0.2743.116 Safari/537.36 Edge/15.15063

This server is running:
Apache/2.4.25 (Win32) OpenSSL/1.0.2j PHP/7.1.2.

B This is the book's first truly dynamic script, in that the web page changes depending on the server running it and the browser viewing it (compare with **A**).

9. Save the file as **predefined.php**, place it in your web directory, and test it in your browser **A**.

TIP If you have problems with this, or any other script, turn to the book's corresponding forum (**LarryUllman.com/forums/**) for assistance.

TIP If possible, run this script using a different browser and/or on another server **B**.

TIP Variable names cannot contain spaces. The underscore is commonly used in lieu of a space.

TIP The most important consideration when creating variables is to use a consistent naming scheme. In this book you'll see that I use all-lowercase letters for my variable names, with underscores separating words (**$first_name**). Some programmers prefer to use capitalization instead: **$FirstName** (known as "camel-case" style).

TIP PHP is very casual in how it treats variables, meaning that you don't need to initialize them (set an immediate value) or declare them (set a specific type), and you can convert a variable among the many types without problem.

Introducing Strings

Now that you've been introduced to the general concept of variables, let's look at variables in detail. The first variable type to delve into is the *string*. A string is merely a quoted chunk of characters: letters, numbers, spaces, punctuation, and so forth. These are all strings:

- 'Tobias'
- "In watermelon sugar"
- '100'
- 'August 2, 2017'

To make a string variable, assign a string value to a valid variable name:

```
$first_name = 'Tobias';
$today = 'August 2, 2011';
```

When creating strings, you can use either single or double quotation marks to encapsulate the characters, just as you would when printing text. Likewise, you must use the same type of quotation mark for the beginning and the end of the string. If that same mark appears within the string, it must be escaped:

```
$var = "Define \"platitude\", please.";
```

Or you can instead use the other quotation mark type:

```
$var = 'Define "platitude", please.';
```

To print out the value of a string, use either **echo** or **print**:

```
echo $first_name;
```

To print the value of string within a context, you must use double quotation marks:

```
echo "Hello, $first_name";
```

You've already worked with strings once—when using the predefined variables in the preceding section, as the values of those variables happened to be strings. In this next example, you'll create and use your own strings.

Script 1.6 String variables are created and their values are sent to the browser in this script.

```
1   <!doctype html>
2   <html lang="en">
3   <head>
4       <meta charset="utf-8">
5       <title>Strings</title>
6   </head>
7   <body>
8   <?php # Script 1.6 - strings.php
9
10  // Create the variables:
11  $first_name = 'Haruki';
12  $last_name = 'Murakami';
13  $book = 'Kafka on the Shore';
14
15  // Print the values:
16  echo "<p>The book <em>$book</em> was
    written by $first_name
    $last_name.</p>";
17
18  ?>
19  </body>
20  </html>
```

To use strings:

1. Begin a new PHP document in your text editor or IDE, to be named **strings.php**, starting with the initial HTML and including the opening PHP tag (**Script 1.6**):

```
<!doctype html>
<html lang="en">
<head>
    <meta charset="utf-8">
    <title>Strings</title>
</head>
<body>
<?php # Script 1.6 - strings.php
```

2. Within the PHP tags, create three variables:

```
$first_name = 'Haruki';
$last_name = 'Murakami';
$book = 'Kafka on the Shore';
```

This rudimentary example creates **$first_name**, **$last_name**, and **$book** variables that will then be printed out in a message.

continues on next page

3. Add an **echo** statement:

```
echo "<p>The book <em>$book
→ </em> was written by
→ $first_name $last_name.</p>";
```

All this script does is print a statement of authorship based on three established variables. A little HTML formatting—the emphasis on the book's title—is thrown in to make it more attractive. Remember to use double quotation marks here for the variable values to be printed out appropriately (more on the importance of double quotation marks at this chapter's end).

4. Complete the PHP block and the HTML page:

```
?>
</body>
</html>
```

5. Save the file as **strings.php**, place it in your web directory, and test it in your browser Ⓐ.

6. If desired, change the values of the three variables, save the file, and run the script again Ⓑ.

TIP If you assign another value to an existing variable (e.g., $book), the new value will overwrite the old one. For example:

```
$book = 'High Fidelity';
$book = 'The Corrections';
/* $book now has a value of
'The Corrections'. */
```

TIP PHP has no set limits on how big a string can be. It's theoretically possible that you'll be limited by the resources of the server, but it's doubtful that you'll ever encounter such a problem.

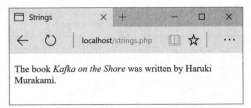

The book *Kafka on the Shore* was written by Haruki Murakami.

Ⓐ The resulting web page is based on printing out the values of three variables.

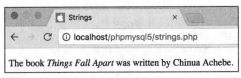

The book *Things Fall Apart* was written by Chinua Achebe.

Ⓑ The output of the script is changed by altering the variables in it.

Script 1.7 Concatenation gives you the ability to append more characters onto a string.

```
1    <!doctype html>
2    <html lang="en">
3    <head>
4       <meta charset="utf-8">
5       <title>Concatenation</title>
6    </head>
7    <body>
8    <?php # Script 1.7 - concat.php
9
10   // Create the variables:
11   $first_name = 'Melissa';
12   $last_name = 'Bank';
13   $author = $first_name . ' ' .
     $last_name;
14
15   $book = 'The Girls\' Guide to Hunting
     and Fishing';
16
17   //Print the values:
18   echo "<p>The book <em>$book</em> was
     written by $author.</p>";
19
20   ?>
21   </body>
22   </html>
```

Concatenating Strings

Concatenation is like addition for strings, whereby characters are added to the end of the string. It is performed using the *concatenation operator*, which is the period (**.**):

$city= 'Seattle';
$state = 'Washington';
$address = $city . $state;

The **$address** variable now has the value *SeattleWashington*, which almost achieves the desired result (*Seattle, Washington*). To improve upon this, you could write

$address = $city . ', ' . $state;

so that a comma and a space are concatenated to the variables as well.

Because of how liberally PHP treats variables, concatenation is possible with strings and numbers. Either of these statements will produce the same result (*Seattle, Washington 98101*):

$address = $city . ', ' . $state .
** ' 98101';**
$address = $city . ', ' . $state .
** ' ' . 98101;**

Let's modify **strings.php** to use this new operator.

To use concatenation:

1. Open **strings.php** (refer to Script 1.6) in your text editor or IDE.

2. After you've established the **$first_name** and **$last_name** variables (lines 11 and 12), add this line (**Script 1.7**):

   $author = $first_name . ' ' .
   →$last_name;

   As a demonstration of concatenation, a new variable—**$author**—will be created as the concatenation of two existing strings and a space in between.

continues on next page

3. Change the **echo** statement to use this new variable:

```
echo "<p>The book <em>$book</em>
→ was written by $author.</p>";
```

Since the two variables have been turned into one, the **echo** statement should be altered accordingly.

4. If desired, change the HTML page title and the values of the first name, last name, and book variables.

5. Save the file as **concat.php**, place it in your web directory, and test it in your browser **Ⓐ**.

> **TIP** PHP has a slew of useful string-specific functions, which you'll see over the course of this book. For example, to calculate how long a string is (how many characters it contains), use strlen():

```
$num = strlen('some string'); // 11
```

> **TIP** You can have PHP convert the case of strings with strtolower(), which makes it entirely lowercase; strtoupper(), which makes it entirely uppercase; ucfirst(), which capitalizes the first character; and ucwords(), which capitalizes the first character of every word.

> **TIP** If you are merely concatenating one value to another, you can use the concatenation assignment operator (.=). The following are equivalent:

```
$title = $title . $subtitle;
$title .= $subtitle;
```

> **TIP** The initial example in this section could be rewritten using either

```
$address = "$city, $state";
```

or

```
$address = $city;
$address .= ',';
$address .= $state;
```

The book *The Girls' Guide to Hunting and Fishing* was written by Melissa Bank.

Ⓐ In this revised script, the end result of concatenation is not apparent to the user.

Using the PHP Manual

The PHP manual—accessible online at **www.php.net/manual**—lists every function and feature of the language. The manual is organized with general concepts (installation, syntax, variables) discussed first and ends with the functions by topic (MySQL, string functions, and so on).

To quickly look up any function in the PHP manual, go to **php.net/functionname** in your browser (for example, **php.net/print**). For each function, the manual indicates the following:

- The versions of PHP the function is available in
- How many and what types of arguments the function takes (optional arguments are wrapped in square brackets)
- What type of value the function returns

The manual also contains a description of the function.

You should be in the habit of checking out the PHP manual whenever you're confused by a function or how it's properly used, or need to learn more about any feature of the language. It's also critically important that you know what version of PHP you're running, since functions and other particulars of PHP do change over time.

Introducing Numbers

In introducing variables, I stated that PHP has both integer and floating-point (decimal) number types. In my experience, though, these two types can be classified under the generic title *numbers* without losing much valuable distinction. Valid numbers in PHP can be anything like

- 8
- 3.14
- 10980843985
- −4.2398508
- 4.4e2

Notice that these values are never quoted—quoted numbers are strings with numeric values—nor do they include commas to indicate thousands. Also, a number is assumed to be positive unless it is preceded by the minus sign (−).

Along with the standard arithmetic operators you can use on numbers (Table 1.1), dozens of functions are built into PHP. Two common ones are **round()** and

number_format(). The former rounds a decimal to the nearest integer:

```
$n = 3.14;
$n = round($n); // 3
```

It can also round to a specified number of decimal places:

```
$n = 3.141592;
$n = round($n, 3); // 3.142
```

The **number_format()** function turns a number into the more commonly written version, grouped into thousands using commas:

```
$n = 20943;
$n = number_format($n); // 20,943
```

This function can also set a specified number of decimal points:

```
$n = 20943;
$n = number_format($n, 2); //
20,943.00
```

To practice with numbers, let's write a mock-up script that performs the calculations you might use in an e-commerce shopping cart.

TABLE 1.1 Arithmetic Operators

Operator	Meaning
+	Addition
−	Subtraction
*	Multiplication
/	Division
%	Modulus
+ +	Increment
− −	Decrement

To use numbers:

1. Begin a new PHP document in your text editor or IDE, to be named **numbers.php** (**Script 1.8**):

```
<!doctype html>
<html lang="en">
<head>
  <meta charset="utf-8">
  <title>Numbers</title>
</head>
<body>
<?php # Script 1.8 - numbers.php
```

2. Establish the requisite variables:

```
$quantity = 30;
$price = 119.95;
$taxrate = .05;
```

This script will use three hard-coded variables on which calculations will be made. Later in the book, you'll see how these values can be dynamically determined (i.e., by user interaction with an HTML form).

3. Perform the calculations:

```
$total = $quantity * $price;
$total = $total + ($total *
→ $taxrate);
```

The first line establishes the order total as the number of widgets purchased multiplied by the price of each widget. The second line then adds the amount of tax to the total (calculated by multiplying the tax rate by the total).

4. Format the total:

```
$total = number_format($total, 2);
```

The **number_format()** function will group the total into thousands and round it to two decimal places. Applying this function will properly format the calculated value.

Script 1.8 The **numbers.php** script performs basic mathematical calculations, like those used in an e-commerce application.

```
1   <!doctype html>
2   <html lang="en">
3   <head>
4     <meta charset="utf-8">
5     <title>Numbers</title>
6   </head>
7   <body>
8   <?php # Script 1.8 - numbers.php
9
10  // Set the variables:
11  $quantity = 30; // Buying 30 widgets.
12  $price = 119.95;
13  $taxrate = .05; // 5% sales tax.
14
15  // Calculate the total:
16  $total = $quantity * $price;
17  $total = $total + ($total * $taxrate);
    // Calculate and add the tax.
18
19  // Format the total:
20  $total = number_format ($total, 2);
21
22  // Print the results:
23  echo '<p>You are purchasing <strong>' .
    $quantity . '</strong> widget(s) at a
    cost of <strong>$' . $price . '</strong>
    each. With tax, the total comes to
    <strong>$' . $total . '</strong>.</p>';
24
25  ?>
26  </body>
27  </html>
```

5. Print the results:

```
echo '<p>You are purchasing
→ <strong>' . $quantity .
→ '</strong> widget(s) at a cost
→ of <strong>$' . $price .
→ '</strong> each. With tax, the
→ total comes to <strong>$' .
→ $total . '</strong>.</p>';
```

The last step in the script is to print out the results. The **echo** statement uses both single-quoted text and concatenated variables in order to print out the full combination of HTML, dollar signs, and variable values. You'll see an alternative approach in the last example of this chapter.

6. Complete the PHP code and the HTML page:

```
?>
</body>
</html>
```

7. Save the file as **numbers.php**, place it in your web directory, and test it in your browser .

8. If desired, change the initial three variables and rerun the script 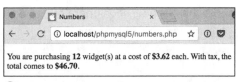.

> **TIP** PHP supports a maximum integer of around two billion on most platforms. With numbers larger than that, PHP will automatically use a floating-point type.

> **TIP** When dealing with arithmetic, the issue of precedence arises—the order in which complex calculations are made. While the PHP manual and other sources tend to list the hierarchy of precedence, I find programming to be safer and more legible when I group clauses in parentheses to force the execution order (see line 17 of Script 1.8).

> **TIP** Computers are notoriously poor at dealing with decimals. For example, the number 2.0 may actually be stored as 1.99999. Most of the time this won't be a problem, but in cases where mathematical precision is paramount, rely on integers, not decimals. The PHP manual has information on this subject, as well as alternative functions for improving computational accuracy.

> **TIP** Many of the mathematical operators also have a corresponding assignment operator, letting you create a shorthand for assigning values. The line
>
> ```
> $total = $total + ($total * $taxrate);
> ```
>
> could be rewritten as
>
> ```
> $total += ($total * $taxrate);
> ```

> **TIP** If you set a `$price` value without using two decimals (e.g., 119.9 or 34), you would want to apply `number_format()` to `$price` before printing it.

> **TIP** New in PHP 7 is the `intdiv()` function, which returns the integer quotient of a division:
>
> ```
> echo intdiv(7, 3); // 2
> ```

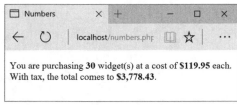

You are purchasing **30** widget(s) at a cost of **$119.95** each. With tax, the total comes to **$3,778.43**.

A The numbers PHP page (Script 1.8) performs calculations based on set values.

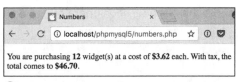

You are purchasing **12** widget(s) at a cost of **$3.62** each. With tax, the total comes to **$46.70**.

B To change the generated web page, alter any or all of the three variables (compare with **A**).

Introducing Constants

Constants, like variables, are used to temporarily store a value, but otherwise, constants and variables differ in many ways. For starters, to create a constant, you use the **define()** function instead of the assignment operator **(=)**:

```
define('NAME', value);
```

Notice that, as a rule of thumb, constants are named using all capitals, although this is not required. Most importantly, constants do not use the initial dollar sign as variables do (because constants are not variables).

A constant is normally assigned a *scalar* value, like a string or a number:

```
define('USERNAME', 'troutocity');
define('PI', 3.14);
```

And unlike variables, a constant's value cannot be changed.

To access a constant's value, like when you want to print it, you cannot put the constant within quotation marks:

```
echo "Hello, USERNAME"; // Won't work!
```

With that code, PHP literally prints *Hello, USERNAME* 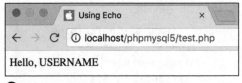 and not the value of the **USERNAME** constant because there's no indication that **USERNAME** is anything other than literal text. Instead, either print the constant by itself:

```
echo 'Hello, ';
echo USERNAME;
```

or use the concatenation operator:

```
echo 'Hello, ' . USERNAME;
```

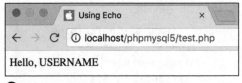

Ⓐ Constants cannot be placed within quoted strings.

PHP runs with several predefined constants, much like the predefined variables used earlier in the chapter. These include **PHP_VERSION** (the version of PHP running) and **PHP_OS** (the operating system of the server). This next script will print those two values, along with the value of a user-defined constant.

To use constants:

1. Begin a new PHP document in your text editor or IDE, to be named **constants.php** (Script 1.9).

```
<!doctype html>
<html lang="en">
<head>
  <meta charset="utf-8">
  <title>Constants</title>
</head>
<body>
<?php # Script 1.9 - constants.php
```

2. Create a new date constant:

```
define('TODAY', 'April 23, 2017');
```

An admittedly trivial use of constants, but this example will illustrate the point. In Chapter 9, "Using PHP with MySQL," you'll see how to use constants to store your database access information.

3. Print out the date, the PHP version, and operating system information:

```
echo '<p>Today is ' . TODAY .
→'.<br>This server is running
→version <strong>' . PHP_VERSION .
→'</strong> of PHP on the
→<strong>' . PHP_OS . '</strong>
→operating system.</p>';
```

Since constants cannot be printed within quotation marks, use the concatenation operator in the **echo** statement.

continues on next page

Script 1.9 Constants are another temporary storage tool you can use in PHP, distinct from variables.

```
1    <!doctype html>
2    <html lang="en">
3    <head>
4       <meta charset="utf-8">
5       <title>Constants</title>
6    </head>
7    <body>
8    <?php # Script 1.9 - constants.php
9
10   // Set today's date as a constant:
11   define('TODAY', 'April 23, 2017');
12
13   // Print a message, using predefined constants and the TODAY constant:
14   echo '<p>Today is ' . TODAY . '.<br>This server is running version <strong>' .
     PHP_VERSION . '</strong> of PHP on the <strong>' . PHP_OS . '</strong> operating
     system.</p>';
15
16   ?>
17   </body>
18   </html>
```

4. Complete the PHP code and the HTML page:

```
?>
</body>
</html>
```

5. Save the file as **constants.php**, place it in your web directory, and test it in your browser **B**.

TIP If possible, run this script on another PHP-enabled server **C**.

TIP The operating system called Darwin **B** is the technical name for macOS.

TIP In Chapter 12, "Cookies and Sessions," you'll learn about another constant, SID (which stands for session ID).

TIP As of PHP 7, you can now create an array constant. You'll learn more about arrays in Chapter 2, "Programming with PHP."

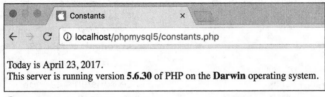

Today is April 23, 2017.
This server is running version **5.6.30** of PHP on the **Darwin** operating system.

B By making use of PHP's constants, you can learn more about your PHP setup.

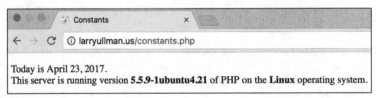

Today is April 23, 2017.
This server is running version **5.5.9-1ubuntu4.21** of PHP on the **Linux** operating system.

C Running the same script (refer to Script 1.9) on different servers garners different results.

Single vs. Double Quotation Marks

In PHP, it's important to understand how single quotation marks differ from double quotation marks. With **echo** and **print**, or when assigning values to strings, you can use either, as in the examples used so far. But there is a key difference between the two types of quotation marks and when you should use which. You've seen this difference already, but it's an important enough concept to merit more discussion.

In PHP, *values enclosed within single quotation marks will be treated literally*, whereas *those within double quotation marks will be interpreted*. In other words, placing variables and special characters (**Table 1.2**) within double quotes will result in their represented values printed, not their literal values. For example, assume that you have

`$var = 'test';`

TABLE 1.2 Escape Sequences

Code	Meaning
\"	Double quotation mark
\'	Single quotation mark
\\	Backslash
\n	Newline
\r	Carriage return
\t	Tab
\$	Dollar sign

The code **echo "var is equal to $var";** will print out *var is equal to test*, but the code **echo 'var is equal to $var';** will print out *var is equal to $var*. Using an escaped dollar sign, the **code echo "\$var is equal to $var";** will print out *$var is equal to test*, whereas the code **echo '\$var is equal to $var';** will print out *\$var is equal to $var* 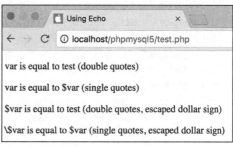.

As these examples should illustrate, double quotation marks will replace a variable's name (**$var**) with its value (*test*) and a special character's code (**\$**) with its represented value (*$*). Single quotes will always display exactly what you type, except for the escaped single quote (**\'**) and the escaped backslash (****), which are printed as a single quotation mark and a single backslash, respectively.

As another example of how the two quotation marks differ, let's modify the **numbers.php** script as an experiment.

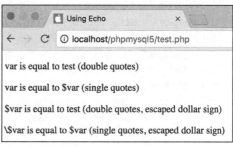

> Using Echo
>
> ← → C ① localhost/phpmysql5/test.php
>
> var is equal to test (double quotes)
>
> var is equal to $var (single quotes)
>
> $var is equal to test (double quotes, escaped dollar sign)
>
> \$var is equal to $var (single quotes, escaped dollar sign)

A How single and double quotation marks affect what gets printed by PHP.

To use single and double quotation marks:

1. Open **numbers.php** (refer to Script 1.8) in your text editor or IDE.

2. Delete the existing **echo** statement (**Script 1.10**).

3. Print a caption and then rewrite the original **echo** statement using double quotation marks:

```
echo "<h3>Using double quotation
→ marks:</h3>";
echo "<p>You are purchasing
→ <strong>$quantity</strong>
→ widget(s) at a cost of
→ <strong>\$$price</strong> each.
→ With tax, the total comes to
→ <strong>\$$total</strong>.</p>\n";
```

In the original script, the results were printed using single quotation marks and concatenation. The same result can be achieved using double quotation marks. When using double quotation marks, the variables can be placed within the string.

There is one catch, though: trying to print a dollar amount as $12.34 (where 12.34 comes from a variable) would suggest that you would code **$$var**. That will not work (for complicated reasons). Instead, escape the initial dollar sign, resulting in **\$$var**, as you see twice in this code. The first dollar sign will be printed, and the second becomes the start of the variable name.

Script 1.10 This, the final script in the chapter, demonstrates the differences between using single and double quotation marks.

```
1   <!doctype html>
2   <html lang="en">
3   <head>
4       <meta charset="utf-8">
5       <title>Quotation Marks</title>
6   </head>
7   <body>
8   <?php # Script 1.10 - quotes.php
9
10  // Set the variables:
11  $quantity = 30; // Buying 30 widgets.
12  $price = 119.95;
13  $taxrate = .05; // 5% sales tax.
14
15  // Calculate the total.
16  $total = $quantity * $price;
17  $total = $total + ($total * $taxrate);
    // Calculate and add the tax.
18
19  // Format the total:
20  $total = number_format ($total, 2);
21
22  // Print the results using double
    quotation marks:
23  echo "<h3>Using double quotation
    marks:</h3>";
24  echo "<p>You are purchasing
    <strong>$quantity</strong> widget(s)
    at a cost of <strong>\$$price
    </strong> each. With tax, the total
    comes to <strong>\$$total</strong>.
    </p>\n";
25
26  // Print the results using single
    quotation marks:
27  echo '<h3>Using single quotation
    marks:</h3>';
28  echo '<p>You are purchasing
    <strong>$quantity</strong> widget(s)
    at a cost of <strong>\$$price
    </strong> each. With tax, the total
    comes to <strong>\$$total</strong>.
    </p>\n';
29
30  ?>
31  </body>
32  </html>
```

4. Repeat the **echo** statements, this time using single quotation marks:

```
echo '<h3>Using single quotation
→ marks:</h3>';
echo '<p>You are purchasing
→ <strong>$quantity</strong>
→ widget(s) at a cost of
→ <strong>\$$price</strong> each.
→ With tax, the total comes to
→ <strong>\$$total</strong>.</p>\n';
```

This **echo** statement is used to highlight the difference between using single or double quotation marks. It will not work as desired, and the resulting page will show you exactly what does happen instead.

5. If you want, change the page's title.

6. Save the file as **quotes.php,** place it in your web directory, and test it in your browser **B**.

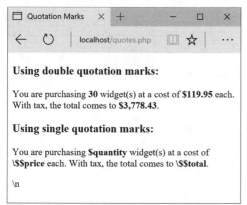

B These results demonstrate when and how you'd use one type of quotation mark as opposed to the other.

7. View the source of the web page to see how using the newline character (**\n**) within each quotation mark type also differs.

You should see that when you place the newline character within double quotation marks it creates a newline in the HTML source. When placed within single quotation marks, the literal characters **** and **n** are printed instead.

TIP Because PHP will attempt to find variables within double quotation marks, using single quotation marks is theoretically faster. If you need to print the value of a variable, though, you must use double quotation marks.

Because valid HTML often includes a lot of double-quoted attributes, it's often easiest to use single quotation marks when printing HTML with PHP:

```
echo '<table class="data">';
```

If you were to print out this HTML using double quotation marks, you would have to escape all of the double quotation marks in the string:

```
echo "<table class=\"data\">";
```

TIP In newer versions of PHP, you can actually use **$$price** and **$$total** without preceding them with a backslash (thanks to some internal magic). In older versions of PHP, you cannot. To guarantee reliable results, regardless of PHP version, I recommend using the **\$$var** syntax when you need to print a dollar sign immediately followed by the value of a variable.

TIP If you're still unclear as to the difference between the types, use double quotation marks and you're less likely to have problems.

Basic Debugging Steps

Debugging is by no means a simple concept to grasp, and unfortunately, it's one that is only truly mastered by doing. The next 50 pages could be dedicated to the subject and you'd still only be able to pick up a fraction of the debugging skills that you'll eventually acquire and need.

The reason I introduce debugging in this somewhat harrowing way is that it's important not to enter into programming with delusions. Sometimes code won't work as expected, you'll inevitably create careless errors, and some days you'll want to pull your hair out, even when using a comparatively user-friendly language such as PHP. In short, prepare to be perplexed and frustrated at times. I've been coding in PHP since 1999, and occasionally I still get stuck in the programming muck. But debugging is a very important skill to have, and one that you will eventually pick up out of necessity and experience. As you begin your PHP programming adventure, I can offer the following basic but concrete debugging tips.

Note that these are just some general debugging techniques, specifically tailored to the beginning PHP programmer. Chapter 8, "Error Handling and Debugging," goes into other techniques in more detail.

To debug a PHP script:

- Make sure you're always running PHP scripts through a URL!

  This is perhaps the most common beginner's mistake. PHP code must be run through the web server application, which means it must be requested via `http://something`. When you see actual PHP code instead of the result of that code's execution, most likely you're not running the PHP script through a URL.

- Know what version of PHP you're running.

  Some problems will arise from the version of PHP in use. Before you ever use any PHP-enabled server, run a `phpinfo.php` script (see Appendix A) or reference the `PHP_VERSION` constant to confirm the version of PHP in use.

- Make sure `display_errors` is on.

  This is a basic PHP configuration setting (also discussed in Appendix A). You can confirm this setting by executing the `phpinfo()` function (just use your browser to search for *display_errors* in the resulting page). For security reasons, PHP may not be set to display the errors that occur. If that's the case, you'll end up seeing blank pages when problems occur. To debug most problems, you'll need to see the errors, so turn this setting on while you're learning. You'll find instructions for doing so in Appendix A.

- Check the HTML source code.

  Sometimes the problem is hidden in the HTML source of the page. In fact, sometimes the PHP error message can be hidden there!

- Trust the error message.

  Another very common beginner's mistake is to not fully read or trust the error that PHP reports. Although an error message can often be cryptic and may seem meaningless, it can't be ignored. At the very least, PHP is normally correct as to the line on which the problem can be found. And if you need to relay that error message to someone else (like when you're asking me for help), do include the entire error message!

- Take a break!

  So many of the programming problems I've encountered over the years, and the vast majority of the toughest ones, have been solved by stepping away from the computer for a while. It's easy to get frustrated and confused, and in such situations, any further steps you take are likely to only make matters worse.

Review and Pursue

Each chapter ends with a "Review and Pursue" section where you'll find questions regarding the material just covered and prompts for ways to expand your knowledge and experience on your own. If you have any problems with these sections, either in answering the questions or pursuing your own endeavors, turn to the book's supporting forum (LarryUllman.com/forums/).

Review

- What tags are used to surround PHP code?

- What extension should a PHP file have?

- What does a page's *encoding* refer to? What impact does the encoding have on the page?

- What PHP functions, or language constructs, can you use to send data to the browser?

- How does using single versus double quotation marks differ in creating or printing strings?

- What does it mean to *escape* a character in a string?

- What are the three comment syntaxes in PHP? Which one can be used over multiple lines?

- What character do all variable names begin with? What characters can come next? What other characters can be used in a variable's name?

- Are variable names case-sensitive or case-insensitive?

- What is the assignment operator?

- How do you create a string variable?

- What is the concatenation operator? What is the concatenation assignment operator?

- How are constants defined and used?

Pursue

- If you don't already know—*for certain*—what version of PHP you're running, check now.

- Look up one of the mentioned string functions in the PHP manual. Then check out some of the other available string functions listed therein.

- Look up one of the mentioned number functions in the PHP manual. Then check out some of the other available number functions listed therein.

- Search the PHP manual for the **$_SERVER** variable to see what other information it contains.

- Create a new script, from scratch, that defines and displays the values of some string variables. Use double quotation marks in the **echo** or **print** statement that outputs the values. For added complexity, include some HTML in the output. Then rewrite the script so that it uses single quotation marks and concatenation instead of double quotation marks.

- Create a new script, from scratch, that defines, manipulates, and displays the values of some numeric variables.

2

Programming with PHP

Now that you have the fundamentals of the PHP scripting language down, it's time to build on those basics and start truly programming. In this chapter you'll begin creating more elaborate scripts while still learning some of the standard constructs, functions, and syntax of the language.

You'll start by creating an HTML form and then learn how you can use PHP to handle the submitted values. From there, the chapter covers conditionals and the remaining operators (Chapter 1, "Introduction to PHP," presented the assignment, concatenation, and mathematical operators), arrays (another variable type), and one last language construct, loops.

In This Chapter

Creating an HTML Form

Handling an HTML form with PHP is an important process in any dynamic web site. Two steps are involved: first you create the HTML form itself, and then you create the corresponding PHP script that will receive and process the form data.

It is outside the realm of this book to go into HTML forms in any detail, but I will lead you through one quick example so that it may be used throughout the chapter. If you're unfamiliar with the basics of an HTML form, including the various types of elements, see an HTML resource for more information.

An HTML form is created using the **form** tags and various elements for taking input. The **form** tags look like

```
<form action="script.php"
→ method="post">
</form>
```

In terms of PHP, the most important attribute of your **form** tag is **action**, which dictates to which page the form data will be sent. The second attribute—**method**—has its own issues (see the "Choosing a Method" sidebar), but *post* is the value you'll use most frequently.

The different inputs—be they text boxes, radio buttons, select menus, check boxes, etc.—are placed within the opening and closing **form** tags. As you'll see in the next section, what kinds of inputs your form has makes little difference to the PHP script handling it. You should, however, pay attention to the names you give your form inputs—they'll be of critical importance when it comes to your PHP code.

Choosing a Method

The **method** attribute of a form dictates how the data is sent to the handling page. The two options—*get* and *post*—refer to the HTTP (Hypertext Transfer Protocol) method to be used. The **GET** method sends the submitted data to the receiving page as a series of name-value pairs appended to the URL—for example,

http://www.example.com/script.php
→ **?name=Homer&gender=M&age=35**

The benefit of using the **GET** method is that the resulting page can be book-marked in the user's browser since it's a complete URL. For that matter, you can also click Back in your browser to return to a **GET** page, or reload it without problems, none of which is true for **POST**. But there is a limit in how much data can be transmitted via **GET**, and this method is less secure since the data is visible.

Generally speaking, *GET is used for requesting information*, like a particular record from a database or the results of a search (searches almost always use **GET**). *The POST method is used when an action is expected*: the updating of a database record or the sending of an email. For these reasons I will primarily use **POST** throughout this book, with noted exceptions.

To create an HTML form:

1. Begin a new HTML document in your text editor or IDE, to be named **form.html** (Script 2.1):

```
<!doctype html>
<html lang="en">
<head>
   <meta charset="utf-8">
   <title>Simple HTML Form</title>
   <style type="text/css">
   label {
      font-weight: bold;
      color: #300ACC;
   }
   </style>
</head>
<body>
<!-- Script 2.1 - form.html -->
<form action="handle_form.php"
 → method="post">
```

The document uses the same basic syntax for an HTML page as in the previous chapter. I have added some inline CSS (Cascading Style Sheets) in order to style the form slightly (specifically, making **label** elements bold and blue).

CSS is the preferred way to handle many formatting and layout issues in an HTML page. You'll see a little bit of CSS here and there in this book; if you're not familiar with the subject, check out a dedicated CSS reference.

Finally, an HTML comment indicates the file's name and number.

continues on next page

Script 2.1 This simple HTML form will be used for several of the examples in this chapter.

```
1    <!doctype html>
2    <html lang="en">
3    <head>
4    <meta charset="utf-8">
5    <title>Simple HTML Form</title>
6    <style type="text/css">
7    label {
8       font-weight: bold;
9       color: #300ACC;
10   }
11   </style>
12   </head>
13   <body>
14   <!-- Script 2.1 - form.html -->
15
16   <form action="handle_form.php" method="post">
17
18   <fieldset><legend>Enter your information in the form below:</legend>
19
20   <p><label>Name: <input type="text" name="name" size="20" maxlength="40"></label></p>
21
22   <p><label>Email Address: <input type="email" name="email" size="40" maxlength="60"></label></p>
23
```

code continues on next page

2. Add the initial **form** tag:

```
<form action="handle_form.php"
→ method="post">
```

Since the **action** attribute dictates to which script the form data will go, you should give it an appropriate name (*handle_form* to correspond with this page: **form.html**) and the **.php** extension (since a PHP script will handle this form's data).

3. Begin the HTML form:

```
<fieldset><legend>Enter your
→ information in the form
→ below:</legend>
```

I'm using the **fieldset** and **legend** HTML tags because they group the form elements nicely (they add a box around the form with a title at the top). This isn't pertinent to the form itself, though.

Script 2.1 *continued*

```
24      <p><label for="gender">Gender: </label><input type="radio" name="gender" value="M"> Male
        <input type="radio" name="gender" value="F"> Female</p>
25
26      <p><label>Age:
27      <select name="age">
28         <option value="0-29">Under 30</option>
29         <option value="30-60">Between 30 and 60</option>
30         <option value="60+">Over 60</option>
31      </select></label></p>
32
33      <p><label>Comments: <textarea name="comments" rows="3" cols="40"></textarea></label></p>
34
35      </fieldset>
36
37      <p align="center"><input type="submit" name="submit" value="Submit My Information"></p>
38
39   </form>
40
41   </body>
42   </html>
```

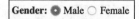

A Two form inputs.

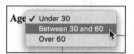

B If multiple radio buttons have the same **name** value, only one can be selected by the user.

C The pull-down menu offers three options, of which only one can be selected (in this example).

4. Add a text and an email input:

```
<p><label>Name: <input type="text"
→ name="name" size="20"
→ maxlength="40"></label></p>
<p><label>Email Address:
→ <input type="email" name="email"
→ size="40" maxlength="60">
→ </label></p>
```

These are just simple text inputs, allowing users to enter their name and email address **A**. The **label** tags just tie each textual label to the associated element.

5. Add a pair of radio buttons:

```
<p><label for="gender">Gender:
→ </label><input type="radio"
→ name="gender" value="M"> Male
→ <input type="radio"
→ name="gender" value="F">
→ Female</p>
```

The radio buttons **B** both have the same name, meaning that only one of the two can be selected. They have different values, though.

6. Add a pull-down menu:

```
<p><label>Age:
<select name="age">
  <option value="0-29">Under 30
  → </option>
  <option value="30-60">Between 30
  → and 60</option>
  <option value="60+">Over 60
  → </option>
</select></label></p>
```

The **select** tag starts the pull-down menu, and then each **option** tag will create another line in the list of choices **C**.

continues on next page

7. Add a text box for comments:

```
<p><label>Comments: <textarea
→ name="comments" rows="3"
→ cols="40"></textarea></label></p>
```

Textareas are different from text inputs; they are presented as a box 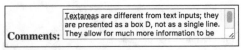, not as a single line. They allow the user to type much more information and are handy for taking user comments.

8. Complete the form:

```
</fieldset>
<p align="center"><input
→ type="submit" name="submit"
→ value="Submit My Information">
→ </p>
```

The first tag closes the **fieldset** that was opened in Step 3. Then a submit button is created and centered using a **p** tag. Finally, the form is closed.

9. Complete the HTML page:

```
</body>
</html>
```

10. Save the file as **form.html**, place it in your web directory, and view it in your browser **E**.

TIP Since this page contains just HTML, it uses an .html extension. It could instead use a .php extension without harm (since code outside of the PHP tags is treated as HTML).

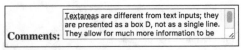

D The textarea form element type allows for lots and lots of text.

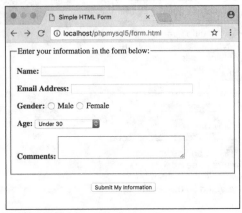

E The complete form, which requests some basic information from the user.

Handling an HTML Form

Now that the HTML form has been created, it's time to write a bare-bones PHP script to handle it. To say that this script will be *handling* the form means that the PHP page will do something with the data it receives (which is the data the user entered in the form). In this chapter, the scripts will simply print the data back to the browser. In later examples, form data will be stored in a MySQL database, compared against previously stored values, sent in emails, and more.

The beauty of PHP—and what makes it so easy to learn and use—is how well it interacts with HTML forms. PHP scripts store the received information in special variables. For example, say you have a form with an input defined like so:

```
<input type="text" name="city">
```

Whatever the user types into that input will be accessible via a PHP variable named `$_REQUEST['city']`. It is very important that the spelling and capitalization match *exactly*! PHP is case-sensitive when it comes to variable names, so `$_REQUEST['city']` will work, but `$_Request['city']` and `$_REQUEST['City']` will have no value.

This next example will be a PHP script that handles the already-created HTML form (Script 2.1). This script will assign the form data to new variables (to be used as shorthand, just like in Script 1.5, `predefined.php`). The script will then print the received values.

To handle an HTML form:

1. Begin a new PHP document in your text editor or IDE, to be named **handle_form.php**, starting with the HTML (**Script 2.2**):

```
<!doctype html>
<html lang="en">
<head>
  <meta charset="utf-8">
  <title>Form Feedback</title>
</head>
<body>
```

2. Add the opening PHP tag and create a shorthand version of the form data variables:

```
<?php # Script 2.2 - handle_form.php
$name = $_REQUEST['name'];
$email = $_REQUEST['email'];
$comments = $_REQUEST['comments'];
```

Following the rules outlined before, the data entered into the first form input, which is called *name*, will be accessible through the variable **$_REQUEST['name']** (**Table 2.1**). The data entered into the email form input, which has a **name** value of *email*, will be accessible through **$_REQUEST['email']**. The same applies to the comments data. Again, the spelling and capitalization of your variables here must exactly match the corresponding **name** values in the HTML form.

At this point, you won't make use of the age, gender, and submit form elements.

Script 2.2 This script receives and prints out the information entered into an HTML form (Script 2.1).

```
1    <!doctype html>
2    <html lang="en">
3    <head>
4      <meta charset="utf-8">
5      <title>Form Feedback</title>
6    </head>
7    <body>
8    <?php # Script 2.2 - handle_form.php
9
10   // Create a shorthand for the form data:
11   $name = $_REQUEST['name'];
12   $email = $_REQUEST['email'];
13   $comments = $_REQUEST['comments'];
14   /* Not used:
15   $_REQUEST['age']
16   $_REQUEST['gender']
17   $_REQUEST['submit']
18   */
19
20   // Print the submitted information:
21   echo "<p>Thank you, <strong>
     $name</strong>, for the following
     comments:</p>
22   <pre>$comments</pre>
23   <p>We will reply to you at <em>$email
     </em>.</p>\n";
24
25   ?>
26   </body>
27   </html>
```

TABLE 2.1 Form Elements to PHP Variables

Element Name	Variable Name
name	$_REQUEST['name ']
email	$_REQUEST['email ']
comments	$_REQUEST['comments ']
age	$_REQUEST['age ']
gender	$_REQUEST['gender ']
submit	$_REQUEST['submit']

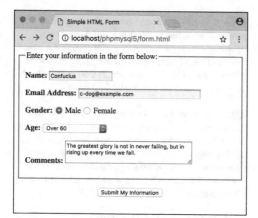

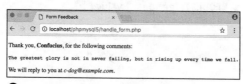

A To test `handle_form.php`, you must load the form through a URL, then fill it out and submit it.

B The script should display results like this.

C If you see the PHP code after submitting the form, the problem is likely that you did not access the form through a URL.

3. Print out the received name, email, and comments values:

```
echo "<p>Thank you, <strong>
→ $name</strong>, for the
→ following comments:</p>
<pre>$comments</pre>
<p>We will reply to you at
→ <em>$email</em>.</p>\n";
```

The submitted values are simply printed out using the **echo** statement, double quotation marks, and a wee bit of HTML formatting.

4. Complete the page:

```
?>
</body>
</html>
```

5. Save the file as **handle_form.php** and place it in the same web directory as **form.html**.

6. Test both documents in your browser by loading **form.html** through a URL (**http://something**) and then filling out **A** and submitting the form **B**.

Because the PHP script must be run through a URL (see Chapter 1), the form must also be run through a URL. Otherwise, when you go to submit the form, you'll see PHP code **C** instead of the proper result **B**.

TIP $_REQUEST is a special variable type, known as a superglobal. It stores all of the data sent to a PHP page through either the GET or POST method, as well as data accessible in cookies. Superglobals will be discussed later in the chapter.

TIP If you have any problems with this script, apply the debugging techniques suggested in Chapter 1. If you still can't solve the problem, check out the extended debugging techniques listed in Chapter 8, "Error Handling and Debugging." If you're still stymied, turn to the book's supporting forum for assistance (LarryUllman.com/forums/).

TIP If the PHP script shows blank spaces where a variable's value should have been printed, it means that the variable has no value. The two most likely causes are 1) you failed to enter a value in the form, or 2) you misspelled or mis-capitalized the variable's name.

TIP If you see any Undefined variable: variablename errors, this is because the variables you refer to have no value and PHP is set on the highest level of error reporting. The previous tip provides suggestions as to why a variable wouldn't have a value. Chapter 8 discusses error reporting in detail.

TIP To see how PHP handles the different form input types, print out the $_REQUEST['age'] and $_REQUEST['gender'] values 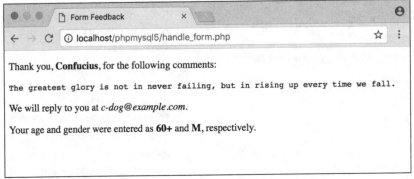.

D The values of gender and age correspond to those defined in the form's HTML.

Conditionals and Operators

PHP's three primary terms for creating conditionals are **if**, **else**, and **elseif**.

Every conditional begins with an **if** clause:

```
if (condition) {
    // Do something!
}
```

An **if** can also have an **else** clause:

```
if (condition) {
} else {
    // Do something else!
}   // Do something!
```

An **elseif** clause allows you to add more conditions:

```
if (condition1) {
    // Do something!
} elseif (condition2) {
    // Do something else!
} else {
    // Do something different!
}
```

If a condition is true, the code in the following braces (**{}**) will be executed. If not, PHP will continue on. If there is a second condition (after an **elseif**), that will be checked for truth. The process will continue—you can use as many **elseif** clauses as you want—until PHP hits an **else**, which will be automatically executed at that point, or until the conditional terminates without an **else**. For this reason, it's important that the **else** always come last and be treated as the default action unless specific criteria—the conditions—are met.

A condition can be true in PHP for any number of reasons. To start, these are true conditions:

- **$var**, if **$var** has a value other than 0, an empty string, **FALSE**, or **NULL**
- **isset($var)**, if **$var** has any value other than **NULL**, including 0, **FALSE**, or an empty string
- **TRUE**, **true**, **True**, etc.

In the second example, a new function, **isset()**, is introduced. This function checks if a variable is "set," meaning that it has a value other than **NULL** (as a reminder, **NULL** is a special type in PHP, representing no set value). You can also use the comparative and logical operators (**Table 2.2**) in conjunction with parentheses to make more complicated expressions.

TABLE 2.2 Comparative and Logical Operators

Symbol	Meaning	Type	Example
==	is equal to	comparison	$x = = $y
!=	is not equal to	comparison	$x != $y
<	less than	comparison	$x < $y
>	greater than	comparison	$x > $y
<=	less than or equal to	comparison	$x <= $y
>=	greater than or equal to	comparison	$x >= $y
!	not	logical	!$x
&&	and	logical	$x && $y
and	and	logical	$x and $y
||	or	logical	$x || $y
or	or	logical	$x or $y
xor	exclusive or	logical	$x xor $y

To use conditionals:

1. Open **handle_form.php** (refer to Script 2.2) in your text editor or IDE, if it is not already.

2. Before the **echo** statement, add a conditional that creates a **$gender** variable (**Script 2.3**):

```php
if (isset($_REQUEST['gender'])) {
    $gender = $_REQUEST['gender'];
} else {
    $gender = NULL;
}
```

This is a simple and effective way to validate a form input (particularly a radio button, check box, or select). If the user checks either gender radio button, then **$_REQUEST['gender']** will have a value, meaning that the condition **isset($_REQUEST['gender'])** is true. In such a case, the shorthand version of this variable—**$gender**—is assigned the value of **$_REQUEST['gender']**, repeating the technique used with **$name**, **$email**, and **$comments**. If the user does not click one of the radio buttons, then this condition is not true, and **$gender** is assigned the value of **NULL**, indicating that it has no value. Notice that **NULL** is not in quotes.

3. After the **echo** statement, add another conditional that prints a message based on **$gender**'s value:

```php
if ($gender == 'M') {
    echo '<p><strong>Good day,
    → Sir!</strong></p>';
} elseif ($gender == 'F') {
    echo '<p><strong>Good day,
    → Madam!</strong></p>';
} else { // No gender selected.
    echo '<p><strong>You forgot to
    → enter your gender!</strong>
    → </p>';
}
```

Script 2.3 In this remade version of **handle_form.php**, two conditionals are used to validate the gender radio buttons.

```php
1   <!doctype html>
2   <html lang="en">
3   <head>
4       <meta charset="utf-8">
5       <title>Form Feedback</title>
6   </head>
7   <body>
8   <?php # Script 2.3 - handle_form.php #2
9
10  // Create a shorthand for the form data:
11  $name = $_REQUEST['name'];
12  $email = $_REQUEST['email'];
13  $comments = $_REQUEST['comments'];
14
15  // Create the $gender variable:
16  if (isset($_REQUEST['gender'])) {
17      $gender = $_REQUEST['gender'];
18  } else {
19      $gender = NULL;
20  }
21
22  // Print the submitted information:
23  echo "<p>Thank you, <strong>$name
    </strong>, for the following comments:
    </p>
24  <pre>$comments</pre>
25  <p>We will reply to you at <em>$email
    </em>.</p>\n";
26
27  // Print a message based upon the gender
    value:
28  if ($gender == 'M') {
29      echo '<p><strong>Good day,
        Sir!</strong></p>';
30  } elseif ($gender == 'F') {
31      echo '<p><strong>Good day,
32  Madam!</strong></p>';
33  } else { // No gender selected.
34      echo '<p><strong>You forgot to
        enter your gender!</strong></p>';
35  }
36
37  ?>
38  </body>
39  </html>
```

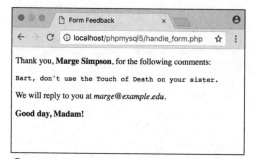

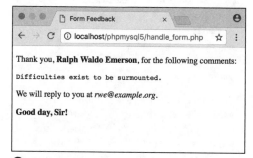

A The gender-based conditional prints a different message for each choice in the form.

B The same script will produce different salutations (compare with **A**) when the gender value changes.

This **if-elseif-else** conditional looks at the value of the **$gender** variable and prints a different message for each possibility. It's very important to remember that the double equals sign (==) means equals, whereas a single equals sign (=) assigns a value. The distinction is important because the condition **$gender == 'M'** may or may not be true, but **$gender = 'M'** will always be true.

Also, the values used here—*M* and *F*—must be exactly the same as those in the HTML form (the values for each radio button). Equality is a case-sensitive comparison with strings, so *m* will not equal *M*.

4. Save the file, place it in your web directory, and test it in your browser **A**, **B**, and **C**.

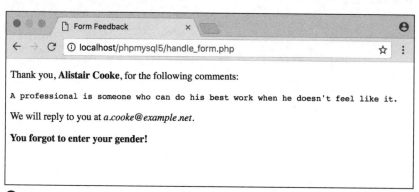

C If no gender was selected, a message is printed indicating the oversight to the user.

TIP Although PHP has no strict formatting rules, it's standard procedure and good programming form to make it clear when one block of code is a subset of a conditional. Indenting the block is the norm.

TIP You can—and frequently will—nest conditionals (place one inside another).

TIP The first conditional in this script (the `isset()`) is a perfect example of how to use a default value. The assumption (the `else`) is that `$gender` has a NULL value unless the one condition is met: that `$_REQUEST['gender']` is set.

TIP The braces used to indicate the beginning and end of a conditional are not required if you are executing only one statement. I recommend that you almost always use them, though, as a matter of clarity.

TIP Both `and` and `or` have two representative operators, with slight technical differences between them. For no particular reason, I tend to use `&&` and `||` instead of `and` and `or`.

TIP XOR is called the exclusive or operator. The conditional `$x xor $y` is true if `$x` is true or if `$y` is true, but not both.

Switch

PHP has another type of conditional, called the **switch**, best used in place of a long **if-elseif-else** conditional. The syntax of **switch** is

```
switch ($variable) {
  case 'value1':
    // Do this.
    break;
  case 'value2':
    // Do this instead.
    break;
default:
  // Do this then.
  break;
}
```

The **switch** conditional compares the value of **$variable** to the different cases. When it finds a match, the following code is executed, up until the **break**. If no match is found, the **default** is executed, assuming it exists (it's optional). The **switch** conditional is limited in its usage in that it can only check a variable's value for equality against certain cases; more complex conditions cannot be easily checked.

Validating Form Data

A critical concept related to handling HTML forms is that of validating form data. In terms of both error management and security, you should absolutely never trust the data being submitted by an HTML form. Whether erroneous data is purposefully malicious or just unintentionally inappropriate, it's up to you—the web architect—to test it against expectations.

Validating form data requires the use of conditionals and any number of functions, operators, and expressions. One standard function to be used is **isset()**, which tests if a variable has a value (including 0, **FALSE**, or an empty string, but not **NULL**). You saw an example of this in the preceding script.

One issue with the **isset()** function is that an empty string tests as true, meaning that **isset()** is not an effective way to validate text inputs and text boxes from an HTML form. To check that a user typed something into textual elements, you can use the **empty()** function. It checks if a variable has an *empty* value: an empty string, 0, **NULL**, or **FALSE**.

The first aim of form validation is seeing if *something* was entered or selected in form elements. The second goal is to ensure that submitted data is of the right type (numeric, string, etc.), of the right format (like an email address), or a specific acceptable value (like **$gender** being equal to either *M* or *F*). Since handling forms is a main use of PHP, validating form data is a point that will be reemphasized time and again in subsequent chapters. But first, let's create a new **handle_form.php** to make sure variables have values before they're referenced (there will be enough changes in this version that simply updating Script 2.3 doesn't make sense).

The NULL Coalescing Operator

New in PHP 7 is the NULL coalescing operator (**??**), which simplifies checking whether a variable is set. Take this common construct (from Script 2.3):

```
if (isset($_REQUEST['gender'])) {
  $gender = $_REQUEST['gender'];
} else {
  $gender = NULL;
}
```

In PHP 7, this could be more succinctly written as

```
$gender = $_REQUEST['gender'] ?? NULL;
```

The meaning is the same: if **$_REQUEST['gender']** has a value, assign that value to **$gender**; otherwise, assign **NULL** to **$gender**.

Because PHP 7 hasn't been widely adopted yet, the book's scripts won't make use of this operator, but feel free to do so if you are running PHP 7 or higher.

To validate your forms:

1. Begin a new PHP script in your text editor or IDE, to be named **handle_form.php**, starting with the initial HTML (**Script 2.4**):

```
<!doctype html>
<html lang="en">
<head>
  <meta charset="utf-8">
  <title>Form Feedback</title>
</head>
<body>
```

2. Within the HTML **head**, add some CSS code:

```
<style type="text/css"
→ title="text/css" media="all">
.error {
  font-weight: bold;
  color: #C00;
}
</style>
```

This code defines one CSS class, called *error*. Any HTML element that has this class name will be formatted in a bold red color (which will be more apparent in your browser than in this black-and-white book).

3. In the PHP block, check if the name was entered:

```
if (!empty($_REQUEST['name'])) {
  $name = $_REQUEST['name'];
} else {
  $name = NULL;
  echo '<p class="error">You
  → forgot to enter your name!</p>';
}
```

Script 2.4 Validating HTML form data before you use it is critical to web security and achieving professional results. Here, conditionals check that every referenced form element has a value.

```
1   <!doctype html>
2   <html lang="en">
3   <head>
4       <meta charset="utf-8">
5       <title>Form Feedback</title>
6       <style type="text/css">
7       .error {
8           font-weight: bold;
9           color: #C00;
10      }
11      </style>
12  </head>
13  <body>
14  <?php # Script 2.4 - handle_form.php #3
15
16  // Validate the name:
17  if (!empty($_REQUEST['name'])) {
18      $name = $_REQUEST['name'];
19  } else {
20      $name = NULL;
21      echo '<p class="error">You forgot to
            enter your name!</p>';
22  }
23
24  // Validate the email:
25  if (!empty($_REQUEST['email'])) {
26      $email = $_REQUEST['email'];
27  } else {
28      $email = NULL;
29      echo '<p class="error">You forgot to
            enter your email address!</p>';
30  }
31
32  // Validate the comments:
33  if (!empty($_REQUEST['comments'])) {
34      $comments = $_REQUEST['comments'];
35  } else {
36      $comments = NULL;
37      echo '<p class="error">You forgot to
            enter your comments!</p>';
38  }
39
```

code continues on next page

```
40    // Validate the gender:
41    if (isset($_REQUEST['gender'])) {
42
43        $gender = $_REQUEST['gender'];
44
45        if ($gender == 'M') {
46            $greeting = '<p><strong>Good day,
              Sir!</strong></p>';
47        } elseif ($gender == 'F') {
48            $greeting = '<p><strong>Good day,
              Madam!</strong></p>';
49        } else { // Unacceptable value.
50            $gender = NULL;
51            echo '<p class="error">Gender
              should be either "M" or "F"!
              </p>';
52        }
53
54    } else { // $_REQUEST['gender']
      is not set.
55        $gender = NULL;
56        echo '<p class="error">You forgot to
          select your gender!</p>';
57    }
58
59    // If everything is OK, print the
      message:
60    if ($name && $email && $gender &&
      $comments) {
61
62        echo "<p>Thank you, <strong>$name
          </strong>, for the following
          comments:</p>
63        <pre>$comments</pre>
64        <p>We will reply to you at <em>$email
          </em>.</p>\n";
65
66        echo $greeting;
67
68    } else { // Missing form value.
69        echo '<p class="error">Please go back
          and fill out the form again.</p>';
70    }
71
72    ?>
73    </body>
74    </html>
```

A simple way to check that a form text input was filled out is to use the **empty()** function. If **$_REQUEST['name']** has a value other than an empty string, 0, **NULL**, or **FALSE**, assume that their name was entered and a shorthand variable is assigned that value. If **$_REQUEST['name']** is empty, the **$name** variable is set to **NULL** and an error message is printed. This error message uses the CSS class.

4. Repeat the same process for the email address and comments:

```
if (!empty($_REQUEST['email'])) {
  $email = $_REQUEST['email'];
} else {
  $email = NULL;
  echo '<p class="error">You
→ forgot to enter your email
→ address!</p>';
}
if (!empty($_REQUEST['comments'])) {
  $comments = $_REQUEST['comments'];
} else {
  $comments = NULL;
  echo '<p class="error">You
→ forgot to enter your
→ comments!</p>';
}
```

Both variables receive the same treatment as **$_REQUEST['name']** in Step 3.

continues on next page

5. Begin validating the gender variable:

```
if (isset($_REQUEST['gender'])) {
    $gender = $_REQUEST['gender'];
```

The validation of the gender is a two-step process. First, check if it has a value or not, using **isset()**. This starts the main **if-else** conditional, which otherwise behaves like those for the name, email address, and comments.

6. Check **$gender** against specific values:

```
if ($gender == 'M') {
    $greeting = '<p><strong>Good
    → day, Sir!</strong></p>';
} elseif ($gender == 'F') {
    $greeting = '<p><strong>Good
    → day, Madam!</strong></p>';
} else { // Unacceptable value.
    $gender = NULL;
    echo '<p class="error">Gender
    → should be either "M" or
    → "F"!</p>';
}
```

Within the gender **if** clause is a nested **if-elseif-else** conditional that tests the variable's value against what's acceptable. This is the second part of the two-step gender validation.

The conditions themselves are the same as those in the last script. If gender does not end up being equal to either *M* or *F*, a problem occurred and an error message will be printed. The **$gender** variable is also set to **NULL** in such cases, because it has an unacceptable value.

If **$gender** does have a valid value, a gender-specific message is assigned to a new variable so that the message can be printed later in the script.

7. Complete the main gender **if-else** conditional:

```
} else { // $_REQUEST['gender']
→ is not set.
    $gender = NULL;
    echo '<p class="error">You
forgot to select your gender!
→ </p>';
}
```

This **else** clause applies if **$_REQUEST['gender']** is not set. The complete, nested conditionals (see lines 41–57 of Script 2.4) successfully check every possibility:

▸ **$_REQUEST['gender']** is not set

▸ **$_REQUEST['gender']** has a value of *M*

▸ **$_REQUEST['gender']** has a value of *F*

▸ **$_REQUEST['gender']** has some other value

You may wonder how this last case may be possible, considering the values are set in the HTML form. If a malicious user creates their own form that gets submitted to your **handle_form.php** script (which is very easy to do), they could give **$_REQUEST['gender']** any value they want.

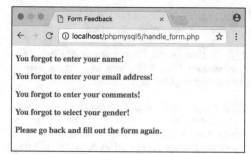

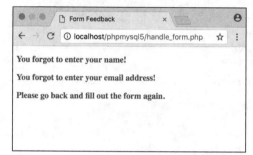

A The script now checks that every form element was filled out (except the age) and reports on those that weren't.

B If you skip even one or two fields, the *Thank you* message is not printed.

8. Print messages indicating the validation results:

```
if ($name && $email && $gender
→ && $comments) {
  echo "<p>Thank you, <strong>
  → $name</strong>, for the
  → following comments:<br>
  <pre>$comments</pre></p>
  <p>We will reply to you at
  → <em>$email</em>.</p>\n";
  echo $greeting;
} else { // Missing form value.
  echo '<p class="error">Please
  → go back and fill out the form
  → again.</p>';
}
```

The main condition is true if every listed variable has a true value. Each variable will have a value if it passed its test but have a value of **NULL** if it didn't. If every variable has a value, the form was completed, so the *Thank you* message will be printed, as will the gender-specific greeting. If any of the variables are **NULL**, the second message will be printed (**A** and **B**).

continues on next page

9. Close the PHP section and complete the HTML page:

```
?>
</body>
</html>
```

10. Save the file as `handle_form.php`, place it in the same web directory as `form.html`, and test it in your browser.

Fill out the form to different levels of completeness to test the new script 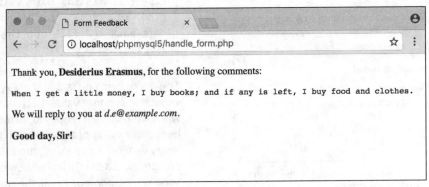.

TIP To test if a submitted value is a number, use the `is_numeric()` function.

TIP In Chapter 14, "Perl-Compatible Regular Expressions," you'll see how to validate form data using regular expressions.

TIP It's considered good form (pun intended) to let users know which fields are required when they're filling out the form and, where applicable, the format of that field (like a date or a phone number).

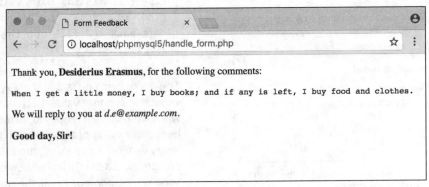

Form Feedback

localhost/phpmysql5/handle_form.php

Thank you, **Desiderius Erasmus**, for the following comments:

`When I get a little money, I buy books; and if any is left, I buy food and clothes.`

We will reply to you at *d.e@example.com*.

Good day, Sir!

Ⓒ If the form was completed properly, the script behaves as it previously had.

TABLE 2.3 Array Example 1: `$artists`

Key	Value
0	The Mynabirds
1	Jeremy Messersmith
2	The Shins
3	Iron and Wine
4	Alexi Murdoch

TABLE 2.4 Array Example 2: `$states`

Key	Value
MD	Maryland
PA	Pennsylvania
IL	Illinois
MO	Missouri
IA	Iowa

Introducing Arrays

Chapter 1 introduced two *scalar* (single-valued) variable types: strings and numbers. Now it's time to learn about another type: the *array*. Unlike strings and numbers, an *array* can hold multiple separate pieces of information. An array is therefore like a list of values, each value being a string or a number or even another array.

Arrays are structured as a series of *key-value* pairs, where one pair is an item or *element* of that array. For each item in the list, there is a *key* (or *index*) associated with it (**Table 2.3**).

PHP supports two kinds of arrays: *indexed*, which use numbers as the keys (as in Table 2.3), and *associative*, which use strings as keys (**Table 2.4**). As in most programming languages, with indexed arrays, arrays will begin with the first index at 0, unless you specify the keys explicitly.

An array follows the same naming rules as any other variable. This means that, offhand, you might not be able to tell that **$var** is an array as opposed to a string or number. The important syntactical difference arises when accessing individual array elements.

To refer to a specific value in an array, start with the array variable name, followed by the key within brackets:

```
$band = $artists[0]; // The Mynabirds
echo $states['MD']; // Maryland
```

You can see that the array keys are used like other values in PHP: numbers (e.g., 0) are never quoted, whereas strings (*MD*) must be.

continues on next page

Because arrays use a different syntax than other variables and can contain multiple values, printing them can be trickier. This will not work **A**:

```php
echo "My list of states: $states";
```

However, printing an individual element's value is simple if it uses indexed (numeric) keys:

```php
echo "The first artist is
→ $artists[0].";
```

But if the array uses strings for the keys, the quotes used to surround the key will muddle the syntax. The following code will cause a parse error **B**:

```php
echo "IL is $states['IL']."; // BAD!
```

To fix this, wrap the array name and key in braces when an array uses strings for its keys **C**:

```php
echo "IL is {$states['IL']}.";
```

If arrays seem slightly familiar to you already, that's because you've already worked with two: **$_SERVER** (in Chapter 1) and **$_REQUEST** (in this chapter). To acquaint you with another array and to practice printing array values directly, one final, but basic, version of the **handle_form.php** page will be created using the more specific **$_POST** array (see the sidebar "Superglobal Arrays").

My list of states: Array

A Attempting to print an array using only the variable's name results in the word *Array* being printed.

Parse error: syntax error, unexpected '' (T_ENCAPSED_AND_WHITESPACE), expecting '-' or identifier (T_STRING) or variable (T_VARIABLE) or number (T_NUM_STRING) in /Users/larry/Sites/test.php on line *18*

B Attempting to print an element in an associative array without using braces results in a parse error.

IL is Illinois.

C Attempting to print an element in an associative array while using braces works as desired.

To use arrays:

1. Begin a new PHP script in your text editor or IDE, to be named **handle_form.php**, starting with the initial HTML (**Script 2.5**):

```
<!doctype html>
<html lang="en">
<head>
    <meta charset="utf-8">
    <title>Form Feedback</title>
</head>
<body>
<?php # Script 2.5 -
→ handle_form.php #4
```

2. Perform some basic form validation:

```
if ( !empty($_POST['name']) &&
→ !empty($_POST['comments']) &&
→ !empty($_POST['email']) ) {
```

In the previous version of this script, the values are accessed by referring to the **$_REQUEST** array. But since these variables come from a form that uses the POST method (see Script 2.1), **$_POST** would be a more exact, and therefore more secure, reference.

This conditional checks that these three text inputs are all not empty. Using the *and* operator (**&&**), the entire conditional is only true if each of the three subconditionals is true.

3. Print the message:

```
echo "<p>Thank you, <strong>
→ {$_POST['name']}</strong>, for
→ the following comments:</p>
<pre>{$_POST['comments']}</pre>
<p>We will reply to you at <em>
→ {$_POST['email']}</em>.</p>\n";
```

continues on next page

Script 2.5 The superglobal variables, like **$_POST** here, are just one type of array you'll use in PHP.

```
1    <!doctype html>
2    <html lang="en">
3    <head>
4        <meta charset="utf-8">
5        <title>Form Feedback</title>
6    </head>
7    <body>
8    <?php # Script 2.5 - handle_form.php #4
9
10   // Print the submitted information:
11   if ( !empty($_POST['name']) && !empty($_POST['comments']) && !empty($_POST['email']) ) {
12       echo "<p>Thank you, <strong>{$_POST['name']}</strong>, for the following
         comments:</p>
13       <pre>{$_POST['comments']}</pre>
14       <p>We will reply to you at <em>{$_POST['email']}</em>.</p>\n";
15   } else { // Missing form value.
16       echo '<p>Please go back and fill out the form again.</p>';
17   }
18   ?>
19   </body>
20   </html>
```

After you comprehend the concept of an array, you still need to master the syntax involved in printing one. When printing an array element that uses a string for its key, use the braces (as in **{$_POST['name']}** here) to avoid parse errors.

4. Complete the conditional begun in Step 2:

```
} else { // Missing form value.
  echo '<p>Please go back and
  → fill out the form again.</p>';
}
```

If any of the three subconditionals in Step 2 is not true (which is to say, if any of the variables has an empty value), then this **else** clause applies and an error message is printed 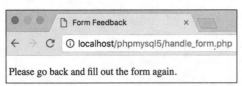.

5. Complete the PHP and HTML code:

```
?>
</body>
</html>
```

6. Save the file as **handle_form.php**, place it in the same web directory as **form.html**, and test it in your browser **E**.

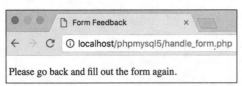

D If any of the three tested form inputs is empty, this generic error message is printed.

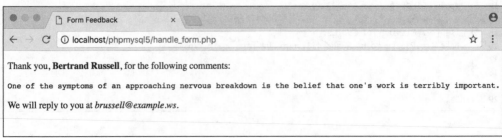

E The fact that the script now uses the **$_POST** array has no effect on the visible result.

TIP Because PHP is lax with its variable structures, an array can even use a combination of numbers and strings as its keys. The only important rule is that the keys of an array must each be unique.

TIP If you find the syntax of accessing superglobal arrays directly to be confusing (e.g., **$_POST['name']**), you can continue to use the shorthand technique at the top of your scripts as you have been:

```
$name = $_POST['name'];
```

In this script, you would then need to change the conditional and the **echo** statement to refer to $name and the other elements.

TIP You only need to use the braces to surround an associated array used within quotation marks. All of these array references are fine:

```
echo $_POST['name'];
echo "The first item is $item[0].";
$total = number_format($cart
→ ['total']);
```

Creating arrays

The preceding example uses a PHP-generated array, but there will frequently be times when you want to create your own. You can define your own array in one of two primary ways. First, you can add an element at a time to build one:

```
$band[] = 'Jemaine';
$band[] = 'Bret';
$band[] = 'Murray';
```

As arrays are indexed starting at 0, **$band[0]** has a value of *Jemaine*; **$band[1]**, *Bret*; and **$band[2]**, *Murray*.

Alternatively, you can specify the key when adding an element. But it's important to understand that if you specify a key and a value already exists indexed with that same key, the new value will overwrite the existing one:

```
$band['fan'] = 'Mel';
$band['fan'] = 'Dave'; // New value
$fruit[2] = 'apple';
$fruit[2] = 'orange'; // New value
```

Instead of adding one element at a time, you can use the **array()** function to build an entire array in one step:

```
$states = array(
  'IA' => 'Iowa',
  'MD' => 'Maryland'
);
```

(As PHP is generally insensitive to white space, you can use this function over multiple lines and indent the array elements for added clarity.)

The **array()** function can be used whether or not you explicitly set the key:

```
$artists = array('Clem Snide',
→'Shins', 'Eels');
```

Or, if you set the first numeric key value, the added values will be keyed incrementally thereafter:

```
$days = array(1 => 'Sun', 'Mon', 'Tue');
echo $days[3]; // Tue
```

The **array()** function is also used to initialize an array prior to referencing it:

```
$tv = array();
$tv[] = 'Flight of the Conchords';
```

Initializing an array (or any variable) in PHP isn't required, but it makes for clearer code and can help avoid errors.

As of PHP 5.4, you can use the short array syntax instead of the **array()** function. These lines are equivalent to the previous examples:

```
$states = [
  'IA' => 'Iowa',
  'MD' => 'Maryland'
];
$artists = ['Clem Snide', 'Shins',
→'Eels'];
$days = [1 => 'Sun', 'Mon', 'Tue'];
$tv = [];
```

Finally, if you want to create an array of sequential numbers, you can use the **range()** function:

```
$ten = range(1, 10);
```

Accessing entire arrays

You've already seen how to access individual array elements using its keys (e.g., **$_POST['email']**). This works when you know exactly what the keys are or if you want to refer to only a single element. To access every array element, use the **foreach** loop:

```
foreach ($array as $value) {
  // Do something with $value.
}
```

continues on next page

The **foreach** loop will iterate through every element in **$array**, assigning each element's value to the **$value** variable. To access both the keys and values, use

```
foreach ($array as $key => $value) {
  echo "The value at $key is $value.";
}
```

(You can use any valid variable name in place of **$key** and **$value**, like just **$k** and **$v**, if you prefer.)

Using arrays, this next script will demonstrate how easy it is to make a set of form pull-down menus for selecting a date 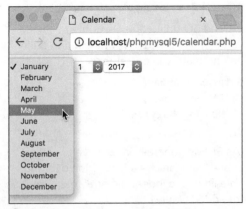.

To create and access arrays:

1. Begin a new PHP document in your text editor or IDE, to be named **calendar.php**, starting with the initial HTML (**Script 2.6**):

```
<!doctype html>
<html lang="en">
<head>
  <meta charset="utf-8">
  <title>Calendar</title>
</head>
<body>
<form action="calendar.php"
→ method="post">
<?php # Script 2.9 - calendar.php #2
```

One thing to note here is that even though the page won't contain a complete HTML form, the form tags are still required to create the pull-down menus.

2. Create an array for the months:

```
$months = [1 => 'January',
→'February', 'March', 'April',
→'May', 'June', 'July', 'August',
→'September', 'October',
→'November', 'December'];
```

Script 2.6 This form uses arrays to dynamically create three pull-down menus.

```
1    <!doctype html>
2    <html lang="en">
3    <head>
4        <meta charset="utf-8">
5        <title>Calendar</title>
6    </head>
7    <body>
8    <form action="calendar.php"
     method="post">
9    <?php # Script 2.6 - calendar.php
10
11   // This script makes three pull-down
     menus
12   // for an HTML form: months, days,
     years.
13
14   // Make the months array:
15   $months = [1 => 'January',
     'February', 'March', 'April',
     'May', 'June', 'July', 'August',
     'September', 'October', 'November',
     'December'];
16
```

code continues on next page

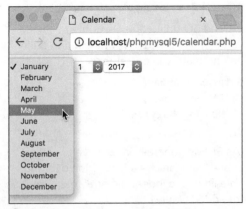

F These pull-down menus will be created using arrays and the **foreach** loop.

Script 2.6 *continued*

```
17    // Make the days and years arrays:
18    $days = range(1, 31);
19    $years = range(2017, 2027);
20
21    // Make the months pull-down menu:
22    echo '<select name="month">';
23    foreach ($months as $key => $value) {
24        echo "<option value=\"$key\">
          $value</option>\n";
25    }
26    echo '</select>';
27
28    // Make the days pull-down menu:
29    echo '<select name="day">';
30    foreach ($days as $value) {
31        echo "<option value=\"$value\">
          $value</option>\n";
32    }
33    echo '</select>';
34
35    // Make the years pull-down menu:
36    echo '<select name="year">';
37    foreach ($years as $value) {
38        echo "<option value=\"$value\">
          $value</option>\n";
39    }
40    echo '</select>';
41
42    ?>
43    </form>
44    </body>
45    </html>
```

```
1  <!doctype html>
2  <html lang="en">
3  <head>
4      <meta charset="utf-8">
5      <title>Calendar</title>
6  </head>
7  <body>
8  <form action="calendar.php" method="post">
9  <select name="month"><option value="1">January</option>
10 <option value="2">February</option>
11 <option value="3">March</option>
12 <option value="4">April</option>
13 <option value="5">May</option>
14 <option value="6">June</option>
15 <option value="7">July</option>
16 <option value="8">August</option>
17 <option value="9">September</option>
18 <option value="10">October</option>
19 <option value="11">November</option>
20 <option value="12">December</option>
21 </select><select name="day"><option value="1">1</option>
22 <option value="2">2</option>
23 <option value="3">3</option>
24 <option value="4">4</option>
25 <option value="5">5</option>
26 <option value="6">6</option>
27 <option value="7">7</option>
28 <option value="8">8</option>
```

G Most of the HTML source was generated by just a few lines of PHP.

This first array will use numbers for the keys, from 1 to 12. Since the value of the first key is specified, the following values will be indexed incrementally (in other words, the **1 =>** code creates an array indexed from 1 to 12, instead of from 0 to 11).

3. Create the arrays for the days of the month and the years:

```
$days = range(1, 31);
$years = range(2017, 2027);
```

Using the **range()** function, you can easily make an array of numbers.

4. Generate the month pull-down menu:

```
echo '<select name="month">';
foreach ($months as $key =>
→ $value) {
  echo "<option value=\"$key\">
  → $value</option>\n";
}
echo '</select>';
```

The **foreach** loop can quickly generate all of the HTML code for the month pull-down menu. Each execution of the loop will create a line of code like **<option value="1">January</option>** **G**.

5. Generate the day and year pull-down menus:

```
echo '<select name="day">';
foreach ($days as $value) {
  echo "<option value=\"$value\">
  → $value</option>\n";
}
```

continues on next page

```
echo '</select>';

// Make the years pull-down menu:
echo '<select name="year">';
foreach ($years as $value) {
   echo "<option value=\"$value\">
   → $value</option>\n";
}
echo '</select>';
```

Unlike the month example, both the day and year pull-down menus will use the same data for the option's value and label (a number, Ⓖ). For that reason, there's no need to also fetch the array's key with each loop iteration.

6. Close the PHP, the form tag, and the HTML page:

```
?>
</form>
</body>
</html>
```

7. Save the file as **calendar.php**, place it in your web directory, and test it in your browser.

TIP To determine the number of elements in an array, use count():

```
$num = count($array);
```

TIP The range() function can also create an array of sequential letters:

```
$alphabet = range('a', 'z');
```

TIP An array's key can be multi-worded strings, such as *first name* or *phone number*.

TIP The is_array() function confirms that a variable is of the array type.

TIP If you see an *Invalid argument supplied for foreach()* error message, that means you are trying to use a foreach loop on a variable that is not an array.

Multidimensional arrays

When introducing arrays, I mentioned that an array's values could be any combination of numbers, strings, and even other arrays. This last option—an array consisting of other arrays—creates a *multidimensional array*.

Multidimensional arrays are much more common than you might expect but remarkably easy to work with. As an example, start with an array of prime numbers:

```
$primes = [2, 3, 5, 7, ...];
```

Then create an array of *sphenic* numbers (don't worry: I had no idea what a sphenic number was either; I had to look it up):

```
$sphenic = [30, 42, 66, 70, ...];
```

These two arrays could be combined into one multidimensional array like so:

```
$numbers = [
   'Primes' => $primes,
   'Sphenic' => $sphenic
];
```

Now, **$numbers** is a multidimensional array. To access the prime numbers subarray, refer to **$numbers['Primes']**. To access the prime number 5, use **$numbers['Primes'][2]** (it's the third element in the array, but the array starts indexing at 0). To print out one of these values, surround the whole construct in braces:

```
echo "The first sphenic number is
→ {$numbers['Sphenic'][0]}.";
```

Of course, you can also access multidimensional arrays using the **foreach** loop, nesting one inside another if necessary. This next example will do just that.

Script 2.7 The multidimensional array is created by using other arrays for its values. Two **foreach** loops, one nested inside the other, can access every array element.

```
1    <!doctype html>
2    <html lang="en">
3    <head>
4       <meta charset="utf-8">
5    <title>Multidimensional Arrays</title>
6    </head>
7    <body>
8    <p>Some North American States,
     Provinces, and Territories:</p>
9    <?php # Script 2.7 - multi.php
10
11   // Create one array:
12   $mexico = [
13      'YU' => 'Yucatan',
14      'BC' => 'Baja California',
15      'OA' => 'Oaxaca'
16   ];
17
```

code continues on next page

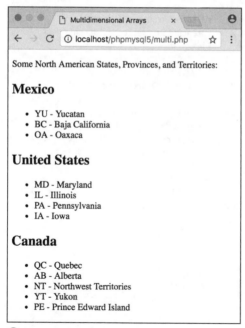

H The end result of running this PHP page (Script 2.7), where each country is printed, followed by an abbreviated list of its states, provinces, and territories.

To use multidimensional arrays:

1. Begin a new PHP document in your text editor or IDE, to be named **multi.php**, beginning with the initial HTML (**Script 2.7**):

```
<!doctype html>
<html lang="en">
<head>
   <meta charset="utf-8">
   <title>Multidimensional
   → Arrays</title>
</head>
<body>
<p>Some North American States,
→ Provinces, and Territories:</p>
<?php # Script 2.7 - multi.php
```

This PHP page will print out some of the states, provinces, and territories found in the three North American countries (Mexico, the United States, and Canada **H**).

2. Create an array of Mexican states:

```
$mexico = [
   'YU' => 'Yucatan',
   'BC' => 'Baja California',
   'OA' => 'Oaxaca'
];
```

This is an associative array, using the state's postal abbreviation as its key. The state's full name is the element's value. This is obviously an incomplete list, just used to demonstrate the concept.

continues on next page

3. Create the second and third arrays:

```
$us = [
   'MD' => 'Maryland',
   'IL' => 'Illinois',
   'PA' => 'Pennsylvania',
   'IA' => 'Iowa'
];
$canada = [
   'QC' => 'Quebec',
   'AB' => 'Alberta',
   'NT' => 'Northwest Territories',
   'YT' => 'Yukon',
   'PE' => 'Prince Edward Island'
];
```

4. Combine all the arrays into one:

```
$n_america = [
   'Mexico' => $mexico,
   'United States' => $us,
   'Canada' => $canada
];
```

You don't have to create three arrays and then assign them to a fourth in order to make the desired multidimensional array, but I think it's easier to read and understand this way (defining a multidimensional array in one step makes for some ugly code).

The **$n_america** array now contains three elements. The key for each element is a string, which is the country's name. The value for each element is the array of states, provinces, and territories found within that country.

5. Begin the primary **foreach** loop:

```
foreach ($n_america as $country
→ => $list) {
   echo "<h2>$country</h2><ul>";
```

Following the syntax outlined earlier, this loop will access every element of **$n_america**. This means that this loop will run three times. Within each

Script 2.7 *continued*

```
18   // Create another array:
19   $us = [
20      'MD' => 'Maryland',
21      'IL' => 'Illinois',
22      'PA' => 'Pennsylvania',
23      'IA' => 'Iowa'
24   ];
25
26   // Create a third array:
27   $canada = [
28      'QC' => 'Quebec',
29      'AB' => 'Alberta',
30      'NT' => 'Northwest Territories',
31      'YT' => 'Yukon',
32      'PE' => 'Prince Edward Island'
33   ];
34
35   // Combine the arrays:
36   $n_america = [
37      'Mexico' => $mexico,
38      'United States' => $us,
39      'Canada' => $canada
40   ];
41
42   // Loop through the countries:
43   foreach ($n_america as $country =>
     $list) {
44
45      // Print a heading:
46      echo "<h2>$country</h2><ul>";
47
48      // Print each state, province,
        or territory:
49      foreach ($list as $k => $v) {
50         echo "<li>$k - $v</li>\n";
51      }
52
53      // Close the list:
54      echo '</ul>';
55
56   } // End of main FOREACH.
57
58   ?>
59   </body>
60   </html>
```

iteration of the loop, the **$country** variable will store the **$n_america** array's key (*Mexico*, *Canada*, or *United States*). Also within each iteration of the loop, the **$list** variable will store the element's value (the equivalent of **$mexico**, **$us**, and **$canada**).

To print out the results, the loop begins by printing the country's name within H2 tags. Because the states and so forth should be displayed as an HTML list, the initial unordered list tag (**<ul>**) is printed as well.

6. Create a second **foreach** loop:

```
foreach ($list as $k => $v) {
  echo "<li>$k - $v</li>\n";
}
```

This loop will run through each subarray (first **$mexico**, then **$us**, and then **$canada**). With each iteration of this loop, **$k** will store the abbreviation and **$v** will store the full name. Both are printed out within HTML list tags. The newline character is also used to better format the HTML source code.

7. Complete the outer **foreach** loop:

```
  echo '</ul>';
} // End of main FOREACH.
```

After the inner **foreach** loop is done, the outer **foreach** loop has to close the unordered list begun in Step 5.

8. Complete the PHP and HTML:

```
?>
</body>
</html>
```

9. Save the file as **multi.php**, place it in your web directory, and test it in your browser ⓗ.

10. If you want, check out the HTML source code to see what PHP created.

TIP Multidimensional arrays can also come from an HTML form. For example, if a form has a series of checkboxes with the name **interests[]**—

```
<input type="checkbox" name=
→"interests[]" value="Music"> Music
<input type="checkbox" name=
→"interests[]" value="Movies"> Movies
<input type="checkbox" name=
→"interests[]" value="Books"> Books
```

—the $_POST variable in the receiving PHP page will be multidimensional. $_POST['interests'] will be an array, with $_POST['interests'][0] storing the value of the first checked box (e.g., Movies), $_POST['interests'][1] storing the second (Books), and so forth. Note that only the checked boxes will get passed to the PHP page.

TIP You can also end up with a multidimensional array if an HTML form's select menu allows for multiple selections:

```
<select name="interests[]"
→ multiple="multiple">
  <option value="Music">Music
  → </option>
  <option value="Movies">Movies
  → </option>
  <option value="Books">Books
  → </option>
  <option value="Napping">Napping
  → </option>
</select>
```

Again, only the selected values will be passed to the PHP page.

Sorting arrays

One of the many advantages arrays have over the other variable types is the ability to sort them. PHP includes several functions you can use for sorting arrays, all simple in syntax:

```
$names = ['Moe', 'Larry', 'Curly'];
sort($names);
```

The sorting functions perform three kinds of sorts. First, you can sort an array by value, discarding the original keys, using **sort()**. It's important to understand that the array's keys will be reset after the sorting process, *so if the key-value relationship is important, you should not use* **sort()**.

Second, you can sort an array by value *while maintaining the keys*, using **asort()**. Third, you can sort an array by key, using **ksort()**. Each of these can sort in reverse order if you change them to **rsort()**, **arsort()**, and **krsort()**, respectively.

To demonstrate the effect sorting arrays will have, this next script will create an array of movie titles and ratings (how much I liked them on a scale of 1 to 10) and then display this list in different ways.

To sort arrays:

1. Begin a new PHP document in your text editor or IDE, to be named **sorting.php**, starting with the initial HTML (**Script 2.8**):

```
<!doctype html>
<html lang="en">
<head>
  <meta charset="utf-8">
  <title>Sorting Arrays</title>
</head>
<body>
```

Arrays and Strings

Because arrays and strings are so commonly used together, PHP has two functions for converting between them:

```
$array = explode(separator, $string);
$string = implode (glue, $array);
```

The key to using and understanding these two functions is the *separator* and *glue* relationships. When turning an array into a string, you establish the glue—the characters or code that will be inserted between the array values in the generated string. Conversely, when turning a string into an array, you specify the separator, which is the token that marks what should become separate array elements. For example, start with a string:

```
$s1 = 'Mon-Tue-Wed-Thu-Fri';
$days_array = explode('-', $s1);
```

The **$days_array** variable is now a five-element array, with *Mon* indexed at **0**, *Tue* indexed at **1**, and so forth.

```
$s2 = implode (', ', $days_array);
```

The **$s2** variable is now a comma-separated list of days: *Mon, Tue, Wed, Thu, Fri*.

Script 2.8 An array is defined and then sorted in two different ways: first by key, then by value (in reverse order).

```
1    <!doctype html>
2    <html lang="en">
3    <head>
4        <meta charset="utf-8">
5        <title>Sorting Arrays</title>
6    </head>
7    <body>
8    <table border="0" cellspacing="3"
     cellpadding="3" align="center">
9    <thead>
10       <tr>
11           <th><h2>Rating</h2></th>
12           <th><h2>Title</h2></th>
13       </tr>
14   </thead>
15   <tbody>
16   <?php # Script 2.8 - sorting.php
17
18   // Create the array:
19   $movies = [
20       'Casablanca' => 10,
21       'To Kill a Mockingbird' => 10,
22       'The English Patient' => 2,
23       'Stranger Than Fiction' => 9,
24       'Story of the Weeping Camel' => 5,
25       'Donnie Darko' => 7
26   ];
27
```

code continues on next page

2. Create an HTML table:

```
<table border="0" cellspacing="3"
  → cellpadding="3" align="center">
<thead>
  <tr>
    <th><h2>Rating</h2></th>
    <th><h2>Title</h2></th>
  </tr>
</thead>
<tbody>
```

To make the ordered list easier to read, it'll be printed within an HTML table. The table is begun here.

3. Add the opening PHP tag and create a new array:

```
<?php # Script 2.8 - sorting.php
$movies = [
    'Casablanca' => 10,
    'To Kill a Mockingbird' => 10,
    'The English Patient' => 2,
    'Stranger Than Fiction' => 9,
    'Story of the Weeping Camel' => 5,
    'Donnie Darko' => 7
];
```

This array uses movie titles as the keys and their respective ratings as their values. This structure will open up several possibilities for sorting the whole list. Feel free to change the movie listings and rankings as you see fit (just don't chastise me for my taste in films).

continues on next page

4. Print out the array as is:

```
echo '<tr><td colspan="2">
→<strong>In their original order:
→</strong></td></tr>';
foreach ($movies as $title =>
→$rating) {
  echo "<tr><td>$rating</td>
  <td>$title</td></tr>\n";
}
```

At this point in the script, the array is in the same order as it was defined. To verify this, print it out. A caption is first printed across both table columns. Then, within the **foreach** loop, the key is printed in the first column and the value in the second. A newline is also printed to improve the readability of the HTML source code.

5. Sort the array alphabetically by title and print it again:

```
ksort($movies);
echo '<tr><td colspan="2">
→<strong>Sorted by title:
→</strong></td></tr>';
foreach ($movies as $title =>
→$rating) {
  echo "<tr><td>$rating</td>
  <td>$title</td></tr>\n";
}
```

The **ksort()** function will sort an array by key, in ascending order, while maintaining the key-value relationship. The rest of the code is a repetition of Step 4.

Script 2.8 *continued*

```
28   // Display the movies in their original
     order:
29   echo '<tr><td colspan="2"><strong>
     In their original order:</strong></td>
     </tr>';
30   foreach ($movies as $title =>
     $rating) {
31       echo "<tr><td>$rating</td>
32       <td>$title</td></tr>\n";
33   }
34
35   // Display the movies sorted by title:
36   ksort($movies);
37   echo '<tr><td colspan="2"><strong>
     Sorted by title:</strong></td></tr>';
38   foreach ($movies as $title =>
     $rating) {
39       echo "<tr><td>$rating</td>
40       <td>$title</td></tr>\n";
41   }
42
43   // Display the movies sorted by rating:
44   arsort($movies);
45   echo '<tr><td colspan="2"><strong>
     Sorted by rating:</strong></td>
     </tr>';
46   foreach ($movies as $title =>
     $rating) {
47       echo "<tr><td>$rating</td>
48       <td>$title</td></tr>\n";
49   }
50
51   ?>
52   </tbody>
53   </table>
54   </body>
55   </html>
```

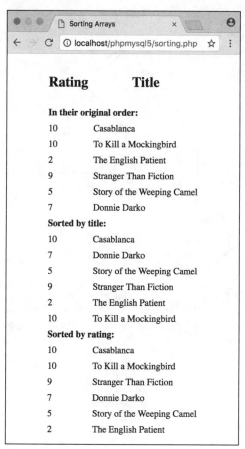

I This page demonstrates different ways arrays can be sorted.

6. Sort the array numerically by descending rating and print again:

```
arsort($movies);
echo '<tr><td colspan="2">
→ <strong>Sorted by rating:
→ </strong></td></tr>';
foreach ($movies as $title =>
→ $rating) {
  echo "<tr><td>$rating</td>
  <td>$title</td></tr>\n";
}
```

To sort by values (the ratings) while maintaining the keys, you would use the **asort()** function. But since the highest-ranking films should be listed first, the order must be reversed, using **arsort()**.

7. Complete the PHP, the table, and the HTML:

```
?>
</tbody>
</table>
</body>
</html>
```

8. Save the file as **sorting.php**, place it in your web directory, and test it in your browser **I**.

TIP To randomize the order of an array, use **shuffle()**.

TIP PHP's **natsort()** function can be used to sort arrays in a more natural order (primarily handling numbers in strings better).

TIP Multidimensional arrays can be sorted in PHP with a little effort. See the PHP manual for more information on the **usort()** function or check out my *PHP Advanced and Object-Oriented Programming: Visual QuickPro Guide* (Peachpit, 2013).

For and While Loops

The last language construct we will discuss in this chapter is the loop. You've already used one, **foreach**, to access every element in an array. The other two types of loops you'll use are **for** and **while**.

The **while** loop looks like this:

```
while (condition) {
    // Do something.
}
```

As long as the *condition* part of the loop is true, the loop will be executed. Once it becomes false, the loop is stopped 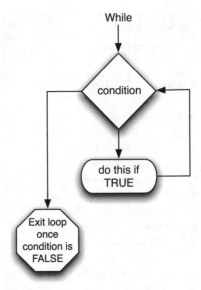. If the condition is never true, the loop will never be executed. The **while** loop will most frequently be used when retrieving results from a database, as you'll see in Chapter 9, "Using PHP with MySQL."

The **for** loop has a more complicated syntax:

```
for (initial expression; condition;
→ closing expression) {
    // Do something.
}
```

Upon first executing the loop, the initial expression is run. Then the condition is checked and, if true, the contents of the loop are executed. After execution, the closing expression is run and the condition is checked again. This process continues until the condition is false 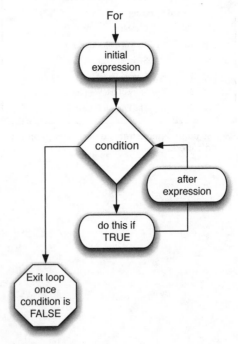. As an example,

```
for ($i = 1; $i <= 10; $i++) {
    echo $i;
}
```

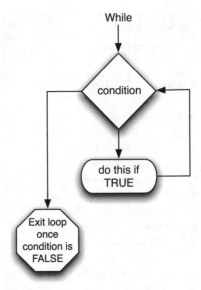

Ⓐ A flowchart representation of how PHP handles a **while** loop.

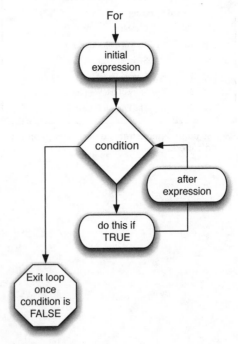

Ⓑ A flowchart representation of how PHP handles the more complex **for** loop.

The first time this loop is run, the **$i** variable is set to the value of 1. Then the condition is checked: is 1 less than or equal to 10? Since this is true, 1 is printed out (**echo $i**). Then, **$i** is incremented to 2 (**$i++**), the condition is checked, and so forth. The result of this script will be the numbers 1 through 10 printed out.

The functionality of both loops is similar enough that **for** and **while** can often be used interchangeably. Still, experience will reveal that the **for** loop is a better choice for doing something *a known number of times*, whereas **while** is used when a condition will be true an *unknown number of times*.

In this chapter's last example, the calendar script created earlier will be rewritten using **for** loops in place of two of the **foreach** loops.

To use loops:

1. Open **calendar.php** (refer to Script 2.6) in your text editor or IDE.

2. Delete the **$days** and **$years** arrays (lines 18–19).

   Using loops, the same result of the two pull-down menus can be achieved without the extra code and memory overhead involved with creating actual arrays. So these two arrays should be deleted, while still keeping the **$months** array.

3. Rewrite the **$days foreach** loop as a **for** loop (Script 2.9):

   ```php
   for ($day = 1; $day <= 31; $day++) {
     echo "<option value=\"$day\">
      $day</option>\n";
   }
   ```

   This standard **for** loop begins by initializing the **$day** variable as 1. It will continue the loop until **$day** is greater than 31, and upon each iteration, **$day** will be incremented by 1. The content of the loop itself (which is executed 31 times) is an **echo** statement.

   continues on next page

Script 2.9 Loops are often used in conjunction with or in lieu of an array. Here, two **for** loops replace the arrays and **foreach** loops used in the script previously.

```
1   <!doctype html>
2   <html lang="en">
3   <head>
4       <meta charset="utf-8">
5       <title>Calendar</title>
6   </head>
7   <body>
8   <form action="calendar.php" method="post">
9   <?php # Script 2.9 - calendar.php #2
10
11  // This script makes three pull-down menus
12  // for an HTML form: months, days, years.
13
14  // Make the months array:
15  $months = [1 => 'January', 'February', 'March', 'April', 'May', 'June', 'July', 'August',
        'September', 'October', 'November', 'December'];
16
```

code continues on next page

4. Rewrite the **$years foreach** loop as a **for** loop:

```
for ($year = 2017; $year <= 2027;
→ $year++) {
  echo "<option value=\"$year\">
  → $year</option>\n";
}
```

The structure of this loop is fundamentally the same as the **$day for** loop, but the **$year** variable is initially set to 2017 instead of 1. As long as **$year** is less than or equal to 2021, the loop will be executed. Within the loop, the **echo** statement is run.

5. Save the file, place it in your web directory, and test it in your browser **C**.

TIP PHP also has a **do...while** loop with a slightly different syntax (check the manual). This loop will always be executed at least once.

TIP When using loops, watch your parameters and conditions to avoid the dreaded infinite loop, which occurs when a loop's condition is never going to be false.

Script 2.9 *continued*

```
17   // Make the months pull-down menu:
18   echo '<select name="month">';
19   foreach ($months as $key => $value) {
20       echo "<option value=\"$key\">$value
         </option>\n";
21   }
22   echo '</select>';
23
24   // Make the days pull-down menu:
25   echo '<select name="day">';
26   for ($day = 1; $day <= 31; $day++) {
27       echo "<option value=\"$day\">$day
         </option>\n";
28   }
29   echo '</select>';
30
31   // Make the years pull-down menu:
32   echo '<select name="year">';
33   for ($year = 2017; $year <= 2027;
     $year++) {
34       echo "<option value=\"$year\">
         $year</option>\n";
35   }
36   echo '</select>';
37
38   ?>
39   </form>
40   </body>
41   </html>
```

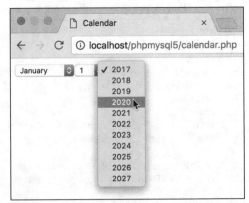

C This calendar form looks the same as it had previously but was created with two fewer arrays (compare Script 2.9 with Script 2.6).

Review and Pursue

If you have any problems with the review questions or the pursue prompts, turn to the book's supporting forum (**LarryUllman.com/forums/**).

Note: Some of these questions and prompts rehash information covered in Chapter 1 in order to reinforce some of the most important points.

Review

- What is the significance of a form's **method** attribute? Of its **action** attribute?

- Why must an HTML form that gets submitted to a PHP script be loaded through a URL? What would happen upon submitting the form if it were not loaded through a URL?

- What are the differences between using single and double quotation marks to delineate strings?

- What control structures were introduced in this chapter?

- What new variable type was introduced in this chapter?

- What operator tests for equality? What is the assignment operator?

- Why are textual form elements validated using **empty()** but other form elements are validated using **isset()**?

- What is the difference between an *indexed* array and an *associative* array?

- With what value do indexed arrays begin (by default)? If an indexed array has ten elements in it, what would the expected index be of the last element in the array?

- What are the *superglobal arrays*? From where do the following superglobals get their values?
  - ▸ **$_GET**
  - ▸ **$_POST**
  - ▸ **$_COOKIE**
  - ▸ **$_REQUEST**
  - ▸ **$_SESSION**
  - ▸ **$_SERVER**
  - ▸ **$_ENV**

- How can you print an individual *indexed* array item? How can you print an individual *associative* array item? Note: There is more than one answer to both questions.

- What does the **count()** function do?

- What impact does printing **\n** have on the browser?

- Generally speaking, when would you use a **while** loop? When would you use a **for** loop? When would you use a **foreach** loop? What is the syntax of each loop type?

- What is the **++** operator? What does it do?

Pursue

- What version of PHP are you using? If you don't know, find out now!

- Create a new form that takes some input from the user (perhaps base it on a form you know you'll need for one of your projects). Then create the PHP script that validates the form data and reports upon the results.

- Rewrite the gender conditional in **handle_form.php** (Script 2.4) as one conditional instead of two nested ones. Hint: You'll need to use the **AND** operator.

- Rewrite **handle_form.php** (Script 2.4) to use **$_POST** instead of **$_REQUEST**.

- Rewrite **handle_form.php** (Script 2.4) so that it validates the age element. Hint: Use the **$gender** validation as a template, this time checking against the corresponding pull-down option values (0–29, 30–60, 60+).

- Rewrite the **echo** statement in the final version of **handle_form.php** (Script 2.5) so that it uses single quotation marks and concatenation instead of double quotation marks.

- If you're using PHP 7 or later, change some of the conditionals to use the NULL coalescing operator instead.

- Look up in the PHP manual one of the array functions introduced in this book. Then check out some of the other array-related functions built into the language.

- Create a new array and then display its elements. Sort the array in different ways and then display the array's contents again.

- Create a form that contains a select menu or series of check boxes that allow for multiple sections. Then, in the handling PHP script, display the selected items along with a count of how many the user selected.

- For added complexity, take the suggested PHP script you just created (that handles multiple selections), and have it display the selections in alphabetical order.

- Learn about form validation in HTML5. This can provide a nicer user experience but does not replace server-side validation, which is always required as client-side validation is easily circumvented.

Creating Dynamic Web Sites

With the fundamentals of PHP under your belt, it's time to begin building truly dynamic web sites. *Dynamic* web sites, as opposed to the static ones on which the web was first built, are easier to maintain, are more responsive to users, and can alter their content in response to differing situations. This chapter introduces three new ideas, all commonly used to create more sophisticated web applications (Chapter 11, "Web Application Development," covers another handful of topics along these same lines).

The first subject involves using external files. This is an important concept, as more complex sites often demand compartmentalizing some HTML or PHP code. Then the chapter returns to the subject of handling HTML forms. You'll learn some new variations on this important and standard aspect of dynamic web sites. Finally, you'll learn how to define and use your own functions.

In This Chapter

Including Multiple Files

To this point, every script in the book has consisted of a single file containing all of the required HTML and PHP code. But as you develop more complex web sites, you'll see that this approach is often not practical. A better way to create dynamic web applications is to divide your scripts and web sites into distinct parts, each part being stored in its own file. Frequently, you will use multiple files to extract the HTML from the PHP or to separate out commonly used processes.

PHP has four functions for incorporating external files: `include()`, `include_once()`, `require()`, and `require_once()`. To use them, your PHP script would have a line like

```
include_once('filename.php');
require('/path/to/filename.html');
```

Using any one of these functions has the end result of taking all the content of the included file and dropping it in the parent script (the one calling the function) at that juncture. An important consideration with included files is that PHP will treat the included code as HTML (i.e., send it directly to the browser) unless the file contains code within the PHP tags.

In terms of functionality, it also doesn't matter what extension the included file uses, be it `.php` or `.html`. However, giving the file a symbolic name and extension helps to convey its purpose (e.g., an included file of HTML might use `.inc.html`). Also, note that you can use either *absolute* or *relative* paths to the included file (see the sidebar for more).

Absolute vs. Relative Paths

When referencing any external item, be it an included file in PHP, a CSS document in HTML, or an image, you have the choice of using either an *absolute* or a *relative* path. An absolute file path references a file starting from the root directory of the computer:

```
include ('C:/php/includes/file.php');
include('/usr/xyz/includes/file.php');
```

Assuming `file.php` exists in the named location, the inclusion will work, no matter the location of the referencing—parent—file, barring any permissions issues. The second example, in case you're not familiar with the syntax, would be a Unix and macOS X absolute path. Absolute paths always start with something like `C:/` or `/`.

A relative path uses the referencing—parent—file as the starting point. To move up one folder, use two periods together. To move into a folder, use its name followed by a slash. So assuming the current script is in the **www/ex1** folder and you want to include something in **www/ex2**, the code would be

```
include('../ex2/file.php');
```

A relative path will remain accurate, even if the site is moved to another server, as long as the files maintain their current relationship to each other.

The **include()** and **require()** functions are exactly the same when working properly but behave differently when they fail. If an **include()** function doesn't work (it cannot include the file for some reason), a warning will be printed to the browser , but the script will continue to run. If **require()** fails, an error is printed and the script is halted .

Both functions also have a ***_once()** version, which guarantees that the file in question is included only once regardless of how many times a script may—presumably inadvertently—attempt to include it.

```
require_once('filename.php');
include_once('filename.php');
```

Because **require_once()** and **include_once()** require extra work from the PHP module (i.e., PHP must first check that the file has not already been included),

it's best not to use these two functions unless a redundant include is likely to occur, which can happen on complex sites.

In this next example, included files will separate the primary HTML formatting from any PHP code. Then, the rest of the examples in this chapter will be able to have the same appearance—as if they are all part of the same web site—without the need to rewrite the common HTML every time. This technique creates a *template system*: an easy way to make large applications consistent and manageable. The focus in these examples is on the PHP code itself; you should also read the "Site Structure" sidebar so that you understand the organizational scheme on the server. If you have any questions about the CSS (Cascading Style Sheets) or HTML used in the example, see a dedicated resource on those topics.

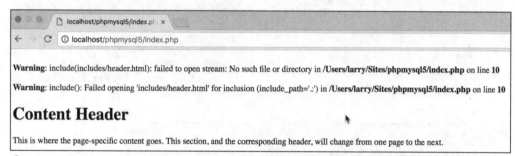

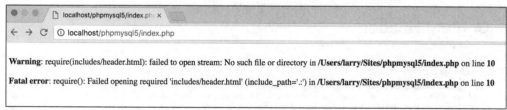

A One failed **include()** call generates these two error messages (assuming that PHP is configured to display errors), but the rest of the page continues to execute.

B The failure of a **require()** function call will print an error and terminate the execution of the script. If PHP is not configured to display errors, then the script will terminate without printing the problem first (i.e., it'd be a blank page).

To include multiple files:

1. Design an HTML page in your text or WYSIWYG editor (**Script 3.1** and 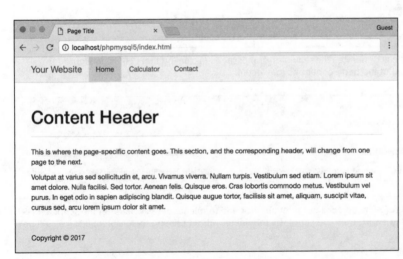).

   To start creating a template for a web site, design the layout like a standard HTML page, independent of any PHP code. For this chapter's example, I've created a simple page using the Bootstrap framework (`http://getbootstrap.com`).

2. Mark where any page-specific content goes.

   Almost every web site has several common elements on each page—header, navigation, advertising, footer, and so on—and one or more page-specific sections. In the HTML page (Script 3.1), enclose the section of the layout that will change from page to page within HTML comments to indicate its status.

   continues on page 80

Site Structure

When you begin using multiple files in your web applications, the overall site structure becomes more important. When laying out your site, you must take into account two primary considerations:

- Ease of maintenance
- Security

Using external files for holding standard procedures (i.e., PHP code), CSS, JavaScript, and the HTML design will greatly improve the ease of maintaining your site because commonly edited code is placed in one central location. I'll frequently make an **includes** or **templates** directory to store these files apart from the main scripts (the ones that are accessed directly in the browser).

I recommend using the `.inc` or `.html` file extension for documents where security is not an issue—such as HTML templates—and `.php` for files that contain more sensitive data, such as database access information. You can also use both `.inc` and `.html` or `.php` so that a file is clearly indicated as an include of a certain type: `db.inc.php` or `header.inc.html`.

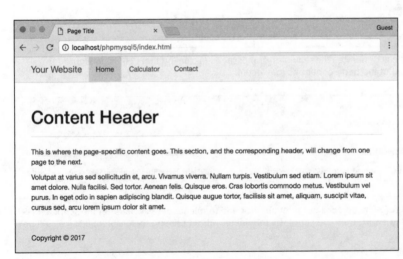

C The HTML and CSS design as it appears in the browser (without using any PHP).

Script 3.1 The HTML template for this chapter's web pages. Download the **sticky-footer-navbar.css** file it uses from the book's supporting web site (**LarryUllman.com**).

```
1    <!DOCTYPE html>
2    <html lang="en">
3    <head>
4    <meta charset="utf-8">
5    <meta http-equiv="X-UA-Compatible" content="IE=edge">
6    <meta name="viewport" content="width=device-width, initial-scale=1">
7    <title>Page Title</title>
8    <link rel="stylesheet" href="https://maxcdn.bootstrapcdn.com/bootstrap/3.3.7/css
     /bootstrap.min.css" integrity="sha384-BVYiiSIFeK1dGmJRAkycuHAHRg32OmUcww7on3RYdg4Va+PmSTsz
     /K68vbdEjh4u" crossorigin="anonymous">
9    <link href="css/sticky-footer-navbar.css" rel="stylesheet">
10   </head>
11   <body>
12   <nav class="navbar navbar-default navbar-fixed-top">
13      <div class="container">
14         <div class="navbar-header"><a class="navbar-brand" href="#">Your Website</a></div>
15         <div id="navbar" class="collapse navbar-collapse">
16            <ul class="nav navbar-nav">
17               <li class="active"><a href="index.php">Home</a></li>
18               <li><a href="calculator.php">Calculator</a></li>
19               <li><a href="#contact">Contact</a></li>
20            </ul>
21         </div>
22      </div>
23   </nav>
24   <div class="container">
25   <!-- Begin page content -->
26      <div class="page-header"><h1>Content Header</h1></div>
27      <p>This is where the page-specific content goes. This section, and the corresponding
        header, will change from one page to the next.</p>
28
29      <p>Volutpat at varius sed sollicitudin et, arcu. Vivamus viverra. Nullam turpis. Vestibulum
        sed etiam. Lorem ipsum sit amet dolore. Nulla facilisi. Sed tortor. Aenean felis. Quisque
        eros. Cras lobortis commodo metus. Vestibulum vel purus. In eget odio in sapien adipiscing
        blandit. Quisque augue tortor, facilisis sit amet, aliquam, suscipit vitae, cursus sed,
        arcu lorem ipsum dolor sit amet.</p>
30   <!-- End page content -->
31   </div>
32   <footer class="footer">
33      <div class="container">
34         <p class="text-muted"><p>Copyright &copy; 2017</p>
35      </div>
36   </footer>
37   </body>
38   </html>
```

3. Copy everything from the first line of the layout's HTML source to just before the page-specific content and paste it in a new document to be named **header.html** (Script 3.2):

```
<!DOCTYPE html>
<html lang="en">
<head>
<meta charset="utf-8">
<meta http-equiv="X-UA-Compatible"
→ content="IE=edge">
<meta name="viewport"
→ content="width=device-width,
→ initial-scale=1">
<title>Page Title</title>
<link rel="stylesheet"
→ href="https://maxcdn
→ .bootstrapcdn.com/bootstrap
→ /3.3.7/css/bootstrap.min.css"
→ integrity="sha384-BVYiiSIF
→ eK1dGmJRAkycuHAHRg32OmUcww7
→ on3RYdg4Va+PmSTsz/K68vbdEjh4u"
→ crossorigin="anonymous">
<link href="css/sticky-footer
→ -navbar.css" rel="stylesheet">
</head>
<body>
<nav class="navbar navbar-default
→ navbar-fixed-top">
  <div class="container">
    <div class="navbar-header">
    → <a class="navbar-brand"
    → href="#">Your Website</a>
    → </div>
    <div id="navbar" class=
    → "collapse navbar-collapse">
      <ul class="nav navbar-nav">
        <li class="active">
        → <a href="index.php">
        → Home</a></li>
        <li><a href="calculator
        → .php">Calculator</a>
        → </li>
        <li><a href="#contact">
        → Contact</a></li>
      </ul>
    </div>
  </div>
</nav>
<div class="container">
<!-- Script 3.2 - header.html -->
```

This first file will contain the initial HTML tags (from **DOCTYPE** through the head and into the beginning of the page body). It also has the code that makes the web site name, plus the horizontal bar of links across the top Ⓒ. All of the page-specific content goes within the DIV that has a **class** value of *container*.

4. Change the page's title line to read

```
<?php echo $page_title; ?>
```

The page title (which appears at the top of the browser Ⓒ) should be changeable on a page-by-page basis. For that to be possible, this value will be based on a PHP variable, which will then be printed out. You'll see how this plays out shortly.

Script 3.2 The initial HTML for each page is stored in a header file.

```
1   <!DOCTYPE html>
2   <html lang="en">
3   <head>
4   <meta charset="utf-8">
5   <meta http-equiv="X-UA-Compatible"
    content="IE=edge">
6   <meta name="viewport"
    content="width=device-width,
    initial-scale=1">
7   <title><?php echo $page_title; ?>
    </title>
```

code continues on next page

```
8    <link rel="stylesheet" href="https://
     maxcdn.bootstrapcdn.com/bootstrap
     /3.3.7/css/bootstrap.min.css"
     integrity="sha384-BVYiiSIFeK1dGmJRAk
     ycuHAHRg320mUcww7on3RYdg4Va+PmSTsz/
     K68vbdEjh4u" crossorigin="anonymous">
9    <link href="css/sticky-footer-navbar
     .css" rel="stylesheet">
10   </head>
11   <body>
12   <nav class="navbar navbar-default
     navbar-fixed-top">
13       <div class="container">
14           <div class="navbar-header">
             <a class="navbar-brand" href="#">
             Your Website</a></div>
15           <div id="navbar" class="collapse
             navbar-collapse">
16               <ul class="nav navbar-nav">
17                   <li class="active"><a
                     href="index.php">Home</a>
                     </li>
18                   <li><a href="calculator
                     .php">Calculator</a></li>
19                   <li><a href="#contact">
                     Contact</a></li>
20               </ul>
21           </div>
22       </div>
23   </nav>
24   <div class="container">
25   <!-- Script 3.2 - header.html -->
```

5. Save the file as **header.html**.

As stated already, included files can use just about any extension for the filename. This file is called **header.html**, indicating that it is the template's header file and that it contains primarily HTML.

6. Copy everything in the original template from the end of the page-specific content to the end of the page and paste it in a new file, to be named **footer.html** (Script 3.3):

```
<!-- Script 3.3 - footer.html -->
</div>
<footer class="footer">
  <div class="container">
    <p class="text-muted">
      → <p>Copyright &copy; 2017</p>
  </div>
</footer>
</body>
</html>
```

The footer file completes the container DIV and creates the footer portion of the page (which will be the same for every page on the site), and then the HTML document itself is completed.

7. Save the file as **footer.html**.

continues on next page

Script 3.3 The concluding HTML for each page is stored in this footer file.

```
1    <!-- Script 3.3 - footer.html -->
2    </div>
3    <footer class="footer">
4        <div class="container">
5            <p class="text-muted"><p>Copyright &copy; 2017</p>
6        </div>
7    </footer>
8    </body>
9    </html>
```

8. Begin a new PHP document in your text editor or IDE, to be named **index.php** (Script 3.4):

```
<?php # Script 3.4 - index.php
```

Since this script will use the included files for most of its HTML, it can begin and end with the PHP tags.

9. Set the **$page_title** variable and include the HTML header:

```
$page_title = 'Welcome to this
→ Site!';
include('includes/header.html');
```

The **$page_title** variable will store the value that appears in the top of the browser window (and therefore is also the default value when a person bookmarks the page). This variable is printed in **header.html** (see Script 3.2). By defining the variable prior to including the header file, the header file will have access to that variable. Remember that this **include()** line has the effect of dropping the contents of the included file into this page at this spot.

The **include()** function call uses a *relative* path to **header.html** (see the sidebar "Absolute vs. Relative Paths"). The syntax states that in the same folder as this file is a folder called **includes** and in that folder is a file named **header.html**.

10. Close the PHP tags and add the page-specific content:

```
?>
<div class="page-header">
→ <h1>Content Header</h1></div>
<p>This is where the page-specific
→ content goes. This section,
→ and the corresponding header,
→ will change from one page to
→ the next.</p>
```

For most pages, PHP will generate this content instead of having static text. This information could be sent to the browser using **echo**, but since there's no dynamic content here, it's easier and more efficient to exit the PHP tags temporarily. (The script and the images have a bit of extra Latin than is shown here, just to fatten up the page.)

Script 3.4 This script generates a complete page by including a template stored in two external files.

```
1    <?php # Script 3.4 - index.php
2    $page_title = 'Welcome to this Site!';
3    include('includes/header.html');
4    ?>
5
6    <div class="page-header"><h1>Content Header</h1></div>
7    <p>This is where the page-specific content goes. This section, and the corresponding header,
     will change from one page to the next.</p>
8
9    <p>Volutpat at varius sed sollicitudin et, arcu. Vivamus viverra. Nullam turpis. Vestibulum
     sed etiam. Lorem ipsum sit amet dolore. Nulla facilisi. Sed tortor. Aenean felis. Quisque
     eros. Cras lobortis commodo metus. Vestibulum vel purus. In eget odio in sapien adipiscing
     blandit. Quisque augue tortor, facilisis sit amet, aliquam, suscipit vitae, cursus sed, arcu
     lorem ipsum dolor sit amet.</p>
10
11   <?php
12   include('includes/footer.html');
13   ?>
```

11. Create a final PHP section and include the footer file:

```php
<?php
include('includes/footer.html');
?>
```

12. Save the file as **index.php** and place it in your web directory.

13. Create an **includes** directory in the same folder as **index.php**. Then place **header.html** and **footer.html** into this **includes** directory.

14. Create a **css** directory in the same folder as **index.php**. Then place **sticky-footer-navbar.css** (part of the downloadable code at **LarryUllman.com**) in it.

Note: To save space, the CSS file for this example—which controls the layout—is not included in the book. You can download the file through the book's supporting web site or do without it (the template will still work; it just won't look as nice).

15. Test the template system by going to the **index.php** page in your browser 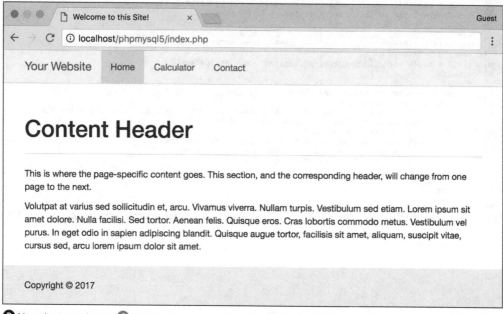.

The **index.php** page is the key script in the template system. You do not need to access any of the included files directly, because **index.php** will take care of incorporating their contents. Since this is a PHP page, you still need to access it through a URL.

continues on next page

Welcome to this Site! ✕   Guest

← → C   ⓘ localhost/phpmysql5/index.php   ⋮

Your Website   Home   Calculator   Contact

Content Header

This is where the page-specific content goes. This section, and the corresponding header, will change from one page to the next.

Volutpat at varius sed sollicitudin et, arcu. Vivamus viverra. Nullam turpis. Vestibulum sed etiam. Lorem ipsum sit amet dolore. Nulla facilisi. Sed tortor. Aenean felis. Quisque eros. Cras lobortis commodo metus. Vestibulum vel purus. In eget odio in sapien adipiscing blandit. Quisque augue tortor, facilisis sit amet, aliquam, suscipit vitae, cursus sed, arcu lorem ipsum dolor sit amet.

Copyright © 2017

ⓓ Now the same layout ⓒ has been created using external files in PHP.

16. If desired, view the HTML source of the page **E**.

TIP In the `php.ini` configuration file, you can adjust the `include_path` setting, which dictates where PHP is and is not allowed to retrieve included files.

TIP As you'll see in Chapter 9, "Using PHP with MySQL," any included file that contains sensitive information (like database access) should ideally be stored outside of the web directory so it can't be viewed within a browser.

TIP Since `require()` has more impact on a script when it fails, it's recommended for mission-critical includes, like those that connect to a database. The `include()` function would be used for less important inclusions.

TIP If a block of PHP code contains only a single executable statement, it's common to place both it and the PHP tags on a single line:

```php
<?php include('filename.html'); ?>
```

```
1   <!DOCTYPE html>
2   <html lang="en">
3     <head>
4       <meta charset="utf-8">
5       <meta http-equiv="X-UA-Compatible" content="IE=edge">
6       <meta name="viewport" content="width=device-width, initial-scale=1">
7       <title>Welcome to this Site!</title>
8       <link rel="stylesheet"
        href="https://maxcdn.bootstrapcdn.com/bootstrap/3.3.7/css/bootstrap.min.css"
        integrity="sha384-BVYiiSIFeK1dGmJRAkycuHAHRg32OmUcww7on3RYdg4Va+PmSTsz/K68vbdEjh4u"
        crossorigin="anonymous">
9       <link href="css/sticky-footer-navbar.css" rel="stylesheet">
10    </head>
11    <body>
12      <nav class="navbar navbar-default navbar-fixed-top">
13        <div class="container">
14          <div class="navbar-header"><a class="navbar-brand" href="#">Your Website</a></div>
15          <div id="navbar" class="collapse navbar-collapse">
16            <ul class="nav navbar-nav">
17              <li class="active"><a href="index.php">Home</a></li>
18              <li><a href="calculator.php">Calculator</a></li>
19              <li><a href="#contact">Contact</a></li>
20            </ul>
21          </div>
22        </div>
23      </nav>
```

E The generated HTML source of the page should replicate the code in the original template (refer to Script 3.1).

Handling HTML Forms, Revisited

A good portion of Chapter 2, "Programming with PHP," involves handling HTML forms with PHP; this makes sense, as a good portion of web programming with PHP is exactly that. All of those examples use two separate files: one that displays the form and another that receives its submitted data. Although there's certainly nothing wrong with this approach, there are advantages to putting the entire process into one script.

To have one page both display and handle a form, a conditional must check which action—display or handle—should be taken:

```
if (/* form has been submitted */) {
  // Handle the form.
} else {
  // Display the form.
}
```

The question, then, is how to determine if the form has been submitted. The answer is simple—after a bit of explanation.

When you have a form that uses the POST method and gets submitted back to the same page, two different types of requests will be made of that script **A**. The first request, which loads the form, will be a GET request. This is the standard request made of most pages. When the form is submitted, a second request of the script will be made, this time a POST request (assuming the form uses the POST method). Hence, you can test for a form's submission by checking the request method, found in the **$_SERVER** array:

```
if ($_SERVER['REQUEST_METHOD'] ==
→ 'POST') {
  // Handle the form.
} else {
  // Display the form.
}
```

continues on next page

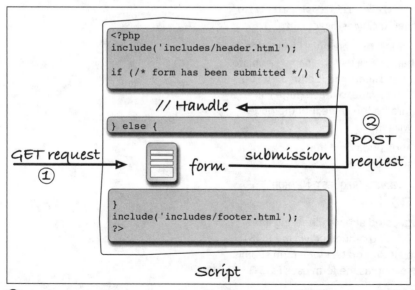

A The interactions between the user and this PHP script on the server involves the user making two requests of this script.

If you want a page to handle a form and then display it again (e.g., to add a record to a database and then give an option to add another), drop the **else** clause:

```
if ($_SERVER['REQUEST_METHOD'] ==
→'POST') {
// Handle the form.
}
// Display the form.
```

Using that code, a script will handle a form if it has been submitted and display the form every time the page is loaded.

To demonstrate having the same page both display and handle a form, let's create a calculator that estimates the cost and time required to take a car trip, based on user-entered values **B**.

To handle HTML forms:

1. Begin a new PHP document in your text editor or IDE, to be named **calculator.php** (**Script 3.5**):

   ```
   <?php # Script 3.5 - calculator.php
   $page_title = 'Trip Cost Calculator';
   include('includes/header.html');
   ```

   This, and all the remaining examples in the chapter, will use the same template system as **index.php** (Script 3.4). The beginning syntax of each page will therefore be the same, but the page titles will differ.

2. Write the conditional that checks for a form submission:

   ```
   if ($_SERVER['REQUEST_METHOD'] ==
   →'POST') {
   ```

   As suggested already, checking if the page is being requested via the POST method is a good test for a form submission (so long as the form uses POST).

continues on page 88

Trip Cost Calculator

Distance (in miles): 225

Ave. Price Per Gallon: ○ 3.00 ● 3.50 ○ 4.00

Fuel Efficiency: [Decent ♦]

[Calculate!]

B The HTML form, completed by the user.

Script 3.5 The `calculator.php` script both displays a simple form and handles the form data; it performs some calculations and reports on the results.

```php
1    <?php # Script 3.5 - calculator.php
2
3    $page_title = 'Trip Cost Calculator';
4    include('includes/header.html');
5
6    // Check for form submission:
7    if ($_SERVER['REQUEST_METHOD'] == 'POST') {
8
9        // Minimal form validation:
10       if (isset($_POST['distance'], $_POST['gallon_price'], $_POST['efficiency']) &&
11        is_numeric($_POST['distance']) && is_numeric($_POST['gallon_price']) &&
          is_numeric($_POST['efficiency']) ) {
12
13           // Calculate the results:
14           $gallons = $_POST['distance'] / $_POST['efficiency'];
15           $dollars = $gallons * $_POST['gallon_price'];
16           $hours = $_POST['distance']/65;
17
18           // Print the results:
19           echo '<div class="page-header"><h1>Total Estimated Cost</h1></div>
20           <p>The total cost of driving ' . $_POST['distance'] . ' miles, averaging ' .
             $_POST['efficiency'] . ' miles per gallon, and paying an average of $' .
             $_POST['gallon_price'] . ' per gallon, is $' . number_format ($dollars, 2) . '.
             If you drive at an average of 65 miles per hour, the trip will take approximately ' .
             number_format($hours, 2) . ' hours.</p>';
21
22       } else { // Invalid submitted values.
23           echo '<div class="page-header"><h1>Error!</h1></div>
24           <p class="text-danger">Please enter a valid distance, price per gallon, and fuel
             efficiency.</p>';
25       }
26
27   } // End of main submission IF.
28
29   // Leave the PHP section and create the HTML form:
30   ?>
31
32   <div class="page-header"><h1>Trip Cost Calculator</h1></div>
33   <form action="calculator.php" method="post">
34       <p>Distance (in miles): <input type="number" name="distance"></p>
35   <p>Ave. Price Per Gallon:    <input type="radio" name="gallon_price" value="3.00"> 3.00
36       <input type="radio" name="gallon_price" value="3.50"> 3.50
37       <input type="radio" name="gallon_price" value="4.00"> 4.00
38   </p>
39       <p>Fuel Efficiency: <select name="efficiency">
40       <option value="10">Terrible</option>
41       <option value="20">Decent</option>
42       <option value="30">Very Good</option>
43       <option value="50">Outstanding</option>
44       </select></p>
45       <p><input type="submit" name="submit" value="Calculate!"></p>
46   </form>
47
48   <?php include('includes/footer.html'); ?>
```

3. Validate the form:

```
if (isset($_POST['distance'],
→ $_POST['gallon_price'],
→ $_POST['efficiency']) &&
is_numeric($_POST['distance']) &&
→ is_numeric($_POST['gallon_price'])
→ && is_numeric($_POST
→ ['efficiency']) ) {
```

The validation here is very simple: it merely checks that three submitted variables are set and are all numeric types. You can certainly elaborate on this, perhaps checking that all values are positive (in fact, Chapter 13, "Security Methods," has a variation on this script that does just that).

If the validation passes all the tests, the calculations will be made; otherwise, the user will be asked to try again.

4. Perform the calculations:

```
$gallons = $_POST['distance'] /
→ $_POST['efficiency'];
$dollars = $gallons * $_POST
→ ['gallon_price'];
$hours = $_POST['distance']/65;
```

The first line calculates the number of gallons of gasoline the trip will take, determined by dividing the distance by the fuel efficiency. The second line calculates the cost of the fuel for the trip, determined by multiplying the number of gallons times the average price per gallon. The third line calculates how long the trip will take, determined by dividing the distance by 65 (representing 65 miles per hour).

5. Print the results:

```
echo '<div class="page-header">
→ <h1>Total Estimated Cost</h1>
→ </div>
<p>The total cost of driving '
→ . $_POST['distance'] . ' miles,
averaging ' . $_POST['efficiency']
→ . ' miles per gallon, and paying
→ an average of $' . $_POST
→ ['gallon_price'] . ' per gallon,
→ is $' . number_format
→ ($dollars, 2) . '. If you drive
→ at an average of 65 miles per
→ hour, the trip will take
→ approximately ' . number_format
→ ($hours, 2) . ' hours.</p>';
```

All of the values are printed out while formatting the cost and hours with the **number_format()** function. Using the concatenation operator (the period) allows the formatted numeric values to be appended to the printed message.

6. Complete the conditionals and close the PHP tag:

```
} else { // Invalid submitted
→ values.
    echo '<div class="page-header">
    → <h1>Error!</h1></div>
    <p class="text-danger">Please
    → enter a valid distance,
    → price per gallon, and fuel
    → efficiency.</p>';
}
} // End of main submission IF.
?>
```

The **else** clause completes the validation conditional (Step 3), printing an error if the submitted values aren't all set and numeric **C**. The final closing curly brace closes the **isset($_SERVER['REQUEST_METHOD'] == 'POST')** conditional. Finally, the PHP section is closed so that the form can be created without using **echo** (see Step 7).

7. Begin the HTML form:

```
<div class="page-header"><h1>Trip
→ Cost Calculator</h1></div>
<form action="calculator.php"
→ method="post">
  <p>Distance (in miles): <input
  → type="number" name="distance">
  → </p>
```

The form itself is fairly obvious, containing only one new trick: the **action** attribute uses this script's name so that the form submits back to this page instead of to another. The first element within the form is a number input—added in HTML5, where the user can enter the distance of the trip.

Error!

Please enter a valid distance, price per gallon, and fuel efficiency.

Trip Cost Calculator

Distance (in miles): [   ]

C If any one of the submitted values is not both set and numeric, an error message is displayed.

8. Complete the form:

```
<p>Ave. Price Per Gallon:
  <input type="radio"
  → name="gallon_price"
  → value="3.00"> 3.00
  <input type="radio"
  → name="gallon_price"
  → value="3.50"> 3.50
  <input type="radio"
  → name="gallon_price"
  → value="4.00"> 4.00
</p>
<p>Fuel Efficiency:
→ <select name="efficiency">
  <option value="10">Terrible
  → </option>
  <option value="20">Decent
  → </option>
  <option value="30">Very
  → Good</option>
  <option value="50">
  → Outstanding</option>
</select></p>
<p><input type="submit"
→ name="submit"
→ value="Calculate!"></p>
</form>
```

The form uses radio buttons to select the average price per gallon (the buttons are wrapped within **span** tags to format them similarly to the other form elements). For the fuel efficiency, the user can select from a drop-down menu of four options. A submit button completes the form.

continues on next page

9. Include the footer file:

```php
<?php include('includes/footer
→ .html'); ?>
```

10. Save the file as **calculator.php**, place it in your web directory, and test it in your browser **D**.

TIP You can also have a form submit back to itself by using no value for the `action` attribute:

```
<form action="" method="post">
```

By doing so, the form will always submit back to this same page, even if you later change the name of the script.

TIP The Bootstrap framework has many ways to make the HTML page and the form more attractive and usable. I've forgone these to save space, but check out the Bootstrap documentation for details.

Total Estimated Cost

The total cost of driving 225 miles, averaging 20 miles per gallon, and paying an average of $3.50 per gallon, is $39.38. If you drive at an average of 65 miles per hour, the trip will take approximately 3.46 hours.

Trip Cost Calculator

Distance (in miles): [   ]

D The page performs the calculations, reports on the results, and then redisplays the form.

Making Sticky Forms

A *sticky form* is simply a standard HTML form that remembers how you filled it out. This is a particularly nice feature for end users, especially if you are requiring them to resubmit a form after filling it out incorrectly in the first place (as in ⓒ in the previous section).

To preset what's entered in any text-type input, including number and email, use its **value** attribute:

```
<input type="text" name="city"
→ value="Innsbruck">
```

To have PHP preset that value, print the appropriate variable (this assumes that the referenced variable exists):

```
<input type="text" name="city"
→ value="<?php echo $city; ?>">
```

This is also a nice example of the benefit of PHP's HTML-embedded nature: you can place PHP code anywhere, including within HTML tags.

To preset the status of radio buttons or check boxes—to pre-check them, add the code **checked="checked"** to their **input** tags. Using PHP, you might write:

```
<input type="radio" name="gender"
→ value="F" <?php if ($gender == 'F') {
echo 'checked="checked"';
} ?>>
```

As you can see, the syntax can quickly get complicated; you may find it easiest to create the form element and then add the PHP code as a second step.

To preset the value of a textarea, print the value between the **textarea** tags:

```
<textarea name="comments" rows="10"
→ cols="50"><?php echo $comments; ?>
→ </textarea>
```

Note that the **textarea** tag does not have a **value** attribute like the standard **text** input.

To preselect a pull-down menu, add **selected="selected"** to the appropriate option. This is easy if you also use PHP to generate the menu:

```
echo '<select name="year">';
for ($y = 2017; $y <= 2027; $y++) {
    echo "<option value=\"$y\"";
    if ($year == $y) {
        echo ' selected="selected"';
    }
    echo ">$y</option>\n";
}
echo '</select>';
```

With this new information in mind, let's rewrite **calculator.php** so that it's sticky. Unlike the earlier examples, the existing values will be present in **$_POST** variables. Also, since it's best not to refer to variables unless they exist, conditionals will check that a variable is set before printing its value.

To make a sticky form:

1. Open **calculator.php** (refer to Script 3.5) in your text editor or IDE, if it is not already open.

continues on next page

2. Change the distance input to read (Script 3.6)

```
<p>Distance (in miles):
→ <input type="number"
→ name="distance" value="<?php if
→ (isset($_POST['distance'])) echo
→ $_POST['distance']; ?>"></p>
```

The first change is to add the **value** attribute to the input. Then, print out the value of the submitted distance variable (**$_POST['distance']**). Since the first time the page is loaded, **$_POST['distance']** has no value, a conditional ensures that the variable is set before attempting to print it. The end result for setting the input's value is the PHP code

```
<?php
if (isset($_POST['distance'])) {
  echo $_POST['distance'];
}
?>
```

This can be condensed to the more minimal form used in the script (you can omit the curly braces if you have only one statement within a conditional block, although I very rarely recommend that you do so).

3. Change the radio buttons to

```
<input type="radio"
→ name="gallon_price"
→ value="3.00" <?php if
→ (isset($_POST['gallon_price']) &&
→ ($_POST['gallon_price'] ==
→ '3.00')) echo 'checked="checked"
→ '; ?>> 3.00
<input type="radio"
→ name="gallon_price" value="3.50"
→ <?php if (isset($_POST['gallon_
→ price']) && ($_POST['gallon_
→ price'] == '3.50')) echo
→ 'checked="checked" '; ?>> 3.50
<input type="radio"
→ name="gallon_price" value="4.00"
→ <?php if (isset($_POST['gallon_
→ price']) && ($_POST['gallon_
→ price'] == '4.00')) echo
→ 'checked="checked" '; ?>> 4.00
```

For each of the three radio buttons, the following code must be added within the **input** tag:

```
<?php if (isset($_POST['gallon_
→ price']) && ($_POST['gallon_
→ price'] == 'XXX')) echo
→ 'checked="checked" '; ?>
```

For each button, the comparison value (*XXX*) gets changed accordingly.

continues on page 94

Script 3.6 The calculator's form now recalls the previously entered and selected values (creating a sticky form).

```
1    <?php # Script 3.5 - calculator.php
2
3    $page_title = 'Trip Cost Calculator';
4    include('includes/header.html');
5
6    // Check for form submission:
7    if ($_SERVER['REQUEST_METHOD'] == 'POST') {
8
9        // Minimal form validation:
10       if (isset($_POST['distance'], $_POST['gallon_price'], $_POST['efficiency']) &&
11       is_numeric($_POST['distance']) && is_numeric($_POST['gallon_price']) &&
         is_numeric($_POST['efficiency']) ) {
```

code continues on next page

Script 3.6 *continued*

```
12
13          // Calculate the results:
14          $gallons = $_POST['distance'] / $_POST['efficiency'];
15          $dollars = $gallons * $_POST['gallon_price'];
16          $hours = $_POST['distance']/65;
17
18          // Print the results:
19          echo '<div class="page-header"><h1>Total Estimated Cost</h1></div>
20          <p>The total cost of driving ' . $_POST['distance'] . ' miles, averaging ' .
            $_POST['efficiency'] . ' miles per gallon, and paying an average of $' . $_POST['gallon_
            price'] . ' per gallon, is $' . number_format ($dollars, 2) . '. If you drive at an
            average of 65 miles per hour, the trip will take approximately ' .
            number_format($hours, 2) . ' hours.</p>';
21
22      } else { // Invalid submitted values.
23          echo '<div class="page-header"><h1>Error!</h1></div>
24          <p class="text-danger">Please enter a valid distance, price per gallon, and fuel
            efficiency.</p>';
25      }
26
27  } // End of main submission IF.
28
29  // Leave the PHP section and create the HTML form:
30  ?>
31
32  <div class="page-header"><h1>Trip Cost Calculator</h1></div>
33  <form action="calculator.php" method="post">
34      <p>Distance (in miles): <input type="number" name="distance" value="<?php if
        (isset($_POST['distance'])) echo $_POST['distance']; ?>"></p>
35      <p>Ave. Price Per Gallon:
36          <input type="radio" name="gallon_price" value="3.00" <?php if
            (isset($_POST['gallon_price']) && ($_POST['gallon_price'] == '3.00'))
            echo 'checked="checked" '; ?>> 3.00
37          <input type="radio" name="gallon_price" value="3.50" <?php if
            (isset($_POST['gallon_price']) && ($_POST['gallon_price'] == '3.50'))
            echo 'checked="checked" '; ?>> 3.50ç
38          <input type="radio" name="gallon_price" value="4.00" <?php if
            (isset($_POST['gallon_price']) && ($_POST['gallon_price'] == '4.00'))
            echo 'checked="checked" '; ?>> 4.00
39      </p>
40      <p>Fuel Efficiency: <select name="efficiency">
41          <option value="10"<?php if (isset($_POST['efficiency']) && ($_POST['efficiency']
            == '10')) echo ' selected="selected"'; ?>>Terrible</option>
42          <option value="20"<?php if (isset($_POST['efficiency']) && ($_POST['efficiency']
            == '20')) echo ' selected="selected"'; ?>>Decent</option>
43          <option value="30"<?php if (isset($_POST['efficiency']) && ($_POST['efficiency']
            == '30')) echo ' selected="selected"'; ?>>Very Good</option>
44          <option value="50"<?php if (isset($_POST['efficiency']) && ($_POST['efficiency']
            == '50')) echo ' selected="selected"'; ?>>Outstanding</option>
45      </select></p>
46      <p><input type="submit" name="submit" value="Calculate!"></p>
47  </form>
48
49  <?php include('includes/footer.html'); ?>
```

4. Change the select menu options to

```
<option value="10"<?php if
→ (isset($_POST['efficiency'])
→ && ($_POST['efficiency']
→ == '10')) echo ' selected=
→ "selected"'; ?>>Terrible
→ </option>
<option value="20"<?php if
→ (isset($_POST['efficiency'])
→ && ($_POST['efficiency']
→ == '20')) echo ' selected=
→ "selected"'; ?>>Decent
→ </option>
<option value="30"<?php if
→ (isset($_POST['efficiency'])
→ && ($_POST['efficiency']
→ == '30')) echo ' selected=
→ "selected"'; ?>>Very Good
→ </option>
<option value="50"<?php if
→ (isset($_POST['efficiency'])
→ && ($_POST['efficiency']
→ == '50')) echo ' selected=
→ "selected"'; ?>>Outstanding
→ </option>
```

For each option, within the opening **option** tag, add the following code:

```
<?php if (isset($_POST
→ ['efficiency']) && ($_POST
→ ['efficiency'] == 'XX')) echo '
→ selected="selected"'; ?>
```

Again, just the specific comparison value (*XX*) must be changed to match each option.

5. Save the file as **calculator.php**, place it in your web directory, and test it in your browser Ⓐ and Ⓑ.

TIP Because the price per gallon and fuel efficiency values are numeric, you can quote or not quote the comparison values within the added conditionals. I choose to quote them, because they're technically strings with numeric values.

TIP Because the added PHP code in this example exists inside the HTML form element tags, error messages may not be obvious. If problems occur, check the HTML source of the page to see if PHP errors are printed within the value attributes and the tags themselves.

TIP You should always double-quote HTML attributes, particularly the value attribute of a text input. If you don't, multiword values like Elliott Smith will appear as just Elliott in the browser.

TIP Some browsers will also remember values entered into forms for you; this is a separate but potentially overlapping issue from using PHP to accomplish this.

Total Estimated Cost

The total cost of driving 425 miles, averaging 30 miles per gallon, and paying an average of $3.50 per gallon, is $49.58. If you drive at an average of 65 miles per hour, the trip will take approximately 6.54 hours.

Trip Cost Calculator

Distance (in miles): 425

Ave. Price Per Gallon: ○ 3.00 ◉ 3.50 ○ 4.00
Fuel Efficiency: [Very Good ⬍]

Ⓐ The form now recalls the previously submitted values...

Error!

Please enter a valid distance, price per gallon, and fuel efficiency.

Trip Cost Calculator

Distance (in miles): [   ]

Ave. Price Per Gallon: ○ 3.00 ○ 3.50 ◉ 4.00
Fuel Efficiency: [Decent   ⬍]

Ⓑ ...whether or not the form was completely filled out.

Creating Your Own Functions

PHP has a lot of built-in functions, addressing almost every need you might have. More importantly, though, PHP has the capability for you to define and use your own functions for whatever purpose. The syntax for making your own function is

```
function function_name() {
   // Function code.
}
```

The name of your function can be any combination of letters, numbers, and the underscore, but it must begin with either a letter or the underscore. You also cannot use an existing function name for your function (*print*, *echo*, *isset*, and so on). One perfectly valid function definition is

```
function do_nothing() {
   // Do nothing!
}
```

In PHP, as mentioned in the first chapter, function names are case-insensitive (unlike variable names), so you could call that function using **do_Nothing()** or **DO_NOTHING()** or **Do_Nothing()**, and so forth, but not **donothing()** or **DoNothing()**.

The code within the function can do nearly anything, from generating HTML to performing calculations to calling other functions.

The most common reasons to create your own functions are as follows:

- To associate repeated code with one function call
- To separate sensitive or complicated processes from other code
- To make common code bits easier to reuse

This chapter runs through a couple of examples, and you'll see some others throughout the rest of the book. For this first example, a function will be defined that outputs the HTML code for generating theoretical ads. This function will then be called twice on the home page **Ⓐ**.

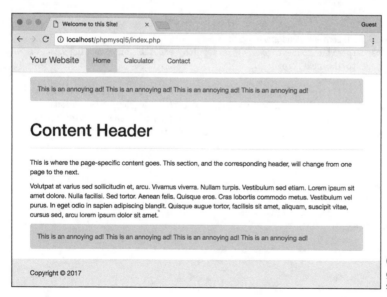

Ⓐ The two "ads" are generated by calling the same user-defined function.

To create your own function:

1. Open **index.php** (Script 3.4) in your text editor or IDE.

2. After the opening PHP tag, begin defining a new function (**Script 3.7**):

```php
function create_ad() {
```

The function to be written here would, in theory, generate the HTML required to add ads to a web page. The function's name clearly states its purpose.

Although not required, it's conventional to place a function definition near the very top of a script or in a separate file.

3. Generate the HTML:

```php
echo '<div class="alert
→ alert-info" role="alert"><p>This
→ is an annoying ad! This is an
→ annoying ad! This is an
→ annoying ad! This is an
→ annoying ad!</p></div>';
```

Script 3.7 This version of the home page has a user-defined function that outputs a theoretical ad. The function is called twice in the script, thus creating two ads.

```php
1    <?php # Script 3.7 - index.php #2
2
3    // This function outputs theoretical HTML
4    // for adding ads to a web page.
5    function create_ad() {
6       echo '<div class="alert alert-info" role="alert"><p>This is an annoying ad! This is
         an annoying ad! This is an annoying ad! This is an annoying ad!</p></div>';
7    } // End of the function definition.
8
9    $page_title = 'Welcome to this Site!';
10   include('includes/header.html');
11
12   // Call the function:
13   create_ad();
14   ?>
15
16   <div class="page-header"><h1>Content Header</h1></div>
17   <p>This is where the page-specific content goes. This section, and the corresponding header,
     will change from one page to the next.</p>
18
19   <p>Volutpat at varius sed sollicitudin et, arcu. Vivamus viverra. Nullam turpis. Vestibulum
     sed etiam. Lorem ipsum sit amet dolore. Nulla facilisi. Sed tortor. Aenean felis. Quisque
     eros. Cras lobortis commodo metus. Vestibulum vel purus. In eget odio in sapien adipiscing
     blandit. Quisque augue tortor, facilisis sit amet, aliquam, suscipit vitae, cursus sed, arcu
     lorem ipsum dolor sit amet.</p>
20
21   <?php
22   // Call the function again:
23   create_ad();
24
25   include('includes/footer.html');
26   ?>
```

In a real function, the code would output actual HTML instead of a paragraph of text. For now, a simple Bootstrap component will suffice. (The actual HTML would be provided by the service you're using to generate and tracks ads.)

4. Close the function definition:

```
} // End of the function
→ definition.
```

It can be helpful to place a comment at the end of a function definition so that you know where a definition starts and stops (it's helpful on longer function definitions, at least).

5. After including the header and before exiting the PHP block, call the function:

```
create_ad();
```

The call to the **create_ad()** function will have the result of inserting the function's output at this point in the script.

6. Just before including the footer, call the function again:

```
create_ad();
```

7. Save the file and test it in your browser **A**.

TIP If you ever see a `call to undefined function function_name` error, this means that you are calling a function that hasn't been defined. This can happen if you misspell the function's name (either when defining or calling it) or if you fail to include the file where the function is defined.

Ave. Price Per Gallon:
Warning: Missing argument 1 for create_gallon_radio(), called in /Users/larry/Sites/phpmysql5/calculator.php on line 55 and defined in **/Users/larry/Sites/phpmysql5/calculator.php** on line **6**

B Failure to send a function the proper number (and sometimes type) of arguments creates an error.

Creating a function that takes arguments

Just like PHP's built-in functions, those you write can take *arguments*. For example, the **strlen()** function takes as an argument the string whose character length will be determined.

A function can take any number of arguments, but the order in which you list them is critical. To allow for arguments, add variables to a function's definition:

```
function print_hello($first, $last) {
    // Function code.
}
```

The variable names you use in the function definition are irrelevant to the rest of the script (more on this in the "Variable Scope" sidebar toward the end of this chapter), but try to use valid, meaningful names.

Once the function is defined, you can then call it as you would any other function in PHP, sending literal values or variables to it:

```
print_hello('Jimmy', 'Stewart');
$surname = 'Stewart';
print_hello('Jimmy', $surname);
```

As with any function in PHP, failure to send the right number of arguments results in an error **B**.

(Technically speaking, an *argument* is the value passed when calling a function; a *parameter* is the variable in the function definition that is assigned the argument value.)

To demonstrate this concept, let's rewrite the calculator form so that a user-defined function creates the price-per-gallon radio buttons. Doing so will help to clean up the messy form code.

To define functions that take arguments:

1. Open **calculator.php** (Script 3.6) in your text editor or IDE.

2. After the initial PHP tag, start defining the **create_gallon_radio()** function (Script 3.8):

```
function create_gallon_radio
→ ($value) {
```

The function will create code like this:

```
<input type="radio"
→ name="gallon_price" value="XXX"
→ checked="checked"> XXX
```

or this:

```
<input type="radio"
→ name="gallon_price"
→ value="XXX"> XXX
```

To be able to dynamically set the value of each radio button, that value must be passed to the function with each call. Therefore, that's the one argument the function takes.

Notice that the variable used in the function definition is not **$_POST['gallon_price']**. The function's parameter variable is particular to this function and has its own name.

continues on page 100

Script 3.8 The **calculator.php** form now uses a function to create the radio buttons. Unlike the **create_ad()** user-defined function, this one takes an argument.

```
1   <?php # Script 3.8 - calculator.php #3
2
3   // This function creates a radio button.
4   // The function takes one argument: the value.
5   // The function also makes the button "sticky."
6   function create_gallon_radio($value) {
7
8       // Start the element:
9       echo '<input type="radio" name="gallon_price" value="' . $value . '"';
10
11      // Check for stickiness:
12      if (isset($_POST['gallon_price']) && ($_POST['gallon_price'] == $value)) {
13          echo ' checked="checked"';
14      }
15
16      // Complete the element:
17      echo "> $value ";
18
19  } // End of create_gallon_radio() function.
20
21  $page_title = 'Trip Cost Calculator';
22  include('includes/header.html');
23
24  // Check for form submission:
25  if ($_SERVER['REQUEST_METHOD'] == 'POST') {
26
27      // Minimal form validation:
28      if (isset($_POST['distance'], $_POST['gallon_price'], $_POST['efficiency']) &&
```

code continues on next page

```
29        is_numeric($_POST['distance']) && is_numeric($_POST['gallon_price']) &&
          is_numeric($_POST['efficiency']) ) {
30
31            // Calculate the results:
32            $gallons = $_POST['distance'] / $_POST['efficiency'];
33            $dollars = $gallons * $_POST['gallon_price'];
34            $hours = $_POST['distance']/65;
35
36            // Print the results:
37            echo '<div class="page-header"><h1>Total Estimated Cost</h1></div>
38            <p>The total cost of driving ' . $_POST['distance'] . ' miles, averaging
              ' . $_POST['efficiency'] . ' miles per gallon, and paying an average of $' .
              $_POST['gallon_price'] . ' per gallon, is $' . number_format ($dollars, 2) . '.
              If you drive at an average of 65 miles per hour, the trip will take approximately
              ' . number_format($hours, 2) . ' hours.</p>';
39
40        } else { // Invalid submitted values.
41            echo '<div class="page-header"><h1>Error!</h1></div>
42            <p class="text-danger">Please enter a valid distance, price per gallon, and fuel
              efficiency.</p>';
43        }
44
45    } // End of main submission IF.
46
47    // Leave the PHP section and create the HTML form:
48    ?>
49
50    <div class="page-header"><h1>Trip Cost Calculator</h1></div>
51    <form action="calculator.php" method="post">
52        <p>Distance (in miles): <input type="number" name="distance" value="<?php if
          (isset($_POST['distance'])) echo $_POST['distance']; ?>"></p>
53        <p>Ave. Price Per Gallon:
54        <?php
55        create_gallon_radio('3.00');
56        create_gallon_radio('3.50');
57        create_gallon_radio('4.00');
58        ?>
59        </p>
60        <p>Fuel Efficiency: <select name="efficiency">
61            <option value="10"<?php if (isset($_POST['efficiency']) && ($_POST['efficiency']
              == '10')) echo ' selected="selected"'; ?>>Terrible</option>
62            <option value="20"<?php if (isset($_POST['efficiency']) && ($_POST['efficiency']
              == '20')) echo ' selected="selected"'; ?>>Decent</option>
63            <option value="30"<?php if (isset($_POST['efficiency']) && ($_POST['efficiency']
              == '30')) echo ' selected="selected"'; ?>>Very Good</option>
64            <option value="50"<?php if (isset($_POST['efficiency']) && ($_POST['efficiency']
              == '50')) echo ' selected="selected"'; ?>>Outstanding</option>
65        </select></p>
66        <p><input type="submit" name="submit" value="Calculate!"></p>
67    </form>
68
69    <?php include('includes/footer.html'); ?>
```

3. Begin creating the radio button element:

```
echo '<input type="radio"
→ name="gallon_price" value="' .
→ $value . '"';
```

This code starts the HTML for the radio button, including its **value** attribute, but does not complete the radio button so that "stickiness" can be addressed next. The value for the input comes from the function argument.

4. Make the input "sticky," if appropriate:

```
if (isset($_POST['gallon_price'])
→ && ($_POST['gallon_price'] ==
→ $value)) {
   echo ' checked="checked"';
}
```

This code is like that in the original form, except now the comparison value comes from the function's argument.

5. Complete the form element and the function:

```
   echo '> $value ";
} // End of create_gallon_radio()
→ function.
```

Finally, the **input** tag is closed and the value is displayed afterward, with a space on either side.

6. Replace the hard-coded radio buttons in the form with three function calls:

```
<?php
create_gallon_radio('3.00');
create_gallon_radio('3.50');
create_gallon_radio('4.00');
?>
```

To create the three buttons, just call the function three times, passing different values for each. The numeric values are quoted here; otherwise, PHP would drop the trailing zeros.

7. Save the file as **calculator.php**, place it in your web directory, and test it in your browser **C**.

Total Estimated Cost

The total cost of driving 685 miles, averaging 20 miles per gallon, and paying an average of $3.00 per gallon, is $102.75. If you drive at an average of 65 miles per hour, the trip will take approximately 10.54 hours.

Trip Cost Calculator

Distance (in miles): 685

Ave. Price Per Gallon: ● 3.00 ○ 3.50 ○ 4.00

Fuel Efficiency: [Decent ◆]

C Although a user-defined function is used to create the radio buttons (see Script 3.8), the result is no different to the user.

Setting default argument values

Another variant on defining your own functions is to preset an argument's value. To do so, assign the parameter a value in the function's definition:

```
function greet($name, $msg = 'Hello') {
   echo "$msg, $name!";
}
```

As the result of setting a default value, that particular argument becomes optional when calling the function. If a value is passed to it, the passed value is used; otherwise, the default value is used.

You can set default values for as many of the parameters as you want, as long as those parameters come last in the function definition. In other words, the required parameters must always be listed first.

With the example function just defined, any of these will work:

```
greet($surname, $message);
greet('Zoe');
greet('Sam', 'Good evening');
```

However, just **greet()** will not work. Also, there's no way to pass **$msg** a value without passing one to **$name** as well (argument values must be passed in order, and you can't skip a required parameter).

To take advantage of default argument values, let's make a better version of the **create_gallon_radio()** function. As originally written, the function only creates radio buttons with a name of *gallon_price*. It'd be better if the function could be used multiple times in a form for multiple radio button groupings (although the function won't be used like that in this script).

To set default argument values:

1. Open **calculator.php** (refer to Script 3.8) in your text editor or IDE, if it is not already.

2. Change the function definition line (line 6) so that it takes a second, optional argument (**Script 3.9**):

```
function create_radio($value,
→ $name = 'gallon_price') {
```

There are two changes here. First, the name of the function is changed to be reflective of its more generic nature. Second, the function now takes a second argument, **$name**, although that argument has a default value, which makes that argument optional when the function is called.

continues on page 103

Script 3.9 The redefined function now assumes a set radio button name unless one is specified when the function is called.

```
1    <?php # Script 3.9 - calculator.php #4
2
3    // This function creates a radio button.
4    // The function takes two arguments: the value and the name.
5    // The function also makes the button "sticky."
6    function create_radio($value, $name = 'gallon_price') {
7
8        // Start the element:
9        echo '<input type="radio" name="' . $name .'" value="' . $value . '"';
10
```

code continues on next page

```
11      // Check for stickiness:
12      if (isset($_POST[$name]) && ($_POST[$name] == $value)) {
13          echo ' checked="checked"';
14      }
15
16      // Complete the element:
17      echo "> $value ";
18
19  } // End of create_gallon_radio() function.
20
21  $page_title = 'Trip Cost Calculator';
22  include('includes/header.html');
23
24  // Check for form submission:
25  if ($_SERVER['REQUEST_METHOD'] == 'POST') {
26
27      // Minimal form validation:
28      if (isset($_POST['distance'], $_POST['gallon_price'], $_POST['efficiency']) &&
29      is_numeric($_POST['distance']) && is_numeric($_POST['gallon_price']) &&
        is_numeric($_POST['efficiency']) ) {
30
31          // Calculate the results:
32          $gallons = $_POST['distance'] / $_POST['efficiency'];
33          $dollars = $gallons * $_POST['gallon_price'];
34          $hours = $_POST['distance']/65;
35
36          // Print the results:
37          echo '<div class="page-header"><h1>Total Estimated Cost</h1></div>
38          <p>The total cost of driving ' . $_POST['distance'] . ' miles, averaging ' .
            $_POST['efficiency'] . ' miles per gallon, and paying an average of $' .
            $_POST['gallon_price'] . ' per gallon, is $' . number_format ($dollars, 2) . '.
            If you drive at an average of 65 miles per hour, the trip will take approximately ' .
            number_format($hours, 2) . ' hours.</p>';
39
40      } else { // Invalid submitted values.
41          echo '<div class="page-header"><h1>Error!</h1></div>
42          <p class="text-danger">Please enter a valid distance, price per gallon, and fuel
            efficiency.</p>';
43      }
44
45  } // End of main submission IF.
46
47  // Leave the PHP section and create the HTML form:
48  ?>
49
50  <div class="page-header"><h1>Trip Cost Calculator</h1></div>
51  <form action="calculator.php" method="post">
52      <p>Distance (in miles): <input type="number" name="distance" value="<?php if
        (isset($_POST['distance'])) echo $_POST['distance']; ?>"></p>
```

code continues on next page

3. Change the function definition so that it uses the **$name** argument in lieu of *gallon_price*:

```
echo '<input type="radio"
→ name="' . $name .'"
→ value="' . $value . '"';
if (isset($_POST[$name]) &&
→ ($_POST[$name] == $value)) {
  echo ' checked="checked"';
}
```

Three changes are necessary. First, **$name** is used for the **name** attribute of the element. Second, the conditional that checks for "stickiness" now uses **$_POST[$name]** twice instead of **$_POST['gallon_price']**.

4. Change the function call lines:

```
create_radio('3.00');
create_radio('3.50');
create_radio('4.00');
```

The function calls must be changed to use the new function name. But because the second argument has a default value, it can be omitted in these calls. The result is the same as executing this call—

```
create_radio('4.00', 'gallon_price');
```

—but now the function could be used to create other radio buttons as well.

continues on next page

Script 3.9 *continued*

```
53    <p>Ave. Price Per Gallon:
54    <?php
55    create_radio('3.00');
56    create_radio('3.50');
57    create_radio('4.00');
58    ?>
59    </p>
60    <p>Fuel Efficiency: <select name="efficiency">
61       <option value="10"<?php if (isset($_POST['efficiency']) && ($_POST['efficiency'] ==
         '10')) echo ' selected="selected"'; ?>>Terrible</option>
62       <option value="20"<?php if (isset($_POST['efficiency']) && ($_POST['efficiency'] ==
         '20')) echo ' selected="selected"'; ?>>Decent</option>
63       <option value="30"<?php if (isset($_POST['efficiency']) && ($_POST['efficiency'] ==
         '30')) echo ' selected="selected"'; ?>>Very Good</option>
64       <option value="50"<?php if (isset($_POST['efficiency']) && ($_POST['efficiency'] ==
         '50')) echo ' selected="selected"'; ?>>Outstanding</option>
65    </select></p>
66    <p><input type="submit" name="submit" value="Calculate!"></p>
67    </form>
68
69    <?php include('includes/footer.html'); ?>
```

5. Save the file, place it in your web directory, and test it in your browser ⓓ.

TIP To pass a function no value for an argument, use either an empty string (''), NULL, or FALSE.

TIP In the PHP manual, brackets ([]) are used to indicate a function's optional parameters ⓔ.

Total Estimated Cost

The total cost of driving 141 miles, averaging 50 miles per gallon, and paying an average of $3.50 per gallon, is $9.87. If you drive at an average of 65 miles per hour, the trip will take approximately 2.17 hours.

Trip Cost Calculator

Distance (in miles): 141

Ave. Price Per Gallon: ○ 3.00 ⬤ 3.50 ○ 4.00

Fuel Efficiency: [Outstanding ⬍]

ⓓ The addition of the second (optional) argument has not affected the functionality of the function.

---

number_format

(PHP 4, PHP 5, PHP 7)

number_format — Format a number with grouped thousands

Description

```
string number_format ( float $number [, int $decimals = 0 ] )
```

ⓔ The PHP manual's description of the **number_format()** function shows that only the first argument is required.

Returning values from a function

The final attribute of a user-defined function to discuss is that of returning values. Some, but not all, functions do this. For example, **print** will return either a 1 or a 0 indicating its success, whereas **echo** will not. As another example, the **number_format()** function returns a string, which is the formatted version of a number (see ⓔ in the previous section).

To have a function return a value, use the **return** statement. This function might return the astrological sign for a given birth month and day:

```
function find_sign($month, $day) {
   // Function code.
   return $sign;
}
```

A function can return a literal value—say a string or a number—or the value of a variable that has been determined within the function.

When calling a function that returns a value, you can assign the function result to a variable:

```
$my_sign = find_sign('October', 23);
```

or use it as an argument when calling another function:

```
echo find_sign('October', 23);
```

Let's update the **calculator.php** script so that it uses a function to determine the cost of the trip.

To have a function return a value:

1. Open **calculator.php** (refer to Script 3.9) in your text editor or IDE, if it is not already.

2. After the first function definition, begin defining a second function (**Script 3.10**):

   ```
   function calculate_trip_cost
   ⟶($miles, $mpg, $ppg) {
   ```

   The **calculate_trip_cost()** function takes three arguments: the distance to be traveled, the average miles per gallon, and the average price per gallon.

continues on page 107

Script 3.10 Another user-defined function is added to the script. It performs the main calculation and returns the result.

```
1    <?php # Script 3.10 - calculator.php #5
2
3    // This function creates a radio button.
4    // The function takes two arguments: the value and the name.
5    // The function also makes the button "sticky".
6    function create_radio($value, $name = 'gallon_price') {
7
8       // Start the element:
9       echo '<input type="radio" name="' . $name .'" value="' . $value . '"';
10
11      // Check for stickiness:
12      if (isset($_POST[$name]) && ($_POST[$name] == $value)) {
13         echo ' checked="checked"';
14      }
15
```

code continues on next page

```
16      // Complete the element:
17      echo "> $value ";
18
19  } // End of create_gallon_radio() function.
20
21  // This function calculates the cost of the trip.
22  // The function takes three arguments: the distance, the fuel efficiency, and the price per
    gallon.
23  // The function returns the total cost.
24  function calculate_trip_cost($miles, $mpg, $ppg) {
25
26      // Get the number of gallons:
27      $gallons = $miles/$mpg;
28
29      // Get the cost of those gallons:
30      $dollars = $gallons * $ppg;
31
32      // Return the formatted cost:
33      return number_format($dollars, 2);
34
35  } // End of calculate_trip_cost() function.
36
37  $page_title = 'Trip Cost Calculator';
38  include('includes/header.html');
39
40  // Check for form submission:
41  if ($_SERVER['REQUEST_METHOD'] == 'POST') {
42
43      // Minimal form validation:
44      if (isset($_POST['distance'], $_POST['gallon_price'], $_POST['efficiency']) &&
45      is_numeric($_POST['distance']) && is_numeric($_POST['gallon_price']) &&
        is_numeric($_POST['efficiency']) ) {
46
47          // Calculate the results:
48          $cost = calculate_trip_cost($_POST['distance'], $_POST['efficiency'],
            $_POST['gallon_price']);
49          $hours = $_POST['distance']/65;
50
51          // Print the results:
52          echo '<div class="page-header"><h1>Total Estimated Cost</h1></div>
53          <p>The total cost of driving ' . $_POST['distance'] . ' miles, averaging ' .
            $_POST['efficiency'] . ' miles per gallon, and paying an average of $' .
            $_POST['gallon_price'] . ' per gallon, is $' . $cost . '. If you drive at
            an average of 65 miles per hour, the trip will take approximately ' .
            number_format($hours, 2) . ' hours.</p>';
54
55      } else { // Invalid submitted values.
56          echo '<div class="page-header"><h1>Error!</h1></div>
57          <p class="text-danger">Please enter a valid distance, price per gallon, and fuel
            efficiency.</p>';
58      }
```

code continues on next page

3. Perform the calculations and return the formatted cost:

```
$gallons = $miles/$mpg;
$dollars = $gallons * $ppg;
return number_format($dollars, 2);
} // End of calculate_trip_cost()
→ function.
```

The first two lines are the same calculations as the script used before, but now they use function variables. The last thing the function does is return a formatted version of the calculated cost.

4. Replace the two lines that calculate the cost (lines 32–33 of Script 3.9) with a function call:

```
$cost = calculate_trip_cost
→ ($_POST['distance'], $_
POST['efficiency'],
→ $_POST['gallon_price']);
```

Invoking the function, while passing it the three required values, will perform the calculation. Since the function returns a value, the results of the function call—the returned value—can be assigned to a variable.

continues on next page

Script 3.10 *continued*

```
59
60   } // End of main submission IF.
61
62   // Leave the PHP section and create the HTML form:
63   ?>
64
65   <div class="page-header"><h1>Trip Cost Calculator</h1></div>
66   <form action="calculator.php" method="post">
67       <p>Distance (in miles): <input type="number" name="distance" value="<?php if
         (isset($_POST['distance'])) echo $_POST['distance']; ?>"></p>
68       <p>Ave. Price Per Gallon:
69       <?php
70       create_radio('3.00');
71       create_radio('3.50');
72       create_radio('4.00');
73       ?>
74       </p>
75       <p>Fuel Efficiency: <select name="efficiency">
76           <option value="10"<?php if (isset($_POST['efficiency']) && ($_POST['efficiency'] ==
             '10')) echo ' selected="selected"'; ?>>Terrible</option>
77           <option value="20"<?php if (isset($_POST['efficiency']) && ($_POST['efficiency'] ==
             '20')) echo ' selected="selected"'; ?>>Decent</option>
78           <option value="30"<?php if (isset($_POST['efficiency']) && ($_POST['efficiency'] ==
             '30')) echo ' selected="selected"'; ?>>Very Good</option>
79           <option value="50"<?php if (isset($_POST['efficiency']) && ($_POST['efficiency'] ==
             '50')) echo ' selected="selected"'; ?>>Outstanding</option>
80       </select></p>
81       <p><input type="submit" name="submit" value="Calculate!"></p>
82   </form>
83
84   <?php include('includes/footer.html'); ?>
```

5. Change the **echo** statement to use the new variable:

```
echo '<div class="page-header">
→ <h1>Total Estimated Cost</h1>
→ </div>
<p>The total cost of driving ' .
→ $_POST['distance'] . ' miles,
→ averaging ' . $_POST['efficiency']
→ . ' miles per gallon, and paying
→ an average of $' . $_POST
→ ['gallon_price'] . ' per gallon,
→ is $' . $cost . '. If you
→ drive at an average of 65
→ miles per hour, the trip will
→ take approximately ' .
→ number_format($hours, 2) . '
→ hours.</p>';
```

The **echo** statement uses the **$cost** variable here, instead of **$dollars** (as in the previous version of the script). Also, since the **$cost** variable is formatted within the function, the **number_format()** function does not need to be applied within the **echo** statement to this variable.

6. Save the file, place it in your web directory, and test it in your browser **F**.

Total Estimated Cost

The total cost of driving 654678 miles, averaging 10 miles per gallon, and paying an average of $4.00 per gallon, is $261,871.20. If you drive at an average of 65 miles per hour, the trip will take approximately 10,071.97 hours.

Trip Cost Calculator

Distance (in miles): 654678

Ave. Price Per Gallon: ○ 3.00 ○ 3.50 ● 4.00

Fuel Efficiency: Terrible ▲▼

F The calculator now uses a user-defined function to calculate and return the trip's cost. But this change has no impact on what the user sees.

TIP The `return` statement terminates the code execution at that point, so any code within a function after an executed `return` will never run.

TIP A function can have multiple `return` statements (e.g., in a `switch` statement or conditional), but only one, at most, will ever be invoked. For example, functions commonly do something like this:

```
function some_function () {
  if (/* condition */) {
    return TRUE;
  } else {
    return FALSE;
  }
}
```

TIP To have a function return multiple values, use the `array()` function—or short array syntax—to return an array of values:

```
return array($var1, $var2);
```

TIP When calling a function that returns an array, use the `list()` function to assign the array elements to individual variables:

```
list($v1, $v2) = some_function();
```

Variable Scope

Every variable in PHP has a *scope* to it, which is to say a realm in which the variable—and therefore its value—can be accessed. For starters, variables have the scope of the page in which they reside. If you define **$var**, the rest of the page can access **$var** but other pages generally cannot.

Since included files act as if they were part of the original (including) script, variables defined before an **include()** line are available to the included file, as you've already seen with **$page_title** and **header.html**. Further, variables defined within the included file are available to the parent (including) script *after* the **include()** line.

User-defined functions have their own scope: variables defined within a function are not available outside of it, and variables defined outside of a function are not available within it. For this reason, a variable inside of a function can have the same name as one outside of it but still be an entirely different variable with a different value. This is a confusing concept for many beginning programmers.

To alter the variable scope within a function, you can use the **global** statement:

```
function function_name() {
    global $var;
}
$var = 20;
function_name(); // Function call.
```

In this example, **$var** inside of the function is now the same as **$var** outside of it. This means that the function **$var** already has a value of 20, and if that value changes inside of the function, the external **$var**'s value will also change.

Another option for circumventing variable scope is to make use of the superglobals: **$_GET**, **$_POST**, **$_REQUEST**, and so forth. These variables are automatically accessible within your functions (hence, they are *super*global). You can also add elements to the **$GLOBALS** array to make them available within a function.

All of that being said, it's almost always best not to use global variables within a function. Functions should be designed so that they receive every value they need as arguments and return whatever value or values need to be returned. Relying on global variables within a function makes them more context dependent and, consequently, less useful.

PHP 7 New Function Features

PHP 7 adds new features to user-defined functions. To start, you can now declare function parameters as scalar types:

```
function greet(string $name) {
```

or

```
function test(bool $testing) {
```

PHP 5 had the ability to declare parameters as arrays or classes (via *type hinting*), and PHP 7 expands this to **bool**, **float**, **int**, and **string**. Failure to call the function without the right type of argument causes an error.

PHP 7 also adds the ability to declare the type of value returned by the function:

```
function greet(string $name): string {
```

That code forces the function to return a string, or creates an error if it doesn't.

PHP 7.1 expands these features a bit more. You can mark a parameter or a return type as "nullable" by preceding it with a question mark:

```
function greet(string ?$name) {
```

That function definition says that if a name value is provided, it must be a string, but you can also provide the value **null** instead. Similarly, this function will return either a string or **null**:

```
function greet(string $name): ?string {
```

Finally, PHP 7.1 adds the ability to indicate that a function returns no value:

```
function test(): void {
   // No return statement!
}
```

Review and Pursue

If you have any problems with the review questions or the pursue prompts, turn to the book's supporting forum (**LarryUllman.com/forums/**).

Review

- What is an *absolute* path? What is a *relative* path?

- What is the difference between **include()** and **require()**?

- What is the difference between **include()** and **include_once()**? Which function should you generally avoid using and why?

- Why does it *not* matter what extension is used for an included file?

- What is the significance of the **$_SERVER['REQUEST_METHOD']** value?

- How do you make the following form elements sticky?
  - ▸ Text input
  - ▸ Select menu
  - ▸ Radio button
  - ▸ Check box
  - ▸ Textarea

- If you have a PHP error caused by code placed within an HTML tag, where must you look to find the error message?

- What is the syntax for defining your own function?

- What is the syntax for defining a function that takes arguments?

- What is the syntax for defining a function that takes arguments with default values? How do default values impact how the function can be called?

- How do you define and call a function that returns a value?

Pursue

- Create a new HTML template for the pages in this chapter. Use that new template as the basis for new header and footer files. By doing so, you should be able to change the look of the entire site without modifying any of the PHP scripts.

- Create a new form and give it the ability to be "sticky." Have the form use a textarea and a check box (neither of which is demonstrated in this chapter).

- Change **calculator.php** so that it uses a constant in lieu of the hard-coded average speed of 65. (As written, the average speed is a "magic number"—a value used in a script without explanation.)

- Better yet, modify **calculator.php** so that the user can enter the average speed or select it from a list of options.

- Update the output of **calculator.php** so that it displays the number of days and hours the trip will take when the number of hours is greater than 24.

- As a more advanced trick, rewrite **calculator.php** so that the **create_radio()** function call is in the script only once but still creates three radio buttons. Hint: Use a loop.

- If you're using PHP 7 or greater, update the function definitions to use parameter and return type declarations. (See the "PHP 7 New Function Features" sidebar and the PHP manual for details.)

- Learn more about the Bootstrap framework to better stylize the calculator form.

Introduction to MySQL

Because this book discusses how to integrate several technologies—primarily PHP, SQL, and MySQL—a solid understanding of each is important before you begin writing PHP scripts that use SQL to interact with MySQL. This chapter is a departure from its predecessors in that it temporarily leaves PHP behind to delve into MySQL.

MySQL is the world's most popular open source database application (according to MySQL's web site, **www.mysql.com**) and is commonly used with PHP. The MySQL software comes with the database server that stores the actual data, different client applications for interacting with the database server, and several utilities. In this chapter, you'll see how to define a simple table using MySQL's allowed data types and other properties. Then you'll learn how to interact with the MySQL server using two different client applications. This information will be the foundation for the SQL taught in the next chapter.

Naming Database Elements

Before you start working with databases, you have to identify your needs. The purpose of the application (or web site, in this case) dictates how the database should be designed. With that in mind, the examples in this chapter and the next will use a database that stores some user registration information.

When creating databases and tables, you should come up with names (formally called *identifiers*) that are clear, meaningful, and easy to type. Also, identifiers

- Should only contain letters, numbers, and the underscore (no spaces)
- Should not be the same as an existing keyword (like an SQL term or a function name)
- Should be treated as case-sensitive
- Cannot be longer than 64 characters (approximately)
- Must be unique within its realm

This last rule means that a table cannot have two columns with the same name and a database cannot have two tables with the same name. You can, however, use the same column name in two different tables in the same database; in fact, you often will do this.

As for the first three rules, I use the word *should*, as these are good policies more than exact requirements. Exceptions can be made to these rules, but the syntax for doing so can be complicated. Abiding by these suggestions is a reasonable limitation and will help avoid complications.

To name a database's elements:

1. Determine the database's name.

   This is the easiest and, arguably, least important step. Just make sure that the database name is unique for that MySQL server. If you're using a hosted server, your web host will likely provide a database name that may or may not include your account or domain name.

   For this first example, the database will be called *sitename*, since the information and techniques could apply to any generic site.

2. Determine the table names.

   The table names just need to be unique within this database, which shouldn't be a problem. For this example, which stores user registration information, the only table will be called *users*.

TABLE 4.1 users Table

Column Name	Example
user_id	834
first_name	Larry
last_name	David
email	ld@example.com
pass	emily07
registration_date	2017-08-31 19:21:03

3. Determine the column names for each table.

The *users* table will have columns to store a user ID, a first name, a last name, an email address, a password, and the registration date. **Table 4.1** shows these columns, with sample data, using proper identifiers. Because MySQL has a function called *password*, I've changed the name of that column to just *pass*. This isn't strictly necessary but is really a good idea.

For the *user_id* column, there are two common approaches. Some use simply *id* as the identifying column name in any table so that all tables have an *id* column. Others use a variation on *tablename_id*: *user_id* or *users_id*.

TIP Chapter 6, "Database Design," discusses database design in more detail, using more complex examples.

TIP To be precise, the length limit for the names of databases, tables, and columns is actually 64 bytes, not characters. While most characters in many languages require 1 byte apiece, it's possible to use a multibyte character in an identifier. But 64 bytes is still a lot of space, so this probably won't be an issue for you.

TIP Whether or not an identifier in MySQL is case-sensitive actually depends on many things, because each database is actually a folder on the server and each table is actually one or more files. On Windows and normally on macOS, database and table names are generally case-insensitive. On Unix and some macOS setups, they are case-sensitive. Column names are always case-insensitive. It's really best, in my opinion, to always use all lowercase letters and work as if case-sensitivity applied.

Choosing Your Column Types

Once you have identified all of the tables and columns that the database will need, you should determine each column's data type. When you're creating a table, MySQL requires that you explicitly state what sort of information each column will contain. There are three primary types, which is true for almost every database application:

- Text (aka *strings*)
- Numbers
- Dates and times

Within each of these, there are many variants—some of which are MySQL specific. Choosing your column types correctly not only dictates what information can be stored and how, but also affects the database's overall performance. **Table 4.2** lists most of the available types for MySQL, how much space they take up, and brief descriptions of each type. Note that some of these limits may change in different versions of MySQL, and the character set (to be discussed in Chapter 6, "Database Design") may also impact the size of the text types.

Many of the types can take an optional *Length* attribute, limiting their size. (The brackets, [ ], indicate an optional parameter to be put in parentheses.) For performance purposes, you should place some restrictions on how much data can be stored in any column. But understand that attempting to insert a string five characters long into a **CHAR(2)** column will result in truncation of the final three characters. Only the first two characters would be stored; the rest would be lost forever. This is true for any field in which the size is set (**CHAR**, **VARCHAR**, **INT**, etc.). Thus, your length should always correspond to the maximum possible value—as a number—or the longest possible string—as text—that might be stored.

The various date types have all sorts of unique behaviors, the most important of which you'll learn about in this book. All the behaviors are documented in the MySQL manual. You'll use the **DATE** and **TIME** fields primarily without modification, so you do not have to worry too much about their intricacies.

There are also two special types—**ENUM** and **SET**—that allow you to define a series of acceptable values for that column. An **ENUM** column can store only one value of a possible several thousand, whereas **SET** allows for several of up to 64 possible values. These are available in MySQL but aren't present in every database application.

TABLE 4.2 MySQL Data Types

Type	Size	Description
CHAR[Length]	Length bytes	A fixed-length field from 0 to 255 characters long
VARCHAR[Length]	String length + 1 or 2 bytes	A variable-length field from 0 to 65,535 characters long
TINYTEXT	String length + 1 bytes	A string with a maximum length of 255 characters
TEXT	String length + 2 bytes	A string with a maximum length of 65,535 characters
MEDIUMTEXT	String length + 3 bytes	A string with a maximum length of 16,777,215 characters
LONGTEXT	String length + 4 bytes	A string with a maximum length of 4,294,967,295 characters
TINYINT[Length]	1 byte	Range of –128 to 127 or 0 to 255 unsigned
SMALLINT[Length]	2 bytes	Range of –32,768 to 32,767 or 0 to 65,535 unsigned
MEDIUMINT[Length]	3 bytes	Range of –8,388,608 to 8,388,607 or 0 to 16,777,215 unsigned
INT[Length]	4 bytes	Range of –2,147,483,648 to 2,147,483,647 or 0 to 4,294,967,295 unsigned
BIGINT[Length]	8 bytes	Range of –9,223,372,036,854,775,808 to 9,223,372,036,854,775,807 or 0 to 18,446,744,073,709,551,615 unsigned
FLOAT[Length, Decimals]	4 bytes	A small number with a floating decimal point
DOUBLE[Length, Decimals]	8 bytes	A large number with a floating decimal point
DECIMAL[Length, Decimals]	Length + 1 or 2 bytes	A **DOUBLE** stored as a string, allowing for a fixed decimal point
DATE	3 bytes	In the format YYYY-MM-DD
DATETIME	8 bytes	In the format YYYY-MM-DD HH:MM:SS
TIMESTAMP	4 bytes	In the format YYYYMMDDHHMMSS; acceptable range starts in 1970 and ends in the year 2038
TIME	3 bytes	In the format of HH:MM:SS
ENUM	1 or 2 bytes	Short for enumeration, which means that each column can have one of several possible values
SET	1, 2, 3, 4, or 8 bytes	Like **ENUM** except that each column can have more than one of several possible values

To select the column types:

1. Identify whether a column should be a text, number, or date/time type (**Table 4.3**).

This is normally an easy and obvious step, but you want to be as specific as possible. For example, the date *2006-08-02* (MySQL format) could be stored as a string—*August 2, 2006*. But if you use the proper date format, you'll have a more useful database (and, as you'll see, there are functions that can turn *2006-08-02* into *August 2, 2006*).

2. Choose the most appropriate subtype for each column (**Table 4.4**).

For this example, *user_id* is set as a **MEDIUMINT**, allowing for up to nearly 17 million values (as an *unsigned*, or non-negative, number). *registration_date* will be a **DATETIME**. It can store both the date and the specific time a user registered. When deciding among the date types, consider whether you'll want to access just the date, the time, or possibly both.

When choosing a subtype, err on the side of storing too much information.

The other fields will be mostly **VARCHAR**, since their lengths will differ from record to record. The only exception is the password column, which will be a fixed-length **CHAR** (you'll see why when inserting records in the next chapter). See the sidebar "**CHAR** vs. **VARCHAR**" for more information on these two types.

CHAR vs. VARCHAR

Both of these types store strings and can be set with a maximum length. The primary difference between the two is that anything stored as a **CHAR** will always be stored as a string the length of the column (using spaces to pad it; these spaces will be removed when you retrieve the stored value from the database). Conversely, strings stored in a **VARCHAR** column will require only as much space as the string itself. So the word *cat* in a **VARCHAR(10)** column requires 4 bytes of space (the length of the string plus 1), but in a **CHAR(10)** column, that same word requires 10 bytes of space. Hence, generally speaking, **VARCHAR** columns tend to require less disk space than **CHAR** columns.

However, databases are normally faster when working with fixed-size columns, which is an argument in favor of **CHAR**. And that same three-letter word—*cat*—in a **CHAR(3)** uses only 3 bytes but in a **VARCHAR(10)** requires 4. So how do you decide which to use?

If a string field will *always* be of a set length (e.g., a state abbreviation), use **CHAR**; otherwise, use **VARCHAR**. You may notice, though, that in some cases MySQL defines a column as the one type—like **CHAR**—even though you created it as the other: **VARCHAR**. This is perfectly normal and is MySQL's way of improving performance.

TABLE 4.3 users Table

Column Name	Type
user_id	number
first_name	text
last_name	text
email	text
pass	text
registration_date	date/time

TABLE 4.4 users Table

Column Name	Type
user_id	MEDIUMINT
first_name	VARCHAR
last_name	VARCHAR
email	VARCHAR
pass	CHAR
registration_date	DATETIME

TABLE 4.5 users Table

Column Name	Type
user_id	MEDIUMINT
first_name	VARCHAR(20)
last_name	VARCHAR(40)
email	VARCHAR(60)
pass	CHAR(128)
registration_date	DATETIME

3. Set the maximum length for text columns (**Table 4.5**).

The size of any field should be restricted to the smallest possible value, based on the largest possible input. For example, if a column stores a state abbreviation, it would be defined as a **CHAR(2)**. Other times you might have to guess: I can't think of any first names longer than about 10 characters, but just to be safe I'll allow for up to 20.

TIP The length attribute for numeric types does not affect the range of values that can be stored in the column. Columns defined as TINYINT(1) or TINYINT(20) can store the exact same values. Instead, for integers, the length dictates the display width; for decimals, the length is the total number of digits that can be stored.

TIP If you need absolute precision when using non-integers, DECIMAL is preferred over FLOAT or DOUBLE.

TIP MySQL has a BOOLEAN type, which is just a TINYINT(1), with 0 meaning FALSE and 1 meaning TRUE.

TIP Many of the data types have synonymous names: INT and INTEGER, DEC and DECIMAL, and so on.

TIP Depending on the version of MySQL in use, the TIMESTAMP field type is automatically set as the current date and time when an INSERT or UPDATE occurs, even if no value is specified for that particular field. If a table has multiple TIMESTAMP columns, only the first one will be updated when an INSERT or UPDATE is performed.

TIP MySQL also has several variants on the text types that allow for storing binary data. These types are BINARY, VARBINARY, TINYBLOB, MEDIUMBLOB, and LONGBLOB. Such types can be used for storing files or encrypted data.

Choosing Other Column Properties

Besides deciding what data types and sizes you should use for your columns, consider a handful of other properties.

First, every column, regardless of type, can be defined as **NOT NULL**. The **NULL** value, in databases and programming, is equivalent to saying that the field has no known value. Ideally, in a properly designed database, every column of every row in every table should have a value, but that isn't always the case. To force a field to have a value, add the **NOT NULL** description to its column type. For example, a required dollar amount can be described as

`cost DECIMAL(5,2) NOT NULL.`

Indexes, Keys, and AUTO_INCREMENT

Two concepts closely related to database design are indexes and keys. An *index* in a database is a way of requesting that the database keep an eye on the values of a specific column or combination of columns (loosely stated). The benefit of an index is improved performance when retrieving records but marginally hindered performance when inserting records or updating them.

A *key* in a database table is integral to the "normalization" process used for designing more complicated databases (see Chapter 6). There are two types of keys: *primary* and *foreign*. Each table should have exactly one primary key, and the primary key in one table is often linked as a foreign key in another.

A table's primary key is an artificial way to refer to a record and must abide by three rules:

1. It must always have a value.
2. That value must never change.
3. That value must be unique for each record in the table.

In the *users* table, *user_id* will be designated as a **PRIMARY KEY**, which is both a description of the column and a directive to MySQL to index it. Since *user_id* is a number—which primary keys almost always will be, the **AUTO_INCREMENT** description is also added to the column, which tells MySQL to use the next-highest number as the *user_id* value for each added record. You'll see what this means in practice when you begin inserting records.

When creating a table, you can also specify a default value for any column, regardless of type. In cases where a majority of the records will have the same value for a column, presetting a default will save you from having to specify a value when inserting new rows (unless that row's value for that column is different from the norm).

```
subscribe ENUM('Yes', 'No') default 'No'
```

With the *subscribe* column, if no value is specified when adding a record, the default will be used.

If a column cannot be **NULL** and does not have a default value, and no value is specified for a new record, that field will be given a default value based on its type. For numeric types, the default value is 0. For most date and time types, the type's version of "zero" will be the default (e.g., *0000-00-00*). The first **TIMESTAMP** column in a table will have a default value of the current date and time. String types use an empty string (`''`) as the default value, except for **ENUM**, whose default value—again, if not otherwise specified—is the first possible enumerated value (*Yes* in the previous example).

The number types can be marked as **UNSIGNED**, which limits the stored data to positive numbers and zero. This also effectively doubles the range of positive numbers that can be stored because no negative numbers will be kept (see Table 4.2). You can also flag the number types as **ZEROFILL**, which means that any extra room will be padded with zeros. **ZEROFILL**s are also automatically **UNSIGNED**.

Finally, when designing a database, you'll need to consider creating indexes, adding keys, and using the **AUTO_INCREMENT** property. Chapter 6 discusses these concepts in greater detail, but in the meantime, check out the sidebar "Indexes, Keys, and **AUTO_INCREMENT**" to learn how they affect the *users* table.

To finish defining your columns:

1. Identify your primary key.

   The primary key is quixotically both arbitrary and critically important. Almost always a number value, the primary key is a unique way to refer to a particular record. For example, your phone number has no inherent value but is unique to you (your home or mobile phone).

   In the *users* table, *user_id* will be the primary key: an arbitrary number used to refer to a row of data. Again, Chapter 6 will go into the concept of primary keys in more detail.

2. Identify which columns cannot have a **NULL** value.

   In this example, every field is required (cannot be **NULL**). As an example of a column that could have **NULL** values, if you stored people's addresses, you might have *address_line1* and *address_line2*, with the latter one being optional. In general, tables that have a lot of **NULL** values suggest a poor design (more on this in...you guessed it...Chapter 6).

   continues on next page

3. Make any numeric type **UNSIGNED** if it won't ever store negative numbers.

user_id, which will be a number, should be **UNSIGNED** so that it's always positive. As a rule, primary keys should always be unsigned. Other examples of **UNSIGNED** numbers would be the price of items in an e-commerce example, a telephone extension for a business, or a zip code.

4. Establish the default value for any column.

None of the columns here logically implies a default value.

5. Confirm the final column definitions (**Table 4.6**).

Before creating the tables, you should revisit the type and range of data you'll store to make sure that your database effectively accounts for everything.

TIP Text columns can also have defined character sets and collations. This will mean more...in Chapter 6.

TIP Default values must always be a static value, not the result of executing a function, with one exception: the default value for a TIMESTAMP column can be assigned as CURRENT_TIMESTAMP.

TIP TEXT columns cannot be assigned default values.

TABLE 4.6 users Table

Column Name	Type
user_id	MEDIUMINT UNSIGNED NOT NULL
first_name	VARCHAR(20) NOT NULL
last_name	VARCHAR(40) NOT NULL
email	VARCHAR(60) NOT NULL
pass	CHAR(128) NOT NULL
registration_date	DATETIME NOT NULL

Accessing MySQL

To create tables, add records, and request information from a database, you need some sort of *client* to communicate with the MySQL server. Later in the book, PHP scripts will act in this role, but being able to use another interface is necessary.

Although oodles of client applications are available, I'll focus on two: the *mysql client* and the web-based phpMyAdmin. A third option, the MySQL Workbench, is not discussed in this book but can be found at the MySQL web site (**https://dev.mysql.com/downloads/workbench/**), should you not be satisfied with these two choices.

The rest of this chapter assumes you have access to a running MySQL server. If you are working on your own computer, see Appendix A, "Installation," for instructions on installing MySQL, starting MySQL, and creating MySQL users, all of which must already be done in order to finish this chapter. If you are using a hosted server, your web host should provide you with the database access. Depending on the hosting, you may be provided with phpMyAdmin but not be able to use the command-line mysql client.

Using the mysql client

The mysql client is normally installed with the rest of the MySQL software. Although the mysql client does not have a pretty graphical interface, it's a reliable, standard tool that's easy to use and behaves consistently on many different operating systems.

The mysql client is accessed from a command-line interface, be it the Terminal application in Linux or macOS **Ⓐ**, or a DOS prompt in Windows **Ⓑ**. If you're not comfortable with command-line interactions, you might find this interface to be challenging, but it becomes easy to use in no time.

To start the application from the command line, type its name and press Return or Enter:

```
mysql
```

Depending on the server (or your computer), you may need to enter the full path to start the application. For example:

- **/Applications/MAMP/Library/bin/** → **mysql** (macOS, using MAMP)

- **C:\xampp\mysql\bin\mysql** (Windows, using XAMPP)

continues on next page

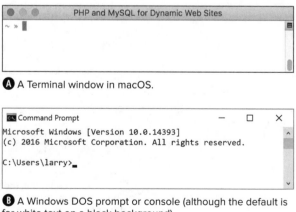

Ⓐ A Terminal window in macOS.

Ⓑ A Windows DOS prompt or console (although the default is for white text on a black background).

When invoking this application, you can add arguments to affect how it runs. The most common arguments are the username, password, and hostname (computer name, URL, or IP address) you want to use to connect. You establish these arguments like so:

```
mysql -u username -h hostname -p
```

The **-p** option will cause the client to prompt you for the password. You can also specify the password on this line if you prefer—by typing it directly after the **-p** prompt—but it will be visible, which is insecure. The **-h hostname** argument is optional, and you can leave it off unless you cannot connect to the MySQL server without it.

Within the mysql client, every statement (SQL command) needs to be terminated by a semicolon. These semicolons are an indication to the client that the query is complete and should be run. The semicolons, a common point of confusion, are not part of the SQL itself. What this also means is that you can continue the same SQL statement over several lines within the mysql client, which makes it easy to read and to edit, should that be necessary.

As a quick demonstration of accessing and using the mysql client, these next steps will show you how to start the mysql client, select a database to use, and quit the client. Before following these steps,

- The MySQL server must be running.
- You must have a username and password with proper access.

Both are explained in Appendix A.

As a side note, in the following steps and throughout the rest of the book, I will continue to provide images using the mysql client on both Windows and macOS. Although the appearance differs, the steps and results will be identical. So in short, don't be concerned about why one image shows the DOS prompt and the next a Terminal.

To use the mysql client:

1. Access your system from a command-line interface.

   On Unix systems and macOS, this is just a matter of bringing up the Terminal or a similar application.

   If you are using Windows and you have installed MySQL on your computer, or press Windows Key+R, type **cmd** in the window **C**, and press Enter (or click OK) to bring up a DOS prompt.

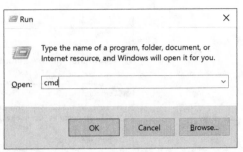

C Executing **cmd** within the Run prompt in Windows is one way to access a DOS prompt interface.

2. Invoke the mysql client, using the appropriate command 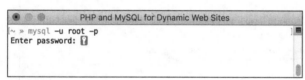.

***/path/to/mysql*/bin/mysql -u**
→ *username* -p

The ***/path/to/mysql*** part of this step will be largely dictated by the operating system you are running and where MySQL was installed. I've already provided two options, based on installations of MAMP on macOS or XAMPP on Windows (both are installed in Appendix A).

The basic premise is that you are running the mysql client, connecting as *username*, and requesting to be prompted for the password. Not to overstate the point, but the username and password values that you use must already be established in MySQL as valid (see Appendix A).

3. Enter the password at the prompt and press Return/Enter.

The password you use here should be for the user you specified in the preceding step. If you used the proper username/password combination (i.e., someone with valid access), you should be greeted as shown in **E**. If access is denied, you're probably not using the correct values (see Appendix A for instructions on creating users).

4. Select the database you want to use **F**.

USE test;

The **USE** command selects the database to be used for every subsequent command. The *test* database is one that MySQL installs by default. Assuming it exists on your server, all users should be able to access it.

continues on next page

```
● ● ●              PHP and MySQL for Dynamic Web Sites
[~ » mysql -u root -p
Enter password:
```

D Access the mysql client by entering the full path to the utility, along with the proper arguments.

```
mysql  -u root -p                                    —    □    ×

Setting environment for using XAMPP for Windows.
larry@LARRYULLMANB008 c:\xampp
# mysql -u root -p
Enter password:
Welcome to the MariaDB monitor.  Commands end with ; or \g.
Your MariaDB connection id is 4
Server version: 10.1.21-MariaDB mariadb.org binary distribution

Copyright (c) 2000, 2016, Oracle, MariaDB Corporation Ab and others.

Type 'help;' or '\h' for help. Type '\c' to clear the current input statement.

MariaDB [(none)]>
```

E If you are successfully able to log in, you'll see a welcome message like this.

5. Quit out of mysql 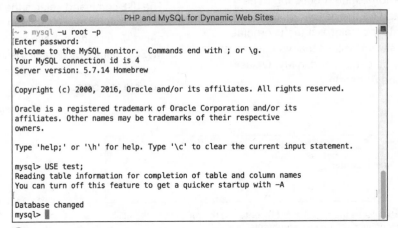.

```
exit
```

You can also use the command **quit** to leave the client. This step—unlike most other commands you enter in the mysql client—does not require a semicolon at the end.

6. Quit the Terminal or DOS console session.

```
exit
```

The command **exit** will terminate the current session. On Windows, it will also close the DOS prompt window.

TIP If you know in advance which database you will want to use, you can simplify matters by starting mysql with

*/path/to/mysql/*bin/mysql -u username -p databasename

TIP To see what else you can do with the mysql client, type

*/path/to/mysql/*bin/mysql --help

TIP The mysql client on most systems allows you to use the up and down arrows to scroll through previously entered commands. If you make a mistake in typing a query, you can scroll up to find it, and then correct the error.

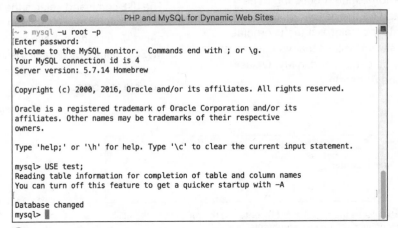

F After getting into the mysql client, run a **USE** command to choose the database with which you want to work.

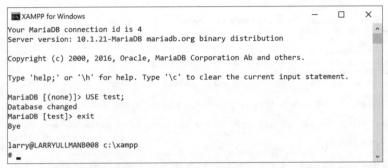

G Type either **exit** or **quit** to terminate your MySQL session and leave the mysql client.

TIP In the mysql client, you can also terminate SQL commands using \G instead of the semicolon. For queries that return results, using \G displays those results as a vertical list, as opposed to a horizontal table, which is sometimes easier to peruse.

TIP If you are in a long statement and make a mistake, cancel the current operation by typing \c and pressing Return or Enter. If mysql thinks a closing single or double quotation mark is missing (as indicated by the '> and "> prompts), you'll need to enter the appropriate quotation mark first.

Using phpMyAdmin

phpMyAdmin (**www.phpmyadmin.net**) is one of the best and most popular applications written in PHP. Its sole purpose is to provide an interface to a MySQL server. It is somewhat easier and more natural to use than the mysql client but requires a PHP installation and must be accessed through a web browser. If you're running MySQL on your own computer, you might find that using the mysql client makes more sense, because installing and configuring

phpMyAdmin constitutes unnecessary extra work (although all-in-one PHP and MySQL installers may do this for you). If you are using a hosted server, your web host is virtually guaranteed to provide phpMyAdmin as the primary way to work with MySQL and the mysql client may not be an option.

Using phpMyAdmin isn't hard, but the next steps run through the basics so that you'll know what to do in the following chapters.

To use phpMyAdmin:

1. Access phpMyAdmin through your web browser 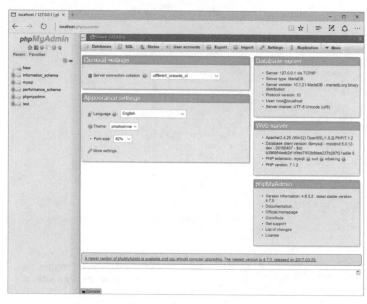.

   The URL you use will depend on your situation. If running web sites on your own computer, this might be **http://localhost/phpMyAdmin/**. If running on a hosted site, your web host will provide you with the proper URL. Likely, phpMyAdmin would be available through the site's control panel (should one exist).

   continues on next page

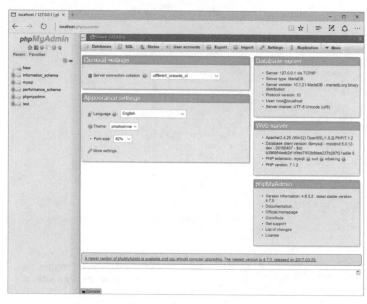

H The first phpMyAdmin page (when connected as a MySQL user who can access multiple databases).

Note that phpMyAdmin will only work if it's been properly configured to connect to MySQL with a valid username/password/hostname combination.

2. If possible and necessary, use the list on the left to select a database to use .

   What options you have here will vary depending on what MySQL user phpMyAdmin is connecting as. That user might have access to one database, several databases, or every database. On a hosted site where you have just one database, that database will probably already be selected for you. On your own computer, with phpMyAdmin connecting as the MySQL root user, you would see a pull-down menu or a simple list of available databases ❶.

3. Click on a table name in the left column to select that table ❶.

   You don't always have to select a table—in fact, you never will if you just use the SQL commands in this book, but doing so can often simplify some tasks.

❶ Use the list of databases on the left side of the window to choose with which database you want to work. This is the equivalent of running a USE *databasename* query within the mysql client.

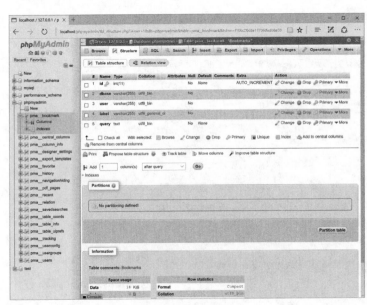

❶ Selecting a table from the left column changes the options on the right side of the page.

4. Use the tabs and links (on the right side of the page) to perform common tasks.

For the most part, the tabs and links are shortcuts to common SQL commands. For example, you can use options on the Browse tab to perform a **SELECT** query and options on the Insert tab to add new records.

5. Use the SQL tab 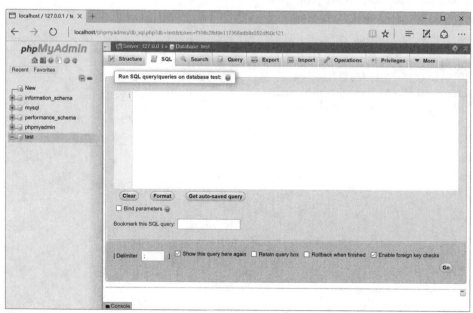 to enter SQL commands.

The next three chapters, and a couple more later in the book, will provide SQL commands that must be run to create, populate, and manipulate tables. These might look like

```
INSERT INTO tablename (col1, col2)
VALUES (x, y)
```

These commands can be run using the mysql client, phpMyAdmin, or any other interface. To run them within phpMyAdmin, just enter them into the SQL tab and click Go.

TIP There's a lot more that can be done with phpMyAdmin, but full coverage would require a chapter in its own right (and a long chapter at that). The information presented here will be enough for you to follow any of the examples in the book, should you not want to use the mysql client.

TIP phpMyAdmin can be configured to use a special database that will record your query history, allow you to bookmark queries, and more. See the phpMyAdmin documentation for details.

TIP One of the best reasons to use php-MyAdmin is to transfer a database from one computer to another. Use options on the Export tab in phpMyAdmin connected to the source computer to create a file of data. Then, on the destination computer, use the Import tab in phpMyAdmin (connected to that MySQL server) to complete the transfer.

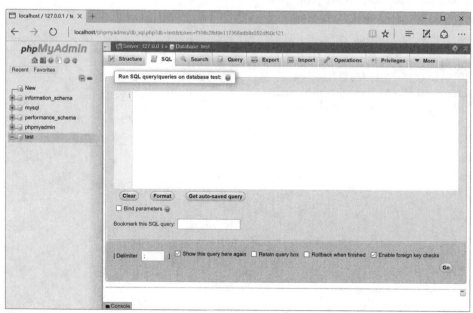

K The SQL tab, in the main part of the window, can be used to run any SQL command.

Review and Pursue

If you have any problems with the review questions or the pursue prompts, turn to the book's supporting forum (LarryUllman.com/forums/).

Review

- What version of MySQL are you using? If you don't know, find out now!

- What characters can be used in database, table, and column names?

- Should you treat database, table, and column names as case-sensitive or case-insensitive?

- What are the three general column types?

- What are the differences between **CHAR** and **VARCHAR**?

- How do you determine what size (in terms of subtype or length) a column should be?

- What are some of the other properties that can be assigned to columns?

- What is a primary key?

- If you're using the command-line mysql client to connect to MySQL, what username and password combination is required?

Pursue

- Find the online MySQL manual for your version of MySQL. Bookmark it!

- Start thinking about what databases you may need for your projects.

- If you haven't yet changed the MySQL root user password (assuming you've installed MySQL on your own computer), use the instructions in Appendix A to do so now.

5

Introduction to SQL

The preceding chapter provided a quick introduction to MySQL. That chapter focused on two topics: using MySQL's rules and data types to define a database, and how to interact with the MySQL server. This chapter moves on to the *lingua franca* of databases: SQL.

SQL, short for Structured Query Language, is a group of special words used exclusively for interacting with databases. SQL is surprisingly easy to learn and use, and yet it's amazingly powerful. In fact, the hardest thing to do in SQL is use it to its full potential!

In this chapter, you'll learn all the SQL you need to know to create tables, populate them, and run other basic queries. The examples will all use the *users* table discussed and designed in the preceding chapter. Also, as with that other chapter, this chapter assumes you have access to a running MySQL server and know how to use a client application to interact with it.

In This Chapter

Creating Databases and Tables

The first logical use of SQL will be to create a database. The syntax for creating a new database is simply

`CREATE DATABASE databasename`

That's all there is to it (as I said, SQL is easy to learn)!

The **CREATE** term is also used for making tables:

```
CREATE TABLE tablename (
column1name description,
column2name description
...)
```

After naming the table, you define each column within parentheses. Each column-description pair should be separated from the next by a comma, although you shouldn't place a comma after the last column definition.

Should you choose to create indexes at this time, you can add those at the end of the creation statement, but you can add indexes at a later time as well. (Indexes are more formally discussed in Chapter 6, "Database Design," but Chapter 4, "Intro-duction to MySQL," introduced the topic.)

In case you were wondering, SQL is *case-insensitive*. However, I make it a habit to capitalize the SQL keywords, as in the preceding example syntax and the following steps. Doing so helps to contrast the SQL terms from the database, table, and column names.

To create databases and tables:

1. Access MySQL using whichever client you prefer.

   Chapter 4 shows how to use two of the most common interfaces—the *mysql* command-line client and *phpMyAdmin*—to communicate with a MySQL server. Using the steps in the previous chapter, you should now connect to MySQL.

   Throughout the rest of this chapter, most of the SQL examples will be entered using the mysql client, but they will work just the same in phpMyAdmin or most other client tools.

2. Create and select the new database :

   ```
   CREATE DATABASE sitename;
   USE sitename;
   ```

   This first line creates the database, assuming that you are connected to MySQL as a user with permission to create new databases. The second line tells MySQL that you want to work within this database from here on out. Remember that within the mysql client, you must terminate every SQL command with a semicolon, although these semicolons aren't technically part of SQL itself. If executing multiple

```
PHP and MySQL for Dynamic Web Sites
mysql> CREATE DATABASE sitename;
Query OK, 1 row affected (0.04 sec)

mysql> USE sitename;
Database changed
mysql>
```

Ⓐ A new database, called *sitename*, is created in MySQL. It is then selected for future queries.

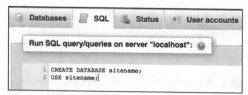

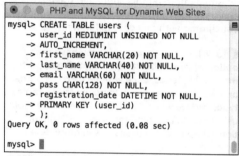

B The same commands for creating and selecting a database can be run within phpMyAdmin's SQL window.

C This **CREATE** SQL command will make the *users* table.

queries at once within phpMyAdmin, they should also be separated by semicolons **B**. If you are running only a single query within phpMyAdmin, no semicolons are necessary.

If you are using a hosting company's MySQL, they will probably create the database for you. In that case, just connect to MySQL and select the database.

3. Create the *users* table **C**:

```
CREATE TABLE users (
user_id MEDIUMINT UNSIGNED NOT NULL
AUTO_INCREMENT,
first_name VARCHAR(20) NOT NULL,
last_name VARCHAR(40) NOT NULL,
email VARCHAR(60) NOT NULL,
pass CHAR(128) NOT NULL,
registration_date DATETIME NOT NULL,
PRIMARY KEY (user_id)
);
```

The *users* table was designed in Chapter 4. There, the names, types, and attributes of each column in the table are determined based on a number of criteria (see that chapter for more information). Here, that information is placed within the **CREATE** table syntax to make the table in the database.

Because the mysql client will not run a query until it encounters a semicolon (or **\G** or **\g**), you can enter statements over multiple lines, as in **C** (by pressing Return or Enter at the end of each line). This often makes a query easier to read and debug. In phpMyAdmin, you can also run queries over multiple lines, although they will not be executed until you click Go.

continues on next page

4. Confirm the existence of the table 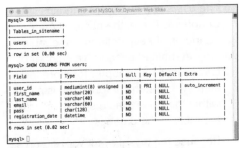 **D**:

```
SHOW TABLES;
SHOW COLUMNS FROM users;
```

The **SHOW** command reveals the tables in a database or the column names and types in a table.

Also, you might notice in **D** that the default value for *user_id* is **NULL**, even though this column was defined as **NOT NULL**. This is correct and has to do with *user_id* being an automatically incremented primary key. MySQL will often make minor changes to a column's definition for better performance or other reasons.

In phpMyAdmin, a database's tables are listed on the left side of the browser window, under the database's name **E**. Click a table's name to view its columns **F**.

> **TIP** The rest of this chapter assumes that you are using the mysql client or other tool and have already selected the sitename database with USE.

> **TIP** The order in which you list the columns when creating a table has no functional impact, but there are stylistic suggestions for how to order them. I normally list the primary-key column first, followed by any foreign-key columns (more on this subject in the next chapter), followed by the rest of the columns, concluding with any date columns.

> **TIP** When creating a table, you have the option of specifying its type. MySQL supports many table types, each with its own strengths and weaknesses. If you do not specify a table type, MySQL will automatically create the table using the default type for that MySQL installation. Chapter 6 discusses this in more detail.

> **TIP** When creating tables and text columns, you have the option to specify its collation and character set. Both come into play when using multiple languages or languages other than the default for the MySQL server. Chapter 6 also covers these subjects.

> **TIP** DESCRIBE `tablename` is the same statement as SHOW COLUMNS FROM `tablename`.

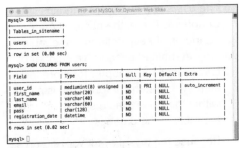

D Confirm the existence of, and columns in, a table using the **SHOW** command.

E phpMyAdmin shows that the *sitename* database contains one table, named *users*.

#	Name	Type	Collation	Attributes	Null	Default	Comments	Extra
☐ 1	user_id 🔑	mediumint(8)		UNSIGNED	No	*None*		AUTO_INCREMENT
☐ 2	first_name	varchar(20)	utf8_general_ci		No	*None*		
☐ 3	last_name	varchar(40)	utf8_general_ci		No	*None*		
☐ 4	email	varchar(60)	utf8_general_ci		No	*None*		
☐ 5	pass	char(128)	utf8_general_ci		No	*None*		
☐ 6	registration_date	datetime			No	*None*		

F phpMyAdmin shows a table's definition on this screen (accessed by clicking the table's name in the left-hand column).

Inserting Records

After a database and its table(s) have been created, you can start populating them using the **INSERT** command. There are two ways that an **INSERT** query can be written. With the first method, you name the columns to be populated:

```
INSERT INTO tablename (column1,
→ column2...) VALUES (value1,
→ value2 ...)
INSERT INTO tablename (column4,
→ column8) VALUES (valueX, valueY)
```

Using this structure, you can add rows of records, populating only the columns that matter. The result will be that any columns not given a value will be treated as **NULL** (or given a default value, if one was defined). Note that if a column cannot have a **NULL** value (it was defined as **NOT NULL**) and does not have a default value, not specifying a value will cause an error or warning 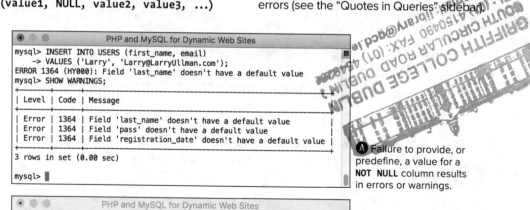.

The second format for inserting records is not to specify any columns at all but to include values for every one:

```
INSERT INTO tablename VALUES
→ (value1, NULL, value2, value3, ...)
```

If you use this second method, you must specify a value, even if it's **NULL**, for every column. If there are six columns in the table, you must list six values. Failure to match the number of values to the number of columns will cause an error **B**. For this and other reasons, the first format of inserting records is generally preferable.

MySQL also allows you to insert multiple rows at one time, separating each record by a comma.

```
INSERT INTO tablename (column1,
→ column4) VALUES (valueA, valueB),
(valueC, valueD),
(valueE, valueF)
```

While you can do this with MySQL, it is not acceptable within the SQL standard and is therefore not supported by all database applications. In MySQL, however, this syntax is faster than using individual **INSERT** queries.

Note that in these examples, placeholders are used for the actual table names, column names, and values. Furthermore, the examples forgo quotation marks. In real queries, you must abide by certain rules to avoid errors (see the "Quotes in Queries" sidebar).

```
PHP and MySQL for Dynamic Web Sites
mysql> INSERT INTO USERS (first_name, email)
    -> VALUES ('Larry', 'Larry@LarryUllman.com');
ERROR 1364 (HY000): Field 'last_name' doesn't have a default value
mysql> SHOW WARNINGS;
+-------+------+-------------------------------------------------------+
| Level | Code | Message                                               |
+-------+------+-------------------------------------------------------+
| Error | 1364 | Field 'last_name' doesn't have a default value        |
| Error | 1364 | Field 'pass' doesn't have a default value             |
| Error | 1364 | Field 'registration_date' doesn't have a default value|
+-------+------+-------------------------------------------------------+
3 rows in set (0.00 sec)

mysql>
```

A Failure to provide, or predefine, a value for a **NOT NULL** column results in errors or warnings.

```
PHP and MySQL for Dynamic Web Sites
mysql> INSERT INTO USERS VALUES
    -> ('Larry', 'Ullman', 'Larry@LarryUllman.com');
ERROR 1136 (21S01): Column count doesn't match value count at row 1
mysql>
```

B Not providing a value for every column in a table, or named in an **INSERT** query, also causes an error.

To insert data into a table:

1. Insert one row of data into the *users* table, naming the columns to be populated **C**:

```
INSERT INTO users
(first_name, last_name, email,
→ pass, registration_date)
VALUES ('Larry', 'Ullman',
→ 'email@example.com',
→ SHA2('mypass', 512), NOW());
```

Again, this syntax—where the specific columns are named—is more foolproof but not always the most convenient. For the first name, last name, and email columns, simple strings are used for the values—and strings must always be quoted.

For the password and registration date columns, two functions are being used to generate the values (see the sidebar "Two MySQL Functions"). The **SHA2()** function will encrypt the password (*mypass* in this example). The **NOW()** function will set the *registration_date* as this moment.

Quotes in Queries

In every SQL command:

- Numeric values shouldn't be quoted.
- String values (for **CHAR**, **VARCHAR**, and **TEXT** column types) must always be quoted.
- Date and time values must always be quoted.
- Functions cannot be quoted.
- The word **NULL** must not be quoted.

Unnecessarily quoting a numeric value normally won't cause problems (although you still shouldn't do it), but misusing quotation marks in the other situations will almost always mess things up. Also, it does not matter if you use single or double quotation marks, as long as you consistently pair them (an opening mark with a matching closing one).

And, as with PHP, if you need to use a quotation mark in a value, either use the other quotation mark type to encapsulate it or escape the mark by preceding it with a backslash:

```
INSERT INTO tablename (last_name)
→ VALUES ('O\'Toole')
```

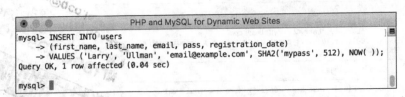

```
PHP and MySQL for Dynamic Web Sites
mysql> INSERT INTO users
    -> (first_name, last_name, email, pass, registration_date)
    -> VALUES ('Larry', 'Ullman', 'email@example.com', SHA2('mypass', 512), NOW( ));
Query OK, 1 row affected (0.04 sec)

mysql>
```

C This query inserts a single record into the *users* table. The *1 row affected* message indicates the success of the insertion.

Two MySQL Functions

Although functions are discussed in more detail later in this chapter, two need to be introduced now: **SHA2()** and **NOW()**.

The **SHA2()** function is one way to encrypt data. This function creates a *hashed* string. Hashing is a type of one-way encryption in that it cannot be reversed (i.e., you cannot decrypt the string). Hashing functions are useful when you need to store sensitive data that need not be viewed in an unencrypted form again. Because the output from **SHA2()** cannot be decrypted, it's obviously not a good choice for sensitive data that should be protected but later seen, like credit card numbers.

The **SHA2()** function takes a second argument indicating the desired length. A longer hash output will be more secure than a shorter one. Given a length of 512, this function returns a string that is always exactly 128 characters long. This is why the *users* table's *pass* column is defined as **CHAR(128)**.

The **NOW()** function is handy for populating date, time, and timestamp columns. It returns the current date and time on the server.

When using any function in an SQL statement, do not place it within quotation marks. You also must not have any spaces between the function's name and the following parentheses (so **NOW()** and not **NOW ()**).

2. Insert one row of data into the *users* table without naming the columns **D**:

```
INSERT INTO users VALUES
(NULL, 'Zoe', 'Isabella',
→ 'email2@example.com',
→ SHA2('mojito', 512), NOW());
```

In this second syntactical example, every column must be provided with a value. The *user_id* column is given a **NULL** value, which will cause MySQL to use the next logical number, per its **AUTO_INCREMENT** description. In other words, the first record will be assigned a *user_id* of 1, the second, 2, and so on.

continues on next page

```
● ● ●                PHP and MySQL for Dynamic Web Sites
mysql> INSERT INTO users VALUES
    -> (NULL, 'Zoe', 'Isabella', 'email2@example.com', SHA2('mojito', 512), NOW());
Query OK, 1 row affected (0.01 sec)

mysql> ▯
```

D Another record is inserted into the table, this time by providing a value for every column in the table.

3. Insert several values into the *users* table **E**:

```
INSERT INTO users
→ (first_name, last_name, email,
→ pass, registration_date) VALUES
('John', 'Lennon',
→ 'john@beatles.com',
→ SHA2('Happin3ss', 512), NOW()),
('Paul', 'McCartney',
→ 'paul@beatles.com',
→ SHA2('letITbe', 512), NOW()),
('George', 'Harrison',
→ 'george@beatles.com ',
→ SHA2('something', 512), NOW()),
('Ringo', 'Starr',
→ 'ringo@beatles.com',
→ SHA2('thisboy', 512), NOW());
```

Since MySQL allows you to insert multiple values at once, you can take advantage of this and fill up the table with records.

4. Continue Steps 1 and 2 until you've thoroughly populated the *users* table.

Throughout the rest of this chapter I will be performing queries based on the records I entered into my database. Should your database not have the same specific records as mine, change the particulars accordingly. The fundamental thinking behind the following queries should still apply regardless of the data, since the *sitename* database has a set column and table structure.

```
                      PHP and MySQL for Dynamic Web Sites
mysql> INSERT INTO users (first_name, last_name, email, pass, registration_date) VALUES
    -> ('John', 'Lennon', 'john@beatles.com', SHA2('Happin3ss', 512), NOW()),
    -> ('Paul', 'McCartney', 'paul@beatles.com', SHA2('letITbe', 512), NOW()),
    -> ('George', 'Harrison', 'george@beatles.com ', SHA2('something', 512), NOW()),
    -> ('Ringo', 'Starr', 'ringo@beatles.com', SHA2('thisboy', 512), NOW());
Query OK, 4 rows affected (0.00 sec)
Records: 4  Duplicates: 0  Warnings: 0

mysql>
```

E This one query—which MySQL allows but other databases will not—inserts several records into the table at once.

TIP On the downloads page of the book's supporting web site (LarryUllman.com), you can download all of the SQL commands for the book. Using some of those commands, you can populate your users table exactly as I have.

TIP The term INTO in INSERT statements is optional in MySQL.

TIP phpMyAdmin's Insert tab allows you to insert records using an HTML form **F**.

TIP Depending on the version of MySQL in use, failure to provide a value for a column that cannot be NULL may issue warnings with the INSERT still working **A** or issue errors with the INSERT failing.

TIP You'll occasionally see uses of the backtick (`) in SQL commands. This character, found on the same key as the tilde (~), is different than a single quotation mark. The backtick is used to safely reference a table or column name that might be the same as an existing keyword.

TIP If MySQL warns you about the previous query, the SHOW WARNINGS command will display the problem **A**.

TIP An interesting variation on INSERT is REPLACE. If the value used for the table's primary key, or a UNIQUE index, already exists, then REPLACE updates that row. If not, REPLACE inserts a new row.

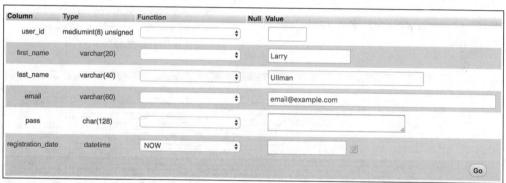

Column	Type	Function	Null	Value
user_id	mediumint(8) unsigned			
first_name	varchar(20)			Larry
last_name	varchar(40)			Ullman
email	varchar(60)			email@example.com
pass	char(128)			
registration_date	datetime	NOW		

F phpMyAdmin's **INSERT** form shows a table's columns and provides text boxes for entering values. The pull-down menu lists functions that can be used, like **NOW()** for the registration date (although the current version does not support **SHA2()**).

Selecting Data

Now that the database has some records in it, you can retrieve the stored information with the most used of all SQL terms, **SELECT**. A **SELECT** query returns rows of records using the syntax

SELECT *which_columns* **FROM** *which_table*

The simplest **SELECT** query is

SELECT * **FROM** *tablename*

The asterisk means that you want to retrieve every column. The alternative would be to specify the columns to be returned, with each separated from the next by a comma:

SELECT *column1, column3* **FROM** *tablename*

There are a few benefits to being explicit about which columns are selected. The first is performance: there's no reason to fetch columns you will not be using. The second is order: you can return columns in an order other than their layout in the table. Third—and you'll see this later in the chapter—naming the columns allows you to manipulate the values in those columns using functions.

To select data from a table:

1. Retrieve all the data from the *users* table **A**:

   SELECT * **FROM** users;

   This very basic SQL command will retrieve every column of every row stored within that table.

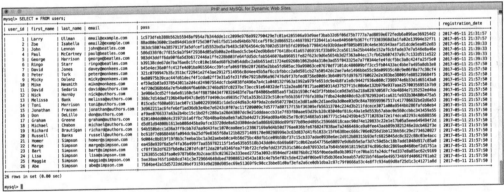

A The **SELECT** * **FROM** *tablename* query returns every column for every record stored in the table.

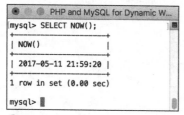

B Only two of the columns for every record in the table are returned by this query.

C Many queries can be run without specifying a database or table. This query selects the result of calling the **NOW()** function, which returns the current date and time (according to MySQL).

2. Retrieve just the first and last names from *users* B:

```
SELECT first_name, last_name
FROM users;
```

Instead of showing the data from every column in the *users* table, you can use the **SELECT** statement to limit the results to only the fields you need.

TIP In phpMyAdmin, options on the Browse tab run a simple SELECT query.

TIP You can actually use SELECT without naming tables or columns—for example, SELECT NOW() C.

TIP The order in which you list columns in your SELECT statement dictates the order in which the values are presented (compare B with D).

TIP With SELECT queries, you can even retrieve the same column multiple times, a feature that enables you to manipulate the column's data in many different ways.

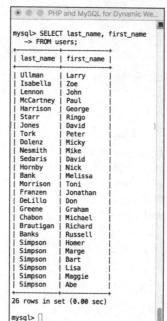

D If a **SELECT** query specifies the columns to be returned, they'll be returned in that order.

Using Conditionals

The **SELECT** query as used thus far will always retrieve every record from a table. But often you'll want to limit what rows are returned, based on certain criteria. This can be accomplished by adding conditionals to **SELECT** queries. Conditionals use the SQL term **WHERE** and are written much as you'd write a conditional in PHP:

SELECT *which_columns* FROM
→ *which_table* WHERE *condition(s)*

Table 5.1 lists the most common operators you would use within a conditional—for example, a simple equality check:

SELECT name FROM people

WHERE birth_date = '2011-01-26'

The operators can be used together, along with parentheses, to create more complex expressions:

SELECT * FROM items WHERE
(price BETWEEN 10.00 AND 20.00) AND
(quantity > 0)
SELECT * FROM cities WHERE
(zip_code = 90210) OR
→ (zip_code = 90211)

This last example could also be written as

SELECT * FROM cities WHERE
zip_code IN (90210, 90211)

To demonstrate using conditionals, let's run some more **SELECT** queries on the *sitename* database. The examples that follow will be just a few of the nearly limitless possibilities. Over the course of this chapter and the entire book, you will see how conditionals are used in all types of queries.

TABLE 5.1 MySQL Operators

Operator	Meaning
=	Equals
<	Less than
>	Greater than
<=	Less than or equal to
>=	Greater than or equal to
!= (also <>)	Not equal to
IS NOT NULL	Has a value
IS NULL	Does not have a value
IS TRUE	Has a true value
IS FALSE	Has a false value
BETWEEN	Within a range
NOT BETWEEN	Outside of a range
IN	Found within a list of values
NOT IN	Not found within a list of values
OR (also ||)	Where one of two conditionals is true
AND (also &&)	Where both conditionals are true
NOT (also !)	Where the condition is not true
XOR	Where *only one* of two conditionals is true

To use conditionals:

1. Select all of the users whose last name is *Simpson* **A**:

   ```
   SELECT * FROM users
   WHERE last_name = 'Simpson';
   ```

   This simple query returns every column of every row whose *last_name* value is *Simpson*. (Again, if the data in your table differs, you can change any of these queries accordingly.)

2. Select just the first names of users whose last name is *Simpson* **B**:

   ```
   SELECT first_name FROM users
   WHERE last_name = 'Simpson';
   ```

   Here, only one column—*first_name*—is being returned for each row. Although it may seem strange, you do not have

to select a column on which you are performing a **WHERE**. The reason for this is that the columns listed after **SELECT** dictate only what *columns* to return and the columns listed in a **WHERE** dictate which *rows* to return.

3. Select every column from every record in the *users* table that does not have an email address **C**:

   ```
   SELECT * FROM users
   WHERE email IS NULL;
   ```

   The **IS NULL** conditional is the same as saying *does not have a value*. Keep in mind that an empty string is different than **NULL** and therefore would not match this condition. An empty string would, however, match

   ```
   SELECT * FROM users WHERE email='';
   ```

continues on next page

A This query returns all of the Simpsons who have registered.

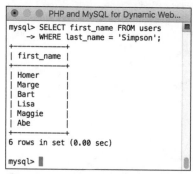

B This query returns just the first names of all the Simpsons who have registered.

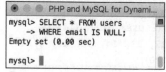

C No records are returned by this query because the email column cannot have a **NULL** value. So this query *did* work; it just matched no records.

4. Select the user ID, first name, and last name of all records in which the password is *mypass* 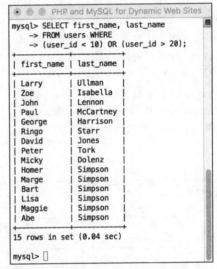:

```
SELECT user_id, first_name,
→ last_name
FROM users
WHERE pass = SHA2('mypass', 512);
```

Since the stored passwords were encrypted with the **SHA2()** function, you can match a password by using that same encryption function in a conditional. **SHA2()** is case-sensitive, so this query will work only if the passwords—stored vs. queried—match exactly. Also note you must use the same length value—512, here—as was used to store the password originally.

5. Select the usernames whose user ID is less than 10 or greater than 20 **E**:

```
SELECT first_name, last_name
FROM users WHERE
(user_id < 10) OR (user_id > 20);
```

This same query could also be written as

```
SELECT first_name, last_name FROM
users WHERE user_id
NOT BETWEEN 10 and 20;
```

or even

```
SELECT first_name, last_name FROM
users WHERE user_id NOT IN
(10, 11, 12, 13, 14, 15, 16, 17,
→ 18, 19, 20);
```

TIP You can perform mathematical calculations within your queries using the mathematic addition (+), subtraction (-), multiplication (*), and division (/) characters.

TIP MySQL supports the keywords TRUE and FALSE, case-insensitive. Internally, TRUE evaluates to 1 and FALSE evaluates to 0. So, in MySQL, TRUE + TRUE equals 2.

```
● ● ●     PHP and MySQL for Dynamic Web Sites
mysql> SELECT user_id, first_name, last_name
    -> FROM users
    -> WHERE pass = SHA2('mypass', 512);
+---------+------------+-----------+
| user_id | first_name | last_name |
+---------+------------+-----------+
|       1 | Larry      | Ullman    |
+---------+------------+-----------+
1 row in set (0.00 sec)

mysql>
```

D Conditionals can make use of functions, like **SHA2()** here.

```
● ● ●     PHP and MySQL for Dynamic Web Sites
mysql> SELECT first_name, last_name
    -> FROM users WHERE
    -> (user_id < 10) OR (user_id > 20);
+------------+-----------+
| first_name | last_name |
+------------+-----------+
| Larry      | Ullman    |
| Zoe        | Isabella  |
| John       | Lennon    |
| Paul       | McCartney |
| George     | Harrison  |
| Ringo      | Starr     |
| David      | Jones     |
| Peter      | Tork      |
| Micky      | Dolenz    |
| Homer      | Simpson   |
| Marge      | Simpson   |
| Bart       | Simpson   |
| Lisa       | Simpson   |
| Maggie     | Simpson   |
| Abe        | Simpson   |
+------------+-----------+
15 rows in set (0.04 sec)

mysql>
```

E This query uses two conditions and the **OR** operator.

Using LIKE and NOT LIKE

Using numbers, dates, and **NULL**s in conditionals is a straightforward process, but strings can be trickier. You can check for string equality with a query such as

```
SELECT * FROM users
WHERE last_name = 'Simpson'
```

However, comparing strings in a more liberal manner requires extra operators and characters. If, for example, you wanted to match a person's last name that could be *Smith* or *Smiths* or *Smithson*, you would need a more flexible conditional. This is where the **LIKE** and **NOT LIKE** terms come in. These are used—primarily with strings—in conjunction with two wildcard characters: the underscore (_), which matches a single character, and the percentage sign (**%**), which matches zero or more characters. In the last-name example, the query would be

```
SELECT * FROM users
WHERE last_name LIKE 'Smith%'
```

That query will return all rows whose *last_name* value begins with *Smith*. Because it's a case-insensitive search by default, it would also apply to names that begin with *smith*.

To use LIKE:

1. Select all the records in which the last name starts with *Bank* :

```
SELECT * FROM users
WHERE last_name LIKE 'Bank%';
```

continues on next page

Ⓐ The **LIKE** SQL term adds flexibility to your conditionals. This query matches any record where the last name value begins with *Bank*.

2. Select the name for every record whose email address is not of the form *something@authors.com* :

```
SELECT first_name, last_name
FROM users WHERE
email NOT LIKE '%@authors.com';
```

To rule out the presence of values in a string, use **NOT LIKE** with the wildcard.

TIP Queries with a LIKE conditional are generally slower because they can't take advantage of indexes. Use LIKE and NOT LIKE only if you absolutely have to.

TIP The wildcard characters can be used at the front and/or back of a string in your queries.

```
SELECT * FROM users WHERE last_name
→ LIKE '_smith%'
```

TIP Although LIKE and NOT LIKE are normally used with strings, they can also be applied to numeric columns.

TIP To use either the literal underscore or the percentage sign in a LIKE or NOT LIKE query, you will need to escape it (by preceding the character with a backslash) so that it is not confused with a wildcard.

TIP The underscore can be used in combination with itself; for example, LIKE '__' would find any two-letter combination.

TIP In Chapter 7, "Advanced SQL and MySQL," you'll learn about FULLTEXT searches, which can be more useful than LIKE searches.

B A **NOT LIKE** conditional returns records based on what a value does not contain.

Sorting Query Results

By default, a **SELECT** query's results will be returned in a meaningless order. For many new to databases, this is an odd concept. To give a meaningful order to a query's results, use an **ORDER BY** clause:

```
SELECT * FROM tablename ORDER BY
→ column
SELECT * FROM orders ORDER BY total
```

The default order when using **ORDER BY** is ascending (abbreviated **ASC**), meaning that numbers increase from small to large, dates go from oldest to most recent, and text is sorted alphabetically. You can reverse this by specifying a descending order (abbreviated **DESC**):

```
SELECT * FROM tablename
ORDER BY column DESC
```

You can even order the returned values by multiple columns:

```
SELECT * FROM tablename
ORDER BY column1, column2
```

You can, and frequently will, use **ORDER BY** with **WHERE** or other clauses. When doing so, place the **ORDER BY** after the conditions:

```
SELECT * FROM tablename WHERE
→ conditions
ORDER BY column
```

To sort data:

1. Select all the users in alphabetical order by last name **A**:

   ```
   SELECT first_name, last_name FROM
   users ORDER BY last_name;
   ```

   If you compare these results with those in **B** in the "Selecting Data" section, you'll see the benefits of using **ORDER BY**.

2. Display all the users in alphabetical order by last name and then first name **B**:

   ```
   SELECT first_name, last_name FROM
   users ORDER BY last_name ASC,
   first_name ASC;
   ```

   continues on next page

```
PHP and MySQL for Dynamic Web Sites
mysql> SELECT first_name, last_name FROM
    -> users ORDER BY last_name;
+------------+-----------+
| first_name | last_name |
+------------+-----------+
| Melissa    | Bank      |
| Russell    | Banks     |
| Richard    | Brautigan |
| Michael    | Chabon    |
| Don        | DeLillo   |
| Micky      | Dolenz    |
| Jonathan   | Franzen   |
| Graham     | Greene    |
| George     | Harrison  |
| Nick       | Hornby    |
| Zoe        | Isabella  |
| David      | Jones     |
| John       | Lennon    |
| Paul       | McCartney |
| Toni       | Morrison  |
| Mike       | Nesmith   |
| David      | Sedaris   |
| Homer      | Simpson   |
| Marge      | Simpson   |
| Bart       | Simpson   |
| Lisa       | Simpson   |
| Maggie     | Simpson   |
| Abe        | Simpson   |
| Ringo      | Starr     |
| Peter      | Tork      |
| Larry      | Ullman    |
+------------+-----------+
26 rows in set (0.00 sec)

mysql>
```

A The records in alphabetical order by last name.

```
PHP and MySQL for Dynamic Web Sites
mysql> SELECT first_name, last_name FROM
    -> users ORDER BY last_name ASC,
    -> first_name ASC;
+------------+-----------+
| first_name | last_name |
+------------+-----------+
| Melissa    | Bank      |
| Russell    | Banks     |
| Richard    | Brautigan |
| Michael    | Chabon    |
| Don        | DeLillo   |
| Micky      | Dolenz    |
| Jonathan   | Franzen   |
| Graham     | Greene    |
| George     | Harrison  |
| Nick       | Hornby    |
| Zoe        | Isabella  |
| David      | Jones     |
| John       | Lennon    |
| Paul       | McCartney |
| Toni       | Morrison  |
| Mike       | Nesmith   |
| David      | Sedaris   |
| Abe        | Simpson   |
| Bart       | Simpson   |
| Homer      | Simpson   |
| Lisa       | Simpson   |
| Maggie     | Simpson   |
| Marge      | Simpson   |
| Ringo      | Starr     |
| Peter      | Tork      |
| Larry      | Ullman    |
+------------+-----------+
26 rows in set (0.00 sec)

mysql>
```

B The records in alphabetical order, first by last name, and then by first name within that.

In this query, the effect would be that every row is returned, first ordered by *last_name*, and then by *first_name* within the *last_name*s. The effect is most evident among the Simpsons.

3. Show all the non-Simpson users by date registered 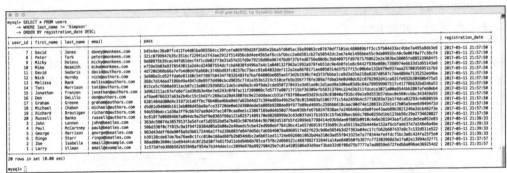:

```
SELECT * FROM users
WHERE last_name != 'Simpson'
ORDER BY registration_date DESC;
```

You can use an **ORDER BY** on any column type, including numbers and dates. The clause can also be used in a query with a conditional, placing the **ORDER BY** after the **WHERE**.

TIP Because MySQL works naturally with any number of languages, the ORDER BY will be based on the collation being used (see Chapter 6).

TIP If the column that you choose to sort on is an ENUM type, the sort will be based on the order of the possible ENUM values when the column was created. For example, if you have the column gender, defined as ENUM('M', 'F'), the clause ORDER BY gender returns the results with the M records first.

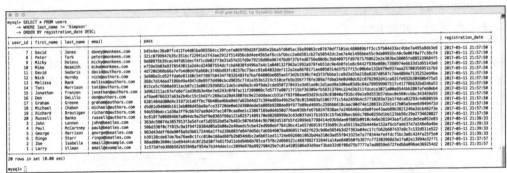

C All of the users not named *Simpson*, displayed by date registered, with the most recent listed first.

Limiting Query Results

Another SQL clause that can be added to most queries is **LIMIT**. In a **SELECT** query, **WHERE** dictates which records to return and **ORDER BY** decides how those records are sorted, but **LIMIT** states how many records to return. It is used like so:

`SELECT * FROM` *tablename* `LIMIT x`

In such queries, only the initial *x* records from the query result will be returned. To return only three matching records, use

`SELECT * FROM` *tablename* `LIMIT 3`

Using this format

`SELECT * FROM` *tablename* `LIMIT x, y`

you can have *y* records returned, starting at *x*. To have records 11 through 20 returned, you would write

`SELECT * FROM` *tablename* `LIMIT 10, 10`

```
PHP and MySQL for Dynamic Web Sites
mysql> SELECT first_name, last_name
    -> FROM users ORDER BY
    -> registration_date DESC LIMIT 5;
+------------+-----------+
| first_name | last_name |
+------------+-----------+
| David      | Jones     |
| Peter      | Tork      |
| Abe        | Simpson   |
| Micky      | Dolenz    |
| Mike       | Nesmith   |
+------------+-----------+
5 rows in set (0.00 sec)

mysql>
```

A Using the **LIMIT** clause, a query can return a specific number of records.

Like arrays in PHP, result sets begin at 0 when it comes to **LIMIT**s, so 10 is the 11th record.

Because **SELECT** does not return results in any meaningful order, you almost always want to apply an **ORDER BY** clause when using **LIMIT**. You can use **LIMIT** with **WHERE** and/or **ORDER BY** clauses, always placing **LIMIT** last:

`SELECT` *which_columns* `FROM` *tablename*
`WHERE` *conditions* `ORDER BY` *column*
`LIMIT x`

To limit the amount of data returned:

1. Select the last five registered users **A**:

   `SELECT first_name, last_name`
   `FROM users ORDER BY`
   `registration_date DESC LIMIT 5;`

   To return the latest of anything, sort the data by date, in descending order. Then, to see just the most recent five, add **LIMIT 5** to the query.

   continues on next page

2. Select the second person to register 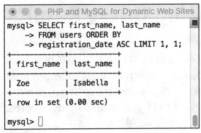:

```
SELECT first_name, last_name
FROM users ORDER BY
registration_date ASC LIMIT 1, 1;
```

This may look strange, but it's just a good application of the information learned so far. First, order all the records by *registration_date* ascending, so the first people to register would be returned first. Then, limit the returned results to start at 1 (which is the second row) and to return just one record.

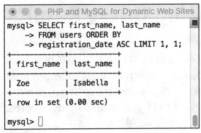

```
PHP and MySQL for Dynamic Web Sites

mysql> SELECT first_name, last_name
    -> FROM users ORDER BY
    -> registration_date ASC LIMIT 1, 1;
+------------+-----------+
| first_name | last_name |
+------------+-----------+
| Zoe        | Isabella  |
+------------+-----------+
1 row in set (0.00 sec)

mysql>
```

B Thanks to the **LIMIT** clause, a query can even return records from the middle of a group, using the **LIMIT** *x, y* format.

TIP The LIMIT *x, y* clause is most frequently used when paginating query results (showing them in blocks over multiple pages). You'll see this in Chapter 10, "Common Programming Techniques."

TIP A LIMIT clause does not improve the execution speed of a query, since MySQL still has to assemble the entire result and then truncate the list. But a LIMIT clause will minimize the amount of data to handle when it comes to the mysql client or your PHP scripts.

TIP The LIMIT term is not part of the SQL standard and is therefore (sadly) not available on all databases.

TIP The LIMIT clause can be used with most types of queries, not just SELECTs.

Updating Data

Once tables contain some data, you have the potential need to edit those existing records. This might be necessary if information was entered incorrectly or if the data changes, such as a last name or email address. The syntax for updating records is

UPDATE *tablename* SET *column=value*

You can alter multiple columns at a single time, separating each from the next by a comma.

UPDATE *tablename* SET *column1=valueA, column5=valueB...*

You will almost always want to use a **WHERE** clause to specify what rows should be updated:

UPDATE *tablename* SET *column2=value* WHERE *column5=value*

If you don't use a **WHERE** clause, the changes would be applied to every record.

Updates, along with deletions, are one of the most important reasons to use a primary key. This value—which should never change—can be a reference point in **WHERE** clauses, even if every other field needs to be altered.

To update a record:

1. Find the primary key for the record to be updated **Ⓐ**:

   SELECT user_id FROM users
   WHERE first_name = 'Michael'
   AND last_name='Chabon';

   In this example, I'll change the email for this author's record. To do so, I must first find that record's primary key, which this query accomplishes.

2. Update the record **Ⓑ**:

   UPDATE users
   SET email='mike@authors.com'
   WHERE user_id = 18;

   To change the email address, use an **UPDATE** query, using the primary key (*user_id*) to specify to which record the update should apply. MySQL will report upon the success of the query and how many rows were affected.

continues on next page

```
● ● ●    PHP and MySQL for Dynamic Web Sites
mysql> SELECT user_id FROM users
    -> WHERE first_name = 'Michael'
    -> AND last_name='Chabon';
+---------+
| user_id |
+---------+
|      18 |
+---------+
1 row in set (0.00 sec)

mysql>
```

Ⓐ Before updating a record, determine which primary key to use in the **UPDATE**'s **WHERE** clause.

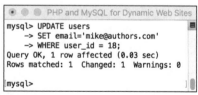

```
● ● ●    PHP and MySQL for Dynamic Web Sites
mysql> UPDATE users
    -> SET email='mike@authors.com'
    -> WHERE user_id = 18;
Query OK, 1 row affected (0.03 sec)
Rows matched: 1  Changed: 1  Warnings: 0

mysql>
```

Ⓑ This query altered the value of one column in just one row.

3. Confirm that the change was made :

```
SELECT * FROM users
WHERE user_id=18;
```

Although MySQL already indicated the update was successful **B**, it can't hurt to select the record again to confirm that the proper changes occurred.

TIP Be extra certain to use a WHERE conditional whenever you use UPDATE unless you want the changes to affect every row.

TIP If you run an update query that doesn't actually change any values (like UPDATE users SET first_name='mike' WHERE user_id=0), you won't see any errors but no rows will be affected **D**.

TIP To protect yourself against accidentally updating too many rows, apply a LIMIT clause to your UPDATEs:

```
UPDATE users SET
→ email='mike@authors.com'
→ WHERE user_id = 18 LIMIT 1
```

TIP You should never perform an UPDATE on a primary-key column, because the primary key value should never change. Altering the value of a primary key could have serious repercussions.

TIP To update a record in phpMyAdmin, you can run an UPDATE query using the SQL window or tab. Alternatively, run a SELECT query to find the record you want to update, and then click the pencil next to the record. This will bring up a form like the insert form, where you can edit the record's current values.

C As a final step, you can confirm the update by selecting the record again.

```
mysql> UPDATE users SET first_name='mike' WHERE user_id=0;
Query OK, 0 rows affected (0.00 sec)
Rows matched: 0  Changed: 0  Warnings: 0

mysql> []
```

D Queries that have no effect still don't count as errors.

Deleting Data

Along with updating existing records, another step you might need to take is to entirely remove a record from the database. To do this, you use the **DELETE** command:

```
DELETE FROM tablename
```

That command as written will delete every record in a table, making it empty again. Once you have deleted a record, there is no way of retrieving it.

In most cases, you'll want to delete individual rows, not all of them. To do so, apply a **WHERE** clause:

```
DELETE FROM tablename WHERE condition
```

To delete a record:

1. Find the primary key for the record to be deleted Ⓐ:

   ```
   SELECT user_id FROM users
   WHERE first_name='Peter'
   AND last_name='Tork';
   ```

   Just as in the **UPDATE** example, I first need to determine which primary key to use for the delete.

2. Preview what will happen when the delete is made Ⓑ:

   ```
   SELECT * FROM users
   WHERE user_id = 8;
   ```

   A good trick for safeguarding against errant deletions is to first run the query using **SELECT** * instead of **DELETE**. The results of this query will represent which row(s) will be affected by the deletion.

   continues on next page

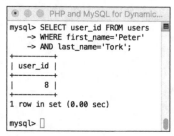

Ⓐ The *user_id* value will be used to refer to this record in a **DELETE** query.

Ⓑ To preview the effect of a **DELETE** query, first run a syntactically similar **SELECT** query.

3. Delete the record 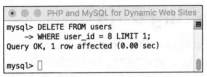:

```
DELETE FROM users
WHERE user_id = 8 LIMIT 1;
```

As with the update, MySQL will report on the successful execution of the query and how many rows were affected. At this point, there is no way of reinstating the deleted records unless you backed up the database beforehand.

Even though the **SELECT** query (Step 2 and ⓑ) returned only the one row, just to be extra careful, a **LIMIT 1** clause is added to the **DELETE** query.

4. Confirm that the change was made 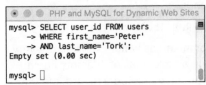:

```
SELECT user_id FROM users
WHERE first_name='Peter'
AND last_name='Tork';
```

TIP The preferred way to empty a table is to use TRUNCATE:

TRUNCATE TABLE *tablename*

TIP To delete all of the data in a table, as well as the table itself, use DROP TABLE:

DROP TABLE *tablename*

TIP To delete an entire database, including every table therein and all of its data, use

DROP DATABASE *databasename*

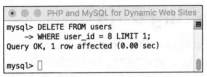

Ⓒ Deleting one record from the table.

Ⓓ The record is no longer part of this table.

Using Functions

To wrap up this chapter, you'll learn about several functions that you can use in your MySQL queries. You have already seen two—**NOW()** and **SHA2()**—but those are just the tip of the iceberg. Most of the functions you'll see here are used with **SELECT** queries to format and alter the returned data, but you may use MySQL functions in other types of queries as well.

To apply a function to a column's values, the query would look like

```
SELECT FUNCTION(column) FROM tablename
```

To apply a function to one column's values while also selecting some other columns, you can write a query like either of these:

- `SELECT *, FUNCTION(column)`
  `→ FROM tablename`

- `SELECT column1, FUNCTION(column2),`
  `→ column3 FROM tablename`

Generally speaking, the latter syntax is preferred, because it returns only the columns you need as opposed to all of them.

Before getting to the actual functions, make note of a couple more things. First, functions are often applied to stored data (i.e., columns) but can also be applied to literal values. Either of these applications of the **UPPER()** function, which capitalizes a string, is valid:

```
SELECT UPPER(first_name) FROM users
SELECT UPPER('this string')
```

Second, while the function names themselves are case-insensitive, I will continue to write them in an all-capitalized format, to help distinguish them from table and column names (I also capitalize SQL terms). Third, an important rule with functions is that *you cannot have spaces between the function name and the opening parenthesis in MySQL*, although spaces within the parentheses are acceptable. And finally, when using functions to format returned data, you'll often want to make uses of *aliases*, a concept discussed in the sidebar.

TIP Just as there are different standards of SQL and different database applications have their own slight variations on the language, some functions are common to all database applications and others are particular to MySQL. This chapter, and the book, concerns itself only with the MySQL functions.

TIP Chapter 7 discusses two more categories of MySQL functions: grouping and encryption.

Text functions

The first group of functions we will discuss are those meant for manipulating text. The most common of the functions in this category are listed in **Table 5.2**. As with most functions, these can be applied to either columns or literal values (both represented by *t*, *t1*, *t2*, etc.).

CONCAT(), perhaps the most useful of the text functions, deserves special attention. The **CONCAT()** function accomplishes concatenation, for which PHP uses the period (see Chapter 1, "Introduction to PHP"). The syntax for concatenation requires you to place, within parentheses, the various values you want assembled, in order and separated by commas:

```
SELECT CONCAT(t1, t2) FROM tablename
```

While you can—and normally will—apply **CONCAT()** to columns, you can also incorporate strings, entered within quotation marks. For example, to format a person's name as *First<SPACE>Last*, you would use

```
SELECT CONCAT(first_name, ' ',
→ last_name)
FROM users
```

Because concatenation normally returns values in a new format, it's an excellent time to use an alias (see the sidebar):

```
SELECT CONCAT(first_name, ' ',
→ last_name)
AS Name FROM users
```

TABLE 5.2 Text Functions

Function	Usage	Returns
CONCAT()	CONCAT(t1, t2, ...)	A new string of the form *t1t2*
CONCAT_WS()	CONCAT_WS(S, t1, t2, ...)	A new string of the form *t1St2S*...
LENGTH()	LENGTH(t)	The number of characters in *t*
LEFT()	LEFT(t, y)	The leftmost *y* characters from *t*
RIGHT()	RIGHT(t, x)	The rightmost *x* characters from *t*
TRIM()	TRIM(t)	*t* with excess spaces from the beginning and end removed
UPPER()	UPPER(t)	*t* capitalized
LOWER()	LOWER(t)	*t* in all-lowercase format
REPLACE()	REPLACE(t1, t2, t3)	The string *t1* with instances of *t2* replaced with *t3*
SUBSTRING()	SUBSTRING(t, x, y)	*y* characters from *t* beginning with *x* (indexed from 1)

```
● ● ●    PHP and MySQL for Dynamic Web Sites
mysql> SELECT CONCAT(last_name, ', ', first_name)
    -> FROM users;
+-------------------------------------+
| CONCAT(last_name, ', ', first_name) |
+-------------------------------------+
| Ullman, Larry                       |
| Isabella, Zoe                       |
| Lennon, John                        |
| McCartney, Paul                     |
| Harrison, George                    |
| Starr, Ringo                        |
| Jones, David                        |
| Dolenz, Micky                       |
| Nesmith, mike                       |
| Sedaris, David                      |
| Hornby, Nick                        |
| Bank, Melissa                       |
| Morrison, Toni                      |
| Franzen, Jonathan                   |
| DeLillo, Don                        |
| Greene, Graham                      |
| Chabon, Michael                     |
| Brautigan, Richard                  |
| Banks, Russell                      |
| Simpson, Homer                      |
| Simpson, Marge                      |
| Simpson, Bart                       |
| Simpson, Lisa                       |
| Simpson, Maggie                     |
| Simpson, Abe                        |
+-------------------------------------+
25 rows in set (0.00 sec)

mysql>
```

Ⓐ This simple concatenation returns every registered user's full name. Notice how the column heading is the use of the CONCAT() function.

To format text:

1. Concatenate the names *without* using an alias Ⓐ:

   ```
   SELECT CONCAT(last_name, ', ',
   → first_name)
   FROM users;
   ```

   This query will demonstrate two things. First, the users' last names, a comma and a space, plus their first names are concatenated together to make one string in the format of *Last, First*. Second, as the figure shows, if you don't use an alias, the returned data's column heading will be the function call. In the mysql client or phpMyAdmin, this is just unsightly; when using PHP to connect to MySQL, this will likely be a problem.

   continues on next page

Aliases

An *alias* is merely a symbolic renaming of an item used in a query, normally applied to tables, columns, or function calls. Aliases are created using the term **AS**:

```
SELECT registration_date AS reg
FROM users
```

Aliases are case-sensitive strings composed of numbers, letters, and the underscore but are normally kept to a very short length. As you'll see in the following examples, aliases are also reflected in the captions for the returned results. For the preceding example, the query results returned will contain one column of data, named *reg* (not *registration_date*).

In MySQL, if you've defined an alias for a table or a column used in a query, the entire query should consistently use that same alias rather than the original name. For example:

```
SELECT first_name AS name FROM
users WHERE name='Sam'
```

This differs from standard SQL, which doesn't support the use of aliases in **WHERE** conditionals.

2. Concatenate the names while using an alias **B**:

```
SELECT CONCAT(last_name, ', ',
→ first_name)
AS Name FROM users ORDER BY Name;
```

To use an alias, just add **AS *aliasname*** after the item to be renamed. The alias will be the new title for the returned data. To make the query a little more interesting, the same alias is also used in the **ORDER BY** clause.

3. Find the longest last name **C**:

```
SELECT LENGTH(last_name) AS L,
last_name FROM users
ORDER BY L DESC LIMIT 1;
```

To determine which registered user's last name is the longest (has the most characters in it), use the **LENGTH()** function. To find the name, select both the last name value and the calculated length, which is given an alias of *L*. To then find the longest name, order all of the results by *L*, in descending order, but return only the first record.

TIP A query like that in Step 3 (also **C**) may be useful for helping to fine-tune your column lengths once your database has some records in it.

TIP MySQL has two functions for performing regular expression searches on text: REGEXP() and NOT REGEXP(). Chapter 14, "Perl-Compatible Regular Expressions," introduces regular expressions using PHP.

TIP CONCAT() has a corollary function called CONCAT_WS(), which stands for with separator. The syntax is CONCAT_WS(separator, t1, t2, ...). The separator will be inserted between each of the listed columns or values. For example, to format a person's full name as First<SPACE>_Middle<SPACE>_Last, you would write

```
SELECT CONCAT_WS(' ', first, middle,
last) AS Name FROM tablename
```

CONCAT_WS() has an added advantage over CONCAT() in that it will ignore columns with NULL values. So that query might return Joe Banks from one record but Jane Sojourner Adams from another.

```
PHP and MySQL for Dynamic Web Sites
mysql> SELECT CONCAT(last_name, ', ', first_name)
    -> AS Name FROM users ORDER BY Name;
+---------------------+
| Name                |
+---------------------+
| Bank, Melissa       |
| Banks, Russell      |
| Brautigan, Richard  |
| Chabon, Michael     |
| DeLillo, Don        |
| Dolenz, Micky       |
| Franzen, Jonathan   |
| Greene, Graham      |
| Harrison, George    |
| Hornby, Nick        |
| Isabella, Zoe       |
| Jones, David        |
| Lennon, John        |
| McCartney, Paul     |
| Morrison, Toni      |
| Nesmith, mike       |
| Sedaris, David      |
| Simpson, Abe        |
| Simpson, Bart       |
| Simpson, Homer      |
| Simpson, Lisa       |
| Simpson, Maggie     |
| Simpson, Marge      |
| Starr, Ringo        |
| Ullman, Larry       |
+---------------------+
25 rows in set (0.00 sec)

mysql>
```

B By using an alias, the returned data is under the column heading of *Name* (compare with **A**).

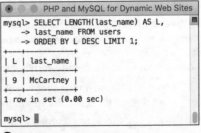

```
PHP and MySQL for Dynamic Web Sites
mysql> SELECT LENGTH(last_name) AS L,
    -> last_name FROM users
    -> ORDER BY L DESC LIMIT 1;
+---+-----------+
| L | last_name |
+---+-----------+
| 9 | McCartney |
+---+-----------+
1 row in set (0.00 sec)

mysql>
```

C By using the **LENGTH()** function, an alias, an **ORDER BY** clause, and a **LIMIT** clause, this query returns the length and value of the longest stored name.

TABLE 5.3 Numeric Functions

Function	Usage	Returns
ABS()	ABS(n)	The absolute value of n
CEILING()	CEILING(n)	The next-highest integer based upon the value of n
FLOOR()	FLOOR(n)	The integer value of n
FORMAT()	FORMAT(n1, n2)	n1 formatted as a number with n2 decimal places and commas inserted every three spaces
MOD()	MOD(n1, n2)	The remainder of dividing n1 by n2
POW()	POW(n1, n2)	n1 to the n2 power
RAND()	RAND()	A random number between 0 and 1.0
ROUND()	ROUND(n1, n2)	n1 rounded to n2 decimal places
SQRT()	SQRT(n)	The square root of n

```
◉ ◯ ◯   PHP and MySQL for Dynamic Web Sites
mysql> SELECT RAND();
+---------------------+
| RAND()              |
+---------------------+
| 0.41631779392838275 |
+---------------------+
1 row in set (0.00 sec)

mysql> SELECT RAND();
+--------------------+
| RAND()             |
+--------------------+
| 0.2314725669393992 |
+--------------------+
1 row in set (0.00 sec)

mysql> █
```

D The **RAND()** function returns a random number between 0 and 1.0.

Numeric functions

Besides the standard math operators that MySQL uses for addition, subtraction, multiplication, and division, there are a couple dozen functions for formatting and performing calculations on numeric values. **Table 5.3** lists the most common of these, some of which will be demonstrated shortly. As with most functions, these can be applied to either columns or literal values (both represented by n, n1, n2, etc.).

I want to specifically highlight three of these functions: **FORMAT()**, **ROUND()**, and **RAND()**. The first—which is not technically number-specific—turns any number into a more conventionally formatted layout. For example, if you stored the cost of a car as 20198.20, **FORMAT(car_cost, 2)** would turn that number into the more common 20,198.20.

ROUND() will take one value, presumably from a column, and round that to a specified number of decimal places. If no decimal places are indicated, it will round the number to the nearest integer. If more decimal places are indicated than exist in the original number, the remaining spaces are padded with zeros (to the right of the decimal point).

The **RAND()** function, as you might infer, is used for returning random numbers **D**:

SELECT RAND()

A further benefit to the **RAND()** function is that it can be used with your queries to return the results in a random order:

SELECT * FROM *tablename*
→ **ORDER BY RAND()**

To use numeric functions:

1. Display a number, formatting the amount as dollars 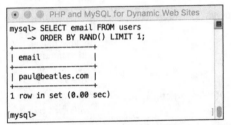:

   SELECT CONCAT('$', FORMAT(5639.6, 2)) AS cost;

   Using the **FORMAT()** function, as just described, with **CONCAT()**, you can turn any number into a currency format as you might display it in a web page.

2. Retrieve a random email address from the table 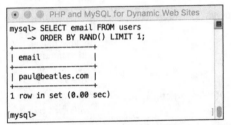:

   SELECT email FROM users ORDER BY RAND() LIMIT 1;

   What happens with this query is: All the email addresses are selected; the order they are in is shuffled (**ORDER BY RAND()**); and then the first one is returned. Running this same query multiple times will produce different random results. Notice that you do not specify a column to which **RAND()** is applied.

TIP Along with the mathematical functions listed here, there are several trigonometric, exponential, and other types of numeric functions available.

TIP The **MOD()** function is the same as using the percent sign:

SELECT MOD(9,2)
SELECT 9%2

It returns the remainder of a division (1 in these examples).

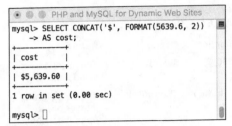

E Using an arbitrary example, this query shows how the **FORMAT()** function works.

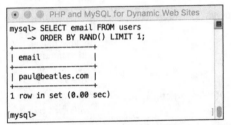

F This query uses the **RAND()** function to select a random record. Subsequent executions of the same query return different random results.

Date and time functions

The date and time column types in MySQL are particularly flexible and useful. But because many database users are not familiar with all the available date and time functions, these options are frequently underused. Whether you want to make calculations based on a date or return only the month name from a value, MySQL has a function for that purpose. **Table 5.4** lists most of these; see the MySQL manual for a complete list. As with most functions, these can be applied to either columns or literal values (both represented by *dt*, short for *datetime*).

MySQL supports two data types that store both a date and a time (**DATETIME** and **TIMESTAMP**), one type that stores just the date (**DATE**), one that stores just the time (**TIME**), and one that stores just a year (**YEAR**). Besides allowing for different types of values, each data type also has its own unique behaviors (again, I recommend reading the MySQL manual's pages on this for all the details). But MySQL is very flexible as to which functions you can use with which type. You can apply a date function to any value that contains a date (i.e., **DATETIME**, **TIMESTAMP**, and **DATE**), or you can apply an hour function to any value that contains the time (i.e., **DATETIME**, **TIMESTAMP**, and **TIME**). MySQL will use the part of the value that it needs and ignore the rest. What you cannot do, however, is apply a date function to a **TIME** value or a time function to a **DATE** or **YEAR** value.

continues on next page

TABLE 5.4 Date and Time Functions

Function	Usage	Returns
DATE()	DATE(dt)	The date value of *dt*
HOUR()	HOUR(dt)	The hour value of *dt*
MINUTE()	MINUTE(dt)	The minute value of *dt*
SECOND()	SECOND(dt)	The second value of *dt*
DAYNAME()	DAYNAME(dt)	The name of the day for *dt*
DAYOFMONTH()	DAYOFMONTH(dt)	The numerical day value of dt
MONTHNAME()	MONTHNAME(dt)	The name of the month of *dt*
MONTH()	MONTH(dt)	The numerical month value of *dt*
YEAR()	YEAR(column)	The year value of *dt*
CURDATE()	CURDATE()	The current date
CURTIME()	CURTIME()	The current time
NOW()	NOW()	The current date and time
UNIX_TIMESTAMP()	UNIX_TIMESTAMP(dt)	The number of seconds since the epoch until the current moment or until the date specified
UTC_TIMESTAMP()	UTC_TIMESTAMP(dt)	The number of seconds since the epoch until the current moment or until the date specified, in Coordinated Universal Time (UTC)

To use date and time functions:

1. Display the date that the last user registered 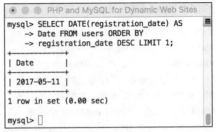:

   SELECT DATE(registration_date) AS Date FROM users ORDER BY registration_date DESC LIMIT 1;

   The **DATE()** function returns the date part of a value. To see the date that the last person registered, an **ORDER BY** clause lists the users, starting with the most recently registered, and this result is limited to just one record.

2. Display the day of the week that the first user registered 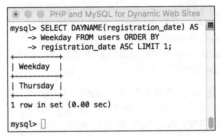:

   SELECT DAYNAME(registration_date) AS Weekday FROM users ORDER BY registration_date ASC LIMIT 1;

   This is like the query in Step 1, but the results are returned in ascending order and the **DAYNAME()** function is applied to the *registration_date* column. This function returns *Sunday*, *Monday*, *Tuesday*, etc., for a given date.

3. Show the current date and time, according to MySQL 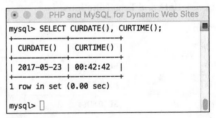:

   SELECT CURDATE(), CURTIME();

   To show what date and time MySQL currently thinks it is, you can select the **CURDATE()** and **CURTIME()** functions, which return these values. This is another example of a query that can be run without referring to a particular table.

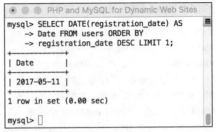

G The date functions can be used to extract information from stored values.

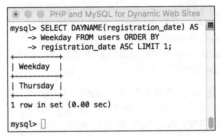

H This query returns the name of the day that a given date represents.

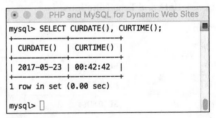

I This query, not run on any specific table, returns the current date and time on the MySQL server.

```
mysql> SELECT LAST_DAY(CURDATE()),
    -> MONTHNAME(CURDATE());
+---------------------+---------------------+
| LAST_DAY(CURDATE()) | MONTHNAME(CURDATE()) |
+---------------------+---------------------+
| 2017-05-31          | May                 |
+---------------------+---------------------+
1 row in set (0.00 sec)

mysql>
```

J Among the many things MySQL can do with date and time types is determine the last date in a month or the name value of a given date.

4. Show the last day of the current month **J**:

SELECT LAST_DAY(CURDATE()), MONTHNAME(CURDATE());

As the last query showed, **CURDATE()** returns the current date on the server. This value can be used as an argument to the **LAST_DAY()** function, which returns the last date in the month for a given date. The **MONTHNAME()** function returns the name of the current month.

TIP The date and time returned by MySQL's date and time functions correspond to those on the server, not to those on the client accessing the database.

TIP Not mentioned in this section or in Table 5.4 are ADDDATE(), SUBDATE(), ADDTIME(), SUBTIME(), and DATEDIFF(). Each can be used to perform arithmetic on date and time values. These can be very useful (for example, to find everyone registered within the past week), but their syntax is cumbersome. As always, see the MySQL manual for more information.

TIP Chapter 6 discusses the concept of time zones in MySQL.

TIP As of MySQL 5.0.2, the server will also prevent invalid dates (e.g., February 31, 2017) from being inserted into a date or date/time column.

Formatting the date and time

There are two additional date and time functions that you might find yourself using more than all the others combined: **DATE_FORMAT()** and **TIME_FORMAT()**. There is some overlap between the two and when you would use one or the other.

DATE_FORMAT() can be used to format both the date and time if a value contains both (e.g., *YYYY-MM-DD HH:MM:SS*). Comparatively, **TIME_FORMAT()** can format only the time value and must be used if only the time value is being stored (e.g., *HH:MM:SS*). The syntax is

SELECT DATE_FORMAT(datetime,
→ formatting)

The *formatting* relies on combinations of key codes and the percent sign to indicate what values you want returned. **Table 5.5** lists the available date- and time-formatting parameters. You can use these in any combination, along with literal characters, such as punctuation, to return a date and time in a more presentable form.

TABLE 5.5 *_FORMAT() Parameters

Term	Usage	Example
%e	Day of the month	1–31
%d	Day of the month, two digit	01–31
%D	Day with suffix	1st–31st
%W	Weekday name	Sunday–Saturday
%a	Abbreviated weekday name	Sun–Sat
%c	Month number	1–12
%m	Month number, two digit	01–12
%M	Month name	January–December
%b	Month name, abbreviated	Jan–Dec
%Y	Year	2002
%y	Year	02
%l (lowercase L)	Hour	1–12
%h	Hour, two digit	01–12
%k	Hour, 24-hour clock	0–23
%H	Hour, 24-hour clock, two digit	00–23
%i	Minutes	00–59
%S	Seconds	00–59
%r	Time	8:17:02 PM
%T	Time, 24-hour clock	20:17:02
%p	AM or PM	AM or PM

Assuming that a column called *the_date* has the date and time of *1996-04-20 11:07:45* stored in it, common formatting tasks and results would be

- Time (11:07:45 AM)
  `TIME_FORMAT(the_date, '%r')`

- Time without seconds (11:07 AM)
  `TIME_FORMAT(the_date, '%l:%i %p')`

- Date (April 20th, 1996)
  `DATE_FORMAT(the_date, '%M %D, %Y')`

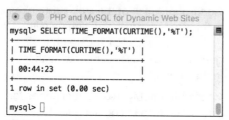

```
● ● ●    PHP and MySQL for Dynamic Web Sites
mysql> SELECT DATE_FORMAT(NOW(),'%M %e, %Y %l:%i');
+--------------------------------------+
| DATE_FORMAT(NOW(),'%M %e, %Y %l:%i') |
+--------------------------------------+
| May 23, 2017 12:44                   |
+--------------------------------------+
1 row in set (0.00 sec)

mysql> []
```

K The current date and time, formatted.

```
● ● ●    PHP and MySQL for Dynamic Web Sites
mysql> SELECT TIME_FORMAT(CURTIME(),'%T');
+-----------------------------+
| TIME_FORMAT(CURTIME(),'%T') |
+-----------------------------+
| 00:44:23                    |
+-----------------------------+
1 row in set (0.00 sec)

mysql> []
```

L The current time in a 24-hour format.

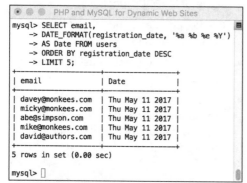

```
● ● ●    PHP and MySQL for Dynamic Web Sites
mysql> SELECT email,
    -> DATE_FORMAT(registration_date, '%a %b %e %Y')
    -> AS Date FROM users
    -> ORDER BY registration_date DESC
    -> LIMIT 5;
+-------------------+------------------+
| email             | Date             |
+-------------------+------------------+
| davey@monkees.com | Thu May 11 2017  |
| micky@monkees.com | Thu May 11 2017  |
| abe@simpson.com   | Thu May 11 2017  |
| mike@monkees.com  | Thu May 11 2017  |
| david@authors.com | Thu May 11 2017  |
+-------------------+------------------+
5 rows in set (0.00 sec)

mysql> []
```

M The `DATE_FORMAT()` function is used to preformat the registration date when selecting records from the *users* table.

To format the date and time:

1. Return the current date and time as *Month DD, YYYY - HH:MM* **K**:

   ```
   SELECT DATE_FORMAT(NOW(),'%M %e,
   →%Y %l:%i');
   ```

   Using the **NOW()** function, which returns the current date and time, you can practice formatting to see what results are returned.

2. Display the current time, using 24-hour notation **L**:

   ```
   SELECT TIME_FORMAT(CURTIME(),'%T');
   ```

3. Select the email address and date registered, ordered by date registered, formatting the date as *Weekday (abbreviated) Month (abbreviated) Day Year*, for the last five registered users **M**:

   ```
   SELECT email,
   DATE_FORMAT(registration_date,
   →'%a %b %e %Y')
   AS Date FROM users
   ORDER BY registration_date DESC
   LIMIT 5;
   ```

   This is just one more example of how you can use these formatting functions to alter the output of an SQL query.

TIP In your web applications, you should almost always use MySQL functions to format any dates coming from the database (as opposed to formatting the dates within PHP after retrieving them from the database).

TIP The only way to access the date or time on the client (the user's machine) is to use JavaScript. It cannot be done with PHP or MySQL.

Review and Pursue

If you have any problems with the review questions or the pursue prompts, turn to the book's supporting forum (LarryUllman.com/forums/).

Review

- What version of MySQL are you using? If you don't know, find out now!

- What SQL command is used to make a new database? What command is used to make a new table in a database?

- What SQL command is used to select the database with which you want to work?

- What SQL commands are used for adding records to a table? Hint: There are multiple options.

- What types of values must be quoted in queries? What types of values shouldn't be quoted?

- What does the asterisk in **SELECT * FROM** *tablename* mean? How do you restrict which columns are returned by a query?

- What does the **NOW()** function do?

- How do you restrict which *rows* are returned by a query?

- How do **LIKE** and **NOT LIKE** differ from simple equality comparisons? Which type of comparison will be faster? What are the two **LIKE** and **NOT LIKE** wildcard characters?

- How do you affect the sorting of the returned records? What is the default sorting method? How do you inverse the sort? What is the syntax for sorting by multiple columns?

- What does the **LIMIT** clause do? How does **LIMIT** *x* differ from **LIMIT** *x, y*?

- What SQL command is used to change the values already stored in a table? How do you change multiple columns at once? How do you restrict to which rows the changes are applied?

- What SQL command is used to delete rows stored in a table? How do you restrict to which rows the deletions are applied?

- What is an SQL alias? How do you create one? Why is an alias useful?

Pursue

- If you haven't done so already, bookmark the version of the MySQL manual that matches the version of MySQL you are running.

- Go through each of the step sequences in this chapter again, coming up with your own queries to execute (that demonstrate similar concepts as those in the steps).

- Check out the MySQL manual pages for operators used in conditionals.

- Check out the MySQL manual pages for some of MySQL's functions.

- Create, populate, and manipulate your own table of data.

- Do some more practice using functions and aliases.

- Check out the MySQL manual pages for the various date and time types. Also check out **ADDDATE()** and other date-related functions.

6

Database Design

Now that you have a basic understanding of databases, SQL, and MySQL, this chapter begins the process of taking that knowledge deeper. The focus in this chapter, as the title states, is real-world database design. Like the work done in Chapter 4, "Introduction to MySQL," much of the effort in this chapter requires paper and pen—and serious thinking about what your applications will need to do.

The chapter begins with thorough coverage of database *normalization*, a vital approach to the design process. After that, the chapter turns to design-related concepts specific to MySQL: working with indexes, table types, language support, times, and foreign key constraints.

In this chapter, you'll explore steps involved in proper database design and how to make the most of MySQL. You'll also plan a couple of multi-table databases. In the next chapter, you'll learn more advanced SQL and MySQL, and use these new databases as examples.

In This Chapter

Normalization

Whenever you are working with a relational database management system such as MySQL, the first step in creating and using a database is to establish the database's structure (also called the database *schema*). Database design, also known as *data modeling*, is crucial for successful long-term management of information. Using a process called *normalization*, you carefully eliminate redundancies and other problems that would undermine the integrity of your database.

The techniques you will learn over the next few pages will help ensure the viability, usefulness, and reliability of your databases. The primary example to be discussed—a forum where users can post messages—will be used more explicitly in Chapter 17, "Example—Message Board," but the principles of normalization apply to any database you might create. (The *sitename* example as created and used in the past two chapters was properly normalized, even though normalization was never discussed.)

Normalization was developed by an IBM researcher named E. F. Codd in the early 1970s (he also invented the relational database). A relational database is merely a collection of data, organized in a particular manner, and Dr. Codd created a series of rules called *normal forms* that help define that organization. This chapter discusses the first three of the normal forms, which are sufficient for most database designs.

Before you begin normalizing your database, you must define the role of the application being developed. Whether it means that you thoroughly discuss the subject with a client or figure it out for yourself, understanding how the information will be accessed dictates the modeling. Thus, this process will require paper and pen rather than the MySQL software itself (although

database design is applicable to any relational database, not just MySQL).

In this example, I want to create a message board where users can post messages and other users can reply. I imagine that users will need to register, and then log in with an email address/password combination to post messages. I also expect that there could be multiple forums for different subjects. I have listed a sample row of data in **Table 6.1**. The database itself will be called *forum*.

TIP One of the best ways to determine what information should be stored in a database is to think about what questions will be asked of the database and what data would be included in the answers.

TIP Always err on the side of storing more information than you might need. It's easy to ignore unnecessary data but impossible to later manufacture data that was never stored in the first place.

TIP Normalization can be hard to learn if you fixate on the little things. Each of the normal forms is defined in a very cryptic way; even when put into layman's terms, they can still be confounding. My best advice is to focus on the big picture as you follow along. Once you've gone through normalization and seen the end result, the overall process should be clear enough.

TABLE 6.1 Sample Forum Data

Item	Example
username	troutster
password	mypass
actual name	Larry Ullman
user email	email@example.com
forum	MySQL
message subject	Question about normalization
message body	I have a question about...
message date	November 2, 2017 12:20 AM

Keys

As briefly mentioned in Chapter 4, *keys* are integral to normalized databases. There are two types of keys: *primary* and *foreign*. A primary key is a unique identifier that has to abide by certain rules. They must

- Always have a value (they cannot be **NULL**)
- Have a value that remains the same (never changes)
- Have a unique value for each record in a table

A good real-world example of a primary key is the U.S. Social Security number: everyone has a unique Social Security number, and that number never changes. Just as the Social Security number is an artificial construct used to identify people, you'll frequently find creating an arbitrary primary key for each table to be the best design practice.

The second type of key is a foreign key. Foreign keys are the representation in Table B of the primary key from Table A. If you have a *cinema* database with a *movies* table and a *directors* table, the primary key from *directors* would be linked as a foreign key in *movies*. You'll see better how this works as the normalization process continues.

The *forum* database is just a simple table as it stands (Table 6.1), but before beginning the normalization process, identify at least one primary key. The foreign keys will come in later steps.

To assign a primary key:

1. Look for any fields that meet the three tests for a primary key.

   In this example (Table 6.1), no column fits all the criteria for a primary key. The username and email address will be unique for each forum user but will not be unique for each record in the database because the same user could post multiple messages. The same subject could be used multiple times as well. The message body will likely be unique for each message but could change (if edited), violating one of the rules of primary keys.

2. If no logical primary key exists, invent one (**Table 6.2**).

   Frequently, you will need to create a primary key because no good solution presents itself. In this example, a *message ID* is manufactured. When you create a primary key that has no other meaning or purpose, it's called a *surrogate* primary key.

TIP As a rule of thumb, I name my primary keys using at least part of the table's name (e.g., message) and the word id. Some database developers like to add the abbreviation pk to the name as well. Some developers just use id.

TIP MySQL allows for only one primary key per table, although you can base a primary key on multiple columns. A multiple-column primary key means the combination of those columns must be unique and never change.

TIP Ideally, your primary key should always be an integer, which results in better MySQL performance.

TABLE 6.2 Sample Forum Data

Item	Example
message ID	325
username	troutster
password	mypass
actual name	Larry Ullman
user email	email@example.com
forum	MySQL
message subject	Question about normalization
message body	I have a question about...
message date	November 2, 2017 12:20 AM

Relationships

Database relationships refer to how the data in one table relates to the data in another. There are three types of relationships between any two tables: *one-to-one*, *one-to-many*, or *many-to-many*. Two tables in a database may also be unrelated.

A relationship is one-to-one if one and only one item in Table A applies to one and only one item in Table B. For example, each U.S. citizen has only one Social Security number, and each Social Security number applies to only one U.S. citizen; no citizen can have two Social Security numbers, and no Social Security number can refer to two citizens.

A relationship is one-to-many if one item in Table A can apply to multiple items in Table B. The terms *on* and *off* will apply to many switches, but each switch can be in only one state or the other. A one-to-many relationship is the most common one between tables in normalized databases.

Finally, a relationship is many-to-many if multiple items in Table A can apply to multiple items in Table B. A book can be written by multiple authors, and authors can write multiple books. Although many-to-many relationships are common in the real word, *you should avoid many-to-many relationships in your design* because they lead to data redundancy and integrity problems. Instead of having many-to-many relationships, properly designed databases use *intermediary tables* that break down one many-to-many relationship into two one-to-many relationships .

Relationships and keys work together in that a key in one table will normally relate to a key in another, as mentioned earlier.

A A many-to-many relationship between two tables will be better represented as two one-to-many relationships those tables have with an intermediary table.

TIP Database modeling uses certain conventions to represent the structure of the database, which I'll follow through a series of images in this chapter. The symbols for the three types of relationships are shown in **B**.

TIP The process of database design results in an ERD (entity-relationship diagram) or ERM (entity-relationship model). This graphical representation of a database uses shapes for tables and columns and the symbols from **B** to represent the relationships.

TIP Many programs are available to help create a database schema, including MySQL Workbench (https://www.mysql.com/products/workbench/). Many of the images in this chapter will come from MySQL Workbench.

TIP The term "relational" in RDBMS actually stems from the tables, which are technically called relations.

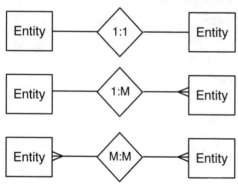

B These symbols, or variations on them, are commonly used to represent relationships in database modeling schemes.

First Normal Form

As already stated, normalizing a database is the process of changing the database's structure according to several rules, called *forms*. Your database should adhere to each rule exactly, and the forms must be followed in order.

Every table in a database must have the following two qualities to be in First Normal Form (1NF):

- Each column must contain only one value (this is sometimes described as being *atomic* or *indivisible*).

- No table can have repeating groups of related data.

A table containing one field for a person's entire address (street, city, state, zip code, country) would *not* be 1NF compliant, because it has multiple values in one column, violating the first property. As for the second, a *movies* table that had columns such as *actor1*, *actor2*, *actor3*, and so on would fail to be 1NF compliant because of the repeating columns all listing the exact same kind of information.

To begin the normalization process, check the existing structure (Table 6.2) for 1NF compliance. Any columns that are not atomic should be broken into multiple columns. If a table has repeating similar columns, then those should be turned into their own, separate table.

To make a database 1NF compliant:

1. Identify any field that contains multiple pieces of information.

   Looking at Table 6.2, one field is not 1NF compliant: *actual name*. The example record contained both the first name and the last name in this one column.

   The *message date* field contains a day, a month, and a year, plus a time, but subdividing past that level of specificity isn't warranted. And, as the end of the previous chapter shows, MySQL can handle dates and times quite nicely using the **DATETIME** type.

   Other examples of problems would be if a table used just one column for multiple phone numbers (mobile, home, work) or stored a person's multiple interests (cooking, dancing, skiing, etc.) in a single column.

2. Break up any fields found in Step 1 into distinct fields (**Table 6.3**).

   To fix this problem for the current example, create separate *first name* and *last name* fields, each containing only one value.

3. Turn any repeating column groups into their own table.

   The *forum* database doesn't have this problem currently, so to demonstrate what would be a violation, consider **Table 6.4**. The repeating columns—the multiple actor fields—introduce two problems. First, there's no getting around the fact that each movie will be

TABLE 6.3 Forum Database, Atomic

Item	Example
message ID	325
username	troutster
password	mypass
first name	Larry
last name	Ullman
user email	email@example.com
forum	MySQL
message subject	Question about normalization
message body	I have a question about...
message date	November 2, 2017 12:20 AM

TABLE 6.4 Movies Table

Column	Value
movie ID	976
movie title	Casablanca
year released	1943
director	Michael Curtiz
actor 1	Humphrey Bogart
actor 2	Ingrid Bergman
actor 3	Peter Lorre

TABLE 6.5 Movies-Actors Table

ID	Movie	Actor First Name	Actor Last Name
1	*Casablanca*	Humphrey	Bogart
2	*Casablanca*	Ingrid	Bergman
3	*Casablanca*	Peter	Lorre
4	*The Maltese Falcon*	Humphrey	Bogart
5	*The Maltese Falcon*	Peter	Lorre

limited to a certain number of actors when stored this way. Even if you add columns *actor 1* through *actor 100*, there will still be that limit (of a hundred). Second, any record that doesn't have the maximum number of actors will have **NULL** values in those extra columns. You should generally avoid columns with **NULL** values in your database schema. As another concern, the actor and director columns are not atomic.

To fix the problems in the *movies* table, a second table would be created (**Table 6.5**). This table uses one row for each actor in a movie, which solves the problems mentioned in the last paragraph. The actor names are also broken up to be atomic. Notice as well that a primary key column should be added to the new table. The notion that each table has a primary key is implicit in the First Normal Form.

4. Double-check that all new columns and tables created in Steps 2 and 3 pass the 1NF test.

TIP The simplest way to think about 1NF is that this rule analyzes a table horizontally: inspect all of the columns within a single row to guarantee specificity and avoid repetition of similar data.

TIP Various resources will describe the normal forms in somewhat different ways, likely with much more technical jargon. What is most important is the spirit—and end result—of the normalization process, not the technical wording of the rules.

Second Normal Form

For a database to be in Second Normal Form (2NF), the database must first already be in 1NF. You must normalize in order. Then, every column in the table that is not a foreign key must be dependent on the primary key. You can normally identify a column that violates this rule when it has non-key values that are the same in multiple rows. Such values should be stored in their own table and related back to the original table through a key.

Going back to the *cinema* example, a *movies* table (Table 6.4) would have the director Martin Scorsese listed 20+ times. This violates the 2NF rule, as the column(s) that store the directors' names would not be keys and would not be dependent on the primary key (the movie ID). The

fix is to create a separate *directors* table that stores the directors' information and assigns each director a primary key. To tie the director back to the movies, the director's primary key would also be a foreign key in the *movies* table.

Looking at Table 6.5 (for actors in movies), both the movie name and the actor names are also in violation of the 2NF rule: they aren't keys and they aren't dependent on the table's primary key. In the end, the *cinema* database in this minimal form requires four tables ●. Each director's name, movie name, and actor's name will be stored only once, and any non-key column in a table is dependent on that table's primary key. In fact, normalization could be summarized as the process of creating more and more tables until potential redundancies have been eliminated.

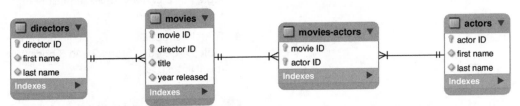

● To make the *cinema* database 2NF compliant (given the information being represented), four tables are necessary. The directors are represented in the *movies* table through the *director ID* key; the movies are represented in the *movies-actors* table through the *movie ID* key; and the actors are represented in the *movies-actors* table through the *actor ID* key.

To make a database 2NF compliant:

1. Identify any non-key columns that aren't dependent on the table's primary key.

   Looking at Table 6.3, the username, first name, last name, email, and forum values are all non-keys (message ID is the only key column currently), and none are dependent on the message ID. Conversely, the message subject, body, and date are also non-keys, but these do depend on the message ID.

2. Create new tables accordingly **D**.

   The most logical modification for the forum database is to make three tables: *users*, *forums*, and *messages*.

   In a visual representation of the database, create a box for each table, with the table name as a header and all its columns (also called its *attributes*) underneath.

3. Assign or create new primary keys **E**.

   Using the techniques described earlier in the chapter, ensure that each new table has a primary key. Here I've added a *user ID* field to the *users* table and a *forum ID* field to *forums*. These are both surrogate primary keys. Because the *username* field in the *users* table and the *name* field in the *forums* table must be unique for each record and must always have a value, you could have them act as the primary keys for their tables. However, this would mean that these values could never change (per the rules of primary keys) and the database would be a little slower, using text-based keys instead of numeric ones.

   continues on next page

D To make the *forum* database 2NF compliant, three tables are necessary.

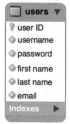 

E Each table needs its own primary key.

4. Create the requisite foreign keys and indicate the relationships **F**.

The final step in achieving 2NF compliance is to incorporate foreign keys to link associated tables. Remember that a primary key in one table will often be a foreign key in another.

With this example, the *user ID* from the *users* table links to the *user ID* column in the *messages* table. Therefore, *users* has a one-to-many relationship with *messages*: each user can post multiple messages, but each message can be posted by only one user.

Also, the two *forum ID* columns are linked, creating a one-to-many relationship between *messages* and *forums*: each message can only be in one forum, but each forum can have multiple messages.

There is no direct relationship between the *users* and *forums* tables.

TIP Another way to test for 2NF is to look at the relationships between tables. The ideal is to create one-to-one or one-to-many situations. Tables that have a many-to-many relationship may need to be restructured.

TIP Looking back at **C**, the movies-actors table is an intermediary table, which turns the many-to-many relationship between movies and actors into two one-to-many relationships. You can often tell a table is acting as an intermediary when all its columns are keys. In fact, in that table, the primary key could be the combination of the movie ID and the actor ID.

TIP A properly normalized database should never have duplicate rows in the same table: two or more rows in which the values in every non–primary key column match.

TIP To simplify how you conceive of the normalization process, remember that 1NF is a matter of inspecting a table horizontally, and 2NF is a vertical analysis: hunting for repeating values over multiple rows.

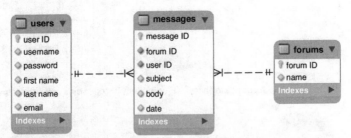

F To relate the three tables, add two foreign keys to the *messages* table, each key representing one of the other two tables.

Third Normal Form

A database is in Third Normal Form (3NF) if it is in 2NF and every non-key column is mutually independent. If you followed the normalization process properly to this point, you may not have 3NF issues. You would know that you have a 3NF violation if changing the value in one column would require changing the value in another. In the *forum* example thus far, there aren't any 3NF problems, but I'll explain a hypothetical situation where this rule would come into play.

Take, as an example, a database about books. After applying the first two normal forms, you might end up with one table listing the books, another listing the authors, and a third acting as an intermediary table between books and authors, since there's a many-to-many relationship there. If the *books* table listed the publisher's name and address, that table would be in violation of 3NF . The publisher's address isn't related to the book, but rather to the publisher itself. In other words, that version of the *books* table has a column that's dependent on a non-key column: the publisher's name.

As I said, the *forum* example is fine as is, but I'll outline the 3NF steps just the same, showing how to fix the books example just mentioned.

To make a database 3NF compliant:

1. Identify any fields in any tables that are interdependent.

    As just stated, what you need to look for are columns that depend more on each other than they do on the record as a whole. In the *forum* database, this isn't an issue. Just looking at the *messages* table, each *subject* will be specific to a *message ID*, each *body* will be specific to that *message ID*, and so forth.

    With a books example, the problematic fields are those in the *books* table that pertain to the publisher.

2. Create new tables accordingly.

    If you found any problematic columns in Step 1, like *address1*, *address2*, *city*, *state*, and *zip* in a *books* example, you would create a separate publishers table. (Addresses would be more complex once you factor international publishers in.)

continues on next page

G This database as currently designed fails the 3NF test.

3. Assign or create new primary keys.

   Every table must have a primary key, so add *publisher ID* to the new tables.

4. Create the requisite foreign keys that link any of the relationships 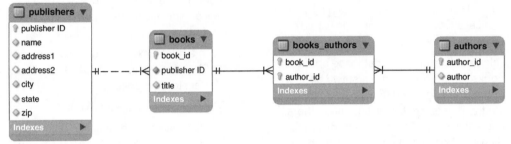.

   Finally, add a *publisher ID* to the *books* table. This effectively links each book to its publisher.

TIP Despite the existence of set rules for how to normalize a database, two different people could normalize the same example in slightly different ways. Database design does allow for personal preference and interpretations. The important thing is that a database has no clear and obvious NF violations. Any NF violation will likely lead to problems down the road.

H Going with a minimal version of a hypothetical *books* database, one new table is created for storing the publisher's information.

Overruling Normalization

As much as ensuring that a database is in 3NF will help guarantee reliability and viability, you won't fully normalize every database with which you work. Before undermining the proper methods, though, understand that doing so may have devastating long-term consequences.

The two primary reasons to overrule normalization are convenience and performance. Fewer tables are easier to manipulate and comprehend than more tables. Further, because of their more intricate nature, normalized databases will most likely be slower for updating, retrieving data from, and modifying. Normalization, in short, is a trade-off between data integrity/scalability and simplicity/speed. On the other hand, there are ways to improve your database's performance but few to remedy corrupted data that can result from poor design.

This chapter includes an example where normalization is ignored: a message's post date and time is stored in one field. As mentioned, because MySQL is so good with dates, there are no dangers to this approach. Another situation where you would overrule normalization is a table that stored a person's preference for a certain setting, such as "receive notifications." If stored as just Y/N or Yes/No (instead of linking to an answers table), there would be many repeating values. But that is fine in this case, since those labels are stable values, not likely to change over time (i.e., it's unlikely that a third option will be invented, or that "Yes" will be renamed, forcing a mass update of half the records in the table).

Practice and experience will teach you how best to model your database, but do try to err on the side of abiding by the normal forms, particularly as you are still mastering the concept.

Reviewing the design

After walking through the normalization process, it's best to review the design one more time. You want to make sure that the database stores all the data you may ever need. Often the creation of new tables, thanks to normalization, implies additional information to record. For example, although the original focus of the *cinema* database was on the movies, now that there are separate *actors* and *directors* tables, additional facts about those people could be reflected in those tables.

With that in mind, although there are many additional columns that could be added to the *forum* database, particularly regarding the user, one more field should be added to the *messages* table. Because one message might be a reply to another, some method of indicating that relationship is required. One solution is to add a *parent_id* column to *messages* **❶**. If a message is a reply, its *parent_id* value will be the *message_id* of the original message (so *message_id* is acting as a foreign key to this same table). If a message has a *parent_id* of 0, then it's a new thread, not a reply **❶**.

continues on next page

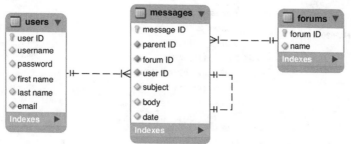

❶ To reflect a message hierarchy, the *parent_id* column is added to *messages*.

message_id	parent_id
3	0
4	0
18	3
19	4
20	18

❶ How the *parent_id* field is used to track message threads.

After making any changes to the tables, you must run through the normal forms one more time to ensure that the database is still normalized. Finally, choose the column types and names, per the steps in Chapter 4 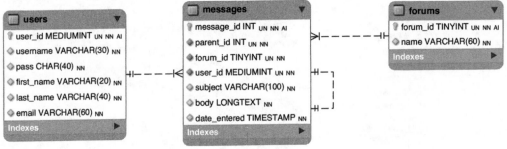. Note that every integer column is **UNSIGNED**, the three primary key columns are also designated as **AUTO_INCREMENT**, and every column is set as **NOT NULL**.

Once the schema is fully developed, it can be created in MySQL, using the commands shown in Chapter 5, "Introduction to SQL." You'll do that later in the chapter, after learning a few more things.

TIP When you have a primary key–foreign key link (like `forum_id` in *forums* to `forum_id` in *messages*), both columns should be of the same type (in this case, **TINYINT UNSIGNED NOT NULL**).

K The final ERD for the *forums* database.

Creating Indexes

Indexes are a special system that databases use to improve the performance of **SELECT** queries. Indexes can be placed on one or more columns, of any data type, effectively telling MySQL to pay attention to those values.

While the maximum number of indexes that a table can have varies, MySQL always guarantees that you can create at least 16 indexes for each table, and each index can incorporate up to 16 columns. Although the need for a multicolumn index may not seem obvious, it will come in handy for searches frequently performed on the same combinations of columns (e.g., first and last name, city and state, etc.).

Although indexes are an integral part of any table, not everything needs to be indexed. An index does improve the speed of reading from databases, but it slows down queries that alter data in a database because the changes need to be recorded in the index.

Indexes are best used on columns that are frequently used

- In the **WHERE** part of a query
- In an **ORDER BY** part of a query
- As the focal point of a **JOIN** (joins are discussed in the next chapter)

Generally speaking, you should *not* index columns that

- Allow for **NULL** values
- Have a very limited range of values (such as just Y/N or 1/0)

MySQL has four types of indexes: **INDEX** (the standard), **UNIQUE** (which requires each row to have a unique value for that column), **FULLTEXT** (for performing **FULLTEXT** searches, also discussed in Chapter 7, "Advanced SQL and MySQL"), and **PRIMARY KEY** (which is just a particular **UNIQUE** index and one you've already been using). Note that a column should only ever have a single index on it, so choose the index type that's most appropriate.

With this in mind, let's continue designing the *forum* database by identifying appropriate indexes. Later in this chapter, the indexes will be defined when the tables are created in the database. To establish an index when creating a table, this clause is added to the **CREATE TABLE** command:

INDEX_TYPE index_name `(columns)`

The index name is optional. If no name is provided, the index will take the name of the column, or columns, to which it is applied. When indexing multiple columns, separate them by commas, and put them in the order from most to least important:

```
INDEX full_name (last_name,
→ first_name)
```

You've already seen the syntax for creating indexes in Chapter 5. This command creates a table with a **PRIMARY KEY** index on the **user_id** field:

```
CREATE TABLE users (
user_id MEDIUMINT UNSIGNED NOT NULL
→ AUTO_INCREMENT,
first_name VARCHAR(20) NOT NULL,
last_name VARCHAR(40) NOT NULL,
email VARCHAR(40) NOT NULL,
pass CHAR(128) NOT NULL,
registration_date DATETIME NOT NULL,
PRIMARY KEY (user_id)
)
```

continues on next page

The last thing you should know about indexes are the implications of indexing multiple columns. If you add an index on *col1*, *col2*, and *col3* (in that order), this effectively creates an index for uses of *col1*, *col1* and *col2* together, or on all three columns together. It does not provide an index for referencing just *col2* or *col3* or those two together.

To create indexes:

1. Add a **PRIMARY KEY** index on all primary keys.

   Each table should always have a primary key and therefore a **PRIMARY KEY** index. With the *forums* database, the specific columns to be indexed as primary keys are *forums.forum_id*, *messages.message_id*, and *users.user_id*. (The syntax *table_name.column_name* is a way to refer to a specific column within a specific table.)

2. Add **UNIQUE** indexes to any columns whose values cannot be duplicated within the table.

   The *forums* database has three columns that should always be unique or else there will be problems: *forums.name*, *users.username*, and *users.email*.

3. Add **FULLTEXT** indexes, if appropriate.

   FULLTEXT indexes and **FULLTEXT** searching are discussed in the next chapter, so I won't discuss this topic any more here, but as you'll discover, there is one **FULLTEXT** index to be used in this database.

4. Add standard indexes to columns frequently used in a **WHERE** clause.

   It requires some experience to know in advance which columns will often be used in **WHERE** clauses and therefore ought to be indexed. With the *forums* database, one common **WHERE** stands out: when a user logs in, she'll provide her email address and password. The query to confirm the user has provided the correct information will be something like this:

   ```
   SELECT * FROM users WHERE
   pass=SHA2('provided_password',
   → 512) AND
   email='provided_email_address'
   ```

   From this query, you can reason that indexing the combination of the email address and password would be beneficial.

5. Add standard indexes to columns frequently used in **ORDER BY** clauses.

   Again, in time such columns will stand out while designing the database. In the *forums* example, there's one column left that would be used in **ORDER BY** clauses that isn't already indexed: *messages.date_entered*. This column will frequently be used in **ORDER BY** clauses, since the site will, by default, show all messages in the order they were entered.

TABLE 6.6 The Forum Database Indexes

Column Name	Table	Index Type
forum_id	forums	PRIMARY
name	forums	UNIQUE
message_id	messages	PRIMARY
forum_id	messages	INDEX
parent_id	messages	INDEX
user_id	messages	INDEX
date_entered	messages	INDEX
user_id	users	PRIMARY
username	users	UNIQUE
pass/email	users	INDEX
email	users	UNIQUE

6. Add standard indexes to columns frequently used in **JOIN**s.

You may not know what a **JOIN** is now (and the topic is thoroughly covered in Chapter 7), but the most obvious candidates are the foreign key columns. Remember that a foreign key in Table B relates to the primary key in Table A. When selecting data from the database, a **JOIN** will be written based on this relationship. For that **JOIN** to be efficient, the foreign key must be indexed (the primary key will already have been indexed). In the *forums* example, three foreign key fields in the messages table ought to be indexed: *forum_id*, *parent_id*, and *user_id*.

Table 6.6 lists all the indexes identified through these steps.

TIP Indexes can be created after you already have a populated table. However, you'll get an error and the index will not be created if you attempt to add a UNIQUE index to a column that has duplicate values.

TIP MySQL uses the term KEY as synonymous for INDEX:

```
KEY full_name (last_name,
→ first_name)
```

TIP You can limit the length of an index to a certain number of characters, such as the first 10:

```
INDEX index_name (column_name(10))
```

You might do so in situations where the first X characters will be sufficiently useful in an ORDER BY clause.

TIP MySQL supports another type of index: SPATIAL. It's used to index columns that store geometric data.

Using Different Table Types

A MySQL feature uncommon in other database applications is the ability to use different types of tables. A table's type is also called its *storage engine*. Each table type supports different features, has its own limits in terms of how much data it can store, and even performs better or worse under certain situations. Still, how you interact with any table type—in terms of running queries—is consistent across them all.

Historically, the most important table type was *MyISAM*. Until version 5.5.5 of MySQL, MyISAM was the default table type on all operating systems (on Windows, the switch to a different default was made in an earlier version of MySQL). MyISAM tables are great for most applications, handling **SELECT**s and **INSERT**s very quickly. The MyISAM storage engine cannot handle *transactions*, though, which is its main drawback (transactions are covered in the next chapter). Between that feature and its lack of row-level *locking* (the entire table must be locked instead), MyISAM tables are more vulnerable to corruption and data loss should a crash occur.

As of MySQL version 5.5.5, MySQL's new default storage engine, on all operating systems, is *InnoDB*. InnoDB tables can be used for transactions and they perform **UPDATE**s nicely. InnoDB tables also support *foreign key constraints* (discussed at the end of the chapter) and row-level locking. But the InnoDB storage engine may be slower than MyISAM and requires more disk space on the server. Also, before MySQL 5.6.4, InnoDB tables do not support **FULLTEXT** indexes (covered in Chapter 7).

All that being said, InnoDB is the default table type in MySQL and is likely the one you'll want to use.

To specify the storage engine when you define a table, add a clause to the end of the creation statement:

```
CREATE TABLE tablename (
column1name COLUMNTYPE,
column2name COLUMNTYPE...
) ENGINE = type
```

If you don't specify a storage engine when creating tables, MySQL will use the default type for that MySQL server.

This feature of MySQL is even more significant because you can mix the table types within the same database. This way, you can best customize each table for optimum features and performance. To continue designing the *forums* database, the next step is to identify the storage engine to be used by each table.

To establish a table's type:

1. Find your MySQL server's available table types **Ⓐ**:

   SHOW ENGINES;

   The **SHOW ENGINES** command, when executed on the MySQL server, will reveal not only the available storage engines but also the default storage engine. It will help to know this information when it's time to choose a table type for your database.

2. If any of your tables requires a **FULLTEXT** index and you're not using MySQL 5.6.4 or greater, make it a MyISAM table.

   Again, **FULLTEXT** indexes and searches are discussed in the next chapter, but I'll say now that the *messages* table in the *forums* example will require a **FULLTEXT** index. Therefore, this table can use InnoDB if you're using MySQL 5.6.4 or greater but must be MyISAM if you're not.

3. If any of your tables requires support for transactions, make it an InnoDB table.

   Yes, again, transactions are discussed in the next chapter, but the storage engines ought to be determined now. Neither the *forums* nor *users* tables in the *forums* database will require transactions.

4. If neither of the above applies to a table, use the default storage engine.

   Table 6.7 identifies the storage engines to be used by the tables in the *forums* database with the caveat that if you're not using MySQL 5.6.4 or greater, the *messages* table should be MyISAM.

TIP **MySQL has several other table types, but MyISAM and InnoDB are the two most important, by far. The MEMORY type creates the table in memory, making it an extremely fast table but with absolutely no permanence.**

TABLE 6.7 The Forum Database Table Types

Table	Table Type
forums	InnoDB
messages	InnoDB
users	InnoDB

```
                              PHP and MySQL for Dynamic Web Sites
mysql> SHOW ENGINES;
+--------------------+---------+----------------------------------------------------------------+--------------+------+------------+
| Engine             | Support | Comment                                                        | Transactions | XA   | Savepoints |
+--------------------+---------+----------------------------------------------------------------+--------------+------+------------+
| InnoDB             | DEFAULT | Supports transactions, row-level locking, and foreign keys     | YES          | YES  | YES        |
| MRG_MYISAM         | YES     | Collection of identical MyISAM tables                          | NO           | NO   | NO         |
| MEMORY             | YES     | Hash based, stored in memory, useful for temporary tables      | NO           | NO   | NO         |
| BLACKHOLE          | YES     | /dev/null storage engine (anything you write to it disappears) | NO           | NO   | NO         |
| MyISAM             | YES     | MyISAM storage engine                                          | NO           | NO   | NO         |
| CSV                | YES     | CSV storage engine                                             | NO           | NO   | NO         |
| ARCHIVE            | YES     | Archive storage engine                                         | NO           | NO   | NO         |
| PERFORMANCE_SCHEMA | YES     | Performance Schema                                             | NO           | NO   | NO         |
| FEDERATED          | NO      | Federated MySQL storage engine                                 | NULL         | NULL | NULL       |
+--------------------+---------+----------------------------------------------------------------+--------------+------+------------+
9 rows in set (0.00 sec)

mysql>
```

Ⓐ To confirm what table types your MySQL installation supports, run this command (in the mysql client, here, or phpMyAdmin).

Languages and MySQL

Chapter 1, "Introduction to PHP," briefly introduced the concept of *encodings*. An HTML page or PHP script can specify its encoding, which dictates what characters, and therefore languages, are supported. The same is true for a MySQL database: by setting your database's encoding, you can impact what characters can be stored in it. To see a list of encodings supported by your version of MySQL, run a **SHOW CHARACTER SET** command Ⓐ. Note that the phrase *character set* is being used in MySQL to mean *encoding* (which I'll generally follow in this section to be consistent with MySQL).

Each character set in MySQL has one or more *collations*. Collation refers to the rules used for comparing characters in a set. It's like alphabetization, but it considers numbers, spaces, and other characters as well. Collation is tied to the character set being used, reflecting both the kinds of characters present in that language and the cultural habits of people who generally use the language. For example, how text is sorted in English is not the same as it is in traditional Spanish or in Arabic. Other considerations include: Are upper- and lowercase versions of a character considered to be the same or different (i.e., is it a case-sensitive comparison)? How do accented characters get sorted? Is a space counted or ignored?

```
                  PHP and MySQL for Dynamic Web Sites
mysql> SHOW CHARACTER SET;
+----------+-----------------------------+--------------------+--------+
| Charset  | Description                 | Default collation  | Maxlen |
+----------+-----------------------------+--------------------+--------+
| big5     | Big5 Traditional Chinese    | big5_chinese_ci    |      2 |
| dec8     | DEC West European           | dec8_swedish_ci    |      1 |
| cp850    | DOS West European           | cp850_general_ci   |      1 |
| hp8      | HP West European            | hp8_english_ci     |      1 |
| koi8r    | KOI8-R Relcom Russian       | koi8r_general_ci   |      1 |
| latin1   | cp1252 West European        | latin1_swedish_ci  |      1 |
| latin2   | ISO 8859-2 Central European | latin2_general_ci  |      1 |
| swe7     | 7bit Swedish                | swe7_swedish_ci    |      1 |
| ascii    | US ASCII                    | ascii_general_ci   |      1 |
| ujis     | EUC-JP Japanese             | ujis_japanese_ci   |      3 |
| sjis     | Shift-JIS Japanese          | sjis_japanese_ci   |      2 |
| hebrew   | ISO 8859-8 Hebrew           | hebrew_general_ci  |      1 |
| tis620   | TIS620 Thai                 | tis620_thai_ci     |      1 |
| euckr    | EUC-KR Korean               | euckr_korean_ci    |      2 |
| koi8u    | KOI8-U Ukrainian            | koi8u_general_ci   |      1 |
| gb2312   | GB2312 Simplified Chinese   | gb2312_chinese_ci  |      2 |
| greek    | ISO 8859-7 Greek            | greek_general_ci   |      1 |
| cp1250   | Windows Central European    | cp1250_general_ci  |      1 |
| gbk      | GBK Simplified Chinese      | gbk_chinese_ci     |      2 |
| latin5   | ISO 8859-9 Turkish          | latin5_turkish_ci  |      1 |
| armscii8 | ARMSCII-8 Armenian          | armscii8_general_ci|      1 |
| utf8     | UTF-8 Unicode               | utf8_general_ci    |      3 |
| ucs2     | UCS-2 Unicode               | ucs2_general_ci    |      2 |
| cp866    | DOS Russian                 | cp866_general_ci   |      1 |
| keybcs2  | DOS Kamenicky Czech-Slovak  | keybcs2_general_ci |      1 |
| macce    | Mac Central European        | macce_general_ci   |      1 |
| macroman | Mac West European           | macroman_general_ci|      1 |
| cp852    | DOS Central European        | cp852_general_ci   |      1 |
| latin7   | ISO 8859-13 Baltic          | latin7_general_ci  |      1 |
| utf8mb4  | UTF-8 Unicode               | utf8mb4_general_ci |      4 |
| cp1251   | Windows Cyrillic            | cp1251_general_ci  |      1 |
| utf16    | UTF-16 Unicode              | utf16_general_ci   |      4 |
| utf16le  | UTF-16LE Unicode            | utf16le_general_ci |      4 |
| cp1256   | Windows Arabic              | cp1256_general_ci  |      1 |
| cp1257   | Windows Baltic              | cp1257_general_ci  |      1 |
| utf32    | UTF-32 Unicode              | utf32_general_ci   |      4 |
| binary   | Binary pseudo charset       | binary             |      1 |
| geostd8  | GEOSTD8 Georgian            | geostd8_general_ci |      1 |
| cp932    | SJIS for Windows Japanese   | cp932_japanese_ci  |      2 |
| eucjpms  | UJIS for Windows Japanese   | eucjpms_japanese_ci|      3 |
| gb18030  | China National Standard GB18030 | gb18030_chinese_ci|   4 |
+----------+-----------------------------+--------------------+--------+
41 rows in set (0.00 sec)

mysql> █
```

Ⓐ The list of character sets supported by this MySQL installation.

To view MySQL's available collations, run this query **B**, replacing *charset* with the proper value from the result in the last query **A**:

SHOW COLLATION LIKE 'charset%'

The results of this query will also indicate the default collation for that character set. The names of collations use a concluding *ci* to indicate case-insensitivity, *cs* for case-sensitivity, and *bin* for binary.

Generally speaking, I recommend using the UTF-8 character set, with its default collation. More importantly, *the character set in use by the database should match that of your PHP scripts*. If you're not using UTF-8 in your PHP scripts, use the matching encoding in the database. If the default collation doesn't adhere to the conventions of the language primarily in use, then adjust the collation accordingly.

In MySQL, the server as a whole, each database, each table, and even every string column can have a defined character set and collation. To set these values when you create a database, use

CREATE DATABASE *name*
CHARACTER SET *charset*
COLLATE *collation*

To set these values when you create a table, use

CREATE TABLE *name* (
column definitions
)
CHARACTER SET *charset*
COLLATE *collation*

continues on next page

```
           PHP and MySQL for Dynamic Web Sites
mysql> SHOW COLLATION LIKE 'utf8%';
+------------------------+---------+-----+---------+----------+---------+
| Collation              | Charset | Id  | Default | Compiled | Sortlen |
+------------------------+---------+-----+---------+----------+---------+
| utf8_general_ci        | utf8    |  33 | Yes     | Yes      |       1 |
| utf8_bin               | utf8    |  83 |         | Yes      |       1 |
| utf8_unicode_ci        | utf8    | 192 |         | Yes      |       8 |
| utf8_icelandic_ci      | utf8    | 193 |         | Yes      |       8 |
| utf8_latvian_ci        | utf8    | 194 |         | Yes      |       8 |
| utf8_romanian_ci       | utf8    | 195 |         | Yes      |       8 |
| utf8_slovenian_ci      | utf8    | 196 |         | Yes      |       8 |
| utf8_polish_ci         | utf8    | 197 |         | Yes      |       8 |
| utf8_estonian_ci       | utf8    | 198 |         | Yes      |       8 |
| utf8_spanish_ci        | utf8    | 199 |         | Yes      |       8 |
| utf8_swedish_ci        | utf8    | 200 |         | Yes      |       8 |
| utf8_turkish_ci        | utf8    | 201 |         | Yes      |       8 |
| utf8_czech_ci          | utf8    | 202 |         | Yes      |       8 |
| utf8_danish_ci         | utf8    | 203 |         | Yes      |       8 |
| utf8_lithuanian_ci     | utf8    | 204 |         | Yes      |       8 |
| utf8_slovak_ci         | utf8    | 205 |         | Yes      |       8 |
| utf8_spanish2_ci       | utf8    | 206 |         | Yes      |       8 |
| utf8_roman_ci          | utf8    | 207 |         | Yes      |       8 |
| utf8_persian_ci        | utf8    | 208 |         | Yes      |       8 |
| utf8_esperanto_ci      | utf8    | 209 |         | Yes      |       8 |
| utf8_hungarian_ci      | utf8    | 210 |         | Yes      |       8 |
| utf8_sinhala_ci        | utf8    | 211 |         | Yes      |       8 |
| utf8_german2_ci        | utf8    | 212 |         | Yes      |       8 |
| utf8_croatian_ci       | utf8    | 213 |         | Yes      |       8 |
| utf8_unicode_520_ci    | utf8    | 214 |         | Yes      |       8 |
| utf8_vietnamese_ci     | utf8    | 215 |         | Yes      |       8 |
| utf8_general_mysql500_ci | utf8  | 223 |         | Yes      |       1 |
| utf8mb4_general_ci     | utf8mb4 |  45 | Yes     | Yes      |       1 |
| utf8mb4_bin            | utf8mb4 |  46 |         | Yes      |       1 |
| utf8mb4_unicode_ci     | utf8mb4 | 224 |         | Yes      |       8 |
| utf8mb4_icelandic_ci   | utf8mb4 | 225 |         | Yes      |       8 |
| utf8mb4_latvian_ci     | utf8mb4 | 226 |         | Yes      |       8 |
| utf8mb4_romanian_ci    | utf8mb4 | 227 |         | Yes      |       8 |
| utf8mb4_slovenian_ci   | utf8mb4 | 228 |         | Yes      |       8 |
| utf8mb4_polish_ci      | utf8mb4 | 229 |         | Yes      |       8 |
| utf8mb4_estonian_ci    | utf8mb4 | 230 |         | Yes      |       8 |
| utf8mb4_spanish_ci     | utf8mb4 | 231 |         | Yes      |       8 |
| utf8mb4_swedish_ci     | utf8mb4 | 232 |         | Yes      |       8 |
| utf8mb4_turkish_ci     | utf8mb4 | 233 |         | Yes      |       8 |
| utf8mb4_czech_ci       | utf8mb4 | 234 |         | Yes      |       8 |
```

B The list of collations available in the UTF-8 character set. The first one, *utf_general_ci*, is the default.

To establish the character set and collation for a column, add the right clause to the column's definition (you'd only use this for text types):

```
CREATE TABLE name (
something TEXT
CHARACTER SET charset
COLLATE collation
...)
```

In each of these cases, both clauses are optional. If omitted, a default character set or collation will be used.

Establishing the character set and collation when you define a database affects what data can be stored; you cannot store a character in a column if its encoding doesn't support that character. A second issue is the encoding used to communicate with MySQL. If you want to store Chinese characters in a table with a Chinese encoding, those characters will need to be transferred using the same encoding. To do so within the mysql client, set the encoding using just

```
CHARSET charset
```

With phpMyAdmin, the encoding to be used is established in the application itself (i.e., written in the configuration file).

At this point in time, every aspect of the database design for the *forums* example has been covered, so let's create that database in MySQL, including its indexes, storage engines, character sets, and collations.

To assign character sets and collations:

1. Access MySQL using whatever client you prefer.

   Like the preceding chapter, this one will also use the mysql client for all of its examples. You are welcome to use phpMyAdmin or other tools as the interface to MySQL.

2. Create the *forum* database **C**:

   ```
   CREATE DATABASE forum
   CHARACTER SET utf8
   COLLATE utf8_general_ci;
   USE forum;
   ```

   Depending on your setup, you may not be allowed to create your own databases. If that's the case, just use the database provided to you and add the following tables to it. Note that in the **CREATE DATABASE** command, the character set and collation are also defined. By doing so at this point, you ensure that every table will use those settings.

3. Create the *forums* table **D**:

   ```
   CREATE TABLE forums (
   forum_id TINYINT UNSIGNED NOT
   → NULL AUTO_INCREMENT,
   name VARCHAR(60) NOT NULL,
   PRIMARY KEY (forum_id),
   UNIQUE (name)
   ) ENGINE = INNODB;
   ```

```
PHP and MySQL for Dynamic Web Sites
mysql> CREATE DATABASE forum
    -> CHARACTER SET utf8
    -> COLLATE utf8_general_ci;
Query OK, 1 row affected (0.02 sec)

mysql> USE forum;
Database changed
mysql>
```

C The first steps are to create and select the database.

```
PHP and MySQL for Dynamic Web Sites
mysql> CREATE TABLE forums (
    -> forum_id TINYINT UNSIGNED NOT NULL AUTO_INCREMENT,
    -> name VARCHAR(60) NOT NULL,
    -> PRIMARY KEY (forum_id),
    -> UNIQUE (name)
    -> ) ENGINE = INNODB;
Query OK, 0 rows affected (0.06 sec)

mysql>
```

D Creating the first table.

It does not matter in what order you create your tables, but I'll make the *forums* table first. Remember that you can enter your SQL queries over multiple lines for convenience.

This table contains only two columns (which will happen frequently in a normalized database). Because I don't expect there to be many forums, the primary key is a really small type (**TINYINT**). If you wanted to add descriptions of each forum, a **VARCHAR(255)** or **TINYTEXT** column could be added to this table. This table uses the InnoDB storage engine.

4. Create the *messages* table **E**:

```
CREATE TABLE messages (
message_id INT UNSIGNED
→ NOT NULL AUTO_INCREMENT,
parent_id INT UNSIGNED
→ NOT NULL DEFAULT 0,
```

```
forum_id TINYINT UNSIGNED
→ NOT NULL,
user_id MEDIUMINT UNSIGNED
→ NOT NULL,
subject VARCHAR(100) NOT NULL,
body LONGTEXT NOT NULL,
date_entered DATETIME NOT NULL,
PRIMARY KEY (message_id),
INDEX (parent_id),
INDEX (forum_id),
INDEX (user_id),
INDEX (date_entered)
) ENGINE = INNODB;
```

The primary key for this table has to be big, since it could have lots and lots of records. The three foreign key columns—*forum_id*, *parent_id*, and *user_id*—will all be the same size and type as their primary key counterparts. The subject is limited to 100 characters and the body of each message can be a lot of text. The *date_entered* field is a **DATETIME** type.

All three tables use the InnoDB storage engine, unless you're using an older version of MySQL, in which case you'll probably need to make this one MyISAM.

5. Create the *users* table **F**:

```
CREATE TABLE users (
user_id MEDIUMINT UNSIGNED
→ NOT NULL AUTO_INCREMENT,
username VARCHAR(30) NOT NULL,
pass CHAR(128) NOT NULL,
first_name VARCHAR(20) NOT NULL,
last_name VARCHAR(40) NOT NULL,
email VARCHAR(60) NOT NULL,
PRIMARY KEY (user_id),
UNIQUE (username),
UNIQUE (email),
INDEX login (pass, email)
) ENGINE = INNODB;
```

```
mysql> CREATE TABLE messages (
    -> message_id INT UNSIGNED NOT NULL AUTO_INCREMENT,
    -> parent_id INT UNSIGNED NOT NULL DEFAULT 0,
    -> forum_id TINYINT UNSIGNED NOT NULL,
    -> user_id MEDIUMINT UNSIGNED NOT NULL,
    -> subject VARCHAR(100) NOT NULL,
    -> body LONGTEXT NOT NULL,
    -> date_entered DATETIME NOT NULL,
    -> PRIMARY KEY (message_id),
    -> INDEX (parent_id),
    -> INDEX (forum_id),
    -> INDEX (user_id),
    -> INDEX (date_entered)
    -> ) ENGINE = INNODB;
Query OK, 0 rows affected (0.02 sec)

mysql>
```

E Creating the second table.

```
mysql> CREATE TABLE users (
    -> user_id MEDIUMINT UNSIGNED NOT NULL AUTO_INCREMENT,
    -> username VARCHAR(30) NOT NULL,
    -> pass CHAR(128) NOT NULL,
    -> first_name VARCHAR(20) NOT NULL,
    -> last_name VARCHAR(40) NOT NULL,
    -> email VARCHAR(60) NOT NULL,
    -> PRIMARY KEY (user_id),
    -> UNIQUE (username),
    -> UNIQUE (email),
    -> INDEX login (pass, email)
    -> ) ENGINE = INNODB;
Query OK, 0 rows affected (0.03 sec)

mysql>
```

F The database's third and final table.

continues on next page

Most of the columns here mimic those in the *sitename* database's *users* table, created in the preceding two chapters. The pass column is defined as **CHAR(128)**, because the **SHA2()** function will be used and it always returns a string 128 characters long (see Chapter 5).

This table uses the InnoDB engine.

6. If desired, confirm the database's structure **G**:

```
SHOW TABLES;
SHOW COLUMNS FROM forums;
SHOW COLUMNS FROM messages;
SHOW COLUMNS FROM users;
```

The **SHOW** command reveals information about a database or a table. This step is optional because MySQL reports on the success of each query as it is entered. Still, it's always nice to remind yourself of a database's structure.

TIP Collations in MySQL can also be specified within a query, to affect the results:

```
SELECT ... ORDER BY column
COLLATE collation
SELECT ... WHERE column LIKE 'value'
COLLATE collation
```

TIP The CONVERT() function can convert text from one character set to another.

TIP You can change the default character set or collation for a database or table using an ALTER command, discussed in Chapter 7.

TIP Because different character sets require more space to represent a string, you will likely need to increase the size of a column for UTF-8 characters. Do this before changing a column's encoding so that no data is lost.

```
                              PHP and MySQL for Dynamic Web Sites
mysql> SHOW TABLES;
+------------------+
| Tables_in_forum  |
+------------------+
| forums           |
| messages         |
| users            |
+------------------+
3 rows in set (0.00 sec)

mysql> SHOW COLUMNS FROM forums;
+----------+-------------------+------+-----+---------+----------------+
| Field    | Type              | Null | Key | Default | Extra          |
+----------+-------------------+------+-----+---------+----------------+
| forum_id | tinyint(3) unsigned| NO  | PRI | NULL    | auto_increment |
| name     | varchar(60)       | NO   | UNI | NULL    |                |
+----------+-------------------+------+-----+---------+----------------+
2 rows in set (0.00 sec)

mysql> SHOW COLUMNS FROM messages;
+--------------+---------------------+------+-----+---------+----------------+
| Field        | Type                | Null | Key | Default | Extra          |
+--------------+---------------------+------+-----+---------+----------------+
| message_id   | int(10) unsigned    | NO   | PRI | NULL    | auto_increment |
| parent_id    | int(10) unsigned    | NO   | MUL | 0       |                |
| forum_id     | tinyint(3) unsigned | NO   | MUL | NULL    |                |
| user_id      | mediumint(8) unsigned| NO  | MUL | NULL    |                |
| subject      | varchar(100)        | NO   |     | NULL    |                |
| body         | longtext            | NO   |     | NULL    |                |
| date_entered | datetime            | NO   | MUL | NULL    |                |
+--------------+---------------------+------+-----+---------+----------------+
7 rows in set (0.00 sec)

mysql> SHOW COLUMNS FROM users;
+------------+---------------------+------+-----+---------+----------------+
| Field      | Type                | Null | Key | Default | Extra          |
+------------+---------------------+------+-----+---------+----------------+
| user_id    | mediumint(8) unsigned| NO  | PRI | NULL    | auto_increment |
| username   | varchar(30)         | NO   | UNI | NULL    |                |
| pass       | char(128)           | NO   | MUL | NULL    |                |
| first_name | varchar(20)         | NO   |     | NULL    |                |
| last_name  | varchar(40)         | NO   |     | NULL    |                |
| email      | varchar(60)         | NO   | UNI | NULL    |                |
+------------+---------------------+------+-----+---------+----------------+
6 rows in set (0.00 sec)

mysql>
```

G Check the structure of any database or table using **SHOW**.

TABLE 6.8 UTC Offsets

City	Time
New York City, U.S.	UTC−4
Cape Town, South Africa	UTC+2
Mumbai, India	UTC+5:30
Auckland, New Zealand	UTC+13
Kathmandu, Nepal	UTC+5:45
Santiago, Chile	UTC[nd]3
Dublin, Ireland	UTC+1

Time Zones and MySQL

Chapter 5 discussed how to use `NOW()` and other date- and time-related functions. That chapter explained that these functions reflect the time on the server. Therefore, values stored in a database using these functions are also storing the server's time. That may not sound like a problem, but say you move your site from one server to another: you export all the data, import it into the other, and everything's fine...unless the two servers are in different time zones, in which case all the dates are now technically off. For some sites, such an alteration wouldn't be a big deal, but what if your site features paid memberships? That means some people's membership might expire several hours early, and for others several hours late! The goal of a database is to reliably store information, and such possibilities simply won't do.

The solution to this particular problem is to store dates and times in a time zone–neutral way. Doing so requires something called UTC (*Coordinated Universal Time*, and, yes, the abbreviation doesn't exactly match the term). UTC, like Greenwich Mean Time (GMT), provides a common point of origin, from which all times in the world can be expressed as UTC plus or minus some hours and minutes (**Table 6.8**).

Fortunately, you don't have to know these values or perform any calculations to determine UTC for your server. Instead, the `UTC_DATE()` function returns the UTC date, `UTC_TIME()` returns the current UTC time, and `UTC_TIMESTAMP()` returns the current date and time.

continues on next page

Once you have stored a UTC time, you can retrieve the time adjusted to reflect the server's or the user's location. To change a date and time from any one time zone to another, use CONVERT_TZ() **Ⓐ**:

CONVERT_TZ(dt, *from*, *to*)

The first argument is a date and time value, like the result of a function or what's stored in a column. The second and third arguments are named time zones. To use this function, the list of time zones must already be stored in MySQL, which may or may not be the case for your installation (see the sidebar). If you see **NULL** results **Ⓑ**, check out the MySQL manual for how to install the time zones on your server.

To use this information, let's start populating the *forums* database, recording the message posted date and time using UTC.

Using Time Zones in MySQL

MySQL does not necessarily install support for time zones by default. To use named time zones, you must make sure that five specific tables in the *mysql* database are populated. While MySQL may not automatically do this for you, it does provide the tools to do this yourself.

This process is just complicated enough that there's not room to discuss it in this book (not for every possible contingency, operating system, etc.). But you can find the instructions by looking up "server time zone support" in the MySQL manual.

If you continue to use time zones in MySQL, you also need to keep this information in the *mysql* database updated. The rules for time zones, in particular when and how they observe daylight saving time, change often enough. Again, the MySQL manual has instructions for updating your time zones.

```
mysql> SELECT CONVERT_TZ(UTC_TIMESTAMP(), 'UTC', 'US/Eastern');
+-------------------------------------------------+
| CONVERT_TZ(UTC_TIMESTAMP(), 'UTC', 'US/Eastern') |
+-------------------------------------------------+
| 2017-05-29 15:12:08                             |
+-------------------------------------------------+
1 row in set (0.00 sec)

mysql>
```

Ⓐ A conversion of the current UTC date and time to the American Eastern Daylight Time (EDT).

```
mysql -u root -p
MariaDB [(none)]> SELECT CONVERT_TZ(UTC_TIMESTAMP(), 'UTC', 'US/Eastern');
+-------------------------------------------------+
| CONVERT_TZ(UTC_TIMESTAMP(), 'UTC', 'US/Eastern') |
+-------------------------------------------------+
| NULL                                            |
+-------------------------------------------------+
1 row in set (0.01 sec)

MariaDB [(none)]>
```

Ⓑ The CONVERT_TZ() function will return **NULL** if it references an invalid time zone or if the time zones haven't been installed in MySQL (which is the case here).

To work with UTC:

1. Access the *forum* database using whatever client you prefer.

   Like the preceding chapter, this one will also use the mysql client for all its examples. You are welcome to use php-MyAdmin or other tools as the interface to MySQL.

2. If necessary, change the encoding to UTF-8 **C**:

   CHARSET utf8;

   Because the database uses UTF-8 as its character set, the communication with the database should use the same. This line, explained in the previous section of the chapter, does exactly that. Note that you only need to do this when using the mysql client. Also, if you're not using UTF-8, change the command accordingly.

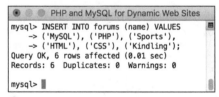

C The character set used to communicate with MySQL should match that used in the database.

```
PHP and MySQL for Dynamic Web Sites
mysql> INSERT INTO forums (name) VALUES
    -> ('MySQL'), ('PHP'), ('Sports'),
    -> ('HTML'), ('CSS'), ('Kindling');
Query OK, 6 rows affected (0.01 sec)
Records: 6  Duplicates: 0  Warnings: 0

mysql>
```

D Adding records to the *forums* table.

3. Add some new records to the *forums* table **D**:

   INSERT INTO forums (name) VALUES ('MySQL'), ('PHP'), ('Sports'), ('HTML'), ('CSS'), ('Kindling');

   Since the *messages* table relies on values retrieved from both the *forums* and *users* tables, those two tables need to be populated first. With this **INSERT** command, only the *name* column must be provided a value (the table's *forum_id* column will be given an automatically incremented integer by MySQL).

4. Add some records to the *users* table **E**:

   INSERT INTO users (username, pass,
   → first_name, last_name, email)
   → VALUES
   ('troutster', SHA2('mypass', 512),
   → 'Larry', 'Ullman',
   → 'lu@example.com'),
   ('funny man', SHA2('monkey', 512),
   → 'David', 'Brent',
   → 'db@example.com'),
   ('Gareth', SHA2('asstmgr', 512),
   → 'Gareth', 'Keenan',
   → 'gk@example.com');
   INSERT INTO users (username, pass,
   → first_name, last_name, email)
   → VALUES
   ('tim', SHA2('psych', 512) , 'Tim',
   → 'Canterbury', 'tc@example.com'),
   ('finchy', SHA2('jerk', 512),
   → 'Chris', 'Finch', '
   → cf@example.com');

continues on next page

```
PHP and MySQL for Dynamic Web Sites
mysql> INSERT INTO users (username, pass, first_name, last_name, email) VALUES
    -> ('tim', SHA2('psych', 512) , 'Tim', 'Canterbury', 'tc@example.com'),
    -> ('finchy', SHA2('jerk', 512), 'Chris', 'Finch', 'cf@example.com');
Query OK, 2 rows affected (0.00 sec)
Records: 2  Duplicates: 0  Warnings: 0

mysql>
```

E Adding records to the *users* table.

If you have any questions about the **INSERT** syntax or use of the **SHA1( )** function here, see Chapter 5.

5. Add new records to the *messages* table 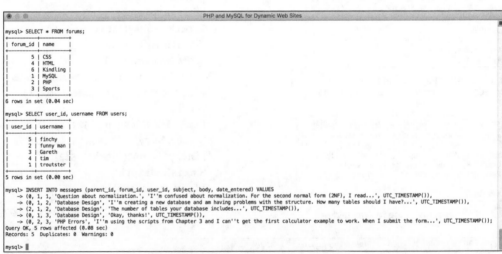:

```
SELECT * FROM forums;
SELECT user_id, username
→ FROM users;
INSERT INTO messages (parent_id,
→ forum_id, user_id, subject,
→ body, date_entered) VALUES
(0, 1, 1, 'Question about
→ normalization.', 'I''m confused
→ about normalization. For the
→ second normal form (2NF), I
→ read...', UTC_TIMESTAMP()),
(0, 1, 2, 'Database Design',
→ 'I''m creating a new database
→ and am having problems with the
→ structure. How many
→ tables should I have?...',
→ UTC_TIMESTAMP()),
(2, 1, 2, 'Database Design',
→ 'The number of tables
→ your database includes...',
→ UTC_TIMESTAMP()),
(0, 1, 3, 'Database Design',
→ 'Okay, thanks!', UTC_TIMESTAMP()),
(0, 2, 3, 'PHP Errors', 'I''m using
→ the scripts from Chapter 3 and
→ I can''t get the first
→ calculator example to work.
→ When I submit the form...',
→ UTC_TIMESTAMP());
```

Because two of the fields in the *messages* table (*forum_id* and *user_id*) relate to values in other tables, you need to know those values before inserting new records into this table. For example, when the *troutster* user creates a new message in the MySQL forum, the **INSERT** will have a *forum_id* of 1 and a *user_id* of 1.

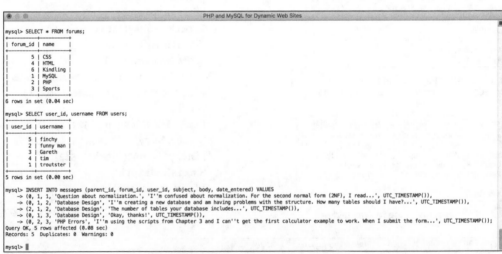

F Populating the *messages* table requires knowing foreign key values from *users* and *forums*.

This is further complicated by the *parent_id* column, which should store the *message_id* to which the new message is a reply. The second message added to the database will have a *message_id* of 2, so replies to that message need a *parent_id* of 2.

With your PHP scripts—once you've created an interface for this database, this process will be much easier, but it's important to comprehend the theory in SQL terms first.

For the *date_entered* field, the value returned by the **UTC_TIMESTAMP()** function will be used. Using the **UTC_TIMESTAMP()** function, the record will store the UTC date and time, not the date and time on the server.

6. Repeat Steps 3–5 to populate the database.

   The rest of the examples in this chapter and the next will use the populated database. You'll probably want to download the SQL commands from the book's corresponding web site, although you can populate the tables with your own examples and then just change the queries in the rest of the chapter accordingly.

7. View the most recent record in the messages table, using the stored date and time 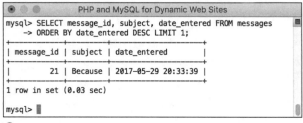:

```
SELECT message_id, subject,
→ date_entered FROM messages
ORDER BY date_entered DESC
→ LIMIT 1;
```

   As you can see in the figure and the table definition, UTC times are stored just the same as non-UTC times. What's not obvious in the figure is that the record just inserted reflects a time four hours ahead of the server (because my particular server is in a time zone four hours behind UTC).

continues on next page

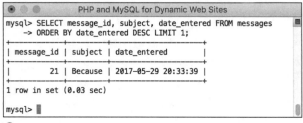

```
        ● ● ●          PHP and MySQL for Dynamic Web Sites
mysql> SELECT message_id, subject, date_entered FROM messages
    -> ORDER BY date_entered DESC LIMIT 1;
+------------+---------+---------------------+
| message_id | subject | date_entered        |
+------------+---------+---------------------+
|         21 | Because | 2017-05-29 20:33:39 |
+------------+---------+---------------------+
1 row in set (0.03 sec)

mysql>
```

G The record that was just inserted, which reflects a time four hours ahead (the server is UTC-4).

8. Retrieve the same record converting the *date_entered* to your time zone 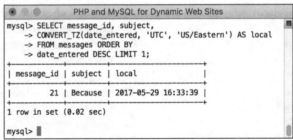:

```
SELECT message_id, subject,
CONVERT_TZ(date_entered,
→'UTC', 'US/Eastern') AS local
FROM messages ORDER BY
date_entered DESC LIMIT 1;
```

Using the **CONVERT_TZ( )** function, you can convert any date and time to a different time zone. For the *from* time zone, use *UTC*. For the *to* time zone, use yours (see the MySQL manual to find the right value to use).

If you get a **NULL** result ⓑ, either the name of one of your time zones is wrong or MySQL hasn't had its time zones loaded yet (see the sidebar).

TIP However you decide to handle dates, the key is to be consistent. If you decide to use UTC, then always use UTC.

TIP UTC is also known as Zulu time, represented by the letter Z.

TIP Besides being time zone and daylight saving time agnostic, UTC is also more accurate. It factors in irregular leap seconds that compensate for the inexact movement of the planet.

```
PHP and MySQL for Dynamic Web Sites

mysql> SELECT message_id, subject,
    -> CONVERT_TZ(date_entered, 'UTC', 'US/Eastern') AS local
    -> FROM messages ORDER BY
    -> date_entered DESC LIMIT 1;
+------------+---------+---------------------+
| message_id | subject | local               |
+------------+---------+---------------------+
|         21 | Because | 2017-05-29 16:33:39 |
+------------+---------+---------------------+
1 row in set (0.02 sec)

mysql>
```

Ⓗ The UTC-stored date and time converted to my local time.

Foreign Key Constraints

A feature of the InnoDB table type, not supported in other storage engines, is the ability to apply *foreign key constraints*. When you have related tables, the foreign key in Table B relates to the primary key in Table A (for ease of understanding, it may help to think of Table B as the child to Table A's parent). For example, in the *forums* database, the *messages.user_id* field is tied to *users.user_id*. If the administrator were to delete a user account, the relationship between those tables would be broken because the *messages* table would have records with a *user_id* value that doesn't exist in *users*. Foreign key constraints set rules as to what should happen when a break would occur, including preventing that break.

The syntax for creating a foreign key constraint is

```
FOREIGN KEY (item_name)
REFERENCES table (column)
```

This goes within a **CREATE TABLE** or **ALTER TABLE** statement.

The item name is the foreign key column in the current table. The *table(column)* clause is a reference to the parent table column to which this foreign key should be constrained. If you just use this minimal constraint definition—only identifying the relationship without stating what should happen when the constraint would be broken—MySQL will throw an error if you attempt to delete the parent record while child records exist **Ⓐ**. MySQL will also throw an error if you attempt to create a child record using a parent ID that doesn't exist **Ⓑ**.

You can dictate what alternative actions should occur by following the previous syntax with one or both of these:

```
ON DELETE action
ON UPDATE action
```

There are five action options, but two—**RESTRICT** and **NO ACTION**—are synonymous and also the default (i.e., the same as if you don't specify the action at all). A third action option—**SET DEFAULT**—doesn't work on InnoDB tables. That leaves **CASCADE** and **SET NULL**. If the action set is **SET NULL**, the removal of a parent record will result in setting the corresponding foreign keys in the child table to **NULL**. If that table defines that column as **NOT NULL**, which it almost always should, deletion of the parent record will trigger an error.

continues on next page

```
● ● ●          PHP and MySQL for Dynamic Web Sites
mysql> DELETE FROM parent WHERE parent_id=1;
ERROR 1451 (23000): Cannot delete or update a parent row: a foreign key
constraint fails (`test`.`child`, CONSTRAINT `child_ibfk_1` FOREIGN KEY
(`parent_id`) REFERENCES `parent` (`parent_id`))
mysql>
```

Ⓐ This error indicates that MySQL is preventing a query from deleting a parent record because the record is constrained to one or more existing children records.

```
● ● ●          PHP and MySQL for Dynamic Web Sites
mysql> INSERT INTO child
    -> (child_id, parent_id)
    -> VALUES (NULL, 12343234);
ERROR 1452 (23000): Cannot add or update a child row: a foreign
key constraint fails (`test`.`child`, CONSTRAINT `child_ibfk_1`
FOREIGN KEY (`parent_id`) REFERENCES `parent` (`parent_id`))
mysql>
```

Ⓑ Foreign key constraints also affect **INSERT** queries.

The **CASCADE** action is the most useful option. It tells the database to apply the same changes to the related table. With this instruction, if you delete the parent record, MySQL will also delete the child records with that parent ID as its foreign key.

Only the InnoDB table type supports foreign key constraints, so both tables in the relationship must be of the InnoDB type. Also, for MySQL to be able to compare the foreign key–primary key values, the related columns must be of equitable types. This means that numeric columns must be the same type and size; text columns must use the same character set and collation.

With the *forums* example, you can create foreign key constraints if you're using version 5.6.4 or greater of MySQL (and you created the *messages* table using the InnoDB storage engine). If you didn't create the *messages* table using the InnoDB storage engine, then it's impossible to use foreign key constraints, as *messages* is the only table related to another—*messages* relates to both *forums* and *users*.

As you may not be able to use foreign key constraints with the existing example, let's instead use a new hypothetical example for banking **C**.

The *customers* table stores all the information particular to a customer. It would logically also store contact information and so forth. The *accounts* table stores the accounts for each customer, including the type—Checking or Savings—and balance. Each customer may have more than one account, but each account is associated with only one customer (for a bit of simplicity). In the real world, the table might also store the date the account was opened and use a **BIGINT** as the balance, thereby representing all transactions in cents instead of dollars with decimals. Finally, the *transactions* table stores every movement of money from one account to another. Again, to make the example a bit easier to follow, the example assumes that only accounts within this same system will interact. Note that the *transactions* table has two one-to-many relationships with *accounts* (not one many-to-many). Each transaction's *to_account_id* value will be associated with a single account, but each account could be the "to" account multiple times. The same applies to the "from" account. Finally, foreign key constraints are applied to preserve the integrity of the data.

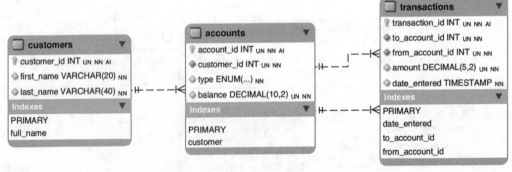

C The *banking* database could be used for virtual banking.

In this next series of steps, you'll create and populate this database, paying attention to the constraints. In the next chapter, this same database will be used to demonstrate transactions and encryption.

To create foreign key constraints:

1. Access MySQL using whatever client you prefer.

   Like the preceding chapter, this one will use the mysql client for all its examples. You are welcome to use phpMyAdmin or other tools as the interface to MySQL.

2. Create the *banking* database 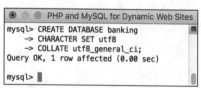:

   ```
   CREATE DATABASE banking
   CHARACTER SET utf8
   COLLATE utf8_general_ci;
   USE banking;
   ```

   As always, depending on your setup, you may not be allowed to create your own databases. If not, just use the database provided to you and add the following tables to it.

3. If necessary, change the communication encoding to UTF-8:

   ```
   CHARSET utf8;
   ```

4. Create the *customers* table ⒠:

   ```
   CREATE TABLE customers (
   customer_id INT UNSIGNED NOT NULL
   → AUTO_INCREMENT,
   first_name VARCHAR(20) NOT NULL,
   last_name VARCHAR(40) NOT NULL,
   PRIMARY KEY (customer_id),
   INDEX full_name (last_name,
   → first_name)
   ) ENGINE = INNODB;
   ```

   The *customers* table just stores the customer's ID—the primary key—and name (in two columns). An index is also placed on the full name, in case it might be used in **ORDER BY** and other query clauses. So that the database can use foreign key constraints, every table will use the InnoDB storage engine.

   continues on next page

```
  ● ● ●        PHP and MySQL for Dynamic Web Sites
mysql> CREATE DATABASE banking
    -> CHARACTER SET utf8
    -> COLLATE utf8_general_ci;
Query OK, 1 row affected (0.00 sec)

mysql>
```

ⓓ A new database is being created for this example.

```
  ● ● ●        PHP and MySQL for Dynamic Web Sites
mysql> CREATE TABLE customers (
    -> customer_id INT UNSIGNED NOT NULL AUTO_INCREMENT,
    -> first_name VARCHAR(20) NOT NULL,
    -> last_name VARCHAR(40) NOT NULL,
    -> PRIMARY KEY (customer_id),
    -> INDEX full_name (last_name, first_name)
    -> ) ENGINE = INNODB;
Query OK, 0 rows affected (0.05 sec)

mysql>
```

ⓔ Creating the *customers* table.

5. Create the *accounts* table **F**:

```
CREATE TABLE accounts (
account_id INT UNSIGNED
→ NOT NULL AUTO_INCREMENT,
customer_id INT UNSIGNED
→ NOT NULL,
type ENUM('Checking', 'Savings')
→ NOT NULL,
balance DECIMAL(10,2) UNSIGNED
→ NOT NULL DEFAULT 0.0,
PRIMARY KEY (account_id),
INDEX (customer_id),
FOREIGN KEY (customer_id)
→ REFERENCES customers
→ (customer_id) ON DELETE NO
→ ACTION ON UPDATE NO ACTION
) ENGINE = INNODB;
```

The *accounts* table stores the account ID, customer ID, account type, and balance. The *customer_id* column has an index on it, since it will be used in **JOIN**s (in Chapter 7). More importantly, the column is constrained to *customers.customer_id*, thereby protecting both tables. Even though **NO ACTION** is the default constraint, I've included it in the definition for added clarity.

Note that you must create the *accounts* table after creating *customers* or else the attempt will fail (due to trying to impose a constraint involving a table that doesn't exist).

```
                    PHP and MySQL for Dynamic Web Sites
mysql> CREATE TABLE accounts (
    -> account_id INT UNSIGNED NOT NULL AUTO_INCREMENT,
    -> customer_id INT UNSIGNED NOT NULL,
    -> type ENUM('Checking', 'Savings') NOT NULL,
    -> balance DECIMAL(10,2) UNSIGNED NOT NULL DEFAULT 0.0,
    -> PRIMARY KEY (account_id),
    -> INDEX (customer_id),
    -> FOREIGN KEY (customer_id) REFERENCES customers (customer_id) ON DELETE NO ACTION ON UPDATE NO ACTION
    -> ) ENGINE = INNODB;
Query OK, 0 rows affected (0.48 sec)

mysql>
```

F Creating the *accounts* table.

6. Create the *transactions* table 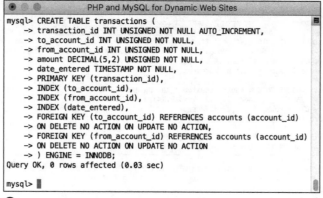:

```
CREATE TABLE transactions (
transaction_id INT UNSIGNED
→ NOT NULL AUTO_INCREMENT,
to_account_id INT UNSIGNED
→ NOT NULL,
from_account_id INT UNSIGNED
→ NOT NULL,
amount DECIMAL(5,2) UNSIGNED
→ NOT NULL,
date_entered TIMESTAMP NOT NULL,
PRIMARY KEY (transaction_id),
INDEX (to_account_id),
INDEX (from_account_id),
INDEX (date_entered),
```

```
FOREIGN KEY (to_account_id)
→ REFERENCES accounts (account_id)
ON DELETE NO ACTION ON UPDATE
→ NO ACTION,
FOREIGN KEY (from_account_id)
→ REFERENCES accounts (account_id)
ON DELETE NO ACTION ON UPDATE
→ NO ACTION
) ENGINE = INNODB;
```

The final table will be used to record all movements of monies among the accounts. To do so, it stores both account IDs (the "to" and "from"), the amount, and the date/time. Indexes are added accordingly, and both account IDs are constrained to the *accounts* table.

continues on next page

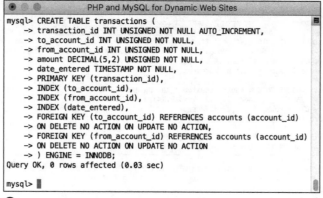

G Creating the third, and final, table: *transactions*.

7. Populate the *customers* and *accounts* tables 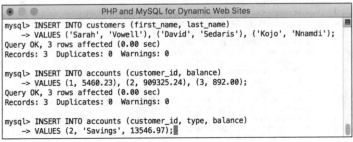:

```
INSERT INTO customers
→(first_name, last_name)
VALUES ('Sarah', 'Vowell'),
→('David', 'Sedaris'),
→('Kojo', 'Nnamdi');
INSERT INTO accounts
→(customer_id, balance)
VALUES (1, 5460.23), (2, 909325.24),
→(3, 892.00);
INSERT INTO accounts
→(customer_id, type, balance)
VALUES (2, 'Savings', 13546.97);
```

First, sample data is entered into the first two tables (the third will be used in the next chapter). Note that because the *accounts.type* column is defined as an **ENUM NOT NULL**, if no value is provided for that column, the first item in the **ENUM** definition—*Checking*—will be used.

8. Attempt to put data into the *accounts* table for which there is no customer 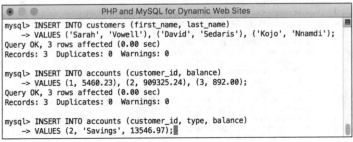:

```
INSERT INTO accounts
→(customer_id, type, balance)
VALUES (10, 'Savings', 200.00);
```

The foreign key constraint present in the *accounts* table will prevent an account being created without a valid customer ID—a pretty useful check in the real world.

```
                    PHP and MySQL for Dynamic Web Sites
mysql> INSERT INTO customers (first_name, last_name)
    -> VALUES ('Sarah', 'Vowell'), ('David', 'Sedaris'), ('Kojo', 'Nnamdi');
Query OK, 3 rows affected (0.00 sec)
Records: 3  Duplicates: 0  Warnings: 0

mysql> INSERT INTO accounts (customer_id, balance)
    -> VALUES (1, 5460.23), (2, 909325.24), (3, 892.00);
Query OK, 3 rows affected (0.00 sec)
Records: 3  Duplicates: 0  Warnings: 0

mysql> INSERT INTO accounts (customer_id, type, balance)
    -> VALUES (2, 'Savings', 13546.97);█
```

 Three records are added to both the *customers* and *accounts* tables.

```
                    PHP and MySQL for Dynamic Web Sites
mysql> INSERT INTO accounts (customer_id, type, balance)
    -> VALUES (10, 'Savings', 200.00);
ERROR 1452 (23000): Cannot add or update a child row: a foreign key
 constraint fails (`test`.`accounts`, CONSTRAINT `accounts_ibfk_1`
FOREIGN KEY (`customer_id`) REFERENCES `customers` (`customer_id`)
ON DELETE NO ACTION ON UPDATE NO ACTION)
mysql> []
```

 Again, as in , the constraint denies the **INSERT** query due to an invalid value from the parent table.

9. Attempt to delete a record from the *customers* table for which there is an *accounts* record 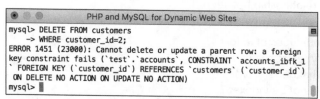:

```
DELETE FROM customers
WHERE customer_id=2;
```

The constraint will also prevent the deletion of customer records when that customer still has an account.

Despite the constraint, you could still delete a customer record if the customer does not have any records in the *accounts* table.

TIP To delete constrained records, you must first delete all the children records, and then the parent record.

TIP Foreign key constraints require that all columns in the constraint be indexed. Normal database design would suggest this is the case, but if the correct indexes do not exist, MySQL will create them when the constraint is defined.

TIP Similar to constraints are triggers. Simply put, a trigger is a way of telling the database "when X happens to this table, do Y." For example, when inserting a record in Table A, another record might be created or updated in Table B. See the MySQL manual for more on triggers.

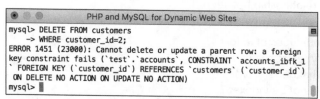

```
mysql> DELETE FROM customers
    -> WHERE customer_id=2;
ERROR 1451 (23000): Cannot delete or update a parent row: a foreign
key constraint fails (`test`.`accounts`, CONSTRAINT `accounts_ibfk_1
` FOREIGN KEY (`customer_id`) REFERENCES `customers` (`customer_id`)
ON DELETE NO ACTION ON UPDATE NO ACTION)
mysql>
```

J Because the customer with an ID of 2 has one or more records in the *accounts* table, the *customers* record cannot be deleted.

Review and Pursue

If you have any problems with the review questions or the pursue prompts, turn to the book's supporting forum (`LarryUllman.com/forums/`).

Review

- Why is normalization important?

- What are the two types of keys?

- What are the three types of table relationships?

- How do you fix the problem of a many-to-many relationship between two tables?

- What are the four types of indexes? What general types of columns *should* be indexed? What general types of columns *should not* be indexed?

- What are the two most common MySQL table types? What is the default table type for your MySQL installation?

- What is a *character set*? What is a *collation*? What impact does the character set have on the database? What impact does the collation have? What character set and collation are you using?

- What is *UTC*? How do you find the UTC time in MySQL? How do you convert from UTC to another time zone's time?

- What are *foreign key constraints*? What table type supports foreign key constraints?

Pursue

- You may want to consider downloading, installing, and learning to use the MySQL Workbench application. It can be quite useful.

- If you don't fully grasp the process of normalization—and that's perfectly understandable—search for additional tutorials online or ask a question in my support forums.

- Design your own database using the information presented here.

Advanced SQL
and MySQL

This, the last chapter dedicated to SQL and MySQL (although most of the rest of the book will use these technologies in some form or another), discusses the higher-end concepts often needed to work with more complicated databases, like those created in the previous chapter. The first such topic is the **JOIN**, a critical SQL term for querying normalized databases with multiple tables. From there, the chapter introduces a category of functions that are specifically used when grouping query results, followed by more complex ways to select values from a table.

In the middle of the chapter, you'll learn how to perform **FULLTEXT** searches, which can add search engine–like functionality to any site. Next up is the **EXPLAIN** command; it provides a way to test the efficiency of your database schema and your queries. The chapter concludes with coverage of transactions and database encryption.

Performing Joins

Because relational databases are more complexly structured, they sometimes require special query statements to retrieve the information you need most. For example, if you wanted to know what messages are in the *MySQL* forum (using the *forum* database created in the previous chapter), you would need to first find the *forum_id* for *MySQL*:

```
SELECT forum_id FROM forums WHERE
→ name='MySQL'
```

Then you would use that number to retrieve all the records from the *messages* table that have that *forum_id*:

```
SELECT * FROM messages WHERE
→ forum_id=1
```

This one simple—and, in a forum, often necessary—task would require two separate queries. By using a *join,* you can perform both requests in a single query.

A join is an SQL query that uses two or more tables and produces a virtual table of results. Whenever you need to simultaneously retrieve information from more than one table, a join is what you'll probably use.

Joins can be written in many ways, but the basic syntax is

```
SELECT what_columns
FROM tableA
JOIN_TYPE tableB
JOIN_CLAUSE
```

Because joins involve multiple tables, the *what_columns* can include columns in any named table. And since joins often return so much information, it's normally best to specify exactly what columns you want returned, instead of selecting them all.

When selecting from multiple tables, you must use the dot syntax (*table.column*) if the tables named in the query have columns with the same name. This is often the case when dealing with relational databases because a primary key from one table may have the same name as a foreign key in another. If you are not explicit when referencing your columns, you'll get an error **A**:

```
SELECT forum_id FROM messages
INNER JOIN forums
ON messages.forum_id=forums.forum_id
```

The two main types of joins are *inner* and *outer*, and there are subtypes within both. As you'll see with outer joins, the order in which you reference the tables does matter.

The join clause is where you indicate the relationship between the joined tables. For example, *forums.forum_id* should equal *messages.forum_id* in the previous code.

You can also use **WHERE** and **ORDER BY** clauses with a join, as you would with any **SELECT** query.

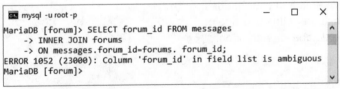

```
mysql -u root -p                                    —   □   ×
MariaDB [forum]> SELECT forum_id FROM messages
    -> INNER JOIN forums
    -> ON messages.forum_id=forums. forum_id;
ERROR 1052 (23000): Column 'forum_id' in field list is ambiguous
MariaDB [forum]>
```

A Generically referring to a column name present in multiple tables will cause an ambiguity error.

As a last note, before getting into joins more specifically, the SQL concept of an *alias*—introduced in Chapter 5, "Introduction to SQL"—will come in handy when writing joins. Often an alias will just be used as a shorthand way of referencing the same table multiple times within the same query. If you don't recall the syntax for creating aliases, or how they're used, revisit that part of Chapter 5.

As in the previous two chapters, this chapter will use the command-line mysql client to execute queries, but you can also use phpMyAdmin or another tool. The chapter assumes you know how to connect to the MySQL server and declare the character set to use, if necessary.

Inner joins

An inner join returns all the records from the named tables wherever a match is made. For example, to find every message posted in the *MySQL* forum, the inner join would be written as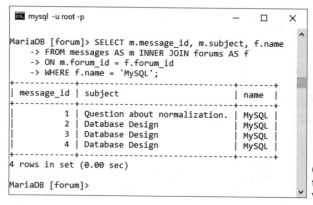

```
SELECT m.message_id, m.subject,
→ f.name
FROM messages AS m INNER JOIN
→ forums AS f
ON m.forum_id = f.forum_id
WHERE f.name = 'MySQL'
```

This join is selecting two columns from the *messages* table (aliased as *m*) and one column from the *forums* table (aliased as *f*) under two conditions. First, the *f.name* column must have a value of *MySQL*. This will return the *forum_id* of 1. Second, the *forum_id* value in the *forums* table must match the *forum_id* value in the *messages* table. Because of the equality comparison being made across both tables (**m.forum_id = f.forum_id**), this is known as an *equijoin*.

As an alternative syntax, if the column in both tables being used in the equality comparison has the same name, you can simplify your query with **USING**:

```
SELECT m.message_id, m.subject,
→ f.name
FROM messages AS m INNER JOIN
→ forums AS f
USING (forum_id)
WHERE f.name = 'MySQL'
```

```
MariaDB [forum]> SELECT m.message_id, m.subject, f.name
    -> FROM messages AS m INNER JOIN forums AS f
    -> ON m.forum_id = f.forum_id
    -> WHERE f.name = 'MySQL';
+------------+-----------------------------+-------+
| message_id | subject                     | name  |
+------------+-----------------------------+-------+
|          1 | Question about normalization. | MySQL |
|          2 | Database Design             | MySQL |
|          3 | Database Design             | MySQL |
|          4 | Database Design             | MySQL |
+------------+-----------------------------+-------+
4 rows in set (0.00 sec)

MariaDB [forum]>
```

B This join returns three columns from two tables where the *forum_id* value—1—represents the *MySQL* forum.

To use inner joins:

1. Connect to MySQL and select the *forum* database.

2. Retrieve the forum name and message subject for every record in the *messages* table :

   ```
   SELECT f.name, m.subject FROM
   → forums
   AS f INNER JOIN messages AS m
   USING (forum_id) ORDER BY f.name;
   ```

   This query will effectively replace the *forum_id* value in the *messages* table with the corresponding *name* value from the *forums* table for each of the records in the *messages* table. The result is that it displays the textual version of the forum name for each message subject.

   Notice that you can still use **ORDER BY** clauses in joins.

3. Retrieve the subject and date entered for every message posted by the user *funny man* 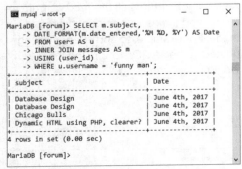:

   ```
   SELECT m.subject,
   DATE_FORMAT(m.date_entered,'%M %D,
   → %Y') AS Date
   FROM users AS u
   INNER JOIN messages AS m
   USING (user_id)
   WHERE u.username = 'funny man';
   ```

   This join also uses two tables: *users* and *messages*. The linking column for the two tables is *user_id*, so that's placed in the **USING** clause. The **WHERE** conditional identifies the user being targeted, and the **DATE_FORMAT()** function will help format the *date_entered* value.

C A basic inner join that returns only two columns of values.

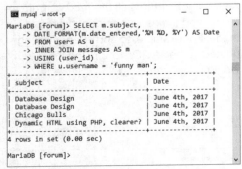

D A slightly more complicated version of an inner join, based on the *users* and *messages* tables.

```
┌─────────────────────────────────────────────┐
│ ▣ mysql -u root -p          —    □    ✕       │
├─────────────────────────────────────────────┤
│ MariaDB [forum]> SELECT f.name FROM forums AS f  ʌ│
│     -> INNER JOIN messages AS m                 │
│     -> USING (forum_id)                         │
│     -> ORDER BY m.date_entered DESC             │
│     -> LIMIT 5;                                 │
│ +------+                                        │
│ | name |                                        │
│ +------+                                        │
│ | CSS  |                                        │
│ | PHP  |                                        │
│ | HTML |                                        │
│ | PHP  |                                        │
│ | PHP  |                                        │
│ +------+                                        │
│ 5 rows in set (0.00 sec)                        │
│                                                 │
│ MariaDB [forum]>                               ∨│
└─────────────────────────────────────────────┘
```

E An **ORDER BY** clause and a **LIMIT** clause are applied to this join, which returns the forums with the five most recent messages.

4. Find the forums that have had the five most recent postings **E**:

```
SELECT f.name FROM forums AS f
INNER JOIN messages AS m
USING (forum_id)
ORDER BY m.date_entered DESC
LIMIT 5;
```

Since the only information that needs to be returned is the forum name, that's the sole column selected by this query. The join is then across the *forums* and *messages* table, linked via the *forum_id*. The query to that point would return every message matched with the forum it's in. That result is then ordered by the *date_entered* column, in descending order, and restricted to just the first five records.

TIP Inner joins can also be written without formally using the phrase **INNER JOIN**. To do so, place a comma between the table names and turn the **ON**, or **USING**, clause into another **WHERE** condition:

```
SELECT m.message_id, m.subject,
→ f.name
FROM messages AS m, forums AS f
WHERE m.forum_id = f.forum_id
AND f.name = 'MySQL'
```

TIP Joins that do not include a join clause (ON or USING) or a WHERE clause (e.g., SELECT * FROM urls INNER JOIN url_associations) are called full joins and will return every record from both tables. This construct can have unwieldy results with larger tables.

TIP A NULL value in a column referenced in an inner join will never be returned, because NULL matches no other value, including NULL.

TIP MySQL's supported join types differ slightly from the SQL standard. For example, SQL supports a CROSS JOIN and an INNER JOIN as two separate things, but in MySQL they are syntactically the same.

Outer Joins

Whereas an inner join returns records based on making matches between two tables, an *outer join* will return records that are matched by both tables, *and will return records that don't match*. In other words, an inner join is exclusive but an outer join is inclusive. There are three outer join subtypes: *left*, *right*, and *full*, with left being the most important. Here is an example of a left join:

```
SELECT f.*, m.subject FROM forums AS f
LEFT JOIN messages AS m
ON f.forum_id = m.forum_id
```

The most important consideration with left joins is which table gets named first. In this example, all the *forums* records will be returned along with all the *messages* information, if a match is made. If no *messages* records match a *forums* row, then **NULL** values will be returned for the selected *messages* columns instead .

As with an inner join, if the column in both tables being used in the equality comparison has the same name, you can simplify your query with **USING**:

```
SELECT f.*, m.subject FROM forums AS f
LEFT JOIN messages AS m
USING (forum_id)
```

A right outer join does the opposite of a left outer join: it returns all the applicable records from the right-hand table, along with matches from the left-hand table. This query is equivalent to the previous one:

```
SELECT f.*, m.subject FROM messages
→ AS m
RIGHT JOIN forums AS f
USING (forum_id)
```

Historically, the left join is preferred over the right.

A full outer join is like a combination of a left outer join and a right outer join. In other words, all the matching records from both

```
◘⊓ mysql -u root -p                              —  □  ✕
MariaDB [forum]> SELECT f.*, m.subject FROM forums AS f
    -> LEFT JOIN messages AS m
    -> ON f.forum_id = m.forum_id;
+----------+-------------+------------------------------------+
| forum_id | name        | subject                            |
+----------+-------------+------------------------------------+
|        5 | CSS         | CSS Resources                      |
|        5 | CSS         | CSS Resources                      |
|        4 | HTML        | HTML vs. XHTML                     |
|        4 | HTML        | HTML vs. XHTML                     |
|        6 | Kindling    | Why?                               |
|        6 | Kindling    | Why? Why? Why?                     |
|        6 | Kindling    | Because                            |
|        7 | Modern Dance| NULL                               |
|        1 | MySQL       | Question about normalization.      |
|        1 | MySQL       | Database Design                    |
|        1 | MySQL       | Database Design                    |
|        1 | MySQL       | Database Design                    |
|        2 | PHP         | PHP Errors                         |
|        2 | PHP         | PHP Errors                         |
|        2 | PHP         | PHP Errors                         |
|        2 | PHP         | PHP Errors                         |
|        2 | PHP         | Dynamic HTML using PHP             |
|        2 | PHP         | Dynamic HTML using PHP             |
|        2 | PHP         | Dynamic HTML using PHP, still not clear |
|        2 | PHP         | Dynamic HTML using PHP, clearer?   |
|        3 | Sports      | Chicago Bulls                      |
|        3 | Sports      | Chicago Bulls                      |
+----------+-------------+------------------------------------+
22 rows in set (0.00 sec)

MariaDB [forum]> _
```

F An outer join returns all the records from the first table listed, with non-matching records from the second table replaced with **NULL** values.

tables will be returned, along with all the records from the left-hand table that do not have matches in the right-hand table, along with all the records from the right-hand table that do not have matches in the left-hand table. MySQL does not directly support the full outer join, but you can replicate that functionality using a left join, a right join, and a **UNION** statement. A full outer join is not often needed, but see the MySQL manual if you're curious about it or *unions*.

To use outer joins:

1. Connect to MySQL and select the *forum* database, if you have not already.

2. Retrieve every username and every message ID posted by those users 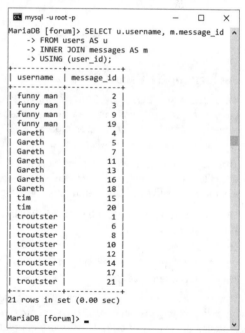:

```
SELECT u.username, m.message_id
FROM users AS u
LEFT JOIN messages AS m
USING (user_id);
```

If you were to run an inner join like this, a user who had not yet posted a message would not be listed 🅗. Hence, an outer join is required to be inclusive of all users. Note that the fully included table (here, *users*) must be the first table listed in a left join.

continues on next page

```
mysql -u root -p                        —   □   ×

MariaDB [forum]> SELECT u.username, m.message_id
    -> FROM users AS u
    -> LEFT JOIN messages AS m
    -> USING (user_id);
+-----------+------------+
| username  | message_id |
+-----------+------------+
| finchy    |       NULL |
| funny man |          2 |
| funny man |          3 |
| funny man |          9 |
| funny man |         19 |
| Gareth    |          4 |
| Gareth    |          5 |
| Gareth    |          7 |
| Gareth    |         11 |
| Gareth    |         13 |
| Gareth    |         16 |
| Gareth    |         18 |
| tim       |         15 |
| tim       |         20 |
| troutster |          1 |
| troutster |          6 |
| troutster |          8 |
| troutster |         10 |
| troutster |         12 |
| troutster |         14 |
| troutster |         17 |
| troutster |         21 |
+-----------+------------+
22 rows in set (0.00 sec)

MariaDB [forum]>
```

🅖 This left join returns for every user, every posted message ID. If a user hasn't posted a message (like *finchy* at the top), the message ID value will be **NULL**.

```
mysql -u root -p                        —   □   ×

MariaDB [forum]> SELECT u.username, m.message_id
    -> FROM users AS u
    -> INNER JOIN messages AS m
    -> USING (user_id);
+-----------+------------+
| username  | message_id |
+-----------+------------+
| funny man |          2 |
| funny man |          3 |
| funny man |          9 |
| funny man |         19 |
| Gareth    |          4 |
| Gareth    |          5 |
| Gareth    |          7 |
| Gareth    |         11 |
| Gareth    |         13 |
| Gareth    |         16 |
| Gareth    |         18 |
| tim       |         15 |
| tim       |         20 |
| troutster |          1 |
| troutster |          6 |
| troutster |          8 |
| troutster |         10 |
| troutster |         12 |
| troutster |         14 |
| troutster |         17 |
| troutster |         21 |
+-----------+------------+
21 rows in set (0.00 sec)

MariaDB [forum]> _
```

🅗 This inner join will not return any users who haven't yet posted messages (see *finchy* at the top of 🅖).

3. Retrieve every forum name and every message submission date in that forum in order of submission date **❶**:

```
SELECT f.name,
DATE_FORMAT(m.date_entered,
→ '%M %D, %Y') AS Date
FROM forums AS f
LEFT JOIN messages AS m
USING (forum_id)
ORDER BY date_entered DESC;
```

This is really just a variation on the join in Step 2, this time swapping the *forums* table for the *users* table.

```
mysql -u root -p                             —  □  ✕
    -> DATE_FORMAT(m.date_entered, '%M %D, %Y') AS Date
    -> FROM forums AS f
    -> LEFT JOIN messages AS m
    -> USING (forum_id)
    -> ORDER BY date_entered DESC;
+--------------+------------------+
| name         | Date             |
+--------------+------------------+
| CSS          | June 4th, 2017   |
| CSS          | June 4th, 2017   |
| HTML         | June 4th, 2017   |
| HTML         | June 4th, 2017   |
| Kindling     | June 4th, 2017   |
| Kindling     | June 4th, 2017   |
| Kindling     | June 4th, 2017   |
| PHP          | June 4th, 2017   |
| PHP          | June 4th, 2017   |
| PHP          | June 4th, 2017   |
| PHP          | June 4th, 2017   |
| PHP          | June 4th, 2017   |
| PHP          | June 4th, 2017   |
| PHP          | June 4th, 2017   |
| Sports       | June 4th, 2017   |
| Sports       | June 4th, 2017   |
| MySQL        | June 4th, 2017   |
| MySQL        | June 4th, 2017   |
| MySQL        | June 4th, 2017   |
| MySQL        | June 4th, 2017   |
| PHP          | June 4th, 2017   |
| Modern Dance | NULL             |
+--------------+------------------+
22 rows in set (0.00 sec)

MariaDB [forum]>
```

❶ This left outer join returns every forum name and the date of every message posted in that forum.

Performing Self-Joins

It's possible with SQL to perform a *self-join*: join a table with itself. For example, with the *messages* table, the *parent_id* column is a way of indicating which postings are replies to other postings. To retrieve a single hierarchy of postings, a **SELECT** query must join the *messages* table with itself, equating *parent_id* with *message_id* in the process.

This may sound confusing or impossible, but it's not. The trick with self-joins is to treat the two references to the same table as if they were single references to two different tables. To pull that off, assign a different alias to each table reference. The already described example would be written like so:

```
SELECT m1.subject, m2.subject AS Reply
FROM messages AS m1
LEFT JOIN messages AS m2
ON m1.message_id=m2.parent_id
WHERE m1.parent_id=0
```

That query first selects every root-level message—those with a 0 *parent_id* value—in the first *messages* table instance, *m1*. Those records are then outer joined with the second *messages* table instance, *m2*. If you run this query yourself, you'll see that the root message's subject is selected, along with the subject of that message's reply, if applicable.

Self-joins aren't the most popular join type, but they can sometimes solve a problem better than most other solutions.

TIP Joins can be created using conditionals involving any columns, not just the primary and foreign keys, although that's the most common basis for comparison.

TIP You can perform joins across multiple databases using the `database.table.column` syntax, as long as every database is on the same server (you cannot do this across a network) and you're connected as a user with permission to access every database involved.

TIP The word OUTER in a left outer join is optional and often omitted. To be formal, you could write

```
SELECT f.name,
DATE_FORMAT(m.date_entered,
→'%M %D, %Y') AS
Date FROM forums AS f
LEFT OUTER JOIN messages AS m
USING (forum_id)
ORDER BY date_entered DESC;
```

Joining three or more tables

There are two more ways joins can be used with which you ought to be familiar: *self-joins*, discussed in the sidebar, and joins on three or more tables.

When joining three or more tables, it helps to remember that a join between two tables creates a virtual table of results. When you add a third table, the join is between this initial virtual table and the third referenced table **J**. The syntax for a three-table join is of the format

```
SELECT what_columns FROM tableA
JOIN_TYPE tableB JOIN_CLAUSE
JOIN_TYPE tableC JOIN_CLAUSE
```

continues on next page

users

user_id	username
1	troutster
2	funny man
3	Gareth
4	tim
5	finchy

messages

message_id	forum_id	user_id	subject
1	1	1	faa
2	1	2	fee
3	1	2	fii
4	1	3	foo
5	2	3	fuu

JOIN virtual table

username	forum_id	subject
troutster	1	faa
funny man	1	fee
Gareth	1	fii
tim	1	foo
finchy	2	fuu

forums

forum_id	name
1	MySQL
2	PHP
3	Sports
4	HTML
5	CSS

JOIN virtual table

username	name	subject
troutster	MySQL	faa
funny man	MySQL	fee
Gareth	MySQL	fii
tim	MySQL	foo
finchy	PHP	fuu

J How a join across three tables works: by first creating a virtual table of results, and then by joining the third table to that.

The join types do not have to be the same in both cases—one could be an inner and the other an outer—and the join clauses are almost certain to be different. You can even add **WHERE**, **ORDER BY**, and **LIMIT** clauses to the end of this. Simply put, to perform a join on more than two tables, just continue to add **JOIN_TYPE tableX JOIN_CLAUSE** sections as needed.

There are three likely problems you'll have with joins that span three or more tables:

- A simple syntax error, especially when you use parentheses to separate out the clauses

- An ambiguous column error, which is common enough among any join type

- A lack of results returned

Should the last of these happen to you, simplify the join down to just two tables to confirm the result, and then try to reapply the additional join clauses to find where the problem is.

To use joins on three tables or more:

1. Connect to MySQL and select the *forum* database, if you have not already.

2. Retrieve the message ID, subject, and forum name for every message posted by the user *troutster* **K**:

```
SELECT m.message_id, m.subject,
→ f.name
FROM users AS u
INNER JOIN messages AS m
USING (user_id)
INNER JOIN forums AS f
USING (forum_id)
WHERE u.username = 'troutster';
```

This join is like one earlier in the chapter, but this one takes things a step further by incorporating a third table.

```
■ mysql -u root -p                                  —   □   ×

MariaDB [forum]> SELECT m.message_id, m.subject, f.name
    -> FROM users AS u
    -> INNER JOIN messages AS m
    -> USING (user_id)
    -> INNER JOIN forums AS f
    -> USING (forum_id)
    -> WHERE u.username = 'troutster';
+------------+------------------------------+----------+
| message_id | subject                      | name     |
+------------+------------------------------+----------+
|          1 | Question about normalization.| MySQL    |
|          6 | PHP Errors                   | PHP      |
|          8 | PHP Errors                   | PHP      |
|         10 | Chicago Bulls                | Sports   |
|         12 | CSS Resources                | CSS      |
|         14 | HTML vs. XHTML               | HTML     |
|         17 | Dynamic HTML using PHP       | PHP      |
|         21 | Because                      | Kindling |
+------------+------------------------------+----------+
8 rows in set (0.00 sec)

MariaDB [forum]>
```

K An inner join across all three tables.

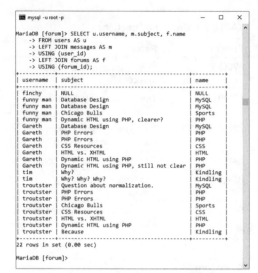

MariaDB [forum]> SELECT u.username, m.subject, f.name
    -> FROM users AS u
    -> LEFT JOIN messages AS m
    -> USING (user_id)
    -> LEFT JOIN forums AS f
    -> USING (forum_id);
+-----------+----------------------------------+----------+
| username | subject | name |
+-----------+----------------------------------+----------+
finchy	NULL	NULL
funny man	Database Design	MySQL
funny man	Database Design	MySQL
funny man	Chicago Bulls	Sports
funny man	Dynamic HTML using PHP, clearer?	PHP
Gareth	Database Design	MySQL
Gareth	PHP Errors	PHP
Gareth	PHP Errors	PHP
Gareth	CSS Resources	CSS
Gareth	HTML vs. XHTML	HTML
Gareth	Dynamic HTML using PHP	PHP
Gareth	Dynamic HTML using PHP, still not clear	PHP
tim	Why?	Kindling
tim	Why? Why? Why?	Kindling
troutster	Question about normalization.	MySQL
troutster	PHP Errors	PHP
troutster	PHP Errors	PHP
troutster	Chicago Bulls	Sports
troutster	CSS Resources	CSS
troutster	HTML vs. XHTML	HTML
troutster	Dynamic HTML using PHP	PHP
troutster	Because	Kindling
+-----------+----------------------------------+----------+
22 rows in set (0.00 sec)

MariaDB [forum]>

L This left join returns for every user, every posted message subject, and every forum name. If a user hasn't posted a message (like *finchy* at the top), his or her subject and forum name values will be **NULL**.

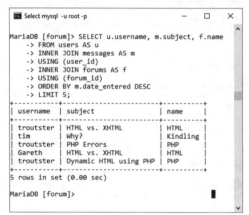

MariaDB [forum]> SELECT u.username, m.subject, f.name
    -> FROM users AS u
    -> INNER JOIN messages AS m
    -> USING (user_id)
    -> INNER JOIN forums AS f
    -> USING (forum_id)
    -> ORDER BY m.date_entered DESC
    -> LIMIT 5;
+-----------+------------------------+----------+
| username | subject | name |
+-----------+------------------------+----------+
troutster	HTML vs. XHTML	HTML
tim	Why?	Kindling
troutster	PHP Errors	PHP
Gareth	HTML vs. XHTML	HTML
troutster	Dynamic HTML using PHP	PHP
+-----------+------------------------+----------+
5 rows in set (0.00 sec)

MariaDB [forum]>

M This inner join returns values from all three tables, with applied **ORDER BY** and **LIMIT** clauses.

3. Retrieve the username, message subject, and forum name for every user **L**:

```
SELECT u.username, m.subject, f.name
FROM users AS u
LEFT JOIN messages AS m
USING (user_id)
LEFT JOIN forums AS f
USING (forum_id);
```

Whereas the query in Step 2 performs two inner joins, this one performs two outer joins. The process behind this query is visually represented by the diagram in **J**.

4. Find the users who have had the five most recent postings, while also selecting the message subject and the forum name **M**:

```
SELECT u.username, m.subject, f.name
FROM users AS u
INNER JOIN messages AS m
USING (user_id)
INNER JOIN forums AS f
USING (forum_id)
ORDER BY m.date_entered DESC
LIMIT 5;
```

To retrieve the username, the message subject, and the forum name, a join across all three tables is required. Since the query is looking only for users who have posted, an inner join is appropriate. The result of the two joins will be every username, with every message they posted, in every forum. That result is then ordered by the message's *date_entered* column, and limited to just the first five records.

Grouping Selected Results

Chapter 5 discussed and demonstrated several different categories of functions you can use in MySQL. Another category, used for more complex queries, is the *grouping* or *aggregate* functions (**Table 7.1**).

Whereas most of the functions covered in Chapter 5 manipulate a single value in a single row at a time (e.g., formatting the value in a date column), what the grouping functions return is based on a value present in a single column over a set of rows. For example, to find the average account balance in the *banking* database, you would run this query **A**:

```
SELECT AVG(balance) FROM accounts
```

To find the smallest and largest account balances, use **B**:

```
SELECT MAX(balance), MIN(balance)
FROM accounts
```

To simply count the number of records in a table (or result set), apply **COUNT()** to either every column or every column that's guaranteed to have a value:

```
SELECT COUNT(*) FROM accounts
```

TABLE 7.1 Grouping Functions

Function	Returns
AVG()	The average of the values in a column
COUNT()	The number of values in a column
GROUP_CONCAT()	The concatenation of a column's values
MAX()	The largest value in a column
MIN()	The smallest value in a column
SUM()	The sum of all the values in a column

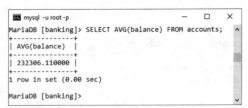

A The **AVG()** function is used to find the average of all the account balances.

B The **MAX()** and **MIN()** functions return the largest and smallest account values found in the table.

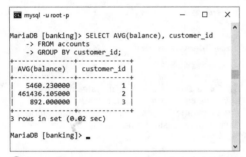

```
mysql -u root -p                                    —   □   ×
MariaDB [banking]> SELECT COUNT(customer_id)
    -> FROM accounts;
+--------------------+
| COUNT(customer_id) |
+--------------------+
|                  4 |
+--------------------+
1 row in set (0.00 sec)

MariaDB [banking]> SELECT COUNT(DISTINCT customer_id)
    -> FROM accounts;
+-----------------------------+
| COUNT(DISTINCT customer_id) |
+-----------------------------+
|                           3 |
+-----------------------------+
1 row in set (0.03 sec)

MariaDB [banking]>
```

C The **COUNT()** function, with or without the **DISTINCT** keyword, simply counts the number of records in a record set.

```
mysql -u root -p                                    —   □   ×
MariaDB [banking]> SELECT AVG(balance), customer_id
    -> FROM accounts
    -> GROUP BY customer_id;
+---------------+-------------+
| AVG(balance)  | customer_id |
+---------------+-------------+
|   5460.230000 |           1 |
| 461436.105000 |           2 |
|    892.000000 |           3 |
+---------------+-------------+
3 rows in set (0.02 sec)

MariaDB [banking]> _
```

D Use the **GROUP BY** clause with an aggregating function to group the aggregate results.

The **AVG()**, **COUNT()**, and **SUM()** functions can also use the **DISTINCT** keyword so that the aggregation applies only to distinct values. For example, **SELECT COUNT(customer_id) FROM accounts** will return the number of accounts, but **SELECT COUNT(DISTINCT customer_ID) FROM accounts** will return the number of customers that have accounts **C**.

The aggregate functions as used on their own return individual values, as in **A**, **B**, and **C**. When the aggregate functions are used with a **GROUP BY** clause, a single aggregate value will be returned for each row in the result set **D**:

```
SELECT AVG(balance), customer_id
FROM accounts
GROUP BY customer_id
```

You can apply combinations of **WHERE**, **ORDER BY**, and **LIMIT** conditions to a **GROUP BY**, structuring your query like this:

```
SELECT what_columns
FROM table
WHERE condition
GROUP BY column
ORDER BY column
LIMIT x, y
```

A **GROUP BY** clause can also be used in a join. Remember that a join returns a new, virtual table of data, so any grouping would then apply to that virtual table.

To group data:

1. Connect to MySQL and select the *banking* database.

2. Count the number of registered customers :

   SELECT COUNT(*) FROM customers;

   COUNT() is perhaps the most popular grouping function. With it, you can quickly count records, like the number of records in the *customers* table here. The **COUNT()** function can be applied to any column that's certain to have a value, such as * (i.e., every column) or *customer_id*, the primary key.

   Notice that not all queries using the aggregate functions necessarily have **GROUP BY** clauses.

3. Find the total balance of all accounts by customer, counting the number of accounts in the process 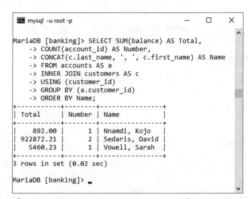:

   SELECT SUM(balance) AS Total,
   COUNT(account_id) AS Number,
   customer_id
   FROM accounts
   GROUP BY (customer_id);

   This query is an extension of that in Step 2, but instead of counting just the customers, it counts the number of accounts associated with each customer and totals the account balances, too.

4. Repeat the query from Step 3, selecting the customer's name instead of their ID 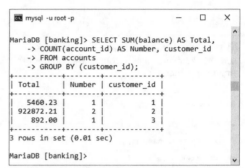:

   SELECT SUM(balance) AS Total,
   COUNT(account_id) AS Number,
   CONCAT(c.last_name, ', ',
   → c.first_name) AS Name
   FROM accounts AS a
   INNER JOIN customers AS c
   USING (customer_id)
   GROUP BY (a.customer_id)
   ORDER BY Name;

E This aggregating query counts the number of records in the *customers* table.

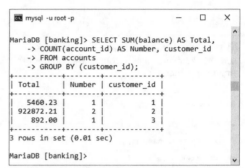

F This **GROUP BY** query aggregates all of the accounts by *customer_id*, returning the sum of each customer's accounts, and the total number of accounts the customer has, in the process.

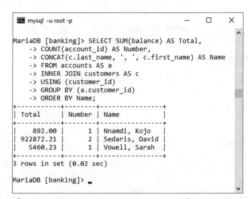

G This **GROUP BY** query is like that in **F**, but also returns the customer's name and sorts the results by name (which requires a join).

To retrieve the customer's name, instead of his or her ID, a join is required: **INNER JOIN customers USING (customer_id)**. Next, aliases are added for easier references, and the **GROUP BY** clause is modified to specify to which *customer_id* field the grouping should be applied. Thanks to the join, the customer's name can be selected as the concatenation of the customer's first and last names, a comma, and a space. And finally, the results can be sorted by the customer's name (note that another reference to the alias is used in the **ORDER BY** clause).

Remember that if you used an outer join instead of an inner join, you could then retrieve customers who did not have account balances.

5. Concatenate each customer's balance into a single string **H**:

```
SELECT GROUP_CONCAT(balance),
CONCAT(c.last_name, ', ',
→ c.first_name) AS Name
FROM accounts AS a
INNER JOIN customers AS c
USING (customer_id)
GROUP BY (a.customer_id)
ORDER BY Name;
```

The **GROUP_CONCAT()** function is a useful and often overlooked aggregating tool. As you can see in the figure, by default this function concatenates values, separating each with a comma.

TIP NULL is a peculiar value, and it's interesting to know that GROUP BY will group NULL values together, since they have the same nonvalue.

TIP You should be careful how you apply the COUNT() function, since it counts only non-NULL values. Be certain to use it either on every column (*) or on columns that will never contain NULL values (like the primary key).

TIP The GROUP BY clause, and the functions listed here, take some time to figure out, and MySQL will report an error whenever your syntax is inapplicable. Experiment within the mysql client or phpMyAdmin to determine the exact wording of any query you might want to run from a PHP script.

TIP A related clause is HAVING, which is like a WHERE condition applied to a group.

TIP You cannot apply SUM() and AVG() to date or time values. Instead, you'll need to convert date and time values to seconds, perform the SUM() or AVG(), and then convert that value back to a date and time.

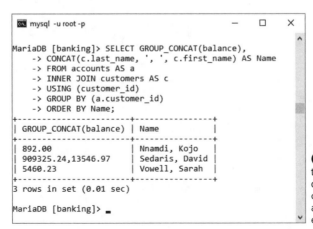

H A variation on the query in **G**, this query retrieves the concatenation of all account balances for each customer.

Advanced Selections

The previous two sections of the chapter present more advanced ways to select data from complex structures. But even with the use of the aggregate functions, the data being selected is comparatively straightforward. Sometimes, though, you'll need to select data conditionally, as if you were using an **if-else** clause within the query itself. This is possible in SQL thanks to the *control flow* and *advanced comparison* functions.

To start, **GREATEST()** returns the largest value in a list 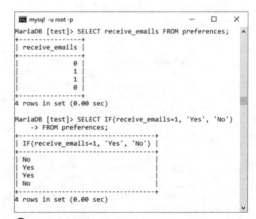:

```
SELECT GREATEST(col1, col2) FROM table
SELECT GREATEST(235, 1209, 59)
```

LEAST() returns the smallest value in a list:

```
SELECT LEAST(col1, col2) FROM table
SELECT LEAST(235, 1209, 59)
```

Note that unlike the aggregate functions, which apply to a list of values found in the same column over multiple rows, the comparison and control flow functions apply to multiple columns within the same row (or list of values).

Another useful comparison function is **COALESCE()**. It returns the first non-**NULL** value in a list:

```
SELECT COALESCE(col1, col2) FROM table
```

If none of the listed items has a value, the function returns **NULL**. You'll see an example in the step sequence that follows.

Whereas **COALESCE()** simply returns the first non-**NULL** value, you can use **IF()** to return any value, based on a condition:

```
SELECT IF(condition, return_if_true,
return_if_false)
```

If the condition is true, the second argument to the function is returned; otherwise, the third argument is returned. As an example, assuming a table stored the value 0 or 1 in a preferences column, a query could select *No* or *Yes* instead **B**:

```
SELECT IF(receive_emails=1, 'Yes', 'No')
FROM preferences
```

As these functions return values, they could even be used in other query types:

```
INSERT INTO prefernces
→ (receive_emails) VALUES
(IF(something='Y', 1, 0))
```

A The **GREATEST()** function returns the biggest value in a list.

B The **IF()** function can dictate the returned value based on a conditional.

The **CASE()** function is a more complicated tool that can be used in different ways. The first approach is to treat **CASE()** like PHP's **switch** conditional:

```
SELECT CASE col1
WHEN value1 THEN return_this
ELSE return_that
END
FROM table
```

The preferences example could be rewritten as

```
SELECT CASE receive_emails
WHEN 1 THEN 'Yes'
ELSE 'NO'
END
FROM preferences
```

The **CASE()** function can have additional **WHEN** clauses. The **ELSE** is also always optional:

```
SELECT CASE receive_emails
WHEN 1 THEN 'Yes'
WHEN 0 THEN 'No'
END
FROM preferences
```

If you're not looking to perform a simple equality test, you can write conditions into a **CASE()** :

```
SELECT message_id,
CASE WHEN date_entered >
→ NOW() THEN 'Future'
ELSE 'PAST'
END AS Posted
FROM messages
```

Again, you can add multiple **WHEN...THEN** clauses, as needed, and omit the **ELSE**, if that's not necessary.

To practice using these functions, let's run a few more queries on the *forum* database. Heads up: they're going to get a little complicated.

```
mysql -u root -p                                    —    □    ×
MariaDB [forum]> SELECT message_id,
    -> CASE WHEN date_entered > NOW() THEN 'Future'
    -> ELSE 'PAST'
    -> END AS Posted
    -> FROM messages;
+------------+--------+
| message_id | Posted |
+------------+--------+
|          1 | PAST   |
|          2 | PAST   |
|          3 | PAST   |
|          4 | PAST   |
|          5 | PAST   |
|          6 | PAST   |
|          7 | PAST   |
|          8 | PAST   |
|          9 | PAST   |
|         10 | PAST   |
|         11 | PAST   |
|         12 | PAST   |
|         13 | PAST   |
|         14 | PAST   |
|         15 | PAST   |
```

C **CASE()** can be used like **IF()** to customize the returned value.

To perform advanced selections:

1. Connect to MySQL and select the *forum* database.

2. For each forum, find the date and time of the most recent post, or return *N/A* if the forum has no posts :

```
SELECT f.name,
COALESCE(MAX(m.date_entered),
→ 'N/A') AS last_post
FROM forums AS f
LEFT JOIN messages AS m
USING (forum_id)
GROUP BY (m.forum_id)
ORDER BY m.date_entered DESC;
```

To start, to find both the forum name and the date of the latest posting in that forum, a join is necessary—specifically, an outer join, as there may be forums without postings. To find the most recent posting in each forum, the aggregating **MAX()** function is applied to the *date_entered* column, and the results must be grouped by the *forum_id* (so that **MAX()** is applied to each subset of postings within each forum).

The results at that point, without the **COALESCE()** function call, would return **NULL** for any forum without any messages in it. The final step is to apply **COALESCE()** so that the string *N/A* is returned should **MAX(m.date_entered)** have a **NULL** value.

3. For each message, append the string *(REPLY)* to the subject if the message is a reply to another message **E**:

```
SELECT message_id,
CASE parent_id WHEN O THEN subject
ELSE CONCAT(subject, ' (Reply) ')
END AS subject
FROM messages;
```

D The **COALESCE()** function is used to turn **NULL** values into the string *N/A* (see the last record).

E Here, the string *(Reply)* is appended to the subject of any message that is a reply to another message.

The records in the *messages* tables that have a *parent_id* other than 0 are replies to existing messages. For these messages, let's append *(REPLY)* to the subject value to indicate that. To accomplish this, a **CASE** statement returns just the subject, unadulterated, if the *parent_id* value equals 0. If the *parent_id* value does not equal 0, the string *(REPLY)* is concatenated to the subject, again thanks to **CASE**. This whole construct is assigned the alias of *subject*, so it's still returned under the original "subject" heading.

4. For each user, find the number of messages they've posted, converting zeros to the string *None* **F**:

```
SELECT u.username,
IF(COUNT(message_id) > 0,
COUNT(message_id), 'None') AS Posts
FROM users AS u
LEFT JOIN messages AS m
USING (user_id)
GROUP BY (u.user_id);
```

This is somewhat of a variation on the query in Step 2. A left join bridges *users* and *messages*, to grab both the username and the count of messages posted. To perform the count, the results are grouped by *users.user_id*. The query to this point would return 0 for every user that has not yet posted **G**. To convert those zeros to the string *None*, while maintaining the non-zero counts, the **IF()** function is applied. That function's first argument establishes the condition if the count is greater than zero. The second argument says that the count should be returned when that condition is true. The third argument says that the string *None* should be returned when that condition is false.

TIP The IFNULL() function can sometimes be used instead of COALESCE(). Its syntax is

```
IFNULL(value, return_if_null)
```

If the first argument, such as a named column, has a NULL value, then the second argument is returned. If argument does not have a NULL value, the value of that argument is returned.

```
mysql -u root -p                          —   □   ×
MariaDB [forum]> SELECT u.username,
    -> IF(COUNT(message_id) > 0,
    -> COUNT(message_id), 'None') AS Posts
    -> FROM users AS u
    -> LEFT JOIN messages AS m
    -> USING (user_id)
    -> GROUP BY (u.user_id);
+----------+-------+
| username | Posts |
+----------+-------+
| troutster | 8    |
| funny man | 4    |
| Gareth    | 7    |
| tim       | 2    |
| finchy    | None |
+----------+-------+
5 rows in set (0.00 sec)

MariaDB [forum]>
```

F Thanks to an **IF()** call, the count of posted messages is displayed as *None* for any user who has not yet posted a message.

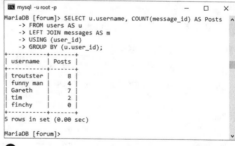

```
mysql -u root -p                          —   □   ×
MariaDB [forum]> SELECT u.username, COUNT(message_id) AS Posts
    -> FROM users AS u
    -> LEFT JOIN messages AS m
    -> USING (user_id)
    -> GROUP BY (u.user_id);
+----------+-------+
| username | Posts |
+----------+-------+
| troutster | 8    |
| funny man | 4    |
| Gareth    | 7    |
| tim       | 2    |
| finchy    | 0    |
+----------+-------+
5 rows in set (0.00 sec)

MariaDB [forum]>
```

G What the query results would look like (compare with **F**) without using **IF()**.

Performing FULLTEXT Searches

In Chapter 5, the **LIKE** keyword was introduced to perform somewhat simple string matches like

```
SELECT * FROM users
WHERE last_name LIKE 'Smith%'
```

This type of conditional is effective enough but is still very limiting. For example, it would not allow you to do Google-like searches using multiple words. For those kinds of situations, you need **FULLTEXT** searches. Over the next several pages, you'll learn everything you need to know about **FULLTEXT** searches and you'll learn some more SQL tricks in the process.

Creating a FULLTEXT Index

To start, **FULLTEXT** searches require a **FULLTEXT** index. This index type, as previewed in Chapter 6, "Database Design," can be created on a MyISAM table, or on an InnoDB table if you are using MySQL 5.6.4 or greater. These next examples will use the *messages* table in the *forum* database. The first step, then, is to add a **FULLTEXT** index on the *body* and *subject* columns. Adding indexes to existing tables requires using the **ALTER** command, as described in the sidebar.

Altering Tables

The **ALTER** SQL term is primarily used to modify the structure of an existing table. Commonly this means adding, deleting, or changing the columns, but it also includes the addition of indexes. An **ALTER** statement can even be used for renaming the table itself. The basic syntax of **ALTER** is

```
ALTER TABLE tablename CLAUSE
```

There are many possible clauses; **Table 7.2** lists the most common ones, where *t* represents the table's name, *c* a column's name, and *i* an index's name. As always, the MySQL manual covers the topic in exhaustive detail.

TABLE 7.2 ALTER TABLE Clauses

Clause	Usage	Meaning
ADD COLUMN	ALTER TABLE t ADD COLUMN c TYPE	Adds a new column to the table
CHANGE COLUMN	ALTER TABLE t CHANGE COLUMN c c TYPE	Changes the data type and properties of a column
DROP COLUMN	ALTER TABLE t DROP COLUMN c	Removes a column from a table, including all of its data
ADD INDEX	ALTER TABLE t ADD INDEX i (c)	Adds a new index on c
DROP INDEX	ALTER TABLE t DROP INDEX i	Removes an existing index
RENAME TO	ALTER TABLE t RENAME TO new_t	Changes the name of a table

You can also change a table's character set and collation using
`ALTER t CONVERT TO CHARACTER SET x COLLATE y`.

To add a FULLTEXT index:

1. Connect to MySQL and select the *forum* database, if you have not already.

2. Confirm the *messages* table's type **A**:

   `SHOW TABLE STATUS\G`

   The `SHOW TABLE STATUS` query returns a fair amount of information about each table in the database, including the table's storage engine. Because so much information is returned by the query, the command concludes with `\G` instead of a semicolon. This tells the mysql client to return the results as a vertical list instead of a table (which is sometimes easier to read). If you're using phpMyAdmin or another interface, you can omit the `\G` (just as you can omit concluding semicolons).

   To just find the information for the *messages* table, you can use the query `SHOW TABLE STATUS LIKE 'messages'`.

3. If the *messages* table does not support **FULLTEXT** indexes, change the storage engine:

   `ALTER TABLE messages ENGINE=MyISAM;`

   This is only necessary if the table isn't currently of the correct type. Acceptable types include MyISAM for any version of MySQL and InnoDB as of MySQL 5.6.4.

   continues on next page

```
mysql -u root -p                              —    □    ×
MariaDB [forum]> SHOW TABLE STATUS\G
ERROR 2006 (HY000): MySQL server has gone away
No connection. Trying to reconnect...
Connection id:    5
Current database: forum

*************************** 1. row ***************************
           Name: forums
         Engine: InnoDB
        Version: 10
     Row_format: Compact
           Rows: 7
 Avg_row_length: 2340
    Data_length: 16384
Max_data_length: 0
   Index_length: 16384
      Data_free: 0
 Auto_increment: 8
    Create_time: 2017-06-04 13:38:55
    Update_time: NULL
     Check_time: NULL
      Collation: utf8_general_ci
       Checksum: NULL
 Create_options:
        Comment:
*************************** 2. row ***************************
           Name: messages
         Engine: InnoDB
        Version: 10
     Row_format: Compact
           Rows: 21
 Avg_row_length: 780
    Data_length: 16384
Max_data_length: 0
   Index_length: 65536
      Data_free: 0
 Auto_increment: 22
    Create_time: 2017-06-04 13:39:16
    Update_time: NULL
     Check_time: NULL
      Collation: utf8_general_ci
       Checksum: NULL
```

A To confirm a table's type, use the `SHOW TABLE STATUS` command.

4. Add the **FULLTEXT** index to the *messages* table **B**:

```
ALTER TABLE messages
ADD FULLTEXT(body, subject);
```

The syntax for adding any index, regardless of type, is **ALTER TABLE tablename ADD INDEX_TYPE index_name (columns)**. The index name is optional.

Here, the *body* and *subject* columns get a **FULLTEXT** index, to be used in **FULLTEXT** searches later in this chapter.

TIP Inserting records into tables with FULLTEXT indexes can be slower because of the complex index that's required.

TIP FULLTEXT searches can successfully be used in a simple search engine. But a FULLTEXT index can be applied only to a single table at a time, so more elaborate sites, with content stored in multiple tables, would benefit from using a more formal search engine.

Performing Basic FULLTEXT Searches

Once you've established a **FULLTEXT** index on a column or columns, you can start querying against it, using **MATCH...AGAINST** in a **WHERE** conditional:

```
SELECT * FROM tablename WHERE
MATCH (columns) AGAINST (terms)
```

MySQL will return matching rows in order of a mathematically calculated relevance, just like a search engine. When doing so, certain rules apply:

- Strings are broken down into their individual keywords.

- Keywords fewer than four characters long are ignored.

- Very popular words, called *stopwords*, are ignored.

- If more than 50 percent of the records match the keywords, no records are returned.

This last fact is problematic to many users as they begin with **FULLTEXT** searches and wonder why no results are returned. When you have a sparsely populated table, there just won't be sufficient records for MySQL to return *relevant* results.

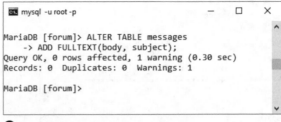

B The **FULLTEXT** index is added to the *messages* table.

To perform FULLTEXT searches:

1. Connect to MySQL and select the *forum* database, if you have not already.

2. Thoroughly populate the *messages* table, focusing on adding lengthy bodies.

   Once again, SQL **INSERT** commands can be downloaded from this book's corresponding site or you can make up your own and adjust the following queries accordingly.

3. Run a simple **FULLTEXT** search on the word *database* 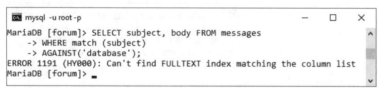:

   ```
   SELECT subject, body FROM messages
   WHERE MATCH (body, subject)
   AGAINST ('database');
   ```

   This is a very simple example that will return some results if at least one and less than 50 percent of the records in the *messages* table have the word "database" in their body or subject. Note that the columns referenced in **MATCH** must be the same as those on which the **FULLTEXT** index was made. In this case, you could use either **body, subject** or **subject, body**, but you could not use just **body** or just **subject** 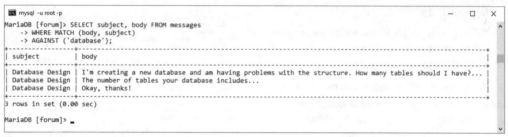.

   continues on next page

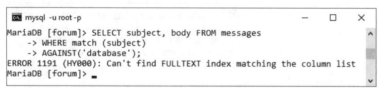

```
mysql -u root -p                                                        —  □  ×
MariaDB [forum]> SELECT subject, body FROM messages
    -> WHERE MATCH (body, subject)
    -> AGAINST ('database');
+-----------------+----------------------------------------------------------------------------+
| subject         | body                                                                       |
+-----------------+----------------------------------------------------------------------------+
| Database Design | I'm creating a new database and am having problems with the structure. How many tables should I have?... |
| Database Design | The number of tables your database includes...                             |
| Database Design | Okay, thanks!                                                              |
+-----------------+----------------------------------------------------------------------------+
3 rows in set (0.00 sec)

MariaDB [forum]> _
```

C A basic **FULLTEXT** search.

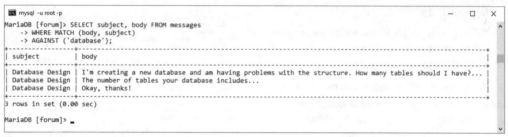

```
mysql -u root -p                               —    □    ×
MariaDB [forum]> SELECT subject, body FROM messages
    -> WHERE match (subject)
    -> AGAINST('database');
ERROR 1191 (HY000): Can't find FULLTEXT index matching the column list
MariaDB [forum]> _
```

D A **FULLTEXT** query can be run only on the same column or combination of columns that the **FULLTEXT** index was created on. With this query, even though the combination of *body* and *subject* has a **FULLTEXT** index, attempting to run the match on just *subject* will fail.

4. Run the same **FULLTEXT** search while also showing the relevance **E**:

```
SELECT subject, body,
MATCH (body, subject)
AGAINST ('database') AS R
FROM messages
WHERE
MATCH (body, subject)
AGAINST ('database')\G
```

If you use the same **MATCH...AGAINST** expression as a selected value, the actual relevance will be returned. As in the previous section of the chapter, to make the results easier to view in the mysql client, the query is terminated using **\G**, thereby returning the results as a vertical list.

5. Run a **FULLTEXT** search using multiple keywords **F**:

```
SELECT subject, body FROM messages
WHERE MATCH (body, subject)
AGAINST ('html xhtml');
```

With this query, a match will be made if the subject or body contains either word. Any record that contains both words will be ranked higher.

TIP Remember that if a FULLTEXT search returns no records, this means either that no matches were made or that over half of the records match.

TIP For sake of simplicity, all the queries in this section are simple SELECT statements. You can certainly use FULLTEXT searches within joins or more complex queries.

TIP MySQL comes with several hundred stopwords already defined. These are part of the application's source code.

TIP The minimum keyword length—four characters by default—is a configuration setting you can change in MySQL.

TIP FULLTEXT searches are case-insensitive by default.

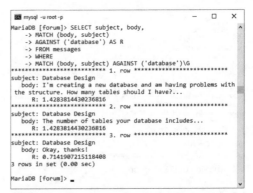

```
mysql -u root -p                                    —    □    ×

MariaDB [forum]> SELECT subject, body,
    -> MATCH (body, subject)
    -> AGAINST ('database') AS R
    -> FROM messages
    -> WHERE
    -> MATCH (body, subject) AGAINST ('database')\G
*************************** 1. row ***************************
subject: Database Design
   body: I'm creating a new database and am having problems with
the structure. How many tables should I have?...
      R: 1.4283814430236816
*************************** 2. row ***************************
subject: Database Design
   body: The number of tables your database includes...
      R: 1.4283814430236816
*************************** 3. row ***************************
subject: Database Design
   body: Okay, thanks!
      R: 0.7141907215118408
3 rows in set (0.00 sec)

MariaDB [forum]>
```

E The relevance of a **FULLTEXT** search can be selected, too. In this case, you'll see that the two records with the word "database" in both the subject and body have higher relevance than the record that contains the word in just the subject.

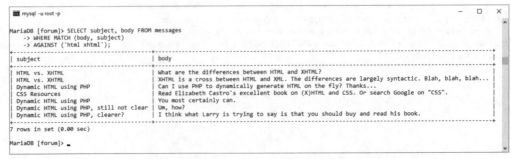

```
mysql -u root -p                                                                                          —    □    ×

MariaDB [forum]> SELECT subject, body FROM messages
    -> WHERE MATCH (body, subject)
    -> AGAINST ('html xhtml');
+---------------------------------------+----------------------------------------------------------------------------+
| subject                               | body                                                                       |
+---------------------------------------+----------------------------------------------------------------------------+
| HTML vs. XHTML                        | What are the differences between HTML and XHTML?                            |
| HTML vs. XHTML                        | XHTML is a cross between HTML and XML. The differences are largely syntactic. Blah, blah, blah... |
| Dynamic HTML using PHP                | Can I use PHP to dynamically generate HTML on the fly? Thanks...            |
| CSS Resources                         | Read Elizabeth Castro's excellent book on (X)HTML and CSS. Or search Google on "CSS". |
| Dynamic HTML using PHP                | You most certainly can.                                                    |
| Dynamic HTML using PHP, still not clear | Um, how?                                                                  |
| Dynamic HTML using PHP, clearer?      | I think what Larry is trying to say is that you should buy and read his book. |
+---------------------------------------+----------------------------------------------------------------------------+
7 rows in set (0.00 sec)

MariaDB [forum]>
```

F Using the **FULLTEXT** search, you can easily find messages that contain multiple keywords.

Performing Boolean FULLTEXT Searches

The basic **FULLTEXT** search is nice, but a more sophisticated **FULLTEXT** search can be accomplished using its Boolean mode. To do so, add the phrase **IN BOOLEAN MODE** to the **AGAINST** clause:

```
SELECT * FROM tablename WHERE
MATCH (columns)
AGAINST ('terms' IN BOOLEAN MODE)
```

Boolean mode has a number of operators (**Table 7.3**) to tweak how each keyword is treated:

```
SELECT * FROM tablename WHERE
MATCH (columns)
AGAINST ('+database -mysql'
→ IN BOOLEAN MODE)
```

In that example, a match will be made if the word *database* is found and *mysql* is not present. Alternatively, the tilde (~) is used as a milder form of the minus sign, meaning that the keyword can be present in a match, but such matches should be considered less relevant.

TABLE 7.3 Boolean Mode Operators

Operator	Meaning
+	Must be present in every match
-	Must not be present in any match
~	Lowers a ranking if present
*	Wildcard
<	Decrease a word's importance
>	Increase a word's importance
" "	Must match the exact phrase
(	Create subexpressions

The wildcard character (*) matches variations on a word, so **cata*** matches *catalog*, *catalina*, and so on. Two operators explicitly state what keywords are more (**>**) or less (**<**) important. Finally, you can use double quotation marks to hunt for exact phrases and parentheses to make subexpressions; just be certain to use single quotation marks to wrap the keywords.

The following query would look for records with the phrase *Web develop* with the word *html* being required and the word *JavaScript* detracting from a match's relevance:

```
SELECT * FROM tablename
WHERE MATCH (columns)
AGAINST('>"Web develop"
→ +html ~JavaScript'
IN BOOLEAN MODE)
```

When using Boolean mode, keep in mind these differences in how **FULLTEXT** searches work:

- If a keyword is not preceded by an operator, the word is optional but a match will be ranked higher if it is present.

- Results will be returned even if more than 50 percent of the records match the search.

- The results are *not* automatically sorted by relevance.

Because of this last fact, you'll also want to sort the returned records by their relevance, as demonstrated in the next sequence of steps. One important rule that's the same with Boolean searches is that the minimum word length (four characters by default) still applies. Trying to require a shorter word using a plus sign (**+php**) still won't work.

To perform FULLTEXT Boolean searches:

1. Connect to MySQL and select the *forum* database, if you have not already.

2. Run a simple **FULLTEXT** search that finds *HTML*, *XHTML*, or *(X)HTML* **Ⓖ**:

   ```
   SELECT subject, body FROM
   messages WHERE MATCH(body, subject)
   AGAINST ('*HTML' IN BOOLEAN MODE)\G
   ```

   The term HTML may appear in messages in many formats, including *HTML*, *XHTML*, or *(X)HTML*. This Boolean mode query will find all of those, thanks to the wildcard character (*).

   To make the results easier to view, I'm using the **\G** trick mentioned earlier in the chapter, which tells the mysql client to return the results vertically, not horizontally.

```
MariaDB [forum]> SELECT subject, body FROM
    -> messages WHERE MATCH(body, subject)
    -> AGAINST ('*HTML' IN BOOLEAN MODE)\G
*************************** 1. row ***************************
subject: HTML vs. XHTML
   body: What are the differences between HTML and XHTML?
*************************** 2. row ***************************
subject: HTML vs. XHTML
   body: XHTML is a cross between HTML and XML. The differences are largely syntactic.
Blah, blah, blah...
*************************** 3. row ***************************
subject: Dynamic HTML using PHP
   body: Can I use PHP to dynamically generate HTML on the fly? Thanks...
*************************** 4. row ***************************
subject: CSS Resources
   body: Read Elizabeth Castro's excellent book on (X)HTML and CSS. Or search Google on
"CSS".
*************************** 5. row ***************************
subject: Dynamic HTML using PHP
   body: You most certainly can.
*************************** 6. row ***************************
subject: Dynamic HTML using PHP, still not clear
   body: Um, how?
*************************** 7. row ***************************
subject: Dynamic HTML using PHP, clearer?
   body: I think what Larry is trying to say is that you should buy and read his book.
7 rows in set (0.00 sec)

MariaDB [forum]>
```

Ⓖ A simple Boolean-mode **FULLTEXT** search.

3. Find matches involving databases, with an emphasis on normal forms **H**:

```
SELECT subject, body FROM messages
WHERE MATCH (body, subject)
AGAINST ('>"normal form*"
→ +database*'
IN BOOLEAN MODE)\G
```

This query first finds all records that have *database*, *databases*, etc. and *normal form*, *normal forms*, etc. in them. The **database*** term is required

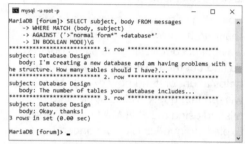

```
mysql -u root -p                              —  □  ×
MariaDB [forum]> SELECT subject, body FROM messages
    -> WHERE MATCH (body, subject)
    -> AGAINST ('>"normal form*" +database*'
    -> IN BOOLEAN MODE)\G
*********************** 1. row ***********************
subject: Database Design
   body: I'm creating a new database and am having problems with t
he structure. How many tables should I have?...
*********************** 2. row ***********************
subject: Database Design
   body: The number of tables your database includes...
*********************** 3. row ***********************
subject: Database Design
   body: Okay, thanks!
3 rows in set (0.00 sec)

MariaDB [forum]> _
```

H This search looks for variations on two different keywords, ranking the one higher than the other.

```
mysql -u root -p                              —  □  ×
MariaDB [forum]> SELECT subject, body,
    -> MATCH (body, subject)
    -> AGAINST ('*HTML >XHTML' IN BOOLEAN MODE) AS R
    -> FROM messages WHERE MATCH (body, subject)
    -> AGAINST ('*HTML >XHTML' IN BOOLEAN MODE)
    -> ORDER BY R DESC\G
*********************** 1. row ***********************
subject: HTML vs. XHTML
   body: What are the differences between HTML and XHTML?
      R: 3.5409445762634277
*********************** 2. row ***********************
subject: HTML vs. XHTML
   body: XHTML is a cross between HTML and XML. The differences ar
e largely syntactic. Blah, blah, blah...
      R: 3.5409445762634277
*********************** 3. row ***********************
subject: Dynamic HTML using PHP
   body: Can I use PHP to dynamically generate HTML on the fly? Th
anks...
      R: 0.45528939366340637
*********************** 4. row ***********************
subject: CSS Resources
   body: Read Elizabeth Castro's excellent book on (X)HTML and CSS
. Or search Google on "CSS".
      R: 0.22764469683170319
*********************** 5. row ***********************
subject: Dynamic HTML using PHP
   body: You most certainly can.
      R: 0.22764469683170319
*********************** 6. row ***********************
subject: Dynamic HTML using PHP, still not clear
   body: Um, how?
      R: 0.22764469683170319
*********************** 7. row ***********************
subject: Dynamic HTML using PHP, clearer?
```

I This modified version of an earlier query selects, and then sorts the results by, the relevance.

(as indicated by the plus sign), but emphasis is given to the normal form clause (which is preceded by the greater-than sign).

4. Repeat the query from Step 2, with a greater importance on XHTML, returning the results in order of relevance **I**:

```
SELECT subject, body,
MATCH (body, subject)
AGAINST ('*HTML >XHTML' IN
→ BOOLEAN MODE) AS R
FROM messages WHERE MATCH
→ (body, subject)
AGAINST ('*HTML >XHTML' IN
→ BOOLEAN MODE)
ORDER BY R DESC\G
```

This is like the earlier query, but now *XHTML* is specifically given extra weight. This query additionally selects the calculated relevance, and the results are returned in that order.

TIP MySQL 5.1.7 added another FULLTEXT search mode: natural language. This is the default mode, if no other mode (like Boolean) is specified.

TIP The WITH QUERY EXPANSION modifier can increase the number of returned results. Such queries perform two searches and return one result set. It bases a second search on terms found in the most relevant results of the initial search. While a WITH QUERY EXPANSION search can find results that would not otherwise have been returned, it can also return results that aren't at all relevant to the original search terms.

Optimizing Queries

Once you have a complete and populated database, and have a sense as to what queries will commonly be run on it, it's a good idea to take some steps to optimize your queries and your database. Doing so will ensure you're getting the best possible performance out of MySQL (and therefore, your site).

To start, the sidebar reemphasizes key design ideas that have already been suggested in this book. Along with these tips are two simple techniques for optimizing existing tables. One way to improve MySQL's performance is to run an **OPTIMIZE** command on occasion. This query will rid a table of any unnecessary overhead, thereby improving the speed of any interactions with it:

`OPTIMIZE TABLE tablename`

Running this command is particularly beneficial after changing a table via an **ALTER** command, or after a table has had lots of **DELETE** queries run on it, leaving virtual gaps among the records.

Second, you can occasionally use the **ANALYZE** command:

`ANALYZE TABLE tablename`

Executing this command updates the indexes on the table, thereby improving their usage in queries. You could execute it whenever massive amounts of data stored in the table changes (e.g., via **UPDATE** or **INSERT** commands).

Speaking of queries, as you're probably realizing by now, there are often many ways of accomplishing the same goal. To find out the most efficient approach, it helps to understand how exactly MySQL will run that query. This can be accomplished using the **EXPLAIN** SQL keyword. Explaining queries is an advanced topic, but I'll introduce the fundamentals here, and you can always see the MySQL manual or search online for more information.

Database Optimization

The performance of your database is primarily dependent on its structure and indexes. When creating databases, try to

- Choose the best storage engine
- Use the smallest data type possible for each column
- Define columns as **NOT NULL** whenever possible
- Use integers as primary keys
- Judiciously define indexes, selecting the correct type and applying them to the right column or columns
- Limit indexes to a certain number of characters, if possible
- Avoid creating too many indexes
- Make sure that columns to be used as the basis of joins are of the same type and, in the case of strings, use the same character set and collation

To explain a query:

1. Find a query that may be resource-intensive.

   Good candidates are queries that do any of the following:

   ▸ Join two or more tables

   ▸ Use groupings and aggregate functions

   ▸ Have **WHERE** clauses

   For example, this query from earlier in the chapter meets two of these criteria:

   ```
   SELECT SUM(balance) AS Total,
   COUNT(account_id) AS Number,
   CONCAT(c.last_name, ', ',
   → c.first_name) AS Name
   FROM accounts AS a
   INNER JOIN customers AS c USING
   → (customer_id)
   GROUP BY (a.customer_id)
   ORDER BY Name;
   ```

2. Connect to MySQL and select the applicable database, if you have not already.

3. Execute the query on the database, prefacing it with **EXPLAIN** Ⓐ:

   ```
   EXPLAIN SELECT SUM(balance)
   → AS Total,
   COUNT(account_id) AS Number,
   CONCAT(c.last_name, ', ',
   → c.first_name) AS Name
   FROM accounts AS a
   INNER JOIN customers AS c USING
   → (customer_id)
   GROUP BY (a.customer_id)
   ORDER BY Name;
   ```

   If you're using the mysql client, you'll find it also helps to use the concluding **\G** trick (instead of the semicolon) to make the output more legible. The output itself will be one row of information for every table used in the query. The tables are listed in the same order that MySQL must access them to execute the query.

   I'll walk through the key parts of the output, but to begin, the *select_type* value should be *SIMPLE* for most **SELECT** queries, and would be different if the query involves a **UNION** or subquery (see the MySQL manual for more on either **UNION**s or subqueries).

continues on next page

```
mysql -u root -p                                                                          —    □    ×
MariaDB [banking]> EXPLAIN SELECT SUM(balance) AS Total,
    -> COUNT(account_id) AS Number,
    -> CONCAT(c.last_name, ', ', c.first_name) AS Name
    -> FROM accounts AS a
    -> INNER JOIN customers AS c USING (customer_id)
    -> GROUP BY (a.customer_id)
    -> ORDER BY Name;
+----+-------------+-------+-------+---------------+-------------+---------+------+------+----------------------------------------------------+
| id | select_type | table | type  | possible_keys | key         | key_len | ref  | rows | Extra                                              |
+----+-------------+-------+-------+---------------+-------------+---------+------+------+----------------------------------------------------+
|  1 | SIMPLE      | c     | index | PRIMARY       | full_name   | 184     | NULL |    3 | Using index; Using temporary; Using filesort       |
|  1 | SIMPLE      | a     | ALL   | customer_id   | NULL        | NULL    | NULL |    4 | Using where; Using join buffer (flat, BNL join)    |
+----+-------------+-------+-------+---------------+-------------+---------+------+------+----------------------------------------------------+
2 rows in set (0.03 sec)

MariaDB [banking]>
```

Ⓐ This **EXPLAIN** output reveals how MySQL will go about processing the query.

4. Check out the *type* value.

Table 7.4 lists the different type values, from best to worst. The MySQL manual discusses what each means in detail, but understand first that *eq_ref* is the best you'll commonly see and *ALL* is the worst. A type of *eq_ref* means that an index is being properly used and an equality comparison is being made.

Note that you'll sometimes see *ALL* because the table has very few records in it, in which case it's more efficient for MySQL to scan the table rather than use an index. This is presumably the case with **Ⓐ**, since the *accounts* table only has four records.

5. Check out the *possible_keys* value.

The *possible_keys* value indicates which indexes exist that MySQL might be able to use to find the corresponding rows in this table. If you have a **NULL** value here, there are no indexes that MySQL thinks would be useful. Therefore, you might benefit from creating an index on that table's applicable columns.

6. Check out the *key*, *key_len*, and *ref* values.

Whereas *possible_keys* indicates what indexes might be usable, *key* says what index MySQL will actually use for that query. Occasionally, you'll find a value here that's not listed in *possible_keys*, which is OK. If no key is being used, that almost always indicates a problem that can be remedied by adding an index or modifying the query.

The *key_len* value indicates the length (i.e., the size) of the key that MySQL used. Generally, shorter is better here, but don't worry about it too much.

The *ref* column indicates which columns MySQL compared to the index named in the key column.

TABLE 7.4 Join Types

Type
system
const
eq_ref
ref
fulltext
ref_or_null
index_merge
unique_subquery
index_subquery
range
index
ALL

7. Check out the *rows* value.

This column provides an estimate of how many rows in the table MySQL thinks it will need to examine. Once again, lower is better. In fact, on a join, a rough estimate of the efficiency can be determined by multiplying all the rows values together.

Often in a join, the number of rows to be examined should go from more to less, as in **B**.

8. Check out the *Extra* value.

Finally, this column reports any additional information about how MySQL will execute the query that may be useful. Two phrases you don't want to find here are *Using filesort* and *Using temporary*. Both mean that extra steps are required to complete the query

(e.g., a **GROUP BY** clause often requires that MySQL create a temporary table).

If *Extra* says anything along the lines of *Impossible X* or *No matching Y*, that means your query has clauses that are always false and can be removed.

9. Modify your table or queries and repeat!

If the output suggests problems with how the query is being executed, you can consider doing any of the following:

- Changing the particulars of the query
- Changing the properties of a table's columns
- Adding or modifying a table's indexes

Remember that the validity of the explanation will depend, in part, on how many rows are in the involved tables (as explained in Step 4, MySQL may skip indexes for small tables). Also understand that not all queries are fixable. Simple **SELECT** queries and even joins can sometimes be improved, but there's little we can do to improve the efficiency of a **GROUP BY** query, considering everything MySQL must do to aggregate data.

```
mysql -u root -p                              -  □  ×
MariaDB [forum]> EXPLAIN SELECT u.username, m.subject, f.name
    -> FROM users AS u
    -> LEFT JOIN messages AS m
    -> USING (user_id)
    -> LEFT JOIN forums AS f
    -> USING (forum_id)\G
*************************** 1. row ***************************
           id: 1
  select_type: SIMPLE
        table: u
         type: index
possible_keys: NULL
          key: username
      key_len: 92
          ref: NULL
         rows: 5
        Extra: Using index
*************************** 2. row ***************************
           id: 1
  select_type: SIMPLE
        table: m
         type: ref
possible_keys: user_id
          key: user_id
      key_len: 3
          ref: forum.u.user_id
         rows: 2
        Extra:
*************************** 3. row ***************************
           id: 1
  select_type: SIMPLE
        table: f
         type: eq_ref
possible_keys: PRIMARY
          key: PRIMARY
      key_len: 1
          ref: forum.m.forum_id
         rows: 1
        Extra: Using where
3 rows in set (0.00 sec)

MariaDB [forum]>
```

B Another explanation of a query, this one a join across three tables.

> **TIP** The EXPLAIN EXTENDED command provides a few more details about a query:
>
> EXPLAIN EXTENDED SELECT...

> **TIP** Problematic queries can also be found by enabling certain MySQL logging features, but that requires administrative control over the MySQL server.

> **TIP** In terms of performance, MySQL deals with more, smaller tables better than it does fewer, larger tables. That being said, a normalized database structure should always be the primary goal.

> **TIP** In MySQL terms, a "big" database has thousands of tables and millions of rows.

Performing Transactions

A *database transaction* is a sequence of queries run during a single session. For example, you might insert a record into one table, insert another record into another table, and maybe run an update. Without using transactions, each individual query takes effect immediately and cannot be undone (the queries, by default, are automatically committed). With transactions, you can set start and stop points and then enact or retract all the queries between those points as needed: if one query failed, all the queries can be undone.

Commercial interactions commonly require transactions, even something as basic as transferring $100 from my bank account to yours. What seems like a simple process requires several steps:

- Confirm that I have $100 in my account.
- Decrease my account by $100.
- Verify the decrease.
- Increase the amount of money in your account by $100.
- Verify that the increase worked.

If any of the steps failed, all of them should be undone. For example, if the money couldn't be deposited in your account, it should be returned to mine until the entire transaction can go through.

The ability to execute transactions depends on the features of the storage engine in use. To perform transactions with MySQL, you must use the InnoDB table type (or storage engine).

To begin a new transaction in the mysql client, type

START TRANSACTION;

Once your transaction has begun, you can now run your queries. Once you have finished, you can either enter COMMIT to enact all the queries or ROLLBACK to undo the effect of all the queries.

After you have either committed or rolled back the queries, the transaction is considered complete, and MySQL returns to an *autocommit* mode. This means that any queries you execute take immediate effect. To start another transaction, just type

START TRANSACTION.

It is important to know that certain types of queries cannot be rolled back. Specifically, those that create, alter, truncate (empty), or delete tables or that create or delete databases cannot be undone. Furthermore, using such a query has the effect of committing and ending the current transaction.

Second, understand that transactions are particular to each connection. One user connected through the mysql client has a different transaction than another mysql client user, both of which are different from a connected PHP script.

Finally, you cannot perform transactions using phpMyAdmin. Each submission of a query through phpMyAdmin's SQL window or tab is an individual and complete transaction, which cannot be undone with subsequent submissions.

With this in mind, let's use transactions with the banking database to perform the already mentioned task.

To perform transactions:

1. Connect to MySQL and select the *banking* database.

2. Begin a transaction and show the table's current values 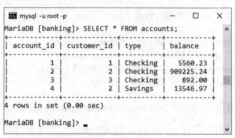:

   ```
   START TRANSACTION;
   SELECT * FROM accounts;
   ```

3. Subtract $100 from David Sedaris's (or any user's) checking account.

   ```
   UPDATE accounts
   SET balance = (balance-100)
   WHERE account_id=2;
   ```

   Using an **UPDATE** query, a little math, and a **WHERE** conditional, you can subtract 100 from a balance. Although MySQL will indicate that one row was affected, the effect is not permanent until the transaction is committed.

4. Add $100 to Sarah Vowell's checking account:

   ```
   UPDATE accounts
   SET balance = (balance+100)
   WHERE account_id=1;
   ```

   This is the opposite of Step 3, as if $100 were being transferred from the one person to the other.

5. Confirm the results 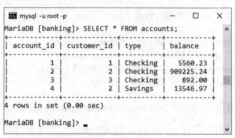:

   ```
   SELECT * FROM accounts;
   ```

   As you can see in the figure, the one balance is 100 more and the other is 100 less than they originally were 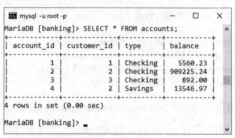.

6. Roll back the transaction:

   ```
   ROLLBACK;
   ```

   To demonstrate how transactions can be undone, let's undo the effects of these queries. The **ROLLBACK** command returns the database to how it was prior to starting the transaction. The command also terminates the transaction, returning MySQL to its autocommit mode.

   continues on next page

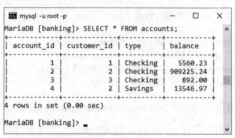

A A transaction is begun and the existing table records are shown.

B Two **UPDATE** queries are executed and the results are viewed.

7. Confirm the results **C**:

```
SELECT * FROM accounts;
```

The query should reveal the contents of the table as they originally were.

8. Repeat Steps 2 through 4.

To see what happens when the transaction is committed, the two **UPDATE** queries will be run again. Be certain to start the transaction first, though, or the queries will automatically take effect!

9. Commit the transaction and confirm the results **D**:

```
COMMIT;
SELECT * FROM accounts;
```

Once you enter **COMMIT**, the entire transaction is permanent, meaning that any changes are now in place. **COMMIT** also ends the transaction, returning MySQL to autocommit mode.

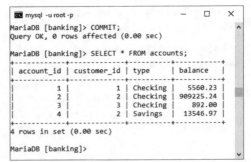

C Because the **ROLLBACK** command was used, the potential effects of the **UPDATE** queries were ignored.

D Invoking the **COMMIT** command makes the transaction's effects permanent.

TIP One of the great features of transactions is that they offer protection should a random event occur, such as a server crash. Either a transaction is executed in its entirety or all the changes are ignored.

TIP To alter MySQL's autocommit nature, type

```
SET AUTOCOMMIT=0;
```

Then you do not need to type START TRANSACTION and no queries will be permanent until you type COMMIT (or use an ALTER, CREATE, etc., query).

TIP You can create *savepoints* in transactions:

```
SAVEPOINT savepoint_name;
```

Then you can roll back to that point:

```
ROLLBACK TO SAVEPOINT savepoint_name;
```

Database Encryption

Up to this point, pseudo-encryption has been accomplished in the database using the **SHA2()** function. In the *sitename* and *forum* databases, the user's password has been stored after running it through **SHA2()**. Although using the function in this way is perfectly fine (and quite common), the function doesn't provide *real* encryption; the **SHA2()** function returns a *representation* of a value, called a *hash*, not an encrypted version of the value. By storing the hashed version of some data, comparisons can still be made later (such as upon login), but the original data cannot be retrieved from the database. If you need to store data in a protected way while still being able to view the data in its original form at some later point, other MySQL functions are necessary.

MySQL has several encryption and decryption functions built into the software. If you require data to be stored in an encrypted form that can be decrypted, you'll want to use **AES_ENCRYPT()** and **AES_DECRYPT()**. The **AES_ENCRYPT()** function is the most secure encryption option.

These functions take two arguments: the data being encrypted or decrypted and a *salt* argument. The salt argument is a string that helps to randomize the encryption. Let's look at the encryption and decryption functions first, and then I'll return to the salt.

To add a record to a table while encrypting the data, the query might look like

```
INSERT INTO users (username, pass)
VALUES ('troutster', AES_ENCRYPT
('mypass', 'nacl19874salt!'))
```

The encrypted data returned by the **AES_ENCRYPT()** function will be in binary format. To store that data in a table, the column must be defined as one of the binary types (e.g., **VARBINARY** or **BLOB**).

To run a login query for the record just inserted (matching a submitted username and password against those in the database), you would write

```
SELECT * FROM users WHERE
username = 'troutster' AND
AES_ENCRYPT('mypass',
 →'nacl19874salt!') = pass
```

Returning to the issue of the *salt*, the exact same salt must be used for both encryption and decryption, which means that the salt must be stored somewhere as well. Contrary to what you might think, it's safe to store the salt in the database, even in the same row as the salted data. This is because the purpose of the salt is to make the encryption process harder to crack (specifically, by a "rainbow" attack). Such attacks are done remotely, using brute force. Conversely, if someone can see everything stored in your database, you have bigger problems to worry about (i.e., all your data has been breached).

Finally, to get the maximum benefit from "salting" the stored data, each piece of stored data should use a salt that's unique, long, and binary.

The MySQL manual recommends running the salt through the **SHA2()** function to increase its length. Use the **UNHEX()** function to convert it to binary:

```
INSERT INTO users (username, pass)
VALUES ('troutster', AES_ENCRYPT
('mypass', UNHEX(SHA2('nacl19874salt!',
 →512))))
```

To put all this together, let's add PIN and salt columns to the *banking.customers* table, and then store an encrypted version of each customer's PIN.

To encrypt and decrypt data:

1. Access MySQL and select the *banking* database:

2. Add the two new columns to the *customers* table 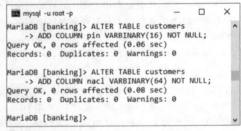:

   ```
   ALTER TABLE customers
   ADD COLUMN pin VARBINARY(16)
   → NOT NULL;
   ALTER TABLE customers
   ADD COLUMN nacl VARBINARY(64)
   → NOT NULL;
   ```

   The first column, *pin*, will store an encrypted version of the user's PIN. For a PIN of four digits, **AES_ENCRYPT()** returns a binary value 16 characters long, so the *pin* column is defined as **VARBINARY(16)**. The second column stores the salt, which will be run through **SHA2()** and **UNHEX()**, resulting in another binary type, this time with a length of 64.

3. Update the first customer's PIN **B**:

   ```
   UPDATE customers SET nacl =
   → UNHEX(SHA2(RAND(), 512))
   → WHERE customer_id=1;
   UPDATE customers SET
   → pin=AES_ENCRYPT(1234, nacl)
   → WHERE customer_id=1;
   ```

The first query updates the customer's record, adding a salt value to the *nacl* column. That random value is obtained by applying the **SHA2()** function to the output from the **RAND()** function. This will create a string 128 characters long, such as *ee26b0dd4af7e749aa1a8ee 3c10ae9923f618980772e473f8819a 5d4940e0db27ac185f8a0e1d5f84f 88bc887fd67b143732c304cc5fa9ad 8e6f57f50028a8ff*. This is then converted to binary using **UNHEX()**.

The second query stores the customer's PIN—1234, using the already-stored *nacl* value as the salt.

```
mysql -u root -p                          —   □   ×

MariaDB [banking]> ALTER TABLE customers
    -> ADD COLUMN pin VARBINARY(16) NOT NULL;
Query OK, 0 rows affected (0.06 sec)
Records: 0  Duplicates: 0  Warnings: 0

MariaDB [banking]> ALTER TABLE customers
    -> ADD COLUMN nacl VARBINARY(64) NOT NULL;
Query OK, 0 rows affected (0.08 sec)
Records: 0  Duplicates: 0  Warnings: 0

MariaDB [banking]>
```

A Two columns are added to the *customers* table.

```
mysql -u root -p                                                                      —   □   ×

MariaDB [banking]> UPDATE customers SET nacl = UNHEX(SHA2(RAND(), 512)) WHERE customer_id=1;
Query OK, 1 row affected (0.00 sec)
Rows matched: 1  Changed: 1  Warnings: 0

MariaDB [banking]> UPDATE customers SET pin=AES_ENCRYPT(1234, nacl) WHERE customer_id=1;
Query OK, 1 row affected (0.00 sec)
Rows matched: 1  Changed: 1  Warnings: 0

MariaDB [banking]> _
```

B A record is updated, using an encryption function to protect the PIN.

4. Retrieve the PIN in an unencrypted form 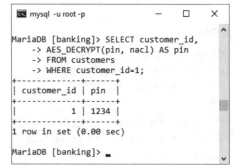:

```sql
SELECT customer_id,
AES_DECRYPT(pin, nacl) AS pin
FROM customers
WHERE customer_id=1;
```

This query returns the decrypted PIN for the customer with a *customer_id* of 1. Any value stored using **AES_ENCRYPT()** can be retrieved (and matched) using **AES_DECRYPT()** if the same salt is used.

```
mysql -u root -p                          —   □   ×

MariaDB [banking]> SELECT customer_id,
    -> AES_DECRYPT(pin, nacl) AS pin
    -> FROM customers
    -> WHERE customer_id=1;
+-------------+------+
| customer_id | pin  |
+-------------+------+
|           1 | 1234 |
+-------------+------+
1 row in set (0.00 sec)

MariaDB [banking]> _
```

C The record has been retrieved, decrypting the PIN in the process.

```
mysql -u root -p                                          —   □   ×

MariaDB [banking]> SELECT * FROM customers
    -> WHERE customer_id=1\G
*************************** 1. row ***************************
customer_id: 1
 first_name: Sarah
  last_name: Vowell
        pin: ■Shä▥ƒ[å¥yΩp√▥╦
       nacl: óMó"üε▥°
c≤0╦E-▥; *î■ä⌠ñn≥      t╓⌐ℝ|)ì╢LV`"╦°▥4>T▥Öí<Ä[!▥·≈ᴸ≤ì╦Wú╢▥
1 row in set (0.00 sec)

MariaDB [banking]> _
```

5. Check out the customer's record without using decryption **D**:

```sql
SELECT * FROM customers
WHERE customer_id=1\G
```

As you can see in the figure, the encrypted version of the PIN and the binary version of the salt are unreadable.

TIP As a rule of thumb, use SHA2() for information that will never need to be viewable, such as passwords and perhaps usernames. Use AES_ENCRYPT() for information that needs to be protected but may need to be viewable at a later date, such as credit card information, Social Security numbers, addresses (perhaps), and so forth.

TIP As a reminder, never storing credit card numbers and other high-risk data is always the safest option.

TIP The same salting technique can be applied to SHA2() and other functions.

TIP Be aware that data sent to the MySQL server, or received from it, could be intercepted and viewed. Better security can be had by using an SSL connection to the MySQL database.

D Encrypted data is stored in an unreadable format (here, as a binary string of data).

Review and Pursue

If you have any problems with the review questions or the pursue prompts, turn to the book's supporting forum (LarryUllman.com/forums/).

Review

- What are the two primary types of joins?

- Why are aliases often used with joins?

- Why is it considered often necessary and at least a best practice to use the *table.column* syntax in joins?

- What impact does the order of tables used have on an outer join?

- How do you create a self-join?

- What are the aggregate functions?

- What impact does the **DISTINCT** keyword have on an aggregate function? What impact does **GROUP BY** have on an aggregate function?

- What kind of index is required to perform **FULLTEXT** searches? What type of storage engine?

- What impact does it have when you conclude a **SELECT** query with \G instead of a semicolon in the mysql client?

- How do **IN BOOLEAN MODE FULLTEXT** searches differ from standard **FULLTEXT** searches?

- What commands can you use to improve a table's performance?

- How do you examine the efficiency of a query?

- Why doesn't the *forum* database support transactions?

- How do you begin a transaction? How do you undo the effects of a transaction in progress? How do you make the effects of the current transaction permanent?

- What kind of column type is required to store the output from the **AES_ENCRYPT()** function?

- What are the important criteria for the salt used in the encryption process?

Pursue

- Come up with more join examples for the *forum* and *banking* databases. Perform inner joins, outer joins, and joins across all three tables.

- Check out the MySQL manual pages if you're curious about the **UNION** SQL command or about subqueries.

- Perform some more grouping exercises on the *banking* or *forum* databases.

- Practice running **FULLTEXT** searches on the *forum* database.

- Examine other queries to see the results.

- Read the MySQL manual pages, and other online tutorials, on explaining queries and optimizing tables.

- Play with transactions some more.

- Research the subjects of salting passwords and rainbow attacks to learn more.

Error Handling and Debugging

If you're working through this book sequentially (which would be for the best), the next subject to learn is how to use PHP and MySQL together. However, that process will undoubtedly generate errors, errors that can be tricky to debug. So before moving on to new concepts, these next few pages address the bane of the programmer: *errors*. As you gain experience, you'll make fewer errors and learn your own debugging methods, but there are plenty of tools and techniques the beginner can use to help ease the learning process.

This chapter has three main threads. One focus is on learning about the various kinds of errors that can occur when developing dynamic websites and what their likely causes are. Second, several debugging techniques are taught, in a step-by-step format. Finally, you'll see different techniques for handling the errors that do occur in the most graceful manner possible.

Error Types and Basic Debugging

When developing web applications with PHP and MySQL, you end up with potential bugs in one of four or more technologies. You could have HTML issues, PHP problems, SQL errors, or MySQL mistakes. The first step in fixing any bug is identifying its source.

HTML problems are often the least disruptive and the easiest to catch. You normally know there's a problem when your layout is all messed up. Some steps for catching and fixing these, as well as general debugging hints, are discussed in the next section.

PHP errors are the ones you'll see most often, since this language will be at the heart of your applications. PHP errors fall into three general areas:

- Syntactical
- Run-time
- Logical

Syntactical, or *parse*, errors are the most common and the easiest to fix. You'll see them if you merely omit a semicolon. Such errors stop the script from executing, and if *display_errors* is on in your PHP configuration, PHP will show an error, including the line PHP thinks it's on . If *display_errors* is off, you'll see a blank page. You'll learn more about *display_errors* later in this chapter.

Run-time errors include those things that don't stop a PHP script from executing (like parse errors do) but do stop the script from doing everything it was supposed to do. Examples include calling a function using the wrong number or types of parameters. With these errors, PHP will normally display a message indicating the exact problem 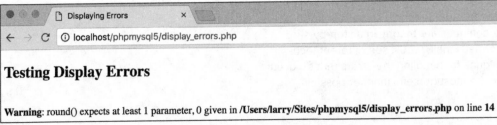 (again, assuming that *display_errors* is on).

The final category of error—logical—is actually the worst, because PHP won't necessarily report it to you. These are out-and-out bugs—problems that aren't obvious and don't stop the execution of a script. Tricks for solving these PHP errors will be demonstrated in just a few pages.

Parse error: parse error in /Users/larry/Sites/phpmysql5/display_errors.php on line 20

A Parse errors—which you've probably seen many times over by now—are the most common sort of PHP error, particularly for beginning programmers.

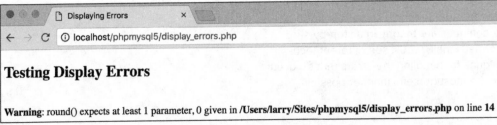

Testing Display Errors

Warning: round() expects at least 1 parameter, 0 given in **/Users/larry/Sites/phpmysql5/display_errors.php** on line **14**

B Misusing a function (calling it with improper parameters) will create errors during the execution of the script.

SQL errors are normally a matter of syntax, and they'll be reported when you try to run the query in MySQL. For example, I've done this too many times **C**:

DELETE * FROM *tablename*

The syntax is just wrong, a confusion with the **SELECT** syntax (**SELECT * FROM** *tablename*). The correct syntax is

DELETE FROM *tablename*

The Right Mentality

Before getting much further, a word regarding errors: they happen to the best of us. Even the author of this book sees more than enough errors in his development duties (but rest assured that the code in this book should be bug-free). Thinking that you'll get to a skill level where errors never occur is a fool's dream, but there are techniques for minimizing errors, and knowing how to quickly catch, handle, and fix errors is a major skill in its own right. So try not to become frustrated as you make errors; instead, bask in the knowledge that you're becoming a better debugger!

Again, MySQL will raise a red flag when you have SQL errors, so these aren't that difficult to find and fix. With modern web sites, the catch is that you don't always have static queries but often ones dynamically generated by PHP. In such cases, if there's an SQL syntax problem, the issue is probably in your PHP code.

Besides reporting on SQL errors, MySQL has its own errors to consider. An inability to access the database is a common one and a showstopper at that **D**. You'll also see errors when you misuse a MySQL function or ambiguously refer to a column in a join. Again, MySQL will report any such error in specific detail. Keep in mind that when a query doesn't return the records or otherwise have the result you expect, that's not a MySQL or SQL error, but rather a logical one. Toward the end of this chapter you'll see how to solve SQL and MySQL problems.

But as you should walk before you can run, the next section covers the fundamentals of debugging dynamic web sites, starting with the basic checks you should make and how to fix HTML problems.

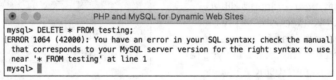

```
mysql> DELETE * FROM testing;
ERROR 1064 (42000): You have an error in your SQL syntax; check the manual
that corresponds to your MySQL server version for the right syntax to use
near '* FROM testing' at line 1
mysql>
```

C MySQL will report any errors found in the syntax of an SQL command.

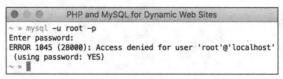

```
~ » mysql -u root -p
Enter password:
ERROR 1045 (28000): Access denied for user 'root'@'localhost'
(using password: YES)
~ »
```

D An inability to connect to a MySQL server or a specific database is a common MySQL error.

Basic debugging steps

This first sequence of steps may seem obvious, but when it comes to debugging, missing one of these steps leads to an unproductive and extremely frustrating debugging experience. And while I'm at it, I should mention that the best piece of general debugging advice is this:

When you get frustrated, step away from the computer!

I have solved almost all of the most perplexing issues I've come across by taking a break, clearing my head, and coming back to the code with fresh eyes. Readers in the book's supporting forum (**LarryUllman.com/forums/**) have frequently found this to be true as well. Trying to forge ahead when you're frustrated tends to make things worse. Much worse.

To begin debugging any problem:

- Make sure that you are running the right page.

  It's altogether too common that you try to fix a problem and no matter what you do, it never goes away. The reason is you've actually been editing a different page than you thought. Verify that the name and location of the file being executed matches that of the file you're editing. In this regard, using an all-in-one IDE, such as Adobe Dreamweaver (**www.adobe.com/go/dreamweaver**), is an advantage.

- Make sure that you have saved your latest changes.

  An unsaved document will continue to have the same problems it had before you edited it (because the edits haven't been enacted). One of the many reasons I like the TextMate (**www.macromates.com**) text editor is that it automatically saves every document when the application loses focus.

- Make sure that you run all PHP pages through the URL.

  Because PHP works through a web server (Apache, IIS, etc.), running any PHP code requires that you access the page through a URL (**http://www.example.com/page.php** or **http://localhost/page.php**). If you double-click a PHP page to open it in a browser (or use the browser's File > Open option), you'll see the PHP code, not the executed result. This also occurs if you load an HTML page without going through a URL (which will work on its own) but then submit the form to a PHP page **E**.

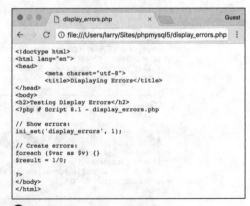

E PHP code will be executed only if run through a URL. This means that forms that submit to a PHP page must also be loaded through **http://**.

- Know what versions of PHP and MySQL you are running.

  Some problems are specific to a certain version of PHP or MySQL. For example, some functions are added in later versions of PHP, and MySQL added significant new features in version 5. Run a **phpinfo()** script 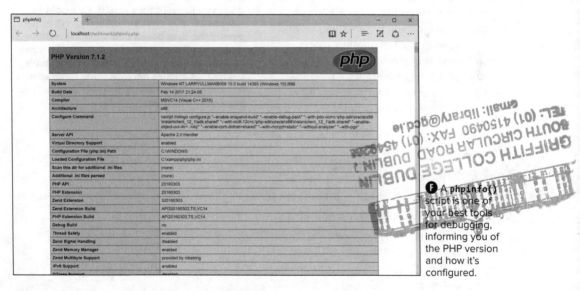 (see Appendix A, "Installation," for a script example) and open a mysql client session 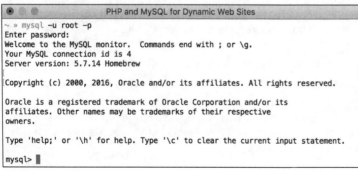 to determine this information. phpMyAdmin will often report on the versions involved as well (but don't confuse the version of phpMyAdmin with the versions of PHP or MySQL).

- Know what web server you are running.

  Similarly, some problems and features are unique to your web serving application—Apache, IIS, or Nginx. You should know which one you are using, and which version, from when you installed the application. If you're using a web host, the hosting company can provide you with this information.

  continues on next page

PHP Version 7.1.2

System	Windows NT LARRYULLMANB006 10.0 build 14393 (Windows 10) i586
Build Date	Feb 14 2017 21:24:05
Compiler	MSVC14 (Visual C++ 2015)
Architecture	x86
Configure Command	cscript /nologo configure.js "--enable-snapshot-build" "--enable-debug-pack" "--with-pdo-oci=c:\php-sdk\oracle\x86\instantclient_12_1\sdk,shared" "--with-oci8-12c=c:\php-sdk\oracle\x86\instantclient_12_1\sdk,shared" "--enable-object-out-dir=../obj/" "--enable-com-dotnet=shared" "--with-mcrypt=static" "--without-analyzer" "--with-pgo"
Server API	Apache 2.0 Handler
Virtual Directory Support	enabled
Configuration File (php.ini) Path	C:\WINDOWS
Loaded Configuration File	C:\xampp\php\php.ini
Scan this dir for additional .ini files	(none)
Additional .ini files parsed	(none)
PHP API	20160303
PHP Extension	20160303
Zend Extension	320160303
Zend Extension Build	API320160303,TS,VC14
PHP Extension Build	API20160303,TS,VC14
Debug Build	no
Thread Safety	enabled
Zend Signal Handling	disabled
Zend Memory Manager	enabled
Zend Multibyte Support	provided by mbstring
IPv6 Support	enabled

F A phpinfo() script is one of your best tools for debugging, informing you of the PHP version and how it's configured.

```
PHP and MySQL for Dynamic Web Sites
~ » mysql -u root -p
Enter password:
Welcome to the MySQL monitor.  Commands end with ; or \g.
Your MySQL connection id is 4
Server version: 5.7.14 Homebrew

Copyright (c) 2000, 2016, Oracle and/or its affiliates. All rights reserved.

Oracle is a registered trademark of Oracle Corporation and/or its
affiliates. Other names may be trademarks of their respective
owners.

Type 'help;' or '\h' for help. Type '\c' to clear the current input statement.

mysql>
```

G When you connect to a MySQL server, it will let you know the version number in use.

- Try executing pages in a different browser.

  Every developer should have and use at least two browsers. If you test your pages in different ones, you'll be able to see if the problem has to do with your script or a particular browser. Normally, only HTML and CSS problems can arise (or disappear) when you switch browsers; rarely will PHP, let alone MySQL or SQL, errors be browser specific.

- If possible, try executing the page using a different web server, version of PHP, and/or version of MySQL.

  PHP and MySQL errors sometimes stem from particular configurations and versions on one server. If something works on one server but not another, then you'll know that the script isn't inherently at fault. From there it's a matter of using **phpinfo()** scripts to see what server settings may be different.

TIP If taking a break is one thing you should do when you become frustrated, here's what you shouldn't do: send off one or multiple panicky and persnickety emails to a writer, to a newsgroup or mailing list, or to anyone else. When it comes to asking for free help from strangers, patience and pleasantries garner much better and faster results.

TIP For that matter, I strongly advise against randomly guessing at solutions. I've seen far too many people only complicate matters further by taking stabs at solutions without a full understanding of what the attempted changes should or should not do.

TIP There's another different realm of errors that you could classify as usage errors: what goes wrong when the site's users don't do what you thought they would. As a golden rule, write your code so that it doesn't break even if the user doesn't do anything right or does everything wrong! In other words, make no assumptions. There's a quote from Doug Linder that applies here: "A good programmer is someone who looks both ways before crossing a one-way street."

Book Errors

If you've followed an example in this book and something's not working right, what should you do?

1. Double-check your code or steps against those in the book.

2. Use the index at the back of the book to see if I reference a script or function in an earlier page (you may have missed an important usage rule or tip).

3. View the PHP manual for a specific function to see if it's available in your version of PHP and to verify how the function is used.

4. Check out the book's errata page (through the supporting website, **LarryUllman.com**) to see if an error in the code does exist and has been reported. Don't post your particular problem there yet, though!

5. Triple-check your code and use all the debugging techniques outlined in this chapter.

6. Search the book's supporting forum to see if others have had this problem and if a solution has already been determined.

7. If all else fails, use the book's supporting forum to ask for assistance. When you do, make sure you include all the pertinent information (version of PHP, version of MySQL, the debugging steps you took and what the results were, etc.).

Debugging HTML

Debugging HTML is relatively easy. The source code is very accessible, most problems are overt, and attempts at fixing the HTML don't normally make things worse (as can happen with PHP). Still, you should follow some basic steps to find and fix an HTML problem.

To debug an HTML error:

- Check the source code.

  If you have an HTML problem, you'll almost always need to check the source code of the page to find it. How you view the source code depends on the browser being used, but normally it's a matter of finding "developer tools" or "view source."

- Use a validation tool 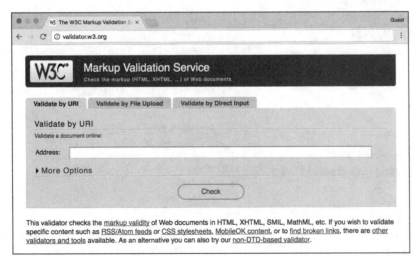.

  Validation tools, like the one at **http://validator.w3.org**, are great for finding mismatched tags, broken tables, and other problems.

- Use a great debugging browser.

  The debugging tools built into browsers have come a long way over the years, and most of them have comparable tools. Find a browser that you like best, that has great debugging tools (look online for tutorials, if you want), and master what it offers.

- Test the page in another browser.

  PHP code is generally browser-independent, meaning you'll get consistent results regardless of the client. Not so with HTML. Sometimes a particular browser has a quirk that affects the rendered page. Running the same page in another browser is the easiest way to know if it's an HTML problem or a browser quirk.

TIP The first step toward fixing any kind of problem is understanding what's causing it. Remember the role each technology—HTML, PHP, SQL, and MySQL—plays as you debug. If your page doesn't look right, that's an HTML problem. If your HTML is dynamically generated by PHP, it's still an HTML problem, but you'll need to work with the PHP code to make it right.

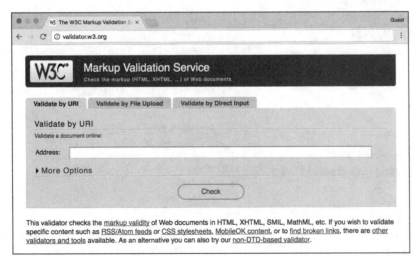

H Validation tools like the one provided by the W3C (World Wide Web Consortium) are good for finding problems and making sure your HTML conforms to standards.

Displaying PHP Errors

PHP provides remarkably useful and descriptive error messages when things go awry. Unfortunately, PHP doesn't show these errors when running using its default configuration. This policy makes sense for live servers, where you don't want the end users seeing PHP-specific error messages, but it also makes everything that much more confusing for the beginning PHP developer. To be able to see PHP's errors, you must turn on the *display_errors* directive, either in an individual script or for the PHP configuration as a whole.

To turn on *display_errors* in a script, use the `ini_set()` function. As its arguments, this function takes a directive name and what setting that directive should have:

```
ini_set('display_errors', 1);
```

Including this line in a script will turn on *display_errors* for that script. The only downside is that if your script has a syntax error that prevents it from running at all, then you'll still see a blank page. To have PHP display errors for the entire server, you'll need to edit its configuration, as discussed in the "Configuring PHP" section of Appendix A.

To turn on display_errors:

1. Create a new PHP document in your text editor or IDE, to be named **display_errors.php** (Script 8.1):

```
<!doctype html>
<html lang="en">
<head>
  <meta charset="utf-8">
  <title>Displaying Errors</title>
</head>
<body>
<h2>Testing Display Errors</h2>
<?php # Script 8.1 -
→ display_errors.php
```

2. After the initial PHP tags, add

```
ini_set('display_errors', 1);
```

From this point in this script forward, any errors that occur will be displayed.

3. Create some errors:

```
foreach ($var as $v) { }
$result = 1/0;
```

To test the *display_errors* setting, the script needs to have at least one error. This first line doesn't even try to do anything, but it's guaranteed to cause an error. There are actually two issues here: first, there's a reference to a variable (**$var**) that doesn't exist; second, a non-array (**$var**) is being used in the **foreach** loop as if it were an array.

The second line is a classic division by zero, which is not allowed in programming languages or in math.

Script 8.1 The `ini_set()` function can be used to tell a PHP script to reveal any errors that might occur.

```
1    <!doctype html>
2    <html lang="en">
3    <head>
4        <meta charset="utf-8">
5        <title>Displaying Errors</title>
6    </head>
7    <body>
8    <h2>Testing Display Errors</h2>
9    <?php # Script 8.1 - display_errors.php
10
11   // Show errors:
12   ini_set('display_errors', 1);
13
14   // Create errors:
15   foreach ($var as $v) {}
16   $result = 1/0;
17
18   ?>
19   </body>
20   </html>
```

4. Complete the page:
```
?>
</body>
</html>
```

5. Save the file as **display_errors.php**, place it in your web directory, and test it in your browser **A**.

6. If you want, change the first line of PHP code to read

```
ini_set('display_errors', 0);
```

Then save and retest the script **B**.

TIP There are limits as to what PHP settings the `ini_set()` function can be used to adjust. See the PHP manual for specifics as to what can and cannot be changed using it.

TIP As a reminder, changing the *display_ errors* setting in a script only works so long as that script runs (i.e., it cannot have any parse errors). To be able to always see any errors that occur, you'll need to enable *display_errors* in PHP's configuration file (again, see the appendix).

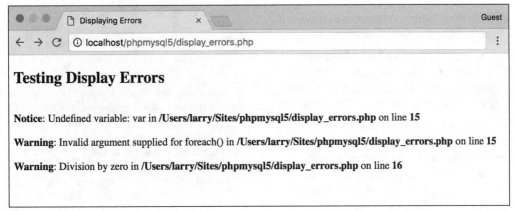

Testing Display Errors

Notice: Undefined variable: var in **/Users/larry/Sites/phpmysql5/display_errors.php** on line **15**

Warning: Invalid argument supplied for foreach() in **/Users/larry/Sites/phpmysql5/display_errors.php** on line **15**

Warning: Division by zero in **/Users/larry/Sites/phpmysql5/display_errors.php** on line **16**

A With *display_errors* turned on (for this script), the page reports the errors when they occur.

Testing Display Errors

B With *display_errors* turned off (for this page), the same errors are no longer reported. Unfortunately, they still exist.

Adjusting Error Reporting in PHP

Once you have PHP set to display the errors that occur, you might want to adjust the level of error reporting. Your PHP installation as a whole, or individual scripts, can be set to report or ignore different types of errors. Table 8.1 lists most of the levels, but they can generally be one of these three kinds:

- *Notices*, which do not stop the execution of a script and may not necessarily be a problem

- *Warnings*, which indicate a problem but don't stop a script's execution

- *Errors*, which stop a script from continuing (including the ever-common parse error, which prevents scripts from running at all)

As a rule of thumb, you'll want PHP to report on any kind of error while you're developing a site but report no specific errors once the site goes live. For security and aesthetic purposes, it's generally unwise for a public user to see PHP's detailed error messages.

Suppressing Errors with @

Individual errors can be suppressed in PHP using the error suppression operator, @. For example, if you don't want PHP to report if it couldn't include a file, you would code

```
@include ('config.inc.php');
```

Or if you don't want to see a "division by zero" error:

```
$x = 8;
$y = 0;
$num = @($x/$y);
```

The @ symbol will work only on expressions, like function calls or mathematical operations. You cannot use @ before conditionals, loops, function definitions, and so forth.

As a rule of thumb, I recommend that @ be used on functions whose execution, should they fail, will not affect the functionality of the script as a whole. Or you can choose not to display PHP's errors by handling them more gracefully yourself (a topic discussed later in this chapter).

TABLE 8.1 Error-Reporting Levels

Number	Constant	Report On
1	E_ERROR	Fatal run-time errors (that stop execution of the script)
2	E_WARNING	Run-time warnings (nonfatal errors)
4	E_PARSE	Parse errors
8	E_NOTICE	Notices (things that could or could not be a problem)
256	E_USER_ERROR	User-generated error messages, generated by the `trigger_error()` function
512	E_USER_WARNING	User-generated warnings, generated by the `trigger_error()` function
1024	E_USER_NOTICE	User-generated notices, generated by the `trigger_error()` function
2048	E_STRICT	Recommendations for compatibility and interoperability
8192	E_DEPRECATED	Warnings about code that won't work in future versions of PHP
32767	E_ALL	All errors, warnings, and recommendations

Script 8.2 This script will demonstrate how error reporting can be manipulated in PHP.

```
1   <!doctype html>
2   <html lang="en">
3   <head>
4       <meta charset="utf-8">
5       <title>Reporting Errors</title>
6   </head>
7   <body>
8   <h2>Testing Error Reporting</h2>
9   <?php # Script 8.2 - report_errors.php
10
11  // Show errors:
12  ini_set('display_errors', 1);
13
14  // Adjust error reporting:
15  error_reporting(E_ALL);
16
17  // Create errors:
18  foreach ($var as $v) {}
19  $result = 1/0;
20
21  ?>
22  </body>
23  </html>
```

Frequently, error messages—particularly those dealing with the database—will reveal certain behind-the-scenes aspects of your web application that are best not shown. Although you hope these will be worked out during the development stage, that may not be the case.

You can universally adjust the level of error reporting following the instructions in Appendix A. Or you can adjust this behavior on a script-by-script basis using the `error_reporting()` function. This function is used to establish what type of errors PHP should report on within a specific page. The function takes either a number or a constant, using the values in Table 8.1 (the PHP manual lists a few others, related to the core of PHP itself).

`error_reporting(0); // Show no errors.`

A setting of 0 turns error reporting off entirely (errors will still occur; you just won't see them anymore). Conversely, `error_reporting(E_ALL)` will tell PHP to report on every error that occurs. The numbers can be added up to customize the level of error reporting, or you could use the bitwise operators—| (or), ~ (not), **&** (and)—with the constants. With the following setting, any non-notice error will be shown:

`error_reporting(E_ALL & ~E_NOTICE);`

To adjust error reporting:

1. Open `display_errors.php` (Script 8.1) in your text editor or IDE, if you haven't already.

   To play around with error reporting levels, use `display_errors.php` as an example.

2. After adjusting the *display_errors* setting, add (**Script 8.2**)

   `error_reporting(E_ALL);`

   continues on next page

For development purposes, have PHP notify you of all errors, notices, warnings, and recommendations. Setting the level of error reporting to **E_ALL** will accomplish that.

Because **E_ALL** is a constant, it's not enclosed in quotation marks.

3. Save the file as **report_errors.php**, place it in your web directory, and run it in your browser 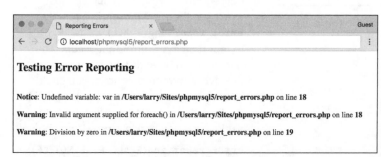.

I also altered the page's title and the heading, but both are immaterial to the point of this exercise.

4. Change the level of error reporting to something different and retest **B** and **C**.

TIP The numeric value of E_ALL in Table 8.1 can differ from one version of PHP to the next.

TIP Because you'll often want to adjust the *display_errors* and *error_reporting* for every page in a web site, you might want to place those lines of code in a separate PHP file that can then be included by other PHP scripts.

TIP The scripts in this book were all written with PHP's error reporting on the highest level (with the intention of catching every possible problem).

TIP The **trigger_error()** function is a way to programmatically generate an error in a PHP script. Its first argument is an error message; its second, optional, argument is a numeric error type, corresponding to the values in Table 8.1. By default the type will be E_USER.

```
if (/* some condition */) {
    trigger_error('Something Bad
    → Happened!');
}
```

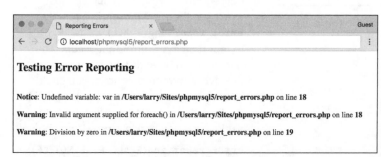

A On the highest level of error reporting, PHP has two warnings and one notice for this page (Script 8.2).

B The same page (Script 8.2) after disabling the reporting of notices.

C The same page again (Script 8.2) with error reporting turned off (set to 0). The result is the same as if *display_errors* were disabled. Of course, the errors still occur; they're just not being reported.

Creating Custom Error Handlers

Another option for error management with your sites is to alter how PHP handles errors. By default, if *display_errors* is enabled and an error is caught (that falls under the level of error reporting), PHP will print the error, in a somewhat simplistic form, within some minimal HTML tags 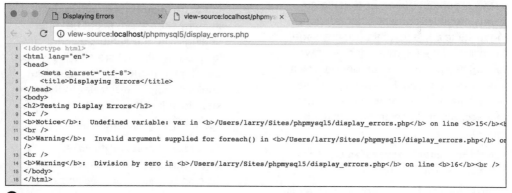.

Some PHP installations will use even more elaborate error reporting 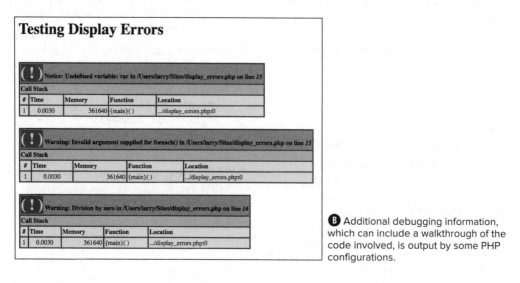.

continues on next page

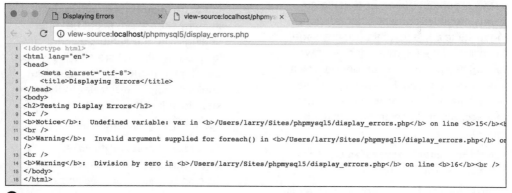

A The HTML source code shows how PHP formats errors by default.

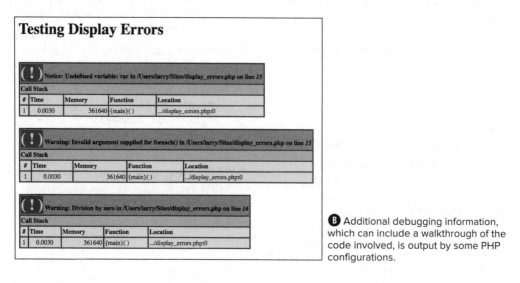

B Additional debugging information, which can include a walkthrough of the code involved, is output by some PHP configurations.

You can override how errors are handled by creating your own function that will be called when errors occur. For example:

```
function report_errors(arguments) {
    // Do whatever here.
}
set_error_handler('report_errors');
```

The PHP `set_error_handler()` function is used to name the user-defined function to be called when an error occurs. The handling function (*report_errors*, in this case) will, at that time, receive several values that can be used in any possible manner.

This function can be written to take up to five arguments. In order, these arguments are an error number (corresponding to Table 8.1), a textual error message, the name of the file where the error was found, the specific line number on which it occurred, and the variables that existed at the time of the error. Defining a function that accepts all these arguments might look like

```
function report_errors($num, $msg,
→ $file, $line, $vars) {...
```

To make use of this concept, we will rewrite the **report_errors.php** file (Script 8.2) one last time.

To create your own error handler:

1. Open **report_errors.php** (Script 8.2) in your text editor or IDE, if you haven't already.

2. Remove the **ini_set()** and **error_reporting()** lines (**Script 8.3**).

   When you establish your own error-handling function, the error reporting levels no longer have any meaning, so the line that adjusts them can be removed. Adjusting the *display_errors* setting is also meaningless, since the error-handling function will control whether or not errors are displayed.

3. Before the script creates the errors, add

   ```
   define('LIVE', FALSE);
   ```

   This constant will be a flag used to indicate if the site is currently live. It's an important distinction, because how you handle errors and what you reveal in the browser should differ greatly when you're developing a site and when a site is live.

   This constant is being set outside of the function for two reasons. First, I want to treat the function as a black box that does what I need it to do without having to go in and tinker with it. Second, in many sites, there might be other settings (like the database connectivity information) that are also live versus development-specific. Conditionals could, therefore, also refer to this constant to adjust those settings.

4. Begin defining the error-handling function:

   ```
   function my_error_handler
   → ($e_number, $e_message,
   → $e_file, $e_line, $e_vars) {
   ```

   The **my_error_handler()** function is set to receive the full five arguments that a custom error handler can.

5. Create the error message using the received values.

   ```
   $message = "An error occurred in
   → script '$e_file' on line
   → $e_line: $e_message\n";
   ```

   The error message will begin by referencing the filename and line number where the error occurred. Added to this is the actual error message. These values are passed to the function when it is called (when an error occurs).

continues on page 258

Script 8.3 By defining your own error-handling function, you can customize how errors are treated in your PHP scripts.

```
1    <!doctype html>
2    <html lang="en">
3    <head>
4        <meta charset="utf-8">
5        <title>Handling Errors</title>
6    </head>
7    <body>
8
9    <h2>Testing Error Handling</h2>
10   <?php # Script 8.3 - handle_errors.php
11
12   // Flag variable for site status:
13   define('LIVE', FALSE);
14
15   // Create the error handler:
16   function my_error_handler($e_number, $e_message, $e_file, $e_line, $e_vars) {
17
18       // Build the error message:
19       $message = "An error occurred in script '$e_file' on line $e_line: $e_message\n";
20
21       // Append $e_vars to  $message:
22       $message .= print_r ($e_vars, 1);
23
24       if (!LIVE) { // Development (print the error).
25           echo '<pre>' . $message . "\n";
26           debug_print_backtrace();
27           echo '</pre><br>';
28       } else { // Don't show the error.
29           echo '<div class="error">A system error occurred. We apologize for the
             inconvenience.</div><br>';
30       }
31
32   } // End of my_error_handler() definition.
33
34   // Use my error handler:
35   set_error_handler('my_error_handler');
36
37   // Create errors:
38   foreach ($var as $v) {}
39   $result = 1/0;
40
41   ?>
42   </body>
43   </html>
```

6. Add any existing variables to the error message:

```php
$message .= print_r($e_vars, 1);
```

The **$e_vars** variable will receive all the variables that exist, and their values, when the error happens. Because this might contain useful debugging information, it's added to the message.

The **print_r()** function is normally used to print out a variable's structure and value; it is particularly useful with arrays. If you call the function with a second argument (1 or TRUE), the result is returned instead of printed. So, this line adds all of the variable information to **$message**.

7. Print a message that will vary, depending on whether or not the site is live:

```php
if (!LIVE) {
  echo '<pre>' . $message . "\n";
  debug_print_backtrace();
  echo '</pre><br>';
} else {
  echo '<div class="error">
  → A system error occurred.
  → We apologize for the
  → inconvenience.</div><br>';
}
```

If the site is not live (if **LIVE** is FALSE), which would be the case while the site is being developed, a detailed error message should be printed **C**. For ease of viewing, the error message is printed within HTML **PRE** tags. Furthermore, a useful debugging function, **debug_print_backtrace()**, is also called. This function returns a slew of information about what functions have been called, what files have been included, and so forth.

If the site is live, a simple mea culpa will be printed, letting the user know that an error occurred but not what the specific problem is **D**. Under this situation, you could also use the **error_log()** function (see the sidebar) to have the detailed error message emailed or written to a log.

8. Complete the function and tell PHP to use it:

```php
}
set_error_handler
→ ('my_error_handler');
```

This second line is the important one, telling PHP to use the custom error handler instead of PHP's default handler.

Handling Errors   ×   +

← → ↻ | localhost/handle_errors.php

Testing Error Handling

```
An error occurred in script 'C:\xampp\htdocs\handle_errors.php' on line 38: Undefined variable: var
Array
(
    [_GET] => Array
        (
        )

    [_POST] => Array
        (
        )

    [_COOKIE] => Array
        (
        )

    [_FILES] => Array
        (
        )
)
```

C During the development phase, detailed error messages are printed in the web browser. (In a more real-world script, with more code, the messages would be more useful.)

Logging PHP Errors

In Script 8.3, errors are handled by simply printing them out in detail or not printing them at all. Another option is to log the errors—making a permanent note of them. For this purpose, the **error_log()** function instructs PHP how to file an error. Its syntax is

```
error_log(message, type,
 destination, extra headers);
```

The *message* value should be the text of the logged error (i.e., **$message** in Script 8.3). The type dictates how the error is logged. The options are the numbers 0, 1, 3, and 4: use the computer's default logging method (0), send it in an email (1), write it to a text file (3), or send it to the web server's logging handler (4).

The destination parameter can be either the name of a file (for log type 3) or an email address (for log type 1). The extra headers argument is used only when sending emails (log type 1). Both the destination and extra headers are optional.

9. Save the file as **handle_errors.php**, place it in your web directory, and test it in your browser ⒞.

10. Change the value of **LIVE** to TRUE, save, and retest the script ⒟.

   To see how the error handler behaves with a live site, change just this one value.

TIP If your PHP page uses special HTML formatting—like CSS tags to affect the layout and font treatment—add this information to your error reporting function.

TIP Obviously in a live site you'll probably need to do more than apologize for the inconvenience (particularly if the error significantly affects the page's functionality). Still, this example demonstrates how you can easily adjust error handling to suit the situation.

TIP If you don't want the error-handling function to report on every notice, error, or warning, you could check the error number value (the first argument sent to the function). For example, to ignore notices when the site is live, you would change the main conditional to

```
if (!LIVE) {
    echo '<pre>' . $message . "\n";
    debug_print_backtrace();
    echo '</pre><br>';
} elseif ($e_number != E_NOTICE) {
    echo '<div class="error">A system
    → error occurred. We apologize
    → for the inconvenience.</div>
    → <br>';
}
```

⒟ Once a site has gone live, more user-friendly (and less revealing) errors are printed. Here, one message is printed for each of the three errors in the script.

PHP Debugging Techniques

When it comes to debugging, what you'll best learn from experience are the causes of certain types of errors. Understanding the common causes will shorten the time it takes to fix errors. To expedite the learning process, **Table 8.2** lists the likely reasons for the most common PHP errors.

The first, and most common, type of error that you'll run across is syntactical and will prevent your scripts from executing. An error like this will result in messages like the one in **Ⓐ**, which every PHP developer has seen too many times. To avoid making this sort of mistake when you program, be sure to

- End every statement (but not language constructs like loops and conditionals) with a semicolon.

- Balance all quotation marks, parentheses, curly braces, and square brackets (each opening character must be closed).

- Be consistent with your quotation marks (single quotes can be closed only with single quotes and double quotes with double quotes).

- Escape, using the backslash, all single- and double-quotation marks within strings, as appropriate.

TABLE 8.2 Common PHP Errors

Error	Likely Cause
Blank Page	HTML problem, or PHP error and *display_errors* or *error_reporting* is off.
Parse error	Missing semicolon; unbalanced curly braces, parentheses, or quotation marks; or use of an unescaped quotation mark in a string.
Empty variable value	Forgot the initial **$**, misspelled or miscapitalized the variable name, or inappropriate variable scope (with functions).
Undefined variable	Reference made to a variable before it is given a value or an empty variable value (see those potential causes).
Call to undefined function	Misspelled function name, PHP is not configured to use that function (like a MySQL function), or document that contains the function definition was not included.
Cannot redeclare function	Two definitions of your own function exist; check within included files.
Headers already sent	White space exists in the script before the PHP tags, data has already been printed, or a file has been included.

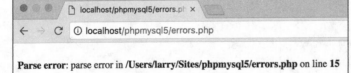

Parse error: parse error in **/Users/larry/Sites/phpmysql5/errors.php** on line **15**

Ⓐ The parse error prevents a script from running because of invalid PHP syntax. This one was caused by omitting a semicolon.

One thing you should also understand about syntactical errors is that just because the PHP error message says the error is occurring on line 12, that doesn't mean the mistake is on that line. At the very least, it is not uncommon for there to be a difference between what PHP thinks is line 12 and what your text editor indicates is line 12. So although PHP's direction is useful in tracking down a problem, treat the line number referenced as more of a starting point than an absolute.

If PHP reports an error on the last line of your document, this is almost always because a mismatched parenthesis, curly brace, or quotation mark was not caught until that moment.

The second type of error you'll encounter results from misusing a function. This error occurs, for example, when a function is called without the proper arguments. This error is discovered by PHP when attempting to execute the code. In later chapters you'll probably see such errors when using the **header()** function, cookies, or sessions.

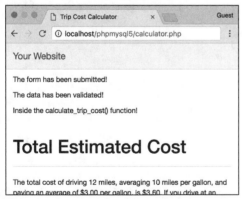

B More complex debugging can be accomplished by leaving yourself notes as to what the script is doing.

To fix errors, you'll need to do a little detective work to see what mistakes were made and where. For starters, though, always thoroughly read and trust the error message PHP offers. Although the referenced line number may not always be correct, a PHP error is very descriptive, normally helpful, and almost always 100 percent correct.

To debug your scripts:

- Turn on *display_errors*.

  Use the earlier steps to enable *display_errors* for a script or, if possible, the entire server, as you develop your applications.

- Use comments.

  Just as you can use comments to document your scripts, you can also use them to rule out problematic lines. If PHP is giving you an error on line 12, then commenting out that line should get rid of the error. If not, then you know the error is elsewhere. Just be careful that you don't introduce more errors by improperly commenting out only a portion of a code block: the syntax of your scripts must be maintained.

- Use the **print** and **echo** functions.

  In more complicated scripts, I frequently use **echo** statements to leave myself notes as to what is happening as the script is executed B. When a script has several steps, it may not be easy to know if the problem is occurring in step 2 or step 5. By using an **echo** statement, you can narrow the problem down to the specific juncture.

continues on next page

- Check what quotation marks are being used for printing variables.

  It's not uncommon for programmers to mistakenly use single quotation marks and then wonder why their variables are not printed properly. Remember that single quotation marks treat text literally and that you must use double quotation marks to print out the values of variables.

- Track variables .

  It is easy for a script not to work because you referred to the wrong variable or the right variable by the wrong name or because the variable does not have the value you would expect. To check for these possibilities, use **print** or **echo** statements to print out the values of variables at important points in your scripts. This is simply a matter of

  ```
  echo "<p>\$var = $var</p>\n";
  ```

  or

  ```
  echo "<p>\$var is $var</p>\n";
  ```

  The first dollar sign is escaped so that the variable's name is printed. The second reference of the variable will print its value.

- Print array values.

  For more complicated variable types (arrays and objects), the **print_r()** and **var_dump()** functions will print out their values without the need for loops. Both functions accomplish the same task, although **var_dump()** is more detailed in its reporting than **print_r()**.

The form has been submitted!

The data has been validated!

$_POST['distance'] is 12.

$_POST['gallon_price'] is 3.00.

$_POST['efficiency'] is 10.

Inside the calculate_trip_cost() function!

$miles is 12.

$mpg is 10.

$ppg is 3.00.

Total Estimated Cost

 Printing the names and values of variables is the easiest way to track them over the course of a script.

Using die() and exit()

Two functions that are often used with error management are **die()** and **exit()** (they're technically language constructs, not functions, but who cares?). When a **die()** or **exit()** is called in your script, the entire script is terminated. Both are useful for stopping a script from continuing should something important—like establishing a database connection—fail to happen. You can also pass to **die()** and **exit()** a string that will be printed out in the browser.

You'll commonly see **die()** or **exit()** used in an **OR** conditional. For example:

```
include('config.inc.php') OR
→ die('Could not open the file.');
```

With a line like that, if PHP could not include the configuration file, the **die()** statement would be executed and the "Could not open the file" message would be printed. You'll see variations on this throughout this book and in the PHP manual, since it's a quick, but potentially excessive, way to handle errors without using a custom error handler.

TIP Many text editors include utilities to check for balanced parentheses, brackets, and quotation marks.

TIP If you cannot find the parse error in a complex script, begin by using the /* */ comments to render the entire PHP code inert. Then continue to uncomment sections at a time (by moving the opening or closing comment characters) and rerun the script until you deduce what lines are causing the error. Watch how you comment out control structures, though; the curly braces must continue to be matched in order to avoid parse errors. For example:

```
if (condition) {
    /* Start comment.
    Inert code.
    End comment. */
}
```

TIP To make the results of **print_r()** more readable in the web browser, wrap it within HTML **<pre>** (preformatted) tags. This one line is one of my favorite debugging tools:

```
echo '<pre>' . print_r ($var, 1) .
→ '</pre>';
```

SQL and MySQL Debugging Techniques

The most common SQL errors are caused by the following issues:

- Unbalanced use of quotation marks or parentheses
- Unescaped apostrophes in column values
- Misspelling a column name, table name, or function
- Ambiguously referring to a column in a join
- Placing a query's clauses (**WHERE**, **GROUP BY**, **ORDER BY**, **LIMIT**) in the wrong order

Furthermore, when using MySQL you can also run across the following:

- Unpredictable or inappropriate query results
- Inability to access the database

Since you'll be running the queries for your dynamic web sites from PHP, you'll need a methodology for debugging SQL and MySQL errors within that context (PHP will not report a problem with your SQL).

Debugging SQL problems

To decide if you are experiencing a MySQL (or SQL) problem rather than a PHP one, you need a system for finding and fixing the issue. Fortunately, the steps you should take to debug MySQL and SQL problems are easy to define and should be followed without thinking. If you ever have any MySQL or SQL errors to debug, just abide by this sequence of steps.

To hammer the point home, this next sequence of steps is probably the most useful debugging technique in this chapter and the entire book. You'll likely need to follow these steps in any PHP-MySQL web application when you're not getting the results you expected.

To debug your SQL queries:

1. Print out any applicable queries in your PHP script **A**.

   As you'll see in the next chapter, SQL queries will often be assigned to a variable, particularly when you use PHP to dynamically create them. Using the code **echo $query** (or whatever the query variable is called) in your PHP scripts, you can send to the browser the exact query being run. Sometimes this step alone will help you see what the real problem is.

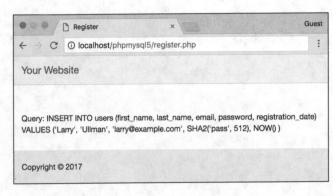

A Knowing exactly what query a PHP script is attempting to execute is the most useful first step for solving SQL and MySQL problems.

2. Run the query in the mysql client or other tool **B**.

The most foolproof method of debugging an SQL or MySQL problem is to run the query used in your PHP scripts through an independent application—the mysql client, phpMyAdmin, or the like. Doing so will give you the same result that the original PHP script receives but without the overhead, hassle, or mystery.

If the independent application returns the expected result but you are still not getting the proper behavior in your PHP script, then you will know that the problem lies within the script itself, not in your SQL command or the MySQL database.

3. If the problem still isn't evident, rewrite the query in its most basic form, and then keep adding dimensions back in until you discover which clause is causing the problem. Continue to use a third-party interface to MySQL to do this (i.e., put away the PHP script until you've got the SQL query working properly).

Sometimes it's difficult to debug a query because there's too much going on. Like commenting out most of a PHP script, taking a query down to its bare minimum structure and slowly building it back up can be the easiest way to debug complex SQL commands.

Debugging access problems

Access-denied error messages are the most common problem beginning developers encounter when using PHP to interact with MySQL. These are among the common solutions:

- Reload MySQL after altering the privileges so that the changes take effect. Either use the mysqladmin tool or run **FLUSH PRIVILEGES** in the mysql client. You must be logged in as a user with the appropriate permissions to do this (see Appendix A for more).

- Double-check the password used. The error message *Access denied for user: 'user@localhost' (Using password: YES)* frequently indicates that the password is wrong or mistyped. (This is not always the cause but is the first thing to check.)

- The error message *Can't connect to...* (error number 2002) indicates that MySQL either is not running or is not running on the socket or TCP/IP port tried by the client.

TIP MySQL keeps its own error logs, which are very useful in solving MySQL problems (like why MySQL won't even start). MySQL's error log will be located in the MySQL data directory and titled `hostname.err`.

TIP The MySQL manual is very detailed, containing SQL examples, function references, and the meanings of error codes. Make the manual your friend and turn to it when confusing errors pop up.

```
                PHP and MySQL for Dynamic Web Sites
mysql>  INSERT INTO users (first_name, last_name, email, password,
registration_date) VALUES ('Larry', 'Ullman', 'larry@example.com',
SHA2('pass', 512), NOW() );
ERROR 1054 (42S22): Unknown column 'password' in 'field list'
mysql> ▊
```

B To understand what result a PHP script is receiving, run the same query through a separate interface. In this case, the problem is the reference to the *password* column, when the table's column is actually called just *pass*.

Review and Pursue

If you have any problems with the review questions or the pursue prompts, turn to the book's supporting forum (**LarryUllman.com/forums/**).

Review

- Why must PHP scripts be run through a URL?

- What version of PHP are you using? What version of MySQL? What version of what web server application are you using? On what operating system?

- What debugging steps should you take if the rendered web page doesn't look right in your browser?

- Do you have *display_errors* enabled on your server? Why is enabling *display_errors* useful on development servers? Why is revealing errors a bad thing on production servers?

- How does the level of *error_reporting* affect PHP scripts? To what level of *error_reporting* is your PHP server set?

- What does the @ operator do?

- What are the benefits of using your own error-handling function? What impact does the error-reporting level have when using your own error-handling function?

- How can **print** or **echo** be used as debugging tools? Hint: There are many correct answers.

- What is the method for fixing PHP-SQL-MySQL bugs?

Pursue

- Learn about the debugging tools built into your favorite browser.

- Enable *display_errors* on your development server, if you can.

- If you can, set PHP's level of error reporting to **E_ALL** on your development server.

- Check out the PHP manual's page for the **debug_print_backtrace()** function to learn more about it.

- Consider using a professional-grade IDE that provides built-in debugging tools.

9

Using PHP with MySQL

Now that you have a sufficient amount of PHP, SQL, and MySQL experience under your belt, it's time to put all the technologies together. PHP's strong integration with MySQL is just one reason so many programmers have embraced it; it's impressive how easily you can use the two together.

This chapter will use the existing *sitename* database—created in Chapter 5, "Introduction to SQL"—to build a PHP interface for interacting with the *users* table. The knowledge taught and the examples used here will be the basis for all your PHP-MySQL web applications, because the principles involved are the same for any PHP-MySQL interaction.

Before heading into this chapter, you should be comfortable with everything covered in the first eight chapters, including the error debugging and handling techniques just taught in the previous chapter. Finally, remember that you need a PHP-enabled web server and access to a running MySQL server to execute the following examples.

In This Chapter

Modifying the Template

Since all the pages in this chapter and the next will be part of the same web application, it'll be worthwhile to use a common template system. Instead of creating a new template from scratch, the layout from Chapter 3, "Creating Dynamic Web Sites," will be used again, with only a minor modification to the header file's navigation links.

To make the header file:

1. Open **header.html** (Script 3.2) in your text editor or IDE.

2. Change the list of links to read as follows (**Script 9.1**):

```
<ul class="nav navbar-nav">
  <li class="active"><a href=
  → "index.php">Home</a></li>
  <li><a href="register.php">
  → Register</a></li>
  <li><a href="view_users.php">
  → View Users</a></li>
  <li><a href="password.php">
  → Change Password</a></li>
</ul>
```

All the examples in this chapter will involve the registration, view users, and change password pages. The date form and calculator links from Chapter 3 can be deleted.

Script 9.1 The site's header file, used for the pages' template, modified with new navigation links.

```
1    <!DOCTYPE html>
2    <html lang="en">
3    <head>
4    <meta charset="utf-8">
5    <meta http-equiv="X-UA-Compatible" content="IE=edge">
6    <meta name="viewport" content="width=device-width, initial-scale=1">
7    <title><?php echo $page_title; ?></title>
8    <link rel="stylesheet" href="https://maxcdn.bootstrapcdn.com/bootstrap/3.3.7/css
     /bootstrap.min.css" integrity="sha384-BVYiiSIFeK1dGmJRAkycuHAHRg32OmUcww7on3RYdg4Va+PmSTsz
     /K68vbdEjh4u" crossorigin="anonymous">
9    <link href="css/sticky-footer-navbar.css" rel="stylesheet">
10   </head>
11   <body>
12   <nav class="navbar navbar-default navbar-fixed-top">
13      <div class="container">
14         <div class="navbar-header"><a class="navbar-brand" href="#">Your Website</a></div>
15         <div id="navbar" class="collapse navbar-collapse">
16         <ul class="nav navbar-nav">
17            <li class="active"><a href="index.php">Home</a></li>
18            <li><a href="register.php">Register</a></li>
19            <li><a href="view_users.php">View Users</a></li>
20            <li><a href="password.php">Change Password</a></li>
21         </ul>
22         </div>
23      </div>
24   </nav>
25   <div class="container">
26   <!-- Script 9.1 - header.html -->
```

3. Save the file as **header.html**.

4. Place the new header file in your web directory, within the **includes** folder, along with **footer.html** (Script 3.3) and **style.css** (available for download from the book's supporting website, **LarryUllman.com**).

5. Test the new header file by running **index.php** in your browser **Ⓐ**.

TIP For a preview of this site's structure, see the sidebar "Organizing Your Documents" in the next section.

TIP Remember that you can use any file extension for your template files, including **.inc** or **.php**.

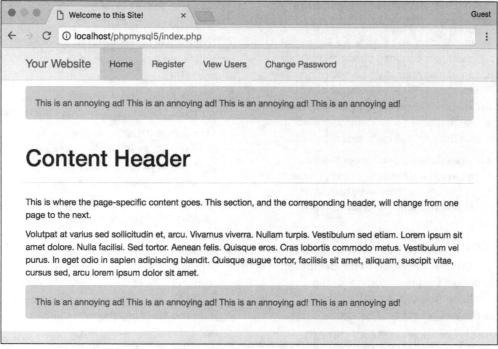

Ⓐ The dynamically generated home page with new navigation links.

Connecting to MySQL

The first step for interacting with MySQL—connecting to the server—requires the appropriately named `mysqli_connect()` function:

```
$dbc = mysqli_connect(hostname,
→ username, password, db_name);
```

The first three arguments sent to the function—*hostname*, *username*, and *password*—are based on the users and privileges established within MySQL (see Appendix A, "Installation," for more information). Commonly (but not always), the host value will be *localhost*.

The fourth argument is the name of the database to use. This is the equivalent of saying `USE databasename` within the mysql client.

If the connection was made, the `$dbc` variable, short for *database connection* (but you can use any name you want, of course), will become a reference point for all your subsequent database interactions. Most of the PHP functions for working with MySQL will take this variable as its first argument.

If a connection problem occurred, you can call `mysqli_connect_error()`, which returns the connection error message. It takes no arguments and so would be called using just

```
mysqli_connect_error();
```

Once you've connected to the database, you should set the encoding for the interaction. You can do so with the `mysqli_set_charset()` function:

```
mysqli_set_charset($dbc, 'utf8');
```

The value used as the encoding—the second argument—should match that of your PHP scripts and the collation of your database (see Chapter 6, "Database Design," for more on MySQL collations). If you fail to do this, all data will be transferred using the default character set, which could cause problems.

To start using PHP with MySQL, let's create a special script that makes the connection. Other PHP scripts that require a MySQL connection can then include this file.

To connect to and select a database:

1. Create a new PHP document in your text editor or IDE, to be named `mysqli_connect.php` (Script 9.2):

   ```
   <?php # Script 9.2 -
   → mysqli_connect.php
   ```

   This file will be included by other PHP scripts, so it doesn't need to contain any HTML.

2. Set the MySQL host, username, password, and database name as constants:

   ```
   define('DB_USER', 'username');
   define('DB_PASSWORD', 'password');
   define('DB_HOST', 'localhost');
   define('DB_NAME', 'sitename');
   ```

   I prefer to establish these values as constants for security reasons (they cannot be changed this way), but that isn't required. In general, setting these values as some sort of variable or constant makes sense so that you can separate the configuration parameters from the functions that use them—but again, this is not obligatory.

When writing your script, change these values to ones that will work on your setup. If you have been provided with a MySQL username/password combination and a database (like for a hosted site), use that information here. Or, if possible, follow the steps in Appendix A to create a user who has access to the *sitename* database, and insert those values here. Whatever you do, don't just use the values written in this book's code unless you know for certain they will work on your server!

3. Connect to MySQL:

```
$dbc = @mysqli_connect (DB_HOST,
→ DB_USER, DB_PASSWORD, DB_NAME)
→ OR die('Could not connect to
→ MySQL: ' . mysqli_connect_
→ error() );
```

The **mysqli_connect()** function, if it successfully connects to MySQL, will return a resource link that corresponds to the open connection. This link will be assigned to the **$dbc** variable so that other functions can make use of this connection.

The function call is preceded by the error suppression operator (**@**). This prevents the PHP error from being displayed in the browser. This is preferable in this specific case, since the error will be handled by the **OR die()** clause.

continues on next page

Script 9.2 The **mysqli_connect.php** script will be used by every other script in this chapter. It establishes a connection to MySQL, selects the database, and sets the encoding.

```
1    <?php # Script 9.2 - mysqli_connect.php
2
3    // This file contains the database access information.
4    // This file also establishes a connection to MySQL,
5    // selects the database, and sets the encoding.
6
7    // Set the database access information as constants:
8    define('DB_USER', 'username');
9    define('DB_PASSWORD', 'password');
10   define('DB_HOST', 'localhost');
11   define('DB_NAME', 'sitename');
12
13   // Make the connection:
14   $dbc = @mysqli_connect(DB_HOST, DB_USER, DB_PASSWORD, DB_NAME) OR die('Could not connect to
     MySQL: ' . mysqli_connect_error() );
15
16   // Set the encoding...
17   mysqli_set_charset($dbc, 'utf8');
```

If the **mysqli_connect()** function cannot return a valid resource link, then the **OR die()** part of the statement is executed (because the first part of the **OR** will be false, so the second part must be true). As discussed in the preceding chapter, the **die()** function terminates the execution of the script. The function can also take as an argument a string that will be printed to the browser. In this case, the string is a combination of *Could not connect to MySQL:* and the specific MySQL error **Ⓐ**. Using this blunt error management system makes debugging much easier as you develop your sites.

4. Set the encoding:

   mysqli_set_charset($dbc, 'utf8');

   The final step in this script is to set the encoding for all future communications.

5. Save the file as **mysqli_connect.php**.

   Since this file contains information—the database access data—that must be kept private, it will use a **.php** extension. With a **.php** extension, even if malicious users ran this script in their browser, they would not see the page's actual content.

   You may also note that I did not include a terminating PHP tag: **?>**. This is allowed in PHP (when the script ends with PHP code), and has a benefit to be explained in subsequent chapters.

6. Ideally, place the file outside of the web document directory **Ⓑ**.

   Because the file contains sensitive MySQL access information, it ought to be stored securely. If you can, place it

Could not connect to MySQL: Access denied for user 'username'@'localhost' (using password: YES)

Ⓐ If there were problems connecting to MySQL, an informative message is displayed and the script is halted.

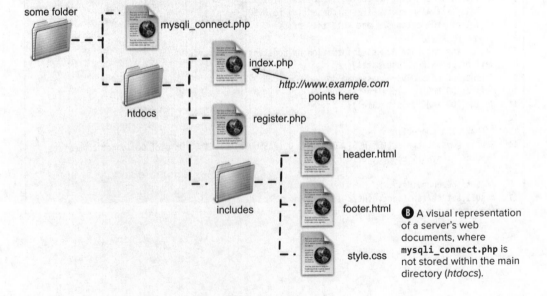

some folder

mysqli_connect.php

index.php

http://www.example.com points here

htdocs

register.php

header.html

includes

footer.html

Ⓑ A visual representation of a server's web documents, where **mysqli_connect.php** is not stored within the main directory (*htdocs*).

style.css

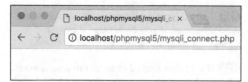

C If the MySQL connection script works properly, the end result will be a blank page (no HTML is generated by the script).

in the directory immediately above or otherwise outside of the web directory. This way, the file will not be accessible from a browser. See the "Organizing Your Documents" sidebar for more.

7. Temporarily place a copy of the script within the web directory and run it in your browser **C**.

   To test the script, you'll want to place a copy on the server so that it's accessible from the browser, which means it must be in the web directory. If the script works properly, the result should be a blank page **C**. If you see an *Access denied...* or similar message **A**, it means that the combination of username, password, and host does not have permission to access the particular database.

8. Remove the temporary copy from the web directory.

Organizing Your Documents

Chapter 3 introduced the concept of *site structure* while developing the first web application. Now that pages will begin using a database connection script, the topic is more important.

Should the database connectivity information (username, password, host, and database) fall into malicious hands, it could be used to steal your information or wreak havoc upon the database as a whole. Therefore, you cannot keep a script like **mysqli_connect.php** too secure.

The best recommendation for securing such a file is to store it outside of the web documents directory. If, for example, the *htdocs* folder in **B** is the root of the web directory (in other words, the URL **www.example.com** leads there), then not storing **mysqli_connect.php** anywhere within the *htdocs* directory means it will never be accessible via the browser. Granted, the source code of PHP scripts is not viewable from the browser (only the data sent to the browser by the script is), but you can never be too careful. If you aren't allowed to place documents outside of the web directory, placing **mysqli_connect.php** in the web directory is less secure, but not the end of the world.

Second, I recommend using a **.php** extension for your connection scripts. A properly configured and working server will execute rather than display code in such a file. Conversely, if you use just **.inc** as your extension, that page's contents would be displayed in the browser if accessed directly.

TIP The same values used in Chapter 5 to log in to the mysql client should work from your PHP scripts.

TIP If you receive an error that claims `mysqli_connect()` is an "undefined function," it means that PHP has not been compiled with support for the Improved MySQL Extension. See the appendix for installation information.

TIP If you see a `Could not connect...` error message when running the script **D**, it likely means that MySQL isn't running.

TIP In case you are curious, **E** shows what would happen if you didn't use @ before `mysqli_connect()` and an error occurred.

TIP If you don't need to select the database when establishing a connection to MySQL, omit that argument from the `mysqli_connect()` function:

`$dbc = mysqli_connect(hostname,`
`→ username, password);`

Then, when appropriate, you can select the database using:

`mysqli_select_db($dbc, db_name);`

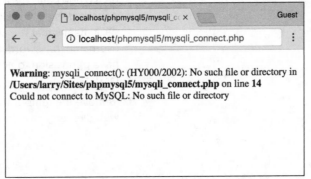

D Another reason why PHP might not be able to connect to MySQL (besides using invalid username/password/hostname/database information) is if MySQL isn't currently running.

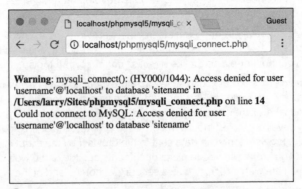

E If you don't use the error suppression operator (@), you'll see both the PHP error and the custom `OR die()` error.

Executing Simple Queries

Once you have successfully connected to and selected a database, you can start executing queries. The queries can be as basic as inserts, updates, and deletions or as involved as complex joins returning numerous rows. Regardless of the SQL command type, the PHP function for executing a query is `mysqli_query()`:

```
result = mysqli_query(dbc, query);
```

The function takes the database connection as its first argument and the query itself as the second. Within the context of a complete PHP script, I normally assign the query to another variable, called **$query** or just **$q**, so running a query might look like

```
$r = mysqli_query($dbc, $q);
```

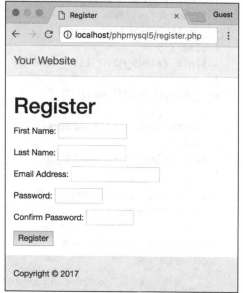

A The registration form.

For simple queries that do not return records, like **INSERT**, **UPDATE**, **DELETE**, etc., the **$r** variable—short for *result*—will be either TRUE or FALSE, depending on whether the query executed successfully. Keep in mind that "executed successfully" means that it ran without error; it doesn't mean that the query's execution necessarily had the desired result; you'll need to test for that.

For complex queries that return records (**SELECT** being the most important of these), **$r** will be a resource link to the results of the query if it worked or be FALSE if it did not. Thus, you can use this code to test if the query successfully ran:

```
$r = mysqli_query($dbc, $q);
if ($r) { // Worked!
```

If the query did not successfully run, some sort of MySQL error must have occurred. To find out what that error was, call the `mysqli_error()` function:

```
echo mysqli_error($dbc);
```

The function's lone argument is the database connection.

One final, albeit optional, step in your script would be to close the existing MySQL connection once you're finished with it:

```
mysqli_close($dbc);
```

This function call is not required, because PHP will automatically close the connection at the end of a script, but it does make for good programming form to incorporate it.

To demonstrate this process, let's create a registration script. It will show the form when first accessed **A**, handle the form submission, and, after validating all the data, insert the registration information into the *users* table of the *sitename* database.

continues on next page

As a forewarning, this script knowingly has a security hole in it (depending on the version of PHP in use, and its settings), to be remedied later in the chapter.

To execute simple queries:

1. Begin a new PHP script in your text editor or IDE, to be named **register.php** (Script 9.3):

```php
<?php # Script 9.3 - register.php
$page_title = 'Register';
include('includes/header.html');
```

The fundamentals of this script—using included files, having the same page both display and handle a form, and creating a sticky form—come from Chapter 3. See that chapter if you're confused about any of these concepts.

2. Create the submission conditional and initialize the **$errors** array:

```php
if ($_SERVER['REQUEST_METHOD'] ==
→ 'POST') {
  $errors = [];
```

This script will both display and handle the HTML form. This first conditional will check for how the script is being requested, to know when to process the form (again, this comes from Chapter 3). The **$errors** variable will be used to store every error message (one for each form input not properly filled out).

3. Validate the first name:

```php
if (empty($_POST['first_name'])) {
  $errors[] = 'You forgot to
  → enter your first name. ';
} else {
  $fn = trim($_POST['first_name']);
}
```

As discussed in Chapter 3, the **empty()** function provides a minimal way of ensuring that a text field was filled out. If the first name field was not filled out, an error message is added to the **$errors** array. Otherwise, **$fn** is set to the submitted value, after trimming off any extraneous spaces. By using this new variable—which is obviously short for *first_name*—it will be syntactically easier to write the query later.

4. Validate the last name and email address:

```php
if (empty($_POST['last_name'])) {
  $errors[] = 'You forgot to
  → enter your last name. ';
} else {
  $ln = trim($_POST['last_name']);
}
if (empty($_POST['email'])) {
  $errors[] = 'You forgot to
  → enter your email address. ';
} else {
  $e = trim($_POST['email']);
}
```

These lines are essentially the same as those validating the first name field. In both cases a new variable will be created, assuming that the minimal validation was passed.

continues on page 279

Script 9.3 The registration script adds a record to the database by running an **INSERT** query.

```php
1    <?php # Script 9.3 - register.php
2    // This script performs an INSERT query to add a record to the users table.
3
4    $page_title = 'Register';
5    include('includes/header.html');
6
7    // Check for form submission:
8    if ($_SERVER['REQUEST_METHOD'] == 'POST') {
9
10       $errors = []; // Initialize an error array.
11
12       // Check for a first name:
13       if (empty($_POST['first_name'])) {
14          $errors[] = 'You forgot to enter your first name.';
15       } else {
16          $fn = trim($_POST['first_name']);
17       }
18
19       // Check for a last name:
20       if (empty($_POST['last_name'])) {
21          $errors[] = 'You forgot to enter your last name.';
22       } else {
23          $ln = trim($_POST['last_name']);
24       }
25
26       // Check for an email address:
27       if (empty($_POST['email'])) {
28          $errors[] = 'You forgot to enter your email address.';
29       } else {
30          $e = trim($_POST['email']);
31       }
32
33       // Check for a password and match against the confirmed password:
34       if (!empty($_POST['pass1'])) {
35          if ($_POST['pass1'] != $_POST['pass2']) {
36             $errors[] = 'Your password did not match the confirmed password.';
37          } else {
38             $p = trim($_POST['pass1']);
39          }
40       } else {
41          $errors[] = 'You forgot to enter your password.';
42       }
43
44       if (empty($errors)) { // If everything's OK.
45
46          // Register the user in the database...
47
```

code continues on next page

```
48        require('../mysqli_connect.php'); // Connect to the db.
49
50        // Make the query:
51        $q = "INSERT INTO users (first_name, last_name, email, pass, registration_date)
          VALUES ('$fn', '$ln', '$e', SHA2('$p', 512), NOW() )";
52        $r = @mysqli_query($dbc, $q); // Run the query.
53        if ($r) { // If it ran OK.
54
55            // Print a message:
56            echo '<h1>Thank you!</h1>
57        <p>You are now registered. In Chapter 12 you will actually be able to log in!
          </p><p><br></p>';
58
59        } else { // If it did not run OK.
60
61            // Public message:
62            echo '<h1>System Error</h1>
63            <p class="error">You could not be registered due to a system error. We apologize for
              any inconvenience.</p>';
64
65            // Debugging message:
66            echo '<p>' . mysqli_error($dbc) . '<br><br>Query: ' . $q . '</p>';
67
68        } // End of if ($r) IF.
69
70        mysqli_close($dbc); // Close the database connection.
71
72        // Include the footer and quit the script:
73        include('includes/footer.html');
74        exit();
75
76    } else { // Report the errors.
77
78        echo '<h1>Error!</h1>
79        <p class="error">The following error(s) occurred:<br>';
80        foreach ($errors as $msg) { // Print each error.
81            echo " - $msg<br>\n";
82        }
83        echo '</p><p>Please try again.</p><p><br></p>';
84
85    } // End of if (empty($errors)) IF.
86
87 } // End of the main Submit conditional.
88 ?>
89 <h1>Register</h1>
90 <form action="register.php" method="post">
91    <p>First Name: <input type="text" name="first_name" size="15" maxlength="20" value="<?php
      if (isset($_POST['first_name'])) echo $_POST['first_name']; ?>"></p>
92    <p>Last Name: <input type="text" name="last_name" size="15" maxlength="40" value="<?php if
      (isset($_POST['last_name'])) echo $_POST['last_name']; ?>"></p>
```

code continues on next page

5. Validate the passwords:

```
if (!empty($_POST['pass1'])) {
    if ($_POST['pass1'] !=
    → $_POST['pass2']) {
        $errors[] = 'Your password
        → did not match the confirmed
        → password. ';
    } else {
        $p = trim($_POST['pass1']);
    }
} else {
    $errors[] = 'You forgot to
    → enter your password. ';
}
```

To validate the password, the script needs to check the *pass1* input for a value and then confirm that the *pass1* value matches the *pass2* value (meaning the password and confirmed password are the same).

6. Check if it's OK to register the user:

```
if (empty($errors)) {
```

If the submitted data passed all the conditions, the **$errors** array will have no values in it (it will be empty), so this condition will be true and it's safe to add the record to the database. If the **$errors** array is not empty, then the appropriate error messages should be printed (see Step 11) and the user given another opportunity to register.

7. Include the database connection:

```
require('../mysqli_connect.php');
```

This line of code will insert the contents of the **mysqli_connect.php** file into this script, thereby creating a connection to MySQL and selecting the database. You may need to change the reference to the location of the file as it is on your server (as written, this line assumes that **mysqli_connect.php** is in the parent folder of the current folder).

8. Add the user to the database:

```
$q = "INSERT INTO users
→ (first_name, last_name, email,
→ pass, registration_date) VALUES
→ ('$fn', '$ln', '$e', SHA2('$p',
→ 512), NOW() )";
$r = @mysqli_query($dbc, $q);
```

The query itself is like those demonstrated in Chapter 5. The **SHA2()** function is used to encrypt the password, and **NOW()** is used to set the registration date as this moment. (In Chapter 13, "Security Methods," you'll learn a PHP solution for hashing and matching the registration password.)

continues on next page

Script 9.3 *continued*

```
93    <p>Email Address: <input type="email" name="email" size="20" maxlength="60" value="<?php if
      (isset($_POST['email'])) echo $_POST['email']; ?>" > </p>
94    <p>Password: <input type="password" name="pass1" size="10" maxlength="20" value="<?php if
      (isset($_POST['pass1'])) echo $_POST['pass1']; ?>" ></p>
95    <p>Confirm Password: <input type="password" name="pass2" size="10" maxlength="20"
      value="<?php if (isset($_POST['pass2'])) echo $_POST['pass2']; ?>" ></p>
96    <p><input type="submit" name="submit" value="Register"></p>
97    </form>
98    <?php include('includes/footer.html'); ?>
```

After assigning the query to a variable, it is run through the **mysqli_query()** function, which sends the SQL command to the MySQL database. As in the **mysqli_connect.php** script, the **mysqli_query()** call is preceded by @ to suppress any ugly errors. If a problem occurs, the error will be handled more directly in the next step.

9. Report on the success of the registration:

```
if ($r) {
   echo '<h1>Thank you!</h1>
<p>You are now registered.
→ In Chapter 12 you will actually
→ be able to log in!</p><p><br>
→ </p>';
} else {
   echo '<h1>System Error</h1>
   <p class="error">You could not
   → be registered due to a system
   → error. We apologize for any
   → inconvenience.</p>';
   echo '<p>' . mysqli_error($dbc)
   → . '<br><br>Query: ' . $q .
   → '</p>';
} // End of if ($r) IF.
```

The **$r** variable, which is assigned the value returned by **mysqli_query()**, can be used in a conditional to test for the successful operation of the query.

If **$r** has a TRUE value, then a *Thank you!* message is displayed 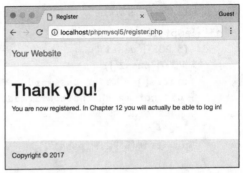. If **$r** has a FALSE value, error messages are printed. For debugging purposes, the error messages will include both the error spit out by MySQL (thanks to the **mysqli_error()** function) and the query that was run 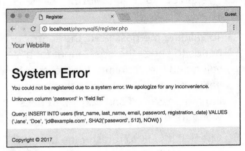. This information is critical to debugging the problem. You would not want to display this kind of information on a live site, however.

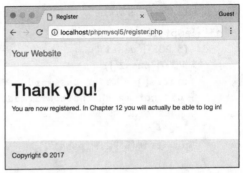

B If the user could be registered in the database, this message is displayed.

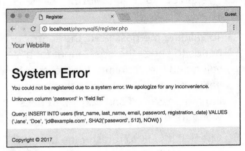

C Any MySQL errors caused by the query will be printed, as will the query that was being run.

Register × Guest

Your Website

Error!

The following error(s) occurred:
- You forgot to enter your last name.
- Your password did not match the confirmed password.

Please try again.

Register

First Name: Jane

Last Name:

Email Address: jd@example.com

Password: ••••••••

Confirm Password:

Register

Copyright © 2017

D Each form validation error is reported to the user so that they may try registering again.

10. Close the database connection and complete the HTML template:

```
mysqli_close($dbc);
include('includes/footer.html');
exit();
```

Closing the connection isn't required but is a good policy. Then the footer is included and the script terminated (thanks to the **exit()** function). If those two lines weren't here, the registration form would be displayed again (which isn't necessary after a successful registration).

11. Print out any error messages and close the submit conditional:

```
} else { // Report the errors.
  echo '<h1>Error!</h1>
  <p class="error">The following
  → error(s) occurred:<br>';
  foreach ($errors as $msg) {
  → // Print each error.
    echo " - $msg<br>\n";
  }
  echo '</p><p>Please try
  → again.</p><p><br></p>';
} // End of if (empty($errors))
→ IF.
} // End of the main Submit
→ conditional.
```

The **else** clause is invoked if there were any errors. In that case, all of the errors are displayed using a **foreach** loop **D**.

The final closing brace closes the main submit conditional. The main conditional is a simple **if**, not an **if-else**, so that the form can be made sticky (again, see Chapter 3).

continues on next page

12. Close the PHP section and begin the HTML form:

```php
?>
<h1>Register</h1>
<form action="register.php"
→ method="post">
  <p>First Name:
  → <input type="text"
  → name="first_name" size="15"
  → maxlength="20" value="<?php if
  → (isset($_POST['first_name']))
  → echo $_POST['first_name']; ?>">
  → </p>
  <p>Last Name: <input type="text"
  → name="last_name" size="15"
  → maxlength="40" value="<?php if
  → (isset($_POST['last_name']))
  → echo $_POST['last_name']; ?>">
  → </p>
```

The form is simple, with one text input for each field in the *users* table (except for the *user_id* and *registration_date* columns, which will automatically be populated). Each input is made sticky, using code like

```php
value="<?php if (isset($_POST['v']))
→ echo $_POST['v']; ?>"
```

Also, I strongly recommend that you use the same name for your form inputs as the corresponding column in the database where that value will be stored. Further, you should set the maximum input length in the form equal to the maximum column length in the database. Such habits help to minimize errors.

13. Complete the HTML form:

```php
  <p>Email Address: <input
  → type="email" name="email"
  → size="20" maxlength="60"
  → value="<?php if
  → (isset($_POST['email'])) echo
  → $_POST['email']; ?>" > </p>
  <p>Password: <input
  → type="password" name="pass1"
  → size="10" maxlength="20"
  → value="<?php if
  → (isset($_POST['pass1'])) echo
  → $_POST['pass1']; ?>" ></p>
  <p>Confirm Password: <input
  → type="password" name="pass2"
  → size="10" maxlength="20"
  → value="<?php if
  → (isset($_POST['pass2'])) echo
  → $_POST['pass2']; ?>" ></p>
  <p><input type="submit"
  → name="submit"
  → value="Register"></p>
</form>
```

This is all much like that in Step 12, with the addition of a submit button.

As a side note, I don't need to follow my **maxlength** recommendation (from Step 12) with the password inputs, because they will be encrypted with **SHA2()**, which always creates a string of a fixed length. And since there are two password inputs, they can't both use the same name as the column in the database.

14. Complete the template:

```php
<?php include('includes/
→ footer.html'); ?>
```

15. Save the file as **register.php**, place it in your web directory, and test it in your browser.

Note that if you use an apostrophe in one of the form values, it will likely break the query 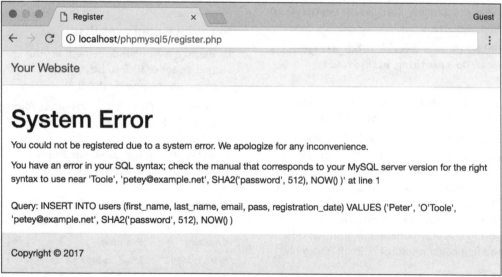 **E**. The section "Ensuring Secure SQL" later in this chapter will show how to protect against this.

TIP After running the script, you can always ensure that it worked by using the mysql client or phpMyAdmin to view the records in the users table.

TIP You should not end your queries with a semicolon in PHP, as you do when using the mysql client. When working with MySQL, this is a common, albeit harmless, mistake to make. When working with other database applications (Oracle, for one), doing so will make your queries unusable.

TIP As a reminder, the mysqli_query() function returns a TRUE value if the query could be executed on the database without error. This does not necessarily mean that the result of the query is what you were expecting. Later scripts will demonstrate how to more accurately gauge the success of a query.

TIP You are not obligated to create a $q variable as I tend to do; you could directly insert your query text into mysqli_query(). However, as the construction of your queries becomes more complex, using a variable will be the only option.

TIP Practically any query you would run in the mysql client can also be executed using mysqli_query().

TIP Another benefit of the Improved MySQL Extension over the standard extension is that the mysqli_multi_query() function lets you execute multiple queries at one time. The syntax for doing so, particularly if the queries return results, is a bit more complicated, so see the PHP manual if you have this need.

E Apostrophes in form values (like the last name here) will conflict with the apostrophes used to delineate values in the query.

Retrieving Query Results

The preceding section of this chapter demonstrates how to execute simple queries on a MySQL database. A *simple query*, as I'm calling it, could be defined as one that begins with **INSERT**, **UPDATE**, **DELETE**, or **ALTER**. What all four of these have in common is that they return no data, just an indication of their success. Conversely, a **SELECT** query generates information—it will return rows of records—that has to be handled by other PHP functions.

The primary tool for handling **SELECT** query results is **mysqli_fetch_array()**, which uses the query result variable (that I've been calling **$r**) and returns one row of data at a time, in an array format. You'll want to use this function within a loop that will continue to access every returned row as long as there are more to be read. The basic construction for reading every record from a query is

```
while ($row = mysqli_fetch_array($r)) {
    // Do something with $row.
}
```

You will almost always want to use a **while** loop to fetch the results from a **SELECT** query.

The **mysqli_fetch_array()** function takes an optional second parameter specifying what type of array is returned: associative, indexed, or both. An associative array allows you to refer to column values by name, whereas an indexed array requires you to use only numbers, starting at 0 for the first column returned. Each parameter

is defined by a constant listed in **Table 9.1**, with **MYSQLI_BOTH** being the default. The **MYSQLI_NUM** setting is marginally faster and uses less memory than the other options. Conversely, **MYSQLI_ASSOC** is more overt (**$row['column']** rather than **$row[3]**) and may continue to work even if the query changes.

An optional step you can take when using **mysqli_fetch_array()** would be to free up the query result resources once you are done using them:

```
mysqli_free_result($r);
```

This line removes the overhead (memory) taken by **$r**. It's an optional step, since PHP will automatically free up the resources at the end of a script, but—like using **mysqli_close()**—it does make for good programming form.

To demonstrate how to handle results returned by a query, let's create a script for viewing all the currently registered users.

To retrieve query results:

1. Begin a new PHP document in your text editor or IDE, to be named **view_users.php** (Script 9.4):

   ```php
   <?php # Script 9.4 - view_users.php
   $page_title = 'View the Current
   → Users';
   include('includes/header.html');
   echo '<h1>Registered Users</h1>';
   ```

TABLE 9.1 mysqli_fetch_array() Constants

Constant	Example
MYSQLI_ASSOC	$row['column']
MYSQLI_NUM	$row[0]
MYSQLI_BOTH	$row[0] or $row['column']

2. Connect to and query the database:

```
require('../mysqli_connect.php');
$q = "SELECT CONCAT(last_name,
→', ', first_name) AS name,
→ DATE_FORMAT(registration_date,
→ '%M %d, %Y') AS dr FROM users
→ ORDER BY registration_date ASC";
$r = @mysqli_query ($dbc, $q);
```

The query here will return two columns
Ⓐ: the users' names (formatted as *Last
Name, First Name*) and the date they
registered (formatted as *Month DD,
YYYY*). Because both columns are formatted using MySQL functions, aliases
are given to the returned results (*name*
and *dr*, accordingly). See Chapter 5 if
you are confused by any of this syntax.

```
● ● ●      PHP and MySQL for Dynamic Web Sites
mysql> SELECT CONCAT(last_name, ', ', first_name) AS
name, DATE_FORMAT(registration_date, '%M %d, %Y') AS
dr FROM users ORDER BY registration_date ASC;
+----------------------+----------------+
| name                 | dr             |
+----------------------+----------------+
| Ullman, Larry        | May 11, 2017   |
| Isabella, Zoe        | May 11, 2017   |
| Lennon, John         | May 11, 2017   |
| McCartney, Paul      | May 11, 2017   |
| Harrison, George     | May 11, 2017   |
| Starr, Ringo         | May 11, 2017   |
| Jones, David         | May 11, 2017   |
| Dolenz, Micky        | May 11, 2017   |
| Nesmith, mike        | May 11, 2017   |
| Sedaris, David       | May 11, 2017   |
| Hornby, Nick         | May 11, 2017   |
| Bank, Melissa        | May 11, 2017   |
| Morrison, Toni       | May 11, 2017   |
| Franzen, Jonathan    | May 11, 2017   |
| DeLillo, Don         | May 11, 2017   |
| Greene, Graham       | May 11, 2017   |
| Chabon, Michael      | May 11, 2017   |
| Brautigan, Richard   | May 11, 2017   |
| Banks, Russell       | May 11, 2017   |
| Simpson, Homer       | May 11, 2017   |
| Simpson, Marge       | May 11, 2017   |
| Simpson, Bart        | May 11, 2017   |
| Simpson, Lisa        | May 11, 2017   |
| Simpson, Maggie      | May 11, 2017   |
| Simpson, Abe         | May 11, 2017   |
| Doe, Jane            | June 26, 2017  |
+----------------------+----------------+
26 rows in set (0.00 sec)

mysql> █
```

Ⓐ The query results as run within the mysql client.

3. Create an HTML table for displaying the
query results:

```
if ($r) {
  echo '<table width="60%">
  <thead>
  <tr>
    <th align="left">Name</th>
    <th align="left">Date
    → Registered</th>
  </tr>
  </thead>
  <tbody>
';
```

If the **$r** variable has a TRUE value,
then the query ran without error and
the results can be displayed. To do that,
start by making a table and a header
row in HTML.

4. Fetch and print each returned record:

```
while ($row = mysqli_fetch_array
→ ($r, MYSQLI_ASSOC)) {
  echo '<tr><td align="left">' .
  → $row['name'] . '</td><td
  → align="left">' . $row['dr'] .
  → '</td></tr>
  ';
}
```

Next, loop through the results using
mysqli_fetch_array() and print each
fetched row. Notice that within the
while loop, the code refers to each
returned value using the proper alias:
$row['name'] and **$row['dr']**. The script
could not refer to **$row['first_name']**
or **$row['date_registered']** because
no such field name was returned Ⓐ.

continues on page 287

Script 9.4 The `view_users.php` script runs a static query on the database and prints all the returned rows.

```
1    <?php # Script 9.4 - view_users.php
2    // This script retrieves all the records from the users table.
3
4    $page_title = 'View the Current Users';
5    include('includes/header.html');
6
7    // Page header:
8    echo '<h1>Registered Users</h1>';
9
10   require('../mysqli_connect.php'); // Connect to the db.
11
12   // Make the query:
13   $q = "SELECT CONCAT(last_name, ', ', first_name) AS name, DATE_FORMAT(registration_date,
     '%M %d, %Y') AS dr FROM users ORDER BY registration_date ASC";
14   $r = @mysqli_query($dbc, $q); // Run the query.
15
16   if ($r) { // If it ran OK, display the records.
17
18       // Table header.
19       echo '<table width="60%">
20       <thead>
21       <tr>
22           <th align="left">Name</th>
23           <th align="left">Date Registered</th>
24       </tr>
25       </thead>
26       <tbody>
27   ';
28
29       // Fetch and print all the records:
30       while ($row = mysqli_fetch_array($r, MYSQLI_ASSOC)) {
31           echo '<tr><td align="left">' . $row['name'] . '</td><td align="left">' . $row['dr'] .
         '</td></tr>
32           ';
33       }
34
35       echo '</tbody></table>'; // Close the table.
36
37       mysqli_free_result($r); // Free up the resources.
38
39   } else { // If it did not run OK.
40
41       // Public message:
42       echo '<p class="error">The current users could not be retrieved. We apologize for any
         inconvenience.</p>';
43
44       // Debugging message:
45       echo '<p>' . mysqli_error($dbc) . '<br><br>Query: ' . $q . '</p>';
46
47   } // End of if ($r) IF.
48
49   mysqli_close($dbc); // Close the database connection.
50
51   include('includes/footer.html');
52   ?>
```

5. Close the HTML table and free up the query resources:

```
echo '</tbody></table>';
mysqli_free_result($r);
```

Again, this is an optional step but a good one to take.

6. Complete the main conditional:

```
} else {
    echo '<p class="error">The
    → current users could not be
    → retrieved. We apologize for
    → any inconvenience.</p>';
    echo '<p>' . mysqli_error($dbc)
    → . '<br><br>Query: ' . $q .
    → '</p>';
} // End of if ($r) IF.
```

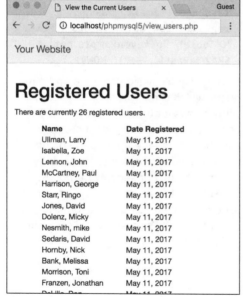

B All of the user records are retrieved from the database and displayed in the browser.

As in the **register.php** example, there are two kinds of error messages here. The first is a generic message, the type you'd show in a live site. The second is much more detailed, printing both the MySQL error and the query—both are critical for debugging purposes.

7. Close the database connection and finish the page:

```
mysqli_close($dbc);
include('includes/footer.html');
?>
```

8. Save the file as **view_users.php**, place it in your web directory, and test it in your browser **B**.

TIP The function `mysqli_fetch_row()` is the equivalent of `mysqli_fetch_array ($r, MYSQLI_NUM);`.

TIP The function `mysqli_fetch_assoc()` is the equivalent of `mysqli_fetch_array ($r, MYSQLI_ASSOC);`.

TIP As with any associative array, when you retrieve records from the database, you must refer to the selected columns or aliases exactly as they are in the database or query. In other words, the keys are case-sensitive.

TIP If you are in a situation where you need to run a second query inside your while loop, be certain to use different variable names for that query. For example, the inner query would use `$r2` and `$row2` instead of `$r` and `$row`. If you don't do this, you'll encounter logical errors.

TIP I sometimes see beginning PHP developers muddle the process of fetching query results. Remember that you must execute the query using `mysqli_query()`, and then use `mysqli_fetch_array()` to retrieve a single row of information. If you have multiple rows to retrieve, use a `while` loop.

Ensuring Secure SQL

Database security with respect to PHP comes down to three broad issues:

- Protecting the MySQL access information
- Not revealing too much about the database
- Being cautious when running queries, particularly those involving user-submitted data

You can accomplish the first objective by securing the MySQL connection script outside of the web directory so that it is never viewable through a browser (see **ⓒ** in "Connecting to MySQL" earlier). I discussed this in some detail earlier in the chapter. The second objective is attained by not letting the user see PHP's error messages or your queries: in these scripts, that information is printed for your debugging purposes; you'd never want to do that on a live site.

For the third objective, there are numerous steps you can and should take, all based on the premise of never trusting user-supplied data. First, validate that some value has been submitted or that it is of the proper type (number, string, etc.). Second, use the Filter extension (discussed in Chapter 13) or regular expressions

(discussed in Chapter 14, "Perl-Compatible Regular Expressions") to make sure that submitted data matches what you would expect it to be. Third, you can typecast some values to guarantee that they're numbers. A fourth recommendation is to run user-submitted data through the `mysqli_real_escape_string()` function. This function makes data safe to use in a query by escaping what could be problematic characters. It's used like so:

```
$safe = mysqli_real_escape_string
→ ($dbc, data);
```

To understand why this is necessary, see **ⓔ** in "Executing Simple Queries" earlier. The use of the apostrophe in the user's last name made the query syntactically invalid:

```
INSERT INTO users (first_name,
→ last_name, email, pass,
→ registration_date) VALUES ('Peter',
→ 'O'Toole', 'petey@example.net',
→ SHA2('aPass8', 512), NOW() )
```

In that example, valid user data broke the query, which is not good. But if your PHP script allows for this possibility, a malicious user can purposefully submit problematic characters—the apostrophe being one example—to hack into, or damage, your database. For security purposes, `mysqli_real_escape_string()` should be used on every text input in a form. To demonstrate this, let's revamp **register.php** (Script 9.3).

To use mysqli_real_escape_string():

1. Open **register.php** (Script 9.3) in your text editor or IDE, if you haven't already.

2. Move the inclusion of the **mysqli_connect.php** file (line 48 in Script 9.3) to just after the main conditional (**Script 9.5**).

   Because the **mysqli_real_escape_string()** function requires a database connection, the **mysqli_connect.php** script must be required earlier in the script.

3. Change the validation routines to use the **mysqli_real_escape_string()** function, replacing each occurrence of **$var = trim($_POST['var'])** with **$var = mysqli_real_escape_string($dbc, trim($_POST['var']))**:

```
$fn = mysqli_real_escape_string
  ➝ ($dbc, trim($_POST['first_name']));
$ln = mysqli_real_escape_string
  ➝ ($dbc, trim($_POST['last_name']));
$e = mysqli_real_escape_string
  ➝ ($dbc, trim($_POST['email']));
$p = mysqli_real_escape_string
  ➝ ($dbc, trim($_POST['pass1']));
```

Instead of just assigning the submitted value to each variable (**$fn, $ln**, etc.), the values will be run through the **mysqli_real_escape_string()** function first. The **trim()** function is still used to get rid of any unnecessary spaces.

continues on page 291

Script 9.5 The **register.php** script now uses the **mysqli_real_escape_string()** function to make submitted data safe to use in a query.

```
1    <?php # Script 9.5 - register.php #2
2    // This script performs an INSERT query to add a record to the users table.
3
4    $page_title = 'Register';
5    include('includes/header.html');
6
7    // Check for form submission:
8    if ($_SERVER['REQUEST_METHOD'] == 'POST') {
9
10       require('../mysqli_connect.php'); // Connect to the db.
11
12       $errors = []; // Initialize an error array.
13
14       // Check for a first name:
15       if (empty($_POST['first_name'])) {
16           $errors[] = 'You forgot to enter your first name.';
17       } else {
18           $fn = mysqli_real_escape_string($dbc, trim($_POST['first_name']));
19       }
20
21       // Check for a last name:
22       if (empty($_POST['last_name'])) {
23           $errors[] = 'You forgot to enter your last name.';
```

code continues on next page

```
24      } else {
25          $ln = mysqli_real_escape_string($dbc, trim($_POST['last_name']));
26      }
27
28      // Check for an email address:
29      if (empty($_POST['email'])) {
30          $errors[] = 'You forgot to enter your email address.';
31      } else {
32          $e = mysqli_real_escape_string($dbc, trim($_POST['email']));
33      }
34
35      // Check for a password and match against the confirmed password:
36      if (!empty($_POST['pass1'])) {
37          if ($_POST['pass1'] != $_POST['pass2']) {
38              $errors[] = 'Your password did not match the confirmed password.';
39          } else {
40              $p = mysqli_real_escape_string($dbc, trim($_POST['pass1']));
41          }
42      } else {
43          $errors[] = 'You forgot to enter your password.';
44      }
45
46      if (empty($errors)) { // If everything's OK.
47
48          // Register the user in the database...
49
50          // Make the query:
51          $q = "INSERT INTO users (first_name, last_name, email, pass, registration_date) VALUES
              ('$fn', '$ln', '$e', SHA2('$p', 512), NOW() )";
52          $r = @mysqli_query ($dbc, $q); // Run the query.
53          if ($r) { // If it ran OK.
54
55              // Print a message:
56              echo '<h1>Thank you!</h1>
57          <p>You are now registered. In Chapter 12 you will actually be able to log in!
              </p><p><br></p>';
58
59          } else { // If it did not run OK.
60
61              // Public message:
62              echo '<h1>System Error</h1>
63          <p class="error">You could not be registered due to a system error. We apologize for
              any inconvenience.</p>';
64
65              // Debugging message:
66              echo '<p>' . mysqli_error($dbc) . '<br><br>Query: ' . $q . '</p>';
67
68          } // End of if ($r) IF.
69
```

code continues on next page

4. Add a second call to `mysqli_close()` before the end of the main conditional:

`mysqli_close($dbc);`

To be consistent, since the database connection is opened as the first step of the main conditional, it should be closed as the last step of this same conditional. It still needs to be closed before including the footer and terminating the script (lines 73 and 74), though.

Script 9.5 *continued*

```
70        mysqli_close($dbc); // Close the database connection.
71
72        // Include the footer and quit the script:
73        include('includes/footer.html');
74        exit();
75
76    } else { // Report the errors.
77
78        echo '<h1>Error!</h1>
79        <p class="error">The following error(s) occurred:<br>';
80        foreach ($errors as $msg) { // Print each error.
81            echo " - $msg<br>\n";
82        }
83        echo '</p><p>Please try again.</p><p><br></p>';
84
85    } // End of if (empty($errors)) IF.
86
87    mysqli_close($dbc); // Close the database connection.
88
89 } // End of the main Submit conditional.
90 ?>
91 <h1>Register</h1>
92 <form action="register.php" method="post">
93    <p>First Name: <input type="text" name="first_name" size="15" maxlength="20" value="<?php
       if (isset($_POST['first_name'])) echo $_POST['first_name']; ?>"></p>
94    <p>Last Name: <input type="text" name="last_name" size="15" maxlength="40" value="<?php
       if (isset($_POST['last_name'])) echo $_POST['last_name']; ?>"></p>
95    <p>Email Address: <input type="email" name="email" size="20" maxlength="60" value="<?php
       if (isset($_POST['email'])) echo $_POST['email']; ?>" > </p>
96    <p>Password: <input type="password" name="pass1" size="10" maxlength="20" value="<?php
       if (isset($_POST['pass1'])) echo $_POST['pass1']; ?>" ></p>
97    <p>Confirm Password: <input type="password" name="pass2" size="10" maxlength="20"
       value="<?php if (isset($_POST['pass2'])) echo $_POST['pass2']; ?>" ></p>
98    <p><input type="submit" name="submit" value="Register"></p>
99 </form>
100 <?php include('includes/footer.html'); ?>
```

5. Save the file as **register.php**, place it in your web directory, and test it in your browser  and 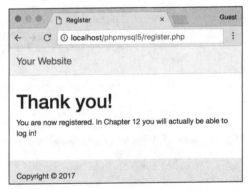.

TIP The `mysqli_real_escape_string()` function escapes a string in accordance with the language being used (i.e., the collation), which is an advantage using this function has over alternative solutions.

TIP If you see results like those in **C**, it means that the `mysqli_real_escape_string()` function cannot access the database (because it has no connection, like `$dbc`).

TIP If you look at the values stored in the database (using the mysql client, phpMyAdmin, or the like), you will not see the apostrophes and other problematic characters stored with preceding backslashes. This is correct. The backslashes keep the problematic characters from breaking the query, but the backslashes are not themselves stored.

A Values with apostrophes in them, like a person's last name, will no longer break the **INSERT** query, thanks to the `mysqli_real_ escape_ string()` function.

B Now the registration process will handle problematic characters and be more secure.

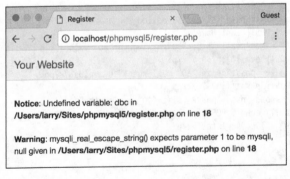

C Since the `mysqli_real_escape_string()` function requires a database connection, using it without that connection (e.g., before including the connection script) can lead to other errors.

Counting Returned Records

The next function to discuss is `mysqli_num_rows()`. This function returns the number of rows retrieved by a **SELECT** query. It takes one argument, the query result variable:

```
$num = mysqli_num_rows($r);
```

Although simple in purpose, this function is very useful. It's necessary if you want to paginate your query results (an example of this can be found in the next chapter). It's also a good idea to use this function before you attempt to fetch any results using a **while** loop (because there's no need to fetch the results if there aren't any, and attempting to do so may cause errors). In this next sequence of steps, let's modify **view_users.php** to list the total number of registered users.

To modify `view_users.php`:

1. Open **view_users.php** (refer to Script 9.4) in your text editor or IDE, if you haven't already.

2. Before the `if ($r)` conditional, add this line (**Script 9.6**):

   ```
   $num = mysqli_num_rows($r);
   ```

   This line will assign the number of rows returned by the query to the **$num** variable.

3. Change the original **$r** conditional to

   ```
   if ($num > 0) {
   ```

   The conditional as it was written before was based on whether the query did or did not successfully run, not whether any records were returned. Now it will be more accurate.

   continues on next page

Script 9.6 Now the **view_users.php** script will display the total number of registered users, thanks to the `mysqli_num_rows()` function.

```
1   <?php # Script 9.6 - view_users.php #2
2   // This script retrieves all the records from the users table.
3
4   $page_title = 'View the Current Users';
5   include('includes/header.html');
6
7   // Page header:
8   echo '<h1>Registered Users</h1>';
9
10  require('../mysqli_connect.php'); // Connect to the db.
11
12  // Make the query:
13  $q = "SELECT CONCAT(last_name, ', ', first_name) AS name, DATE_FORMAT(registration_date,
       '%M %d, %Y') AS dr FROM users ORDER BY registration_date ASC";
14  $r = @mysqli_query($dbc, $q); // Run the query.
15
16  // Count the number of returned rows:
17  $num = mysqli_num_rows($r);
18
```

code continues on next page

4. Before creating the HTML table, print the number of registered users:

```
echo "<p>There are currently
→ $num registered users.</p>\n";
```

Script 9.6 *continued*

```
19   if ($num > 0) { // If it ran OK, display the records.
20
21       // Print how many users there are:
22       echo "<p>There are currently $num registered users.</p>\n";
23
24       // Table header.
25       echo '<table width="60%">
26       <thead>
27       <tr>
28           <th align="left">Name</th>
29           <th align="left">Date Registered</th>
30       </tr>
31       </thead>
32       <tbody>
33       ';
34
35       // Fetch and print all the records:
36       while ($row = mysqli_fetch_array($r, MYSQLI_ASSOC)) {
37           echo '<tr><td align="left">' . $row['name'] . '</td><td align="left">' . $row['dr'] .
             '</td></tr>
38           ';
39       }
40
41       echo '</tbody></table>'; // Close the table.
42
43       mysqli_free_result($r); // Free up the resources.
44
45   } else { // If no records were returned.
46
47       echo '<p class="error">There are currently no registered users.</p>';
48
49   }
50
51   mysqli_close($dbc); // Close the database connection.
52
53   include('includes/footer.html');
54   ?>
```

Modifying `register.php`

The `mysqli_num_rows()` function could be applied to `register.php` to prevent someone from registering with the same email address multiple times. Although the **UNIQUE** index on that column in the database will prevent that from happening, such attempts will create a MySQL error. To avoid this using PHP, run a **SELECT** query to confirm that the email address isn't currently registered. That query would be simply

```
SELECT user_id FROM users WHERE
→ email='$e'
```

You would run this query (using the `mysqli_query()` function) and then call `mysqli_num_rows()`. If `mysqli_num_rows()` returns 0, you know that the email address hasn't already been registered and it's safe to run the **INSERT**.

5. Change the **else** part of the main conditional to read

   ```
   echo '<p class="error">There are
   → currently no registered users.
   → </p>';
   ```

   The original conditional was based on whether the query worked. Hopefully, you've successfully debugged the query so that it is working and the original error messages are no longer needed. Now the error message just indicates if no records were returned.

6. Save the file as **view_users.php**, place it in your web directory, and test it in your browser 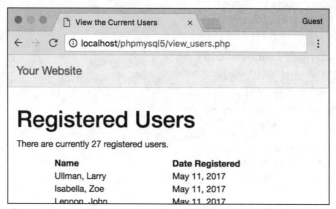.

Ⓐ The number of registered users is now displayed at the top of the page.

Updating Records with PHP

The last technique in this chapter shows how to update database records through a PHP script. Doing so requires an **UPDATE** query, and its successful execution can be verified with PHP's `mysqli_affected_rows()` function.

While the `mysqli_num_rows()` function will return the number of rows generated by a **SELECT** query, `mysqli_affected_rows()` returns the number of rows affected by an **INSERT**, **UPDATE**, or **DELETE** query. It's used like so:

`$num = mysqli_affected_rows($dbc);`

Unlike `mysqli_num_rows()`, the one argument the function takes is the database connection (`$dbc`), not the results of the previous query (`$r`).

The following example will be a script that allows registered users to change their password. It demonstrates two important ideas:

- Checking a submitted username and password against registered values (the key to a login system as well)

- Updating database records using the primary key as a reference

As with the registration example, this one PHP script will both display the form  and handle it.

Ⓐ The form for changing a user's password.

To update records with PHP:

1. Begin a new PHP script in your text editor or IDE, to be named **password.php** (Script 9.7):

```
<?php # Script 9.7 - password.php
$page_title = 'Change Your
→ Password';
include('includes/header.html');
```

2. Start the main conditional:

```
if ($_SERVER['REQUEST_METHOD'] ==
→ 'POST') {
```

Since this page both displays and handles the form, it'll use the standard conditional to check for the form's submission.

3. Include the database connection and create an array for storing errors:

```
require('../mysqli_connect.php');
$errors = [];
```

The initial part of this script mimics the registration form.

4. Validate the email address and current password fields:

```
if (empty($_POST['email'])) {
  $errors[] = 'You forgot to
  → enter your email address. ';
} else {
  $e = mysqli_real_escape_string
  → ($dbc, trim($_POST['email']));
}
if (empty($_POST['pass'])) {
  $errors[] = 'You forgot to
  → enter your current password. ';
} else {
  $p = mysqli_real_escape_string
  → ($dbc, trim($_POST['pass']));
}
```

The form Ⓐ has four inputs: the email address, the current password, and two for the new password. The process for validating each of these is the same as it is in **register.php**. Any data that passes the validation test will be trimmed and run through the **mysqli_real_escape_string()** function so that it is safe to use in a query.

continues on page 299

Script 9.7 The **password.php** script runs an **UPDATE** query on the database and uses the **mysqli_affected_rows()** function to confirm the change.

```
1    <?php # Script 9.7 - password.php
2    // This page lets a user change their password.
3
4    $page_title = 'Change Your Password';
5    include('includes/header.html');
6
7    // Check for form submission:
8    if ($_SERVER['REQUEST_METHOD'] == 'POST') {
9
10       require('../mysqli_connect.php'); // Connect to the db.
11
12       $errors = []; // Initialize an error array.
13
14       // Check for an email address:
```

code continues on next page

```
15      if (empty($_POST['email'])) {
16          $errors[] = 'You forgot to enter your email address.';
17      } else {
18          $e = mysqli_real_escape_string($dbc, trim($_POST['email']));
19      }
20
21      // Check for the current password:
22      if (empty($_POST['pass'])) {
23          $errors[] = 'You forgot to enter your current password.';
24      } else {
25          $p = mysqli_real_escape_string($dbc, trim($_POST['pass']));
26      }
27
28      // Check for a new password and match
29      // against the confirmed password:
30      if (!empty($_POST['pass1'])) {
31          if ($_POST['pass1'] != $_POST['pass2']) {
32              $errors[] = 'Your new password did not match the confirmed password.';
33          } else {
34              $np = mysqli_real_escape_string($dbc, trim($_POST['pass1']));
35          }
36      } else {
37          $errors[] = 'You forgot to enter your new password.';
38      }
39
40      if (empty($errors)) { // If everything's OK.
41
42          // Check that they've entered the right email address/password combination:
43          $q = "SELECT user_id FROM users WHERE (email='$e' AND pass=SHA2('$p', 512) )";
44          $r = @mysqli_query($dbc, $q);
45          $num = @mysqli_num_rows($r);
46          if ($num == 1) { // Match was made.
47
48              // Get the user_id:
49              $row = mysqli_fetch_array($r, MYSQLI_NUM);
50
51              // Make the UPDATE query:
52              $q = "UPDATE users SET pass=SHA2('$np', 512) WHERE user_id=$row[0]";
53              $r = @mysqli_query($dbc, $q);
54
55              if (mysqli_affected_rows($dbc) == 1) { // If it ran OK.
56
57                  // Print a message.
58                  echo '<h1>Thank you!</h1>
59                  <p>Your password has been updated. In Chapter 12 you will actually be able to log
                    in!</p><p><br></p>';
60
61              } else { // If it did not run OK.
62
```

code continues on page 300

5. Validate the new password:

```php
if (!empty($_POST['pass1'])) {
  if ($_POST['pass1'] !=
  →$_POST['pass2']) {
    $errors[] = 'Your new
    →password did not match the
    →confirmed password. ';
  } else {
    $np = mysqli_real_escape_
    →string($dbc, trim
    →($_POST['pass1']));
  }
} else {
  $errors[] = 'You forgot to
  →enter your new password. ';
}
```

This code is also exactly like that in the registration script, except that a valid new password is assigned to a variable called **$np** (because **$p** represents the current password).

6. If all the tests are passed, retrieve the user's ID:

```php
if (empty($errors)) {
  $q = "SELECT user_id FROM users
  WHERE (email='$e' AND pass=SHA2
  →('$p', 512) )";
  $r = @mysqli_query($dbc, $q);
  $num = @mysqli_num_rows($r);
```

This first query will return just the *user_id* field for the record that matches the submitted email address and password **B**. To compare the submitted password against the stored one, encrypt it again with the **SHA1()** function. If the user is registered and has correctly entered both the email address and password, exactly one column from one row will be selected (since the email value must be unique across all rows). Finally, this one record is assigned as an array (of one element) to the **$row** variable.

If this part of the script doesn't work for you, apply the standard debugging methods: remove the error suppression operators (@) so that you can see what errors, if any, occur; use the **mysqli_error()** function to report any MySQL errors; and print, then run the query using another interface **B**.

7. Update the database for the new password:

```php
$q = "UPDATE users SET pass=SHA2
→('$np', 512) WHERE user_id=$row
→[0]";
$r = @mysqli_query($dbc, $q);
```

This query will change the password—using the new submitted value—where the *user_id* column is equal to the number retrieved from the previous query.

continues on page 301

```
● ● ●  PHP and MySQL for Dyna...
mysql> SELECT user_id FROM users
WHERE (email='email@example.com'
AND pass=SHA2('password', 512) );
+---------+
| user_id |
+---------+
|       1 |
+---------+
1 row in set (0.00 sec)

mysql> ▮
```

B The result when running the **SELECT** query from the script (the first of two queries it has) within the mysql client.

```
63              // Public message:
64              echo '<h1>System Error</h1>
65              <p class="error">Your password could not be changed due to a system error.
                We apologize for any inconvenience.</p>';
66
67              // Debugging message:
68              echo '<p>' . mysqli_error($dbc) . '<br><br>Query: ' . $q . '</p>';
69
70          }
71
72          mysqli_close($dbc); // Close the database connection.
73
74          // Include the footer and quit the script (to not show the form).
75          include('includes/footer.html');
76          exit();
77
78      } else { // Invalid email address/password combination.
79          echo '<h1>Error!</h1>
80          <p class="error">The email address and password do not match those on file.</p>';
81      }
82
83  } else { // Report the errors.
84
85      echo '<h1>Error!</h1>
86      <p class="error">The following error(s) occurred:<br>';
87      foreach ($errors as $msg) { // Print each error.
88          echo " - $msg<br>\n";
89      }
90      echo '</p><p>Please try again.</p><p><br></p>';
91
92  } // End of if (empty($errors)) IF.
93
94  mysqli_close($dbc); // Close the database connection.
95
96  } // End of the main Submit conditional.
97  ?>
98  <h1>Change Your Password</h1>
99  <form action="password.php" method="post">
100     <p>Email Address: <input type="email" name="email" size="20" maxlength="60" value="<?php
        if (isset($_POST['email'])) echo $_POST['email']; ?>" > </p>
101     <p>Current Password: <input type="password" name="pass" size="10" maxlength="20"
        value="<?php if (isset($_POST['pass'])) echo $_POST['pass']; ?>" ></p>
102     <p>New Password: <input type="password" name="pass1" size="10" maxlength="20" value="<?php
        if (isset($_POST['pass1'])) echo $_POST['pass1']; ?>" ></p>
103     <p>Confirm New Password: <input type="password" name="pass2" size="10" maxlength="20"
        value="<?php if (isset($_POST['pass2'])) echo $_POST['pass2']; ?>" ></p>
104     <p><input type="submit" name="submit" value="Change Password"></p>
105 </form>
106 <?php include('includes/footer.html'); ?>
```

8. Check the results of the query:

```php
if (mysqli_affected_rows($dbc) ==
→ 1) {
  echo '<h1>Thank you!</h1>
  <p>Your password has been
  → updated. In Chapter 12 you
  → will actually be able to log
  → in!</p><p><br></p>';
} else { // If it did not run OK.
  echo '<h1>System Error</h1>
  <p class="error">Your password
  → could not be changed due to a
  → system error. We apologize
  → for any inconvenience.</p>';
  echo '<p>' . mysqli_error($dbc)
  → . '<br><br>Query: ' . $q .
  → '</p>';
}
```

This part of the script again works like **register.php**. In this case, if **mysqli_affected_rows()** returns the number 1, the record has been updated, and a success message will be printed. If not, both a public, generic message and a more useful debugging message will be printed.

9. Close the database connection, include the footer, and terminate the script:

```php
mysqli_close($dbc);
include('includes/footer.html');
exit();
```

At this point in the script, the **UPDATE** query has been run. It either worked or it did not (because of a system error). In both cases, there's no need to show the form again, so the footer is included (to complete the page) and the script is terminated, using the **exit()** function. Prior to that, just to be thorough, the database connection is closed.

10. Complete the **if ($num == 1)** conditional:

```php
} else {
  echo '<h1>Error!</h1>
  <p class="error">The email
  → address and password do not
  → match those on file.</p>';
}
```

If **mysqli_num_rows()** does not return a value of 1, then the submitted email address and password do not match those in the database and this error is printed. In this case, the form will be displayed again so that the user can enter the correct information.

11. Print any validation error messages:

```php
} else {
  echo '<h1>Error!</h1>
  <p class="error">The following
  → error(s) occurred:<br>';
  foreach ($errors as $msg) {
    echo " - $msg<br>\n";
  }
  echo '</p><p>Please try again.
  → </p><p><br></p>';
} // End of if (empty($errors)) IF.
```

This **else** clause applies if the **$errors** array is not empty (which means that the form data did not pass all the validation tests). As in the registration page, the errors will be printed.

12. Close the database connection and complete the PHP code:

```php
  mysqli_close($dbc);
}
?>
```

continues on next page

13. Display the form:

```
<h1>Change Your Password</h1>
<form action="password.php"
method="post">
  <p>Email Address: <input
  → type="email" name="email"
  → size="20" maxlength="60"
  → value="<?php if
  → (isset($_POST['email']))
  → echo $_POST['email']; ?>" >
  → </p>
  <p>Current Password: <input
  → type="password" name="pass"
  → size="10" maxlength="20"
  → value="<?php if
  → (isset($_POST['pass'])) echo
  → $_POST['pass']; ?>" ></p>
  <p>New Password: <input
  → type="password" name="pass1"
  → size="10" maxlength="20"
  → value="<?php if
  → (isset($_POST['pass1'])) echo
  → $_POST['pass1']; ?>" ></p>
  <p>Confirm New Password:
  → <input type="password"
  → name="pass2" size="10"
  → maxlength="20" value="<?php
  → if (isset($_POST['pass2'])) echo
  → $_POST['pass2']; ?>" ></p>
  <p><input type="submit"
  → name="submit" value="Change
  → Password"></p>
</form>
```

The form takes three different inputs of type password—the current password, the new one, and a confirmation of the new password—and one email input for the email address. Every input is sticky, too.

14. Include the footer file:

```
<?php include('includes/
→ footer.html'); ?>
```

15. Save the file as **password.php**, place it in your web directory, and test it in your browser **C** and **D**.

C The password was changed in the database.

D If the entered email address and password don't match those on file, the password will not be updated.

TIP If you delete every record from a table using the command TRUNCATE tablename, mysqli_affected_rows() will return 0, even if the query was successful and every row was removed. This is just a quirk.

TIP If an UPDATE query runs but does not actually change the value of any column (for example, a password is replaced with the same password), mysqli_affected_rows() will return 0.

TIP The mysqli_affected_rows() conditional used here could (and maybe should) also be applied to the register.php script to confirm that one record was added. That would be a more exacting condition to check than if ($r).

Review and Pursue

If you have any problems with the review questions or the pursue prompts, turn to the book's supporting forum (`LarryUllman.com/forums/`).

Review

- What version of PHP are you using? What version of MySQL? Does your PHP-MySQL combination support the Improved MySQL Extension?

- What is the most important sequence of steps for debugging PHP-MySQL problems (explicitly covered at the end of Chapter 8, "Error Handling and Debugging")?

- What hostname, username, and password combination do you, specifically, use to connect to MySQL?

- What PHP code is used to connect to a MySQL server, select the database, and establish the encoding?

- What encoding are you using? Why is it necessary for the PHP scripts to use the same encoding that is used to interact with MySQL as is used for storing the text in the database?

- Why is it preferable to store the `mysqli_connect.php` script outside of the web root directory? And what is the web root directory?

- Why shouldn't live sites show MySQL errors and the queries being run?

- What syntax will you almost always use to handle the results of a **SELECT** query? What syntax could you use if the **SELECT** query returns only a single row?

- Why is it important to use the `mysqli_real_escape_string()` function?

- After what kind of queries would you use the `mysqli_num_rows()` function?

- After what types of queries would you use the `mysqli_affected_rows()` function?

Pursue

- If you don't remember how the template system works, or how to use the `include()` function, revisit Chapter 3.

- Use the information covered in Chapter 8 to apply your own custom error handler to this site's examples.

- Change the use of `mysqli_num_rows()` in **view_users.php** so that it's called only if the query had a TRUE result.

- Apply the `mysqli_num_rows()` function to **register.php**, as suggested in the "Modifying register.php" sidebar.

- Apply the `mysqli_affected_rows()` function to **register.php** to confirm that the **INSERT** worked.

- If you want, create scripts that interact with the *banking* database. Easy projects to begin with include viewing all customers, viewing all accounts (do a **JOIN** to also show the customer's name), and adding to or subtracting from an account's balance.

Common Programming Techniques

Now that you have a little PHP and MySQL interaction under your belt, it's time to kick things up a notch. This chapter is like Chapter 3, "Creating Dynamic Web Sites," in that it covers myriad independent topics. But what these have in common is that they demonstrate common PHP-MySQL programming techniques. You won't learn any new functions here; instead, you'll see how to use the knowledge you already possess to create standard web functionality.

The examples themselves will broaden the application started in the preceding chapter by adding new, popular features. You'll see several tricks for managing database information, in particular editing and deleting records using PHP. At the same time, a couple of new ways of passing data to your PHP pages will be introduced. The final sections of the chapter add features to the **view_users.php** page.

In This Chapter

Sending Values to a Script

In the examples so far, all the data received in the PHP script came from what the user entered in a form. There are, however, two different ways you can pass variables and values to a PHP script, both worth knowing.

The first method is to make use of HTML's **hidden** input type:

```
<input type="hidden" name="do"
→ value="this">
```

If this code is anywhere between the **form** tags, the variable **$_POST['do']** will have a value of *this* in the handling PHP script, assuming that the form uses the POST method. If the form uses the GET method, then **$_GET['do']** would have that value. With that in mind, you can skip the creation of the form and just directly append a *name=value* pair to the URL:

www.example.com/page.php?do=this

Again, with this specific example, **page.php** receives a variable called **$_GET['do']** with a value of *this*.

To demonstrate this GET method trick, a new version of the **view_users.php** script, first created in the previous chapter, will be written. This one will provide links to pages that will allow you to edit or delete an existing user's record. The links will pass the user's ID to the handling pages, both of which will also be written in this chapter.

To manually send values to a PHP script:

1. Open **view_users.php** (Script 9.6) in your text editor or IDE.

2. Change the SQL query to read (Script 10.1)

   ```
   $q = "SELECT last_name,
   → first_name, DATE_FORMAT
   → (registration_date, '%M %d, %Y')
   → AS dr, user_id FROM users ORDER
   → BY registration_date ASC";
   ```

   The query has been changed in a couple of ways. First, the first and last names are selected separately, not concatenated together. Second, the *user_id* is also now being selected, since that value will be necessary in creating the links.

continues on page 308

Script 10.1 The **view_users.php** script, started in Chapter 9, "Using PHP with MySQL," now modified so that it presents Edit and Delete links, passing the user's ID number along in each URL.

```
1    <?php # Script 10.1 - view_users.php #3
2    // This script retrieves all the records from the users table.
3    // This new version links to edit and delete pages.
4
5    $page_title = 'View the Current Users';
6    include('includes/header.html');
7    echo '<h1>Registered Users</h1>';
8
9    require('../mysqli_connect.php');
10
11   // Define the query:
```

code continues on next page

```
12   $q = "SELECT last_name, first_name, DATE_FORMAT(registration_date, '%M %d, %Y') AS dr,
     user_id FROM users ORDER BY registration_date ASC";
13   $r = @mysqli_query($dbc, $q);
14
15   // Count the number of returned rows:
16   $num = mysqli_num_rows($r);
17
18   if ($num > 0) { // If it ran OK, display the records.
19
20       // Print how many users there are:
21       echo "<p>There are currently $num registered users.</p>\n";
22
23       // Table header:
24       echo '<table width="60%">
25       <thead>
26       <tr>
27         <th align="left"><strong>Edit</strong></th>
28         <th align="left"><strong>Delete</strong></th>
29         <th align="left"><strong>Last Name</strong></th>
30         <th align="left"><strong>First Name</strong></th>
31         <th align="left"><strong>Date Registered</strong></th>
32       </tr>
33       </thead>
34       <tbody>
35       ';
36
37       // Fetch and print all the records:
38       while ($row = mysqli_fetch_array($r, MYSQLI_ASSOC)) {
39           echo '<tr>
40             <td align="left"><a href="edit_user.php?id=' . $row['user_id'] .
                 '">Edit</a></td>
41             <td align="left"><a href="delete_user.php?id=' . $row['user_id'] .
                 '">Delete</a></td>
42             <td align="left">' . $row['last_name'] . '</td>
43             <td align="left">' . $row['first_name'] . '</td>
44             <td align="left">' . $row['dr'] . '</td>
45           </tr>
46           ';
47       }
48
49       echo '</tbody></table>';
50       mysqli_free_result($r);
51
52   } else { // If no records were returned.
53       echo '<p class="error">There are currently no registered users.</p>';
54   }
55
56   mysqli_close($dbc);
57
58   include('includes/footer.html');
59   ?>
```

3. Add three more columns to the main table:

```
echo '<table width="60%">
<thead>
<tr>
  <th align="left"><strong>Edit
  ↪ </strong></th>
  <th align="left"><strong>
  ↪ Delete</strong></th>
  <th align="left"><strong>
  ↪ Last Name</strong></th>
  <th align="left"><strong>
  ↪ First Name</strong></th>
  <th align="left"><strong>
  ↪ Date Registered</strong></th>
</tr>
</thead>
<tbody>
';
```

In the previous version of the script, there were only two columns: one for the name and another for the date the user registered. The name column has been separated into its two parts and two new columns have been added: one for the *Edit* link and another for the *Delete* link.

4. Change the **echo** statement within the **while** loop to match the table's new structure:

```
echo '<tr>
  <td align="left">
  ↪ <a href="edit_user.php?id=' .
  ↪ $row['user_id'] . '">Edit</a>
  ↪ </td>
  <td align="left">
  ↪ <a href="delete_user.php?id='
  ↪ . $row['user_id'] . '">Delete
  ↪ </a></td>
  <td align="left">' .
  ↪ $row['last_name'] . '</td>
  <td align="left">' .
  ↪ $row['first_name'] . '</td>
  <td align="left">' . $row['dr']
  ↪ . '</td>
</tr>
';
```

For each record returned from the database, this line will print out a row with five columns. The last three columns are obvious and easy to create; just refer to the returned column name.

For the first two columns, which provide links to edit or delete the user, the syntax is slightly more complicated. The desired end result is HTML code like **<a href="edit_user.php?id=X">Edit </a>**, where *X* is the user's ID. Knowing this, all the PHP code has to do is print **$row['user_id']** for *X*, being mindful of the quotation marks to avoid parse errors.

Because the HTML attributes use a lot of double quotation marks and this **echo** statement requires a lot of variables to be printed, I find it easiest to use single quotes for the HTML and then to concatenate the variables to the printed text.

5. Save the file as **view_users.php**, place it in your web directory, and run it in your browser **Ⓐ**.

There's no point in clicking the new links, though, because those scripts have not yet been created.

6. If you want, view the HTML source of the page to see each dynamically generated link **Ⓑ**.

TIP To append multiple variables to a URL, use this syntax: page.php?name1=value1& name2=value2&name3=value3. It's simply a matter of using the ampersand, plus another name-value pair.

TIP One trick to adding variables to URLs is that strings should be encoded to ensure that the value is handled properly. For example, the space in the string Elliott Smith would be problematic. The solution then is to use the urlencode( ) function:

```
$url = 'page.php?name=' .
→ urlencode('Elliott Smith');
```

You only need to do this when programmatically adding values to a URL. When a form uses the GET method, it automatically encodes the data.

Registered Users

There are currently 26 registered users.

Edit	Delete	Last Name	First Name	Date Registered
Edit	Delete	Ullman	Larry	May 11, 2017
Edit	Delete	Isabella	Zoe	May 11, 2017
Edit	Delete	Lennon	John	May 11, 2017
Edit	Delete	McCartney	Paul	May 11, 2017
Edit	Delete	Harrison	George	May 11, 2017
Edit	Delete	Starr	Ringo	May 11, 2017
Edit	Delete	Jones	David	May 11, 2017
Edit	Delete	Dolenz	Micky	May 11, 2017
Edit	Delete	Nesmith	mike	May 11, 2017
Edit	Delete	Sedaris	David	May 11, 2017
Edit	Delete	Hornby	Nick	May 11, 2017

Ⓐ The revised version of the **view_users.php** page, with new columns and links.

```
<tr>
    <td align="left"><a href="edit_user.php?id=2">Edit</a></td>
    <td align="left"><a href="delete_user.php?id=2">Delete</a></td>
    <td align="left">Isabella</td>
    <td align="left">Zoe</td>
    <td align="left">May 11, 2017</td>
</tr>
<tr>
    <td align="left"><a href="edit_user.php?id=3">Edit</a></td>
    <td align="left"><a href="delete_user.php?id=3">Delete</a></td>
    <td align="left">Lennon</td>
    <td align="left">John</td>
    <td align="left">May 11, 2017</td>
</tr>
```

Ⓑ Part of the HTML source of the page (see **Ⓐ**) shows how the user's ID is added to each link's URL.

Using Hidden Form Inputs

In the preceding example, a new version of the **view_users.php** script was written. It now includes links to the **edit_user.php** and **delete_user.php** pages, passing each a user's ID through the URL. This next example, **delete_user.php**, will take the passed user ID and allow the administrator to delete that user. Although you could have this page simply execute a **DELETE** query as soon as the page is accessed, to prevent an inadvertent deletion there should be multiple steps 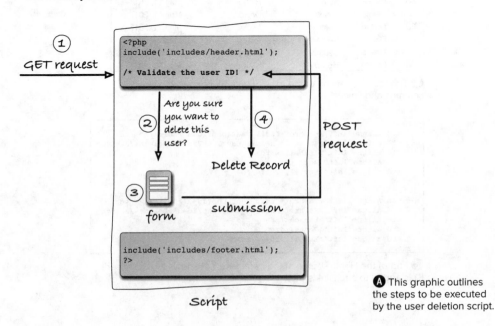:

1. The page must check that it received a numeric user ID.

2. A message will confirm that this user should be deleted.

3. The user ID will be stored in a hidden form input.

4. Upon submission of this form, the user will actually be deleted.

To use hidden form inputs:

1. Begin a new PHP document in your text editor or IDE, to be named **delete_user.php** (Script 10.2):

   ```php
   <?php # Script 10.2 -
   → delete_user.php
   ```

2. Include the page header:

   ```php
   $page_title = 'Delete a User';
   include('includes/header.html');
   echo '<h1>Delete a User</h1>';
   ```

   This document will use the same template system as the other pages in the application. See Chapter 9 and Chapter 3 for clarification, if needed.

3. Check for a valid user ID value:

Ⓐ This graphic outlines the steps to be executed by the user deletion script.

```
if ( (isset($_GET['id'])) &&
→ (is_numeric($_GET['id'])) )
→ { // From view_users.php
   $id = $_GET['id'];
} elseif ( (isset($_POST['id'])) &&
→ (is_numeric($_POST['id'])) )
→ { // Form submission.
   $id = $_POST['id'];
} else { // No valid ID, kill the
→ script.
   echo '<p class="error">This
   → page has been accessed in
   → error.</p>';
   include('includes/footer.html');
   exit();
}
```

This script relies on having a valid user ID, to be used in a **DELETE** query's **WHERE** clause. The first time this page is accessed, the user ID should be passed in the URL (the page's URL will end with **delete_user.php?id=X**) after clicking the *Delete* link in the **view_users.php** page. The first **if** condition checks for such a value and that the value is numeric.

As you will see, the script will then store the user ID value in a hidden form input. When the form is submitted (back to this same page), the script will receive the ID through **$_POST**. The second condition checks this and, again, that the ID value is numeric.

continues on page 313

Script 10.2 This script expects a user ID to be passed to it through the URL. It then presents a confirmation form and deletes the user upon submission.

```
1    <?php # Script 10.2 - delete_user.php
2    // This page is for deleting a user record.
3    // This page is accessed through view_users.php.
4
5    $page_title = 'Delete a User';
6    include('includes/header.html');
7    echo '<h1>Delete a User</h1>';
8
9    // Check for a valid user ID, through GET or POST:
10   if ( (isset($_GET['id'])) && (is_numeric($_GET['id'])) ) { // From view_users.php
11       $id = $_GET['id'];
12   } elseif ( (isset($_POST['id'])) && (is_numeric($_POST['id'])) ) { // Form submission.
13       $id = $_POST['id'];
14   } else { // No valid ID, kill the script.
15       echo '<p class="error">This page has been accessed in error.</p>';
16       include('includes/footer.html');
17       exit();
18   }
19
20   require('../mysqli_connect.php');
21
22   // Check if the form has been submitted:
23   if ($_SERVER['REQUEST_METHOD'] == 'POST') {
24
25       if ($_POST['sure'] == 'Yes') { // Delete the record.
```

code continues on next page

```
26
27          // Make the query:
28          $q = "DELETE FROM users WHERE user_id=$id LIMIT 1";
29          $r = @mysqli_query($dbc, $q);
30          if (mysqli_affected_rows($dbc) == 1) { // If it ran OK.
31
32              // Print a message:
33              echo '<p>The user has been deleted.</p>';
34
35          } else { // If the query did not run OK.
36              echo '<p class="error">The user could not be deleted due to a system error.</p>';
                // Public message.
37              echo '<p>' . mysqli_error($dbc) . '<br>Query: ' . $q . '</p>'; // Debugging message.
38          }
39
40      } else { // No confirmation of deletion.
41          echo '<p>The user has NOT been deleted.</p>';
42      }
43
44  } else { // Show the form.
45
46      // Retrieve the user's information:
47      $q = "SELECT CONCAT(last_name, ', ', first_name) FROM users WHERE user_id=$id";
48      $r = @mysqli_query($dbc, $q);
49
50      if (mysqli_num_rows($r) == 1) { // Valid user ID, show the form.
51
52          // Get the user's information:
53          $row = mysqli_fetch_array($r, MYSQLI_NUM);
54
55          // Display the record being deleted:
56          echo "<h3>Name: $row[0]</h3>
57          Are you sure you want to delete this user?";
58
59          // Create the form:
60          echo '<form action="delete_user.php" method="post">
61  <input type="radio" name="sure" value="Yes"> Yes
62  <input type="radio" name="sure" value="No" checked="checked"> No
63  <input type="submit" name="submit" value="Submit">
64  <input type="hidden" name="id" value="' . $id . '">
65  </form>';
66
67      } else { // Not a valid user ID.
68          echo '<p class="error">This page has been accessed in error.</p>';
69      }
70
71  } // End of the main submission conditional.
72
73  mysqli_close($dbc);
74
75  include('includes/footer.html');
76  ?>
```

If neither of these conditions is TRUE, then the page cannot proceed, so an error message is displayed and the script's execution is terminated **B**.

4. Include the MySQL connection script:

```
require_once('../mysqli_connect
→ .php');
```

Both of this script's processes—showing the form and handling the form—require a database connection, so this line is outside of the main submit conditional (Step 5).

5. Begin the main submit conditional:

```
if ($_SERVER['REQUEST_METHOD'] ==
→ 'POST') {
```

To test for a form submission, the script uses the same conditional first explained in Chapter 3 (and also used in Chapter 9).

B If the page does not receive a number ID value, this error is shown.

Delete a User

Name: Doe, Jane

Are you sure you want to delete this user?

○ Yes ● No Submit

C The page confirms the user deletion using this simple form.

6. Delete the user, if appropriate:

```
if ($_POST['sure'] == 'Yes') {
  $q = "DELETE FROM users WHERE
  → user_id=$id LIMIT 1";
  $r = @mysqli_query($dbc, $q);
```

The form **C** will force the user to click a radio button to confirm the deletion. This little requirement prevents any accidents. Thus, the handling process first checks that the correct radio button was selected. If so, a basic **DELETE** query is defined, using the user's ID in the **WHERE** clause. A **LIMIT** clause is added to the query as an extra precaution.

7. Check if the deletion worked and respond accordingly:

```
if (mysqli_affected_rows($dbc) ==
→ 1) {
  echo '<p>The user has been
  → deleted.</p>';
} else {
  echo '<p class="error">The user
  → could not be deleted due to
  → a system error.</p>'; //
  → Public message.
  echo '<p>' . mysqli_error($dbc)
  → . '<br>Query: ' . $q . '</p>';
}
```

The `mysqli_affected_rows()` function checks that exactly one row was affected by the **DELETE** query. If so, a happy message is displayed **D**. If not, an error message is sent out.

continues on next page

Delete a User

The user has been deleted.

D If you select *Yes* in the form (see **C**) and click Submit, this should be the result.

Keep in mind that it's possible that no rows were affected without a MySQL error occurring. For example, suppose the query tries to delete the record where the user ID is equal to 42000 (and that record doesn't exist). In that case, no rows will be deleted but no MySQL error will occur. Still, because of the checks made when the form is first loaded, it would take a fair amount of hacking by the user to get to that point.

8. Complete the `$_POST['sure']` conditional:

```
} else {
  echo '<p>The user has NOT been
  → deleted.</p>';
}
```

If the user did not explicitly select the *Yes* button, the user will *not* be deleted and this message will be displayed **E**.

9. Begin the `else` clause of the main submit conditional:

```
} else {
```

The page will either handle the form or display it. Most of the code prior to this takes effect if the form has been submitted (if `$_SERVER['REQUEST_METHOD']` equals *POST*). The code from here on takes effect if the form has not yet been submitted, in which case the form should be displayed.

10. Retrieve the information for the user being deleted:

```
$q = "SELECT CONCAT(last_name, ',
→ ', first_name) FROM users WHERE
→ user_id=$id";
$r = @mysqli_query($dbc, $q);
if (mysqli_num_rows($r) == 1) {
$row = mysqli_fetch_array($r,
→ MYSQL_NUM);
```

To confirm that the script received a valid user ID and to state exactly who is being deleted (refer back to **C**), the to-be-deleted user's name is retrieved from the database **F**.

The conditional—checking that a single row was returned—ensures that a valid user ID was provided to the script. If so, that one record is fetched into the `$row` variable.

11. Display the record being deleted:

```
echo "<h3>Name: $row[0]</h3>
Are you sure you want to delete
→ this user? ";
```

To help prevent accidental deletions of the wrong record, the name of the user to be deleted is first displayed. That value is available in `$row[0]`, because the `mysqli_fetch_array()` function (in Step 10) uses the `MYSQL_NUM` constant, thereby assigning the returned record to `$row` as an indexed array. The user's name is the first, and only, column in the returned record, so it's indexed at 0 (as arrays normally begin indexing at 0).

Delete a User

The user has NOT been deleted.

E If you do not select *Yes* in the form, no database changes are made.

```
● ● ●      PHP and MySQL for Dynamic Web Sites
mysql> mysql> SELECT CONCAT(last_name, ', ', first_name)
  FROM users WHERE =12;_id
+------------------------------------+
| CONCAT(last_name, ', ', first_name) |
+------------------------------------+
| Hornby, Nick                        |
+------------------------------------+
1 row in set (0.00 sec)

mysql> █
```

F Running the same **SELECT** query in the mysql client.

12. Create the form:

```
echo '<form action="delete_
→ user.php" method="post">
<input type="radio" name="sure"
→ value="Yes"> Yes
<input type="radio" name="sure"
→ value="No" checked="checked"> No
<input type="submit" name="submit"
→ value="Submit">
<input type="hidden" name="id"
→ value="' . $id . '">
</form>';
```

The form posts back to this same page. It contains two radio buttons, with the same name but different values, a submit button, and a hidden input. The most important step here is that the user ID (**$id**) is stored as a hidden form input so that the handling process can also access this value **G**.

13. Complete the **mysqli_num_rows( )** conditional:

```
} else {
  echo '<p class="error">This page
→ has been accessed in error.
→ </p>';
}
```

If no record was returned by the **SELECT** query (because an invalid user ID was submitted), this message is displayed.

If you see this message when you test this script but don't understand why, apply the standard debugging steps outlined at the end of Chapter 8, "Error Handling and Debugging."

14. Complete the PHP page:

```
}
mysqli_close($dbc);
include('includes/footer.html');
?>
```

The closing brace finishes the main submission conditional. Then the MySQL connection is closed and the footer is included.

15. Save the file as **delete_user.php** and place it in your web directory (it should be in the same directory as **view_users.php**).

16. Run the page by first clicking a *Delete* link in the **view_users.php** page.

TIP Hidden form elements don't display in the web browser but are still present in the HTML source code **G**. For this reason, never store anything there that must be kept truly secure.

TIP Using hidden form inputs and appending values to a URL are just two ways to make data available to other PHP pages. Two more methods—cookies and sessions—are thoroughly covered in Chapter 12, "Cookies and Sessions."

```
<!-- Script 9.1 - header.html --><h1>Delete a User</h1><h3>Name: Hornby, Nick</h3>
        Are you sure you want to delete this user?<form action="delete_user.php"
method="post">
    <input type="radio" name="sure" value="Yes"> Yes
    <input type="radio" name="sure" value="No" checked="checked"> No
    <input type="submit" name="submit" value="Submit">
    <input type="hidden" name="id" value="12">
    </form><!-- Script 3.3 - footer.html -->
</div>
```

G The user ID is stored as a hidden input so that it's available when the form is submitted.

Editing Existing Records

A common practice with database-driven websites is having a system in place so that you can easily edit existing records. This concept seems daunting to many beginning programmers, but the process is surprisingly straightforward. For the following example—editing registered user records—the process combines skills this book has already taught:

- Making sticky forms
- Using hidden inputs
- Validating registration data
- Executing simple queries

This next example is generally very similar to **delete_user.php** and will also be linked from the **view_users.php** script (when a person clicks *Edit*). A form will be displayed with the user's current information, allowing for those values to be changed **Ⓐ**. Once the form is submitted, if the data passes all the validation routines an **UPDATE** query will be run to update the database.

To edit an existing database record:

1. Begin a new PHP document in your text editor or IDE, to be named **edit_user.php** (Script 10.3):

```php
<?php # Script 10.3 -
→ edit_user.php
$page_title = 'Edit a User';
include('includes/header.html');
echo '<h1>Edit a User</h1>';
```

Edit a User

First Name: Richard

Last Name: Brautigan

Email Address: richard@authors.com

Submit

Ⓐ The form for editing a user's record.

Script 10.3 The **edit_user.php** page first displays the user's current information in a form. Upon submission of the form, the record will be updated in the database.

```php
1    <?php # Script 10.3 - edit_user.php
2    // This page is for editing a user record.
3    // This page is accessed through view_users.php.
4
5    $page_title = 'Edit a User';
6    include('includes/header.html');
7    echo '<h1>Edit a User</h1>';
8
9    // Check for a valid user ID, through GET or POST:
10   if ( (isset($_GET['id'])) && (is_numeric($_GET['id'])) ) { // From view_users.php
11       $id = $_GET['id'];
12   } elseif ( (isset($_POST['id'])) && (is_numeric($_POST['id'])) ) { // Form submission.
13       $id = $_POST['id'];
14   } else { // No valid ID, kill the script.
15       echo '<p class="error">This page has been accessed in error.</p>';
```

code continues on next page

```
16      include('includes/footer.html');
17      exit();
18 }
19
20 require('../mysqli_connect.php');
21
22 // Check if the form has been submitted:
23 if ($_SERVER['REQUEST_METHOD'] ==
   'POST') {
24
25     $errors = [];
26
27     // Check for a first name:
28     if (empty($_POST['first_name'])) {
29         $errors[] = 'You forgot to enter
           your first name.';
30     } else {
31         $fn = mysqli_real_escape_
           string($dbc, trim($_POST
           ['first_name']));
32     }
33
34     // Check for a last name:
35     if (empty($_POST['last_name'])) {
36         $errors[] = 'You forgot to enter
           your last name.';
37     } else {
38         $ln = mysqli_real_
           escape_string($dbc,
           trim($_POST['last_name']));
39     }
40
41     // Check for an email address:
42     if (empty($_POST['email'])) {
43         $errors[] = 'You forgot to enter
           your email address.';
44     } else {
45         $e = mysqli_real_escape_string
           ($dbc, trim($_POST['email']));
46     }
47
48     if (empty($errors)) { // If
       everything's OK.
49
50         //  Test for unique email address:
51         $q = "SELECT user_id FROM users
           WHERE email='$e' AND user_id !=
           $id";
52         $r = @mysqli_query($dbc, $q);
53         if (mysqli_num_rows($r) == 0) {
54
```

code continues on next page

2. Check for a valid user ID value:

```
if ( (isset($_GET['id'])) &&
→ (is_numeric($_GET['id'])) ) {
    $id = $_GET['id'];
} elseif ( (isset($_POST['id'])) &&
→ (is_numeric($_POST['id'])) ) {
    $id = $_POST['id'];
} else { // No valid ID, kill the
→ script.
    echo '<p class="error">This page
→ has been accessed in error.
→ </p>';
    include('includes/footer.html');
    exit();
}
```

This validation routine is exactly the same as that in **delete_user.php**, confirming that a numeric user ID has been received, whether the page has first been accessed from **view_users.php** (the first condition) or upon submission of the form (the second condition).

3. Include the MySQL connection script and begin the main submit conditional:

```
require_once('../mysqli_
→ connect.php');
if ($_SERVER['REQUEST_METHOD'] ==
→ 'POST') {
$errors = [];
```

Like the registration examples you have already done, this script makes use of an array to track errors.

4. Validate the first name:

```
if (empty($_POST['first_name'])) {
    $errors[] = 'You forgot to
→ enter your first name.';
} else {
    $fn = mysqli_real_escape_
→ string($dbc, trim
→ ($_POST['first_name']));
}
```

continues on next page

The form Ⓐ is like a registration page but without the password fields (see the second tip). The form data can therefore be validated by applying the same techniques used in a registration script. As with a registration example, the validated data is trimmed and then run through `mysqli_real_escape_string()` for security.

Script 10.3 *continued*

```
55          // Make the query:
56          $q = "UPDATE users SET first_name='$fn', last_name='$ln', email='$e'
            WHERE user_id=$id LIMIT 1";
57          $r = @mysqli_query($dbc, $q);
58          if (mysqli_affected_rows($dbc) == 1) { // If it ran OK.
59
60              // Print a message:
61              echo '<p>The user has been edited.</p>';
62
63          } else { // If it did not run OK.
64              echo '<p class="error">The user could not be edited due to a system error.
                We apologize for any inconvenience.</p>'; // Public message.
65              echo '<p>' . mysqli_error($dbc) . '<br>Query: ' . $q . '</p>';
                // Debugging message.
66          }
67
68      } else { // Already registered.
69          echo '<p class="error">The email address has already been registered.</p>';
70      }
71
72  } else { // Report the errors.
73
74      echo '<p class="error">The following error(s) occurred:<br>';
75      foreach ($errors as $msg) { // Print each error.
76          echo " - $msg<br>\n";
77      }
78      echo '</p><p>Please try again.</p>';
79
80  } // End of if (empty($errors)) IF.
81
82  } // End of submit conditional.
83
84  // Always show the form...
85
86  // Retrieve the user's information:
87  $q = "SELECT first_name, last_name, email FROM users WHERE user_id=$id";
88  $r = @mysqli_query($dbc, $q);
```

code continues on next page

```
89
90   if (mysqli_num_rows($r) == 1) { // Valid
     user ID, show the form.
91
92       // Get the user's information:
93       $row = mysqli_fetch_array($r,
         MYSQLI_NUM);
94
95       // Create the form:
96       echo '<form action="edit_user.php"
         method="post">
97   <p>First Name: <input type="text"
     name="first_name" size="15"
     maxlength="15" value="' . $row[0] .
     '"></p>
98   <p>Last Name: <input type="text"
     name="last_name" size="15"
     maxlength="30" value="' . $row[1] .
     '"></p>
99   <p>Email Address: <input type="email"
     name="email" size="20" maxlength="60"
     value="' . $row[2] . '"> </p>
100  <p><input type="submit" name="submit"
     value="Submit"></p>
101  <input type="hidden" name="id" value="'
     . $id . '">
102  </form>';
103
104  } else { // Not a valid user ID.
105      echo '<p class="error">This page has
     been accessed in error.</p>';
106  }
107
108  mysqli_close($dbc);
109
110  include('includes/footer.html');
111  ?>
```

5. Validate the last name and email address:

```
if (empty($_POST['last_name'])) {
    $errors[] = 'You forgot to
→ enter your last name.';
} else {
    $ln = mysqli_real_escape_
→ string($dbc, trim
→ ($_POST['last_name']));
}

// Check for an email address:
if (empty($_POST['email'])) {
    $errors[] = 'You forgot to
→ enter your email address.';
} else {
    $e = mysqli_real_escape_
→ string($dbc, trim($_POST
→ ['email']));
}
```

6. If there were no errors, check that the submitted email address is not already in use:

```
if (empty($errors)) {
    $q = "SELECT user_id FROM users
→ WHERE email='$e' AND user_id
→ != $id";
    $r = @mysqli_query($dbc, $q);
    if (mysqli_num_rows($r) == 0) {
```

The integrity of the database and of the application as a whole partially depends on having unique email address values in the *users* table. That requirement guarantees that the login system, which uses a combination of the email address and password (to be developed in Chapter 12), works. Because the form allows for altering the user's email address (see Ⓐ), special steps must be taken to ensure uniqueness of that value across every database record. To understand this query, let's consider two possibilities.

continues on next page

In the first, the user's email address is being changed. In this case you just need to run a query making sure that that particular email address isn't already registered: **SELECT user_id FROM users WHERE email='$e'**.

In the second possibility, the user's email address will remain the same. In this case, it's OK if the email address is already in use, because it's already in use *for this user*.

To write one query that will work for both possibilities, don't check to see if the email address is being used, but rather see if it's being used by *anyone else*—hence:

SELECT user_id FROM users WHERE email='$e' AND user_id != $id

If this query returns no records, it's safe to run the **UPDATE** query.

7. Update the database:

```
$q = "UPDATE users SET
→ first_name='$fn', last_name=
→ '$ln', email='$e' WHERE
→ user_id=$id LIMIT 1";
$r = @mysqli_query($dbc, $q);
```

The **UPDATE** query is like examples you could have seen in Chapter 5, "Introduction to SQL." The query updates three fields—first name, last name, and email address—using the values submitted by the form. This system works because the form is preset with the existing values. So, if you edit the first name in the form but nothing else, the first name value in the database is updated using this new value, but the last name and email address values are "updated" using their current values. This system is much easier than trying to determine which form values have changed and updating just those in the database.

8. Report on the results of the update:

```
if (mysqli_affected_rows($dbc) ==
→ 1) {
  echo '<p>The user has been
  → edited.</p>';
} else {
  echo '<p class="error">The user
  → could not be edited due to a
  → system error. We apologize
  → for any inconvenience.</p>';
  echo '<p>' . mysqli_error($dbc)
  → . '<br>Query: ' . $q . '</p>';
}
```

The **mysqli_affected_rows()** function will return the number of rows in the database affected by the most recent query. If any of the three form values was altered, then this function will return the value 1. This conditional tests for that and prints a message indicating success or failure.

Keep in mind that the **mysqli_affected_rows()** function will return a value of 0 if an **UPDATE** command successfully ran but didn't actually affect any records. Therefore, if you submit this form without changing any of the form values, a system error is displayed, which may not technically be correct. Once you have this script effectively working, you could change the error message to indicate that no alterations were made if **mysqli_affected_rows()** returns 0.

9. Complete the email conditional:

```
} else { // Already registered.
  echo '<p class="error">The
  → email address has already
  → been registered.</p>';

}
```

This **else** completes the conditional that checked whether an email address was already being used by another user. If so, that message is printed.

10. Complete the **$errors** conditional:

```
} else { // Report the errors.
  echo '<p class="error">The
  → following error(s)
  → occurred:<br>';
  foreach ($errors as $msg) {
  → // Print each error.
    echo " - $msg<br>\n";
  }
  echo '</p><p>Please try again.
  → </p>';
} // End of if (empty($errors)) IF.
```

The **else** is used to report any errors in the form (namely, a lack of a first name, last name, or email address), just like in the registration script.

11. Complete the submission conditional:

```
} // End of submit conditional.
```

The final closing brace completes the main submit conditional. In this example, the form will be displayed whenever the page is accessed. After submitting the form, the database will be updated, and the form will be shown again, now displaying the latest information.

12. Retrieve the information for the user being edited:

```
$q = "SELECT first_name,
→ last_name, email FROM users
→ WHERE user_id=$id";
$r = @mysqli_query($dbc, $q);
if (mysqli_num_rows($r) == 1) {
$row = mysqli_fetch_array($r,
→ MYSQLI_NUM);
```

To populate the form elements, the current information for the user must be retrieved from the database. This query is like the one in **delete_user.php**. The conditional—checking that a single row was returned—ensures that a valid user ID was provided.

13. Display the form:

```
echo '<form action="edit_user.php"
→ method="post">
<p>First Name: <input type="text"
→ name="first_name" size="15"
→ maxlength="15" value="' .
→ $row[0] . '"></p>
<p>Last Name: <input type="text"
→ name="last_name" size="15"
→ maxlength="30" value="' .
→ $row[1] . '"></p>
<p>Email Address: <input
→ type="email" name="email"
→ size="20" maxlength="60"
→ value="' . $row[2] . '"> </p>
<p><input type="submit"
→ name="submit" value="Submit">
→ </p>
<input type="hidden" name="id"
→ value="' . $id . '">
</form>';
```

The form has but three text inputs, each of which is made sticky using the data retrieved from the database. Again, the user ID (**$id**) is stored as a hidden form input so that the handling process can also access this value.

14. Complete the **mysqli_num_rows()** conditional:

```
} else {
  echo '<p class="error">This
  → page has been accessed in error.
  → </p>';
}
```

continues on next page

If no record was returned from the database because an invalid user ID was submitted, this message is displayed.

15. Complete the PHP page:

```
mysqli_close($dbc);
include('includes/footer.html');
?>
```

16. Save the file as **edit_user.php** and place it in your web directory (in the same folder as **view_users.php**).

17. Run the page by first clicking an *Edit* link in the **view_users.php** page **B** and **C**.

TIP As written, the sticky form always shows the values retrieved from the database. This means that if an error occurs, the database values will be used, not the ones the user just entered (if those are different). To change this behavior, the sticky form would have to check for the presence of $_POST variables, using those if they exist, or the database values if not.

TIP This edit page does not include the functionality to change the password. That concept was already demonstrated in **password.php** (Script 9.7). If you would like to incorporate that functionality here, keep in mind that you cannot display the current password, since it is stored in a hashed format (i.e., it's not decryptable). Instead, just present two boxes for changing the password (the new password input and a confirmation). If these values are submitted, update the password in the database as well. If these inputs are left blank, do not update the password in the database.

Edit a User

The user has been edited.

First Name: Richard

Last Name: Brautigan

Email Address: rich@authors.com

Submit

B The new values are displayed in the form after successfully updating the database (compare with the form values in **A**).

Edit a User

The email address has already been registered.

First Name: Richard

Last Name: Brautigan

Email Address: richard@authors.com

Submit

C If you try to change a record to an existing email address or if you omit an input, errors are reported.

Paginating Query Results

Pagination is a concept you're familiar with even if you don't know the term. When you use a search engine like Google, it displays the results as a series of pages and not as one long list. The `view_users.php` script could benefit from this feature.

Paginating query results makes extensive use of the **LIMIT** SQL clause introduced in Chapter 5. **LIMIT** restricts which subset of the matched records is returned. To paginate the returned results of a query, each iteration of the page will run the same query using different **LIMIT** parameters. The first page viewing will request the first *X* records; the second page viewing, the second group of *X* records; and so forth. To make this work, two values must be passed from page to page in the URL, like the user IDs passed from the `view_users.php` page. The first value is the total number of pages to be displayed. The second value is an indicator of which records the page should display with this iteration (i.e., where to begin fetching records).

Registered Users

Edit	Delete	Last Name	First Name	Date Registered
Edit	Delete	Ullman	Larry	May 11, 2017
Edit	Delete	Isabella	Zoe	May 11, 2017
Edit	Delete	Lennon	John	May 11, 2017
Edit	Delete	McCartney	Paul	May 11, 2017
Edit	Delete	Harrison	George	May 11, 2017
Edit	Delete	Starr	Ringo	May 11, 2017
Edit	Delete	Jones	David	May 11, 2017
Edit	Delete	Dolenz	Micky	May 11, 2017
Edit	Delete	Nesmith	mike	May 11, 2017
Edit	Delete	Sedaris	David	May 11, 2017

1 2 3 Next

Ⓐ Alternating the table row colors makes this list of users more legible (every other row has a light gray background).

Another, more cosmetic technique will be demonstrated here: displaying each row of the table—each returned record—using an alternating background color Ⓐ. This effect will be achieved with ease, using the ternary operator (see the sidebar "The Ternary Operator").

There's a lot of good, new information to be covered here, so to make it easier to follow along, let's write this version from scratch instead of trying to modify Script 10.1.

To paginate `view_users.php`:

1. Begin a new PHP document in your text editor or IDE, to be named `view_users.php` (Script 10.4):

   ```php
   <?php # Script 10.4 -
   → view_users.php #4
   $page_title = 'View the Current
   → Users';
   include('includes/header.html');
   echo '<h1>Registered Users</h1>';
   require_once('../mysqli_
   → connect.php');
   ```

2. Set the number of records to display per page:

   ```php
   $display = 10;
   ```

   By establishing this value as a variable here, you'll make it easy to change the number of records displayed on each page later. Also, this value will be used multiple times in this script, so it's best represented as a single variable (you could also represent this value as a constant, if you'd rather).

   continues on next page

3. Check if the number of required pages has been already determined:

```
if (isset($_GET['p']) &&
→ is_numeric($_GET['p'])) {
  $pages = $_GET['p'];
} else {
```

For this script to display the users over several page viewings, it will need to determine how many total pages of results will be required. The first time the script is run, this number must be calculated. For every subsequent call to this page, the total number of pages will be passed to the script in the URL, making it available in **$_GET['p']**. If this variable is set and is numeric, its value will be assigned to the **$pages** variable.

If not, then the number of pages will need to be calculated.

4. Count the number of records in the database:

```
$q = "SELECT COUNT(user_id) FROM
→ users";
$r = @mysqli_query($dbc, $q);
$row = @mysqli_fetch_array($r,
→ MYSQLI_NUM);
$records = $row[0];
```

Using the **COUNT( )** function, introduced in Chapter 7, "Advanced SQL and MySQL," you can easily find the number of records in the *users* table (i.e., the number of records to be paginated). This query will return a single row with a single column: the number of records **B**.

continues on page 326

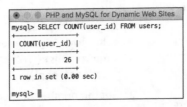

```
● ● ●    PHP and MySQL for Dynamic Web Sites
mysql> SELECT COUNT(user_id) FROM users;
+----------------+
| COUNT(user_id) |
+----------------+
|             26 |
+----------------+
1 row in set (0.00 sec)
mysql> █
```

B The result of running the counting query in the mysql client.

The Ternary Operator

This example uses an operator not introduced before, called the *ternary* operator. Its structure is

(condition) ? *valueT* : *valueF*

The condition in parentheses will be evaluated; if it is TRUE, the first value will be returned (*valueT*). If the condition is FALSE, the second value (*valueF*) will be returned.

Because the ternary operator returns a value, the entire structure is often used to assign a value to a variable or used as an argument for a function. For example, the line

```
echo (isset($var)) ? 'SET' : 'NOT SET';
```

will print out *SET* or *NOT SET*, depending on the status of the variable **$var**.

In this version of the **view_users.php** script, the ternary operator is used to toggle the value of a variable between two options. The variable itself will then be used to dictate the background color of each record in the table. There are certainly other ways to set this value, but the ternary operator is the most concise.

Script 10.4 This new version of `view_users.php` incorporates pagination so that the users are listed over multiple browser pages.

```php
1    <?php # Script 10.4 - #4
2    // This script retrieves all the records from the users table.
3    // This new version paginates the query results.
4
5    $page_title = 'View the Current Users';
6    include('includes/header.html');
7    echo '<h1>Registered Users</h1>';
8
9    require_once ('../mysqli_connect.php');
10
11   // Number of records to show per page:
12   $display = 10;
13
14   // Determine how many pages there are...
15   if (isset($_GET['p']) && is_numeric($_GET['p'])) { // Already been determined.
16
17       $pages = $_GET['p'];
18
19   } else { // Need to determine.
20
21       // Count the number of records:
22       $q = "SELECT COUNT(user_id) FROM users";
23       $r = @mysqli_query($dbc, $q);
24       $row = @mysqli_fetch_array($r, MYSQLI_NUM);
25       $records = $row[0];
26
27       // Calculate the number of pages...
28       if ($records > $display) { // More than 1 page.
29           $pages = ceil ($records/$display);
30       } else {
31           $pages = 1;
32       }
33
34   } // End of p IF.
35
36   // Determine where in the database to start returning results...
37   if (isset($_GET['s']) && is_numeric($_GET['s'])) {
38       $start = $_GET['s'];
39   } else {
40       $start = 0;
41   }
42
43   // Define the query:
44   $q = "SELECT last_name, first_name, DATE_FORMAT(registration_date, '%M %d, %Y') AS dr,
         user_id FROM users ORDER BY registration_date ASC LIMIT $start, $display";
45   $r = @mysqli_query($dbc, $q);
46
47   // Table header:
48   echo '<table width="60%">
49   <thead>
50   <tr>
```

code continues on next page

5. Mathematically calculate how many pages are required:

```
if ($records > $display) {
  $pages = ceil ($records/$display);
} else {
  $pages = 1;
}
```

The number of pages required to display all the records is based on the total number of records to be shown and the number to display per page (as assigned to the **$display** variable). If there are more records in the result set than there are records to be displayed per page, multiple pages will be required. To calculate exactly how many pages, take the next highest integer from the division of the two (the **ceil()** function returns the next highest integer). For example, if there are 25 records returned and 10 are being displayed per page, then 3 pages are required (the first page will display 10, the second page 10, and the third page 5). If **$records** is not greater than **$display**, only one page is necessary.

6. Complete the number of pages **if-else**:

```
} // End of p IF.
```

7. Determine the starting point in the database:

```
if (isset($_GET['s']) &&
→ is_numeric($_GET['s'])) {
  $start = $_GET['s'];
} else {
  $start = 0;
}
```

The second parameter that the script will receive—on subsequent viewings of the page—will be the starting record. This corresponds to the first number in a **LIMIT x, y** clause. Upon initially calling the script, the first ten records—0 through 9—should be retrieved (because **$display** has a value of 10). The second page would show records 10 through 19; the third, 20 through 29; and so forth.

continues on page 328

Script 10.4 *continued*

```
51      <th align="left"><strong>Edit</strong></th>
52      <th align="left"><strong>Delete</strong></th>
53      <th align="left"><strong>Last Name</strong></th>
54      <th align="left"><strong>First Name</strong></th>
55      <th align="left"><strong>Date Registered</strong></th>
56   </tr>
57   </thead>
58   <tbody>
59   ';
60
61   // Fetch and print all the records....
62
63   $bg = '#eeeeee'; // Set the initial background color.
64
65   while ($row = mysqli_fetch_array($r, MYSQLI_ASSOC)) {
66
67       $bg = ($bg=='#eeeeee' ? '#ffffff' : '#eeeeee'); // Switch the background color.
```

code continues on next page

```
68
69     echo '<tr bgcolor="' . $bg . '">
70         <td align="left"><a href="edit_user.php?id=' . $row['user_id'] . '">Edit</a></td>
71         <td align="left"><a href="delete_user.php?id=' . $row['user_id'] . '">Delete</a></td>
72         <td align="left">' . $row['last_name'] . '</td>
73         <td align="left">' . $row['first_name'] . '</td>
74         <td align="left">' . $row['dr'] . '</td>
75     </tr>
76     ';
77
78 } // End of WHILE loop.
79
80 echo '</tbody></table>';
81 mysqli_free_result($r);
82 mysqli_close($dbc);
83
84 // Make the links to other pages, if necessary.
85 if ($pages > 1) {
86
87     // Add some spacing and start a paragraph:
88     echo '<br><p>';
89
90     // Determine what page the script is on:
91     $current_page = ($start/$display) + 1;
92
93     // If it's not the first page, make a Previous link:
94     if ($current_page != 1) {
95         echo '<a href="view_users.php?s=' . ($start - $display) . '&p=' . $pages .
             '">Previous</a> ';
96     }
97
98     // Make all the numbered pages:
99     for ($i = 1; $i <= $pages; $i++) {
100         if ($i != $current_page) {
101             echo '<a href="view_users.php?s=' . (($display * ($i - 1))) . '&p=' . $pages .
                 '">' . $i . '</a> ';
102         } else {
103             echo $i . ' ';
104         }
105     } // End of FOR loop.
106
107     // If it's not the last page, make a Next button:
108     if ($current_page != $pages) {
109         echo '<a href="view_users.php?s=' . ($start + $display) . '&p=' . $pages .
             '">Next</a>';
110     }
111
112     echo '</p>'; // Close the paragraph.
113
114 } // End of links section.
115
116 include('includes/footer.html');
117 ?>
```

The first time this page is accessed, the **$_GET['s']** variable will not be set, and so **$start** should be 0 (the first record in a **LIMIT** clause is indexed at 0). Subsequent pages will receive the **$_GET['s']** variable from the URL, and it will be assigned to **$start**.

8. Write the **SELECT** query with a **LIMIT** clause:

```
$q = "SELECT last_name,
→ first_name, DATE_FORMAT
→ (registration_date, '%M %d, %Y')
→ AS dr, user_id
FROM users
ORDER BY registration_date ASC
LIMIT $start, $display";
$r = @mysqli_query($dbc, $q);
```

The **LIMIT** clause dictates with which record to begin retrieving (**$start**) and how many to return (**$display**) from that point. The first time the page is run, the query will be **SELECT last_name, first_name ... LIMIT 0, 10**. Clicking to the next page will result in **SELECT last_name, first_name ... LIMIT 10, 10**.

9. Create the HTML table header:

```
echo '<table width="60%">
<thead>
<tr>
  <th align="left"><strong>Edit
  → </strong></th>
  <th align="left"><strong>
  → Delete</strong></th>
  <th align="left"><strong>
  → Last Name</strong></th>
  <th align="left"><strong>
  → First Name</strong></th>
  <th align="left"><strong>
  → Date Registered</strong></th>
</tr>
</thead>
<tbody>
';
```

To simplify this script a bit, I'm assuming that there are records to be displayed. To be more formal, this script, prior to creating the table, would invoke the **mysqli_num_rows()** function and have a conditional that confirms that some records were returned.

10. Initialize the background color variable:

```
$bg = '#eeeeee';
```

To make each row have its own background color, we use a variable to store that color. To start, the **$bg** variable is assigned a value of *#eeeeee*, a light gray. This color will alternate with white (*#ffffff*).

11. Begin the **while** loop that retrieves every record, and then swap the background color:

```
while ($row = mysqli_fetch_array
→ ($r, MYSQLI_ASSOC)) {
$bg = ($bg= ='#eeeeee' ? '#ffffff'
→ : '#eeeeee');
```

The background color used by each row in the table is assigned to the **$bg** variable. Because the background color should alternate, this one line of code will, upon each iteration of the loop, assign the opposite color to **$bg**. If **$bg** is equal to *#eeeeee*, then it will be assigned the value of *#ffffff*, and vice versa (again, see the sidebar for the syntax and explanation of the ternary operator). For the first row fetched, **$bg** is initially equal to *#eeeeee* (see Step 10) and will therefore be assigned *#ffffff*, making a white background. For the second row, **$bg** is not equal to *#eeeeee*, so it will be assigned that value, making a gray background.

12. Print the records in a table row:

```
echo '<tr bgcolor="' . $bg . '">
    <td align="left"><a href="edit_
    → user.php?id=' . $row['user_id']
    → . '">Edit</a></td>
    <td align="left">
    → <a href="delete_user.php?id='
    → . $row['user_id'] .
    → '">Delete</a></td>
    <td align="left">' .
    → $row['last_name'] . '</td>
    <td align="left">' .
    → $row['first_name'] . '</td>
    <td align="left">' .
    → $row['dr'] . '</td>
</tr>
';
```

This code differs in only one way from that in the previous version of this script: the initial **TR** tag now includes the **bgcolor** attribute, whose value will be the **$bg** variable (so *#eeeeee* and *#ffffff*, alternating).

13. Complete the **while** loop and the table, free up the query result resources, and close the database connection:

```
} // End of WHILE loop.
echo '</tbody></table>';
mysqli_free_result($r);
mysqli_close($dbc);
```

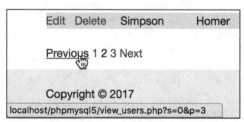

⊙ The *Previous* link will appear only if the current page is not the first one (compare with **Ⓐ**).

14. Begin a section for displaying links to other pages, if necessary:

```
if ($pages > 1) {
    echo '<br><p>';
```

If the script requires multiple pages to display all the records, it needs the appropriate links at the bottom of the page **Ⓐ**.

15. Determine the current page being viewed:

```
$current_page = ($start/$display)
→ + 1;
```

To make the links, the script must first determine the current page. This can be calculated as the starting number divided by the display number, plus 1. For example, on the second viewing of this page, **$start** will be 10 (because on the first instance, **$start** is 0), making the **$current_page** value 2: (10/10) + 1 = 2.

16. Create a link to the previous page, if necessary:

```
if ($current_page != 1) {
    echo '<a href="view_users.
    → php?s=' . ($start - $display)
    → . '&p=' . $pages . '">Previous
    → </a> ';
}
```

If the current page is not the first page, it should also have a *Previous* link to the earlier result set **⊙**. This isn't strictly necessary, but it is nice.

Each link will be made up of the script name, plus the starting point and the number of pages. The starting point for the previous page will be the current starting point minus the number being displayed. These values must be passed in every link, or the pagination will fail.

continues on next page

17. Make the numeric links:

```
for ($i = 1; $i <= $pages; $i++) {
  if ($i != $current_page) {
    echo '<a href="view_
    → users.php?s=' . (($display *
    → ($i - 1))) . '&p=' . $pages
    → . '">' . $i . '</a> ';
  } else {
    echo $i . ' ';
  }
} // End of FOR loop.
```

The bulk of the links will be created by looping from 1 to the total number of pages. Each page will be linked except for the current one. For each link, the starting point value, *s*, will be calculated by multiplying the number of records to display per page times one less than $i. For example, on page 3, $i - 1 is 2, meaning *s* will be 20.

18. Create a *Next* link:

```
if ($current_page != $pages) {
  echo '<a href="view_
  → users.php?s=' . ($start +
  → $display) . '&p=' . $pages .
  → '">Next</a>';
}
```

Finally, a *Next* page link will be displayed, assuming this is not the final page **D**.

19. Complete the page:

```
    echo '</p>';
  } // End of links section.
include('includes/footer.html');
?>
```

20. Save the file as **view_users.php**, place it in your web directory, and test it in your browser.

TIP This example paginates a simple query, but if you want to paginate a more complex query, like the results of a search, it's not that much more complicated. The main difference is that whatever terms are used in the query must be passed from page to page in the links. If the main query is not exactly the same from one viewing of the page to the next, the pagination will fail.

TIP If you run this example and the pagination doesn't match the number of results that should be returned (for example, the counting query indicates there are 150 records but the pagination only creates 3 pages, with 10 records on each), it's most likely because the main query and the COUNT() query are too different. These two queries will never be the same, but they must perform the same join (if applicable) and have the same WHERE and/or GROUP BY clauses to be accurate.

TIP No error handling has been included in this script, since I know the queries function as written. If you have problems, remember your MySQL/SQL debugging steps: print the query, run it using the mysql client or phpMyAdmin to confirm the results, and invoke the `mysqli_error()` function as needed.

Edit	Delete	O'Toole	Peter
Previous 1 2 3			
Copyright © 2017			

D The final results page will not display a *Next* link (compare with **A** and **C**).

Making Sortable Displays

There's another common feature that could be added to **view_users.php**. In its current state, the list of users is displayed in order by the date they registered. It would be nice to be able to view them by name as well.

From a MySQL perspective, accomplishing this task is easy: just change the **ORDER BY** clause of the **SELECT** query. Therefore, adding a sorting feature to the script merely requires additional PHP code that will change the **ORDER BY** clause. A logical way to do this is to link the column headings so that clicking them changes the display order. As you hopefully can guess, this involves using the GET method to pass a parameter back to this page indicating the preferred sort order.

To make sortable links:

1. Open **view_users.php** (Script 10.4) in your text editor or IDE, if you haven't already.

2. After determining the starting point (**$s**), define a **$sort** variable (**Script 10.5**):

   ```
   $sort = (isset($_GET['sort'])) ?
   $_GET['sort'] : 'rd';
   ```

   The **$sort** variable will be used to determine how the query results are to be ordered. This line uses the ternary operator (see the sidebar in the previous section of the chapter) to assign a value to **$sort**. If **$_GET['sort']** is set, which will be the case after the user clicks any link, then **$sort** should be assigned that value. If **$_GET['sort']** is not set, then **$sort** is assigned a default value of *rd* (short for *registration date*).

continues on page 333

Script 10.5 This latest version of the **view_users.php** script creates clickable links out of the table's column headings.

```
1   <?php # Script 10.5 - #5
2   // This script retrieves all the records from the users table.
3   // This new version allows the results to be sorted in different ways.
4
5   $page_title = 'View the Current Users';
6   include('includes/header.html');
7   echo '<h1>Registered Users</h1>';
8
9   require('../mysqli_connect.php');
10
11  // Number of records to show per page:
12  $display = 10;
13
14  // Determine how many pages there are...
15  if (isset($_GET['p']) && is_numeric($_GET['p'])) { // Already been determined.
16      $pages = $_GET['p'];
17  } else { // Need to determine.
18      // Count the number of records:
19      $q = "SELECT COUNT(user_id) FROM users";
20      $r = @mysqli_query($dbc, $q);
21      $row = @mysqli_fetch_array($r, MYSQLI_NUM);
22      $records = $row[0];
23      // Calculate the number of pages...
```

code continues on next page

```
24      if ($records > $display) { // More than 1 page.
25          $pages = ceil ($records/$display);
26      } else {
27          $pages = 1;
28      }
29  } // End of p IF.
30
31  // Determine where in the database to start returning results...
32  if (isset($_GET['s']) && is_numeric($_GET['s'])) {
33      $start = $_GET['s'];
34  } else {
35      $start = 0;
36  }
37
38  // Determine the sort...
39  // Default is by registration date.
40  $sort = (isset($_GET['sort'])) ? $_GET['sort'] : 'rd';
41
42  // Determine the sorting order:
43  switch ($sort) {
44      case 'ln':
45          $order_by = 'last_name ASC';
46          break;
47      case 'fn':
48          $order_by = 'first_name ASC';
49          break;
50      case 'rd':
51          $order_by = 'registration_date ASC';
52          break;
53      default:
54          $order_by = 'registration_date ASC';
55          $sort = 'rd';
56          break;
57  }
58
59  // Define the query:
60  $q = "SELECT last_name, first_name, DATE_FORMAT(registration_date, '%M %d, %Y') AS dr,
    user_id FROM users ORDER BY $order_by LIMIT $start, $display";
61  $r = @mysqli_query($dbc, $q); // Run the query.
62
63  // Table header:
64  echo '<table width="60%">
65  <thead>
66  <tr>
67      <th align="left"><strong>Edit</strong></th>
68      <th align="left"><strong>Delete</strong></th>
69      <th align="left"><strong><a href="view_users.php?sort=ln">Last Name</a></strong>
    </th>
70      <th align="left"><strong><a href="view_users.php?sort=fn">First Name</a></strong>
    </th>
71      <th align="left"><strong><a href="view_users.php?sort=rd">Date Registered</a>
    </strong></th>
72  </tr>
73  </thead>
74  <tbody>
75  ';
```

code continues on page 334

3. Determine how the results should be ordered:

```
switch ($sort) {
  case 'ln':
    $order_by = 'last_name ASC';
    break;
  case 'fn':
    $order_by = 'first_name ASC';
    break;
  case 'rd':
    $order_by =
      'registration_date ASC';
    break;
  default:
    $order_by =
      'registration_date ASC';
    $sort = 'rd';
    break;
}
```

The **switch** checks **$sort** against several expected values. If, for example, it is equal to *ln*, then the results should be ordered by the last name in ascending order. The assigned **$order_by** variable will be used in the SQL query.

If **$sort** has a value of *fn*, then the results should be in ascending order by first name. If the value is *rd*, then the results will be in ascending order of registration date. This is also the default case. Having this default case here protects against a malicious user changing the value of **$_GET['sort']** to something that could break the query.

4. Modify the query to use the new **$order_by** variable:

```
$q = "SELECT last_name,
  first_name, DATE_FORMAT
  (registration_date, '%M %d, %Y')
  AS dr, user_id
FROM users
ORDER BY $order_by
LIMIT $start, $display";
```

By this point, the **$order_by** variable has a value indicating how the returned results should be ordered (for example, *registration_date ASC*), so it can be easily added to the query. Remember that the **ORDER BY** clause comes before the **LIMIT** clause. If the resulting query doesn't run properly for you, print it out and inspect its syntax.

5. Modify the table header **echo** statement to create links out of the column headings:

```
echo '<table width="60%">
<thead>
<tr>
  <th align="left"><strong>Edit
    </strong></th>
  <th align="left">
    <strong>Delete</strong></th>
  <th align="left"><strong>
    <a href="view_users.php?sort=
    ln">Last Name</a></strong>
    </th>
  <th align="left"><strong>
    <a href="view_users.php?sort=
    fn">First Name</a></strong>
    </th>
  <th align="left"><strong>
    <a href="view_users.php?sort=
    rd">Date Registered</a>
    </strong></th>
</tr>
</thead>
<tbody>
';
```

To turn the column headings into clickable links, just surround them with the **A** tag. The value of the **href** attribute for each link corresponds to the acceptable values for **$_GET['sort']** (see the **switch** in Step 3).

continues on page 335

```
76
77   // Fetch and print all the records....
78   $bg = '#eeeeee';
79   while ($row = mysqli_fetch_array($r, MYSQLI_ASSOC)) {
80       $bg = ($bg=='#eeeeee' ? '#ffffff' : '#eeeeee');
81           echo '<tr bgcolor="' . $bg . '">
82           <td align="left"><a href="edit_user.php?id=' . $row['user_id'] . '">Edit</a></td>
83           <td align="left"><a href="delete_user.php?id=' . $row['user_id'] . '">Delete</a></td>
84           <td align="left">' . $row['last_name'] . '</td>
85           <td align="left">' . $row['first_name'] . '</td>
86           <td align="left">' . $row['dr'] . '</td>
87       </tr>
88       ';
89   } // End of WHILE loop.
90
91   echo '</tbody></table>';
92   mysqli_free_result($r);
93   mysqli_close($dbc);
94
95   // Make the links to other pages, if necessary.
96   if ($pages > 1) {
97
98       echo '<br><p>';
99       $current_page = ($start/$display) + 1;
100
101       // If it's not the first page, make a Previous button:
102       if ($current_page != 1) {
103           echo '<a href="view_users.php?s=' . ($start - $display) . '&p=' . $pages .
               '&sort=' . $sort . '">Previous</a> ';
104       }
105
106       // Make all the numbered pages:
107       for ($i = 1; $i <= $pages; $i++) {
108           if ($i != $current_page) {
109               echo '<a href="view_users.php?s=' . (($display * ($i - 1))) . '&p=' . $pages .
                   '&sort=' . $sort . '">' . $i . '</a> ';
110           } else {
111               echo $i . ' ';
112           }
113       } // End of FOR loop.
114
115       // If it's not the last page, make a Next button:
116       if ($current_page != $pages) {
117           echo '<a href="view_users.php?s=' . ($start + $display) . '&p=' . $pages .
               '&sort=' . $sort . '">Next</a>';
118       }
119
120       echo '</p>'; // Close the paragraph.
121
122   } // End of links section.
123
124   include('includes/footer.html');
125   ?>
```

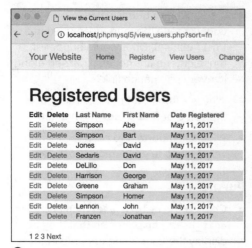

A After clicking the *First Name* column, the results are shown in ascending order by first name.

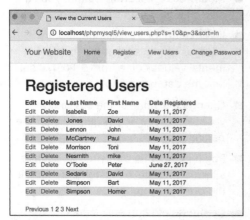

B After clicking the *Last Name* column, and then clicking to the second paginated display, the page shows the second group of results in ascending order by last name.

6. Modify the **echo** statement that creates the *Previous* link so that the sort value is also passed:

```
echo '<a href="view_users.php?s='
→ . ($start - $display) . '&p='
→ . $pages . '&sort=' . $sort .
→ '">Previous</a> ';
```

Add another *name=value* pair to the *Previous* link so that the sort order is also sent to each page of results. If you don't, then the pagination will fail, because the **ORDER BY** clause will differ from one page to the next.

7. Repeat Step 6 for the numbered pages and the *Next* link:

```
echo '<a href="view_users.php?s='
→ . (($display * ($i - 1))) . '&p='
→ . $pages . '&sort=' . $sort .
→ '">' . $i . '</a> ';
echo '<a href="view_users.php?s='
→ . ($start + $display) . '&p='
→ . $pages . '&sort=' . $sort .
→ '">Next</a>';
```

8. Save the file as **view_users.php**, place it in your web directory, and run it in your browser **A** and **B**.

> **TIP** An important security concept was also demonstrated in this example. Instead of using the value of $_GET['sort'] directly in the query, it's checked against assumed values in a **switch**. If, for some reason, $_GET['sort'] has a value other than would be expected, the query uses a default sorting order. The point is this: don't make assumptions about received data, and don't use unvalidated data in an **SQL** query.

Review and Pursue

If you have any problems with the review questions or the pursue prompts, turn to the book's supporting forum (LarryUllman.com/forums/).

Review

- What is the standard sequence of steps for debugging PHP-MySQL problems (explicitly conveyed at the end of Chapter 8)?

- What are the two ways of passing values to a PHP script (aside from user input)?

- What security measures do the **delete_user.php** and **edit_user.php** scripts take to prevent malicious or accidental deletions?

- Why is it safe to use the **$id** value in queries without running it through **mysqli_real_escape_string()** first?

- In what situation will the **mysqli_affected_rows()** function return a false negative (i.e., report that no records were affected despite the fact that the query ran without error)?

- What is the ternary operator? How is it used?

- What two values are required to properly paginate query results?

- How do you alter a query so that its results are paginated?

- If a paginated query is based on additional criteria (beyond those used in a **LIMIT** clause), what would happen if those criteria are not also passed along in every pagination link?

- Why is it important not to directly use the value of **$_GET['sort']** in a query?

- Why is it important to pass the sorting value along in each pagination link?

Pursue

- Change the **delete_user.php** and **edit_user.php** pages so that they both display the user being affected in the browser window's title bar.

- Modify **edit_user.php** so that you can also change a user's password.

- If you're up for a challenge, modify **edit_user.php** so that the form elements' values come from **$_POST**, if set, and the database if not.

- Change the value of the **$display** variable in **view_users.php** to alter the pagination.

- Paginate another query result, such as a list of accounts or customers found in the *banking* database.

- Create delete and edit scripts for the *banking* database. You'll have to factor in the foreign key constraints in place, which limit, for example, the deletion of customers that still have accounts.

11

Web Application Development

The preceding two chapters focus on using PHP and MySQL together (which is, after all, the primary point of this book). But there's still a lot of PHP-centric material to be covered. Taking a quick break from using PHP with MySQL, this chapter covers a handful of techniques that are often used in more complex web applications.

The first topic covered in this chapter is sending email using PHP. It's a very common thing to do and is surprisingly simple (assuming that the server is properly set up). After that, the chapter has examples that cover: handling file uploads through an HTML form, using PHP and JavaScript together, and how to use the **header()** function to manipulate the browser. The chapter concludes by touching on some of the date and time functions available in PHP.

In This Chapter

Sending Email

One of my absolute favorite things about PHP is how easy it is to send an email. On a properly configured server, the process is as simple as using the `mail()` function:

```
mail(to, subject, body, [headers]);
```

The *to* value should be an email address or a series of addresses, separated by commas. Any of these are allowed:

- email@example.com

- email1@example.com, email2@example.com

- Actual Name <email@example.com>

- Actual Name <email@example.com>, This Name <email2@example.com>

The *subject* value will create the email's subject line, and *body* is where you put the contents of the email. To make things more legible, variables are often assigned values and then used in the `mail()` function call:

```
$to = 'email@example.com';
$subject = 'This is the subject';
$body = 'This is the body.
It goes over multiple lines.';
mail($to, $subject, $body);
```

As you can see in the assignment to the **$body** variable, you can create an email message that goes over multiple lines by having the text do exactly that within the quotation marks. You can also use the newline character (**\n**) within double quotation marks to accomplish this:

```
$body = "This is the body.\nIt goes
→ over multiple lines.";
```

This is all very straightforward, and there are only a couple of caveats. First, the subject line cannot contain the newline character (**\n**). Second, each line of the body should be no longer than 70 characters in

PHP `mail()` Dependencies

PHP's **mail()** function doesn't actually send the email itself. Instead, it tells the mail server running on the computer to do so. What this means is that the computer on which PHP is running must have a working mail server for this function to work.

If you have a computer running a Unix variant or if you are running your website through a professional host, this should not be a problem. But if you are running PHP on your own desktop or laptop computer, you'll probably need to make adjustments.

If you are running Windows and have an Internet service provider (ISP) that provides you with an SMTP server (like *smtp.comcast.net*), this information can be set in the **php.ini** file (see Appendix A, "Installation"). Unfortunately, this will only work if your ISP does not require authentication—a username and password combination—to use the SMTP server. Otherwise, you'll need to install an SMTP server on your computer. There are plenty available; just search the Internet for *free windows smtp server* and you'll see some options. The XAMPP application, which Appendix A recommends you use, includes the Mercury mail server.

If you are running macOS, you'll need to enable the built-in SMTP server (either sendmail or postfix, depending on the specific version you are running). You can find instructions online for doing so (search with *enable sendmail "macOS"*). If you're using MAMP, per the recommendation in Appendix A, search online for sending email with MAMP.

length (this is more of a recommendation than a requirement). You can accomplish this using the **wordwrap()** function. It will insert a newline into a string every *X* number of characters. To wrap text to 70 characters, use

```
$body = wordwrap($body, 70);
```

The **mail()** function takes a fourth, optional parameter for additional headers. This is where you could set the From, Reply-To, Cc, Bcc, and similar settings. For example:

```
mail($to, $subject, $body,
→ 'From: reader@example.com');
```

To use multiple headers of different types in your email, separate each with **\r\n**:

```
$headers = "From: John@example.com
→ \r\n";
$headers .= "Cc: Jane@example.com,
→ Joe@example.com\r\n";
mail($to, $subject, $body, $headers);
```

Although this fourth argument is optional, it is advised that you always include a From value (although that can also be established in PHP's configuration file).

A A standard contact form.

To use the **mail()** function, let's create a page that shows a contact form **A** and then handles the form submission, validating the data and sending it along in an email. This example will also provide a nice tip you'll sometimes use on pages with sticky forms.

Note two things before running this script: First, for this example to work, the computer on which PHP is running must have a working mail server. If you're using a hosted site, this shouldn't be an issue; on your own computer, you'll likely need to take preparatory steps (see the accompanying sidebar). I will say in advance that these steps can be daunting for the beginner; it will likely be easiest and most gratifying to use a hosted site for this particular script.

Second, this example, while functional, could be manipulated by bad people, allowing them to send spam through your contact form (not just to you but to anyone). The steps for preventing such attacks are provided in Chapter 13, "Security Methods." Following along and testing this example is just fine; relying on it as your long-term contact form solution is a bad idea.

To send email:

1. Begin a new PHP script in your text editor or IDE, to be named **email.php** (Script 11.1):

```
<!doctype html>
<html lang="en">
<head>
  <meta charset="utf-8">
  <title>Contact Me</title>
</head>
<body>
<h1>Contact Me</h1>
<?php # Script 11.1 - email.php
```

continues on next page

None of the examples in this chapter will use a template, like those in the past two chapters, so it starts with the standard HTML.

2. Create the conditional for checking if the form has been submitted and validate the form data:

```
if ($_SERVER['REQUEST_METHOD'] ==
→'POST') {
  if (!empty($_POST['name']) &&
→!empty($_POST['email']) &&
→!empty($_POST['comments']) ) {
```

The form contains three text inputs (technically, one is a textarea). The **empty()** function will confirm that something was entered into each. In Chapter 13, you'll learn how to use the **Filter** extension to confirm that the supplied email address has a valid format.

3. Create the body of the email:

```
$body = "Name: {$_POST['name']}\n\n
→Comments: {$_POST['comments']}";
$body = wordwrap($body, 70);
```

The email's body will start with the prompt *Name:*, followed by the name entered into the form. Then the same treatment is given to the comments. The **wordwrap()** function then formats the whole body so that each line is only 70 characters long.

4. Send the email and print a message in the browser:

```
mail('your_email@example.com',
→'Contact Form Submission',
→$body, "From: {$_POST['email']}");
echo '<p><em>Thank you for
→contacting me. I will reply
→some day.</em></p>';
```

Assuming the server is properly configured, this one line will send the email. You will need to change the *to* value to your actual email address. The *From* value will be the email address from the form. The subject will be a literal string.

There's no easy way of confirming that the email was successfully sent, let alone received, but a generic message is printed.

5. Clear the **$_POST** array;

```
$_POST = [];
```

In this example, the form will always be shown, even upon successful submission. The form will be sticky in case the user omitted something 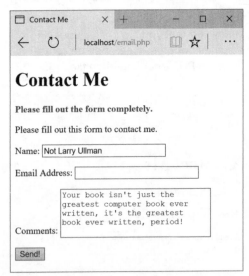. However, if the mail was sent, there's no need to show the values in the form again. To avoid that, the **$_POST** array can be cleared of its values using the short array syntax.

continues on page 342

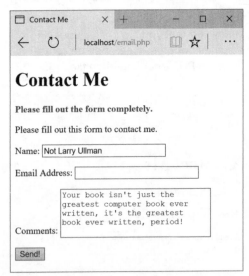

B The contact form will remember the user-supplied values.

Script 11.1 This page displays a contact form that, upon submission, will send an email with the form data to an email address.

```php
1    <!doctype html>
2    <html lang="en">
3    <head>
4        <meta charset="utf-8">
5        <title>Contact Me</title>
6    </head>
7    <body>
8    <h1>Contact Me</h1>
9    <?php # Script 11.1 - email.php
10
11   // Check for form submission:
12   if ($_SERVER['REQUEST_METHOD'] == 'POST') {
13
14       // Minimal form validation:
15       if (!empty($_POST['name']) && !empty($_POST['email']) && !empty($_POST['comments']) ) {
16
17           // Create the body:
18           $body = "Name: {$_POST['name']}\n\nComments: {$_POST['comments']}";
19
20           // Make it no longer than 70 characters long:
21           $body = wordwrap($body, 70);
22
23           // Send the email:
24           mail('your_email@example.com', 'Contact Form Submission', $body,
                 "From: {$_POST['email']}");
25
26           // Print a message:
27           echo '<p><em>Thank you for contacting me. I will reply some day.</em></p>';
28
29           // Clear $_POST (so that the form's not sticky):
30           $_POST = [];
31
32       } else {
33           echo '<p style="font-weight: bold; color: #C00">Please fill out the form completely.
                 </p>';
34       }
35
36   } // End of main isset() IF.
37
38   // Create the HTML form:
39   ?>
40   <p>Please fill out this form to contact me.</p>
41   <form action="email.php" method="post">
42       <p>Name: <input type="text" name="name" size="30" maxlength="60" value="<?php if
             (isset($_POST['name'])) echo $_POST['name']; ?>"></p>
43       <p>Email Address: <input type="email" name="email" size="30" maxlength="80" value="<?php if
             (isset($_POST['email'])) echo $_POST['email']; ?>"></p>
44       <p>Comments: <textarea name="comments" rows="5" cols="30"><?php if
             (isset($_POST['comments'])) echo $_POST['comments']; ?></textarea></p>
45       <p><input type="submit" name="submit" value="Send!"></p>
46   </form>
47   </body>
48   </html>
```

6. Complete the conditionals:

```
    } else {
      echo '<p style="font-weight:
      → bold; color: #C00">
      → Please fill out the form
      → completely.</p>';
    }
} // End of main isset() IF.
?>
```

The error message contains some inline CSS so that the error appears as red and bold.

7. Begin the form:

```
<p>Please fill out this form to
→ contact me.</p>
<form action="email.php"
→ method="post">
  <p>Name: <input type="text"
  → name="name" size="30"
  → maxlength="60" value="<?php
  → if (isset($_POST['name'])) echo
  → $_POST['name']; ?>"></p>
  <p>Email Address: <input
  → type="email" name="email"
  → size="30" maxlength="80"
  → value="<?php if (isset($_POST
  → ['email'])) echo $_POST
  → ['email']; ?>"></p>
```

The form will submit back to this same page using the POST method. The first two inputs are of type text; both are made sticky by checking if the corresponding **$_POST** variable has a value. If so, that value is printed as the current value for that input. Because the **$_POST** array is cleared out in Step 5, **$_POST['name']** and the like will not be set when this form is viewed again, after its previous successful completion and submission.

8. Complete the form:

```
  <p>Comments: <textarea
  → name="comments" rows="5"
  → cols="30"><?php if (isset
  → ($_POST['comments'])) echo
  → $_POST['comments'];
  → ?></textarea></p>
  <p><input type="submit"
  → name="submit" value="Send!">
  → </p>
</form>
```

The comments input is a textarea, which does not use a **value** attribute. Instead, to be made sticky, the value is printed between the opening and closing **textarea** tags.

9. Complete the HTML page:

```
</body>
</html>
```

10. Save the file as **email.php**, place it in your web directory, and test it in your browser **C**.

Contact Me

Thank you for contacting me. I will reply some day.

Please fill out this form to contact me.

Name: [_____]

Email Address: [_____]

[   ]

Comments: [   ]

[Send!]

C Successful completion and submission of the form.

11. Check your email to confirm that you received the message 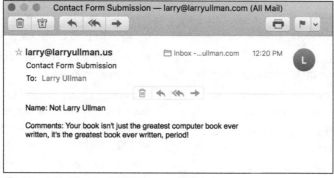.

If you don't actually get the email, you'll need to do some debugging work. With this example, you should confirm with your host (if using a hosted site) or yourself (if running PHP on your server) that there's a working mail server installed. You should also test this using different email addresses (for both the *to* and *from* values). Also, watch that your spam filter isn't eating up the message.

TIP The `mail()` function takes an optional fifth argument, for additional parameters to be sent to the mail-sending application.

TIP The `mail()` function returns a 1 or a 0 indicating the success of the function call. This is not the same thing as the email successfully being sent or received. Again, you cannot easily test for either using PHP.

TIP Although it's easy to send a simple message with the `mail()` function, sending HTML emails or emails with attachments involves more work. I discuss how you can do both in my book *PHP 5 Advanced: Visual QuickPro Guide* (Peachpit Press, 2007).

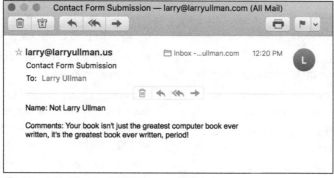

> Contact Form Submission — larry@larryullman.com (All Mail)
>
> ☆ **larry@larryullman.us**   📁 Inbox -...ullman.com   12:20 PM
> Contact Form Submission
> To: Larry Ullman
>
> Name: Not Larry Ullman
>
> Comments: Your book isn't just the greatest computer book ever written, it's the greatest book ever written, period!

D The resulting email (from the data in **A**, albeit using a different From address).

Handling File Uploads

Chapters 2, "Programming with PHP," and 3, "Creating Dynamic Web Sites," go over the basics of handling HTML forms with PHP. For the most part, every type of form element can be handled the same in PHP, with one exception: file uploads. The process of uploading a file has two dimensions. First the HTML form must be displayed, with the proper code to allow for file uploads. Upon submission of the form, the server will first store the uploaded file in a temporary directory, so the next step is for the PHP script to copy the uploaded file to its final destination.

For this process to work, several things must be in place:

- PHP must run with the correct settings.

- A temporary storage directory must exist with the correct permissions.

- The final storage directory must exist with the correct permissions.

The next section will cover the server setup to allow for file uploads; then I'll show you how to create a PHP script that does the uploading.

Allowing for file uploads

As I said, certain settings must be established for PHP to be able to handle file uploads. I'll first discuss why or when you'd need to make these adjustments before walking you through the steps.

The first issue is PHP itself. There are several settings in PHP's configuration file (**php.ini**) that dictate how PHP handles uploads, specifically stating how large of a file can be uploaded and where the upload should temporarily be stored (**Table 11.1**). Generally speaking, you'll need to edit this file if any of these conditions apply:

- *file_uploads* is disabled.

- PHP has no temporary directory to use.

- You will be uploading very large files (larger than 2 MB).

If you don't have access to your **php.ini** file—if you're using a hosted site, for example—presumably the host has already configured PHP to allow for file uploads.

The second issue is the location of, and permissions on, the temporary directory. This is where PHP will store the uploaded file until your PHP script moves it to its final destination. If you installed PHP on your

TABLE 11.1 File Upload Configurations

Setting	Value Type	Importance
file_uploads	Boolean	Enables PHP support for file uploads
max_input_time	integer	Indicates how long, in seconds, a PHP script is allowed to run
post_max_size	integer	Size, in bytes, of the total allowed **POST** data
upload_max_filesize	integer	Size, in bytes, of the largest possible file upload allowed
upload_tmp_dir	string	Indicates where uploaded files should be temporarily stored

own Windows computer, you might need to take steps here. macOS and Unix users need not worry about this—a temporary directory already exists for such purposes (a special directory called **/tmp**).

Finally, the destination folder must be created and have the proper permissions established on it. This is a step that *everyone* must take for *every* application that handles file uploads. Because there are important security issues involved in this step, please also make sure that you read and understand the sidebar "Secure Folder Permissions."

With all of this in mind, let's go through the steps.

Secure Folder Permissions

There's normally a trade-off between security and convenience. With this example, it'd be more convenient to place the *uploads* folder within the web document directory (the convenience arises with respect to how easily the uploaded images can be viewed in the browser), but doing that is less secure.

For PHP to be able to place files in the *uploads* folder, it needs to have write permissions on that directory. On most servers, PHP is running as the same user as the web server itself. On a hosted server, this means that all X number of sites being hosted are running as the same user. Creating a folder that PHP can write to means creating a folder that *everyone* can write to. Literally anyone with a site hosted on the server can now move, copy, or write files to your *uploads* folder (assuming that they know it exists). This even means that a malicious user could copy a troublesome PHP script to your *uploads* directory. However, since the *uploads* directory in this example is not within the web directory, such a PHP script cannot be run in a browser. It's less convenient to do things this way, but more secure.

If you must keep the *uploads* folder publicly accessible, and if you're using the Apache web server, you could limit access to the *uploads* folder using an **.htaccess** file. Basically, you would state that only image files in the folder be publicly viewable, meaning that even if a PHP script were to be placed there, it could not be executed. Or, because you'll learn how to use *proxy scripts* later in this chapter, you could deny all external access to that folder. Information on how to use **.htaccess** files can be found in Appendix A.

Sometimes even the most conservative programmer will make security concessions. The important point is that you're aware of the potential concerns and that you do the most you can to minimize the danger.

To prepare the server:

1. Run the **phpinfo()** function to confirm your server settings **A**.

   The **phpinfo()** function prints out a slew of information about your PHP setup. It's one of the most important functions in PHP, if not the most (in my opinion). Search for the settings listed in Table 11.1 and confirm their values. Make sure that *file_uploads* has a value of *On* and that the limit for *upload_max_filesize* (2 MB, by default) and *post_max_size* (8 MB) won't be a restriction for you. If you are running PHP on Windows, see whether *upload_tmp_dir* has a value. If it doesn't, that might be a problem (you'll know for certain after running the PHP script that handles the file upload). For non-Windows users, if this value says *no value*, that's perfectly fine.

   By the way, another advantage of using an all-in-one installer, such as XAMPP for Windows or MAMP for macOS, is that the installer should properly configure these settings, too.

2. If necessary, open **php.ini** in your text editor.

   If there's anything you saw in Step 1 that needs to be changed, or if something happens when you go to handle a file upload using PHP, you'll need to edit the **php.ini** file. To find this file, see the *Configuration File (php.ini) path* value in the **phpinfo()** output. This indicates exactly where this file is on your computer (also see Appendix A for more).

   If you are not allowed to edit your **php.ini** file (if, for instance, you're using a hosted server), then presumably any necessary edits would have already been made to allow for file uploads. If not, you'll need to request these changes from your hosting company (which may or may not agree to make them).

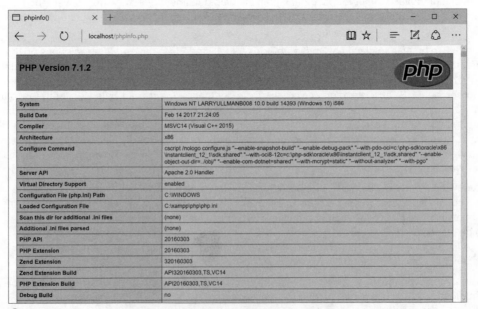

PHP Version 7.1.2	
System	Windows NT LARRYULLMANB008 10.0 build 14393 (Windows 10) i586
Build Date	Feb 14 2017 21:24:05
Compiler	MSVC14 (Visual C++ 2015)
Architecture	x86
Configure Command	cscript /nologo configure.js "--enable-snapshot-build" "--enable-debug-pack" "--with-pdo-oci=c:\php-sdk\oracle\x86\instantclient_12_1\sdk,shared" "--with-oci8-12c=c:\php-sdk\oracle\x86\instantclient_12_1\sdk,shared" "--enable-object-out-dir=../obj/" "--enable-com-dotnet=shared" "--with-mcrypt=static" "--without-analyzer" "--with-pgo"
Server API	Apache 2.0 Handler
Virtual Directory Support	enabled
Configuration File (php.ini) Path	C:\WINDOWS
Loaded Configuration File	C:\xampp\php\php.ini
Scan this dir for additional .ini files	(none)
Additional .ini files parsed	(none)
PHP API	20160303
PHP Extension	20160303
Zend Extension	320160303
Zend Extension Build	API320160303,TS,VC14
PHP Extension Build	API20160303,TS,VC14
Debug Build	no

A A **phpinfo()** script returns all the information regarding your PHP setup, including all the file-upload handling stuff.

3. Search the **php.ini** file for the configuration to be changed and make any edits **B**.

   For example, in the File Uploads section, you'll see these three lines:

   ```
   file_uploads = On
   ;upload_tmp_dir =
   upload_max_filesize = 2M
   ```

   The first line dictates whether or not uploads are allowed. The second states where the uploaded files should be temporarily stored. On most operating systems, including macOS and Unix, this setting can be left commented out (preceded by a semicolon) without any problem.

   If you are running Windows and need to create a temporary directory, set this value to **C:\tmp**, making sure that the line is *not* preceded by a semicolon. Again, using XAMPP on Windows 7, I did not need to create a temporary directory, so you may be able to get away without one too.

   Finally, a maximum upload file size is set (the *M* is shorthand for *megabytes* in configuration settings).

4. Save the **php.ini** file and restart your web server.

   How you restart your web server depends on the operating system and web-serving application being used. See Appendix A for instructions.

5. Confirm the changes by rerunning the **phpinfo()** script.

   Before going any further, confirm that the necessary changes have been enacted by repeating Step 1.

continues on next page

```
805   ;;;;;;;;;;;;;;;;;
806   ; File Uploads ;
807   ;;;;;;;;;;;;;;;;;
808
809   ; Whether to allow HTTP file uploads.
810   ; http://php.net/file-uploads
811   file_uploads = On
812
813   ; Temporary directory for HTTP uploaded files (will use system default if not
814   ; specified).
815   ; http://php.net/upload-tmp-dir
816   ;upload_tmp_dir =
817
818   ; Maximum allowed size for uploaded files.
819   ; http://php.net/upload-max-filesize
820   upload_max_filesize = 2M
821
822   ; Maximum number of files that can be uploaded via a single request
823   max_file_uploads = 20
```

B The File Uploads subsection of the **php.ini** file.

6. If you are running Windows and need to create a temporary directory, add a **tmp** folder within **C:** and make sure that everyone can write to that directory **C**.

PHP, through your web server, will temporarily store the uploaded file in the *upload_tmp_dir*. For this to work, the web user (if your web server runs as a particular user) must have permission to write to the folder.

In all likelihood, you may not have to change the permissions, but to do so, depending on what version of Windows you are running, you can normally adjust the permissions by right-clicking the folder and selecting Properties. Within the Properties window there should be a Security tab, where you can set permissions. It may also be under Sharing. Windows uses a more lax permissions system, so you probably won't have to change anything unless the folder is deliberately restricted.

macOS and Unix users can skip this step since the temporary directory—**/tmp**—has open permissions already. XAMPP on Windows also creates its own temp directory for you.

7. Create a new directory, called *uploads*, in a directory outside of the web root directory.

All of the uploaded files will be permanently stored in the *uploads* directory. If you'll be placing your PHP script in the **C:\xampp\htdocs\ch11** directory, then create a **C:\xampp\uploads** directory. Or if the files are going in **/Users/~<username>/Sites/ch11**, make a **/Users/~<username>/uploads** folder. Figure **D** shows the structure you should establish, and the sidebar discusses why this step is necessary.

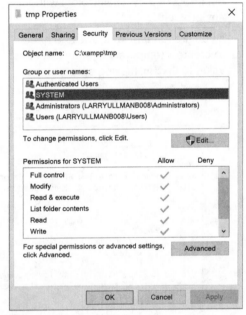

C Windows users need to make sure that the **C:\tmp** (or whatever directory is used) is writable by PHP.

D Assuming that *htdocs* is the web root directory (**http://www.example.com** or **http://localhost** points there), then the *uploads* directory needs to be placed outside of it.

some folder

uploads

htdocs

http://www.example.com points here

images.php

show_image.php

upload_image.php

function.js

js

8. Set the permissions on the *uploads* directory so that the web server can write to it.

Again, Windows users can use the Properties window to make these changes, although it may not be necessary. And macOS users can...

A. Select the folder in the Finder.

B. Press Command+I.

C. Allow everyone to Read & Write, under the Sharing & Permissions panel **E**.

If you're using a hosted site, the host likely provides a control panel through which you can tweak a folder's settings, or you might be able to do this within your FTP application.

Depending on your operating system, you may be able to upload files without first taking this step. You can try the following script before altering the permissions, just to see. If you see messages like those in **F**, then you will need to make some adjustments.

TIP Unix users can use the chmod command to adjust a folder's permissions. The proper permissions in Unix terms can be either 755 or 777.

TIP Because of the time it can take to upload a large file, you may also need to change the max_input_time value in the php.ini file or temporarily bypass it using the set_time_limit() function in your script.

TIP File and directory permissions can be complicated stuff, particularly if you've never dealt with them before. If you have problems with these steps or the next script, search the web or turn to the book's corresponding forum (www.LarryUllman.com/forums/).

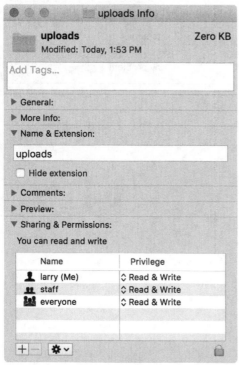

E Adjusting the properties on the *uploads* folder in macOS.

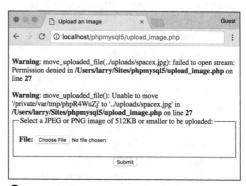

F If PHP could not move the uploaded image over to the *uploads* folder because of a permissions issue, you'll see an error message like this one. Fix the permissions on *uploads* to correct this.

Uploading files with PHP

Now that the server has (hopefully) been set up to properly allow for file uploads, you can create the PHP script that does the actual file handling. There are two parts to such a script: the HTML form and the PHP code.

The required syntax for a form to handle a file upload has three parts:

```
<form enctype="multipart/form-data"
→ action="script.php" method="post">
<input type="hidden"
→ name="MAX_FILE_SIZE" value="30000">
File <input type="file"
→ name="upload">
```

The **enctype** part of the initial **form** tag indicates that the form should be able to handle multiple types of data, including files. If you want to accept file uploads, you must include this **enctype**! Also note that the form *must use* the POST method. The **MAX_FILE_SIZE** hidden input is a form restriction on how large the chosen file can be, in bytes, and must come before the file input. Although it's easy for a user to circumvent this restriction, it should still be used. Finally, the file input type will create the proper button in the form (**G** and **H**).

Upon form submission, the uploaded file can be accessed using the **$_FILES** super-global. The **variable** will be an array of values, listed in **Table 11.2**.

Once the file has been received by the PHP script, the **move_uploaded_file()** function can transfer it from the temporary directory to its permanent location.

```
move_uploaded_file
→ (temporary_filename,
→ /path/to/destination/filename);
```

This next script will let the user select a file on his or her computer and will then store

G The file input as it appears in Edge on Windows.

H The file input as it appears in Google Chrome on macOS.

TABLE 11.2 The $_FILES Array

Index	Meaning
name	The original name of the file (as it was on the user's computer)
type	The MIME type of the file, as provided by the browser
size	The size of the uploaded file in bytes
tmp_name	The temporary filename of the uploaded file as it was stored on the server
error	The error code associated with any problem

Script 11.2 This script allows the user to upload an image file from their computer to the server.

```
1    <!doctype html>
2    <html lang="en">
3    <head>
4        <meta charset="utf-8">
5        <title>Upload an Image</title>
6        <style type="text/css" title="text/
     css" media="all">
7        .error {
8            font-weight: bold;
9            color: #C00;
10       }
11       </style>
12   </head>
13   <body>
14   <?php # Script 11.2 - upload_image.php
15
16   // Check if the form has been submitted:
17   if ($_SERVER['REQUEST_METHOD'] ==
     'POST') {
18
19       // Check for an uploaded file:
20       if (isset($_FILES['upload'])) {
21
22           // Validate the type. Should be
             JPEG or PNG.
23           $allowed = ['image/pjpeg', 'image/
             jpeg', 'image/JPG', 'image/X-
             PNG', 'image/PNG', 'image/png',
             'image/x-png'];
24           if (in_array($_FILES['upload']
             ['type'], $allowed)) {
25
26               // Move the file over.
27               if (move_uploaded_file ($_
                 FILES['upload']['tmp_name'],
                 "../uploads/{$_FILES['upload']
                 ['name']}")) {
28                   echo '<p><em>The file has
                     been uploaded!</em></p>';
29               } // End of move... IF.
30
31           } else { // Invalid type.
32               echo '<p class="error">Please
                 upload a JPEG or PNG image.
                 </p>';
33           }
34
35       } // End of isset($_FILES['upload']) IF.
36
37       // Check for an error:
38       if ($_FILES['upload']['error'] > 0) {
39           echo '<p class="error">The file
             could not be uploaded because:
             <strong>';
```

code continues on next page

it in the *uploads* directory. The script will check that the file is of an image type, specifically a JPEG or PNG. In the next section of this chapter, another script will list, and create links to, the uploaded images.

To handle file uploads in PHP:

1. Create a new PHP document in your text editor or IDE, to be named **upload_image.php** (Script 11.2):

```
<!doctype html>
<html lang="en">
<head>
  <meta charset="utf-8">
  <title>Upload an Image</title>
  <style>
  .error {
    font-weight: bold;
    color: #C00;
  }
  </style>
</head>
<body>
<?php # Script 11.2 -
→ upload_image.php
```

This script will make use of one CSS class to format any errors.

2. Check if the form has been submitted and that a file was selected:

```
if ($_SERVER['REQUEST_METHOD'] ==
→ 'POST') {
  if (isset($_FILES['upload'])) {
```

continues on next page

Since this form will have no other fields to be validated ❶, this is the only conditional required. You could also validate the size of the uploaded file to determine if it fits within the acceptable range (refer to the `$_FILES['upload']['size']` value).

3. Check that the uploaded file is of the proper type:

```
$allowed = ['image/pjpeg',
→'image/jpeg', 'image/JPG',
→'image/X-PNG', 'image/PNG',
→'image/png', 'image/x-png'];
if (in_array($_FILES['upload']
→['type'], $allowed)) {
```

The file's type is its *MIME* type, indicating what kind of file it is. The browser can determine and may provide this information, depending on the properties of the selected file.

To validate the file's type, first create an array of allowed options. The list of allowed types is based on accepting JPEGs and PNGs. Some browsers have variations on the MIME types, so those are included here as well. If the uploaded file's type is in this array, the file is valid and should be handled.

Script 11.2 *continued*

```
40
41        // Print a message based upon the
          error.
42        switch ($_FILES['upload']
          ['error']) {
43            case 1:
44                print 'The file exceeds the
                  upload_max_filesize setting
                  in php.ini.';
45                break;
46            case 2:
47                print 'The file exceeds the
                  MAX_FILE_SIZE setting in
                  the HTML form.';
48                break;
49            case 3:
50                print 'The file was only
                  partially uploaded.';
51                break;
52            case 4:
53                print 'No file was
                  uploaded.';
54                break;
55            case 6:
56                print 'No temporary folder
                  was available.';
57                break;
58            case 7:
59                print 'Unable to write to
                  the disk.';
60                break;
61            case 8:
62                print 'File upload
                  stopped.';
63                break;
64            default:
65                print 'A system error
                  occurred.';
```

code continues on next page

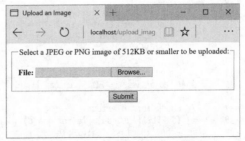

❶ This very basic HTML form only takes one input: a file.

Script 11.2 *continued*

```
66              break;
67         } // End of switch.
68
69         print '</strong></p>';
70
71     } // End of error IF.
72
73     // Delete the file if it still
       exists:
74     if (file_exists ($_FILES['upload']
       ['tmp_name']) && is_file($_
       FILES['upload']['tmp_name']) ) {
75         unlink ($_FILES['upload']
           ['tmp_name']);
76     }
77
78 } // End of the submitted conditional.
79 ?>
80
81 <form enctype="multipart/form-data"
   action="upload_image.php" method="post">
82
83     <input type="hidden" name="MAX_FILE_
       SIZE" value="524288">
84
85     <fieldset><legend>Select a JPEG or
       PNG image of 512KB or smaller to be
       uploaded:</legend>
86
87     <p><strong>File:</strong> <input
       type="file" name="upload"></p>
88
89     </fieldset>
90     <div align="center"><input
       type="submit" name="submit"
       value="Submit"></div>
91
92 </form>
93 </body>
94 </html>
```

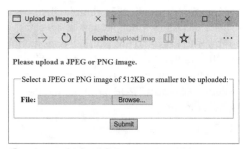

Ⓘ If the user uploads a file that's not a JPEG or PNG, this is the result.

4. Copy the file to its new location on the server:

```
if (move_uploaded_file
→ ($_FILES['upload']['tmp_name'],
→ "../uploads/{$_FILES['upload']
→ ['name']}")) {
    echo '<p><em>The file has been
    → uploaded!</em></p>';
} // End of move... IF.
```

The **move_uploaded_file()** function will move the file from its temporary to its permanent location (in the *uploads* folder). The file will retain its original name. Generally it's best to rename uploaded files—for security purposes—but doing so requires a database or other system for tracking the original and new filenames.

As a rule, you should always use a conditional to confirm that a file was successfully moved, rather than just assuming that the move worked.

5. Complete the image type and **isset ($_FILES['upload'])** conditionals:

```
    } else { // Invalid type
      echo '<p class="error">
      → Please upload a JPEG or PNG
      → image.</p>';
    }
} // End of isset($_FILES
→ ['upload']) IF.
```

The first **else** clause completes the **if** begun in Step 3. It applies if a file was uploaded but it wasn't of the right MIME type Ⓘ.

6. Check for, and report on, any errors:

```
if ($_FILES['upload'][ 'error'] >
→ 0) {
    echo '<p class="error">The file
    → could not be uploaded because:
    → <strong>';
```

continues on next page

If an error occurred, then **$_FILES ['upload']['error']** will have a value greater than 0. In such cases, this script will report what the error was.

7. Begin a **switch** that prints a more detailed error:

```
switch ($_FILES['upload']['error']) {
  case 1:
    print 'The file exceeds the
    → upload_max_filesize setting
    → in php.ini.';
    break;
  case 2:
    print 'The file exceeds the
    → MAX_FILE_SIZE setting in the
    → HTML form.';
    break;
  case 3:
    print 'The file was only
    → partially uploaded.';
    break;
  case 4:
    print 'No file was uploaded.';
    break;
```

There are several possible reasons a file could not be uploaded and moved. The first and most obvious one is if the permissions are not set properly on the destination directory. In such a case, you'll see an appropriate error message (see **F** in the previous section of the chapter). PHP will often also store an error number in the **$_FILES['upload'] ['error']** variable. The numbers correspond to specific problems, from 0 to 4, plus 6 through 8 (oddly enough, there is no 5). The **switch** conditional here prints out the problem according to the error number. The **default** case is added for future support (if different numbers are added in later versions of PHP).

For the most part, these errors are useful to you, the developer, and not things you'd indicate to the average user.

8. Complete the **switch**:

```
  case 6:
    print 'No temporary folder
    → was available. ';
    break;
  case 7:
    print 'Unable to write to
    → the disk. ';
    break;
  case 8:
    print 'File upload stopped. ';
    break;
  default:
    print 'A system error
    → occurred. ';
    break;
} // End of switch.
```

9. Complete the error **if** conditional:

```
    print '</strong></p>';
} // End of error IF.
```

10. Delete the temporary file if it still exists:

```
if (file_exists ($_FILES['upload']
→ ['tmp_name']) && is_file($_FILES
→ ['upload'][ 'tmp_name']) ) {
  unlink ($_FILES['upload']
  → ['tmp_name']);
}
```

If the file was uploaded but it could not be moved to its final destination or some other error occurred, then that file is still sitting on the server in its temporary location. To remove it, apply the **unlink()** function. Just to be safe, prior to applying **unlink()**, a conditional checks that the file exists and that it is a file (because the **file_exists()** function will return TRUE if the named item is a directory).

11. Complete the PHP section:

```
} // End of the submitted
conditional.
?>
```

12. Create the HTML form:

```
<form enctype="multipart/
→ form-data" action="upload_
→ image.php" method="post">
  <input type="hidden"
  → name="MAX_FILE_SIZE"
  → value="524288">
  <fieldset><legend>Select a JPEG
  → or PNG image of 512KB or
  → smaller to be uploaded:
  → </legend>
  <p><strong>File:</strong>
  → <input type="file"
  → name="upload"></p>
  </fieldset>
  <div align="center"><input
  → type="submit" name="submit"
  → value="Submit"></div>
</form>
```

This form is very simple , but it contains the three necessary parts for file uploads: the form's **enctype** attribute, the **MAX_FILE_SIZE** hidden input, and the file input.

13. Complete the HTML page:

```
</body>
</html>
```

14. Save the file as **upload_image.php**, place it in your web directory, and test it in your browser (Ⓚ and Ⓛ).

If you want, you can confirm that the script works by checking the contents of the *uploads* directory.

TIP Omitting the **enctype** form attribute is a common reason for file uploads to mysteriously fail.

TIP The existence of an uploaded file can also be validated with the **is_uploaded_file()** function.

TIP Windows users must use either forward slashes or double backslashes to refer to directories (so C:\\ or C:/ but not C:\). This is because the backslash is the escape character in PHP.

TIP The **move_uploaded_file()** function will overwrite an existing file without warning if the new and existing files both have the same name.

TIP The **MAX_FILE_SIZE** is a restriction in the browser as to how large a file can be, although not all browsers abide by this restriction. The PHP configuration file has its own restrictions. You can also validate the uploaded file size within the receiving PHP script.

TIP In Chapter 13, you'll learn a method for improving the security of this script by validating the uploaded file's type more reliably.

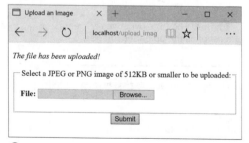

Ⓚ The result upon successfully uploading and moving a file.

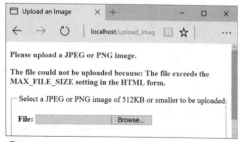

Ⓛ The result upon attempting to upload a file that is too large.

PHP and JavaScript

Although PHP and JavaScript are fundamentally different technologies, they can be used together to make better websites. The most significant difference between the two languages is that JavaScript is primarily client-side (meaning it runs in the browser) and PHP is always server-side. Therefore, JavaScript can do such things as detect the size of the browser window, create pop-up windows, and react to mouseovers, whereas PHP can do nothing like these things. Conversely, PHP can interact with MySQL on the server, but (browser-based) JavaScript cannot.

Although PHP cannot do certain things that JavaScript can, PHP can be used to create JavaScript, just as PHP can create

HTML. To be clear, in a browser, JavaScript is incorporated by and interacts with HTML, but PHP can dynamically generate JavaScript code, just as you've been using PHP to dynamically generate HTML.

To demonstrate this, we will create one PHP script that lists all the images uploaded by the **upload_image.php** script **Ⓐ**. The PHP script will also create each image name as a clickable link. The links themselves will call a JavaScript function **Ⓑ** that creates a pop-up window. The pop-up window will show the clicked image. This example will in no way be a thorough discussion of JavaScript, but it does adequately demonstrate how the various technologies—PHP, HTML, and JavaScript—can be used together. In Chapter 15, "Introducing jQuery," you'll learn how to use the jQuery JavaScript framework to add all sorts of functionality to PHP-based scripts.

Ⓐ This PHP page dynamically creates a list of all the uploaded images.

```
▲ <li>
      <a href="javascript:create_window('IMG_7952.jpg',1280,960)">IMG_7952.jpg</a>
  </li>
▲ <li>
      <a href="javascript:create_window('bravo.jpg',4896,3264)">bravo.jpg</a>
  </li>
```

Ⓑ Each image's name is linked as a call to a JavaScript function. The function call's parameters are created by PHP.

Creating the JavaScript File

Even though JavaScript and PHP are two different languages, they are similar enough that it's possible to dabble with JavaScript without any formal training. Before we create the JavaScript code for this example, I'll explain a few of the fundamentals.

First, JavaScript code can be added to an HTML page in one of two ways: inline or through an external file. To add inline JavaScript, place the JavaScript code between HTML **script** tags:

```
<script>
// Actual JavaScript code.
</script>
```

To use an external JavaScript file, add an **src** attribute to the **script** tag:

```
<script src="somefile.js"></script>
```

Your HTML pages can have multiple uses of the **script** tag, but each can only include an external file or have some JavaScript code—not both.

In both uses, before HTML5 the **script** tag would include a **type** attribute with a value of *text/javascript*. As of HTML5, that's no longer required.

JavaScript files use a **.js** extension. The file should use the same encoding (as set in your text editor or IDE) as the HTML script that will include the file. You can indicate the file's encoding in the **script** tag:

```
<script charset="utf-8"
→ src="somefile.js">
</script>
```

Whether you place your JavaScript code within **script** tags or in an external file, there are no opening and closing JavaScript tags, like the opening and closing PHP tags.

Next, know that variables in JavaScript are case-sensitive, just like PHP, but variables in JavaScript do not begin with dollar signs.

Finally, one of the main differences between JavaScript and PHP is that JavaScript is an object-oriented programming (OOP) language. Whereas PHP can be used in both a procedural approach, as most of this book demonstrates, and an object-oriented approach (introduced in Chapter 16, "An OOP Primer"), JavaScript is only ever an object-oriented language. This means you'll see the "dot" syntax like *something.something()* or *something.something.something*.

That's enough of the basics; in the following script, I'll explain the particulars of each bit of code in sufficient detail. In this next sequence of steps, you'll create a separate JavaScript file that will define one JavaScript function. The function itself will take three arguments—an image's name, its width, and its height. The function will use these values to create a pop-up window specifically for that image.

To create JavaScript with PHP:

1. Begin a new JavaScript document in your text editor or IDE, to be named **function.js** (Script 11.3):

```
// Script 11.3 - function.js
```

Again, there are no opening JavaScript tags here; you can just start writing JavaScript code. Comments in JavaScript can use either the single line (**//**) or multiline (**/* */**) syntax.

2. Begin the JavaScript function:

```
function create_window(image,
→ width, height) {
```

The JavaScript **create_window()** function will accept three parameters: the image's name, its width, and its height. Each of these will be passed to this function when the user clicks a link. The exact values of the image name, width, and height will be determined by PHP.

The syntax for creating a function in JavaScript is like a user-defined function in PHP, except that the variables do not have initial dollar signs.

3. Add 10 pixels to the received **width** and **height** values:

```
width = width + 10;
height = height + 10;
```

Script 11.3 The **function.js** script defines a JavaScript function for creating the pop-up window that will show an individual image.

```
1    // Script 11.3 - function.js
2
3    // Make a pop-up window function:
4    function create_window(image, width, height) {
5
6      // Add some pixels to the width and height:
7      width = width + 10;
8      height = height + 10;
9
10     // If the window is already open,
11     // resize it to the new dimensions:
12     if (window.popup && !window.popup.closed) {
13        window.popup.resizeTo(width, height);
14     }
15
16     // Set the window properties:
17     var specs = "location=no,scrollbars=no,menubar=no,toolbar=no,resizable=yes,left=0,top=0,
       width=" + width + ",height=" + height;
18
19     // Set the URL:
20     var url = "show_image.php?image=" + image;
21
22     // Create the pop-up window:
23     popup = window.open(url, "ImageWindow", specs);
24     popup.focus();
25
26  } // End of function.
```

Some pixels will be added to the width and height values to create a window slightly larger than the image itself. Math in JavaScript uses the same operators as in pretty much every language.

4. Resize the pop-up window if it is already open:

```
if (window.popup &&
→ !window.popup.closed) {
  window.popup.resizeTo(width,
    → height);
}
```

Later in the function, a window will be created, associated with the **popup** variable. If the user clicks one image name, creating the pop-up window, and then clicks another image's name without having closed the first pop-up window, the new image will be displayed in a mis-sized window. To prevent that, a bit of code here first checks if the pop-up window exists and if it is not closed. If both conditions are TRUE (the window is already open), the window will be resized according to the new image dimensions. This is accomplished by calling the **resizeTo()** method of the **popup** object (a *method* is the OOP term for a function).

C The pop-up window created by JavaScript.

5. Determine the properties of the pop-up window:

```
var specs = "location=no,
→ scrollbars=no, menubar=no,
→ toolbar=no,resizable=yes,left=0,
→ top=0,width=" +width +
→ ",height=" + height;
```

This line creates a new JavaScript variable with a name of **specs**. The **var** keyword before the variable name is the preferred way to create variables within a function (specifically, it creates a variable *local* to the function). Note that the **image**, **width**, and **height** variables didn't use this keyword, since they were created as the arguments to a function.

This variable will be used to establish the properties of the pop-up window. The window will have no location bar, scroll bars, menus, or toolbars; it should be resizable; it will be located in the upper-left corner of the screen; and it will have a width of **width** and a height of **height** **C**.

With strings in JavaScript, the plus sign is used to perform concatenation (whereas PHP uses the period).

6. Define the URL:

```
var url = "show_image.php?image="
→ + image;
```

This code sets the URL of the pop-up window—the page the window should load. That page is **show_image.php**, to be created later in this chapter. The **show_image.php** script expects to receive an image's name in the URL, so the value of the **url** variable is *show_image.php?image=* plus the name of the image concatenated to the end **C**.

continues on next page

7. Create the pop-up window:

```
popup = window.open(url,
→ "ImageWindow", specs);
popup.focus();
```

Finally, the pop-up window is created using the **open()** method of the **window** object. The **window** object is a global JavaScript object created by the browser to refer to the open windows. The **open()** method's first argument is the page to load, the second is the title to be given to the window, and the third is a list of properties. Note that the creation of this window is assigned to the **popup** variable. Because this variable's creation does not begin with the keyword **var**, **popup** will be a global variable. This is necessary for multiple calls of this function to reference that same variable.

Finally, focus is given to the new window, meaning it should appear above the current window.

8. Save the script as **function.js**.

9. Place the script, or a copy, in the **js** folder of your web directory.

JavaScript, like CSS, ought to be separated out when organizing your web directory. Normally, external JavaScript files are placed in a folder named *js*, *javascript*, or *scripts*.

Creating the PHP Script

Now that the JavaScript code required by the page has been created, it's time to create the PHP script itself (which will output the HTML that calls the JavaScript function). The purpose of this script is to list all the images already uploaded by **upload_image.php**. To do this, PHP needs to dynamically retrieve the contents of the **uploads** directory. That can be done via the **scandir()** function. It returns an array listing the files in a given directory (it was added in PHP 5).

The PHP script must link each displayed image name as a call to the just-defined JavaScript function. That function expects to receive three arguments: the image's name, its width, and its height. For PHP to find these last two values, the script will use the **getimagesize()** function. It returns an array of information for a given image (Table 11.3).

TABLE 11.3 The **getimagesize()** Array

Element	Value	Example
0	image's width in pixels	423
1	image's height in pixels	368
2	image's type	2 (representing JPG)
3	appropriate HTML **img** tag data	height="368" width="423"
mime	image's MIME type	image/png

To create JavaScript with PHP:

1. Begin a new PHP document in your text editor or IDE, to be named **images.php** (Script 11.4):

```
<!doctype html>
<html lang="en">
<head>
    <meta charset="utf-8">
    <title>Images</title>
```

2. Include the JavaScript file:

```
<script charset="utf-8"
→ src="js/function.js"></script>
```

You can use the **script** tags anywhere in an HTML page, but inclusions of external files are commonly performed in the document's head. The reference

to **function.js** assumes that the file will be found in the **js** directory, with the **js** directory being in the same directory as this current script (see **D** under "Handling File Uploads").

3. Complete the HTML head and begin the body:

```
</head>
<body>
<p>Click on an image to view it
→ in a separate window.</p>
```

4. Begin an HTML unordered list:

```
<ul>
```

To make things simple, this script displays each image as an item in an unordered list.

continues on next page

Script 11.4 The **images.php** script uses JavaScript and PHP to create links to images stored on the server. The images will be viewable through **show_image.php** (Script 11.5).

```
1    <!doctype html>
2    <html lang="en">
3    <head>
4       <meta charset="utf-8">
5       <title>Images</title>
6       <script charset="utf-8" src="js/function.js"></script>
7    </head>
8    <body>
9    <p>Click on an image to view it in a separate window.</p>
10   <ul>
11   <?php # Script 11.4 - images.php
12   // This script lists the images in the uploads directory.
13
14   $dir = '../uploads'; // Define the directory to view.
15
16   $files = scandir($dir); // Read all the images into an array.
17
18   // Display each image caption as a link to the JavaScript function:
19   foreach ($files as $image) {
20
21      if (substr($image, 0, 1) != '.') { // Ignore anything starting with a period.
22
```

code continues on next page

5. Start the PHP code and create an array of images by referring to the *uploads* directory:

```php
<?php # Script 11.4 - images.php
$dir = '../uploads ';
$files = scandir($dir);
```

This script will automatically list and link all of the images stored in the *uploads* folder (presumably put there by **upload_image.php**, Script 11.3). The code begins by defining the directory as a variable so that it's easier to refer to. Then the **scandir()** function, which returns an array of files and directories found within a folder, assigns that information to an array called **$files**.

6. Begin looping through the **$files** array:

```php
foreach ($files as $image) {
    if (substr($image, 0, 1) !=
    →'. ') {
```

This loop will go through every image in the array and create a list item for it. Within the loop, there is one conditional that checks if the first character in the file's name is a period. On non-Windows systems, hidden files start with a period, the current directory is referred to using just a single period, and two periods refers to the parent directory. Since these might be included in **$files**, they need to be weeded out.

7. Get the image information and encode its name:

```php
$image_size = getimagesize
→("$dir/$image");
$image_name = urlencode($image);
```

The **getimagesize()** function returns an array of information about an image (Table 11.3). The values returned by this function will be used to set the width and height sent to the **create_window()** JavaScript function.

Next, the **urlencode()** function makes a string safe to pass in a URL. Because the image name may contain characters not allowed in a URL (and it will be passed in the URL when invoking **show_image.php**), the name should be encoded.

Script 11.4 *continued*

```
23          // Get the image's size in pixels:
24          $image_size = getimagesize("$dir/$image");
25
26          // Make the image's name URL-safe:
27          $image_name = urlencode($image);
28
29          // Print the information:
30          echo "<li><a href=\"javascript:create_window('$image_name',$image_size[0],
            $image_size[1])\">$image</a></li>\n";
31
32      } // End of the IF.
33
34  } // End of the foreach loop.
35  ?>
36  </ul>
37  </body>
38  </html>
```

8. Print the list item:

```
echo "<li><a href=\"javascript:
→ create_window('$image_name',
→ $image_size[0],$image_size[1])\">
→ $image</a></li>\n";
```

Finally, the loop creates the HTML list item, consisting of the linked image name. The link itself is a call to the JavaScript `create_window()` function. In order to execute the JavaScript function from within HTML, preface it with `javascript:`. (There's much more to calling JavaScript from within HTML, but just use this syntax for now.)

The function's three arguments are the image's name, its width, and its height. Because the image's name will be a string, it must be wrapped in quotation marks.

9. Complete the **if** conditional, the **foreach** loop, and the PHP section:

```
    } // End of the IF.
} // End of the foreach loop.
?>
```

10. Complete the unordered list and the HTML page:

```
</ul>
</body>
</html>
```

11. Save the file as **images.php**, place it in your web directory (in the same directory as **upload_image.php**), and test it in your browser **Ⓐ**.

Note that clicking the links will not work yet because **show_image.php**—the page the pop-up window attempts to load—hasn't been created.

12. View the source code to see the dynamically generated links **Ⓑ**.

Notice how the parameters to each function call are appropriate to the specific image.

TIP Different browsers will handle the sizing and display of the window differently. In my tests, for example, Google Chrome always required that the window be at least a certain width, and Internet Explorer would pad the displayed image on all four sides.

TIP Some versions of Windows create a **Thumbs.db** file in a folder of images. You might want to check for this value in the conditional in Step 6 that weeds out some returned items. That code would be

```
if ( (substr($image, 0, 1) != '. ')
→ && ($image != 'Thumbs.db') ) {
```

TIP Not to belabor the point, but almost everything web developers do with JavaScript (for example, resize or move the browser window) cannot be done using server-side PHP.

TIP There is a little overlap between the PHP and JavaScript. Both can set and read cookies, create HTML, and do some browser detection.

Understanding HTTP Headers

The **images.php** script, just created, displays a list of image names, each of which is linked to a JavaScript function call. That JavaScript function creates a pop-up window which loads a PHP script that will reveal the image. This may sound like a lot of work for little effort, but there's a method to my madness. A trivial reason for this approach is that JavaScript is required to create a window sized to fit the image (as opposed to creating a pop-up window of any size, with the image in it). More importantly, because the images are being stored in the **uploads** directory, ideally stored outside of the web root directory, the images cannot be viewed directly in the browser using either of the following:

```
http://www.example.com/uploads
↪/image.png
```

or

```
<img src="image.png">
```

The reason neither of these will work is that files and folders located outside of the web root directory are, by definition, unavailable via a browser. This is a good thing, because it allows you to safeguard content, providing it only when appropriate. To make that content available through a browser, you need to create a *proxy script* in PHP. A proxy script just fulfills a role, such as providing a file (displaying an image is the same thing as providing a file to the browser). Thus, given the proxy script **proxy.php**, the previous examples could be made to work using either **Ⓐ**:

```
http://www.example.com/proxy.php?
↪image=image.png
```

or

```
<img src="proxy.php?image=image.png">
```

This, of course, is exactly what's being done with **show_image.php**, linked in the **create_window()** JavaScript function. But how does **proxy.php**, or **show_image.php**, work? The answer lies in an understanding of *HTTP headers*.

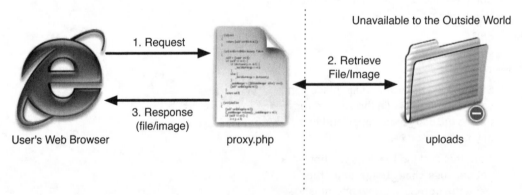

Unavailable to the Outside World

1. Request

2. Retrieve File/Image

3. Response (file/image)

User's Web Browser   proxy.php   uploads

Ⓐ A proxy script is able to provide access to content on the server that would otherwise be unavailable.

HTTP (Hypertext Transfer Protocol) is the technology at the heart of the web and defines the way clients and servers communicate. When a browser requests a page, it receives a series of HTTP headers in return. This happens behind the scenes; most users aren't aware of this at all.

PHP's built-in `header()` function can be used to take advantage of this protocol. The most common example of this will be demonstrated in the next chapter, when the `header()` function will be used to redirect the browser from the current page to another. Here, you'll use it to send files to the browser.

In theory, the `header()` function is easy to use. Its syntax is

`header(header string);`

The list of possible header strings is quite long, since headers are used for everything from redirecting the browser, to sending files, to creating cookies, to controlling page caching, and much, much more. Starting with something simple, to use `header()` to redirect the browser, type

`header('Location:`
` → http://www.example.com/page.php');`

That line will send the browser from the page it's on over to that other URL. You'll see examples of this in the next chapter.

In this next example, which will send an image file to the browser, three header calls are used. The first is *Content-Type*. This indicates to the browser what kind of data is about to follow. The *Content-Type* value matches the data's MIME type. This line lets the browser know it's about to receive a PDF file:

`header("Content-Type:application`
` → /pdf\n");`

Next, you can use *Content-Disposition*, which tells the browser how to treat the data:

`header("Content-Disposition:`
` → attachment; filename=\"somefile`
` → .pdf\"\n");`

The *attachment* value will prompt the browser to download the file **B**. An alternative is to use *inline*, which tells the browser to display the data, assuming that the browser can. The `filename` attribute is just that: it tells the browser the name associated with the data. Some browsers abide by this instruction; others do not.

A third header to use for downloading files is *Content-Length*. This is a value, in bytes, corresponding to the amount of data to be sent.

`header("Content-Length: 4096\n");`

continues on next page

| What do you want to do with IMG_7952.jpg (276 KB)? From: localhost | Save | Save as | Cancel | ✕ |

B Edge prompts the user to download the file because of the *attachment Content-Disposition* value.

That's the basics with respect to using the **header()** function. Before getting to the example, note that if a script uses multiple **header()** calls, each should be terminated by a newline (**\n**), as in the preceding code snippets. More importantly, the absolutely critical thing to remember about the **header()** function is that it must be called before *anything* is sent to the browser. This includes HTML or even blank spaces. If your code has any **echo** or **print** statements, has blank lines outside of PHP tags, or includes files that do any of these things before calling **header()**, you'll see an error message like that shown in **C**.

To use the header() function:

1. Begin a new PHP document in your text editor or IDE, to be named **show_image.php** (Script 11.5):

   ```
   <?php # Script 11.5 -
   → show_image.php
   $name = FALSE;
   ```

   Because this script will use the **header()** function, nothing—absolutely nothing—can be sent to the browser. That means no HTML, not even a blank line, tab, or space before the opening PHP tag.

   The **$name** variable will be used as a flag, indicating whether all the validation routines have been passed.

2. Check for an image name:

   ```
   if (isset($_GET['image'])) {
   ```

   The script needs to receive a valid image name in the URL. This should be appended to the URL in the JavaScript function that calls this page (see **function.js**, Script 11.3).

3. Validate the image's extension:

   ```
   $ext = strtolower(
   → substr($_GET['image'], -4));
     if (($ext == '.jpg') OR
     → ($ext =='jpeg') OR
     → ($ext == '.png')) {
   ```

   The next check is that the file to be sent to the browser has a **.jpeg**, **.jpg**, or **.png** extension. This way the script won't try to send something bad to the user. For example, if a malicious user changed the address in the pop-up window from **http://www.example.com/show_image.php?image=image.png** to **http://www.example.com/show_image.php?image=../../../path/to/something/important**, this conditional would catch, and prevent, that hack.

   To validate the extension, the **substr()** function returns the last four characters from the image's name (the **-4** accomplishes this). The extension is also run through the **strtolower()** function so that **.PNG** and **.png** are treated the same. Then a conditional checks to see if **$ext** is equal to any of the three allowed values.

Warning: Cannot modify header information - headers already sent by (output started at /Users/larryullman/Sites/phpmysql4/proxy.php:2) in **/Users/larryullman/Sites/phpmysql4/proxy.php** on line **3**

Warning: Cannot modify header information - headers already sent by (output started at /Users/larryullman/Sites/phpmysql4/proxy.php:2) in **/Users/larryullman/Sites/phpmysql4/proxy.php** on line **4**

C The *headers already sent* error means that the browser was sent something—HTML, plain text, even a space—prior to using the **header()** function.

Script 11.5 This script retrieves an image from the server and sends it to the browser, using HTTP headers.

```
1    <?php # Script 11.5 - show_image.php
2    // This page displays an image.
3
4    $name = FALSE; // Flag variable:
5
6    // Check for an image name in the URL:
7    if (isset($_GET['image'])) {
8
9        // Make sure it has an image's
         extension:
10       $ext = strtolower ( substr
         ($_GET['image'], -4));
11
12       if (($ext == '.jpg') OR ($ext ==
         'jpeg') OR ($ext == '.png')) {
13
14           // Full image path:
15           $image = "../uploads/
             {$_GET['image']}";
16
17           // Check that the image exists
             and is a file:
18           if (file_exists($image) &&
             (is_file($image))) {
19
20               // Set the name as this image:
21               $name = $_GET['image'];
22
23           } // End of file_exists() IF.
24
25       } // End of $ext IF.
26
27   } // End of isset($_GET['image']) IF.
28
29   // If there was a problem, use the
     default image:
30   if (!$name) {
31       $image = 'images/unavailable.png';
32       $name = 'unavailable.png';
33   }
34
35   // Get the image information:
36   $info = getimagesize($image);
37   $fs = filesize($image);
38
39   // Send the content information:
40   header ("Content-Type:
     {$info['mime']}\n");
41   header ("Content-Disposition: inline;
     filename=\"$name\"\n");
42   header ("Content-Length: $fs\n");
43
44   // Send the file:
45   readfile($image);
```

4. Check that the image is a file on the server:

```
$image = "../uploads/{$_GET
→['image']} ";
if (file_exists($image) &&
→(is_file($image))) {
```

Before attempting to send the image to the browser, make sure that it exists and that it is a file (as opposed to a directory). As a security measure, the image's full path is defined as a combination of *../uploads* and the received image name.

5. Set the value of the flag variable to the image's name:

```
$name = $_GET['image'];
```

Once the image has passed all of these tests, the **$name** variable is assigned the value of the image.

6. Complete the conditionals begun in Steps 2, 3, and 4:

```
        } // End of file_exists() IF.
      } // End of $ext IF.
    } // End of isset($_GET['image']) IF.
```

There are no **else** clauses for any of these three conditions. If all three conditions aren't TRUE, then the flag variable **$name** will still have a FALSE value.

continues on next page

7. If no valid image was received by this page, use a default image:

```
if (!$name) {
  $image = 'images/unavailable.png';
  $name = 'unavailable.png';
}
```

If the image doesn't exist, if it isn't a file, or if it doesn't have the proper extension, then the $name variable will still have a value of FALSE. In such cases, a default image will be used instead . The image itself can be downloaded from the book's corresponding website (**LarryUllman.com**, found with all the downloadable code) and should be placed in an **images** folder. The **images** folder should be in the same directory as this script, not in the same directory as the **uploads** folder.

8. Retrieve the image's information:

```
$info = getimagesize($image);
$fs = filesize($image);
```

To send a file to the browser, the script needs to know the file's MIME type and size. An image file's type can be found using **getimagesize()**. The file's size, in bytes, is found using **filesize()**. Because the **$image** variable represents either **../uploads/{$_GET['image']}** or **images/unavailable.png**, these lines will work on both the correct and the unavailable image.

9. Send the file:

```
header("Content-Type: {$info
→['mime']}\n");
header("Content-Disposition:
→inline; filename=\"$name\"\n");
header("Content-Length: $fs\n");
readfile($image);
```

These **header()** calls will send the file data to the browser. The first line uses the image's MIME type for the value of the *Content-Type* header. The second line tells the browser the name of the file and that it should be displayed in the browser (*inline*). The last **header()** function indicates how much data is to be expected.

The file data itself is sent using the **readfile()** function, which reads in a file and immediately sends the content to the browser.

10. Save the file as **show_image.php**, place it in your web directory, in the same folder as **images.php**, and test it in your browser by clicking a link in **images.php** .

D This image will be shown whenever there's a problem with showing the requested image.

E This image is displayed by having PHP send the file to the browser.

Notice that this page contains no HTML. It only sends an image file to the browser. Also note that I omitted the terminating PHP tag. This is acceptable, and in certain situations like this, preferred. If you included the closing PHP tag, and you inadvertently had an extra space or blank line after that tag, the browser could have problems displaying the image (because the browser will have received the image data of *X* length, matching the *Content-Length* header, plus a bit of extra data).

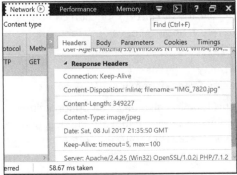

F Browser debugging tools, like those in Edge shown here, include the ability to see what headers were sent by a page and/or server. This can be useful debugging information.

TIP I cannot stress strongly enough that nothing can be sent to the browser before using the header() function. Even an included file that has a blank line after the closing PHP tag will make the header() function unusable.

TIP To avoid problems when using header(), you can call the headers_sent() function first. It returns a Boolean value indicating if something has already been sent to the browser:

```
if (!headers_sent()) {
    // Use the header() function.
} else {
    // Do something else.
}
```

Output buffering, demonstrated in Chapter 18, "Example—User Registration," can also prevent problems when using header().

TIP Debugging scripts like this, where PHP sends data, not text, to the browser, can be challenging. For help, use one of the many developer plug-ins for the Edge browser **F**.

TIP You can also indicate to the browser the page's encoding using PHP and the header() function:

```
<?php header('Content-Type:
→ text/html; charset=UTF-8'); ?>
```

This can be more effective than using a META tag, but it does require the page to be a PHP script. If using this, it must be the first line in the page, before any HTML.

TIP A proxy script can send to the browser only a single file (or image) at a time.

Date and Time Functions

Chapter 5, "Introduction to SQL," demonstrates a handful of great date and time functions that MySQL supports. Naturally, PHP has its own date and time functions. To start, there's `date_default_timezone_set()`. This function is used to establish the default time zone (which can also be set in PHP's configuration file).

```
date_default_timezone_set(tz);
```

The *tz* value is a string like *America/New_York* or *Pacific/Auckland*. There are too many to list here (Africa alone has over 50), but see the PHP manual for them all. Note that as of PHP 5.1, the default time zone must be set, either in a script or in PHP's configuration file, prior to calling any of the date and time functions, or else you'll see a warning.

Next up, the `checkdate()` function takes a month, a day, and a year and returns a Boolean value indicating whether that date exists (or existed). It even considers leap years. This function can be used to ensure that a user supplied a valid date (birth date or other):

```
if (checkdate(month, day, year)) { // OK!
```

Perhaps the most frequently used function is the aptly named `date()`. It returns the date and/or time as a formatted string. It takes two arguments:

```
date(format, [timestamp]);
```

The timestamp is an optional argument representing the number of seconds since the Unix epoch (midnight on January 1, 1970) for the date in question. It allows you to get information, like the day of the week, for a particular date. If a timestamp is not specified, PHP will just use the current time on the server.

There are myriad formatting parameters available (**Table 11.4**), and they can be used in conjunction with literal text. For example:

```
echo date('F j, Y'); // January 26, 2018
echo date('H:i'); // 23:14
echo date('D'); // Fri
```

You can find the timestamp for a particular date using the `mktime()` function:

```
$stamp = mktime(hour, minute,
 → second, month, day, year);
```

If called with no arguments, `mktime()` returns the current timestamp, which is the same as calling the `time()` function.

Finally, the `getdate()` function can be used to return an array of values (**Table 11.5**) for a date and time. For example:

```
$today = getdate();
echo $today['month']; // October
```

This function also takes an optional timestamp argument. If that argument is not used, `getdate()` returns information for the current date and time.

TABLE 11.4 Date() Function Formatting

Character	Meaning	Example
Y	Year as 4 digits	2017
y	Year as 2 digits	11
L	Is it a leap year?	1 (for yes)
n	Month as 1 or 2 digits	2
m	Month as 2 digits	02
F	Month	February
M	Month as 3 letters	Feb
j	Day of the month as 1 or 2 digits	8
d	Day of the month as 2 digits	08
l (lowercase L)	Day of the week	Monday
D	Day of the week as 3 letters	Mon
w	Day of the week as a single digit	0 (Sunday)
z	Day of the year: 0 to 365	189
t	Number of days in the month	31
S	English ordinal suffix for a day, as 2 characters	rd
g	Hour; 12-hour format as 1 or 2 digits	6
G	Hour; 24-hour format as 1 or 2 digits	18
h	Hour; 12-hour format as 2 digits	06
H	Hour; 24-hour format as 2 digits	18
i	Minutes	45
s	Seconds	18
u	Microseconds	1234
a	am or pm	am
A	AM or PM	PM
U	Seconds since the epoch	1499550481
e	Timezone	UTC
I (capital i)	Is it daylight savings?	1 (for yes)
O	Difference from GMT	+0600

These are just a handful of the many date and time functions PHP has. For more, see the PHP manual. To practice working with these functions, let's modify `images.php` (Script 11.4) in a couple of ways. First, the script will show each image's uploaded date and time. Second, while a change is being made to the layout, the script will show each image's file size, too 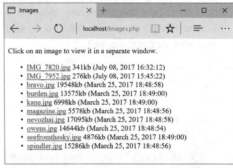.

A The revised `images.php` shows two more pieces of information about each image.

TABLE 11.5 The getdate() Array

Key	Value	Example
year	year	2017
mon	month	11
month	month name	November
mday	day of the month	24
weekday	day of the week	Thursday
hours	hours	11
minutes	minutes	56
seconds	seconds	47

To use the date and time functions:

1. Open **images.php** (Script 11.4) in your text editor or IDE, if you haven't already.

2. As the first line of code after the opening PHP tag, establish the time zone (Script 11.6):

   ```
   date_default_timezone_set
   → ('America/New_York');
   ```

   Before calling any of the date and time functions, the time zone must be established. To find your time zone, see **www.php.net/timezones**.

3. Within the **foreach** loop, after getting the image's dimensions, calculate its file size:

   ```
   $file_size = round( (filesize
   → ("$dir/$image")) / 1024) . "kb";
   ```

   The **filesize()** function was first used in the **show_image.php** script. It returns the size of a file in bytes. To calculate the kilobytes of a file, divide this number by 1,024 (the number of bytes in a kilobyte) and round it off.

4. On the next line, determine the image's modification date and time:

   ```
   $image_date = date("F d, Y H:i:s",
   → filemtime("$dir/$image"));
   ```

   To find a file's modification date and time, call the **filemtime()** function, providing the function with the file, or directory, to be examined. This function returns a timestamp, which can then be used as the second argument to the **date()**, which will format the timestamp accordingly.

If you're perplexed by what's happening here, you can break the code into two steps:

```
$filemtime = filemtime
→ ("$dir/$image");
$image_date = date("F d, Y H:i:s
→ ", $filemtime);
```

5. Change the **echo** statement so that it also prints the file size and modification date:

   ```
   echo "<li><a href=\"javascript:
   → create_window('$image_name',
   → $image_size[0],$image_size[1])\">
   → $image</a> $file_size
   → ($image_date)</li>\n";
   ```

   Both are printed outside of the **A** tag, so they aren't part of the links.

6. Save the file as **images.php**, place it in your web directory, and test it in your browser.

TIP The **date()** function has some parameters that are used for informative purposes, not formatting. For example, **date('L')** returns 1 or 0 indicating if it's a leap year; **date('t')** returns the number of days in the current month; and **date('I')** returns a 1 if it's currently daylight saving time.

TIP PHP's date functions reflect the time on the server (because PHP runs on the server); you'll need to use JavaScript if you want to determine the date and time on the user's computer.

TIP In Chapter 16, you'll learn how to use the new **DateTime** class to work with dates and times in PHP.

Script 11.6 This modified version of `images.php` (Script 11.4) uses PHP's date and time functions to report some information to the user.

```php
1    <!doctype html>
2    <html lang="en">
3    <head>
4       <meta charset="utf-8">
5       <title>Images</title>
6       <script charset="utf-8" src="js/function.js"></script>
7    </head>
8    <body>
9    <p>Click on an image to view it in a separate window.</p>
10   <ul>
11   <?php # Script 11.6 - images.php
12   // This script lists the images in the uploads directory.
13   // This version now shows each image's file size and uploaded date and time.
14
15   // Set the default timezone:
16   date_default_timezone_set('America/New_York');
17
18   $dir = '../uploads'; // Define the directory to view.
19
20   $files = scandir($dir); // Read all the images into an array.
21
22   // Display each image caption as a link to the JavaScript function:
23   foreach ($files as $image) {
24
25      if (substr($image, 0, 1) != '.') { // Ignore anything starting with a period.
26
27         // Get the image's size in pixels:
28         $image_size = getimagesize("$dir/$image");
29
30         // Calculate the image's size in kilobytes:
31         $file_size = round( (filesize("$dir/$image")) / 1024) . "kb";
32
33         // Determine the image's upload date and time:
34         $image_date = date("F d, Y H:i:s", filemtime("$dir/$image"));
35
36         // Make the image's name URL-safe:
37         $image_name = urlencode($image);
38
39         // Print the information:
40         echo "<li><a href=\"javascript:create_window('$image_name',$image_size[0],
             $image_size[1])\">$image</a> $file_size ($image_date)</li>\n";
41
42      } // End of the IF.
43
44   } // End of the foreach loop.
45
46   ?>
47   </ul>
48   </body>
49   </html>
```

Performing Transactions

Switching gears for the last example in this chapter, let's see how to perform database transactions using a PHP script. Chapter 7, "Advanced SQL and MySQL," demonstrates how to perform transactions using the mysql client. A database transaction is a sequence of steps that can be guaranteed to all execute or all fail. This is accomplished by committing or rolling back the previously made queries.

To perform transactions with a PHP script, first disable the autocommit behavior:

```
mysqli_autocommit($dbc, FALSE);
```

Next, execute queries as you otherwise would:

```
$r = @mysqli_query($dbc, $q);
```

Then, based on the results of the query, either commit the transactions or roll them back:

```
mysqli_commit($dbc);
```

or

```
mysqli_rollback($dbc);
```

As an example of this, the following script performs a transfer of funds from one bank account to another: just a web version of the mysql example used in Chapter 7 Ⓐ.

To handle file uploads in PHP:

1. Create a new PHP document in your text editor or IDE, to be named **transfer.php** (Script 11.7):

```
<!doctype html>
<html lang="en">
<head>
  <meta charset="utf-8">
  <title>Transfer Funds</title>
</head>
<body>
<h1>Transfer Funds</h1>
<?php # Script 11.7 - transfer.php
```

2. Create a database connection:

```
$dbc = mysqli_connect('localhost',
→'root', 'password', 'banking') OR
→ die('Could not connect to MySQL:
→' . mysqli_connect_error() );
```

This example uses the *banking* database. You'll need to update the code to use the proper username and password for your setup.

continues on page 376

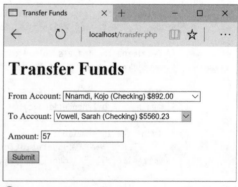

Ⓐ The funds transfer form.

```
1    <!doctype html>
2    <html lang="en">
3    <head>
4       <meta charset="utf-8">
5       <title>Transfer Funds</title>
6    </head>
7    <body>
8    <h1>Transfer Funds</h1>
9    <?php # Script 11.7 - transfer.php
10   // This page performs a transfer of funds from one account to another.
11   // This page uses transactions.
12
13   // Always need the database connection:
14   $dbc = mysqli_connect('localhost', 'root', 'password', 'banking') OR die('Could not connect to
     MySQL: ' . mysqli_connect_error() );
15
16   // Check if the form has been submitted:
17   if ($_SERVER['REQUEST_METHOD'] == 'POST') {
18
19       // Minimal form validation:
20       if (isset($_POST['from'], $_POST['to'], $_POST['amount']) &&
21        is_numeric($_POST['from']) && is_numeric($_POST['to']) && is_numeric($_POST['amount']) ) {
22
23           $from = $_POST['from'];
24           $to = $_POST['to'];
25           $amount = $_POST['amount'];
26
27           // Make sure enough funds are available:
28           $q = "SELECT balance FROM accounts WHERE account_id=$from";
29           $r = @mysqli_query($dbc, $q);
30           $row = mysqli_fetch_array($r, MYSQLI_ASSOC);
31           if ($amount > $row['balance']) {
32               echo '<p class="error">Insufficient funds to complete the transfer.</p>';
33           } else {
34               // Turn autocommit off:
35               mysqli_autocommit($dbc, FALSE);
36
37               $q = "UPDATE accounts SET balance=balance-$amount WHERE account_id=$from";
38               $r = @mysqli_query($dbc, $q);
39               if (mysqli_affected_rows($dbc) == 1) { // If it ran OK.
40
41                   $q = "UPDATE accounts SET balance=balance+$amount WHERE account_id=$to";
42                   $r = @mysqli_query($dbc, $q);
43                   if (mysqli_affected_rows($dbc) == 1) { // If it ran OK.
44
45                       mysqli_commit($dbc);
46                       echo '<p>The transfer was a success!</p>';
47
```

code continues on page 377

3. Check if the form has been submitted and that the minimum requirements are met:

```
if ($_SERVER['REQUEST_METHOD'] ==
→ 'POST') {
  if (isset($_POST['from'], $_POST
  → ['to'], $_POST['amount']) &&
  is_numeric($_POST['from']) &&
  → is_numeric($_POST['to']) &&
  → is_numeric($_POST['amount'])
  → ) {
    $from = $_POST['from'];
    $to = $_POST['to'];
    $amount = $_POST['amount'];
```

The form only has three inputs. The most minimal validation of them confirms that all three have a numeric value. If so, three variables are assigned the values to make referring to them easier.

The "Review and Pursue" section at the end of the chapter will make several recommendations for improving this script, such as checking that a positive amount is being transferred.

4. Make sure there are enough funds to be transferred:

```
$q = "SELECT balance FROM accounts
→ WHERE account_id=$from";
$r = @mysqli_query($dbc, $q);
$row = mysqli_fetch_array($r,
→ MYSQLI_ASSOC);
if ($amount > $row['balance']) {
  echo '<p class="error">
  → Insufficient funds to
  → complete the transfer.</p>';
} else {
```

There's no point in attempting to transfer more funds than are available, so this script first checks that the amount being transferred is not greater than the amount in the account. If it is, an *insufficient funds* message is shown .

5. Turn autocommit off and update the "from" account:

```
mysqli_autocommit($dbc, FALSE);
$q = "UPDATE accounts SET
→ balance=balance-$amount WHERE
→ account_id=$from";
$r = @mysqli_query($dbc, $q);
if (mysqli_affected_rows($dbc)
→ == 1) {
```

This is the same query as in Chapter 7. If one row was affected, the query worked successfully.

6. Update the "to" account:

```
$q = "UPDATE accounts SET
→ balance=balance+$amount WHERE
→ account_id=$to";
$r = @mysqli_query($dbc, $q);
if (mysqli_affected_rows($dbc)
→ == 1) {
```

This is the corollary query, adding funds to the other account.

continues on page 378

 Trying to transfer more money than the "from" account has results in an error.

```
48              } else {
49                  mysqli_rollback($dbc);
50                  echo '<p>The transfer could not be made due to a system error. We apologize
    for any inconvenience.</p>'; // Public message.
51                  echo '<p>' . mysqli_error($dbc) . '<br>Query: ' . $q . '</p>'; // Debugging
    message.
52              }
53
54          } else {
55              mysqli_rollback($dbc);
56              echo '<p>The transfer could not be made due to a system error. We apologize for
                any inconvenience.</p>'; // Public message.
57              echo '<p>' . mysqli_error($dbc) . '<br>Query: ' . $q . '</p>';
                // Debugging message.
58          }
59
60      }
61
62  } else { // Invalid submitted values.
63      echo '<p>Please select a valid "from" and "to" account and enter a numeric amount to
        transfer.</p>';
64  }
65
66  } // End of submit conditional.
67
68  // Always show the form...
69
70  // Get all the accounts and balances as OPTIONs for the SELECT menus:
71  $q = "SELECT account_id, CONCAT(last_name, ', ', first_name) AS name, type, balance FROM
    accounts LEFT JOIN customers USING (customer_id) ORDER BY name";
72  $r = @mysqli_query($dbc, $q);
73  $options = '';
74  while ($row = mysqli_fetch_array($r, MYSQLI_ASSOC)) {
75      $options .= "<option value=\"{$row['account_id']}\">{$row['name']} ({$row['type']})
        \${$row['balance']}</option>\n";
76  }
77
78  // Create the form:
79  echo '<form action="transfer.php" method="post">
80  <p>From Account: <select name="from">' . $options . '</select></p>
81  <p>To Account: <select name="to">' . $options . '</select></p>
82  <p>Amount: <input type="number" name="amount" step="0.01" min="1"></p>
83  <p><input type="submit" name="submit" value="Submit"></p>
84  </form>';
85
86  mysqli_close($dbc);
87  ?>
88  </body>
89  </html>
```

7. Commit the transactions and indicate success:

```
mysqli_commit($dbc);
echo '<p>The transfer was a
→ success!</p>';
```

If both queries affected one row, the transactions can be committed and the message shown **C**.

8. Upon error, roll back the transaction and print a message:

```
} else {
  mysqli_rollback($dbc);
  echo '<p>The transfer could
→ not be made due to a system
→ error. We apologize for any
→ inconvenience.</p>'; // Public
→ message.
    echo '<p>' . mysqli_
→ error($dbc) . '<br>Query:
→' . $q . '</p>'; //
→ Debugging message.
}
} else {
  mysqli_rollback($dbc);
  echo '<p>The transfer could not
→ be made due to a system
→ error. We apologize for any
→ inconvenience.</p>'; // Public
→ message.
  echo '<p>' . mysqli_error($dbc)
→ . '<br>Query: ' . $q . '</p>';
→ // Debugging message.
}
```

This completes the conditionals begun in Step 6 and Step 5, respectively.

9. Complete the validation and form submission conditionals:

```
  } else { // Invalid submitted
→ values.
    echo '<p>Please select a
→ valid "from" and "to"
```

```
→ account and enter a numeric
→ amount to transfer.</p>';
  }
} // End of submit conditional.
```

10. Retrieve every account:

```
$q = "SELECT account_id, CONCAT
→ (last_name, ', ', first_name) AS
→ name, type, balance FROM
→ accounts LEFT JOIN customers
→ USING (customer_id) ORDER BY
→ name";
$r = @mysqli_query($dbc, $q);
$options = '';
while ($row = mysqli_fetch_array
→ ($r, MYSQLI_ASSOC)) {
  $options .= "<option value=\"
→ {$row['account_id']}\">
→ {$row['name']} ({$row['type']})
→ \${$row['balance']}</option>\n";
}
```

As the form has two identical select menus **A**, it'll be most efficient to retrieve the accounts once and reuse that information. To do that, a query fetches each customer's name, account type, balance, and account ID **D**.

C A successful transfer of funds!

This information is then used to dynamically build up the series of HTML options to be used in the select menus. The account ID is the value and the other three columns are used in the displayed text **E**.

11. Create the HTML form:

```
echo '<form action="transfer.php"
→ method="post">
<p>From Account: <select
→ name="from">' . $options .
→ '</select></p>
<p>To Account: <select name="to">'
→ . $options . '</select></p>
<p>Amount: <input type="number"
→ name="amount" step="0.01"
→ min="1"></p>
<p><input type="submit"
→ name="submit"
→ value="Submit"></p>
</form>';
```

```
●  ●  ●           PHP and MySQL for Dynamic Web Sites
mysql> SELECT account_id, CONCAT(last_name, ', ', first_name)
AS name, type, balance FROM accounts LEFT JOIN customers USING
(customer_id) ORDER BY name;
+------------+----------------+----------+-----------+
| account_id | name           | type     | balance   |
+------------+----------------+----------+-----------+
|          3 | Nnamdi, Kojo   | Checking |   1000.00 |
|          4 | Sedaris, David | Savings  |  13438.97 |
|          2 | Sedaris, David | Checking | 909325.24 |
|          1 | Vowell, Sarah  | Checking |   5460.23 |
+------------+----------------+----------+-----------+
4 rows in set (0.00 sec)

mysql> ▌
```

D The same query run through the mysql client.

```
◢ <p>
    From Account:
◢ <select name="from">
  ▷ <option value="3">Nnamdi, Kojo (Checking) $1017....</option>
  ▷ <option value="2">Sedaris, David (Checking) $909...</option>
  ▷ <option value="4">Sedaris, David (Savings) $1342...</option>
  ▷ <option value="1">Vowell, Sarah (Checking) $5560...</option>
  </select>
</p>
◢ <p>
    To Account:
◢ <select name="to">
  ▷ <option value="3">Nnamdi, Kojo (Checking) $1017....</option>
  ▷ <option value="2">Sedaris, David (Checking) $909...</option>
  ▷ <option value="4">Sedaris, David (Savings) $1342...</option>
  ▷ <option value="1">Vowell, Sarah (Checking) $5560...</option>
  </select>
</p>
```

The form only has two select menus and the amount being transferred. In theory the HTML5 number input type ensures only a numeric value is entered. The **min** attribute requires a minimum value of 1, and the **step** value allows a decimal value to be entered.

12. Close the database connection:

```
mysqli_close($dbc);
```

13. Complete the PHP and HTML page:

```
?>
</body>
</html>
```

14. Save the file as **transfer.php**, place it in your web directory, and test it in your browser.

TIP To state what is hopefully obvious, a script that actually transfers funds from one account to another would have layers upon layers upon layers of security added to it.

TIP The client-side validation provided by the number input type—requiring a positive transfer amount—is nice, but all client-side validation is easily circumvented. Server-side validation matters most.

TIP Although it's not a problem that this script allows for a "transfer" from an account to itself, you can prevent that using validation in the PHP code. Smart JavaScript code could also make it impossible to select the same account in both menus.

E The HTML source of the select menus.

Review and Pursue

If you have any problems with the review questions or the pursue prompts, turn to the book's supporting forum (LarryUllman.com/forums/).

Review

- What function is used to send email? What are the function's arguments? What does the server need to send email?
- Does it make a difference whether \n is used within single or double quotation marks?
- Can you easily know for certain if, or when, a recipient received an email sent by PHP?
- What debugging steps can you take if you aren't receiving any email that should be sent from a PHP script?
- How do folder permissions come into play for handling uploaded files?
- What two directories are used in handling file uploads?
- What additional attribute must be made to the opening **form** tag in order to handle a file upload?
- What is a MIME type?
- In what ways are PHP and JavaScript alike? How are they different?
- What tag is used to add JavaScript to an HTML page?
- What does the **var** keyword mean in JavaScript?
- What is the concatenation operator in JavaScript?
- What does the PHP **header()** function do?
- What do *headers already sent* error messages mean?
- What is a *proxy script*? When might a proxy script be necessary?
- What does the **readfile()** function do?

- How do you start a MySQL transaction in a PHP script? How do you commit the changes? How do you roll back the changes?

Pursue

- Create a more custom contact form. Have the PHP script also send a more custom email, including any other data requested by the form.
- Search online using the keywords *php email spam filters* to learn techniques for improving the successful delivery of PHP-sent email (i.e., to minimize the chances of spam filters eating legitimate emails).
- Make a variation on **upload_image.php** that supports the uploading of different file types. Create a corresponding version of **show_image.php**. Note: You'll need to do some research on MIME types to complete these challenges.
- If you're feeling adventurous, come up with a system (probably a database) for renaming—and storing data about—uploaded files.
- Check out the PHP manual page for the **glob()** function, which can be used instead of **scandir()**.
- Add validations to the transfers script to prevent a negative transfer or the selection of the same account for both the "to" and "from."
- If you'd like to learn another advanced database trick, look into locking and unlocking MySQL tables and rows. Ideally the transfers script would lock the "from" account, thereby preventing multiple simultaneous transfers from making the balance negative.
- A lot of information and new functions were introduced in this chapter. Check out the PHP manual for some of them to learn more.

Cookies and Sessions

The Hypertext Transfer Protocol (HTTP) is a *stateless* technology, meaning that each HTML page is an unrelated entity. HTTP has no method for tracking users or retaining variables as a person traverses a site. Without the server being able to track a user, there can be no shopping carts or custom website personalization. Using a server-side technology like PHP, you can overcome the statelessness of the web. The two best PHP tools for this purpose are *cookies* and *sessions*.

The key difference between cookies and sessions is that cookies store data in the user's browser and sessions store data on the server itself. Sessions are generally more secure than cookies and can store much more information. Because both technologies are easy to use with PHP and are worth knowing, this chapter covers both cookies and sessions. The examples for demonstrating this information will be a login system, based on the existing *site-name* database.

Making a Login Page

A login process involves just a few components **Ⓐ**:

- A form for submitting the login information
- A validation routine that confirms the necessary information was submitted
- A database query that compares the submitted information against the stored information
- Cookies or sessions to store data that reflects a successful login

Subsequent pages can then have checks to confirm that the user is logged in (to limit access to that page or add features). There is also, of course, a logging-out process, which involves clearing the cookies or session data that represent a logged-in status.

To start all this, let's take some of these common elements and place them into separate files. Then the pages that require this functionality can include the necessary files. Breaking up the logic this way will make some of the following scripts easier to read and write, as well as cut down on their redundancies.

You'll define two includable files. This first script will contain the bulk of a login page, including the header, the error reporting, the form, and the footer **Ⓑ**.

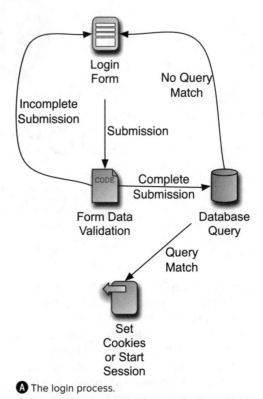

Ⓐ The login process.

Ⓑ The login form and page.

To make a login page:

1. Begin a new PHP page in your text editor or IDE, to be named **login_page.inc.php** (Script 12.1):

   ```
   <?php # Script 12.1 -
   → login_page.inc.php
   ```

2. Include the header:

   ```
   $page_title = 'Login';
   include('includes/header.html');
   ```

   This chapter will make use of the same template system first created in Chapter 3, "Creating Dynamic Web Sites," then modified in Chapter 9, "Using PHP with MySQL."

3. Print any error messages, if they exist:

   ```
   if (isset($errors) &&
   → !empty($errors)) {
      echo '<h1>Error!</h1>
      <p class="error">The following
      → error(s) occurred:<br>';
      foreach ($errors as $msg) {
         echo " - $msg<br>\n";
      }
      echo '</p><p>Please try again.
      → </p>';
   }
   ```

continues on next page

Script 12.1 The **login_page.inc.php** script creates the complete login page, including the form, and reports any errors. It will be included by other pages that need to show the login page.

```
1    <?php # Script 12.1 - login_page.inc.php
2    // This page prints any errors associated with logging in
3    // and it creates the entire login page, including the form.
4
5    // Include the header:
6    $page_title = 'Login';
7    include('includes/header.html');
8
9    // Print any error messages, if they exist:
10   if (isset($errors) && !empty($errors)) {
11       echo '<h1>Error!</h1>
12       <p class="error">The following error(s) occurred:<br>';
13       foreach ($errors as $msg) {
14           echo " - $msg<br>\n";
15       }
16       echo '</p><p>Please try again.</p>';
17   }
18
19   // Display the form:
20   ?><h1>Login</h1>
21   <form action="login.php" method="post">
22       <p>Email Address: <input type="email" name="email" size="20" maxlength="60"> </p>
23       <p>Password: <input type="password" name="pass" size="20" maxlength="20"></p>
24       <p><input type="submit" name="submit" value="Login"></p>
25   </form>
26
27   <?php include('includes/footer.html'); ?>
```

This code was also developed back in Chapter 9, although an additional **isset()** clause has been added as an extra precaution. If any errors exist (in the **$errors** array variable), they'll be printed .

4. Display the form:

```
?><h1>Login</h1>
<form action="login.php"
→ method="post">
  <p>Email Address: <input
  → type="email" name="email"
  → size="20" maxlength="60"> </p>
  <p>Password: <input
  → type="password" name="pass"
  → size="20" maxlength="20"></p>
  <p><input type="submit"
  → name="submit" value="Login">
  → </p>
</form>
```

The HTML form needs only two text inputs: one for an email address and a second for the password. The names of the inputs match those in the *users* table of the *sitename* database (which this login system is based on).

To make it easier to create the HTML form, the PHP section is closed first. The form is not sticky, but you could easily add code to accomplish that.

5. Complete the page:

```
<?php include('includes/footer
→ .html'); ?>
```

6. Save the file as **login_page.inc.php** and place it in your web directory (in the **includes** folder, along with the files from Chapter 3 and Chapter 9: **header.html** and **footer.html**).

The page will use an **.inc.php** extension to indicate both that it's an includable file and that it contains PHP code.

C As with other scripts in this book, form errors are displayed above the form itself.

TIP It may seem illogical that this script includes the header and footer file from within the **includes** directory when this script will also be within that same directory. This code works because this script will be included by pages within the main directory; thus the include references are with respect to the parent file, not this one.

Making the Login Functions

Along with the login page that was stored in **login_page.inc.php**, there's a bit of functionality that will be common to several scripts in this chapter. In this next script, also to be included by other pages in the login/logout system, two functions will be defined.

First, many pages will end up redirecting the user from one page to another. For example, upon successfully logging in, the user will be taken to **loggedin.php**. If a user accesses **loggedin.php** and they aren't logged in, they should be taken to **index.php**. Redirection uses the **header()** function, introduced in Chapter 11, "Web Application Development." The syntax for redirection is

```
header ('Location: http://www.example
→ .com/page.php');
```

Because this function will send the browser to **page.php**, the current script should be terminated using **exit()** immediately after this:

```
header ('Location: http://www.example
→ .com/page.php');
exit();
```

If you don't call **exit()**, the current script will continue to run (just not in the browser).

The location value in the **header()** call should be an absolute URL (**www.example.com/page.php** instead of just **page.php**). You can hard-code this value into every **header()** call or, better yet, have PHP dynamically determine it. The first function in this next script will do just that, and then redirect the user to that absolute URL.

The other bit of code that will be used by multiple scripts in this chapter validates the login form. This is a three-step process:

1. Confirm that an email address was provided.

2. Confirm that a password was provided.

3. Confirm that the provided email address and password match those stored in the database (during the registration process).

This next script will define two different functions. The details of how each function works will be explained in the steps that follow.

To create the login functions:

1. Begin a new PHP document in your text editor or IDE, to be named **login_functions.inc.php** (Script 12.2):

   ```
   <?php # Script 12.2 -
   → login_functions.inc.php
   ```

   Since this file will be included by other files, it does not need to contain any HTML.

2. Begin defining a new function:

   ```
   function redirect_user($page =
   → 'index.php') {
   ```

   The **redirect_user()** function will create an absolute URL that's correct for the site running these scripts, and then redirect the user to that page. The benefit of doing this dynamically (as opposed to just hard-coding **http://www.example.com/page.php**) is that you can develop your code on one server, such as your own computer, and then move it to another server without ever needing to change this code.

   The function takes one optional argument: the final destination page name. The default value is *index.php*.

   continues on next page

3. Start defining the URL:

```
$url = 'http://' . $_SERVER
→['HTTP_HOST'] . dirname
→($_SERVER['PHP_SELF']);
```

To start, **$url** is assigned the value of *http://* plus the hostname (which could be either *localhost* or *www.example.com*). To this is added the name of the current directory using the **dirname()** function, in case the redirection is taking place within a subfolder. **$_SERVER['PHP_SELF']** refers to the current script (which will be the one calling this function), including the directory name. That whole value might be */somedir/page.php*. The **dirname()** function will return just the directory part from that value (i.e., */somedir/*).

4. Remove any ending slashes from the URL:

```
$url = rtrim($url, '/\\');
```

Because the existence of a subfolder might add an extra slash (*/*) or back-slash (**, for Windows), the function needs to remove that. To do so, apply the **rtrim()** function. By default, this function removes spaces from the right side of a string. If provided with a list of characters to remove as the second argument, it'll chop those off instead. The characters to be removed are */* and **. But since the backslash is the escape character in PHP, you need to use ** to refer to a single backslash. With this one line of code, if **$url** concludes with either of these characters, the **rtrim()** function will remove them.

Script 12.2 The `login_functions.inc.php` script defines two functions that will be used by different scripts in the login/logout process.

```
1   <?php # Script 12.2 - login_functions.
    inc.php
2   // This page defines two functions
    used by the login/logout process.
3
4   /* This function determines an absolute
    URL and redirects the user there.
5    * The function takes one argument: the
    page to be redirected to.
6    * The argument defaults to index.php.
7    */
8   function redirect_user($page =
    'index.php') {
9
10      // Start defining the URL...
11      // URL is http:// plus the host name
        plus the current directory:
12      $url = 'http://' . $_SERVER
        ['HTTP_HOST'] . dirname
        ($_SERVER['PHP_SELF']);
13
14      // Remove any trailing slashes:
15      $url = rtrim($url, '/\\');
16
17      // Add the page:
18      $url .= '/' . $page;
19
20      // Redirect the user:
21      header("Location: $url");
22      exit(); // Quit the script.
23
24  } // End of redirect_user() function.
25
26
27  /* This function validates the form data
    (the email address and password).
28   * If both are present, the database is
    queried.
29   * The function requires a database
    connection.
30   * The function returns an array of
    information, including:
31   * - a TRUE/FALSE variable indicating
    success
32   * - an array of either errors or the
    database result
33   */
34  function check_login($dbc, $email = '',
    $pass = '') {
35
```

code continues on next page

```
36      $errors = []; // Initialize error
        array.
37
38      // Validate the email address:
39      if (empty($email)) {
40          $errors[] = 'You forgot to enter
            your email address.';
41      } else {
42          $e = mysqli_real_escape_string
            ($dbc, trim($email));
43      }
44
45      // Validate the password:
46      if (empty($pass)) {
47          $errors[] = 'You forgot to enter
            your password.';
48      } else {
49          $p = mysqli_real_escape_string
            ($dbc, trim($pass));
50      }
51
52      if (empty($errors)) { // If
        everything's OK.
53
54          // Retrieve the user_id and
            first_name for that email/password
            combination:
55          $q = "SELECT user_id, first_name
            FROM users WHERE email='$e' AND
            pass=SHA2('$p', 512)";
56          $r = @mysqli_query($dbc, $q);
            // Run the query.
57
58          // Check the result:
59          if (mysqli_num_rows($r) == 1) {
60
61              // Fetch the record:
62              $row = mysqli_fetch_array($r,
                MYSQLI_ASSOC);
63
64              // Return true and the record:
65              return [true, $row];
66
67          } else { // Not a match!
68              $errors[] = 'The email address
                and password entered do not
                match those on file.';
69          }
70
71      } // End of empty($errors) IF.
72
73      // Return false and the errors:
74      return [false, $errors];
75
76  } // End of check_login() function.
```

5. Append the specific page to the URL:

`$url .= '/' . $page;`

Next, the specific page name is concatenated to the **$url**. It's preceded by a slash because any trailing slashes were removed in Step 4 and you can't have **www.example.compage.php** as the URL.

This may all seem to be quite complicated, but it's a very effective way to ensure that the redirection works no matter on what server, or from what directory, the script is being run (as long as the redirection is taking place within that directory).

6. Redirect the user and complete the function:

> **`header("Location: $url");`**
> **`exit(); // Quit the script.`**
> **`} // End of redirect_user() function.`**

The final steps are to send a *Location* header and terminate the execution of the script.

7. Begin a new function:

> **`function check_login($dbc,`**
> → **`$email = '', $pass = '') {`**

This function will validate the login information. It takes three arguments: the database connection, which is required; the email address, which is optional; and the password, which is also optional.

Although this function could access **$_POST['email']** and **$_POST['pass']** directly, it's better if the function is passed these values, making the function more independent.

continues on next page

8. Validate the email address and password:

```
$errors = []; // Initialize error
→ array.
if (empty($email)) {
  $errors[] = 'You forgot to
  → enter your email address.';
} else {
  $e = mysqli_real_escape_string
  → ($dbc, trim($email));
}
if (empty($pass)) {
  $errors[] = 'You forgot to
  → enter your password.';
} else {
  $p = mysqli_real_escape_string
  → ($dbc, trim($pass));
}
```

This validation routine is similar to that used in the registration page. If any problems occur, they'll be added to the **$errors** array, which will eventually be used on the login page (see **C** under "Making a Login Page"). Note that this **$errors** array is *local* to the function. Even though it has the same name, this is not the same **$errors** variable that is used in the login page. Code later in the function will return this **$errors** variable's value, and code in the scripts that call this function will then assign this returned value to the proper, global **$errors** array, usable on the login page.

9. If no errors occurred, run the database query:

```
if (empty($errors)) {
  $q = "SELECT user_id, first_
  → name FROM users WHERE email=
  → '$e' AND pass=SHA2('$p', 512)";
  $r = @mysqli_query($dbc, $q);
```

The query selects the *user_id* and *first_ name* values from the database where

the submitted email address (from the form) matches the stored email address and the **SHA2()** version of the submitted password matches the stored password **A**.

Keep in mind this approach works only if both the registration and login scripts encrypt or hash the password using the exact same method. In Chapter 13, "Security Methods," you'll learn how to securely hash passwords using just PHP.

10. Check the results of the query:

```
if (mysqli_num_rows($r) == 1) {
  $row = mysqli_fetch_array
  → ($r, MYSQLI_ASSOC);
  return [true, $row];
```

If the query returned one row, then the login information was correct. The results are then fetched into **$row**. The final step in a successful login is to return two pieces of information back to the requesting script: the Boolean *true*, indicating that the login was a success, and the data fetched from MySQL. Using the short array syntax (or the **array()** function), both the Boolean value and the **$row** array can be returned by this function.

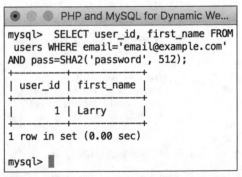

```
mysql> SELECT user_id, first_name FROM
 users WHERE email='email@example.com'
AND pass=SHA2('password', 512);
+---------+------------+
| user_id | first_name |
+---------+------------+
|       1 | Larry      |
+---------+------------+
1 row in set (0.00 sec)

mysql>
```

A The results of the login query, shown in the mysql client, if the user submitted the proper email address/password combination.

11. If no record was selected by the query, create an error:

```
} else { // Not a match!
    $errors[] = 'The email address
    → and password entered do not
    → match those on file.';
}
```

If the query did not return one row, then an error message is added to the array. It will end up being displayed on the login page **B**.

12. Complete the conditional begun in Step 9 and complete the function:

```
} // End of empty($errors) IF.
return [false, $errors];
} // End of check_login() function.
```

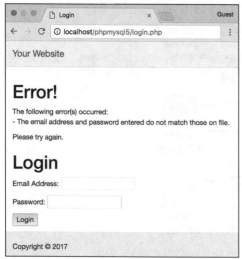

B If the user entered an email address and password, but they don't match the values stored in the database, this is the result in the browser.

The final step is for the function to return a value of *false*, indicating that login failed, and to return the `$errors` array, which stores the reason(s) for failure. This `return` statement can be placed here—at the end of the function instead of within a conditional—because the function will only get to this point if the login failed. If the login succeeded, the `return` line in Step 10 will stop the function from continuing (a function stops as soon as it executes a `return`).

13. Save the file as `login_functions.inc.php` and place it in your web directory (in the `includes` folder, along with `header.html`, `footer.html`, and `login_page.inc.php`).

This page will also use an `.inc.php` extension to indicate both that it's an includable file and that it contains PHP code.

As with some other includable files created in this book (although not `login_page.inc.php`), the closing PHP tag—`?>`—is omitted. Doing so prevents potential complications that can arise should an includable file have an errant blank space or line after the closing tag.

> **TIP** The scripts in this chapter include no debugging code (like the MySQL error or query). If you have problems with these scripts, apply the debugging techniques outlined in Chapter 8, "Error Handling and Debugging."

> **TIP** You can add name-value pairs to the URL in a `header()` call to pass values to the target page:
> ```
> $url .= '?name=' . urlencode(value);
> ```

Using Cookies

Cookies are a way for a server to store information on the user's machine. This is one way that a site can remember or track a user over the course of a visit. Think of a cookie as being like a name tag: you tell the server your name and it gives you a sticker to wear. Then it can know who you are by referring back to that name tag **A**.

In this section, you will learn how to set a cookie, retrieve information from a stored cookie, alter a cookie's settings, and then delete a cookie.

Setting cookies

The most important thing to understand about cookies is that they must be sent from the server to the client prior to *any other information*. Should the server attempt to send a cookie after the browser has already received HTML—even an extraneous white space—an error message will result and the cookie will not be sent **B**. This is by far the most common cookie-related error, but it is easily fixed. If you see such a message:

1. Note the script and line number following *output started at*.

2. Open that script and head to that line number.

3. Remove the blank space, line, text, HTML, or whatever that is outputted by that line.

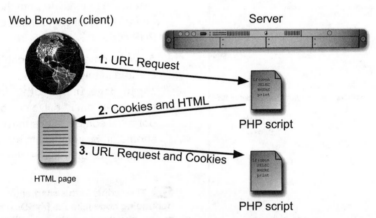

A How cookies are sent back and forth between the server and the client.

> **Warning**: Cannot modify header information - headers already sent by (output started at /Users/larryullman/Sites/phpmysql4/includes/login_functions.inc.php:80) in **/Users/larryullman/Sites/phpmysql4/login.php** on line **22**

B The *headers already sent...* error message is all too common when creating cookies. Pay attention to what the error message says in order to find and fix the problem.

Testing for Cookies

To effectively program using cookies, you need to be able to accurately test for their presence. The best way to do so is to have your browser ask what to do when receiving a cookie. In such a case, the browser will prompt you with the cookie information each time PHP attempts to send a cookie.

Different versions of different browsers on different platforms all define their cookie-handling policies in different places. Search online for instructions for your browser of choice.

Alternatively, most debugging tools built into browsers provide a way to view cookies. This information is normally located under an "Application" or "Network" section. Again, search online for the particulars for your browser.

Cookies are sent via the **setcookie()** function:

```
setcookie(name, value);
setcookie('name', 'Nicole');
```

The second line of code will send a cookie to the browser with a name of *name* and a value of *Nicole* 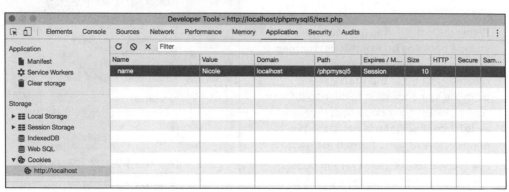.

You can continue to send more cookies to the browser with subsequent uses of the **setcookie()** function:

```
setcookie('ID', 263);
setcookie('email', 'email@example.com');
```

As for the cookies name, it's best not to use white spaces or punctuation, and pay attention to the exact case used.

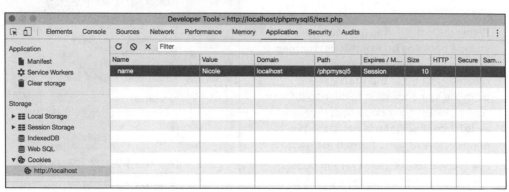

Name	Value	Domain	Path	Expires / M...	Size	HTTP	Secure	Sam...
name	Nicole	localhost	/phpmysql5	Session	10			

C Viewing a received cookie in Google Chrome's developer tools.

To send a cookie:

1. Begin a new PHP document in your text editor or IDE, to be named **login.php** (Script 12.3):

   ```
   <?php # Script 12.3 - login.php
   ```

   For this example, let's make a **login.php** script that works in conjunction with the scripts from Chapter 9. This script will also require the two files created at the beginning of the chapter.

2. If the form has been submitted, include the two helper files:

   ```
   if ($_SERVER['REQUEST_METHOD'] ==
   → 'POST') {
     require('includes/login_
     → functions.inc.php');
     require('../mysqli_connect.php');
   ```

   This script will do two things: handle the form submission and display the form. This conditional checks for the submission.

   Within the conditional, the script must include both **login_functions.inc.php** and **mysqli_connect.php** (which was created in Chapter 9 and should still be in the same location relative to this script; change your code here if your **mysqli_connect.php** is not in the parent directory of the current directory).

   I've chosen to use **require()** in both cases, instead of **include()**, because a failure to include either of these scripts makes the login process impossible.

Script 12.3 Upon a successful login, the **login.php** script creates two cookies and redirects the user.

```
1    <?php # Script 12.3 - login.php
2    // This page processes the login form
     submission.
3    // Upon successful login, the user is
     redirected.
4    // Two included files are necessary.
5    // Send NOTHING to the web browser
     prior to the setcookie() lines!
6
7    // Check if the form has been submitted:
8    if ($_SERVER['REQUEST_METHOD'] ==
     'POST') {
9
10       // For processing the login:
11       require('includes/login_functions.
         inc.php');
12
13       // Need the database connection:
14       require('../mysqli_connect.php');
15
16       // Check the login:
17       list($check, $data) =
         check_login($dbc, $_POST['email'],
         $_POST['pass']);
18
19       if ($check) { // OK!
20
21           // Set the cookies:
22           setcookie('user_id',
             $data['user_id']);
23           setcookie('first_name',
             $data['first_name']);
24
25           // Redirect:
26           redirect_user('loggedin.php');
27
28       } else { // Unsuccessful!
29
30           // Assign $data to $errors for
             error reporting
31           // in the login_page.inc.php file.
32           $errors = $data;
33
34       }
35
36       mysqli_close($dbc); // Close the
         database connection.
37
38   } // End of the main submit conditional.
39
40   // Create the page:
41   include('includes/login_page.inc.php');
42   ?>
```

3. Validate the form data:

```
list($check, $data) =
→ check_login($dbc, $_
→ POST['email'], $_POST['pass']);
```

After including both files, the **check_login()** function can be called. It's passed the database connection (which comes from **mysqli_connect.php**), along with the email address and the password (both of which come from the form). As an added precaution, the script could confirm that both variables are set and not empty prior to invoking the function.

This function returns an array of two elements: a Boolean value and an array (of user data or errors). To assign those returned values to variables, apply the **list()** function. The first value returned by the function (the Boolean) will be assigned to **$check**. The second value returned (either the **$row** or **$errors** array) will be assigned to **$data**.

4. If the user entered the correct information, log them in:

```
if ($check) { // OK!
  setcookie('user_id',
   → $data['user_id']);
  setcookie('first_name',
   → $data['first_name']);
```

The **$check** variable indicates the success of the login attempt. If it has a TRUE value, then **$data** contains the user's ID and first name. These two values can be used in cookies.

Generally speaking, you should never store a database table's primary key value, such as **$data['user_id']**, in a cookie, because cookies can be manipulated easily. In this situation, it's not going to be a problem since the *user_id* value isn't actually used anywhere in the site (it's being stored in the cookie for demonstration purposes).

5. Redirect the user to another page:

```
redirect_user('loggedin.php');
```

Using the function defined earlier in the chapter, the user will be redirected to another script upon a successful login. The specific page to be redirected to is **loggedin.php**.

6. Complete the **$check** conditional (started in Step 4) and then close the database connection:

```
} else {
  $errors = $data;
}
mysqli_close($dbc);
```

If **$check** has a FALSE value, then the **$data** variable is storing the errors generated within the **check_login()** function. If so, the errors should be assigned to the **$errors** variable, because that's what the code in the script that displays the login page—**login_page.inc.php**—is expecting.

continues on next page

7. Complete the main submit conditional and include the login page:

```
}
include('includes/login_
→ page.inc.php');
?>
```

This **login.php** script itself primarily performs validation, by calling the **check_login()** function, and handles the cookies and redirection. The **login_page.inc.php** file contains the login page itself, so it just needs to be included.

8. Save the file as **login.php**, place it in your web directory (in the same folder as the files from Chapter 9), and load this page in your browser (see **B** under "Making a Login Page").

TIP If you want, you can submit the form erroneously, but you cannot correctly log in yet, as the final destination—loggedin.php—hasn't been written.

TIP Cookies are limited to about 4 KB of total data, and each browser can remember a limited number of cookies from any one site. This limit is 50 cookies for most of the current browsers (but if you're sending out 50 different cookies, you may want to rethink how you do things).

TIP The setcookie() function is one of the few functions in PHP that could have different results in different browsers, since each browser treats cookies in its own way. Be sure to test your web sites in multiple browsers on different platforms to ensure consistency.

TIP If the first two included files send anything to the browser or even have blank lines or spaces after the closing PHP tag, you'll see a *headers already sent* error. This is why neither includes the terminating PHP tag.

Accessing cookies

To retrieve a value from a cookie, you only need to refer to the **$_COOKIE** superglobal, using the appropriate cookie name as the key (as you would with any array). For example, to retrieve the value of the cookie established with the line

```
setcookie('username', 'Trout');
```

you would refer to **$_COOKIE['username']**.

In the following example, the cookies set by the **login.php** script will be accessed in two ways. First, a check will be made that the user is logged in (otherwise, that user shouldn't be accessing this page). Second, the user will be greeted by his or her first name, which was stored in a cookie.

To access a cookie:

1. Begin a new PHP document in your text editor or IDE, to be named **loggedin.php** (Script 12.4):

```
<?php # Script 12.4 - loggedin.php
```

The user will be redirected to this page after successfully logging in. The script will greet the user by first name, using the cookie.

2. Check for the presence of a cookie:

```
if (!isset($_COOKIE['user_id'])) {
```

Since a user shouldn't be able to access this page unless he or she is logged in, check for a cookie that should have been set (in **login.php**).

Script 12.4 The `loggedin.php` script prints a greeting to a user thanks to a stored cookie.

```
1    <?php # Script 12.4 - loggedin.php
2    // The user is redirected here from
     login.php.
3
4    // If no cookie is present, redirect the
     user:
5    if (!isset($_COOKIE['user_id'])) {
6
7        // Need the functions:
8        require('includes/login_functions.
         inc.php');
9        redirect_user();
10
11   }
12
13   // Set the page title and include the
     HTML header:
14   $page_title = 'Logged In!';
15   include('includes/header.html');
16
17   // Print a customized message:
18   echo "<h1>Logged In!</h1>
19   <p>You are now logged in,
     {$_COOKIE['first_name']}!</p>
20   <p><a href=\"logout.php\">Logout</a>
     </p>";
21
22   include('includes/footer.html');
23   ?>
```

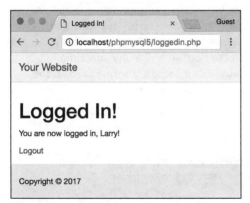

D If you used the correct email address and password, you'll see this page after logging in.

3. Redirect any user who is not logged in:

   ```
   require('includes/login_
   → functions.inc.php');
   redirect_user();
   }
   ```

   If the user is not logged in, he or she will be automatically redirected to the main page. This is a simple way to limit access to content.

4. Include the page header:

   ```
   $page_title = 'Logged In! ';
   include('includes/header.html');
   ```

5. Welcome the user, referencing the cookie:

   ```
   echo "<h1>Logged In!</h1>
   <p>You are now logged in,
   → {$_COOKIE['first_name']}!</p>
   <p><a href=\"logout.php\">Logout
   → </a></p>";
   ```

   To greet the user by name, refer to the `$_COOKIE['first_name']` variable, enclosed within braces to avoid parse errors. A link to the logout page (to be written later in the chapter) is also printed.

6. Complete the HTML page:

   ```
   include('includes/footer.html');
   ?>
   ```

7. Save the file as **loggedin.php**, place it in your web directory (in the same folder as **login.php**), and test it in your browser by logging in through **login.php D**.

   Since these examples use the same database as those in Chapter 9, you should be able to log in using the registered username and password submitted at that time.

   continues on next page

8. Use your browser's developer tools to see the cookies being set 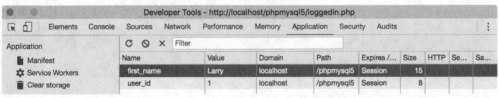, change the cookie settings for your browser, and test again.

> **TIP** Some browsers (e.g., Internet Explorer) will not adhere to your cookie-prompting preferences for cookies sent over localhost.

> **TIP** A cookie is not accessible until the setting page (e.g., login.php) has been reloaded or another page has been accessed (in other words, you cannot set and access a cookie in the same page).

> **TIP** If users decline a cookie or have their browser set not to accept them, they will automatically be redirected to the home page in this example, even if they successfully logged in. For this reason, you may want to let users know that cookies are required.

> **TIP** The European Union (EU) has laws with respect to user privacy and cookies. If your site serves EU users, take the time to research what steps you ought to take to be compliant.

Setting cookie parameters

Although passing just the name and value arguments to the `setcookie()` function will suffice, you ought to be aware of the other arguments available. The function can take up to five more parameters, each of which will alter the definition of the cookie.

```
setcookie(name, value, expiration,
→ path, host, secure, httponly);
```

The *expiration* argument is used to set a definitive length of time for a cookie to

exist, specified in seconds since the *epoch* (the epoch is midnight on January 1, 1970). If it is not set or if it's set to a value of 0, the cookie will continue to be functional until the user closes the browser. These cookies are said to last for the browser session (also indicated in).

To set a specific expiration time, add a number of minutes or hours to the current moment, retrieved using the `time()` function. The following line will set the expiration time of the cookie to be 30 minutes (60 seconds times 30 minutes) from the current moment:

```
setcookie(name, value, time()+1800);
```

The *path* and *host* arguments are used to limit a cookie to a specific folder within a web site (the path) or to a specific host (**www.example.com** or *192.168.0.1*). For example, you could restrict a cookie to exist only while a user is within the *admin* folder of a domain (and the *admin* folder's subfolders):

```
setcookie(name, value, expire,
→ '/admin/');
```

Setting the path to **/** will make the cookie visible within an entire domain (web site). Setting the domain to **.example.com** will make the cookie visible within an entire domain and every subdomain (**www.example.com**, **admin.example.com**, **pages.example.com**, etc.).

The *secure* value dictates that a cookie should be sent only over a secure HTTPS

E The two generated cookies.

connection. A 1 indicates that a secure connection must be used, and a 0 says that a standard connection is fine.

```
setcookie(name, value, expire,
→ path, host, 1);
```

If your site is using a secure connection, you ought to restrict any cookies to HTTPS as well.

Finally, added in PHP 5.2 is the *httponly* argument. A Boolean value is used to make the cookie only accessible through HTTP (and HTTPS). Enforcing this restriction will make the cookie more secure (preventing some hack attempts) but is not supported by all browsers as of this writing.

```
setcookie(name, value, expire, path,
→ host, secure, TRUE);
```

As with all functions that take arguments, you must pass the **setcookie()** values in order. To skip any parameter, use **NULL**, 0, or an empty string; don't use **FALSE**. The expiration and secure values are both integers and are therefore not quoted.

To demonstrate this information, let's add an expiration setting to the login cookies so that they last for only one hour.

To set a cookie's parameters:

1. Open **login.php** in your text editor (refer to Script 12.3), if you haven't already.

2. Change the two **setcookie()** lines to include an expiration date that's 60 minutes away (**Script 12.5**):

```
setcookie('user_id', $data
→ ['user_id'], time()+3600,
→ '/', '', 0, 0);
setcookie('first_name', $data
→ ['first_name'], time()+3600,
→ '/', '', 0, 0);
```

continues on next page

Script 12.5 The **login.php** script now uses every argument the **setcookie()** function can take.

```
1   <?php # Script 12.5 - login.php #2
2   // This page processes the login form submission.
3   // The script now adds extra parameters to the setcookie() lines.
4
5   // Check if the form has been submitted:
6   if ($_SERVER['REQUEST_METHOD'] == 'POST') {
7
8       // Need two helper files:
9       require('includes/login_functions.inc.php');
10      require('../mysqli_connect.php');
11
12      // Check the login:
13      list ($check, $data) = check_login($dbc, $_POST['email'], $_POST['pass']);
14
15      if ($check) { // OK!
16
17          // Set the cookies:
18          setcookie('user_id', $data['user_id'], time()+3600, '/', '', 0, 0);
19          setcookie('first_name', $data['first_name'], time()+3600, '/', '', 0, 0);
20
21          // Redirect:
22          redirect_user('loggedin.php');
```

code continues on next page

With the expiration date set to `time()` **+ 3600** (60 minutes times 60 seconds), the cookie will continue to exist for an hour after it is set. Next, the *path*, *host*, and *secure* parameters are then set to logical defaults.

For the final parameter, which accepts a Boolean value, you can also use 0 to represent FALSE (PHP will handle the conversion for you). Doing so is a good idea, since using *false* in any of the cookie arguments can cause problems.

3. Save the script, place it in your web directory, and test it in your browser by logging in 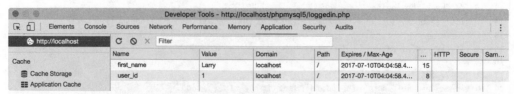 **F**.

TIP Some browsers have difficulties with cookies that do not list every argument. Explicitly stating every parameter—even as an empty string—will achieve more reliable results across all browsers.

TIP Here are some general guidelines for cookie expirations: If the cookie should last as long as the user's session, do not set an expiration time; if the cookie should continue to exist after the user has closed and reopened his or her browser, set an expiration time weeks or months ahead; and if the cookie can constitute a security risk, set an expiration time of an hour or fraction thereof so that the cookie does not continue to exist too long after a user has left his or her browser.

Script 12.5 *continued*

```
23
24        } else { // Unsuccessful!
25
26            // Assign $data to $errors for
              login_page.inc.php:
27            $errors = $data;
28
29        }
30
31        mysqli_close($dbc); // Close the
          database connection.
32
33    } // End of the main submit conditional.
34
35    // Create the page:
36    include('includes/login_page.inc.php');
37    ?>
```

TIP For security purposes, you could set a 5- or 10-minute expiration time on a cookie and have the cookie re-sent with every new page the user visits (assuming that the cookie exists). This way, the cookie will continue to persist as long as the user is active but will automatically die 5 or 10 minutes after the user's last action.

TIP E-commerce and other privacy-related web applications should use an SSL (Secure Sockets Layer) connection for all transactions, including the cookie.

TIP Be careful with cookies created by scripts within a directory. If the path isn't specified, then that cookie will be available to other scripts only within that same directory.

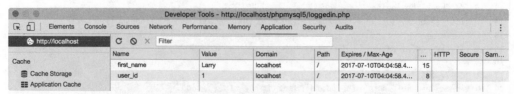

F Changes to the `setcookie()` parameters, like an expiration date and time, will be reflected in the cookie sent to the browser (compare with **E**).

Script 12.6 The `logout.php` script deletes the previously established cookies.

```
1   <?php # Script 12.6 - logout.php
2   // This page lets the user logout.
3
4   // If no cookie is present, redirect the
    user:
5   if (!isset($_COOKIE['user_id'])) {
6
7       // Need the function:
8       require('includes/login_functions.
        inc.php');
9       redirect_user();
10
11  } else { // Delete the cookies:
12      setcookie('user_id', '',
        time()-3600, '/', '', 0, 0);
13      setcookie('first_name', '',
        time()-3600, '/', '', 0, 0);
14  }
15
16  // Set the page title and include the
    HTML header:
17  $page_title = 'Logged Out!';
18  include('includes/header.html');
19
20  // Print a customized message:
21  echo "<h1>Logged Out!</h1>
22  <p>You are now logged out,
    {$_COOKIE['first_name']}!</p>";
23
24  include('includes/footer.html');
25  ?>
```

Deleting cookies

The final thing to understand about using cookies is how to delete one. Although a cookie will automatically expire when the user's browser is closed or when the expiration date/time is met, often you'll want to manually delete the cookie instead. For example, in web sites that have login capabilities, you will want to delete any cookies when the user logs out.

Although the **setcookie()** function can take up to seven arguments, only one is required: the cookie name. If you send a cookie that consists of a name without a value, it will have the same effect as deleting the existing cookie of the same name. For example, to create the cookie *first_name*, you use this line:

setcookie('first_name', 'Tyler');

To delete the *first_name* cookie, you would code

setcookie('first_name');

As an added precaution, you can also set an expiration date that's in the past:

setcookie('first_name', '', time()-3600);

To demonstrate all of this, let's add a logout capability to the site. The link to the logout page appears on **loggedin.php**. As an added feature, the header file will be altered so that a *Logout* link appears when the user is logged in and a *Login* link appears when the user is logged out.

To delete a cookie:

1. Begin a new PHP document in your text editor or IDE, to be named **logout.php** (Script 12.6):

   <?php # Script 12.6 - logout.php

   continues on next page

2. Check for the existence of a *user_id* cookie; if it is not present, redirect the user:

```
if (!isset($_COOKIE['user_id'])) {
  require('includes/login_
  → functions.inc.php');
  redirect_user();
```

As with **loggedin.php**, if the user is not already logged in, this page should redirect the user to the home page. There's no point in trying to log out a user who isn't logged in!

3. Delete the cookies, if they exist:

```
} else { // Delete the cookies:
  setcookie('user_id', '',
  → time()-3600, '/', '', 0, 0);
  setcookie('first_name', '',
  → time()-3600, '/', '', 0, 0);
}
```

If the user is logged in, these two cookies will effectively delete the existing ones. Except for the value and the expiration, the other arguments should have the same values as they do when the cookies were created.

4. Make the remainder of the PHP page:

```
$page_title = 'Logged Out!';
include('includes/header.html');
echo "<h1>Logged Out!</h1>
<p>You are now logged out,
→ {$_COOKIE['first_name']}!</p>";
include('includes/footer.html');
?>
```

The page itself is also much like the **loggedin.php** page. Although it may seem odd that you can still refer to the *first_name* cookie (that was just deleted in this script), it makes perfect sense considering the process:

A. This page is requested by the client.

B. The server reads the available cookies from the client's browser.

C. The page is run and does its thing (including sending new cookies that delete the existing ones).

Thus, in short, the original *first_name* cookie data is available to this script when it first runs. The set of cookies sent by this page—the delete cookies—aren't available to this page, so the original values are still usable.

5. Save the file as **logout.php** and place it in your web directory (in the same folder as **login.php**).

To create the logout link:

1. Open **header.html** (refer to Script 9.1) in your text editor or IDE.

2. Add a final navigation item (**Script 12.7**):

```
<li><?php
if ( (isset($_COOKIE['user_id']))
→ && (basename($_SERVER['PHP_SELF'])
→ != 'logout.php') ) {
  echo '<a href="logout.php">
  → Logout</a>';
} else {
  echo '<a href="login.php">
  → Login</a>';
}
?></li>
```

continues on page 402

Script 12.7 The **header.html** file now displays either a *Login* or a *Logout* link, depending on the user's current status.

```
1    <!DOCTYPE html>
2    <html lang="en">
3    <head>
4    <meta charset="utf-8">
5    <meta http-equiv="X-UA-Compatible" content="IE=edge">
6    <meta name="viewport" content="width=device-width, initial-scale=1">
7    <title><?php echo $page_title; ?></title>
8    <link rel="stylesheet" href="https://maxcdn.bootstrapcdn.com/bootstrap/3.3.7/css/bootstrap.
     min.css" integrity="sha384-BVYiiSIFeK1dGmJRAkycuHAHRg32OmUcww7on3RYdg4Va+PmSTsz/K68vbdEjh4u"
     crossorigin="anonymous">
9    <link href="css/sticky-footer-navbar.css" rel="stylesheet">
10   </head>
11   <body>
12   <nav class="navbar navbar-default navbar-fixed-top">
13      <div class="container">
14         <div class="navbar-header"><a class="navbar-brand" href="#">Your Website</a></div>
15         <div id="navbar" class="collapse navbar-collapse">
16         <ul class="nav navbar-nav">
17            <li class="active"><a href="index.php">Home</a></li>
18            <li><a href="register.php">Register</a></li>
19            <li><a href="view_users.php">View Users</a></li>
20            <li><a href="password.php">Change Password</a></li>
21   <li><?php // Create a login/logout link:
22   if ( (isset($_COOKIE['user_id'])) && (basename($_SERVER['PHP_SELF']) != 'logout.php')
     ) {
23      echo '<a href="logout.php">Logout</a>';
24   } else {
25      echo '<a href="login.php">Login</a>';
26   }
27   ?></li>
28         </ul>
29         </div>
30      </div>
31   </nav>
32   <div class="container">
33   <!-- Script 12.7 - header.html -->
```

Instead of having a permanent login link in the navigation area, it should display a *Login* link if the user is not logged in 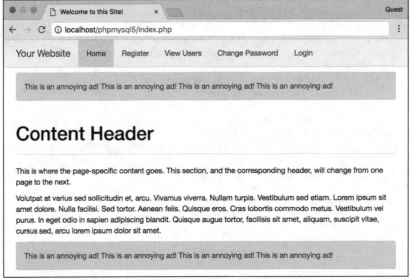 or a *Logout* link if the user is 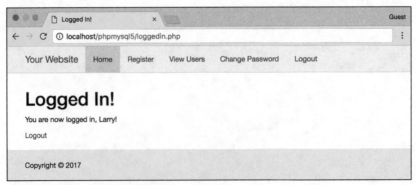. The preceding conditional will accomplish just that, depending on the presence of a cookie.

For that condition, if the cookie is set, the user is logged in and can be shown the logout link. If the cookie is not set, the user should be shown the login link. There is one catch, however: because the **logout.php** script would ordinarily display a logout link (because the cookie exists when the page is first being viewed), the conditional has to also check that the current page is not the **logout.php** script. An easy way to dynamically determine the current page is to apply the **basename()** function to **$_SERVER['PHP_SELF']**.

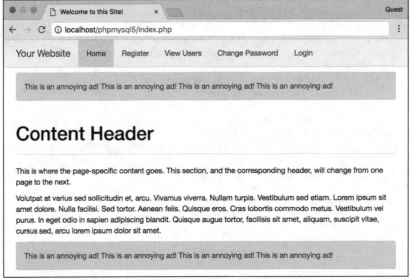

G The home page with a *Login* link.

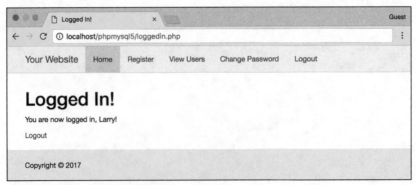

H After the user logs in, the page now has a *Logout* link.

3. Save the file, place it in your web directory (within the **includes** folder), and test the login/logout process in your browser .

TIP Due to a bug in how Internet Explorer on Windows handles cookies, you may need to set the host parameter to `false` in order to get the logout process to work when developing on your own computer (i.e., through localhost).

TIP When deleting a cookie, you should always use the same parameters that set the cookie (aside from the value and expiration, naturally). If you set the host and path in the creation cookie, use them again in the deletion cookie.

TIP To hammer the point home, remember that the deletion of a cookie does not take effect until the page has been reloaded or another page has been accessed. In other words, the cookie will still be available to a page after that page has deleted it.

Guest

localhost/phpmysql5/logout.php

Your Website   Home   Register   View Users   Change Password   Login

Logged Out!

You are now logged out, Larry!

Copyright © 2017

① The result after logging out.

Using Sessions

Another method of making data available to multiple pages of a web site is to use *sessions*. The premise of a session is that data is stored on the server, not in the browser, and a session identifier is used to locate a particular user's record (i.e., the session data). This session identifier is normally stored in the user's browser via a cookie, but the sensitive data itself—like the user's ID, name, and so on—always remains on the server.

The question may arise: why use sessions at all when cookies work just fine? First, sessions are likely more secure in that all of the recorded information is stored on the server and not continually sent back and forth between the server and the client. Second, you can store more data in a session. Third, some users reject cookies or turn them off completely. Sessions, while designed to work with a cookie, can function without them, too.

To demonstrate sessions—and to compare them with cookies—let's rewrite the previous set of scripts.

Setting session variables

The most important rule with respect to sessions is that each page that will use them must begin by calling the **session_start()** function. This function tells PHP to either begin a new session or access an existing one. This function must be called before anything is sent to the browser!

The first time this function is used, **session_start()** will attempt to send a cookie with a name of *PHPSESSID* (the default session name) and a value of something like *a61f8670baa8e90a30c878df89a2074b* (32 hexadecimal letters, the session ID). Because of this attempt to send a cookie, **session_start()** must be called before any data is sent to the browser, as is the case when using the **setcookie()** and **header()** functions.

Sessions vs. Cookies

This chapter has examples accomplishing the same tasks—logging in and logging out—using both cookies and sessions. Obviously, both are easy to use in PHP, but the true question is when to use one or the other.

Sessions have the following advantages over cookies:

- They are generally more secure (because the data is being retained on the server).
- They allow for more data to be stored.
- They can be used without cookies.

Whereas cookies have the following advantages over sessions:

- They are easier to program.
- They require less of the server.
- They can be made to last far longer.

In general, to store and retrieve just a couple of small pieces of information, or to store information for a longer duration, use cookies. For most of your web applications, though, you'll use sessions.

Once the session has been started, values can be registered to the session using the normal array syntax, using the **$_SESSION** superglobal:

```php
$_SESSION['key'] = value;
$_SESSION['name'] = 'Roxanne';
$_SESSION['id'] = 48;
```

Let's update the **login.php** script with this in mind.

To begin a session:

1. Open **login.php** (refer to Script 12.5) in your text editor or IDE.

2. Replace the **setcookie()** lines (18–19) with these lines (**Script 12.8**):

   ```php
   session_start();
   $_SESSION['user_id'] =
   → $data['user_id'];
   $_SESSION['first_name'] =
   → $data['first_name'];
   ```

continues on next page

Script 12.8 This version of the **login.php** script uses sessions instead of cookies.

```php
1    <?php # Script 12.8 - login.php #3
2    // This page processes the login form submission.
3    // The script now uses sessions.
4
5    // Check if the form has been submitted:
6    if ($_SERVER['REQUEST_METHOD'] == 'POST') {
7
8        // Need two helper files:
9        require('includes/login_functions.inc.php');
10       require('../mysqli_connect.php');
11
12       // Check the login:
13       list ($check, $data) = check_login($dbc, $_POST['email'], $_POST['pass']);
14
15       if ($check) { // OK!
16
17           // Set the session data:
18           session_start();
19           $_SESSION['user_id'] = $data['user_id'];
20           $_SESSION['first_name'] = $data['first_name'];
21
22           // Redirect:
23           redirect_user('loggedin.php');
24
25       } else { // Unsuccessful!
26
27           // Assign $data to $errors for login_page.inc.php:
28           $errors = $data;
29
30       }
31
32       mysqli_close($dbc); // Close the database connection.
33
34   } // End of the main submit conditional.
35
36   // Create the page:
37   include('includes/login_page.inc.php');
38   ?>
```

The first step is to begin the session. Since there are no **echo** statements, inclusions of HTML files, or even blank spaces in the script so far, it will be safe to use **session_start()** at this point in the script (although the function call could be placed at the top of the script as well). Then, two *key-value* pairs are added to the **$_SESSION** superglobal array to register the user's first name and user ID to the session.

3. Save the page as **login.php**, place it in your web directory, and test it in your browser **A**.

   Although **loggedin.php** and the header and script will need to be rewritten, you can still test the login script and see the resulting cookie **B**. The **loggedin.php** page should redirect you back to the home page, though, since it's still checking for the presence of a **$_COOKIE** variable.

TIP Because sessions will normally send and read cookies, you should always try to begin them as early in the script as possible. Doing so will help you avoid the problem of attempting to send a cookie after the headers (HTML or white space) have already been sent.

TIP If you want, you can set **session. auto_start** in the **php.ini** file to 1, making it unnecessary to use **session_start()** on each page. This does put a greater toll on the server and, for that reason, shouldn't be used without some consideration of the circumstances.

TIP You can store arrays in sessions (making **$_SESSION** a multidimensional array), just as you can store strings or numbers. You cannot store resources (e.g., a database connection) in a session, however.

A The login form remains unchanged to the end user, but the underlying functionality now uses sessions.

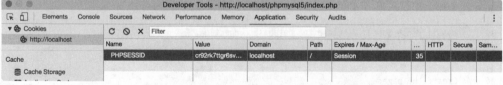

B This cookie, created by PHP's **session_start()** function, stores the session ID in the user's browser.

Accessing session variables

Once a session has been started and variables have been registered to it, you can create other scripts that will access those variables. To do so, each script must first enable sessions using **session_start()**.

This function will give the current script access to the previously started session (if it can read the *PHPSESSID* value stored in the cookie) or create a new session if it cannot. Understand that if the current session ID cannot be found and a new session ID is

generated, none of the data stored under the old session ID will be available. I mention this here because if you're having problems with sessions, checking the session ID value to see if it changes from one page to the next is the first debugging step.

Assuming that there was no problem accessing the current session, to then refer to a session variable, use **$_SESSION['var']**, as you would refer to any other array.

To access session variables:

1. Open **loggedin.php** (refer to Script 12.4) in your text editor or IDE.

2. Add a call to the **session_start()** function (**Script 12.9**):

   session_start();

   Every PHP script that either sets or accesses session variables must use the **session_start()** function. This line must be called before the **header.html** file is included and before anything is sent to the browser.

3. Replace the references to **$_COOKIE** with **$_SESSION** (lines 5 and 19 of the original file):

   if (!isset($_SESSION['user_id'])) {

   and

   echo "<h1>Logged In!</h1>
   <p>You are now logged in,
   → {$_SESSION['first_name']}!</p>
   <p><a href=\"logout.php\">Logout
   → </a></p>";

   Switching a script from cookies to sessions requires only that you change uses of **$_COOKIE** to **$_SESSION** (assuming that the same names were used).

continues on next page

Script 12.9 The **loggedin.php** script is updated so that it refers to **$_SESSION** and not **$_COOKIE** (changes are required on two lines).

```
1   <?php # Script 12.9 - loggedin.php #2
2   // The user is redirected here from
    login.php.
3
4   session_start(); // Start the
    session.
5
6   // If no session value is present,
    redirect the user:
7   if (!isset($_SESSION['user_id'])) {
8
9       // Need the functions:
10      require('includes/login_functions.
        inc.php');
11      redirect_user();
12
13  }
14
15  // Set the page title and include the
    HTML header:
16  $page_title = 'Logged In!';
17  include('includes/header.html');
18
19  // Print a customized message:
20  echo "<h1>Logged In!</h1>
21  <p>You are now logged in,
    {$_SESSION['first_name']}!</p>
22  <p><a href=\"logout.php\">Logout</a>
    </p>";
23
24  include('includes/footer.html');
25  ?>
```

4. Save the file as **loggedin.php**, place it in your web directory, and test it in your browser 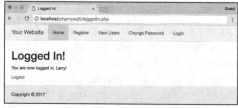.

5. Replace the reference to **$_COOKIE** with **$_SESSION** in **header.html** (from Script 12.7 to **Script 12.10**):

```
if (isset($_SESSION['user_id'])) {
```

C After logging in, the user is redirected to **loggedin.php**, which will welcome the user by name using the stored session value.

Script 12.10 The **header.html** file now also references **$_SESSION** instead of **$_COOKIE**.

```
1    <!DOCTYPE html>
2    <html lang="en">
3    <head>
4    <meta charset="utf-8">
5    <meta http-equiv="X-UA-Compatible" content="IE=edge">
6    <meta name="viewport" content="width=device-width, initial-scale=1">
7    <title><?php echo $page_title; ?></title>
8    <link rel="stylesheet" href="https://maxcdn.bootstrapcdn.com/bootstrap/3.3.7/css/bootstrap.
     min.css" integrity="sha384-BVYiiSIFeK1dGmJRAkycuHAHRg32OmUcww7on3RYdg4Va+PmSTsz/K68vbdEjh4u"
     crossorigin="anonymous">
9    <link href="css/sticky-footer-navbar.css" rel="stylesheet">
10   </head>
11   <body>
12   <nav class="navbar navbar-default navbar-fixed-top">
13     <div class="container">
14       <div class="navbar-header"><a class="navbar-brand" href="#">Your Website</a></div>
15       <div id="navbar" class="collapse navbar-collapse">
16       <ul class="nav navbar-nav">
17         <li class="active"><a href="index.php">Home</a></li>
18         <li><a href="register.php">Register</a></li>
19         <li><a href="view_users.php">View Users</a></li>
20         <li><a href="password.php">Change Password</a></li>
21   <li><?php // Create a login/logout link:
22   if (isset($_SESSION['user_id'])) {
23      echo '<a href="logout.php">Logout</a>';
24   } else {
25      echo '<a href="login.php">Login</a>';
26   }
27   ?></li>
28         </ul>
29       </div>
30     </div>
31   </nav>
32   <div class="container">
33   <!-- Script 12.10 - header.html -->
```

For the *Login/Logout* links to function properly (notice the incorrect link in **C**), the reference to the cookie variable within the header file must be switched over to sessions. The header file does not need to call the `session_start()` function, since it will be included by pages that do.

Note that this conditional does not need to check if the current page is the logout page, because session data behaves differently than cookie data (I'll explain this further in the next section of the chapter).

6. Save the header file, place it in your web directory (in the **includes** folder), and test it in your browser **D**.

TIP For the Login/Logout links to work on the other pages (`register.php`, `index.php`, etc.), you'll need to add the `session_start()` command to each of those.

TIP As a reminder of what I already said, if you have an application where the session data does not seem to be accessible from one page to the next, it could be because a new session is being created on each page. To check for this, compare the session ID (the last few characters of the value will suffice) to see if it is the same. You can see the session's ID by viewing the session cookie as it is sent or by invoking the `session_id()` function:

`echo session_id();`

TIP Session variables are available as soon as you've established them. So, unlike when using cookies, you can assign a value to `$_SESSION['var']` and then refer to `$_SESSION['var']` later in that same script.

TIP The `session_status()` function, added in PHP 5.4, returns a constant indicating the session status: `PHP_SESSION_DISABLED`, `PHP_SESSION_NONE`, and `PHP_SESSION_ACTIVE`.

Deleting session variables

When using sessions, you ought to create a method of deleting the session data. In the current example, this would be necessary when the user logs out.

Whereas a cookie system only requires that another cookie be sent to destroy the existing cookie, sessions are slightly more demanding, since there are both the cookie on the client and the data on the server to consider.

To delete an individual session variable, use the **unset()** function (which works with any variable in PHP):

`unset($_SESSION['var']);`

But to delete every session variable, you shouldn't use **unset()**; instead, reset the `$_SESSION` array:

`$_SESSION = [];`

continues on next page

D With the header file altered for sessions, the proper *Login/Logout* links will be displayed (compare with **C**).

Finally, to remove all of the session data from the server, call **session_destroy()**:

session_destroy();

Note that prior to using any of these methods, the page must begin with **session_start()** so that the existing session is accessed. Let's update the **logout.php** script to clean out the session data.

To delete a session:

1. Open **logout.php** (Script 12.6) in your text editor or IDE.

2. Immediately after the opening PHP line, start the session (**Script 12.11**):

   session_start();

   Anytime you are using sessions, you must call the **session_start()** function, preferably at the very beginning of a page. This is true even if you are deleting a session.

3. Change the conditional so that it checks for the presence of a session variable:

   if (!isset($_SESSION['user_id'])) {

   As with the **logout.php** script in the cookie examples, if the user is not currently logged in, he or she will be redirected.

4. Replace the **setcookie()** lines (that delete the cookies) with

   $_SESSION = [];
   session_destroy();
   setcookie('PHPSESSID', '',
   → time()-3600, '/', '', 0, 0);

   The first line here will reset the entire **$_SESSION** variable as a new array, erasing its existing values. The second line removes the data from the server, and the third sends a cookie to delete the existing session cookie in the browser.

Script 12.11 Destroying a session, as you would in a logout page, requires special syntax to delete the session cookie and the session data on the server, as well as to clear out the **$_SESSION** array.

```
1    <?php # Script 12.11 - logout.php #2
2    // This page lets the user logout.
3    // This version uses sessions.
4
5    session_start(); // Access the
     existing session.
6
7    // If no session variable exists,
     redirect the user:
8    if (!isset($_SESSION['user_id'])) {
9
10       // Need the functions:
11       require('includes/login_functions.
         inc.php');
12       redirect_user();
13
14   } else { // Cancel the session:
15
16       $_SESSION = []; // Clear the
         variables.
17       session_destroy(); // Destroy the
         session itself.
18       setcookie('PHPSESSID', '', time()-
         3600, '/', '', 0, 0); // Destroy
         the cookie.
19
20   }
21
22   // Set the page title and include the
     HTML header:
23   $page_title = 'Logged Out!';
24   include('includes/header.html');
25
26   // Print a customized message:
27   echo "<h1>Logged Out!</h1>
28   <p>You are now logged out!</p>";
29
30   include('includes/footer.html');
31   ?>
```

Garbage Collection

Garbage collection with respect to sessions is the process of the server automatically deleting the session files (where the actual data is stored). Creating a logout system that destroys a session is ideal, but there's no guarantee all users will formally log out as they should. For this reason, PHP includes a cleanup process.

Whenever the `session_start()` function is called, PHP's garbage collection kicks in, checking the last modification date of each session (a session is modified whenever variables are set or retrieved). Two settings dictate garbage collection: *session.gc_maxlifetime* and *session.gc_probability*. The first states after how many seconds of inactivity a session is considered idle and will therefore be deleted. The second setting determines the probability that garbage collection is performed, on a scale of 1 to 100. With the default settings, each call to `session_start()` has a 1 percent chance of invoking garbage collection. If PHP does start the cleanup, any sessions that have not been used in more than 1,440 seconds will be deleted.

You can change these settings using the `ini_set()` function, although be careful in doing so. Too frequent or too probable garbage collection can bog down the server and inadvertently end the sessions of slower users.

5. Remove the reference to **$_COOKIE** in the message:

```
echo "<h1>Logged Out!</h1>
<p>You are now logged out!</p>";
```

Unlike when using the cookie version of the **logout.php** script, you cannot refer to the user by first name anymore, since all of that data has been deleted.

6. Save the file as **logout.php**, place it in your web directory, and test it in your browser **E**.

TIP The **header.html** file only needs to check if **$_SESSION['user_id']** is set, and not if the page is the logout page, because by the time the header file is included by **logout. php**, all of the session data will have already been destroyed. The destruction of session data applies immediately, unlike with cookies.

TIP Never set **$_SESSION** equal to NULL and never use **unset($_SESSION)**. Either could cause problems on some servers.

TIP In case it's not absolutely clear what's going on, there exist three kinds of information within a session: the session identifier (which is stored in a cookie by default), the session data (which is stored in a text file on the server), and the **$_SESSION** array (which is how a script accesses the session data in the text file). Just deleting the cookie doesn't remove the data file, and vice versa. Clearing out the **$_SESSION** array would erase the data from the text file, but the file itself would still exist, as would the cookie. The three steps outlined in this logout script effectively remove all traces of the session.

| Your Website | Home | Register | View Users |

Logged Out!

You are now logged out!

E The logout page (now featuring sessions).

Improving Session Security

Because important information is normally stored in a session (you should never store sensitive data in a cookie), security becomes more of an issue. With sessions there are two areas to pay attention to: the session ID, which is a reference point to the session data, and the session data itself, stored on the server. A malicious person is far more likely to hack into a session through the session ID than the data on the server, so I'll focus on that side of things here. In the tips at the end of this section I mention two ways to protect the session data itself.

The session ID is the key to the session data. By default, PHP will store this in a cookie, which is preferable from a security standpoint. It is possible in PHP to use sessions without cookies, but that leaves the application vulnerable to *session*

Changing the Session Behavior

As part of PHP's support for sessions, there are over 20 different configuration options you can set for how PHP handles sessions. For the full list, see the PHP manual, but I'll highlight a few of the most important ones here. Note two rules about changing the session settings:

1. All changes must be made before calling **session_start()**.
2. The same changes must be made on every page that uses sessions.

Most of the settings can be set within a PHP script using the **ini_set()** function (discussed in Chapter 8):

```
ini_set(parameter, new_setting);
```

For example, to require the use of a session cookie (as mentioned, sessions can work without cookies but it's less secure), use

```
ini_set('session.use_only_cookies', 1);
```

Another change you can make is to the name of the session (perhaps to use a more user-friendly one). To do so, call the **session_name()** function:

```
session_name('YourSession');
```

The benefits of creating your own session name are twofold: it's marginally more secure and it may be better received by the end user (since the session name is the cookie name the end user will see). The **session_name()** function can also be used when deleting the session cookie:

```
setcookie(session_name(),'', time()-3600);
```

If not provided with an argument, this function instead returns the current session name.

Finally, there's also the **session_set_cookie_params()** function. It's used to tweak the settings of the session cookie:

```
session_set_cookie_params(expire, path, host, secure, httponly);
```

Note that the expiration time of the cookie refers only to the longevity of the cookie in the browser, not to how long the session data will be stored on the server.

Script 12.12 This final version of the **login.php** script also stores an encrypted form of the user's *HTTP_USER_AGENT* (the browser and operating system of the client) in a session.

```php
1   <?php # Script 12.12 - login.php #4
2   // This page processes the login form
    submission.
3   // The script now stores the HTTP_
    USER_AGENT value for added security.
4
5   // Check if the form has been submitted:
6   if ($_SERVER['REQUEST_METHOD'] ==
    'POST') {
7
8       // Need two helper files:
9       require('includes/login_functions.
        inc.php');
10      require('../mysqli_connect.php');
11
12      // Check the login:
13      list ($check, $data) = check_
        login($dbc, $_POST['email'],
        $_POST['pass']);
14
15      if ($check) { // OK!
16
17          // Set the session data:
18          session_start();
19          $_SESSION['user_id'] =
            $data['user_id'];
20          $_SESSION['first_name'] =
            $data['first_name'];
21
22          // Store the HTTP_USER_AGENT:
23          $_SESSION['agent'] = sha1
            ($_SERVER['HTTP_USER_AGENT']);
24
25          // Redirect:
26          redirect_user('loggedin.php');
27
28      } else { // Unsuccessful!
29
30          // Assign $data to $errors for
            login_page.inc.php:
31          $errors = $data;
32
33      }
34
35      mysqli_close($dbc); // Close the
        database connection.
36
37  } // End of the main submit conditional.
38
39  // Create the page:
40  include('includes/login_page.inc.php');
41  ?>
```

hijacking: If malicious user Alice can learn user Bob's session ID, Alice can easily trick a server into thinking that Bob's session ID is also *Alice's* session ID. At that point, Alice would be riding the coattails of Bob's session and would have access to Bob's data. Storing the session ID in a cookie makes it somewhat harder to steal.

One method of preventing hijacking is to store some sort of user identifier in the session, and then to repeatedly double-check this value. The *HTTP_USER_AGENT*—a combination of the browser and operating system being used—is a likely candidate for this purpose. This adds a layer of security in that one person could hijack another user's session only if they are both running the exact same browser and operating system. As a demonstration of this, let's modify the examples one last time.

To use sessions more securely:

1. Open **login.php** (refer to Script 12.8) in your text editor or IDE.

2. After assigning the other session variables, also store the *HTTP_USER_AGENT* value (**Script 12.12**):

   **$_SESSION['agent'] = sha1
   ($_SERVER['HTTP_USER_AGENT']);**

   The *HTTP_USER_AGENT* is part of the **$_SERVER** array (you may recall using it way back in Chapter 1, "Introduction to PHP"). It will have a value like *Mozilla/4.0 (compatible; MSIE 8.0; Windows NT 6.1...)*.

   continues on next page

Instead of you storing this value in the session as is, it'll be run through the **sha1()** function for slightly improved security. That function returns a 32-character hexadecimal string (called a *hash*) based on a value. In theory, no two strings will have the same **sha1()** result.

3. Save the file and place it in your web directory.

4. Open **loggedin.php** (Script 12.9) in your text editor or IDE.

5. Change the **!isset($_SESSION['user_id'])** conditional to (**Script 12.13**):

   **if (!isset($_SESSION['agent']) OR
   → ($_SESSION['agent'] != sha1
   → ($_SERVER['HTTP_USER_AGENT']))) {**

   This conditional checks two things. First, it sees if the **$_SESSION['agent']** variable is not set (this part is just as it was before, although *agent* is being used instead of *user_id*). The second part of the conditional checks if the **sha1()** version of **$_SERVER['HTTP_USER_AGENT']** does not equal the value stored in **$_SESSION['agent']**. If either of these conditions is true, the user will be redirected.

6. Save this file, place it in your web directory, and test in your browser by logging in.

Script 12.13 This **loggedin.php** script now confirms that users accessing this page have the same *HTTP_USER_AGENT* as they did when they logged in.

```
1   <?php # Script 12.13 - loggedin.php #3
2   // The user is redirected here from
    login.php.
3
4   session_start(); // Start the session.
5
6   // If no session value is present,
    redirect the user:
7   // Also validate the HTTP_USER_AGENT!
8   if (!isset($_SESSION['agent'])
    OR ($_SESSION['agent'] != md5($_
    SERVER['HTTP_USER_AGENT']) )) {
9
10      // Need the functions:
11      require('includes/login_functions.
        inc.php');
12      redirect_user();
13
14  }
15
16  // Set the page title and include the
    HTML header:
17  $page_title = 'Logged In!';
18  include('includes/header.html');
19
20  // Print a customized message:
21  echo "<h1>Logged In!</h1>
22  <p>You are now logged in,
    {$_SESSION['first_name']}!</p>
23  <p><a href=\"logout.php\">Logout</a>
    </p>";
24
25  include('includes/footer.html');
26  ?>
```

Preventing Session Fixation

Another specific kind of session attack is known as *session fixation*. This approach is the opposite of *session hijacking*. Instead of malicious user Alice finding and using Bob's session ID, she creates her own session ID (perhaps by logging in legitimately), and then gets Bob to access the site using that session. The hope is that Bob would then do something that would unknowingly benefit Alice.

You can help protect against these types of attacks by changing the session ID after a user logs in. The `session_regenerate_id()` does just that, providing a new session ID to refer to the current session data. You can use this function on sites for which security is paramount (like e-commerce or online banking) or in situations when it'd be particularly bad if certain users (i.e., administrators) had their sessions manipulated.

TIP For critical uses of sessions, require the use of cookies and transmit them over a secure connection, if at all possible. You can even set PHP to only use cookies by setting `session.use_only_cookies` to 1.

TIP By default, a server stores every session file for every site within the same temporary directory, meaning any site could theoretically read any other site's session data. If you are using a server shared with other domains, changing the `session.save_path` from its default setting will be more secure. For example, it'd be better if you stored your site's session data in a dedicated directory particular to your site.

TIP The session data itself can also be stored in a database rather than a text file. This is a more secure, but more programming-intensive, option. I show how to do this in my book *PHP 5 Advanced: Visual QuickPro Guide*.

TIP The user's IP address (the network address from which the user is connecting) is not a good unique identifier, for two reasons. First, a user's IP address can, and normally does, change frequently (ISPs dynamically assign them for short periods of time). Second, many users accessing a site from the same network (like a home network or an office) could all have the same IP address.

Review and Pursue

If you have any problems with the review questions or the pursue prompts, turn to the book's supporting forum (LarryUllman.com/forums/).

Review

- What code is used to redirect the user's browser from one page to the next?
- What does the *headers already sent* error message mean?
- What value does $_SERVER['HTTP_HOST'] store? What value does $_SERVER['PHP_SELF'] store?
- What does the dirname() function do?
- What does the rtrim() function do? What arguments can it take?
- How do you write a function that returns multiple values? How do you call such a function?
- What arguments can the setcookie() function take?
- How do you reference values previously stored in a cookie?
- How do you delete an existing cookie?
- Are cookies available immediately after being sent (on the same page)? Why can you still refer to a cookie (on the same page) after it is deleted?
- What debugging steps can you take when you have problems with cookies?
- What does the basename() function do?
- How do you begin a session?
- How do you reference values previously stored in a session?
- Is session data available immediately after being assigned (on the same page)?
- How do you terminate a session?
- What debugging steps can you take when you have problems with sessions?

Pursue

- If you have not already done so, learn how to view cookie data in your browser. When developing sites that use cookies, enable the option so that the browser prompts you when cookies are received.
- Make the login form sticky.
- Add code to the handling of the $errors variable on the login page that uses a foreach loop if $errors is an array, or just prints the value of $errors otherwise.
- Modify the redirect_user() function so that it can be used to redirect the user to a page within another directory.
- Implement another cookie example, such as storing a user's preference in the cookie, and then base a look or feature of a page on the stored value (when present).
- Change the code in logout.php (Script 12.11) so that it uses the session_name() function to dynamically set the name value of the session cookie being deleted.
- Implement another session example, if you'd like more practice with sessions (you'll get more practice later in the book, too).
- Check out the PHP manual pages for any new function introduced in this chapter with which you're not comfortable.
- Check out the PHP manual pages on cookies and sessions (two separate sections) to learn more. Also read some of the user-submitted comments for additional tips.

13

Security Methods

The security of your web applications is such an important topic that it really cannot be overstressed. Although security-related issues have been mentioned throughout this book, this chapter will help to fill in certain gaps, finalize other points, and teach several new things.

The topics discussed here include preventing spam, typecasting variables, preventing cross-site scripting (XSS) and SQL injection attacks, using the Filter extension, validating uploaded files by type, and managing passwords in PHP. This chapter will use six examples to best demonstrate these concepts. Some other common security issues and best practices will be mentioned in sidebars as well.

In This Chapter

Preventing Spam

Spam is nothing short of a plague, cluttering up the Internet and email inboxes. There are steps you can take to avoid receiving spam at your email accounts, but in this book the focus is on preventing spam being sent through your PHP scripts.

Chapter 11, "Web Application Development," shows how easy it is to send email using PHP's **mail()** function. The example there, a contact form, took some information from the user  and sent it to an email address. Although it may seem like there's no harm in this system, it contains a security hole. But first, here's some background on what an email actually is.

Regardless of how an email is sent, how it's formatted, and what it looks like when it's received, an email contains two parts: a header and a body. The header includes such information as the *to* and *from* addresses, the subject, the date, and more . Each item in the header is on its own line, in the format *Name: value*. The body of the email is exactly what you think it is: the actual body text of the email.

In looking at PHP's **mail()** function—

mail(*to, subject, body* [*,headers*]);

—you can see that one of the arguments goes straight to the email's body and the rest appear in its header. To send spam to *your address* (as in Chapter 11's example), all a person would have to do is enter the

A A simple, standard HTML contact form.

B The raw source version of the email sent by the contact form **A**.

A Security Approach

The most important concept to understand about security is that it's not a binary state: don't think of a website or script as being either *secure* or *not secure*. Security isn't a switch that you turn on and off; it's a scale that you can move up and down. When you program, think about what you can do to make your site *more secure* and what you've done that makes it *less secure*. Also, keep in mind that improved security normally comes at a cost of convenience (both to you, the programmer, and to the end user) and performance. Increased security normally means more code, more checks, and more required of the server. When developing web applications, the goal is to achieve a level of security that's appropriate for the particular situation. And then err on the side of being a tad too secure, just to be prudent.

TABLE 13.1 Spam Tip-offs

Strings
content-type:
mime-version:
multipart-mixed:
content-transfer-encoding:
bcc:
cc:
to:
\r
\n
%0a
%0d

spam message into the comments section of the form **Ⓐ**. That's bad enough, but to send spam to *anyone else* at the same time, all the user would have to do is add *Bcc: poorsap@example.org*, followed by some sort of line terminator (like a newline or carriage return), to the email's header. With the example as is, this just means entering the following into the *from* value of the contact form: *me@example.com\n Bcc:poorsap@example.org*.

You might think that safeguarding everything that goes into an email's header would be sufficiently safe, but because an email is just one document, bad input in a body can impact the header, too.

You can apply a couple of preventive techniques to this contact form. First, validate any email addresses by using regular expressions, covered in Chapter 14, "Perl-Compatible Regular Expressions," or by using the Filter extension, discussed in just a few pages. Second, now that you know what an evildoer must enter to send spam (**Table 13.1**), watch for those characters and strings in form values. If a value contains anything from that list, don't use that value in a sent email. (The last four values in Table 13.1 are all different ways of creating newlines.)

In this next example, a modification of the email script from Chapter 11, I'll define a function that scrubs all potentially dangerous characters from provided data. Two new PHP functions will be used as well: **str_replace()** and **array_map()**. Both will be explained in detail in the steps that follow.

To prevent spam:

1. Open **email.php** (Script 11.1) in your text editor or IDE.

   To complete this spam-purification, the email script needs to be modified.

2. After checking for the form submission, begin defining a function (**Script 13.1**):

   ```
   function spam_scrubber($value) {
   ```

   This function will take one argument: a string. Normally, I would define functions at the top of the script, or in a separate file, but to make things simpler, I will define it within the submission-handling block of code.

3. Create a list of really bad things that wouldn't be in a legitimate contact form submission:

   ```
   $very_bad = ['to:', 'cc:', 'bcc:',
   → 'content-type:', 'mime-version:',
   → 'multipart-mixed:',
   → 'content-transfer-encoding:'];
   ```

   Any of these strings should not be present in an honest contact form submission (it's possible someone might legitimately use *to:* in their comments, but unlikely). If any of these strings are present, then this is a spam attempt. To make it easier to test for them, you place them in an array, which will be looped through (Step 4). The comparison in Step 4 will be case-insensitive, so each of the dangerous strings is written in all lowercase letters.

4. Loop through the array. If a very bad thing is found, return an empty string instead:

   ```
   foreach ($very_bad as $v) {
       if (stripos($value, $v) !==
       → false) return '';
   }
   ```

The **foreach** loop will access each item in the **$very_bad** array one at a time, assigning each item to **$v**. Within the loop, the **stripos()** function will check if the item is in the string provided to this function as **$value**. The **stripos()** function performs a case-insensitive search (so it would match *bcc:*, *Bcc:*, *bCC:*, etc.). The function returns a Boolean TRUE if the needle is found in the haystack (e.g., looking for occurrences of **$v** in **$value**). The conditional therefore says that if that function's results do not equal FALSE (i.e., **$v** was found in **$value**), return an empty string.

Therefore, for each of the dangerous character strings, the first time that any of them is found in the submitted value, the function will return an empty string and terminate (functions automatically stop executing once they hit a **return**).

5. Replace any newline characters with spaces:

   ```
   $value = str_replace(["\r", "\n",
   → "%0a", "%0d"], ' ', $value);
   ```

   Newline characters, which are represented by **\r**, **\n** , **%0a**, and **%0d**, may or may not be problematic. A newline character is required to send spam (or else you can't create the proper header) but will also appear if a user just hits Enter or Return while typing in a textarea box. For this reason, any found newlines will just be replaced by a space. This means that the submitted value could lose some of its formatting, but that's a reasonable price to pay to stop spam.

continues on page 422

Script 13.1 This version of the script can now safely send emails without concern for spam. Any problematic characters will be caught by the **spam_scrubber()** function.

```
1    <!doctype html>
2    <html lang="en">
3    <head>
4        <meta charset="utf-8">
5        <title>Contact Me</title>
6    </head>
7    <body>
8    <h1>Contact Me</h1>
9    <?php # Script 13.1 - email.php #2
10   // This version now scrubs dangerous strings from the submitted input.
11
12   // Check for form submission:
13   if ($_SERVER['REQUEST_METHOD'] == 'POST') {
14
15       /* The function takes one argument: a string.
16        * The function returns a clean version of the string.
17        * The clean version may be either an empty string or
18        * just the removal of all newline characters.
19        */
20       function spam_scrubber($value) {
21
22           // List of very bad values:
23           $very_bad = ['to:', 'cc:', 'bcc:', 'content-type:', 'mime-version:',
                 'multipart-mixed:', 'content-transfer-encoding:'];
24
25           // If any of the very bad strings are in
26           // the submitted value, return an empty string:
27           foreach ($very_bad as $v) {
28               if (stripos($value, $v) !== false) return '';
29           }
30
31           // Replace any newline characters with spaces:
32           $value = str_replace(["\r", "\n", "%0a", "%0d"], ' ', $value);
33
34           // Return the value:
35           return trim($value);
36
37       } // End of spam_scrubber() function.
38
39       // Clean the form data:
40       $scrubbed = array_map('spam_scrubber', $_POST);
41
42       // Minimal form validation:
43       if (!empty($scrubbed['name']) && !empty($scrubbed['email']) &&
             !empty($scrubbed['comments']) ) {
44
45           // Create the body:
46           $body = "Name: {$scrubbed['name']}\n\nComments: {$scrubbed['comments']}";
47
48           // Make it no longer than 70 characters long:
49           $body = wordwrap($body, 70);
```

code continues on next page

The **str_replace()** function looks through the value in the third argument and replaces any occurrences of the characters in the first argument with the character or characters in the second. Or as the PHP manual puts it:

```
mixed str_replace(mixed $search,
→ mixed $replace, mixed $subject)
```

This function is very flexible in that it can take strings or arrays for its three arguments (the *mixed* means it accepts a mix of argument types). Hence, this line of code in the script assigns to the **$value** variable its original value, with

any newline characters replaced by a single space.

There is a case-insensitive version of this function, but it's not necessary here, as, for example, **\r** is a carriage return but **\R** is not.

6. Return the value and complete the function:

```
    return trim($value);
} // End of spam_scrubber()
→ function.
```

Finally, this function returns the value, trimmed of any leading and ending spaces. Keep in mind that the function

Script 13.1 *continued*

```
50
51        // Send the email:
52        mail('your_email@example.com', 'Contact Form Submission', $body, "From:
          {$scrubbed['email']}");
53
54        // Print a message:
55        echo '<p><em>Thank you for contacting me. I will reply some day.</em></p>';
56
57        // Clear $scrubbed (so that the form's not sticky):
58        $scrubbed = [];
59
60    } else {
61        echo '<p style="font-weight: bold; color: #C00">Please fill out the form completely.
          </p>';
62    }
63
64 } // End of main isset() IF.
65
66 // Create the HTML form:
67 ?>
68 <p>Please fill out this form to contact me.</p>
69 <form action="email.php" method="post">
70    <p>Name: <input type="text" name="name" size="30" maxlength="60" value="<?php if
       (isset($scrubbed['name'])) echo $scrubbed['name']; ?>"></p>
71    <p>Email Address: <input type="email" name="email" size="30" maxlength="80"
       value="<?php if (isset($scrubbed['email'])) echo $scrubbed['email']; ?>"></p>
72    <p>Comments: <textarea name="comments" rows="5" cols="30"><?php if
       (isset($scrubbed['comments'])) echo $scrubbed['comments']; ?></textarea></p>
73    <p><input type="submit" name="submit" value="Send!"></p>
74 </form>
75 </body>
76 </html>
```

will get to this point only if none of the very bad things was found.

7. After the function definition, invoke the **spam_scrubber()** function:

```
$scrubbed = array_map
→ ('spam_scrubber', $_POST);
```

This approach is beautiful in its simplicity! The **array_map()** function has two required arguments. The first is the name of the function to call. In this case, that's *spam_scrubber* (without the parentheses, because you're providing the function's *name*, not calling the function). The second argument is an array.

What **array_map()** does is apply the named function once for each array element, sending each array element's value to that function call. In this script, **$_POST** has four elements—*name*, *email*, *comments*, and *submit*—meaning that the **spam_scrubber()** function will be called four times, thanks to **array_map()**. After this line of code, the **$scrubbed** array will end up with four elements: **$scrubbed['name']** will have the value of **$_POST['name']** after

running it through **spam_scrubber()**, **$scrubbed['email']** will have the same value as **$_POST['email']** after running it through **spam_scrubber()**, and so forth.

This one line of code then takes an entire array of potentially tainted data (**$_POST**), cleans it using **spam_scrubber()**, and assigns the result to a new variable. Here's the most important thing about this technique: from here on out, the script must use the **$scrubbed** array (which is clean), not **$_POST** (which is still potentially dirty).

8. Change the form validation to use this new array:

```
if (!empty($scrubbed['name']) &&
→ !empty($scrubbed['email']) &&
→ !empty($scrubbed['comments']) ) {
```

Each of these elements could have an empty value for two reasons: first, if the user left them empty; second, if the user entered one of the bad strings in the field **C**, which would be turned into an empty string by the **spam_scrubber()** function **D**.

continues on next page

C The presence of *cc:* in the comments field will prevent this submission from being sent in an email **D**.

D The email was not sent because of the very bad characters used in the comments, which gets turned into an empty string by the spam prevention function.

9. Change the creation of the **$body** variable so that it uses the clean values:

```
$body="Name:
→ {$scrubbed['name']}\n\nComments:
→ {$scrubbed['comments']}";
```

10. Change the invocation of the `mail()` function to use the clean email address:

```
mail('your_email@example.com',
→ 'Contact Form Submission', $body,
→ "From: {$scrubbed['email']}");
```

Remember to use your own email address in the `mail()` call, or you'll never get the message!

11. Change line 30 (of the original script) to clear the **$scrubbed** array instead of the **$_POST** array:

```
$scrubbed = [];
```

This line wipes out the form data upon successful submission.

12. Change the form so that it uses the **$scrubbed** version of the values:

```
<p>Name: <input type="text"
→ name="name" size="30"
→ maxlength="60" value="<?php if
→ (isset($scrubbed['name'])) echo
→ $scrubbed['name']; ?>"></p>
<p>Email Address: <input
→ type="email" name="email"
→ size="30" maxlength="80"
→ value="<?php if (isset($scrubbed
→ ['email'])) echo $scrubbed
→ ['email']; ?>"></p>
<p>Comments: <textarea
→ name="comments" rows="5"
cols="30"><?php if (isset($scrubbed
→ ['comments'])) echo $scrubbed
→ ['comments']; ?></textarea></p>
```

13. Save the script as **email.php**, place it in your web directory, and test it in your browser **E** and **F**.

E Although the comments field contains newline characters (created by pressing Enter or Return), the email will still be sent **F**.

F The received email, with the newlines in the comments **E** turned into spaces.

TIP Using the `array_map()` function as I have in this example is convenient but not without its downsides. First, it blindly applies the `spam_scrubber()` function to the entire `$_POST` array, even to the submit button. This isn't harmful, but it is unnecessary. Second, any multidimensional arrays within `$_POST` will be lost. In this specific example, that's not a problem, but it is something to be aware of.

TIP To prevent automated submissions to any form, you could use a CAPTCHA test. These are prompts that can only be understood by humans (in theory). Although this is commonly accomplished using an image of random characters, the same thing can be achieved using a question like "What is two plus two?" or "On what continent is China?" Checking for the correct answer to this question would then be part of the validation routine.

Validating Data by Type

For the most part, the form validation used in this book thus far has been rather minimal, often just checking whether a variable has any value at all. In many situations, this is the best you can do. For example, there's no perfect test for what a valid street address is or what a user might enter in a comments field. Still, much of the data you'll work with can be validated in stricter ways. In the next chapter, the sophisticated concept of regular expressions will demonstrate just that. But here I'll cover the more approachable ways you can validate some data by type.

PHP supports many types of data: strings, numbers (integers and floats), arrays, and so on. For each of these, there's a specific function that checks if a variable is of that type (**Table 13.2**). You've already seen the **is_numeric()** function in action in earlier chapters, and **is_array()** is great for confirming a variable is acceptable to use in a **foreach** loop. Each function returns TRUE if the submitted variable is of a certain type and FALSE otherwise.

continues on next page

TABLE 13.2 Type Validation Functions

Function	Checks For
is_array()	Arrays
is_bool()	Booleans (**TRUE**, **FALSE**)
is_float()	Floating-point numbers
is_int()	Integers
is_null()	**NULL**s
is_numeric()	Numeric values, even as a string (e.g., **'20'**)
is_resource()	Resources, like a database connection
is_scalar()	Scalar (single-valued) variables
is_string()	Strings

Two Validation Approaches

A large part of security is based on validation: if data comes from outside of the server—from HTML forms, the URL, cookies—it can't be trusted. (A higher level of security also validates any data coming from outside of the *script*, including sessions and databases.) There are two types of validation: *whitelist* and *blacklist*. In the Widget Cost Calculator in this chapter, we know that all values must be positive, that they must all be numbers, and that the quantity must be an integer (the other two numbers could be integers or floats; it makes no difference). Typecasting forces the inputs to be numbers, and a check confirms that they are positive. At this point, the assumption is that the input is valid. This is a whitelist approach: these values are good; anything else is bad.

The preventing spam example uses a blacklist approach. That script knows exactly which characters are bad and invalidates input that contains them. All other input is considered to be good.

Many security experts prefer the whitelist approach, but it can't always be used. Each example will dictate which approach will work best, but it's important to use one or the other. Don't just assume that data is safe without some sort of validation.

In PHP, you can even change a variable's type after it's been assigned a value. Doing so is called *typecasting*, and you accomplish it by entering the destination type in parentheses before the variable's name:

```
$var = 20.2;
echo (int) $var; // 20
```

Depending on the original and destination types, PHP will convert the variable's value accordingly:

```
$var = 20;
echo (float) $var; // 20.0
```

With numeric values, the conversion is straightforward, but with other variable types, more complex rules apply:

```
$var = 'trout';
echo (int) $var; // 0
```

In most circumstances, you don't need to cast a variable from one type to another, since PHP will often automatically do so as needed. But forcibly casting a variable's type can be a good security measure in your web applications. To show how you might use this notion, let's create a calculator script for determining the total purchase price of an item 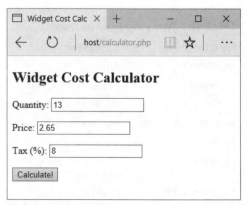.

Before getting into this example, let's think a moment about the role HTML5 plays here. HTML5 supports built-in client-side validation **B**. For example, the `email.php` script (Script 13.1) won't allow the form to be submitted with a syntactically invalid email address. This is great in terms of the user experience; however, it's not a true security measure. It's rather easy for a malicious user to bypass client-side validation by manipulating the HTML source code in the browser or by submitting data to your server directly without using the form at all.

Although you can and should take advantage of the client-side validation HTML5 offers, never rely on it as a security method!

A The HTML form takes three inputs: a quantity, a price, and a tax rate.

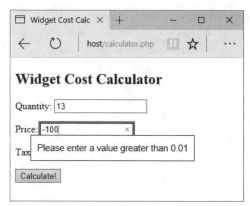

B HTML5 validation rules prevent invalid data from being submitted.

And in case you're curious, the easiest way for you as the developer to bypass the HTML5 validation (for testing purposes) is to add the **novalidate** attribute to the opening form tag:

```
<form action="calculator.php"
→ method="post" novalidate>
```

To use typecasting:

1. Begin a new PHP document in your text editor or IDE, to be named **calculator.php** (Script 13.2):

```
<!doctype html>
<html lang="en">
<head>
  <meta charset="utf-8">
  <title>Widget Cost
  → Calculator</title>
</head>
<body>
<?php # Script 13.2 -
→ calculator.php
```

2. Check if the form has been submitted:

```
if ($_SERVER['REQUEST_METHOD'] ==
→ 'POST') {
```

Like many previous examples, this one script will both display the HTML form and handle its submission.

3. Cast all the variables to a specific type:

```
$quantity = (int) $_POST
→ ['quantity'];
$price = (float) $_POST['price'];
$tax = (float) $_POST['tax'];
```

The form itself has three number boxes Ⓐ. Although the HTML5 validation requires each be a number, that check cannot be relied on for security purposes.

For the calculation to be reliable, the quantity must be an integer, and both price and tax are acceptable as floats (i.e., could contain decimal points). To force these constraints, cast each one to a specific type in PHP.

continues on next page

Script 13.2 By *typecasting* variables, this script more definitively validates that data is of the correct format.

```
1    <!doctype html>
2    <html lang="en">
3    <head>
4       <meta charset="utf-8">
5       <title>Widget Cost Calculator</title>
6    </head>
7    <body>
8    <?php # Script 13.2 - calculator.php
9    // This script calculates an order total based upon three form values.
10
11   // Check if the form has been submitted:
12   if ($_SERVER['REQUEST_METHOD'] == 'POST') {
13
14       // Cast all the variables to a specific type:
15       $quantity = (int) $_POST['quantity'];
16       $price = (float) $_POST['price'];
17       $tax = (float) $_POST['tax'];
18
```

code continues on next page

4. Check if the variables have proper values:

```
if ( ($quantity > 0) &&
→ ($price > 0) && ($tax > 0) ) {
```

For this calculator to work, the three variables must be specific types (see Step 3). More importantly, they must all be positive numbers. This conditional checks for that prior to performing the calculations. Note that, per the rules of typecasting, if the posted values are not numbers, they will be cast to 0 and therefore not pass this conditional.

Again, the HTML5 validation also ensures that values greater than 0 are entered in the form, but you cannot assume the client-side validation applied.

5. Calculate and print the results:

```
$total = $quantity * $price;
$total += $total * ($tax/100);
echo '<p>The total cost of
→ purchasing ' . $quantity . '
→ widget(s) at $' . number_format
→ ($price, 2) . ' each, plus tax,
→ is $' . number_format
→ ($total, 2) . '.</p>';
```

Script 13.2 *continued*

```
19        // All variables should be positive!
20        if ( ($quantity > 0) && ($price > 0) && ($tax > 0) ) {
21
22            // Calculate the total:
23            $total = $quantity * $price;
24            $total += $total * ($tax/100);
25
26            // Print the result:
27            echo '<p>The total cost of purchasing ' . $quantity . ' widget(s) at $' . number_
                 format($price, 2) . ' each, plus tax, is $' . number_format($total, 2) . '.</p>';
28
29        } else { // Invalid submitted values.
30            echo '<p style="font-weight: bold; color: #C00">Please enter a valid quantity, price,
                 and tax rate.</p>';
31        }
32
33    } // End of main isset() IF.
34
35    // Leave the PHP section and create the HTML form.
36    ?>
37    <h2>Widget Cost Calculator</h2>
38    <form action="calculator.php" method="post">
39        <p>Quantity: <input type="number" name="quantity" step="1" min="1" value="<?php if
           (isset($quantity)) echo $quantity; ?>"></p>
40        <p>Price: <input type="number" name="price" step=".01" min="0.01" value="<?php if
           (isset($price)) echo $price; ?>"></p>
41        <p>Tax (%): <input type="text" name="tax" step=".01" min="0.01" value="<?php if
           (isset($tax)) echo $tax; ?>"></p>
42        <p><input type="submit" name="submit" value="Calculate!"></p>
43    </form>
44    </body>
45    </html>
```

To calculate the total, first the quantity is multiplied by the price. To apply the tax to the total, the value of the total times the tax divided by 100 (e.g., 6.5% becomes .065) is then added, using the addition assignment shortcut operator. The `number_format()` function is used to print both the price and total values in the proper format **C**.

6. Complete the conditionals:

```
} else { // Invalid submitted
→ values.
  echo '<p style="font-weight:
  → bold; color: #C00">Please
  → enter a valid quantity,
  → price, and tax rate.</p>';
}

} // End of main isset() IF.
```

A little CSS is used to create a bold, red error message, should there be a problem.

C The results of the calculation when the form is properly completed.

7. Begin the HTML form:

```
<h2>Widget Cost Calculator</h2>
<form action="calculator.php"
→ method="post">
  <p>Quantity: <input
  → type="number" name="quantity"
  → step="1" min="1" value="<?php
  → if (isset($quantity)) echo
  → $quantity; ?>"></p>
```

The HTML form is simple and posts back to this same page. The inputs will have a sticky quality, so the user can see what was previously entered. For example, by referring to **$quantity** instead of **$_POST['quantity']**, the form will reflect the value for each input *as it was typecast*.

To add in client-side validation, each number input requires a minimum value of either 1 or .01. Integer inputs like the quantity use a step value of 1; the decimal inputs will use .01.

8. Complete the HTML form:

```
  <p>Price: <input type="number"
  → name="price" step=".01"
  → min="0.01" value="<?php if
  → (isset($price)) echo $price;
  → ?>"></p>
  <p>Tax (%): <input type="text"
  → name="tax" step=".01" min="0.01"
  → value="<?php if (isset($tax))
  → echo $tax; ?>"></p>
  <p><input type="submit"
  → name="submit"
  → value="Calculate!"></p>
</form>
```

continues on next page

9. Complete the HTML page:

```
</body>
</html>
```

10. Save the file as `calculator.php`, place it in your web directory, and test it in your browser 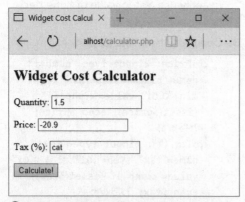 D and E.

TIP You should definitely use typecasting when working with numbers within **SQL** queries. Numbers aren't quoted in queries, so if a string is somehow used in a number's place, there will be an SQL syntax error. If you typecast such variables to an integer or float first, the query may not work (in terms of returning a record) but will still be syntactically valid. You'll frequently see this in this book's last three chapters.

TIP As I implied, regular expressions are a more advanced method of data validation and are sometimes your best bet. But using type-based validation, when feasible, will certainly be faster (in terms of processor speed) and less prone to programmer error (did I mention that regular expressions are complex?).

TIP The rules of how values are converted from one data type to another are somewhat complicated. If you want to get into the details, see the PHP manual.

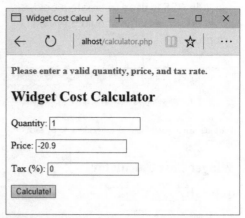

D If invalid values are entered, such as floats for the quantity or strings for the tax...

E ...they'll be cast into more appropriate formats. The negative price will also keep this calculation from being made (although the casting won't change that value).

Validating Files by Type

Chapter 11 includes an example of handling file uploads in PHP. Because uploading files allows users to place a more potent type of content on your server (compared with just the text sent via a form), you cannot be too mindful of security when it comes to handling them. In that particular example, the uploaded file was validated by checking its MIME type. Specifically, with an uploaded file, **$_FILES['upload']['type']** refers to the MIME type provided by the uploading browser. This is a good start, but it's easy for a malicious user to trick the browser into providing a false MIME type. A more reliable way of confirming a file's type is to use the Fileinfo extension.

Added in PHP 5.3, the Fileinfo extension determines a file's type (and encoding) by hunting for "magic bytes" or "magic numbers" within the file. For example, the data that makes up a GIF image must begin with the ASCII code that represents either *GIF89a* or *GIF87a*; the data that makes up a PDF file starts with *%PDF*.

To use Fileinfo, start by creating a Fileinfo resource:

```
$fileinfo = finfo_open(kind);
```

The *kind* value will be one of several constants, indicating the type of resource you want to create. To determine a file's type, the constant is **FILEINFO_MIME_TYPE**:

```
$fileinfo = finfo_open
→ (FILEINFO_MIME_TYPE);
```

Next, call the **finfo_file()** function, providing the Fileinfo resource and a reference to the file you want to examine:

```
finfo_file($fileinfo, $filename);
```

This function returns the file's MIME type (given the already created resource), based on the file's actual magic bytes.

Finally, once you're done, you should close the Fileinfo resource:

```
finfo_close($fileinfo);
```

Our next script will use this information to confirm that an uploaded file is an RTF (Rich Text Format). Note that you'll be able to test this example only if you are using version 5.3 of PHP or later.

To validate files by type:

1. Begin a new PHP script in your text editor or IDE, to be named **upload_rtf.php** (Script 13.3):

   ```
   <!doctype html>
   <html lang="en">
   <head>
       <meta charset="utf-8">
       <title>Upload an RTF Document
       → </title>
   </head>
   <body>
   <?php # Script 13.3 -
   → upload_rtf.php
   ```

2. Check if the form has been submitted:

   ```
   if ($_SERVER['REQUEST_METHOD'] ==
   → 'POST') {
   ```

   This same script will both display and handle the form.

   continues on page 433

Script 13.3 Using the Fileinfo extension, this script does a good job of confirming an uploaded file's type.

```
1    <!doctype html>
2    <html lang="en">
3    <head>
4      <meta charset="utf-8">
5      <title>Upload an RTF Document</title>
6    </head>
7    <body>
8    <?php # Script 13.3 - upload_rtf.php
9
10   // Check if the form has been submitted:
11   if ($_SERVER['REQUEST_METHOD'] == 'POST') {
12
13       // Check for an uploaded file:
14       if (isset($_FILES['upload']) && file_exists($_FILES['upload']['tmp_name'])) {
15
16           // Validate the type. Should be RTF.
17           // Create the resource:
18           $fileinfo = finfo_open(FILEINFO_MIME_TYPE);
19
20           // Check the file:
21           if (finfo_file($fileinfo, $_FILES['upload']['tmp_name']) == 'text/rtf') {
22
23               // Indicate it's okay!
24               echo '<p><em>The file would be acceptable!</em></p>';
25
26               // In theory, move the file over. In reality, delete the file:
27               unlink($_FILES['upload']['tmp_name']);
28
29           } else { // Invalid type.
30               echo '<p style="font-weight: bold; color: #C00">Please upload an RTF document.</p>';
31           }
32
33           // Close the resource:
34           finfo_close($fileinfo);
35
36       } // End of isset($_FILES['upload']) IF.
37
38       // Add file upload error handling, if desired.
39
40   } // End of the submitted conditional.
41   ?>
42
43   <form enctype="multipart/form-data" action="upload_rtf.php" method="post">
44       <input type="hidden" name="MAX_FILE_SIZE" value="524288">
45       <fieldset><legend>Select an RTF document of 512KB or smaller to be uploaded:</legend>
46       <p><strong>File:</strong> <input type="file" name="upload"></p>
47       </fieldset>
48       <div align="center"><input type="submit" name="submit" value="Submit"></div>
49   </form>
50   </body>
51   </html>
```

3. Check for an uploaded file:

```
if (isset($_FILES['upload']) &&
→ file_exists($_FILES['upload']
→ ['tmp_name'])) {
```

This script first confirms that the **$_FILES['upload']** variable is set, which would be the case after a form submission. The conditional then confirms that the uploaded file exists (by default, in the temporary directory). This clause prevents attempts to validate the file's type should the upload have failed (e.g., because the selected file was too large).

4. Create the Fileinfo resource:

```
$fileinfo = finfo_open
→ (FILEINFO_MIME_TYPE);
```

This line, as already explained, creates a Fileinfo resource whose specific purpose is to retrieve a file's MIME type.

5. Check the file's type:

```
if (finfo_file($fileinfo,
→ $_FILES['upload']['tmp_name']) ==
→ 'text/rtf') {
    echo '<p><em>The file would be
→ acceptable!</em></p>';
```

If the **finfo_file()** function returns a value of *text/rtf* for the uploaded file, then the file has the proper type for the purposes of this script. In that case, a message is printed Ⓐ.

6. Delete the uploaded file:

```
unlink($_FILES['upload']['tmp_name']);
```

In a real-world example, the script would now move the file over to its final destination on the server. Because this script is simply for the purpose of validating a file's type, the file can be removed instead.

7. Complete the type conditional:

```
} else { // Invalid type.
    echo '<p style="font-weight:
→ bold; color: #C00">Please
→ upload an RTF document.</p>';
}
```

If the uploaded file's MIME type is not *text/rtf*, the script will print an error message Ⓑ.

8. Close the Fileinfo resource:

```
finfo_close($fileinfo);
```

The final step is to close the open Fileinfo resource once it's no longer needed.

continues on next page

Ⓐ If the selected and uploaded document has a valid RTF MIME type, the user will see this result.

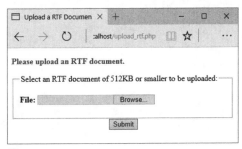

Ⓑ Uploaded files without the proper MIME type are rejected.

9. Complete the remaining conditionals:

```
    } // End of isset($_FILES
    ➞['upload']) IF.
} // End of the submitted
➞ conditional.
?>
```

You could also add debugging information, such as the related uploaded error message, if an error occurs.

10. Create the form:

```
<form enctype="multipart
➞/form-data" action="upload_rtf
➞.php" method="post">
    <input type="hidden" name=
    ➞"MAX_FILE_SIZE" value="524288">
    <fieldset><legend>Select an RTF
    ➞ document of 512KB or smaller
    ➞ to be uploaded:</legend>
    <p><strong>File:</strong> <input
    ➞ type="file" name="upload"></p>
    </fieldset>
    <div align="center"><input
    ➞ type="submit" name="submit"
    ➞ value="Submit"></div>
</form>
```

The form uses the proper **enctype** attribute, has a **MAX_FILE_SIZE** recommendation in a hidden form input, and uses a file input type: the three requirements for accepting file uploads. That's all there is to this example (as in **Ⓐ** and **Ⓑ**).

11. Complete the page:

```
</body>
</html>
```

12. Save the file as **upload_rtf.php**, place it in your web directory, and test it in your browser.

> **TIP** The same Fileinfo resource can be applied to multiple files. Just close the resource after the script is done with the resource.

Preventing XSS Attacks

HTML is simply plain text, like **`<strong>`**, which is given special meaning by browsers (as by making text bold). Because of this fact, your website's user could easily put HTML in their form data, like in the comments field in the email example. What may seem trivial ends up being a significant concern, however.

Many dynamically driven web applications take the information submitted by a user, store it in a database, and then redisplay that information on another page. Think of a forum, as just one example. At the very least, if a user enters HTML code in their data, such code could throw off the layout and aesthetic of your site. Taking this a step further, JavaScript is also just plain text, but text that has special meaning—*executable* meaning—within a browser. If malicious code entered into a form were redisplayed in a browser **Ⓐ**, it could create pop-up windows **Ⓑ**, steal cookies, or

redirect the browser to other sites. Such attacks are referred to as *cross-site scripting* (XSS). As in the email example, where you need to look for and nullify bad strings found in data, prevention of XSS attacks is accomplished by addressing any potentially dangerous PHP, HTML, or JavaScript.

PHP includes a handful of functions for handling HTML and other code found within strings. These include the following:

- **`htmlspecialchars()`**, which turns **&**, ', ", **<**, and **>** into an HTML *entity* format (*&*, *"*, etc.)

- **`htmlentities()`**, which turns all applicable characters into their HTML entity format

- **`strip_tags()`**, which removes all HTML and PHP tags

These three functions are roughly listed in order from least disruptive to most. Which function you'll want to use depends on the application at hand. To demonstrate how these functions work and differ, let's create a simple PHP page that takes some text and runs it through these functions, printing the results **Ⓒ**.

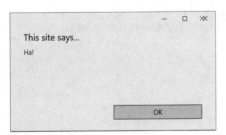

Ⓐ The malicious and savvy user can enter HTML, CSS, and JavaScript into textual form fields.

Ⓒ Thanks to the **`htmlentities()`** and **`strip_tags()`** functions, malicious code entered into a form field **Ⓐ** can be rendered inert.

Ⓑ The JavaScript entered into the comments field **Ⓐ** would create this alert window when the comments were displayed in the browser.

To prevent XSS attacks:

1. Begin a new PHP document in your text editor or IDE, to be named **xss.php** (Script 13.4):

```
<!doctype html>
<html lang="en">
<head>
  <meta charset="utf-8">
  <title>XSS Attacks</title>
</head>
<body>
<?php # Script 13.4 - xss.php
```

2. Check for the form submission and print the received data in its original format:

```
if ($_SERVER['REQUEST_METHOD'] ==
→ 'POST') {
    echo "<h2>Original</h2><p>
    → {$_POST['data']}</p>";
```

In order for us to compare and contrast what was originally received with the result after applying the functions, the original value must first be printed.

3. Apply the **htmlentities()** function, printing the results:

```
echo '<h2>After htmlentities()
→ </h2><p>' . htmlentities
→ ($_POST['data']). '</p>';
```

So that submitted information does not mess up a page or hack the browser, it's run through the **htmlentities()** function. With this function, any HTML entity will be translated; for instance, < and > will become *<* and *>*, respectively.

Script 13.4 Applying the **htmlentities()** and **strip_tags()** functions to submitted text can prevent XSS attacks.

```
1    <!doctype html>
2    <html lang="en">
3    <head>
4       <meta charset="utf-8">
5       <title>XSS Attacks</title>
6    </head>
7    <body>
8    <?php # Script 13.4 - xss.php
9
10   if ($_SERVER['REQUEST_METHOD'] == 'POST') {
11
12       // Apply the different functions, printing the results:
13       echo "<h2>Original</h2><p>{$_POST['data']}</p>";
14       echo '<h2>After htmlentities()</h2><p>' . htmlentities($_POST['data']). '</p>';
15       echo '<h2>After strip_tags()</h2><p>' . strip_tags($_POST['data']). '</p>';
16
17   }
18   // Display the form:
19   ?>
20   <form action="xss.php" method="post">
21       <p>Do your worst! <textarea name="data" rows="3" cols="40"></textarea></p>
22       <div align="center"><input type="submit" name="submit" value="Submit"></div>
23   </form>
24   </body>
25   </html>
```

4. Apply the **strip_tags()** function, printing the results:

```
echo '<h2>After strip_tags()
→ </h2><p>' . strip_tags
→ ($_POST['data']). '</p>';
```

The **strip_tags()** function completely takes out any HTML, JavaScript, or PHP tags. It's therefore the most foolproof function to use on submitted data.

5. Complete the PHP section:

```
}
?>
```

```
8  <h2>Original</h2><p>Time to unleash the
   wrath of JavaScript! <script>alert('Ha');
   </script></p><h2>After htmlentities()
   </h2><p>Time to unleash the wrath of
   JavaScript! &lt;script&gt;alert('Ha');&lt;
   /script&gt;</p><h2>After strip_tags()
   </h2><p>Time to unleash the wrath of
   JavaScript! alert('Ha');</p><form
   action="xss.php" method="post">
```

D This snippet of the page's HTML source **C** shows the original, submitted value, the value after using **html_entities()**, and the value after using **strip_tags()**.

6. Display the HTML form:

```
<form action="xss.php" method="post">
  <p>Do your worst! <textarea
  → name="data" rows="3" cols="40">
  → </textarea></p>
  <div align="center"><input
  → type="submit" name="submit"
  → value="Submit"></div>
</form>
```

The form **A** has only one field for the user to complete: a textarea.

7. Complete the page:

```
</body>
</html>
```

8. Save the page as **xss.php**, place it in your web directory, and test it in your browser.

9. View the source code of the page to see the full effect of these functions **D**.

TIP Both **htmlspecialchars()** and **htmlentities()** take an optional parameter indicating how quotation marks should be handled. See the PHP manual for specifics.

TIP The **strip_tags()** function takes an optional parameter indicating what tags should not be stripped.

```
$var = strip_tags($var, '<p><br>');
```

TIP Unrelated to security but quite useful is the **nl2br()** function. It turns every return (such as those entered into a textarea) into an HTML **
** tag.

Using the Filter Extension

Earlier, this chapter introduced the concept of *typecasting*, which is a good way to force a variable to be of the right type. In the next chapter, you'll learn about *regular expressions*, which can validate both the type of data and its specific contents or format. PHP 5.2 introduced the Filter extension (**www.php.net/filter**), an important tool that bridges the gap between the relatively simple approach of typecasting and the more complex concept of regular expressions.

The Filter extension can be used for one of two purposes: *validating* data or *sanitizing* it. A validation process, as you know well by now, confirms that data matches expectations. Sanitization, by comparison, alters data by removing inappropriate characters to make the data meet expectations.

The most important function in the Filter extension is `filter_var()`:

`filter_var(variable, filter[,options]);`

The function's first argument is the variable to be filtered, the second is the filter to apply, and the optional third argument is for adding additional criteria. **Table 13.3** lists the validation filters, each of which is represented as a constant.

For example, to confirm that a variable has a decimal value, you would use

```
if (filter_var($var,
→ FILTER_VALIDATE_FLOAT)) {
```

A couple of filters take an optional parameter, the most common being the **FILTER_VALIDATE_INT** filter, which has *min_range* and *max_range* options for controlling the smallest and largest acceptable values. For example, this next bit of code confirms that the **$age** variable is an integer between 1 and 120 (inclusive):

```
if (filter_var($var,
→ FILTER_VALIDATE_INT, ['min_range'
→ => 1, 'max_range' => 120])) {
```

To sanitize data, you'll still use the `filter_var()` function, but use one of the sanitization filters as listed in **Table 13.4**.

TABLE 13.3 Validation Filters

Constant
FILTER_VALIDATE_BOOLEAN
FILTER_VALIDATE_EMAIL
FILTER_VALIDATE_FLOAT
FILTER_VALIDATE_INT
FILTER_VALIDATE_IP
FILTER_VALIDATE_MAC
FILTER_VALIDATE_REGEXP
FILTER_VALIDATE_URL

TABLE 13.4 Sanitization Filters

Constant
FILTER_SANITIZE_EMAIL
FILTER_SANITIZE_ENCODED
FILTER_SANITIZE_MAGIC_QUOTES
FILTER_SANITIZE_NUMBER_FLOAT
FILTER_SANITIZE_NUMBER_INT
FILTER_SANITIZE_FULL_SPECIAL_CHARS
FILTER_SANITIZE_SPECIAL_CHARS
FILTER_SANITIZE_STRING
FILTER_SANITIZE_STRIPPED
FILTER_SANITIZE_URL
FILTER_UNSAFE_RAW

Many of the filters duplicate other PHP functions. For example, **FILTER_SANITIZE_MAGIC_QUOTES** is the same as applying **addslashes()**, **FILTER_SANITIZE_SPECIAL_CHARS** can be used in lieu of **htmlspecialchars()**, and **FILTER_SANITIZE_STRING()** can be used as a replacement for **strip_tags()**. The PHP manual lists several additional flags, as constants, that can be used as the optional third argument to affect how each filter behaves. As an example of applying a sanitizing filter, this code is equivalent to how **strip_tags()** is used in **xss.php** (Script 13.4):

```
echo '<h2>After strip_tags()</h2><p>'
→ . filter_var($_POST['data'],
→ FILTER_SANITIZE_STRING) . '</p>';
```

If you get hooked on using the Filter extension, you may appreciate the consistency of being able to use it for all data sanitization, even when functions such as **strip_tags()** exist.

So you can practice this, the next example will update **calculator.php** (Script 13.2) so that it sanitizes all the incoming data.

To use the Filter extension:

1. Open **calculator.php** (Script 13.2) in your text editor or IDE.

2. Change the assignment of the **$quantity** variable to (**Script 13.5**)

```
$quantity = (isset($_POST
→['quantity'])) ? filter_var
→($_POST['quantity'],
→ FILTER_VALIDATE_INT,
→['min_range' => 1]) : NULL;
```

This version of the script will improve on its predecessor in a couple of ways. First, each POST variable is checked for existence using **isset()**, instead of assuming the variable exists. If the variable is not set, then **$quantity** is assigned **NULL**. If the variable is set, it's run through **filter_var()**, sanitizing the value as an integer greater than 1.

continues on page 441

Script 13.5 Using the Filter extension, this script sanitizes incoming data rather than typecasting it, as in the earlier version of the script.

```
1    <!doctype html>
2    <html lang="en">
3    <head>
4        <meta charset="utf-8">
5        <title>Widget Cost Calculator</title>
6    </head>
7    <body>
8    <?php # Script 13.5 - calculator.php #2
9    // This version of the script uses the Filter extension instead of typecasting.
10
11   // Check if the form has been submitted:
12   if ($_SERVER['REQUEST_METHOD'] == 'POST') {
13
```

code continues on next page

```
14      // Sanitize the variables:
15      $quantity = (isset($_POST['quantity'])) ? filter_var($_POST['quantity'],
        FILTER_VALIDATE_INT, ['min_range' => 1]) : NULL;
16      $price = (isset($_POST['price'])) ? filter_var($_POST['price'],
        FILTER_SANITIZE_NUMBER_FLOAT, FILTER_FLAG_ALLOW_FRACTION) : NULL;
17      $tax = (isset($_POST['tax'])) ? filter_var($_POST['tax'],
        FILTER_SANITIZE_NUMBER_FLOAT, FILTER_FLAG_ALLOW_FRACTION) : NULL;
18
19      // All variables should be positive!
20      if ( ($quantity > 0) && ($price > 0) && ($tax > 0) ) {
21
22          // Calculate the total:
23          $total = $quantity * $price;
24          $total += $total * ($tax/100);
25
26          // Print the result:
27          echo '<p>The total cost of purchasing ' . $quantity . ' widget(s) at $' . number_
            format($price, 2) . ' each, plus tax, is $' . number_format($total, 2) . '.</p>';
28
29      } else { // Invalid submitted values.
30          echo '<p style="font-weight: bold; color: #C00">Please enter a valid quantity, price,
            and tax rate.</p>';
31      }
32
33  } // End of main isset() IF.
34
35  // Leave the PHP section and create the HTML form.
36  ?>
37  <h2>Widget Cost Calculator</h2>
38  <form action="calculator.php" method="post">
39      <p>Quantity: <input type="number" name="quantity" step="1" min="1" value="<?php if
        (isset($quantity)) echo $quantity; ?>"></p>
40      <p>Price: <input type="number" name="price" step=".01" min="0.01" value="<?php if
        (isset($price)) echo $price; ?>"></p>
41      <p>Tax (%): <input type="text" name="tax" step=".01" min="0.01" value="<?php if
        (isset($tax)) echo $tax; ?>"></p>
42      <p><input type="submit" name="submit" value="Calculate!"></p>
43  </form>
44  </body>
45  </html>
```

The sanitized value is then assigned to **$quantity**. All this code is written using the ternary operator, introduced in Chapter 10, "Common Programming Techniques," for brevity's sake. As an **if-else** conditional, the same code would be written as:

```
if (isset($_POST['quantity'])) {
    $quantity = filter_var($_POST
    →['quantity'], FILTER_VALIDATE_
    →INT, ['min_range' => 1]);
} else {
    $quantity = NULL;
}
```

3. Change the assignment of the **$price** variable to

```
$price = (isset($_POST['price'])) ?
→filter_var($_POST['price'],
→FILTER_SANITIZE_NUMBER_FLOAT,
→FILTER_FLAG_ALLOW_FRACTION) :
→NULL;
```

This code is a repetition of that in Step 2, except that the sanitizing filter insists that the data be a float. The additional argument, **FILTER_FLAG_ALLOW_FRACTION**, says that it's acceptable for the value to use a decimal point.

4. Change the assignment of the **$tax** variable to

```
$tax = (isset($_POST['tax'])) ?
→filter_var($_POST['tax'], FILTER_
→SANITIZE_NUMBER_FLOAT, FILTER_
→FLAG_ALLOW_FRACTION) : NULL;
```

This is a repetition of the code in Step 3.

5. Save the page, place it in your web directory, and test it in your browser **Ⓐ** and **Ⓑ**.

TIP The filter_has_var() function confirms whether a variable with a given name exists.

TIP The filter_input_array() function allows you to apply an array of filters to an array of variables in one step. For details (and perhaps to be blown away), see the PHP manual.

Ⓐ Invalid values in submitted form data…

Ⓑ …will be nullified by the Filter extension (as opposed to typecasting, which, for example, converted the string *cat* to the number 0).

Preventing SQL Injection Attacks

Another type of attack that malicious users can attempt is *SQL injection*. As the name implies, SQL injection is an attempt to insert bad code into a site's SQL queries. One aim of such attacks is that they would create a syntactically invalid query, thereby revealing something about the script or database in the resulting error message **A**. An even bigger aspiration is that the injection attack could alter, destroy, or expose the stored data.

Fortunately, SQL injection attacks are rather easy to prevent. Start by validating all data to be used in queries (and perform typecasting, or apply the Filter extension, whenever possible). Second, use a function like `mysqli_real_escape_string()`, which makes data safe to use in queries. This function was introduced in Chapter 9, "Using PHP with MySQL." Third, don't show detailed errors on live sites.

An alternative to using `mysqli_real_escape_string()` is to use *prepared statements*. Prepared statements were added to MySQL in version 4.1, and PHP

System Error

You could not be registered due to a system error. We apologize for any inconvenience.

You have an error in your SQL syntax; check the manual that corresponds to your MySQL server version for the right syntax to use near ';DELETE TABLE user', 'Ullman', 'email@example.com', SHA2('password', 512), NOW()' at line 1

Query: INSERT INTO users (first_name, last_name, email, pass, registration_date) VALUES (';DELETE TABLE user', 'Ullman', 'email@example.com', SHA2('password', 512), NOW())

A If a site reveals a detailed error message and doesn't properly handle problematic characters in submitted values, hackers can learn a lot about your server.

Prepared Statement Performance

Prepared statements can be more secure than running queries in the old-fashioned way, but they may also be faster. If a PHP script sends the same query to MySQL multiple times, using different values each time, prepared statements can really speed things up. In such cases, the query itself is only sent to MySQL and parsed once. Then, the values are sent to MySQL separately.

As a trivial example, the following code would run 100 queries in MySQL:

```
$q = 'INSERT INTO counter (num) VALUES (?)';
$stmt = mysqli_prepare($dbc, $q);
mysqli_stmt_bind_param($stmt, 'i', $n);
for ($n = 1; $n <= 100; $n++) {
mysqli_stmt_execute($stmt);
}
```

Even though the query is being run 100 times, the full text is only being transferred to, and parsed by, MySQL once. MySQL versions 5.1.17 and later include a caching mechanism that may also improve the performance of other uses of prepared statements.

---

can use them as of version 5. When you are not using prepared statements, the entire query, including the SQL syntax and the specific values, is sent to MySQL as one long string. MySQL then parses and executes it. With a prepared query, the SQL syntax is sent to MySQL first, where it is parsed, making sure it's syntactically valid (e.g., confirming that the query does not refer to tables or columns that don't exist). Then the specific values are sent separately; MySQL assembles the query using those values, and then executes it. The benefits of prepared statements are important: greater security and potentially better performance. I'll focus on the security aspect here, but see the sidebar for a discussion of performance.

Prepared statements can be created out of any **INSERT**, **UPDATE**, **DELETE**, or **SELECT** query. Begin by defining your query, marking *placeholders* using question marks. As an example, take the **SELECT** query from **edit_user.php** (Script 10.3):

```
$q = "SELECT first_name, last_name,
→ email FROM users WHERE user_id=$id";
```

As a prepared statement, this query becomes

```
$q = "SELECT first_name, last_name,
→ email FROM users WHERE user_id=?";
```

Next, *prepare* the statement in MySQL, assigning the results to a PHP variable:

```
$stmt = mysqli_prepare($dbc, $q);
```

TABLE 13.5 Bound Value Types

Letter	Represents
d	Decimal
i	Integer
b	Blob (binary data)
s	All other types

At this point, MySQL will parse the query, but it won't execute it.

Next, you *bind* PHP variables to the query's placeholders. In other words, you state that one variable should be used for the first question mark, another variable for the next question mark, and so on. Continuing with the same example, you would code

```
mysqli_stmt_bind_param($stmt, 'i', $id);
```

The *i* part of the command indicates what kind of value should be expected, using the characters listed in **Table 13.5**. In this case, the query expects to receive one integer. As another example, here's how the login query from Chapter 12, "Cookies and Sessions," would be handled:

```
$q = "SELECT user_id, first_name
→ FROM users WHERE email=? AND
→ pass=SHA2(?, 512)";
$stmt = mysqli_prepare($dbc, $q);
mysqli_stmt_bind_param($stmt, 'ss',
→ $e, $p);
```

In this example, something interesting is also revealed: even though both the email address and password values are strings, *they are not placed within quotes* in the query. This is another difference between a prepared statement and a standard query.

Once the statement has been bound, you can assign values to the PHP variables (if that hasn't happened already) and then execute the statement. Using the login example, that'd be

```
$e = 'email@example.com';
$p = 'mypass';
mysqli_stmt_execute($stmt);
```

The values of **$e** and **$p** will be used when the prepared statement is executed.

continues on next page

To see this process in action, let's write a script that adds a post to the *messages* table in the *forum* database (created in Chapter 6, "Database Design"). I'll also use the opportunity to demonstrate a couple of the other prepared statement-related functions.

To use prepared statements:

1. Begin a new PHP script in your text editor or IDE, to be named **post_message.php** (Script 13.6):

   ```
   <!doctype html>
   <html lang="en">
   <head>
     <meta charset="utf-8">
     <title>Post a Message</title>
   </head>
   <body>
   <?php # Script 13.6 -
   → post_message.php
   ```

2. Check for form submission and connect to the *forum* database:

   ```
   if ($_SERVER['REQUEST_METHOD'] ==
   → 'POST') {
       $dbc = mysqli_connect
       → ('localhost', 'username',
       → 'password', 'forum');
   ```

   Note that, for brevity's sake, I'm omitting basic data validation and error reporting. Although a real site (a more realized version of this script can be found in Chapter 17, "Example—Message Board") would check that the message subject and body aren't empty and that the various ID values are positive integers, this script will still be relatively safe, thanks to the security offered by prepared statements.

   This example will use the *forum* database, created in Chapter 6.

continues on page 446

continues on page 446

Script 13.6 This script, which represents a simplified version of a message posting page, uses prepared statements as a way of preventing SQL injection attacks.

```
1    <!doctype html>
2    <html lang="en">
3    <head>
4       <meta charset="utf-8">
5       <title>Post a Message</title>
6    </head>
7    <body>
8    <?php # Script 13.6 - post_message.php
9
10   if ($_SERVER['REQUEST_METHOD'] == 'POST') {
11
12       // Validate the data (omitted)!
13
14       // Connect to the database:
15       $dbc = mysqli_connect('localhost', 'username', 'password', 'forum');
16
17       // Make the query:
18       $q = 'INSERT INTO messages (forum_id, parent_id, user_id, subject, body,
             date_entered) VALUES (?, ?, ?, ?, ?, NOW())';
19
```

code continues on next page

```
20      // Prepare the statement:
21      $stmt = mysqli_prepare($dbc, $q);
22
23      // Bind the variables:
24      mysqli_stmt_bind_param($stmt, 'iiiss', $forum_id, $parent_id, $user_id, $subject,
        $body);
25
26      // Assign the values to variables:
27      $forum_id = (int) $_POST['forum_id'];
28      $parent_id = (int) $_POST['parent_id'];
29      $user_id = 3; // The user_id value would normally come from the session.
30      $subject = strip_tags($_POST['subject']);
31      $body = strip_tags($_POST['body']);
32
33      // Execute the query:
34      mysqli_stmt_execute($stmt);
35
36      // Print a message based upon the result:
37      if (mysqli_stmt_affected_rows($stmt) == 1) {
38          echo '<p>Your message has been posted.</p>';
39      } else {
40          echo '<p style="font-weight: bold; color: #C00">Your message could not be posted.</p>';
41          echo '<p>' . mysqli_stmt_error($stmt) . '</p>';
42      }
43
44      // Close the statement:
45      mysqli_stmt_close($stmt);
46
47      // Close the connection:
48      mysqli_close($dbc);
49
50  } // End of submission IF.
51
52  // Display the form:
53  ?>
54  <form action="post_message.php" method="post">
55
56      <fieldset><legend>Post a message:</legend>
57
58      <p><strong>Subject</strong>: <input name="subject" type="text" size="30" maxlength="100">
        </p>
59
60      <p><strong>Body</strong>: <textarea name="body" rows="3" cols="40"></textarea></p>
61
62      </fieldset>
63      <div align="center"><input type="submit" name="submit" value="Submit"></div>
64      <input type="hidden" name="forum_id" value="1">
65      <input type="hidden" name="parent_id" value="0">
66
67  </form>
68  </body>
69  </html>
```

3. Define and prepare the query:

```
$q = 'INSERT INTO messages
→(forum_id, parent_id, user_id,
→subject, body, date_entered)
VALUES (?, ?, ?, ?, ?, NOW())';
$stmt = mysqli_prepare($dbc, $q);
```

This syntax has already been explained. The query is defined, using placeholders for values to be assigned later. Then the **mysqli_prepare()** function sends this to MySQL, assigning the result to **$stmt**.

The query itself was first used in Chapter 6. It populates six fields in the *messages* table. The value for the **date_entered** column will be the result of the **NOW()** function, not a bound value.

4. Bind the appropriate variables and create a list of values to be inserted:

```
mysqli_stmt_bind_param($stmt,
→'iiiss', $forum_id, $parent_id,
→$user_id, $subject, $body);
$forum_id = (int) $_POST
→['forum_id'];
$parent_id = (int) $_POST
→['parent_id'];
$user_id = 3;
$subject = strip_tags($_POST
→['subject']);
$body = strip_tags($_POST['body']);
```

The first line says that three integers and two strings will be used in the prepared statement. The values will be found in the variables to follow.

For those variables, the subject and body values come straight from the form 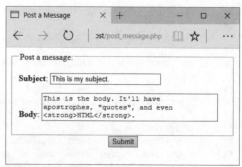, after running them through **strip_tags()** to remove any potentially dangerous code. The forum ID and parent ID (which indicates if the message

is a reply to an existing message or not) also come from the form. They'll be typecast to integers (for added security, you would confirm that they're positive numbers after typecasting them, or you could use the Filter extension).

The user ID value, in a real script, would come from the session, where it would be stored when the user logged in.

5. Execute the query:

```
mysqli_stmt_execute($stmt);
```

Finally, the prepared statement is executed.

6. Print the results of the execution and complete the loop:

```
if (mysqli_stmt_affected_rows
→($stmt) == 1) {
  echo '<p>Your message has been
  →posted.</p>';
} else {
  echo '<p style="font-weight:
  →bold; color: #C00">Your
  →message could not be posted.
  →</p>';
  echo '<p>' . mysqli_stmt_error
  →($stmt) . '</p>';
}
```

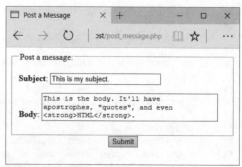

B The simple HTML form.

The successful insertion of a record can be confirmed using the **mysqli_stmt_affected_rows()** function, which works as you expect it would (returning the number of affected rows). In that case, a simple message is printed **C**. If a problem occurred, the **mysqli_stmt_error()** function returns the specific MySQL error message. This is for your debugging purposes, not to be used in a live site. That being said, often the PHP error message is more useful than that returned by **mysqli_stmt_error()** **D**.

7. Close the statement and the database connection:

```
mysqli_stmt_close($stmt);
mysqli_close($dbc);
```

The first function closes the prepared statement, freeing up the resources. At this point, **$stmt** no longer has a value. The second function closes the database connection.

8. Complete the PHP section:

```
} // End of submission IF.
?>
```

9. Begin the form:

```
<form action="post_message.php"
→ method="post">
```

```
<fieldset><legend>Post a
→ message:</legend>
<p><strong>Subject</strong>:
→ <input name="subject"
→ type="text" size="30"
→ maxlength="100"></p>
<p><strong>Body</strong>:
→ <textarea name="body" rows="3"
→ cols="40"></textarea></p>
</fieldset>
```

The form begins with just a subject text input and a textarea for the message's body.

10. Complete the form:

```
<div align="center"><input
→ type="submit" name="submit"
→ value="Submit"></div>
<input type="hidden"
→ name="forum_id" value="1">
<input type="hidden"
→ name="parent_id" value="0">
```

The form contains two fields the user would fill out and two hidden inputs that store values the query needs. In a real version of this script, the **forum_id** and **parent_id** values would be determined dynamically.

continues on next page

C If one record in the database was affected by the query, this will be the result.

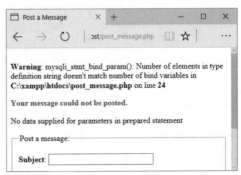

D Error reporting with prepared statements can be confounding sometimes!

11. Complete the page:

```
</body>
</html>
```

12. Save the file as **post_message.php**, place it in your web directory, and test it in your browser **E**.

TIP There are two kinds of prepared statements. Here I have demonstrated bound parameters, where PHP variables are bound to a query. The other type is bound results, where the results of a query are bound to PHP variables.

```
mysql -u root -p                                          —    □    ×
MariaDB [forum]> SELECT * FROM messages ORDER BY date_entered DESC LIMIT 1\G
*************************** 1. row ***************************
  message_id: 22
   parent_id: 0
    forum_id: 1
     user_id: 3
     subject: This is my subject.
        body: This is the body. It'll have apostrophes, "quotes", and even HTML.
date_entered: 2017-07-16 14:49:14
1 row in set (0.06 sec)

MariaDB [forum]>
```

E Selecting the most recent entry in the *messages* table confirms that the prepared statement (Script 13.6) worked. Notice that the HTML was stripped out of the post but the quotes are still present.

Securing Passwords with PHP

How secure a user account system is will depend largely on how passwords are handled. Passwords can be stored on the server in three ways:

- In plain text, which is a terrible thing to do
- In an encrypted format, which can be decrypted
- In a hashed format, which can't be decrypted

If you store passwords in an encrypted format, it's safe from prying eyes and can be retrieved when necessary. But if someone gets onto your server and can find your code for performing the decryption, that person will be able to view every user's password. And it turns out that you don't need passwords to be decryptable; it doesn't matter whether anyone can ever see the plain text in its original form again.

An alternative is to create a hash of the password. A hash is a representation of data. For example, MD5 is a hashing algorithm that's been around for years. The MD5 hash of the word *password* is *5f4dcc3b5aa765d61d8327deb882cf99*; the MD5 hash of the word *omnivore* is *04f7696e917f292f99925f80fcdb1db1*. You can create a hash out of any piece of data, and, in theory, no two pieces of data have the same hash.

continues on next page

Preventing Brute-Force Attacks

In a brute-force attack, a malicious user tries to log in to a secure system by making lots of attempts in the hopes of eventual success. It's not a sophisticated type of attack, hence the name "brute force." For example, if you have a login process that requires a username and password, there is a limit to the possible number of username/password combinations. That limit may be in the billions or trillions, but still, it's a finite number. Using algorithms and automated processes, brute-force attacks repeatedly try combinations until they succeed.

The best way to prevent brute-force attacks from succeeding is requiring users to register long passwords. Although requiring a combination of characters, numbers, and symbols prevents dictionary attacks, using longer passwords requires exponentially more computing power to crack.

Also, don't give indications as to why a login failed: saying that a username and password combination isn't correct gives away nothing, but saying that a username isn't right or that the password isn't right for that username says too much.

To stop a brute-force attack in its tracks, you could also limit the number of incorrect login attempts by a given IP address. IP addresses do change frequently, but in a brute-force attack, the same IP address—or pool of IP addresses—would be trying to log in multiple times in a matter of minutes. You would have to track incorrect logins by IP address, and then, after *X* number of invalid attempts, block that IP address for, say, 24 hours. Or, if you didn't want to go that far, you could use an "incremental delay" defense: each incorrect login from the same IP address creates an added delay in the response (use PHP's `sleep()` function to create the delay). Humans might not notice or be bothered by such delays, but automated attacks most certainly would.

Storing the hash version of a password is more secure in that it can't be decrypted. If hackers get your data, the best they can do is create hashes of common words in the hopes that they find the matching hash (this is called a dictionary attack). But storing a hash still makes logging in possible. When a user logs in, the hashed version of the user's login password just needs to equal the already stored hashed version. If the two hashes equate, the submitted password is correct.

Once you've decided to hash the passwords, you'll need to choose what hashing algorithm (or formula) to use and where the hashing should take place. By the latter

More Security Recommendations

This chapter covers many specific techniques for improving your web security. Here are a handful of other recommendations:

- Do your best to limit what information is requested from the user and what the site stores. The less information handled by the site in any way, the less data you have to worry about being stolen.

- Make it your job to study, follow, and abide by security recommendations. Don't just rely on the advice of one chapter, one book, or one author.

- Don't retain user-supplied names for uploaded files.

- Watch how database references are used. For example, if a person's user ID is that user's primary key from the database and this is stored in a cookie (as in Chapter 12), a malicious user just needs to change that cookie value to access another user's account.

- Don't show detailed error messages (this point was repeated in Chapter 8, "Error Handling and Debugging").

- Use cryptography (this is discussed in Chapter 7, "Advanced SQL and MySQL," with respect to the database, and in my book *PHP 5 Advanced: Visual QuickPro Guide* (Peachpit Press, 2007) with respect to the server).

- Don't store credit card numbers, social security numbers, banking information, and the like. The only exception to this would be if you have deep enough pockets to pay for the best security and to cover the lawsuits that arise when this data is stolen from your site (which will inevitably happen).

- Use SSL. A secure connection is one of the best protections a server can offer a user.

- Reliably and consistently protect every page and directory that needs it. Never assume that people won't find sensitive areas just because there's no link to them. If access to a page or directory should be limited, make sure it is.

My final recommendation is to be aware of your own limitations. As the programmer, you probably approach a script thinking how it *should be* used. This is not the same as to how it *will be* used, either accidentally or on purpose. Try to break your site to see what happens. Do bad things; do the wrong thing. Have other people try to break it, too (it's normally easy to find such volunteers). When you code, if you assume that no one will ever use a page properly, it'll be much more secure than if you assume people always will.

I mean that you can hash the password either in the database or in your PHP code.

Since Chapter 5, "Introduction to SQL," the MySQL **SHA2()** function has been used for passwords. Normally I recommend having the database do as much as possible, but PHP now has a sophisticated hashing function —**password_hash()**—added to the language as of PHP 5.5. This means you must have a current version of PHP to use it (as of this writing, the most current version is only 5.5.3).

If you aren't running PHP 5.5 or greater, you can use an external library found at **https://github.com/ircmaxell/password_compat**. This library was created by Anthony Ferrara (**http://blog.ircmaxell.com/**) and is the basis for the version implemented in PHP 5.5. The library requires PHP 5.3.7 or greater.

This code hashes passwords securely using this new function:

```
$hash = password_hash($password,
→ PASSWORD_DEFAULT);
```

The function automatically creates and uses a proper salt. When provided with the **PASSWORD_DEFAULT** constant as the second argument, it also selects and uses the best, most secure hashing algorithm available.

To verify a password upon login, use the **password_verify()** function. Its first argument is the submitted, unhashed password. The second is the stored, hashed password:

```
if (password_verify($password, $hash)) {
    /* Valid */
} else {
    /* Invalid */
}
```

To use this, let's update the registration and login process for the *sitename* database in a series of three steps:

1. Change the pass column type in the database.

2. Update the registration script to use PHP's **password_hash()** function.

3. Update the login script to use PHP's **password_verify()** function.

Note that changing the hashing mechanism renders all currently stored passwords in the database unusable (i.e., you'd never just casually change the password-handling methodology on a live site).

To update the database:

1. Connect to MySQL and select the *sitename* database, if you have not already.

2. Change the *users.pass* column's type **A**:

   ```
   ALTER TABLE users MODIFY COLUMN
   → pass VARCHAR(256) NOT NULL;
   ```

continues on next page

PHP and MySQL for Dynamic Web Sites

```
mysql> ALTER TABLE users MODIFY COLUMN pass VARCHAR(256) NOT NULL;
Query OK, 0 rows affected (0.08 sec)
Records: 0  Duplicates: 0  Warnings: 0
```

A To change a column's type, use a modify query.

The **ALTER TABLE** query lets you change an existing table, and the **MODIFY COLUMN** part of the query is how you change a column's definition. The column is being converted to a **VARCHAR** up to 256 characters in length, and it cannot have null values.

3. Wipe out all the existing passwords **B**:

```
UPDATE users SET pass= ' ';
```

Since the existing passwords won't work with the PHP-based hashing (when someone attempts to log in), they might as well be erased. Because the column does not allow for null values, an empty string is assigned instead.

To update the registration process:

1. Open **register.php** (refer to Script 9.5) in your text editor or IDE.

2. Change the assignment of the **$p** variable (line 32) so it uses PHP for the hashing (**Script 13.7**):

```
$p = password_hash(trim($_POST
→['pass1']), PASSWORD_DEFAULT);
```

continues on page 454

```
PHP and MySQL for Dynamic Web Sites
mysql> UPDATE users SET pass= ' ';
Query OK, 26 rows affected (0.01 sec)
Rows matched: 26  Changed: 26  Warnings: 0

mysql>
```

B The existing passwords are eliminated using this query.

Script 13.7 The updated registration page now hashes the password using PHP instead of MySQL.

```
1   <?php # Script 13.7 - register.php #3
2   // This script performs an INSERT query to add a record to the users table.
3
4   $page_title = 'Register';
5   include('includes/header.html');
6
7   // Check for form submission:
8   if ($_SERVER['REQUEST_METHOD'] == 'POST') {
9
10      require('../mysqli_connect.php'); // Connect to the db.
11
12      $errors = []; // Initialize an error array.
13
14      // Check for a first name:
15      if (empty($_POST['first_name'])) {
16          $errors[] = 'You forgot to enter your first name.';
17      } else {
18          $fn = mysqli_real_escape_string($dbc, trim($_POST['first_name']));
19      }
20
21      // Check for a last name:
22      if (empty($_POST['last_name'])) {
23          $errors[] = 'You forgot to enter your last name.';
24      } else {
25          $ln = mysqli_real_escape_string($dbc, trim($_POST['last_name']));
26      }
27
```

code continues on next page

```
28      // Check for an email address:
29      if (empty($_POST['email'])) {
30          $errors[] = 'You forgot to enter your email address.';
31      } else {
32          $e = mysqli_real_escape_string($dbc, trim($_POST['email']));
33      }
34
35      // Check for a password and match against the confirmed password:
36      if (!empty($_POST['pass1'])) {
37          if ($_POST['pass1'] != $_POST['pass2']) {
38              $errors[] = 'Your password did not match the confirmed password.';
39          } else {
40              $p = password_hash(trim($_POST['pass1']), PASSWORD_DEFAULT);
41          }
42      } else {
43          $errors[] = 'You forgot to enter your password.';
44      }
45
46      if (empty($errors)) { // If everything's OK.
47
48          // Register the user in the database...
49
50          // Make the query:
51          $q = "INSERT INTO users (first_name, last_name, email, pass, registration_date)
                VALUES ('$fn', '$ln', '$e', '$p', NOW() )";
52          $r = @mysqli_query($dbc, $q); // Run the query.
53          if ($r) { // If it ran OK.
54
55              // Print a message:
56              echo '<h1>Thank you!</h1>
57          <p>You are now registered. In Chapter 12 you will actually be able to log in!
            </p><p><br></p>';
58
59          } else { // If it did not run OK.
60
61              // Public message:
62              echo '<h1>System Error</h1>
63              <p class="error">You could not be registered due to a system error. We apologize for
                any inconvenience.</p>';
64
65              // Debugging message:
66              echo '<p>' . mysqli_error($dbc) . '<br><br>Query: ' . $q . '</p>';
67
68          } // End of if ($r) IF.
69
70          mysqli_close($dbc); // Close the database connection.
71
72          // Include the footer and quit the script:
73          include('includes/footer.html');
74          exit();
75
```

code continues on next page

The hashed password does not need to be run through the **mysqli_real_escape_string()** function since no hashed value could contain any problematic characters.

3. Update the **INSERT** query so it no longer uses the MySQL **SHA2()** function:

```
$q = "INSERT INTO users
→(first_name, last_name, email,
→pass, registration_date) VALUES
→('$fn', '$ln', '$e', '$p', NOW() )";
```

The query now just uses **$p** as the value being stored.

4. Save the file as **register.php**, place it in your web directory, and test it in your browser **C** and **D**.

You'll need to place it in the same directory with the other site files from Chapter 9 (and also this chapter).

C To the user, the registration should look and function the same as before.

```
PHP and MySQL for Dynamic Web Sites
mysql> SELECT * FROM users ORDER BY registration_date DESC LIMIT 1\G
*************************** 1. row ***************************
        user_id: 29
     first_name: Password
      last_name: Hash
          email: password@example.net
           pass: $2y$10$AANu2HqvThx1TbQ9l0EPRuhhGFZ6UulQTU.RW1Qutwp1NfBI90ojq
registration_date: 2017-07-16 20:51:00
1 row in set (0.00 sec)

mysql>
```

D Fetching the registered user from the database shows the hashed password.

Script 13.7 *continued*

```
76      } else { // Report the errors.
77
78          echo '<h1>Error!</h1>
79          <p class="error">The following
            error(s) occurred:<br>';
80          foreach ($errors as $msg) { //
            Print each error.
81              echo " - $msg<br>\n";
82          }
83          echo '</p><p>Please try again.
            </p><p><br></p>';
84
85      } // End of if (empty($errors)) IF.
86
87      mysqli_close($dbc); // Close the
        database connection.
88
89  } // End of the main Submit conditional.
90  ?>
91  <h1>Register</h1>
92  <form action="register.php"
    method="post">
93      <p>First Name: <input type="text"
        name="first_name" size="15"
        maxlength="20" value="<?php if
        (isset($_POST['first_name'])) echo
        $_POST['first_name']; ?>"></p>
94      <p>Last Name: <input type="text"
        name="last_name" size="15"
        maxlength="40" value="<?php if
        (isset($_POST['last_name'])) echo
        $_POST['last_name']; ?>"></p>
95      <p>Email Address: <input type="email"
        name="email" size="20" maxlength="60"
        value="<?php if (isset($_
        POST['email'])) echo $_POST['email'];
        ?>" > </p>
96      <p>Password: <input type="password"
        name="pass1" size="10" maxlength="20"
        value="<?php if (isset($_
        POST['pass1'])) echo $_POST['pass1'];
        ?>" ></p>
97      <p>Confirm Password: <input
        type="password" name="pass2"
        size="10" maxlength="20" value="<?php
        if (isset($_POST['pass2'])) echo
        $_POST['pass2']; ?>" ></p>
98      <p><input type="submit" name="submit"
        value="Register"></p>
99  </form>
100 <?php include('includes/footer.html'); ?>
```

To update the login process:

1. Open **login_functions.inc.php** (refer to Script 12.2) in your text editor or IDE.

2. Change the assignment to the **$p** variable so it no longer uses **mysqli_real_escape_string()** (Script 13.8):

   $p = trim($pass);

   The password won't be used in the query so it need not be escaped. In fact, for a match to be made, it shouldn't be!

   The **trim()** function is still applied as the password is trimmed upon registration, too.

3. Change the **SELECT** query so that it only uses the email address in the conditional and also retrieves the stored password:

   $q = "SELECT user_id, first_name,
   → pass FROM users WHERE email='$e'";

   Because the password must now be verified in PHP, it must be retrieved by the query. The conditional only checks that the email address exists.

continues on page 457

Script 13.8 The updated login functions script now verifies the user's password using PHP instead of MySQL.

```
1    <?php # Script 13.8 - login_functions.inc.php #2
2    // This page defines two functions used by the login/logout process.
3
4    /* This function determines an absolute URL and redirects the user there.
5     * The function takes one argument: the page to be redirected to.
6     * The argument defaults to index.php.
7     */
8    function redirect_user($page = 'index.php') {
9
10       // Start defining the URL...
11       // URL is http:// plus the host name plus the current directory:
12       $url = 'http://' . $_SERVER['HTTP_HOST'] . dirname($_SERVER['PHP_SELF']);
13
14       // Remove any trailing slashes:
15       $url = rtrim($url, '/\\');
16
17       // Add the page:
18       $url .= '/' . $page;
19
20       // Redirect the user:
21       header("Location: $url");
22       exit(); // Quit the script.
23
24    } // End of redirect_user() function.
25
26
27    /* This function validates the form data (the email address and password).
28     * If both are present, the database is queried.
29     * The function requires a database connection.
30     * The function returns an array of information, including:
31     * - a TRUE/FALSE variable indicating success
```

code continues on next page

```
32       * - an array of either errors or the database result
33       */
34    function check_login($dbc, $email = '', $pass = '') {
35
36       $errors = []; // Initialize error array.
37
38       // Validate the email address:
39       if (empty($email)) {
40          $errors[] = 'You forgot to enter your email address.';
41       } else {
42          $e = mysqli_real_escape_string($dbc, trim($email));
43       }
44
45       // Validate the password:
46       if (empty($pass)) {
47          $errors[] = 'You forgot to enter your password.';
48       } else {
49          $p = trim($pass);
50       }
51
52       if (empty($errors)) { // If everything's OK.
53
54          // Retrieve the user_id and first_name for that email/password combination:
55          $q = "SELECT user_id, first_name FROM users WHERE email='$e'";
56          $r = @mysqli_query($dbc, $q); // Run the query.
57
58          // Check the result:
59          if (mysqli_num_rows($r) == 1) {
60
61             // Fetch the record:
62             $row = mysqli_fetch_array($r, MYSQLI_ASSOC);
63
64             // Check the password:
65             if (password_verify($p, $row['pass'])) {
66                unset($row['pass']);
67                return [true, $row];
68             } else {
69                $errors[] = 'The email address and password entered do not match those on
                   file.';
70             }
71
72          } else { // Not a match!
73             $errors[] = 'The email address and password entered do not match those on file.';
74          }
75
76       } // End of empty($errors) IF.
77
78       // Return false and the errors:
79       return [false, $errors];
80
81    } // End of check_login() function.
```

4. Replace this line (line 65 of Script 12.2)—

```
return [true, $row];
```

with the new logic:

```
if (password_verify($p, $row
→['pass'])) {
  unset($row['pass']);
  return [true, $row];
} else {
  $errors[] = 'The email address
  → and password entered do not
  → match those on file.';
}
```

The previous version of this function returned the value TRUE plus the user ID and first name if the query returned one row. Now the logic needs to be expanded since the retrieval of a single row only confirms the email address exists.

After fetching the row of data, the conditional invokes **password_verify()**, comparing the just-submitted password against the previously stored password. If **password_verify()** returns a true value, the **check_login()** function can return true and **$row** as it did before. However, as **$row** now also includes the fetched password, that should be removed—unset—from the variable first.

If the password wasn't a match, the same generic error message is returned. As you learned in the "Preventing Brute-Force Attacks" sidebar, it's best not to be too specific as to why a login attempt failed.

5. Save the page as **login_functions.inc.php**, place it in your web directory (in the **includes** folder), and test it in your browser **E**.

TIP Many sites today are ensuring even better security by not using a password at all, instead using single-access tokens. Search online to learn more.

E The login with the new hashing mechanism worked! (Note that the user was registered with a first name of "Password.")

Review and Pursue

If you have any problems with the review questions or the pursue prompts, turn to the book's supporting forum (LarryUllman.com/forums/).

Review

- What are some of the inappropriate strings and characters that could be indicators of potential spam attempts?
- What does the **stripos()** function do? What is its syntax?
- What does the **str_replace()** function do? What is its syntax?
- What does the **array_map()** function do? What is its syntax?
- What is *typecasting*? How do you typecast a variable in PHP?
- What function is used to move an uploaded file to its final destination on the server?
- What is the Fileinfo extension? How is it used?
- What does the **htmlspecialchars()** function do?
- What does the **htmlentities()** function do?
- What does the **strip_tags()** function do?
- What function converts newline characters into HTML break tags?
- What is the most important function in the Filter extension? How is it used?
- What are prepared statements? What benefits might prepared statements have over the standard method of querying a database?
- What is the syntax for using prepared statements?
- How do you hash a password in PHP?
- How do you check a previously hashed password in PHP?

Pursue

- If you haven't applied the Filter function (for email validation) and the **spam_scrubber()** function to a contact form used on one of your sites, do so now!
- Change **calculator.php** to allow for no tax rate.
- Update **calculator.php**, from Chapter 3, "Creating Dynamic Web Sites," so that it also uses typecasting or the Filter extension. (As a reminder, that calculator determined the cost of a car trip, based on the distance, average miles per gallon, and average price paid per gallon.)
- Modify **upload_rtf.php** so that it reports the actual MIME type for the uploaded file, should it not be *text/rtf*.
- Create a PHP script that reports the MIME type of any uploaded file.
- Apply the **strip_tags()** function to a previous script in the book, such as the registration example, to prevent inappropriate code from being stored in the database.
- Apply the Filter function to the login process in Chapter 12 to guarantee that the submitted email address meets the email address format, prior to using it in a query.
- Apply the Filter function, or typecasting, to the **delete_user.php** and **edit_user.php** scripts from Chapter 10.
- Apply the Fileinfo extension to the **show_image.php** script from Chapter 11.
- Add more stringent validation to the registration script, including using the Filter extension for the email address and requiring a longer password.
- Update the registration and login scripts to use prepared statements.

Perl-Compatible Regular Expressions

Regular expressions are an amazingly powerful—but often taxing—tool available in most of today's programming languages and even in many applications. Think of regular expressions as an elaborate system of matching patterns. You first write the pattern and then use one of PHP's built-in functions to apply the pattern to a value (regular expressions are applied to strings, even if that means a string with a numeric value). Whereas a string function could see if the name *John* is in some text, a regular expression could just as easily find *John*, *Jon*, and *Jonathon*.

Because the regular expression syntax is so complex, while the functions that use them are simple, the focus in this chapter will be on mastering the syntax in little bites. The PHP code will be very simple; later chapters will better incorporate regular expressions into real-world scripts.

Creating a Test Script

Regular expressions are a matter of applying patterns to values. The application of the pattern to a value is accomplished using one of a handful of functions; the most important is **preg_match()**. This function returns a 0 or 1, indicating whether the pattern matched the string. Its basic syntax is

```
preg_match(pattern, subject);
```

The **preg_match()** function will stop once it finds a single match. If you need to find all the matches, use **preg_match_all()**. That function will be discussed toward the end of the chapter.

When providing the pattern to **preg_match()**, it needs to be placed within quotation marks, since it'll be a string. Because many escaped characters within double quotation marks have special meaning (like **\n**), I advocate using single quotation marks to define your patterns.

Second, within the quotation marks, the pattern needs to be encased within *delimiters*. The delimiter can be any character that's not alphanumeric or the backslash, and the same character must be used to mark the beginning and end of the pattern. Commonly, you'll see forward slashes used. To see if the word *cat* contains the letter *a*, you would code (spoiler alert: it does)

```
if (preg_match('/a/', 'cat')) {
```

If you need to match a forward slash in the pattern, use a different delimiter, like the pipe (|) or an exclamation mark (!).

The bulk of this chapter covers all the rules for defining patterns. To best learn by example, let's start by creating a simple PHP script that takes a pattern and a string **Ⓐ** and returns the regular expression result **Ⓑ**.

Ⓐ The HTML form, which will be used for practicing regular expressions.

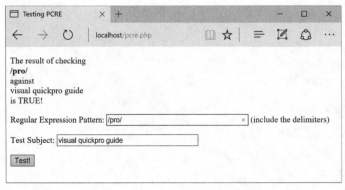

Ⓑ The script will print what values were used in the regular expression and what the result was. The form will also be made sticky to remember previously submitted values.

To match a pattern:

1. Begin a new PHP document in your text editor or IDE, to be named **pcre.php** (Script 14.1).

```
<html lang="en">
<head>
  <meta charset="utf-8">
  <title>Testing PCRE</title>
</head>
<body>
<?php # Script 14.1 - pcre.php
```

2. Check for the form submission:

```
if ($_SERVER['REQUEST_METHOD'] ==
→ 'POST') {
```

3. Treat the incoming values:

```
$pattern = trim($_POST['pattern']);
$subject = trim($_POST['subject']);
```

continues on next page

Script 14.1 The complex regular expression syntax will be best taught and demonstrated using this PHP script.

```
1    <!doctype html>
2    <html lang="en">
3    <head>
4        <meta charset="utf-8">
5        <title>Testing PCRE</title>
6    </head>
7    <body>
8    <?php # Script 14.1 - pcre.php
9    // This script takes a submitted string and checks it against a submitted pattern.
10
11   if ($_SERVER['REQUEST_METHOD'] == 'POST') {
12
13       // Trim the strings:
14       $pattern = trim($_POST['pattern']);
15       $subject = trim($_POST['subject']);
16
17       // Print a caption:
18       echo "<p>The result of checking<br><strong>$pattern</strong><br>against<br>$subject<br>is
     ";
19
20       // Test:
21       if (preg_match($pattern, $subject) ) {
22           echo 'TRUE!</p>';
23       } else {
24           echo 'FALSE!</p>';
25       }
26
27   } // End of submission IF.
28   // Display the HTML form.
29   ?>
30   <form action="pcre.php" method="post">
31       <p>Regular Expression Pattern: <input type="text" name="pattern" value="<?php if
     (isset($pattern)) echo htmlentities($pattern); ?>" size="40"> (include the delimiters)</p>
32       <p>Test Subject: <input type="text" name="subject" value="<?php if (isset($subject)) echo
     htmlentities($subject); ?>" size="40"></p>
33       <input type="submit" name="submit" value="Test!">
34   </form>
35   </body>
36   </html>
```

The form will submit two values to this same script. Both should be trimmed, just to make sure the presence of any extraneous spaces doesn't skew the results. I've omitted a check that each input isn't empty, but you could include that if you wanted.

4. Print a caption:

```
echo "<p>The result of checking
→ <br><strong>$pattern</strong>
→ <br>against<br>$subject<br>is ";
```

As you can see B, the form-handling part of this script will start by printing the values submitted.

5. Run the regular expression:

```
if (preg_match($pattern,
→ $subject) ) {
    echo 'TRUE!</p>';
} else {
    echo 'FALSE!</p>';
}
```

To test the pattern against the string, feed both to the **preg_match()** function. If this function returns 1, that means a match was made, this condition will

be TRUE, and the word *TRUE* will be printed. If no match was made, the condition will be FALSE and that will be stated C.

6. Complete the submission conditional and the PHP block:

```
} // End of submission IF.
?>
```

7. Create the HTML form:

```
<form action="pcre.php"
→ method="post">
  <p>Regular Expression
  → Pattern: <input type="text"
  → name="pattern" value="<?php
  → if (isset($pattern)) echo
  → htmlentities($pattern);
  → ?>" size="40"> (include the
  → delimiters)</p>
  <p>Test Subject: <input
  → type="text" name="subject"
  → value="<?php if (isset
  → ($subject)) echo htmlentities
  → ($subject); ?>" size="40"></p>
  <input type="submit"
  → name="submit" value="Test!">
</form>
```

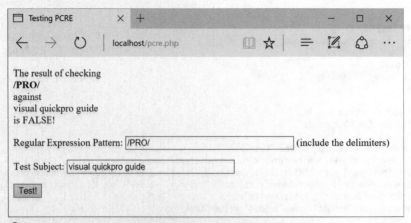

C If the pattern does not match the string, this will be the result. This submission and response also convey that regular expressions are case-sensitive by default.

The form contains two text boxes, both of which are sticky (using the trimmed version of the values). Because the two values might include quotation marks and other characters that would conflict with the form's "stickiness," each variable's value is sent through `htmlentities()`, too.

8. Complete the HTML page:

```
</body>
</html>
```

9. Save the file as **pcre.php**, place it in your web directory, and test it in your browser.

Although you don't know the rules for creating patterns yet, you could use any other literal value. Remember to use delimiters around the pattern or you'll see an error message 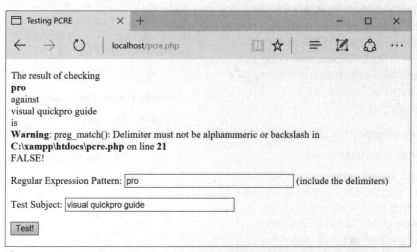.

TIP Many text editors allow you to use regular expressions to match and replace patterns within and throughout several documents.

TIP The PCRE functions all use the established locale. A locale reflects a computer's designated country and language, among other settings.

TIP Previous versions of PHP supported another type of regular expressions called POSIX. These have since been dropped from the language.

D If you fail to wrap the pattern in matching delimiters, you'll see an error message.

Defining Simple Patterns

Using one of PHP's regular expression functions is really easy; defining patterns to use is hard. There are lots of rules for creating a pattern. You can use these rules separately or in combination, making your pattern either quite simple or very complex. To start, then, you'll see what characters are used to define a simple pattern. As a formatting rule, I'll define patterns in **bold** and will indicate what the pattern matches in *italics*. Just to keep things cleaner. the patterns in these explanations won't be placed within delimiters or quotes (both are needed when used within `preg_match()`).

The first type of character you will use for defining patterns is a *literal*. A literal is a value that is written exactly as it is interpreted. For example, the pattern **a** will match the letter *a*, **ab** will match *ab*, and so forth. Therefore, assuming a case-insensitive search is performed, **rom** will match any of the following strings, since they all contain *rom*:

- CD-ROM
- Rommel crossed the desert.
- I'm writing a roman à clef.

Along with literals, your patterns will use *meta-characters*. These are special symbols that have a meaning beyond their literal value (**Table 14.1**). While **a** simply means *a*, the period (.) will match any single character except for a newline (. matches *a*, *b*, *c*, the underscore, a space, etc., just not **\n**). To match any meta-character, you will need to escape it, much as you escape a quotation mark to print it. Hence **\.** will match the period itself. So **1.99** matches *1.99* or *1B99* or *1299* (a 1

followed by any character followed by 99) but **1\.99** only matches *1.99*.

Two meta-characters specify where certain characters must be found. There is the caret (**^**), which marks the beginning of a pattern. There is also the dollar sign (**$**), which marks the conclusion of a pattern. Accordingly, **^a** will match any string beginning with an *a*, whereas **a$** will correspond to any string ending with an *a*. Therefore, **^a$** will only match *a* (a string that both begins and ends with *a*).

These two meta-characters—the caret and the dollar sign—are crucial to *validation*, because validation normally requires checking the value of an entire string, not just the presence of one string in another. For example, using an email-matching pattern without those two characters will match any string containing an email address. Using an email-matching pattern that begins with a caret and ends with a dollar sign will match a string that contains *only* a valid email address.

TABLE 14.1 Meta-Characters

Character	Meaning
\	Escape character
^	Indicates the beginning of a string
$	Indicates the end of a string
.	Any single character except newline
|	Alternatives (or)
[	Start of a class
]	End of a class
(	Start of a subpattern
)	End of a subpattern
{	Start of a quantifier
}	End of a quantifier

Regular expressions also make use of the pipe (|) as the equivalent of *or*: **a|b** will match strings containing either *a* or *b*. (Using the pipe within patterns is called *alternation* or *branching*.) So **yes|no** accepts either of those two words in their entirety (the alternation is *not* just between the two letters surrounding it: *s* and *n*).

Once you comprehend the basic symbols, then you can begin to use parentheses to group characters into more involved patterns. Grouping works as you might expect: **(abc)** will match *abc*, **(trout)** will match *trout*. Think of parentheses as being used to establish a new literal of a larger size. Because of precedence rules in PCRE, **yes|no** and **(yes)|(no)** are equivalent. But **(even|heavy) handed** will match either *even handed* or *heavy handed*.

To use simple patterns:

1. Load **pcre.php** in your browser, if you haven't already.

2. Check whether a string contains the letters *cat* **A**.

   To do so, use the literal *cat* as the pattern and any number of strings as the subject. Any of the following would be a match: *catalog*, *catastrophe*, *my cat left*. For the time being, use all lower-case letters, since *cat* will not match *Cat* **B**.

   Remember to use delimiters around the pattern as well (see the figures).

continues on next page

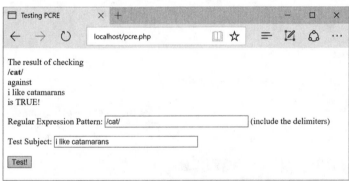

A Looking for a cat in a string.

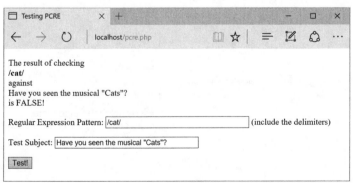

B PCRE performs a case-sensitive comparison by default.

3. Check whether a string starts with *cat* 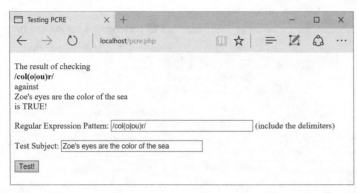.

To have a pattern apply to the start of a string, use the caret as the first character (**^cat**). The sentence *my cat left* will not be a match now.

4. Check whether a string contains the word *color* or *colour* 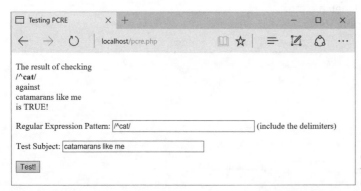.

The pattern to look for the American or British spelling of this word is **col(o|ou)r**. The first three letters—*col*—must be present. This needs to be followed by either an *o* or *ou*. Finally, an *r* is required.

TIP If you are looking to match an exact string within another string, use the `strstr()` function, which is faster than regular expressions. In fact, as a rule of thumb, you should use regular expressions only if the task at hand cannot be accomplished using any other function or technique.

TIP You can escape a lot of characters in a pattern using **\Q** and **\E**. Every character within those will be treated literally (so **\Q$2.99?\E** matches $2.99?).

TIP To match a single backslash, you have to use ****. The reason is that matching a backslash in a regular expression requires you to escape the backslash, resulting in ****. Then to use a backslash in a PHP string, it also has to be escaped, so escaping both backslashes means a total of four.

C The caret in a pattern means that the match has to be found at the start of the string.

D By using the pipe metacharacter, the performed search can be more flexible.

Using Quantifiers

You've just seen and practiced with a couple of the meta-characters, the most important of which are the caret and the dollar sign. Next, there are three meta-characters that allow for multiple occurrences: **a*** will match zero or more *a*'s (no *a*'s, *a*, *aa*, *aaa*, etc.); a+ matches one or more *a*'s (*a*, *aa*, *aaa*, etc., but there must be at least one); and **a?** will match up to one *a* (*a* or no *a*'s)

TABLE 14.2 Quantifiers

Character	Meaning
?	0 or 1
*	0 or more
+	1 or more
{x}	Exactly x occurrences
{x,y}	Between x and y (inclusive)
{x,}	At least x occurrences

A The plus sign, when used as a quantifier, requires that one or more of a thing be present.

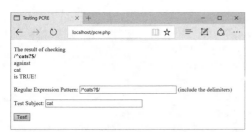

B You can check for the plural form of many words by adding *s?* to the pattern.

match). These meta-characters all act as quantifiers in your patterns, as do the curly braces. **Table 14.2** lists all the quantifiers.

To match a certain quantity of a thing, put the quantity between braces ({}), stating a specific number, just a minimum, or both a minimum and a maximum. Thus, **a{3}** will match *aaa*; **a{3,}** will match *aaa*, *aaaa*, etc. (three or more *a*'s); and **a{3,5}** will match just *aaa*, *aaaa*, and *aaaaa* (between three and five).

Note that quantifiers apply to the thing that came before it, so **a?** matches zero or one *a*'s, **ab?** matches an *a* followed by zero or one *b*'s, but **(ab)?** matches zero or one *ab*'s. Therefore, to match *color* or *colour*, you could also use **colou?r** as the pattern.

To use quantifiers:

1. Load **pcre.php** in your browser, if you haven't already.

2. Check whether a string contains the letters *c* and *t*, with one or more letters in between **A**.

   To do so, use **c.+t** as the pattern and any number of strings as the subject. Remember that the period matches any character (except for the newline). Each of the following would be a match: *cat*, *count*, *coefficient*, etc. The word *doctor* would not match, since there are no letters between the *c* and the *t* (although *doctor* would match **c.*t**).

3. Check whether a string matches either *cat* or *cats* **B**.

continues on next page

To start, if you want to make an exact match, use both the caret and the dollar sign. Then you'd have the literal text *cat*, followed by an *s*, followed by a question mark (representing 0 or 1 *s*'s). The final pattern—**^cats?$**—matches *cat* or *cats* but not *my cat left* or *I like cats*.

4. Check whether a string ends with *.33*, *.333*, or *.3333* 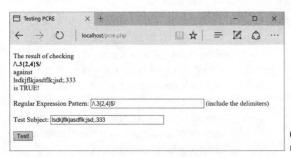.

To find a period, escape it with a backslash: **\\.**. To find a three, use a literal **3**. To find a range of 3's, use the braces (**{}**). Putting this together, the pattern is **\\.3{2,4}**. Because the string should end with this (nothing else can follow), conclude the pattern with a dollar sign: **\\.3{2,4}$**.

Admittedly, this is kind of a silly example (I'm not sure when you'd need to do exactly this), but it does demonstrate several things. This pattern will match lots of things—*12.333, varmit.3333, .33, look .33*—but not *12.3* or *12.334*.

5. Match a five-digit number 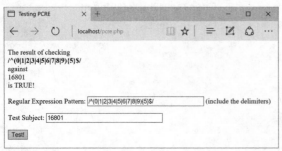.

A number can be any one of the numbers 0 through 9, so the heart of the pattern is **(0|1|2|3|4|5|6|7|8|9)**. Plainly said, this means a number is a 0 or a 1 or a 2 or a 3.... To make it a five-digit number, follow this with a quantifier: **(0|1|2|3|4|5|6|7|8|9){5}**. Finally, to match this exactly (as opposed to matching a five-digit number within a string), use the caret and the dollar sign: **^(0|1|2|3|4|5|6|7|8|9){5}$**.

This, of course, is one way to match a U.S. zip code, a very useful pattern.

TIP When using braces to specify a number of characters, you must always include the minimum number. The maximum is optional: **a{3}** and **a{3,}** are acceptable, but **a{,3}** is not.

TIP Although learning how to write and execute your own regular expressions demonstrates good dedication to programming, numerous working examples are available already by searching the Internet.

The result of checking
/\.3{2,4}$/
against
lsdkjflkjasdflk;jsd;.333
is TRUE!

Regular Expression Pattern: /\.3{2,4}$/ (include the delimiters)

Test Subject: lsdkjflkjasdflk;jsd;.333

Test!

C The braces let you dictate the acceptable range of quantities present.

The result of checking
/^(0|1|2|3|4|5|6|7|8|9){5}$/
against
16801
is TRUE!

Regular Expression Pattern: /^(0|1|2|3|4|5|6|7|8|9){5}$/ (include the delimiters)

Test Subject: 16801

Test!

D The proper test for confirming that a number contains five digits.

Using Character Classes

As the last example demonstrated (**D** in the previous section), relying solely on literals in a pattern can be tiresome. Having to write out all those digits to match any number is silly. Imagine if you wanted to match any four-letter word: ^(a|b|c|d...){4}$ (and that doesn't even take into account uppercase letters)! To make these common references easier, you can use *character classes*.

Classes are created by placing characters within brackets (**[]**). For example, you can match any one vowel with **[aeiou]**. This is equivalent to **(a|e|i|o|u)**. Or you can use the hyphen to indicate a range of characters: **[a-z]** is any single lowercase letter and **[A-Z]** is any uppercase, **[A-Za-z]** is any letter in general, and **[0-9]** matches any digit. As an example, **[a-z]{3}** would match *abc*, *def*, *oiw*, etc.

Within classes, most of the meta-characters are treated literally, except for four. The backslash is still the escape, but the caret (^) is a negation operator when used as the first character in the class. So [^aeiou] will match any non-vowel. The only other meta-character within a class is the dash, which indicates a range. (If the dash is used as the last character in a class, it's a literal dash.) And, of course, the closing bracket (]) still has meaning as the terminator of the class.

Naturally, a class can have both ranges and literal characters. A person's first name, which can contain letters, spaces, apostrophes, and periods, could be represented by **[A-z '.]** (again, the period doesn't need to be escaped within the class, since it loses its meta-meaning there).

Along with creating your own classes, there are six already-defined classes that have their own shortcuts (**Table 14.3**). The digit and space classes are easy to understand. The term *word* doesn't mean "word" in the language sense but rather as in a string unbroken by spaces or punctuation.

Using this information, the five-digit number (aka, zip code) pattern could more easily be written as ^**[0-9]{5}$** or ^**\d{5}$**. As another example, **can\s?not** will match both *can not* and *cannot* (the word *can*, followed by zero or one space characters, followed by *not*).

TABLE 14.3 Character Classes

Class	Shortcut	Meaning
[0-9]	\d	Any digit
[\f\r\t\n\v]	\s	Any white space
[A-Za-z0-9_]	\w	Any word character
[^0-9]	\D	Not a digit
[^\f\r\t\n\v]	\S	Not white space
[^A-Za-z0-9_]	\W	Not a word character

To use character classes:

1. Load **pcre.php** in your browser, if you haven't already.

2. Check whether a string is formatted as a valid U.S. zip code **A**.

   A U.S. zip code always starts with five digits (^\d{5}). But a valid zip code could also have a dash followed by another four digits (-\d{4}$). To make this last part optional, use the question mark (the 0 or 1 quantifier). This complete pattern is then ^(\d{5})(-\d{4})?$. To make it all clearer, the first part of the pattern (matching the five digits) is also grouped in parentheses, although this isn't required in this case.

3. Check whether a string contains no spaces **B**.

The \S character class shortcut will match non-space characters. To make sure that the entire string contains no spaces, use the caret and the dollar sign: ^\S$. If you don't use those, then all the pattern is confirming is that the subject contains at least one non-space character.

4. Validate an email address **C**.

   The pattern ^[\w.-]+@[\w.-]+\.[A-Za-z]{2,6}$ provides for reasonably good email validation. It's wrapped in the caret and the dollar sign, so the string must be a valid email address and nothing more. An email address starts with letters, numbers, and the underscore (represented by \w), plus a period (.) and a dash. This first block will match *larryullman*, *larry77*, *larry.ullman*, *larry-ullman*, and so on. Next, all email addresses include one

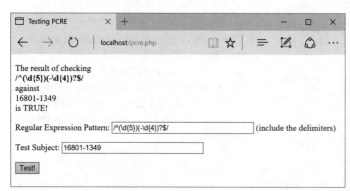

A The pattern to match a U.S. zip code, in either the five-digit or five-plus-four format.

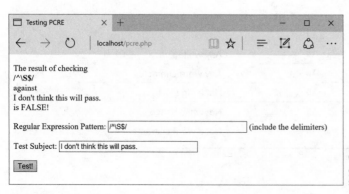

B The no-white-space shortcut can be used to ensure that a submitting string is contiguous.

and only one @. After that, there can be any number of letters, numbers, periods, and dashes. This is the domain name: *larryullman*, *smith-jones*, *amazon.co* (as in *amazon.co.uk*), etc. Finally, all email addresses conclude with one period and between two and six letters. This accounts for *.com*, *.edu*, *.info*, *.travel*, and so forth.

TIP I think that the zip code example is a great demonstration of how complex and useful regular expressions are. One pattern accurately tests for both formats of the zip code, which is fantastic. But when you put this into your PHP code, with quotes and delimiters, it's not easily understood:

```
if (preg_match ('/^(\d{5})(-\d{4})?$/',
→ $zip)) {
```

That certainly looks like gibberish, right?

TIP This email address validation pattern is pretty good, although not perfect. It will allow some invalid addresses to pass through (like ones starting with a period or containing multiple periods together). However, a 100 percent foolproof validation pattern is ridiculously long, and frequently using regular expressions is really a matter of trying to exclude the bulk of invalid entries without inadvertently excluding any valid ones.

TIP Regular expressions, particularly PCRE ones, can be extremely complex. When you're starting out, it's just as likely that your use of them will break the validation routines rather than improve them. That's why practicing like this is important.

C A pretty good and reliable validation for email addresses.

Using Boundaries

Boundaries are shortcuts for helping to find, um, boundaries. In a way, you've already seen this: using the caret and the dollar sign to match the beginning or end of a value. But what if you wanted to match boundaries within a value?

The clearest boundary is between a word and a non-word. A "word" in this case is not *cat*, *month*, or *zeitgeist*, but in the **\w** shortcut sense: the letters A through Z (both upper- and lowercase), plus the numbers 0 through 9, and the underscore. To use words as boundaries, we have the **\b** shortcut. To use non-word characters as boundaries, we have **\B**. So the pattern **\bfor\b** matches *they've come for you* but doesn't match *force* or *forebode*. Therefore, **\bfor\B** would match *force* but not *they've come for you* or *informal*.

Finding All Matches

Going back to the PHP functions used with Perl-compatible regular expressions, **preg_match()** has been used just to see whether or not a pattern matches a value. But the script hasn't been reporting what, exactly, in the value did match the pattern. You can find out this information by providing a variable as a third argument to the function:

preg_match(pattern, subject, $match);

The **$match** variable will contain the first match found (because this function only returns the first match in a value). To find every match, use **preg_match_all()**. Its syntax is the same:

preg_match_all(pattern, subject, → $matches);

This function will return the number of matches made, or FALSE if none were found. It will also assign to **$matches** every match made. Let's update the PHP script to print the returned matches, and then run a couple of more tests.

To report all matches:

1. Open **pcre.php** (Script 14.1) in your text editor or IDE, if you haven't already.

2. Change the invocation of **preg_match()** to (Script 14.2)

   if (preg_match_all($pattern, → $subject, $matches)) {

   There are two changes here. First, the actual function being called is different. Second, the third argument is provided a variable name that will be assigned every match.

3. After printing the value *TRUE*, print the contents of **$matches**:

   echo '<pre>' . print_r($matches, → 1) . '</pre>';

Script 14.2 To reveal exactly what values in a string match which patterns, this revised version of the script will print each match. You can retrieve the matches by naming a variable as the third argument in **preg_match()** or **preg_match_all()**.

```
1    <!doctype html>
2    <html lang="en">
3    <head>
4    <meta charset="utf-8">
5    <title>Testing PCRE</title>
6    </head>
7    <body>
8    <?php # Script 14.2 - matches.php
9    // This script takes a submitted string
     and checks it against a submitted
     pattern.
10   // This version prints every match made.
11
12   if ($_SERVER['REQUEST_METHOD'] == 'POST')
     {
13
14   // Trim the strings:
15   $pattern = trim($_POST['pattern']);
16   $subject = trim($_POST['subject']);
17
18   // Print a caption:
19   echo "<p>The result of
     checking<br><strong>$pattern</strong><br>
     against<br>$subject<br>is ";
20
21   // Test:
22   if (preg_match_all($pattern,
     $subject, $matches) ) {
23       echo 'TRUE!</p>';
24
25       // Print the matches:
26       echo '<pre>' . print_r($matches,
         1) . '</pre>';
27
28   } else {
29       echo 'FALSE!</p>';
30   }
31
32   } // End of submission IF.
33   // Display the HTML form.
34   ?>
35   <form action="matches.php"
     method="post">
```

code continues on next page

```
36    <p>Regular Expression Pattern:
      <input type="text" name="pattern"
      value="<?php if (isset($pattern)) echo
      htmlentities($pattern); ?>" size="40">
      (include the delimiters)</p>
37    <p>Test Subject: <textarea
      name="subject" rows="5"
      cols="40"><?php if (isset($subject))
      echo htmlentities($subject);
      ?></textarea></p>
38    <input type="submit" name="submit"
      value="Test!">
39    </form>
40    </body>
41    </html>
```

Using **print_r()** to output the contents of the variable is the easiest way to know what's in **$matches** (you could use a **foreach** loop instead). As you'll see when you run this script, this variable will be an array whose first element is an array of matches made.

4. Change the form's **action** attribute to *matches.php*:

   <form action="matches.php"
   → method="post">

   This script will be renamed, so the **action** attribute must be changed, too.

5. Change the subject input to be a textarea:

   <p>Test Subject: <textarea
   → name="subject" rows="5"
   → cols="40"><?php if (isset
   → ($subject)) echo htmlentities
   → ($subject); ?></textarea></p>

   To be able to enter in more text for the subject, this element will become a textarea.

continues on next page

Being Less Greedy

A key component to Perl-compatible regular expressions is the concept of *greediness*. By default, PCRE will attempt to match as much as possible. For example, the pattern <.+> matches any HTML tag. When tested on a string like *<a href="page.php">Link</a>*, it will actually match that entire string, from the opening < to the closing one. This string contains three possible matches, though: the entire string, the opening tag (from *<a* to *">*), and the closing tag (*</a>*).

To overrule greediness, make the match *lazy*. A lazy match will contain as little data as possible. Any quantifier can be made lazy by following it with the question mark. For example, the pattern <.+?> would return two matches in the preceding string: the opening tag and the closing tag. It would not return the whole string as a match. (This is one of the confusing aspects of the regular expression syntax: the same character—here, the question mark—can have different meanings depending on its context.)

Another way to make patterns less greedy is to use negative classes. The pattern <[^>]+> matches everything between the opening and closing <> except for a closing >. So using this pattern would have the same result as using <.+?>. This pattern would also match strings that contain newline characters, which the period excludes.

6. Save the file as **matches.php**, place it in your web directory, and test it in your browser.

For the first test, use **for** as the pattern and *This is a formulaic test for informal matches.* as the subject . It may not be proper English, but it's a good test subject.

For the second test, change the pattern to **for.*** 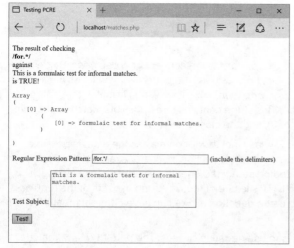. The result may surprise you, the cause of which is discussed in the sidebar "Being Less Greedy." To make this search less greedy, the pattern could be changed to **for.*?**, whose results would be the same as those in 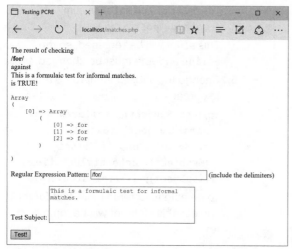.

Ⓐ This first test returns three matches, since the literal text *for* was found three times.

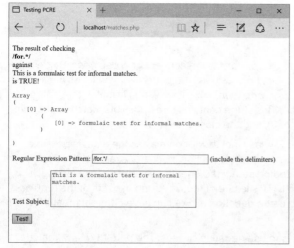

Ⓑ Because regular expressions are "greedy" by default (see the sidebar), this pattern finds only one match in the string. That match happens to start with the first instance of *for* and continues until the end of the string.

For the third test, use **for[\S]***, or, more simply **for\S*** 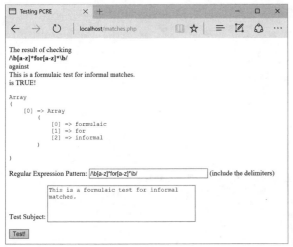. This has the effect of making the match stop as soon as a white space character is found (because the pattern wants to match *for* followed by any number of non–white space characters).

For the final test, use **\b[a-z]*for[a-z]*\b** as the pattern **D**. This pattern makes use of boundaries, discussed in the sidebar "Using Boundaries," earlier in the chapter.

TIP The `preg_split()` function will take a string and break it into an array using a regular expression pattern.

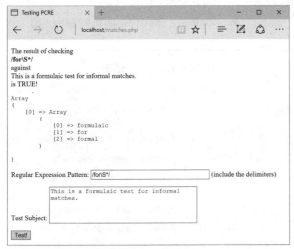

C This revised pattern matches strings that begin with *for* and end on a word.

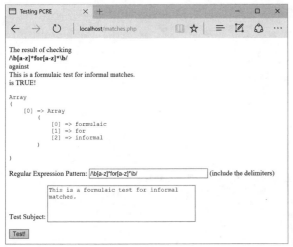

D Unlike the pattern in **C**, this one matches entire words that contain *for* (*informal* here, *formal* in **C**).

Using Modifiers

The majority of the special characters you can use in regular expression patterns are introduced in this chapter. One final type of special character is the pattern modifier. **Table 14.4** lists these. Pattern modifiers are different from the other meta-characters in that they are placed after the closing delimiter.

Of these modifiers, the most important is *i*, which enables case-insensitive searches. All the examples using variations on *for* (in the previous sequence of steps) would not match the word *For*. However, /**for.*/i** would be a match. Note that I am including the delimiters in that pattern, since the modifier goes after the closing delimiter. Similarly, the last step in the previous sequence referenced the sidebar "Being Less Greedy" and stated how **for.*?** would perform a lazy search. So would /**for.*/U**.

The multiline mode is interesting in that you can make the caret and the dollar sign behave differently. By default, each applies to the entire value. In multiline mode, the caret matches the beginning of any line and the dollar sign matches the end of any line.

To use modifiers:

1. Load **matches.php** in your browser, if you haven't already.

2. Validate a list of email addresses 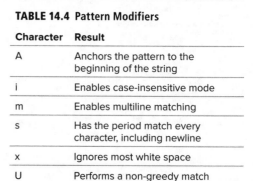.

TABLE 14.4 Pattern Modifiers

Character	Result
A	Anchors the pattern to the beginning of the string
i	Enables case-insensitive mode
m	Enables multiline matching
s	Has the period match every character, including newline
x	Ignores most white space
U	Performs a non-greedy match

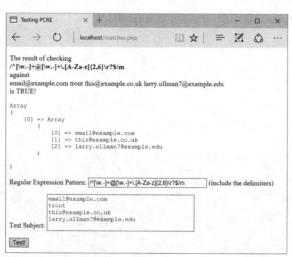

Ⓐ A list of email addresses, one per line, can be validated using the multiline mode. Each valid address is stored in **$matches**.

To do so, use /^[\w.-]+@[\w.-]+\.[A-Za-z]{2,6}\r?$/m as the pattern. You'll see that I've added an optional carriage return (\r?) before the dollar sign. This is necessary because some of the lines will contain returns and others won't. And in multiline mode, the dollar sign matches the end of a line. (To be more flexible, you could use \s? instead.)

3. Validate a list of U.S. zip codes **B**.

Very similar to the example in Step 2, the pattern is now /^(\d{5})(-\d{4})?\s?$/m. You'll see that I'm using the more flexible \s? instead of \r?.

You'll also notice when you try this yourself (or in **B**) that the **$matches** variable contains a lot more information now. This will be explained in the next section of the chapter.

TIP To always match the start or end of a pattern, regardless of the multiline setting, you can use shortcuts. Within the pattern, the shortcut \A will match only the very beginning of the value, \z matches the very end, and \Z matches any line end, like $ in single-line mode.

TIP It's probably best to use the Filter extension, covered in Chapter 13, "Security Methods," to validate an email address or a URL. But if you have to validate a list of either, the Filter extension won't cut it, and regular expressions will be required.

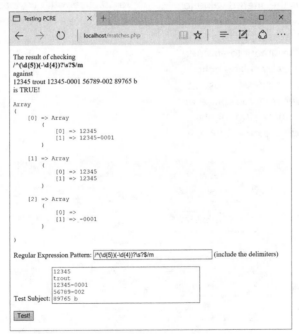

B Validating a list of zip codes, one per line.

Matching and Replacing Patterns

The last subject to discuss in this chapter is how to match and replace patterns in a value. Although **preg_match()** and **preg_match_all()** will find things for you, if you want to do a search and replace, you'll need to use **preg_replace()**. Its syntax is

```
preg_replace(pattern, replacement,
→ subject);
```

This function takes an optional fourth argument limiting the number of replacements made.

To replace all instances of *cat* with *dog*, you would use

```
$str = preg_replace('/cat/', 'dog',
→ 'I like my cat');
```

This function returns the altered value (or unaltered value if no matches were made), so you'll likely want to assign it to a variable or use it as an argument to another function (like printing it by calling **echo**). Also, as a reminder, the above is just an example: you'd never want to replace one literal string with another using regular expressions; use **str_replace()** instead.

There is a related concept to discuss that is involved with this function: *back referencing*. In a zip code–matching pattern—**^(\d{5})(-\d{4})?$**—there are two groups within parentheses: the first five digits and the optional dash plus four-digit extension. Within a regular expression pattern, PHP will automatically number parenthetical groupings beginning at 1. Back referencing allows you to refer to each individual section by using **$** plus the corresponding number. For example, if you match the zip code *94710-0001* with this pattern, referring back to **$2** will give you *-0001*. The code **$0** refers to the whole initial string. This is why Ⓑ in the previous section shows entire zip code matches in **$matches[0]**, the matching first five digits in **$matches[1]**, and any matching dash plus four digits in **$matches[2]**.

To practice with this, let's modify Script 14.2 to also take a replacement input Ⓐ.

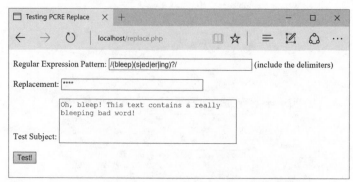

Ⓐ One use of **preg_replace()** would be to replace variations on inappropriate words with symbols representing their omission.

To match and replace patterns:

1. Open **matches.php** (Script 14.2) in your text editor or IDE, if you haven't already.

2. Add a reference to a third incoming variable (**Script 14.3**):

   $replace = trim($_POST['replace']);

   As you can see in **A**, the third form input (added between the existing two) takes the replacement value. That value is also trimmed to get rid of any extraneous spaces.

3. Change the caption:

   ```
   echo "<p>The result of replacing
   → <br><strong>$pattern</strong>
   → <br>with<br>$replace<br>in<br>
   → $subject<br><br>";
   ```

   The caption will print all the incoming values prior to applying **preg_replace()**.

4. Change the regular expression conditional so that it calls **preg_replace()** only if a match is made:

   ```
   if (preg_match($pattern,
   → $subject) ) {
       echo preg_replace($pattern,
       → $replace, $subject) .'</p>';
   } else {
       echo 'The pattern was not
       → found!</p>';
   }
   ```

   You can call **preg_replace()** without running **preg_match()** first. If no match was made, then no replacement will occur. But to make it clear when a match is or is not being made (which is always good to confirm, considering how tricky regular expressions are), the **preg_match()** function will be applied first. If it returns a TRUE value, then **preg_replace()** is called, printing the results **B**. Otherwise, a message is printed indicating that no match was made **C**.

continues on page 481

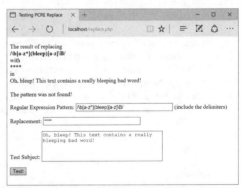

B The resulting text has uses of bleep, bleeps, bleeped, bleeper, and bleeping replaced with ****.

C If the pattern is not found within the subject, the subject will not be changed.

Script 14.3 To test the `preg_replace()` function, which replaces a matched pattern in a string with another value, you can use this third version of the PCRE test script.

```
1    <!doctype html>
2    <html lang="en">
3    <head>
4        <meta charset="utf-8">
5        <title>Testing PCRE Replace</title>
6    </head>
7    <body>
8    <?php # Script 14.3 - replace.php
9    // This script takes a submitted string and checks it against a submitted pattern.
10   // This version replaces one value with another.
11
12   if ($_SERVER['REQUEST_METHOD'] == 'POST') {
13
14       // Trim the strings:
15       $pattern = trim($_POST['pattern']);
16       $subject = trim($_POST['subject']);
17       $replace = trim($_POST['replace']);
18
19       // Print a caption:
20       echo "<p>The result of replacing<br><strong>$pattern</strong><br>with<br>$replace<br>in<br>
         $subject<br><br>";
21
22       // Check for a match:
23       if (preg_match($pattern, $subject) ) {
24           echo preg_replace($pattern, $replace, $subject) . '</p>';
25       } else {
26           echo 'The pattern was not found!</p>';
27       }
28
29   } // End of submission IF.
30   // Display the HTML form.
31   ?>
32   <form action="replace.php" method="post">
33       <p>Regular Expression Pattern: <input type="text" name="pattern" value="<?php if
         (isset($pattern)) echo htmlentities($pattern); ?>" size="40"> (include the delimiters)</p>
34       <p>Replacement: <input type="text" name="replace" value="<?php if (isset($replace))
         echo htmlentities($replace); ?>" size="40"></p>
35       <p>Test Subject: <textarea name="subject" rows="5" cols="40"><?php if (isset($subject))
         echo htmlentities($subject); ?></textarea></p>
36       <input type="submit" name="submit" value="Test!">
37   </form>
38   </body>
39   </html>
```

5. Change the form's **action** attribute to *replace.php*:

```
<form action="replace.php"
→ method="post">
```

This file will be renamed, so this value needs to be changed accordingly.

6. Add a text input for the replacement string:

```
<p>Replacement: <input
→ type="text" name="replace"
→ value="<?php if (isset($replace))
→ echo htmlentities($replace); ?>"
→ size="40"></p>
```

7. Save the file as **replace.php**, place it in your web directory, and test it in your browser **D**.

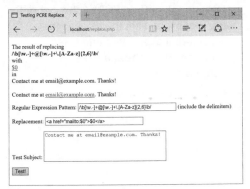

D Another use of **preg_replace()** is dynamically turning email addresses into clickable links. See the HTML source code for the full effect of the replacement.

As a good example, you can turn an email address found within some text into its HTML link equivalent: **<a href="mailto:email@example. com">email@example.com</a>**. The pattern for matching an email address should be familiar by now: **^[\w.-]+@[\w.-]+\.[A-Za-z]{2,6}$**. However, because the email address could be found within some text, the caret and dollar sign need to be replaced by the word boundaries shortcut: **\b**. The final pattern is therefore **/\b[\w.-]+@[\w.-]+\.[A-Za-z]{2,6}\b/**.

To refer to this matched email address, you can refer to **$0** (because **$0** refers to the entire match, whether or not parentheses are used). So the replacement value would be *<a href="mailto:$0"> $0</a>*. Because HTML is involved here, look at the HTML source code of the resulting page for the best idea of what happened.

TIP Back references can even be used within the pattern. For example, if a pattern included a grouping (i.e., a subpattern), that would be repeated.

TIP I've introduced, somewhat quickly, the bulk of the PCRE syntax here, but there's much more to it. Once you've mastered all this, you can consider moving on to anchors, named subpatterns, comments, lookarounds, possessive quantifiers, and more.

Review and Pursue

If you have any problems with the review questions or the pursue prompts, turn to the book's supporting forum (`LarryUllman.com/forums/`).

Review

- What function is used to match a regular expression? What function is used to find all matches of a regular expression? What function is used to replace matches of a regular expression?

- What characters can you use and not use to delineate a regular expression?

- How do you match a literal character or string of characters?

- What are meta-characters? How do you escape a meta-character?

- What meta-character do you use to bind a pattern to the beginning of a string? To the end?

- How do you create subpatterns (aka groupings)?

- What are the quantifiers? How do you require 0 or 1 of a character or string? 0 or more? 1 or more? Precisely *X* occurrences? A range of occurrences? A minimum of occurrences?

- What are character classes?

- What meta-characters still have meaning within character classes?

- What shortcut represents the "any digit" character class? The "any white space" class? "Any word"? What shortcuts represent the opposite of these?

- What are boundaries? How do you create boundaries in patterns?

- How do you make matches "lazy"? And what does that mean anyway?

- What are the pattern modifiers?

- What is *back referencing*? How does it work?

Pursue

- Search online for a PCRE "cheat sheet" (PHP or otherwise) that lists all the meaningful characters and classes. Print the cheat sheet and keep it beside your computer.

- Practice, practice, practice!

Introducing
jQuery

As JavaScript has developed into a more valuable language over the past two decades, its meaningful usage has become commonplace in today's web sites. Accordingly, many PHP developers are expected to know a bit of JavaScript as well. Often this means learning jQuery, a popular JavaScript framework.

Although this chapter cannot present full coverage of JavaScript or jQuery, you'll learn more than enough to be able to add to your PHP-based projects the features that users have come to expect. In the process, you'll also learn some basics of programming in JavaScript in general, and get a sense of into which areas of jQuery you may want to further delve.

In This Chapter

What Is jQuery?

To grasp jQuery, you must have a solid sense of what JavaScript is. As discussed in Chapter 11, "Web Application Development," JavaScript is a programming language that's primarily used to add dynamic features to HTML pages. Unlike PHP, which always runs on the server, JavaScript generally runs on the client (JavaScript is starting to be used as a server-side tool, too, although that's still more on the fringe). PHP, precisely because it is server-side, is browser-agnostic for the most part; very few things you'll do in PHP will have different results from one browser to the next. Conversely, precisely because it's running in the browser, JavaScript code often has to be customized for the variations in browsers. For many years, this was the bane of the web developer: creating reliable cross-browser code. Overcoming this hurdle is one of the many strengths of jQuery (**www.jquery.com** Ⓐ).

jQuery is a JavaScript framework. A framework is defined as a library of code whose use can expedite and simplify development. The core of the jQuery framework can handle all key JavaScript functionality, as you'll see in this chapter. But the framework is extendable via plug-ins to provide other features, such as the ability to create a dynamic, paginated, sortable table of data. In fact, several useful user interface tools have been wrapped inside their own bundle, jQuery UI (**www.jqueryui.com** Ⓑ). There's also jQuery Mobile (**www.jquerymobile.com**), which supports a touch interface and other features commonly used on smartphones and tablets.

Ⓐ The home page for the jQuery JavaScript framework.

Ⓑ The home page for the jQuery User Interface library (jQuery UI), which works in conjunction with jQuery.

Debugging JavaScript

To this point, you may not have thought it so wonderful that PHP dumped all its errors into your browser, shoving your mistakes in your face. Until now. When HTML pages have JavaScript errors, you rarely are notified. To debug problematic JavaScript code, the first thing you'll need to do is see what actual errors exist.

The first tool you'll need when programming in JavaScript is a good debugging browser. For years, Firefox (**www.mozilla.com**) was the clear champion in this regard, with Opera (**www.opera.com**) and Google Chrome (**www.google.com/chrome/**) close behind.

By now, all the major browsers, including Microsoft's Internet Explorer and Edge, include a solid set of developer tools. Look online for instructions on using the developer tools built into your favorite browser.

While researching, you may want to also see what additional extensions exist for your browser. Running your JavaScript-enabled pages in-browser with excellent developer tools or extensions will make it easier for you to debug any problems that occur.

Many JavaScript frameworks are out there, and in no way am I claiming jQuery is the best. I do use jQuery frequently, however, and it quickly earned a place as one of the premier JavaScript frameworks. As you'll soon see, jQuery has a simple, albeit cryptic, syntax, and by using it, you can manipulate the Document Object Model (DOM) with aplomb. This is to say that you can easily reference elements within an HTML page, thereby grabbing the values of form inputs, adding or removing any kind of HTML element, changing element properties, and so forth.

Before getting into the particulars of using jQuery, I want you to understand that jQuery is just a JavaScript framework, meaning that what you'll actually be doing over the next several pages is JavaScript programming. JavaScript as a language, though similar in some ways to PHP, differs in other ways, such as how variables are created, what character is used to perform concatenation, and so forth. Moreover, JavaScript is an *object-oriented language*, meaning the syntax you'll sometimes see will be that much different than the procedural PHP programming you've done to this point (the next chapter introduces object-oriented programming [OOP] in PHP). Because you'll inevitably have problems—like simply omitting a closing brace—you'llneed to know a bit about how to debug JavaScript. For a quick introduction to that subject, see the sidebar.

For examples of server-side JavaScript, check out Node (**www.nodejs.org**).

Incorporating jQuery

JavaScript is built into all graphical browsers by default, meaning no special steps must be taken to include JavaScript in an HTML page (users have the option of disabling JavaScript, although statistically few do). jQuery is a framework of code, though; to use it, a page must first incorporate the jQuery library. Including any external JavaScript file in an HTML page involves the **script** tag, providing the name of the external file as the value of its **src** attribute:

```
<script src="file.js"></script>
```

The jQuery framework file will have a name like **jquery-X.Y.Z.min.js**, where *X.Y.Z* is the version number (3.2.1 as of this writing). The *min* part of the file's name indicates that the JavaScript file has been *minified*. *Minification* is the removal of spaces, newlines, and comments from code. The result is code that's barely legible 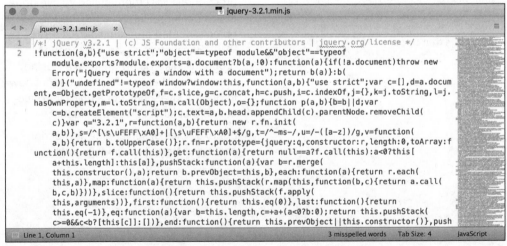 but still completely functional. The benefit of minified code is that it will load in the browser slightly faster because it will be a marginally smaller file size.

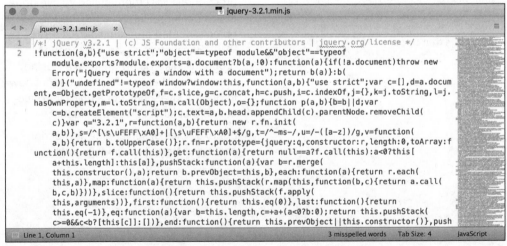

A What the minified jQuery code looks like.

The following set of steps will walk you through installing the jQuery library on your server and incorporating it into an HTML page; see the sidebar for an alternative approach.

To incorporate jQuery:

1. Load **www.jquery.com** in your browser.

2. At the top of the page, click *Download jQuery*.

3. On the resulting page, download the compressed, production version **B**.

4. If the JavaScript loads directly instead of being downloaded, save the page on your computer.

Because the resulting file is just JavaScript, it may load directly in your browser **A**. If so, save the file as **jquery-X.Y.Z.min.js**, where *X.Y.Z* is the actual version number.

continues on next page

---

jQuery

For help when upgrading jQuery, please see the <u>upgrade guide</u> most relevant to your version. We also recommend using the <u>jQuery Migrate plugin</u>.

Download the compressed, production jQuery 3.2.1

<u>Download the uncompressed, development jQuery 3.2.1</u>

<u>Download the map file for jQuery 3.2.1</u>

B The links for downloading the current version of jQuery.

Using Hosted jQuery

This chapter recommends that you download a copy of jQuery and place it in your web directory. Upon doing so, you just need to update the **script** tag to point to the location of the jQuery file on your site. I want to mention an alternative solution, though: using a *hosted* version of jQuery. By this, I mean that instead of using a version of the jQuery library stored on your own web server, you could use a version stored elsewhere online. For example, Google provides copies of many JavaScript frameworks for public use (**http://code.google.com/apis/libraries/**). To use Google's copy of the jQuery library, you'd use the following code:

```
<script src="https://ajax.googleapis.com/ajax/libs/jquery/3.2.1/jquery.min.js">
→ </script>
```

If you use Google's hosted version of jQuery, your site (i.e., your site's visitors) will likely see a performance boost, due to Google's Content Delivery Network (CDN) and the way browsers cache media.

On the other hand, using a hosted version makes your site's functionality dependent on another site's uptime. And your site is more vulnerable from a security perspective since it's assuming the other site is serving the jQuery library and not a virus. All that being said, it's fairly safe to say that Google's uptime and security model is probably better than yours (or mine)!

5. Move the downloaded file to a **js** folder within your web server directory.

All the JavaScript files to be used by this chapter's examples will be placed within a subdirectory named **js**.

6. Begin a new HTML document in your text editor or IDE, to be named **test.html** (Script 15.1):

```
<!doctype html>
<html lang="en">
<head>
  <meta charset="utf-8">
  <title>Testing jQuery</title>
</head>
<body>
  <!-- Script 15.1 - test.html -->
</body>
</html>
```

This very first example will simply test the incorporation and basic use of the jQuery library.

7. Within the HTML head, include jQuery:

```
<script src="js/jquery-3.2.1.min.
  js"></script>
```

The **script** tag is used to include a JavaScript file. Conventionally, **script** tags are placed within the HTML page's head, although that's not required (or always the case). The value of the **src** attribute needs to match the name and location of your jQuery library. In this case, the assumption is that this HTML page is in the same directory as the **js** folder, created as part of Step 5.

8. Save the file as **test.html**.

Because this script won't be executing any PHP, it uses the **.html** extension.

9. If you want, load the page in your browser and check for errors.

As this is just an HTML page, you can load it directly in a browser, without going through a URL. You can then use your browser's error console or other development tools (see the "Debugging JavaScript" sidebar) to check that no errors occurred in loading the JavaScript file.

Script 15.1 This blank HTML page shows how the jQuery library can be included.

```
1   <!doctype html>
2   <html lang="en">
3   <head>
4       <meta charset="utf-8">
5       <title>Testing jQuery</title>
6       <script src="js/jquery-3.2.1.min.js">
        </script>
7   </head>
8   <body>
9       <!-- Script 15.1 - test.html -->
10  </body>
11  </html>
```

Using jQuery

Once you successfully have jQuery incorporated into an HTML page, you can begin using it. jQuery, or any JavaScript code, can be written between opening and closing **script** tags:

```
<script>
// JavaScript goes here.
</script>
```

(Note that in JavaScript, the double slashes create comments, just as in PHP.)

Alternatively, you can place jQuery and JavaScript code within a separate file, and then include that file using the **script** tags, just as you included the jQuery library. This is the route to be used in this chapter, to further separate the JavaScript from the HTML.

To be clear, an HTML page can have multiple uses of the **script** tags, and the same **script** tag cannot both include an external file and contain JavaScript code.

The code placed within a **script** tag will be executed as soon as the browser encounters it. This is often problematic, though, because JavaScript is frequently used to interact with the DOM; if immediately executed JavaScript code references a DOM element, the code will fail, since that DOM element will not have been encountered by the browser at that point 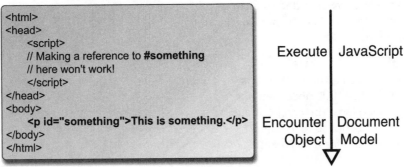. The only reliable way to reference DOM elements is after the browser has knowledge of the entire DOM.

In standard JavaScript, you can have code be executed after the page is completely loaded by referencing **window.onload**. In jQuery, the preferred method is to confirm that the web document is *ready*:

```
$(document).ready(some_function);
```

As mentioned already, the jQuery syntax can seem especially strange for the uninitiated, so I'll explain this in detail. First of all, the code **$(something)** is how elements and such within the browser are selected in jQuery. In this case, the item being selected is the entire HTML document. To this selection, the **ready()** function is applied. It takes one argument: a function to be called. Note that the argument is a reference to the function: its name, without quotation marks. Separately, **some_function()** would have to be defined, wherein the actual work—which should be done when the document is loaded—takes place.

continues on next page

HTML Page   Browser Load

A A browser reads a page as the HTML is loaded, meaning that JavaScript code cannot reference DOM elements until the browser has seen them all.

An alternative syntax is to use an *anonymous function*, which is a function definition without a name. Anonymous functions are common to JavaScript (anonymous functions are possible in PHP, too, but less common). To create an anonymous function, the function's definition is placed in line, in lieu of the function's name:

```
$(document).ready(function() {
    // Function code.
});
```

Because the need to execute code when the browser is ready is so common, this whole construct is often simplified in jQuery to just:

```
$(function() {
    // Function code.
});
```

The syntax is unusual, especially the **});** at the end, so be mindful of this as you program. As with any programming language, incorrect JavaScript syntax will make the code inoperable.

To test jQuery, this next sequence of steps will create a JavaScript alert once the document is ready **B**. After you have this simple test working, you can safely begin using jQuery more practically.

To use jQuery:

1. Create a new JavaScript document in your text editor or IDE, to be named **test.js** (Script 15.2):

   // Script 15.2 - test.js

   A JavaScript file has no **script** tags—those are in the HTML document—or other opening tags. You can just begin entering JavaScript code. Again, a double slash creates a comment.

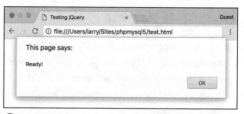

B This JavaScript alert is created once jQuery recognizes that the HTML document is ready in the browser.

Script 15.2 This simple JavaScript file creates an alert to test successful incorporation and use of the jQuery library.

```
1    // Script 15.2 - test.js
2    // This script is included by test.html.
3    // This script just creates an alert to
     test jQuery.
4
5    // Do something when the document is
     ready:
6    $(function() {
7
8        // Alert!
9        alert('Ready!');
10
11   });
```

2. Create an alert when the document is ready:

```
$(function() {
alert('Ready!');
});
```

This is just the syntax already explained, with a call to **alert()** in place of the *Function code* comment shown earlier. The **alert()** function takes a string as its argument, which will be used in the presented alert box **B**.

3. Save the file as **test.js** in your web server's **js** directory.

4. Open **test.html** (Script 15.1) in your text editor or IDE.

The next step is to update the HTML page so that it includes the new JavaScript file.

Script 15.3 The updated test HTML page loads a new JavaScript file.

```
1   <!doctype html>
2   <html lang="en">
3   <head>
4       <meta charset="utf-8">
5       <title>Testing jQuery</title>
6       <script src="js/jquery-3.2.1.min.js">
        </script>
7       <script src="js/test.js"></script>
8   </head>
9   <body>
10      <!-- Script 15.3 - test.html #2 -->
11  </body>
12  </html>
```

5. After including the jQuery library, include the new JavaScript file (**Script 15.3**):

```
<script src="js/test.js"></script>
```

Assuming that the **test.js** JavaScript file is placed in the same directory as the jQuery library, with the same relative location to **test.html**, this code will successfully incorporate it.

6. Save the HTML page and test it in your browser **B**.

If you do not see the alert window, you'll need to debug the JavaScript code.

TIP Technically, in OOP, a function is called a method. For the duration of this chapter, I'll continue to use the term "function," as it's likely to be more familiar to you.

TIP The code **$()** is shorthand for calling the **jQuery()** function.

TIP jQuery's "ready" status is slightly different than JavaScript's **onload**: the latter also waits for the loading of images and other media, whereas jQuery's ready status is triggered by the full loading of the DOM.

Selecting Page Elements

Once you've got basic jQuery functionality working, the next thing to learn is how to select page elements. Being able to do so will allow you to hide and show images or blocks of text, manipulate forms, and more.

You've already seen how to select the web document itself: **$(document)**. To select other page elements, use *CSS selectors* in place of **document**:

- **#something** selects the element with an **id** value of *something*.

- **.something** selects every element with a **class** value of *something*.

- **something** selects every element of *something* type (e.g., **p** selects every paragraph).

Those three rules are more than enough to get you started, but know that unlike **document**, each of these gets placed within quotation marks. For example, the code **$('a')** selects every link and **$('#caption')** selects the element with an **id** value of *caption*. By definition, no two elements in a single HTML page should have the same identifying value; thus, to reference individual elements on the page, **#something** is the easiest solution.

These rules can be combined as well:

- **$('img.landscape')** selects every image with a **class** of *landscape*.

- **$('#register input')** selects every input element found within an element that has an **id** of *register*.

For the next jQuery example, a JavaScript-driven version of the Widget Cost Calculator form, like the one from Chapter 13, "Security Methods," will be developed. In these next few steps, the HTML page will be created, with the appropriate elements, classes, and unique identifiers to be easily manipulated by jQuery **A**.

To create the HTML form:

1. Open **test.html** (Script 15.3) in your text editor or IDE, if you haven't already.

   Since this file is already jQuery enhanced, it'll be easiest to just update it.

2. Change the page's title (**Script 15.4**):

   ```
   <title>Widget Cost Calculator
   → </title>
   ```

3. After the page title, incorporate a CSS file:

   ```
   <link rel="stylesheet"
   → href="css/style.css">
   ```

   To make the form a bit more attractive, some CSS code will style it. You can find the CSS file in the book's corresponding downloads at **LarryUllman.com**.

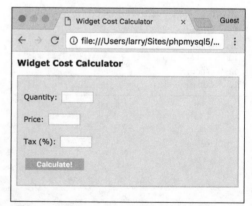

A The Widget Cost Calculator as an HTML form.

The CSS file also defines two significant classes—*error* and *errorMessage*, to be manipulated by jQuery later in the chapter. The first turns everything red; the second italicizes text (but the class will be more meaningful as a way of identifying a group of similar items). In time, you'll see how these classes are used.

4. Change the second **script** tag so that it references **calculator.js**, not **test.js**:

```
<script src="js/calculator.js">
→ </script>
```

The JavaScript for this example will go in **calculator.js**, to be written subsequently. It will be stored in the same **js** folder as the other JavaScript documents.

5. Within the HTML body, create an empty paragraph and begin a form:

```
<h1>Widget Cost Calculator</h1>
<p id="results"></p>
<form action="calculator.php"
→ method="post" id="calculator">
```

The paragraph with the **id** of *results* but no content will be used later in the chapter to present the results of the calculations. It has a unique **id** value, for easy reference. The form, too, has a unique **id** value. The form, in theory, would be submitted to **calculator.php** (a separate script, not actually written in this chapter), but that submission will be interrupted by JavaScript.

continues on next page

Script 15.4 In this HTML page is a form with three textual inputs for performing a calculation.

```
1   <!doctype html>
2   <html lang="en">
3   <head>
4       <meta charset="utf-8">
5       <title>Widget Cost Calculator</title>
6       <link rel="stylesheet" href="css/style.css">
7       <script src="js/jquery-3.2.1.min.js"></script>
8       <script src="js/calculator.js"></script>
9   </head>
10  <body>
11      <!-- Script 15.4 - calculator.html -->
12      <h1>Widget Cost Calculator</h1>
13      <p id="results"></p>
14      <form action="calculator.php" method="post" id="calculator">
15          <p id="quantityP">Quantity: <input type="number" name="quantity" id="quantity"
            step="1" min="1"></p>
16          <p id="priceP">Price: <input type="number" name="price" id="price" step="0.01"
            min="0.01"></p>
17          <p id="taxP">Tax (%): <input type="number" name="tax" id="tax" step="0.01"
            min="0.01"></p>
18          <p><input type="submit" name="submit" id="submit" value="Calculate!"></p>
19      </form>
20  </body>
21  </html>
```

6. Create the first form element:

```
<p id="quantityP">Quantity:
→ <input type="number"
→ name="quantity" id="quantity"
→ step="1" min="1"></p>
```

Each form input, as originally written in Chapter 13, involved the textual prompt, the element itself, and a paragraph surrounding both. To the paragraph and form input, unique **id** values are added.

Note that I tend to use "camel-case" style names—*quantityP*—in object-oriented languages such as JavaScript. This approach just better follows OOP conventions (conversely, I would use *quantity_p* in procedural PHP code).

7. Create the remaining two form elements:

```
<p id="priceP">Price:
→ <input type="number"
→ name="price" id="price"
→ step="0.01" min="0.01"></p>
<p id="taxP">Tax (%):
→ <input type="number" name="tax"
→ id="tax" step="0.01" min="0.01">
→ </p>
```

8. Complete the form and the HTML page:

```
  <p><input type="submit"
→ name="submit" id="submit"
→ value="Calculate!"></p>
</form>
</body>
</html>
```

The submit button also has a unique **id**, but that's for the benefit of the CSS; it won't actually be referenced in the JavaScript.

9. Save the page as **calculator.html** and load it in your browser **Ⓐ**.

Even though the second JavaScript file, **calculator.js**, has not yet been written, the form is still loadable.

TIP jQuery has its own additional, custom selectors, allowing you to select page elements in more sophisticated ways. For examples, see the jQuery manual.

Event Handling

JavaScript, like PHP, is often used to respond to events. Differently, though, events in JavaScript terms are primarily user actions within the browser, such as the following:

- Moving the cursor over an image or piece of text
- Clicking a link
- Changing the value of a form element
- Submitting a form

To handle events in JavaScript, you apply an *event listener* (also called an *event handler*) to an element; you tell JavaScript that when A event happens to B element, the C function should be called. In jQuery, event listeners are assigned using the syntax

selection.*eventType*(*function*);

The *selection* part would be like **$('.something')** or **$('a')**: whatever element or elements to which the event listener should be applied. The *eventType* value will differ based on the selection. Common values are *change*, *focus*, *mouseover*, *click*, *submit*, and *select*: different events can be triggered by different HTML elements. In jQuery, these are all actually the names of functions being called on the selection. These functions take one argument: a function to be called when the event occurs on that selection. Commonly, the function to be invoked is written inline, anonymously. For example, to handle the event of any image being moused-over, you would code

```
$('img').mouseover(function() {
  // Do this!
});
```

This construct should look familiar—**test.js** assigns an event handler that listens for the *ready* event occurring on the HTML document.

Let's take this new information and apply it to the HTML page already begun. At this point, an event listener can be added to the form so that its submission can be handled. In this case, the form's three inputs will be minimally validated, the total calculation will be performed, and the results of the calculation displayed in an alert 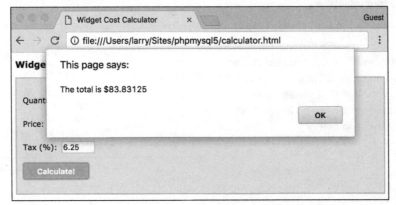. To do all this, you need to know one more thing: to fetch the values entered into the textual form inputs requires the **val()** function. It returns the value for the selection, as you'll see in these next steps.

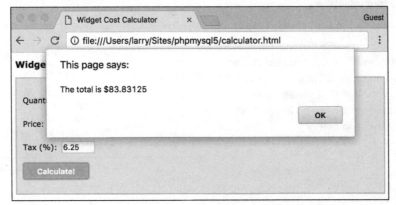

A The calculations are displayed using an alert box (for now).

To handle the form submission:

1. Open **test.js** in your text editor or IDE.

   Since the **test.js** file already has the proper syntax for executing code when the browser is ready, it'll be easiest and most foolproof to start with it.

2. Remove the existing **alert()** call (Script 15.5).

   All the following code will go in place of the original **alert()**.

3. In place of the **alert()** call, add an event handler to the form's submission:

   **$('#calculator').submit(function() {
   }); // End of form submission.**

   The selector grabs a reference to the form, which has an **id** value of *calculator*. To this selection the **submit()** function is applied, so that when the form is submitted, the inline anonymous function will be called. Because the syntax can be so tricky, my recommendation is to add this block of code, and then write the contents of the anonymous function—found in the following steps. Note that this and the following code go within the existing **$(document).ready() {}** block.

4. Within the new anonymous function, initialize four variables:

   var quantity, price, tax, total;

   In JavaScript, the **var** keyword is used to declare a variable. It can also declare multiple variables at once, if separated by commas. Note that variables in JavaScript do not have an initial dollar sign, like those in PHP.

Script 15.5 This JavaScript file is included by **calculator.html** (Script 15.4). Upon submission of the form, the form's values are validated and a calculation performed.

```
1    // Script 15.5 - calculator.js
2    // This script is included by
     calculator.html.
3    // This script handles and validates the
     form submission.
4
5    // Do something when the document is
     ready:
6    $(function() {
7
8        // Assign an event handler to the
         form:
9        $('#calculator').submit(function() {
10
11           // Initialize some variables:
12           var quantity, price, tax, total;
13
14           // Validate the quantity:
15           if ($('#quantity').val() > 0) {
16
17               // Get the quantity:
18               quantity = $('#quantity').
                 val();
19
20           } else { // Invalid quantity!
21
22               // Alert the user:
23               alert('Please enter a valid
                 quantity!');
24
25           }
26
27           // Validate the price:
28           if ($('#price').val() > 0) {
29               price = $('#price').val();
30           } else {
31               alert('Please enter a valid
                 price!');
32           }
33
34           // Validate the tax:
35           if ($('#tax').val() > 0) {
36               tax = $('#tax').val();
37           } else {
```

code continues on next page

```
38              alert('Please enter a valid
            tax!');
39          }
40
41          // If appropriate, perform the
            calculations:
42          if (quantity && price && tax) {
43
44              total = quantity * price;
45              total += total * (tax/100);
46
47              // Display the results:
48              alert('The total is $' +
                total);
49
50          }
51
52          // Return false to prevent an
            actual form submission:
53          return false;
54
55      }); // End of form submission.
56
57  }); // End of document ready.
```

5. Validate the quantity:

```
if ($('#quantity').val() > 0) {
  quantity = $('#quantity').val();
} else {
  alert('Please enter a valid
  → quantity!');
}
```

For each of the three form inputs, the value needs to be a number greater than zero. The value entered can be found by calling the **val()** function on the selected element. If the returned value is greater than zero, then the value is assigned to the local variable **quantity**. Otherwise, an alert box indicates the problem to the user 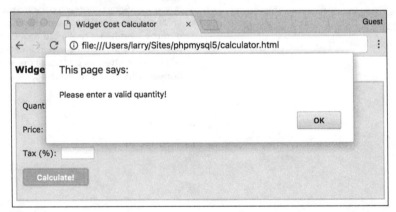. This is admittedly a tedious use of alerts; you'll learn a smoother approach in the next section of the chapter.

As a reminder, HTML5 will also validate the inputs in supported browsers. To disable that while testing, add **novalidate** to the opening **form** tag:

```
<form action="calculator.php"
→ method="post" id="calculator"
→ novalidate>
```

continues on next page

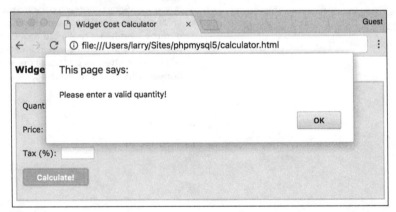

B If a form element does not have a positive numeric value, an alert box indicates the error.

6. Repeat the validation for the other two form inputs:

```
if ($('#price').val() > 0) {
   price = $('#price').val();
} else {
   alert('Please enter a valid
   → price!');
}
if ($('#tax').val() > 0) {
   tax = $('#tax').val();
} else {
   alert('Please enter a valid
   → tax!');
}
```

7. If all three variables have valid values, perform the calculations:

```
if (quantity && price && tax) {
   total = quantity * price;
   total += total * (tax/100);
```

This code should be fairly obvious by now: it looks almost exactly as it would in PHP, save for the lack of dollar signs in front of each variable's name.

8. Report the total:

```
alert('The total is $' + total);
```

Again, a crude alert window will be used to display the results of the calculation Ⓐ. As you can see in this code, the plus sign performs concatenation in JavaScript.

9. Complete the conditional begun in Step 7 and return the value **false**:

```
}
return false;
```

Having the function return **false** prevents the form from being submitted to the script that's identified as the form's **action**.

10. Save the page as **calculator.js** (in the **js** folder) and test the calculator in your browser.

Note that if you already had **calculator.html** loaded in your browser, you'll need to refresh the browser to load the updated JavaScript.

TIP There are many jQuery plug-ins specifically intended for validating forms, but I wanted to keep this simple (and explain core JavaScript concepts in the process).

TIP It is possible to format numbers in JavaScript—for example, so they always contain two decimals—but it's not easily done. For this reason, and because I didn't want to detract from the more important information being covered, the results of the calculation may not always look as good as they should.

TIP With jQuery, if the browser supports it, the JavaScript code will perform the calculations. If the user has JavaScript disabled, or if the user has a really old browser, the JavaScript will not take effect and the form will be submitted as per usual (here, to the nonexistent **calculator.php**).

DOM Manipulation

One of the most critical uses of JavaScript in general, and jQuery in particular, is manipulation of the DOM: changing, in any way, the contents of the browser. Normally, DOM manipulation is manifested by altering what the user sees; how easily you can do this in jQuery is one of its strengths.

Once you've selected the element or elements to be manipulated, applying any number of jQuery functions to the selection will change its properties. For starters, the **hide()** and **show()** functions ...um...hide and show the selection. Thus, to hide a form (perhaps after the user has successfully completed it), you would use

```
$('#actualFormId').hide();
```

Similar to **show()** and **hide()** are **fadeIn()** and **fadeOut()**. These functions also reveal or hide the selection, but do so with a bit of effect added in.

Another way to impact the DOM is to change the CSS classes that apply to a selection. The **addClass()** function applies a CSS class and **removeClass()** removes one. The following code adds the *emphasis* class to a specific blockquote and removes it from all paragraphs:

```
$('#blockquoteID').addClass
  → ('emphasis');
$('p').removeClass('emphasis');
```

The **toggleClass()** function can be used to toggle the application of a class to a selection.

The already mentioned functions generally change the *properties* of the page's elements, but you can also change the *contents* of those elements. In the previous section, you used the **val()** function, which returns the value of a form element. But when provided with an argument, **val()** assigns a new value to that form element:

```
$('#something').val('cat');
```

Similarly, the **html()** function returns the HTML contents of an element and **text()** returns the textual contents. Both functions can also take arguments used to assign new HTML and text, accordingly.

continues on next page

Let's use all this information to finish off the widget cost calculator. A few key changes will be made:

- Errors will be indicated by applying the *error* class.
- Errors will also be indicated by hiding or showing error messages 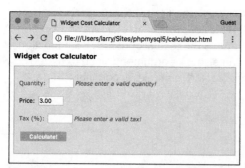.
- The final total will be written to the page 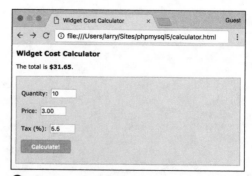.
- Alerts will not be used.

There are a couple of ways of showing and hiding error messages. The simplest, to be implemented here, is to manually add the messages to the form and then toggle their visibility using JavaScript. Accordingly, these steps begin by updating the HTML page.

To manipulate the DOM:

1. Open **calculator.html** in your text editor or IDE, if you haven't already.

2. Between the quantity form element and its closing paragraph tag, add an error message (**Script 15.6**):

```
<p id="quantityP">Quantity:
→ <input type="number"
→ name="quantity" id="quantity"
→ step="1" min="1"><span
→ class="errorMessage"
→ id="quantityError">Please enter
→ a valid quantity!</span></p>
```

Now following the input is a textual error, which also has a unique **id**. The span containing the error also uses the *errorMessage* class. This impacts the message's formatting, thanks to the external CSS document, and makes it easier for jQuery to globally hide all error messages upon first loading the page.

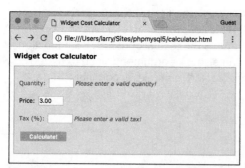

A Error messages are now displayed next to the problematic form inputs.

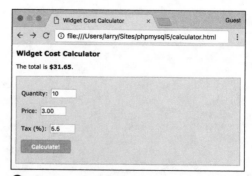

B The results of the calculations are now displayed above the form.

3. Repeat Step 2 for the other two form inputs:

```
<p id="priceP">Price:
→ <input type="number"
→ name="price" id="price"
→ step="0.01" min="0.01"><span
→ class="errorMessage"
→ id="priceError">Please enter a
→ valid price!</span></p>
<p id="taxP">Tax (%): <input
→ type="number" name="tax" id="tax"
→ step="0.01" min="0.01"></p>
<p><input type="submit"
→ name="submit" id="submit"
→ value="Calculate!"><span
→ class="errorMessage"
→ id="taxError">Please enter a
→ valid tax!</span></p>
```

continues on next page

Script 15.6 The updated HTML page has hardcoded error messages beside the key form inputs.

```
1    <!doctype html>
2    <html lang="en">
3    <head>
4        <meta charset="utf-8">
5        <title>Widget Cost Calculator</title>
6        <link rel="stylesheet" href="css/style.css" type="text/css" media="screen">
7        <script src="js/jquery-3.2.1.min.js"></script>
8        <script src="js/calculator.js"></script>
9    </head>
10   <body>
11       <!-- Script 15.6 - calculator.html #2 -->
12   <h1>Widget Cost Calculator</h1>
13   <p id="results"></p>
14   <form action="calculator.php" method="post" id="calculator">
15       <p id="quantityP">Quantity: <input type="number" name="quantity" id="quantity"
         step="1" min="1"><span class="errorMessage" id="quantityError">Please enter a valid
         quantity!</span></p>
16       <p id="priceP">Price: <input type="number" name="price" id="price" step="0.01"
         min="0.01"><span class="errorMessage" id="priceError">Please enter a valid price!
         </span></p>
17       <p id="taxP">Tax (%): <input type="number" name="tax" id="tax" step="0.01"
         min="0.01"><span class="errorMessage" id="taxError">Please enter a valid tax!
         </span></ </p>
18       <p><input type="submit" name="submit" id="submit" value="Calculate!"> p>
19   </form>
20   </body>
21   </html>
```

4. Save the file.

5. Open **calculator.js** in your text editor or IDE, if it is not already open.

6. Remove all existing **alert()** calls (**Script 15.7**).

7. Before the submit event handler, hide every element with the *error-Message* class:

```
$('.errorMessage').hide();
```

The selector grabs a reference to any element of any type that has a class of *errorMessage*. In the HTML form, this applies only to the three **span** tags.

8. In the **if** clause code after assigning a value to the local **quantity** variable, remove the *error* class and hide the error message:

```
$('#quantityP').removeClass
→ ('error');
$('#quantityError').hide();
```

As you'll see in Step 9, when the user enters an invalid quantity, the quantity paragraph (with an **id** value of *quantityP*) will be assigned the *error* class and the quantity error message (i.e., *#quantityError*) will be shown. If the user entered an invalid quantity but then entered a valid one, those two effects must be undone, using the code shown here.

continues on page 504

Script 15.7 Using jQuery, the JavaScript code now manipulates the DOM instead of using **alert()** calls.

```
1    // Script 15.7 - calculator.js #2
2    // This script is included by calculator.html.
3    // This script handles and validates the form submission.
4
5    // Do something when the document is ready:
6    $(function() {
7
8        // Hide all error messages:
9        $('.errorMessage').hide();
10
11       // Assign an event handler to the form:
12       $('#calculator').submit(function() {
13
14           // Initialize some variables:
15           var quantity, price, tax, total;
16
17           // Validate the quantity:
18           if ($('#quantity').val() > 0) {
19
20               // Get the quantity:
21               quantity = $('#quantity').val();
22
23               // Clear an error, if one existed:
24               $('#quantityP').removeClass('error');
25
```

code continues on next page

```
26          // Hide the error message, if it was visible:
27          $('#quantityError').hide();
28
29      } else { // Invalid quantity!
30
31          // Add an error class:
32          $('#quantityP').addClass('error');
33
34          // Show the error message:
35          $('#quantityError').show();
36
37      }
38
39      // Validate the price:
40      if ($('#price').val() > 0) {
41          price = $('#price').val();
42          $('#priceP').removeClass('error');
43          $('#priceError').hide();
44      } else {
45          $('#priceP').addClass('error');
46          $('#priceError').show();
47      }
48
49      // Validate the tax:
50      if ($('#tax').val() > 0) {
51          tax = $('#tax').val();
52          $('#taxP').removeClass('error');
53          $('#taxError').hide();
54      } else {
55          $('#taxP').addClass('error');
56          $('#taxError').show();
57      }
58
59      // If appropriate, perform the calculations:
60      if (quantity && price && tax) {
61
62          total = quantity * price;
63          total += total * (tax/100);
64
65          // Display the results:
66          $('#results').html('The total is <strong>$' + total + '</strong>.');
67
68      }
69
70      // Return false to prevent an actual form submission:
71      return false;
72
73    }); // End of form submission.
74
75 }); // End of document ready.
```

In the case that an invalid quantity was never submitted, the quantity paragraph will not have the *error* class and the quantity error message will still be hidden. In situations where jQuery is asked to do something that's not possible, such as hiding an already hidden element, jQuery just ignores the request.

9. If the quantity is not valid, add the *error* class and show the error message:

```
$('#quantityP').addClass('error');
$('#quantityError').show();
```

This code does the opposite of that in Step 8. Note that it goes within the **else** clause.

10. Repeat Steps 8 and 9 for the price, making that **if-else** read:

```
if ($('#price').val() > 0) {
  price = $('#price').val();
  $('#priceP').removeClass('error');
  $('#priceError').hide();
} else {
  $('#priceP').addClass('error');
  $('#priceError').show();
}
```

11. Repeat Steps 8 and 9 for the tax, making that **if-else** read:

```
if ($('#tax').val() > 0) {
  tax = $('#tax').val();
  $('#taxP').removeClass('error');
  $('#taxError').hide();
} else {
  $('#taxP').addClass('error');
  $('#taxError').show();
}
```

12. After calculating the total, within the same **if** clause, update the *results* paragraph:

```
$('#results').html('The total is
 → <strong>$' + total + '</strong>.');
```

Instead of using an alert box, you can write the total message to the HTML page dynamically. One way of doing so is by changing the text or HTML of an element on the page. The page already has an empty paragraph for this purpose, with an **id** value of *results*. To change the text found within the paragraph, you would apply the **text()** function. To change the HTML found within the paragraph, use **html()** instead.

13. Save the page as **calculator.js** (in the **js** folder) and test the calculator in your browser.

Again, remember that you must reload the HTML page (because both the HTML and the JavaScript have been updated).

TIP jQuery will not throw an error if you attempt to select page elements that don't exist. jQuery will also not throw an error if you call a function on nonexistent elements.

TIP In JavaScript, as in other OOP languages, you can "chain" function calls together, performing multiple actions at one time. This code reveals a previously hidden paragraph, adds a new class, and changes its textual content, all in one line:

```
$('#pId').show().addClass('thisClass').
 → text('Hello, world! ');
```

TIP You can change the attributes of a selection using the **attr()** function. Its first argument is the attribute to be impacted; the second, the new value. For example, the following code will disable a submit button by adding the property **disabled="disabled"**:

```
$('#submitButtonId').attr('disabled',
 → 'disabled');
```

TIP You can add, move, or remove elements using the **prepend()**, **append()**, **remove()**, and other functions. See the jQuery manual for specifics.

Using Ajax

Along with DOM manipulation, another key use of JavaScript and jQuery is *Ajax*. The term Ajax was first coined in 2005, although browser support was mixed for years. Come 2017, Ajax is a standard feature of many dynamic web sites, and its straightforward use is supported by all the major browsers. But what is Ajax?

Ajax can mean many things, involving several different technologies and approaches, but at the end of the day, Ajax is simply the use of JavaScript to perform a server-side request unbeknownst to the user. In a standard request model—which is to say pretty much every other example in this book—the user may begin on, say, `login.html`. Upon submission of the form, the browser will be taken to perhaps `login.php`, where the actual form validation is done, the registration in the database takes place, and the results are displayed **Ⓐ**. (Even if the same PHP script both displays and handles a form, the standard request model requires two separate and overt requests of that same page.)

continues on next page

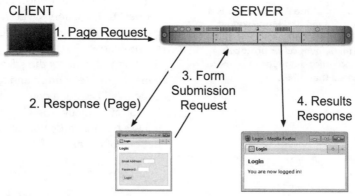

Ⓐ A standard client-server request model, with the browser constantly reloading entire HTML pages.

With the Ajax model, the form submission will be *hijacked* by JavaScript, which will in turn send the form data to a server-side PHP script. That PHP script does whatever validation and other tasks necessary, and then returns only data to the client-side JavaScript, indicating the results of the operation. The client-side JavaScript then uses the returned data to update the HTML page **B**. Although there are more steps, the user will be unaware of most of them and will be able to continue interacting with the HTML page while this process takes place.

TIP The foundation of the Ajax process is a JavaScript object of type XMLHttpRequest, sometimes abbreviated XHR. However, the request can be made over other protocols besides HTTP and other data types are more commonly returned than XML.

Creating the form

Incorporating Ajax into a web site results in an improved user experience, more similar to how desktop applications behave. There can also be better performance, with less data transmitted back and forth (e.g., an entire second page of HTML, like **login.php**, does not need to be transmitted).

You already know much of the information required for performing Ajax transactions: form validation with JavaScript, form validation with PHP, and using JavaScript to update the DOM. The last bit of knowledge you need is how to perform the actual Ajax request using jQuery. Over the next several pages, you'll create the HTML form, the server-side PHP script, and the intermediary JavaScript, all for the sake of handling a login form. To shorten and simplify the code a bit, I've cut a couple of corners, but I'll indicate exactly when I do so, and every cut will be in an area you could easily flesh out on your own.

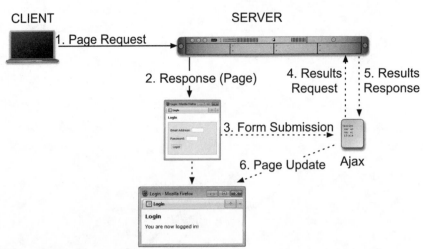

B With Ajax, server requests are made behind the scenes, and the browser can be updated without reloading.

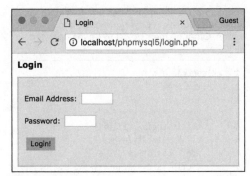

C The login form.

D Error messages are revealed beside each form element.

Creating the form

The login form simply needs two inputs: one for an email address and another for a password **C**. The form will use the same techniques for displaying errors and indicating results as **calculator.html D**.

To create the form:

1. Begin a new PHP document in your text editor or IDE, to be named **login.php** (Script 15.8):

   ```
   <!doctype html>
   <html lang="en">
   <head>
     <meta charset="utf-8">
     <title>Login</title>
     <link rel="stylesheet"
     → href="css/style.css">
   ```

   This will actually be a PHP script, not just an HTML file. The page uses the same external CSS file as **calculator.html**.

2. Incorporate the jQuery library and a second JavaScript file:

   ```
   <script src="js/jquery-3.2.1.min.
   → js"></script>
   <script src="js/login.js"></script>
   ```

   The page will use the same jQuery library as **calculator.html**. The page-specific JavaScript will go in **login.js**. Both will be stored in the **js** folder, found in the same directory as this script.

   continues on next page

3. Complete the HTML head and begin the body:

```
</head>
<body>
   <!-- Script 15.8 - login.php -->
<h1>Login</h1>
<p id="results"></p>
```

Within the body, before the form, is an empty paragraph with an **id** of *results*, to be dynamically populated with jQuery later 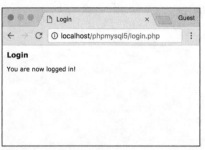.

4. Create the form:

```
<form action="login.php"
→ method="post" id="login">
  <p id="emailP">Email
  → Address: <input type="email"
  → name="email" id="email"><span
  → class="errorMessage"
  → id="emailError">Please enter
  → your email address!</span></p>
  <p id="passwordP">Password:
  → <input type="password"
  → name="password"
  → id="password"><span
  → class="errorMessage"
  → id="passwordError">Please
  → enter your password!</span>
  → </p>
  <p><input type="submit"
  → name="submit" value="Login!">
  → </p>
</form>
```

This form is quite like that in **calculator.html**. Both form elements are wrapped within paragraphs that have unique **id** values, making it easy for jQuery to apply the *error* class when needed. Both elements are followed by the default error message, to be hidden and shown by jQuery as warranted.

Script 15.8 The login form has one text input for the email address, a password input, and a submit button. Other elements exist to be manipulated by jQuery.

```
1    <!doctype html>
2    <html lang="en">
3    <head>
4        <meta charset="utf-8">
5        <title>Login</title>
6        <link rel="stylesheet"
         href="css/style.css">
7        <script src="js/jquery-3.2.1.min.js">
         </script>
8        <script src="js/login.js"></script>
9    </head>
10   <body>
11       <!-- Script 15.8 - login.php -->
12   <h1>Login</h1>
13   <p id="results"></p>
14   <form action="login.php" method="post"
     id="login">
15       <p id="emailP">Email Address:
         <input type="email" name="email"
         id="email"><span class="errorMessage"
         id="emailError">Please enter your
         email address!</span></p>
16       <p id="passwordP">Password:
         <input type="password"
         name="password" id="password">
         <span class="errorMessage"
         id="passwordError">Please enter your
         password!</span></p>
17       <p><input type="submit" name="submit"
         value="Login!"></p>
18   </form>
19   </body>
20   </html>
```

 Upon successfully logging in, the form will disappear and a message will appear just under the header.

5. Complete the HTML page:

```
</body>
</html>
```

6. Save the page as **login.php** and load it in your browser.

Remember that this is a PHP script, so it must be accessed through a URL (*http://something*).

Creating the server-side script

The previous sequence of steps goes through creating the client side of the process: the HTML form. Next, I'm going to skip ahead and look at the server side: the PHP script that handles the form data. This script must do two things:

1. Validate the submitted data.

2. Return a string indicating the results.

For simplicity's sake, the PHP script will merely compare the submitted values against hardcoded ones, but you could easily modify this code to perform a database query instead.

In terms of the Ajax process, the important thing is that this PHP script only ever returns a single string **F**, without any HTML or other markup **G**. This is mandatory, because the entire output of the PHP script is what the JavaScript performing the Ajax request will receive. And, as you'll see in the JavaScript for this example, the PHP script's output will be the basis for the error reporting and DOM manipulation to be performed.

F The results of the server-side PHP script when a proper request is made.

G The HTML source of the server-side PHP script shows that the only output is a simple string, without any HTML at all.

To handle the Ajax request:

1. Begin a new PHP document in your text editor or IDE, to be named **login_ajax.php** (Script 15.9):

```
<?php # Script 15.9 -
→ login_ajax.php
```

Again, this script is not meant to be executed directly, so it contains no HTML.

2. Validate that an email address and a password were received in the URL:

```
if (isset($_GET['email'],
→ $_GET['password'])) {
```

A GET request will be made of this script; therefore, the first thing the code does is confirm that both an email address and a password were passed to it.

3. Validate that the submitted email address is of the proper syntax:

```
if (filter_var($_GET['email'],
→ FILTER_VALIDATE_EMAIL)) {
```

Using the Filter extension, the provided email address is also checked for basic syntax.

4. If the submitted values are correct, indicate success:

```
if ( ($_GET['email'] ==
→ 'email@example.com') && ($_GET
→ ['password'] == 'testpass') ) {
  echo 'CORRECT';
```

As already mentioned, this code just compares the submitted values against two static strings. You could easily swap out this code for a database query, like those in Chapter 12, "Cookies and Sessions." At this point you could also set a cookie or begin a session (although see the following tip for the "gotchas" involved with doing so).

Script 15.9 This PHP script will receive the Ajax request from JavaScript. It performs some validation and returns simple strings to indicate the results.

```
1   <?php # Script 15.9 - login_ajax.php
2   // This script is called via Ajax from
    login.php.
3   // The script expects to receive two
    values in the URL: an email address and
    a password.
4   // The script returns a string
    indicating the results.
5
6   // Need two pieces of information:
7   if (isset($_GET['email'],
    $_GET['password'])) {
8
9       // Need a valid email address:
10      if (filter_var($_GET['email'],
        FILTER_VALIDATE_EMAIL)) {
11
12          // Must match specific values:
13          if ( ($_GET['email'] ==
            'email@example.com') &&
            ($_GET['password'] == 'testpass')
            ) {
14
15              // Set a cookie, if you want,
                or start a session.
16
17              // Indicate success:
18              echo 'CORRECT';
19
20          } else { // Mismatch!
21              echo 'INCORRECT';
22          }
23
24      } else { // Invalid email address!
25          echo 'INVALID_EMAIL';
26      }
27
28  } else { // Missing one of the two
    variables!
29      echo 'INCOMPLETE';
30  }
31
32  ?>
```

Most importantly, the script simply echoes the word *CORRECT*, without any other HTML (**F** and **G**).

5. Complete the three conditionals:

```
    } else {
        echo 'INCORRECT';
    }
} else {
    echo 'INVALID_EMAIL';
}
} else {
    echo 'INCOMPLETE';
}
```

These three **else** clauses complete the conditionals begun in Steps 2, 3, and 4. Each simply prints a string indicating a certain status. The JavaScript associated with the login form, to be written next, will take different actions based on each of the possible results.

6. Complete the PHP page:

```
?>
```

7. Save the file as **login_ajax.php**, and place it in the same folder of your web directory as **login.php**.

The two files must be in the same directory for the Ajax request to work.

TIP It's perfectly acceptable for the server-side PHP script in an Ajax process to set cookies or begin a session. Keep in mind, however, that the page in the browser has already been loaded, meaning that page cannot access cookies or sessions created after the fact. You'll need to use JavaScript to update the page after creating a cookie or starting a session, but subsequent pages loaded in the browser will have full access to cookie or session data.

Creating the JavaScript

The final step is to create the JavaScript that interrupts the form submission, sends the data to the server-side PHP script, reads the PHP script's results, and updates the DOM accordingly. This is the "glue" between the client-side HTML form and the server-side PHP. All the JavaScript form validation and DOM manipulation will be quite similar to what you've already seen in this chapter. Two new concepts will be introduced.

First, you'll need to know how to create a *generic object* in JavaScript. In this case, one object will represent the data to be sent to the PHP script and another will represent the options for the Ajax request. Here is how you create a new object in JavaScript:

```
var objectName = new Object();
```

The next chapter gets into OOP in more detail, but understand now that this just creates a new variable of type *Object*. The capital letter "O" **Object** is a blank template in JavaScript (since JavaScript is an object-oriented language, most variables are objects of some type). Once you've created the object, you can add values to it using the syntax:

```
objectName.property = value;
```

If you're new to JavaScript or OOP, it may help to think of the generic object as being like an indexed array, with a name and a corresponding value.

The second new piece of information is the usage of jQuery's **ajax()** function. This function performs an Ajax request. It takes as its lone argument the request's settings. As part of the jQuery library, it's invoked like so:

```
$.ajax(settings);
```

That's the basic premise; the particulars will be discussed in detail in the following code.

To perform an Ajax request:

1. Begin a new JavaScript file in your text editor or IDE, to be named **login.js** (**Script 15.10**):

   `// Script 15.10 - login.js`

2. Add the jQuery code for handling the "ready" state of the document:

   ```
   $(function() {
   });
   ```

   The JavaScript needs to start with this code in order to set the table once the browser is ready. Because of the complicated syntax, I think it's best to add this entire block of code first and then place all the subsequent code within the braces.

3. Hide every element that has the *errorMessage* class:

   `$('.errorMessage').hide();`

   The selector grabs a reference to any element of any type that has a **class** of *errorMessage*. In the HTML form, this applies only to the three **span** tags. Those will be hidden by this code as soon as the DOM is loaded.

4. Create an event listener for the form's submission:

   ```
   $('#login').submit(function() {
   });
   ```

   This code is virtually the same as that in the calculator form. All the remaining code will go within these braces.

continues on page 514

Script 15.10 The JavaScript code in this file performs an Ajax request of a server-side script and updates the DOM based on the returned response.

```
1    // Script 15.10 - login.js
2    // This script is included by login.php.
3    // This script handles and validates the
     form submission.
4    // This script then makes an Ajax
     request of login_ajax.php.
5
6    // Do something when the document is
     ready:
7    $(function() {
8
9        // Hide all error messages:
10       $('.errorMessage').hide();
11
12       // Assign an event handler to the
         form:
13       $('#login').submit(function() {
14
15           // Initialize some variables:
16           var email, password;
17
18           // Validate the email address:
19           if ($('#email').val().length
             >= 6) {
20
21               // Get the email address:
22               email = $('#email').val();
23
24               // Clear an error, if one
                 existed:
25               $('#emailP').removeClass
                 ('error');
26
27               // Hide the error message,
                 if it was visible:
28               $('#emailError').hide();
29
30           } else { // Invalid email address!
31
32               // Add an error class:
33               $('#emailP').addClass
                 ('error');
34
35               // Show the error message:
36               $('#emailError').show();
37
38           }
```

code continues on next page

```
39
40        // Validate the password:
41        if ($('#password').val().length > 0) {
42            password = $('#password').val();
43            $('#passwordP').removeClass('error');
44            $('#passwordError').hide();
45        } else {
46            $('#passwordP').addClass('error');
47            $('#passwordError').show();
48        }
49
50        // If appropriate, perform the Ajax request:
51        if (email && password) {
52
53            // Create an object for the form data:
54            var data = new Object();
55            data.email = email;
56            data.password = password;
57
58            // Create an object of Ajax options:
59            var options = new Object();
60
61            // Establish each setting:
62            options.data = data;
63            options.dataType = 'text';
64            options.type = 'get';
65            options.success = function(response) {
66
67                // Worked:
68                if (response == 'CORRECT') {
69
70                    // Hide the form:
71                    $('#login').hide();
72
73                    // Show a message:
74                    $('#results').removeClass('error');
75                    $('#results').text('You are now logged in!');
76
77                } else if (response == 'INCORRECT') {
78                    $('#results').text('The submitted credentials do not match those on file!');
79                    $('#results').addClass('error');
80                } else if (response == 'INCOMPLETE') {
81                    $('#results').text('Please provide an email address and a password!');
82                    $('#results').addClass('error');
83                } else if (response == 'INVALID_EMAIL') {
84                    $('#results').text('Please provide your email address!');
85                    $('#results').addClass('error');
86                }
87
```

code continues on next page

5. Initialize two variables:

```
var email, password;
```

These two variables will act as local representations of the form data.

6. Validate the email address:

```
if ($('#email').val().length >= 6) {
   email = $('#email').val();
   $('#emailP').removeClass('error');
   $('#emailError').hide();
```

The calculator form validated that all the numbers were greater than zero, which isn't an appropriate validation for the login form. Instead, the conditional confirms that the string length of the value of the email input is greater than or equal to 6 (six characters being the absolute minimum required for a valid email address, such as *a@b.cc*). You could also use regular expressions in JavaScript to perform more stringent validation, but I'm trying to keep this simple (and the server-side PHP script will validate the email address as well, as you've already seen).

If the email address value passes the minimal validation, it's assigned to the local variable. Next, the *error* class is removed from the paragraph, in case it was added previously, and the email-specific error is hidden, in case it was shown previously.

Script 15.10 *continued*

```
88          }; // End of success.
89          options.url =
            'login_ajax.php';
90
91          // Perform the request:
92          $.ajax(options);
93
94      } // End of email && password IF.
95
96      // Return false to prevent an
            actual form submission:
97      return false;
98
99  }); // End of form submission.
100
101 }); // End of document ready.
```

7. Complete the email address conditional:

```
} else {
  $('#emailP').addClass('error');
  $('#emailError').show();
}
```

This code completes the conditional begun in Step 6. The code is the same as that used in **calculator.html**, adding the *error* class to the entire paragraph and showing the error message **D**.

8. Validate the password:

```
if ($('#password').val().length >
→ 0) {
  password = $('#password').val();
  $('#passwordP').removeClass
  → ('error');
  $('#passwordError').hide();
} else {
  $('#passwordP').addClass('error');
  $('#passwordError').show();
}
```

For the password, the minimum length would likely be determined by the registration process. As a placeholder, this code just confirms a positive string length. Otherwise, this code is essentially the same as that in the previous two steps.

9. If both values were received, store them in a new object:

```
if (email && password) {
  var data = new Object();
  data.email = email;
  data.password = password;
```

The premise behind this code was explained before these steps. First a new, generic object is created. Then a property of that object named *email* is created and then assigned the value of the email address. Finally, a property named *password* is created and then assigned the value of the entered password. If it helps to imagine this code in PHP terms, the equivalent would be

```
$data = array();
$data['email'] = $email;
$data['password'] = $password;
```

10. Create a new object for the Ajax options, and establish the first three settings:

```
var options = new Object();
options.data = data;
options.dataType = 'text';
options.type = 'get';
```

Here, another generic object is created. Next, a property named *data* is assigned the value of the **data** object. This property of the **options** object stores the data being passed to the PHP script as part of the Ajax request.

continues on next page

The second setting is the data type expected back from the server-side request. As the PHP script **login_ajax.php** returns (i.e., prints) a simple string, the value here is *text*. The **dataType** setting impacts how the JavaScript will attempt to work with the returned response; it needs to match what the actual server response will be.

The *type* setting is the type of request being made, with *get* and *post* the two most common. A GET request is the default, so it does not need to be assigned here, but the code is being explicit anyway.

To be clear, because of the name of the properties in the **data** object—*email* and *password*—and because of the *type* value of *get*, the **login_ajax.php** script will receive **$_GET['email']** and **$_GET['password']**. If you were to change the names of the properties in **data**, or the value of **options.type**, the server-side PHP script would receive the Ajax data in different superglobal variables.

11. Begin defining what should happen upon a successful Ajax request:

```
options.success = function
→ (response) {
}; // End of success.
```

The **success** property defines what the JavaScript should do when the Ajax query works. By "work," I mean that the JavaScript can perform a request of the server-side page and receive a result. For what should *actually* happen, an anonymous function is assigned to this property. In this step, the anonymous function is defined and the assignment line is completed. The code in subsequent steps will go between these curly brackets.

As you can see, the anonymous function takes one argument: the response from the server-side script, assigned to the **response** variable. As already explained, the response received by the JavaScript will be the entirety of whatever is outputted by the PHP script.

12. Within the anonymous function created in Step 11, if the server response equals *CORRECT*, hide the form and update the page:

```
if (response == 'CORRECT') {
  $('#login').hide();
  $('#results').removeClass('error');
  $('#results').text('You are now
  → logged in!');
```

When the user submits the correct credentials—*email@example.com* and *testpass*, **login_ajax.php** will return the string *CORRECT*. In that case, the JavaScript will hide the entire login form and assign a string to the *results* paragraph, indicating such ⓔ. Because incorrect submissions may have added the *error* class to this paragraph (see Step 13), that class is also removed here.

13. If the server response equals *INCORRECT*, indicate an error:

```
} else if (response == 'INCORRECT') {
  $('#results').text('The submitted
  → credentials do not match those
  → on file! ');
  $('#results').addClass('error');
```

When the user submits a password and a syntactically valid email address but does not provide the correct specific values, the server-side PHP script will return the string *INCORRECT*. In that case, a different string is assigned to the *results* paragraph and the *error* class is applied to the paragraph as well 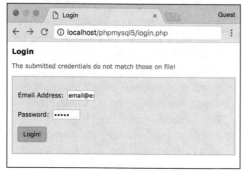.

14. Add clauses for the other two possible server responses:

```
} else if (response ==
→'INCOMPLETE') {
  $('#results').text('Please
  →provide an email address and
  →a password! ');
  $('#results').addClass('error');
} else if (response ==
→'INVALID_EMAIL') {
  $('#results').text('Please
  →provide your email address!
  →');
  $('#results').addClass('error');
}
```

These are repetitions of the code in Step 13, with different messages. This is the end of the code that goes within the **success** property's anonymous function.

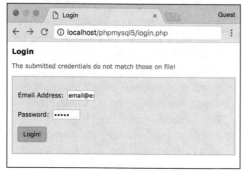

① The results upon providing invalid login credentials.

15. Add the **url** property and make the request:

```
options.url = 'login_ajax.php';
$.ajax(options);
```

The **url** property of the Ajax object names the actual server-side script to which the request should be sent. As long as **login.php** and **login_ajax.php** are in the same directory, this reference will work.

Finally, after establishing all of the request options, the request is performed.

16. Complete the conditional begun in Step 9 and return **false**:

```
} // End of email && password IF.
return false;
```

If the **email** and **password** variables do not have TRUE values, no Ajax request is made (i.e., that conditional has no **else** clause). Finally, the value **false** is returned here to prevent the actual submission of the form.

17. Save the page as **login.js** (in the **js** folder) and test the login form in your browser.

TIP Here's a debugging tip: it often helps to run the server-side script directly **①** to confirm that it works (e.g., that it doesn't contain a parse or other error).

TIP An improvement you could make to this process would be to have the server-side PHP script respond in JSON (JavaScript Object Notation) format instead. Search online for details on returning JSON from a PHP script and using JSON in JavaScript.

TIP Because JavaScript can be disabled by users, you can never rely strictly on JavaScript form validation. You must always also use server-side PHP validation to protect your web site.

Review and Pursue

If you have any problems with the review questions or the pursue prompts, turn to the book's supporting forum (`LarryUllman.com/forums/`).

Review

- What is JavaScript? How does JavaScript compare to PHP?
- What is jQuery? What is the relationship between jQuery and JavaScript?
- How is an external JavaScript file incorporated into an HTML page? How is JavaScript code placed within the HTML page itself?
- Why is it important to wait until the entire DOM has been loaded to execute JavaScript code that references DOM elements?
- Why are unique identifiers in the DOM necessary?
- In jQuery, how do you select elements of a given tag type? How do you select elements that have a certain class? How do you select a specific element?
- In jQuery, how do you add an event listener to a page element (or elements)? What *is* an event listener?
- Why must you reload HTML pages after altering their JavaScript?
- What are some of the jQuery functions you can use to manipulate the DOM?
- What is Ajax? Why is Ajax a "good thing"?
- Why must an HTML page that performs a server-side request be loaded through a URL?
- How do you create a generic object in JavaScript?
- What impact does the Ajax request's **type** property have? What impact do the names of the properties in the **data** object have?

Pursue

- Head to the jQuery web site and start perusing the jQuery documentation.
- Check out jQuery UI and what it can do for your HTML pages.
- Use the jQuery documentation, or simply search online, for some of jQuery's plug-ins. Attempt to use one or more of them in an HTML page.
- Once you feel comfortable with the Ajax process, search online for information about performing Ajax requests using *JSON* to represent the data transmitted back to the JavaScript.
- See what happens when you reference a DOM element in JavaScript before the entire DOM has been loaded. Witnessing this should help you recognize what's happening when you inevitably and accidentally fail to wait until the browser is ready before referencing the DOM.
- Update **calculator.js** so that the *results* paragraph is initially cleared on each form submission. By doing so, the results of previous submissions won't be shown upon subsequent invalid submissions.
- Modify **login_ajax.php** so that it uses a database to confirm successful login.
- Modify **login_ajax.php** so that it sends a cookie or begins a session. Create a secondary PHP script that accesses the created cookie or session.
- Modify **login.php** so that it also performs the login validation, should the user have JavaScript disabled. Hint: This is simpler than you might think— just use PHP to handle the form submission (in the same file) as if JavaScript were not present at all.

16

An OOP Primer

PHP is somewhat unusual as a language in that it can be used both *procedurally*, as most of this book demonstrates, and as an *object-oriented programming* (OOP) language. There are merits to both approaches, and you ought to be familiar with each (in due time, at least).

Unfortunately, mastery of OOP requires lots of time and information: my *PHP Advanced and Object-Oriented Programming: Visual QuickPro Guide* (Peachpit Press) spends 200 pages on the subject! Still, one of the great things about OOP is that you can *use* it without fully *knowing* it. You'll see what this means shortly.

This chapter is a primer for OOP in PHP. Some of the examples will replicate procedural ones already shown in the book to best compare and contrast the two approaches. Various sidebars and tips will mention other uses of OOP in PHP, many of which will not have procedural equivalents.

Fundamentals and Syntax

If you've never done any object-oriented programming, both the concept and the syntax can be quite foreign. Simply put, all applications, or scripts, involve *taking actions with information*: validating it, manipulating it, storing it in a database, and so forth. Philosophically, procedural programming is written with a focus on the actions: do this, then this, then this; OOP is data-centric, focusing more on the kinds of information being used.

OOP fundamentals

OOP in PHP begins with the definition of a *class*, which is a template for a particular type of data: an employee, a user, a page of content, and so forth. A class definition contains both variables and functions. Syntactically, a variable in a class definition is called an *attribute* or *property*, and a function in a class definition is called a *method*. Combined, the attributes and methods are the *members* of the class.

As a theoretical example, you might have a class called *Car*. Note that class names conventionally begin with an uppercase letter. The properties of a **Car** would include **make**, **model**, **year**, **odometer**, and so forth: all information that can be known about a car. A **Car**'s properties can be set, changed, and retrieved, and the values of the properties distinguish *this* **Car** from *that* **Car**. A **Car**'s methods—the things that the car can do—would include **start()**, **drive()**, **park()**, and **turnOff()**. These actions are common to all **Car**s.

OOP vs. Procedural

Discussions as to the merits of OOP vs. procedural programming can quickly escalate to verbal wars, with each side fiercely advocating for their approach. PHP is somewhat unique in that you have a choice (by comparison, C is strictly a procedural language and Java object-oriented). In my opinion, each programming style has its strengths and weaknesses, but neither is "better" than the other.

Procedural programming is arguably faster to learn and use, particularly for smaller projects. But procedural code can be harder to maintain and expand, especially in more complicated sites, and has the potential to be buggier.

Code written using OOP, on the other hand, may be easier to maintain, specifically on larger projects, and may be more appropriate in team environments. But OOP is harder to master, and when not done well, is that much more challenging to remedy.

In time, you'll naturally come up with your own opinions and preferences. The real lesson, to me, is to take advantage of the fact that PHP allows for both syntaxes, and not to limit yourself to just one style regardless of the situation.

In the introduction to this chapter, I stated that you can *use* OOP without really *knowing* it. By that I mean that it's very easy, and common enough, to use an existing class definition for your own needs. In fact, the reusability of code—particularly code created by others—is one of the key benefits of OOP. What takes a lot of effort, at least to do it right, is to master the design process: understanding what members to define and, more importantly, how to implement sophisticated OOP concepts such as

- Inheritance
- Access control
- Overriding methods
- Scope resolution
- Abstraction
- And so on

When you're interested in learning how to properly create your own classes, you can read more about these subjects in my *PHP Advanced and Object-Oriented Programming: Visual QuickPro Guide*, among other resources, but in this chapter, let's focus on using existing classes instead of creating your own custom ones.

OOP syntax in PHP

Let's say someone has gone through the process of designing and defining a **Car** class. Most classes are not used directly; rather, you create an *instance* of that class—a specific variable of the class's type. That instance is called an *object*. In PHP, an instance is created using the **new** keyword:

```
$obj = new ClassName();
$mine = new Car();
```

Whereas the code **$name = 'Larry'** creates a variable of type **string**, this code creates a variable of type **Car**. Everything that's part of **Car**'s definition—every property (i.e., variable) and method (i.e., function)—is now embedded in **$mine**.

Behind the scenes (i.e., in the class definition), a special method called the *constructor* is automatically invoked when a new object of that type is generated. The constructor normally provides whatever initial setup would be required by the subsequent usage of that object. For example, the **MySQLi** class's constructor establishes a connection to the database and the **DateTime** class's constructor creates a reference to an exact date and time (both the **MySQLi** and **DateTime** classes will be explicitly used in this chapter).

If the constructor takes arguments, like any function can, those may be provided when the object is created:

```
$mine = new Car('Honda', 'Fit', 2008);
```

Once you have an object, you reference its properties (i.e., variables) and call its methods (i.e., functions) using the syntax **$object_name->member_name**:

```
$mine->color = 'Purple';
$mine->start();
```

The first line (theoretically) assigns the value *Purple* to the object's **color** property. The second line invokes the object's **start()** method. As with any function call, the parentheses are required. If the method takes arguments, those can be provided, too:

```
$mine->drive('Forward');
```

continues on next page

Sometimes you'll use an object's properties as you would any other variable:

```
$mine->odometer += 20;
echo "My car currently has
→ $mine->odometer miles on it.";
```

If an object's method returns a value, the method can be invoked in the same manner as any function that returns a value:

```
// The fill() method takes a
→ number of
// gallons being added and returns
// how full the tank is:
$tank = $mine->fill(8.5);
```

And that's really enough to know about OOP to start using it. As you'll see, the examples over the next few pages will replicate functionality explained earlier in the book so that the contrasting approaches to the same end result should help you better understand what's going on.

TIP In documentation, you'll see the `ClassName::method_name()` syntax. This is a way of specifying to which class a method belongs.

TIP One of the major changes in PHP 5.3 was support for namespaces. Namespaces, in layman's terms, provide a way to group multiple class definitions under a single title. Namespaces are useful for organizing code, as well as preventing conflicts (e.g., differentiating between my `Car` class and your `Car` class).

TIP Classes can also have their own constants, just as they have their own variables and functions. Class constants are normally used without an instance of that class, as in

```
echo ClassName::CONSTANT_NAME;
```

More OOP Classes

There are more OOP classes defined in PHP than just those illustrated in this chapter, although I think the **MySQLi** and **DateTime** classes are the two most obviously accessible and usable. The largest body of classes can be found in the *Standard PHP Library* (SPL), built into PHP as of version 5.0, and greatly expanded in version 5.3.

The SPL provides high-end classes in several categories: exception handling, *iterators* (loops that can work on any collection of data), custom data types, and more. The SPL is definitely for more advanced PHP programmers and is most beneficial for otherwise strongly or entirely OOP-based code.

There are several good classes defined for internationalization purposes, too (**www.php.net/intl**). These classes define some of the functionality originally intended as part of the now-defunct PHP 6, including the ability to sort words, format numbers, and so forth, in a manner customized to the given *locale* (a locale is a combination of the language, cultural habits, and other unique choices for a region).

Working with MySQL

Just as you can write PHP code in both procedural and object-oriented styles, the MySQL Improved extension can similarly be used either way to interact with a database. Chapter 9, "Using PHP with MySQL," introduced the basics of the procedural approach. As a comparison, this chapter will run through the same functionality using OOP.

There are three defined classes that you will use in this chapter:

- **MySQLi**, the primary class, provides a database connection, a querying method, and more.

- **MySQLi_Result** is used to handle the results of **SELECT** queries (among others).

- **MySQLi_Stmt** is for performing prepared statements (introduced in Chapter 13, "Security Methods").

For each, I'll explain the basic usage and walk you through an example script. For a full listing of all the possibilities—all the properties and methods of each class—see the PHP manual.

Creating a connection

As with the procedural approach, creating a connection is the first step in interacting with MySQL when using object notation. With the **MySQLi** class, a connection is established when the object is instantiated (i.e., when the object is created), by passing the appropriate connection values to the constructor:

```
$mysqli = new MySQLi(hostname,
username, password, database);
```

Even though this is OOP, you would use the same MySQL values as you would when programming procedurally, or when connecting to MySQL using the command-line client or other interface.

If a connection could not be made, the **connect_error** property will store the reason why 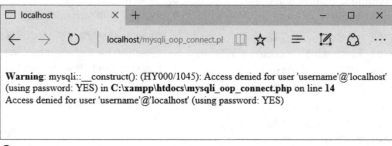:

```
if ($mysqli->connect_error) {
  echo $mysqli->connect_error;
}
```

Next, you should establish the character set:

```
$mysqli->set_charset(charset);
$mysqli->set_charset('utf8');
```

continues on next page

A A MySQL connection error.

At this point, you're ready to execute your queries, to be covered next.

After executing the queries, call the **close()** method to close the database connection:

```
$mysqli->close();
```

To be extra tidy, you can delete the object, too:

```
unset($mysqli);
```

To practice this, let's write a PHP script that connects to MySQL. Because the subsequent two scripts will be updates of scripts from Chapter 9 and will use the same template as Chapter 9, you'll want to place these next three scripts in the same web directories you used for Chapter 9.

To make an OOP MySQL connection:

1. Begin a new PHP script in your text editor or IDE, to be named **mysqli_oop_connect.php** (Script 16.1):

```
<?php # Script 16.1 -
→ mysqli_oop_connect.php
```

This script will largely follow the same approach as **mysqli_connect.php** in Chapter 9. It will contain no HTML.

2. Set the database connection parameters as constants:

```
DEFINE('DB_USER', 'username');
DEFINE('DB_PASSWORD', 'password');
DEFINE('DB_HOST', 'localhost');
DEFINE('DB_NAME', 'sitename');
```

As always, you'll need to change the particulars to be correct for your server. As with Chapter 9, this chapter's examples will make use of the *sitename* database.

3. Create a **MySQLi** object:

```
$mysqli = new MySQLi(DB_HOST,
→ DB_USER, DB_PASSWORD, DB_NAME);
```

This is the syntax already explained, using the constants as the values to be passed to the constructor.

4. If an error occurred, show it:

```
if ($mysqli->connect_error) {
  echo $mysqli->connect_error;
  unset($mysqli);
```

If the **MySQLi** object's **connect_error** property has a value, it means that the script could not establish a connection to the database. In that case, the connection error is displayed Ⓐ, and the object variable is unset, since it's useless.

5. If a connection was made, establish the encoding:

```
} else {
  $mysqli->set_charset('utf8');
}
```

Remember that the encoding used to communicate with MySQL needs to match the encoding set by the HTML pages and by the database.

6. Save the script as **mysqli_oop_connect.php**.

As with most files in this book that are meant to be included by other scripts, this one omits the closing PHP tag.

7. Ideally, place the file outside of the web document directory.

Because the file contains sensitive MySQL access information, it ought to be stored securely. If you can, place it in the directory immediately above or otherwise outside of the web directory (see Chapter 9 for particulars).

Again, the following two scripts will use the template that Chapter 9 used, so you should store this connection script in the same directory as **mysqli_connect.php** from Chapter 9.

8. Temporarily place a copy of the script within the web directory and run it in your browser.

To test the script, you'll want to place a copy on the server so that it's accessible from the browser (which means it must be in the web directory). If the script works properly, the result should be a blank page. If you see an *Access denied...* or similar message Ⓐ, it means that the combination of username, password, and host does not have permission to access the particular database.

9. Remove the temporary copy from the web directory.

Script 16.1 This script creates a new **MySQLi** object, through which database interactions will take place.

```
1    <?php # Script 16.1 - mysqli_oop_connect.php
2    // This file contains the database access information.
3    // This file also establishes a connection to MySQL,
4    // selects the database, and sets the encoding.
5    // The MySQL interactions use OOP!
6
7    // Set the database access information as constants:
8    DEFINE('DB_USER', 'username');
9    DEFINE('DB_PASSWORD', 'password');
10   DEFINE('DB_HOST', 'localhost');
11   DEFINE('DB_NAME', 'sitename');
12
13   // Make the connection:
14   $mysqli = new MySQLi(DB_HOST, DB_USER, DB_PASSWORD, DB_NAME);
15
16   // Verify the connection:
17   if ($mysqli->connect_error) {
18       echo $mysqli->connect_error;
19       unset($mysqli);
20   } else { // Establish the encoding.
21       $mysqli->set_charset('utf8');
22   }
```

TIP You can use `print_r()` to learn about, and debug, objects in PHP code **B**:

```
echo '<pre>' . print_r($mysqli, 1) .
→ '</pre>';
```

TIP Since the `$mysqli` object is unset if no connection is made, any script that needs it can be written to test for a successful connection by just using

```
if (isset($mysqli)) { // Do whatever.
```

For brevity's sake, this test is omitted in subsequent scripts, but know it's possible.

TIP The MySQLi constructor takes two more arguments: the port to use and the socket. When running MAMP or XAMPP (see Appendix A, "Installation"), you may need to provide the port.

TIP The `MySQLi::character_set_name()` method returns the current character set. The `MySQLi::get_charset()` method returns the character set, collation, and more.

TIP You can change the database used by the current connection via the `select_db()` method:

```
$mysqli->select_db(dbname);
```

Executing simple queries

Once you've successfully established a connection to the MySQL server, you can begin using the **MySQLi** object to query the database. For that, call the appropriately named **query()** method:

```
$mysqli->query(query);
```

Its lone argument is the SQL command to be executed, which I normally assign to a separate variable beforehand:

```
$q = 'SELECT * FROM tablename';
$mysqli->query($q);
```

You can test for the query's error-free execution by using the method call as a condition:

```
if ($mysqli->query($q)) { // Worked!
```

```
mysqli Object
(
    [affected_rows] => 0
    [client_info] => mysqlnd 5.0.12-dev - 20150407 - $Id: b39
    [client_version] => 50012
    [connect_errno] => 0
    [connect_error] =>
    [errno] => 0
    [error] =>
    [error_list] => Array
        (
        )

    [field_count] => 0
    [host_info] => localhost via TCP/IP
    [info] =>
    [insert_id] => 0
    [server_info] => 5.5.5-10.1.21-MariaDB
    [server_version] => 50505
    [stat] => Uptime: 629  Threads: 1  Questions: 2  Slow que
    [sqlstate] => 00000
    [protocol_version] => 10
    [thread_id] => 5
    [warning_count] => 0
)
```

B Using `print_r()` on an object, perhaps wrapped within preformatted tags to make its output easier to read, reveals the object's many property names and values.

Alternatively, you can check the **error** property :

```
if ($mysqli->error) { // Did not work!
  echo $mysqli->error;
}
```

If the query just executed was an **INSERT**, you can retrieve the automatically generated primary key value via the **insert_id** property:

```
$id = $mysqli->insert_id;
```

If the query just executed was an **UPDATE**, **INSERT**, or **DELETE**, you can retrieve the number of affected rows—how many rows were updated, inserted, or deleted—from the **affected_rows** property:

```
echo "$mysqli->affected_rows rows
→ were affected by the query.";
```

The last thing to know, before executing any queries, is how to *sanctify* data used in the query. To do so, apply the **real_escape_method()** to a string variable beforehand:

```
$var = $mysqli->real_escape_
→ string($var);
```

This is equivalent to invoking **mysqli_real_escape_string()**, and it prevents apostrophes and other problematic characters from breaking the syntax of the SQL command.

Using all this information, the next set of steps will rewrite **register.php** (Script 13.7) from Chapter 13 using OOP.

To execute simple queries:

1. Open **register.php** (Script 13.7) in your text editor or IDE.

2. Change the inclusion of the MySQL connection script to (**Script 16.2**)

   ```
   require('../mysqli_oop_connect.php');
   ```

   Assuming that **mysqli_oop_connect.php** is in the directory above this one, this code will work. If your directory structure differs, change the reference to the file accordingly.

continues on next page

C A problem with a query results in a MySQL error.

3. Change each use of `mysqli_real_escape_string()` to: `$mysqli->real_escape_string()`:

```
$fn = $mysqli->real_escape_string
→ (trim($_POST['first_name']));
$ln = $mysqli->real_escape_string
→ (trim($_POST['last_name']));
$e = $mysqli->real_escape_string
→ (trim($_POST['email']));
```

Three pieces of data—all strings, naturally—are escaped for added protection in the query. Because the script now uses the MySQL Improved extension using an object-oriented approach, these four lines should be changed.

4. Update how the query is executed (line 52 of the original script):

```
$mysqli->query($q);
```

To execute a query on the database using OOP, call the object's **query()** method, providing it with the query to be run.

5. Change the confirmation of the query's execution to read (originally line 53)

```
if ($mysqli->affected_rows == 1) {
```

The previous version of the script used the result variable to confirm that the query worked:

```
if ($r) {
```

Here, the conditional more formally asserts that the number of affected rows equals 1.

continues on page 530

Script 16.2 This updated version of the registration script uses the MySQL Improved extension via OOP.

```
1    <?php # Script 16.2 - register.php #4
2    // This script performs an INSERT query to add a record to the users table.
3
4    $page_title = 'Register';
5    include('includes/header.html');
6
7    // Check for form submission:
8    if ($_SERVER['REQUEST_METHOD'] == 'POST') {
9
10       require('mysqli_oop_connect.php'); // Connect to the db.
11
12       $errors = []; // Initialize an error array.
13
14       // Check for a first name:
15       if (empty($_POST['first_name'])) {
16           $errors[] = 'You forgot to enter your first name.';
17       } else {
18           $fn = $mysqli->real_escape_string(trim($_POST['first_name']));
19       }
20
21       // Check for a last name:
22       if (empty($_POST['last_name'])) {
23           $errors[] = 'You forgot to enter your last name.';
24       } else {
```

code continues on next page

```
25          $ln = $mysqli->real_escape_string(trim($_POST['last_name']));
26      }
27
28      // Check for an email address:
29      if (empty($_POST['email'])) {
30          $errors[] = 'You forgot to enter your email address.';
31      } else {
32          $e = $mysqli->real_escape_string(trim($_POST['email']));
33      }
34
35      // Check for a password and match against the confirmed password:
36      if (!empty($_POST['pass1'])) {
37          if ($_POST['pass1'] != $_POST['pass2']) {
38              $errors[] = 'Your password did not match the confirmed password.';
39          } else {
40              $p = password_hash(trim($_POST['pass1']), PASSWORD_DEFAULT);
41          }
42      } else {
43          $errors[] = 'You forgot to enter your password.';
44      }
45
46      if (empty($errors)) { // If everything's OK.
47
48          // Register the user in the database...
49
50          // Make the query:
51          $q = "INSERT INTO users (first_name, last_name, email, pass, registration_date)
          VALUES ('$fn', '$ln', '$e', '$p', NOW() )";
52          $r = @$mysqli->query($q); // Run the query.
53          if ($mysqli->affected_rows == 1) { // If it ran OK.
54
55              // Print a message:
56              echo '<h1>Thank you!</h1>
57              <p>You are now registered. In Chapter 12 you will actually be able to log in!
              </p><p><br></p>';
58
59          } else { // If it did not run OK.
60
61              // Public message:
62              echo '<h1>System Error</h1>
63              <p class="error">You could not be registered due to a system error. We apologize for
              any inconvenience.</p>';
64
65              // Debugging message:
66              echo '<p>' . $mysqli->error . '<br><br>Query: ' . $q . '</p>';
67
68          } // End of if ($r) IF.
69
```

code continues on next page

6. Update the debugging error message to use the object (line 66 of the original script):

```
echo '<p>' . $mysqli->error .
→'<br><br>Query: ' . $q . '</p>';
```

Instead of invoking the **mysqli_error()** function, the **error** property of the object will store the database reported problem ⓒ.

7. Finally, change both instances where the database connection is closed to

```
$mysqli->close();
unset($mysqli);
```

The first line closes the connection. The second line removes the variable from existence. This step frees up the used memory and though not obligatory, is a professional touch.

Script 16.2 *continued*

```
70      $mysqli->close(); // Close the database connection.
71      unset($mysqli);
72
73      // Include the footer and quit the script:
74      include('includes/footer.html');
75      exit();
76
77   } else { // Report the errors.
78
79      echo '<h1>Error!</h1>
80      <p class="error">The following error(s) occurred:<br>';
81      foreach ($errors as $msg) { // Print each error.
82         echo " - $msg<br>\n";
83      }
84      echo '</p><p>Please try again.</p><p><br></p>';
85
86   } // End of if (empty($errors)) IF.
87
88      $mysqli->close(); // Close the database connection.
89      unset($mysqli);
90
91 } // End of the main Submit conditional.
92 ?>
93 <h1>Register</h1>
94 <form action="register.php" method="post">
95    <p>First Name: <input type="text" name="first_name" size="15" maxlength="20" value="<?php
       if (isset($_POST['first_name'])) echo $_POST['first_name']; ?>"></p>
96    <p>Last Name: <input type="text" name="last_name" size="15" maxlength="40" value="<?php if
       (isset($_POST['last_name'])) echo $_POST['last_name']; ?>"></p>
97    <p>Email Address: <input type="email" name="email" size="20" maxlength="60" value="<?php if
       (isset($_POST['email'])) echo $_POST['email']; ?>" > </p>
98    <p>Password: <input type="password" name="pass1" size="10" maxlength="20" value="<?php if
       (isset($_POST['pass1'])) echo $_POST['pass1']; ?>" ></p>
99    <p>Confirm Password: <input type="password" name="pass2" size="10" maxlength="20"
       value="<?php if (isset($_POST['pass2'])) echo $_POST['pass2']; ?>" ></p>
100   <p><input type="submit" name="submit" value="Register"></p>
101 </form>
102 <?php include('includes/footer.html'); ?>
```

The original script closed the database connection in two places; make sure you update both.

8. Save the script, place it in your web directory, and test it in your browser **D**.

Fetching results

The previous section demonstrated how to execute "simple" queries, which is how I categorize queries that don't return rows of results. When executing **SELECT** queries, the code is a bit different, because you have to handle the query's results. First, after establishing the **MySQLi** object, you run the query on the database using the **query()** method. If the query is expected to return a result set, assign the results of the method invocation to another variable:

```
$q = 'SELECT * FROM tablename';
$result = $mysqli->query($q);
```

The **$result** variable will be an object of type **MySQLi_Result**: just as some functions return a string or an integer, **MySQLi::query()** will return a **MySQLi_Result** object. Its **num_rows** property will reflect the number of records in the query result:

```
if ($result->num_rows > 0) {
  // Handle the results.
```

If you have only one row returned by the query, you can just call the **fetch_array()** method to get it:

```
$row = $result->fetch_array();
```

This method, like the procedural **mysqli_fetch_array()** counterpart, takes a constant as an optional argument to indicate whether the returned row should be treated as an associative array (**MYSQLI_ASSOC**), an indexed array (**MYSQLI_NUM**), or both (**MYSQLI_BOTH**). **MYSQLI_BOTH** is the default value.

When you have multiple records to fetch, you can do so using a loop:

```
while ($row = $result->fetch_array
→ (MYSQLI_NUM)) {
  // Use $row.
}
```

With that code, **$row** within the loop will be an array, meaning you access individual columns using either **$row[0]** or **$row['column']** (assuming you're using the appropriate constant). If you're really enjoying the OOP syntax, you can use the **fetch_object()** method instead, thereby creating an object instead of an array:

```
$q = 'SELECT user_id, first_name
→ FROM users';
$result = $mysqli->query($q);
while ($row = $result->fetch_object
→ ()) {
  // Use $row->user_id
  // Use $row->first_name
}
```

continues on next page

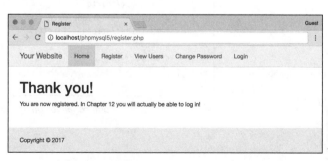

D If all of the code was updated as appropriate, the registration script should work as it did before.

Once you're done with the results, you should free the resources they required:

`$result->free();`

Let's take this information to update **view_users.php** (Script 9.6).

To retrieve query results:

1. Open **view_users.php** (Script 9.6) in your text editor or IDE.

   I've chosen to update this version since it's shorter, but feel free to update a later version of the same script if you'd rather.

2. Change the inclusion of the MySQL connection script to (**Script 16.3**)

   `require('../mysqli_oop_connect.php');`

   Again, the path needs to be correct for your setup.

3. Change the execution of the query to (originally line 14)

   `$r = $mysqli->query($q);`

   Regardless of the type of query being executed, the same **MySQLi::query()** method is called. Here, though, the results of executing the query are assigned to a new variable, which will be an object of type **MySQLi_Result**.

   For brevity, I'm calling this variable just **$r**, but you can use the more formal **$result**, if you'd prefer.

Script 16.3 The **MySQLi** and **MySQLi_Result** classes are used in this script to fetch records from the database.

```
1    <?php # Script 16.3 - view_users.php #6
2    // This script retrieves all the records
     from the users table.
3    // This is an OOP version of the script
     from Chapter 10.
4
5    $page_title = 'View the Current Users';
6    include('includes/header.html');
7
8    // Page header:
9    echo '<h1>Registered Users</h1>';
10
11   require('../mysqli_oop_connect.php');
     // Connect to the db.
12
13   // Make the query:
14   $q = "SELECT CONCAT(last_name,
     ', ', first_name) AS name, DATE_
     FORMAT(registration_date, '%M %d, %Y')
     AS dr FROM users ORDER BY registration_
     date ASC";
15   $r = $mysqli->query($q);
     // Run the query.
16
17   // Count the number of returned rows:
18   $num = $r->num_rows;
19
20   if ($num > 0) { // If it ran OK, display
     the records.
21
22       // Print how many users there are:
23       echo "<p>There are currently $num
         registered users.</p>\n";
24
25       // Table header.
26       echo '<table width="60%">
27       <thead>
28       <tr><td align="left"><strong>Name
         </strong></td><td
         align="left"><strong>Date
         Registered</strong></td></tr>
29       </thead>
30       <tbody>
31       ';
32
```

code continues on next page

```
33      // Fetch and print all the records:
34      while ($row = $r->fetch_
        object()) {
35          echo '<tr><td align="left">'
            . $row->name . '</td><td
            align="left">' . $row->dr .
            '</td></tr>
36          ';
37      }
38
39      echo '</tbody></table>';
        // Close the table.
40
41      $r->free(); // Free up the
        resources.
42      unset($r);
43
44  } else { // If no records were returned.
45
46      echo '<p class="error">There are
        currently no registered users.</p>';
47
48  }
49
50  // Close the database connection.
51  $mysqli->close();
52  unset($mysqli);
53
54  include('includes/footer.html');
55  ?>
```

4. Alter how the number of returned rows is determined to (line 17 of the original script):

   $num = $r->num_rows;

   The result object's **num_rows** property reflects the number of records returned by the query. This value is assigned to the variable **$num**, as before.

   Note that this is a *property*, not a *method* (it's **$r->num_rows**, not **$r->num_rows()**).

5. Change the **while** loop to read

   while ($row = $r->fetch_object()) {

   The change here is that the **MySQLi_Result** object's **fetch_object()** function is called instead of invoking **mysqli_fetch_array()**.

6. Within the **while** loop, change how each column's value is printed:

   echo '<tr><td align="left">' .
   → $row->name . '</td>
   → <td align="left">' . $row->dr .
   → '</td></tr>
   ';

   Since the **$row** variable is now an object, object notation, instead of array notation, must be used to refer to the columns in each row: **$row->name** and **$row->dr** instead of **$row['name']** and **$row['dr']**.

7. Change how the resources are freed:

   $r->free();
   unset($r);

   To free the memory taken by the returned results, call the **MySQLi_Result** object's **free()** method. Furthermore, since that object won't be used anymore in the script, it can be unset.

continues on next page

8. Update how the database connection is closed:

```
$mysqli->close();
unset($mysqli);
```

9. Save the script, place it in your web directory, and test it in your browser **E**.

TIP The real benefit of using the `fetch_object()` method is that you can have the results fetched as a particular type of object. For example, say you have defined a `Car` class in PHP and a script fetches all the stored information about cars from the database. In the PHP script, each record can be fetched as an object of the `Car` class type. By doing so, you'll have created a PHP `Car` object, whose data is populated from the database record, but you can still invoke the methods of the `Car` class.

Prepared statements

Chapter 13 introduced another way of executing queries: using *prepared statements*. Prepared statements can offer improved security, and possibly even better performance, over the standard approach to running queries. Naturally, you can execute prepared statements using the MySQL Improved extension as objects. The steps are the same: after creating a

`MySQLi` object (and therefore a connection to the database), you

- Prepare the query
- Bind the parameters
- Execute the query

In actual code that looks like:

```
$q = 'INSERT INTO tablename
  (this, that) VALUES (?, ?)';
$stmt = $mysqli->prepare($q);
$stmt->bind_param('si', $this, $that);
$this = 'Larry';
$that = 234;
$stmt->execute();
```

The `MySQLi::prepare()` method returns an object of type `MySQLi_Stmt`. That object has a few key properties:

- `affected_rows` stores how many rows were affected by the statement, normally applicable to **INSERT**, **UPDATE**, and **DELETE** queries.

- `num_rows` reflects the number of records in the result set for a **SELECT** query.

- `insert_id` stores the automatically generated ID value for the previous **INSERT** query.

- `error` represents any error that might have occurred.

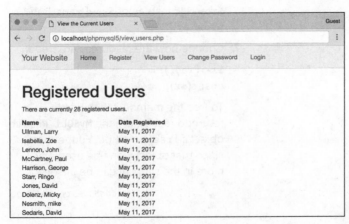

E The object-oriented version of `view_users.php` (Script 16.3) looks the same as the original procedural version.

Once you're done executing the prepared statement, you should close the statement:

```
$stmt->close();
```

Let's apply this information by updating **post_message.php** (Script 13.6). This is a standalone script that uses the *forum* database and isn't, in Chapter 13 or this chapter, tied to any other scripts.

To execute prepared statements:

1. Open **post_message.php** (Script 13.6) in your text editor or IDE.

2. Change the creation of the database connection to (**Script 16.4**)

   ```
   $mysqli = new MySQLi('localhost',
   →'username', 'password', 'forum');
   $mysqli->set_charset('utf8');
   ```

The previous version of the script did not use a separate connection script, and neither will this one. Make sure your values are correct for connecting to the *forum* database on your server.

3. Alter the preparation of the query to read (line 21 of the original script):

   ```
   $stmt = $mysqli->prepare($q);
   ```

   The **MySQLi::prepare()** method prepares a statement, taking the query as its lone argument. It returns an object of type **MySQLi_Stmt**, assigned to **$stmt** here.

4. Change the binding of parameters to

   ```
   $stmt->bind_param('iiiss',
   →$forum_id, $parent_id, $user_id,
   →$subject, $body);
   ```

continues on page 537

Script 16.4 In this version of a script from Chapter 13, the **MySQLi_Stmt** class is used to execute a prepared statement.

```
1   <!doctype html>
2   <html lang="en">
3   <head>
4      <meta charset="utf-8">
5      <title>Post a Message</title>
6   </head>
7   <body>
8   <?php # Script 16.4 - post_message.php #2
9   // This is an OOP version of the script from Chapter 13.
10
11  if ($_SERVER['REQUEST_METHOD'] == 'POST') {
12
13     // Validate the data (omitted)!
14
15     // Connect to the database:
16     $mysqli = new MySQLi('localhost', 'username', 'password', 'forum');
17     $mysqli->set_charset('utf8');
18
19     // Make the query:
20     $q = 'INSERT INTO messages (forum_id, parent_id, user_id, subject, body,
           date_entered) VALUES (?, ?, ?, ?, ?, NOW())';
21
22     // Prepare the statement:
23     $stmt = $mysqli->prepare($q);
```

code continues on next page

```
24
25      // Bind the variables:
26      $stmt->bind_param('iiiss', $forum_id, $parent_id, $user_id, $subject, $body);
27
28      // Assign the values to variables:
29      $forum_id = (int) $_POST['forum_id'];
30      $parent_id = (int) $_POST['parent_id'];
31      $user_id = 3; // The user_id value would normally come from the session.
32      $subject = strip_tags($_POST['subject']);
33      $body = strip_tags($_POST['body']);
34
35      // Execute the query:
36      $stmt->execute();
37
38      // Print a message based upon the result:
39      if ($stmt->affected_rows == 1) {
40          echo '<p>Your message has been posted.</p>';
41      } else {
42          echo '<p style="font-weight: bold; color: #C00">Your message could not be posted.</p>';
43          echo '<p>' . $stmt->error . '</p>';
44      }
45
46      // Close the statement:
47      $stmt->close();
48      unset($stmt);
49
50      // Close the connection:
51      $mysqli->close();
52      unset($mysqli);
53
54  } // End of submission IF.
55
56  // Display the form:
57  ?>
58  <form action="post_message.php" method="post">
59
60      <fieldset><legend>Post a message:</legend>
61
62      <p><strong>Subject</strong>: <input name="subject" type="text" size="30" maxlength="100">
        </p>
63
64      <p><strong>Body</strong>: <textarea name="body" rows="3" cols="40"></textarea></p>
65
66      </fieldset>
67      <div align="center"><input type="submit" name="submit" value="Submit"></div>
68      <input type="hidden" name="forum_id" value="1">
69      <input type="hidden" name="parent_id" value="0">
70
71  </form>
72  </body>
73  </html>
```

F The HTML form for posting a new message.

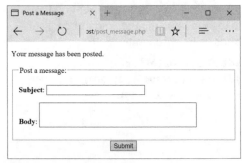

G The new message has been successfully stored in the database.

This code change is simply from `mysqli_stmt_bind_param($stmt...` to `$stmt->bind_param(...`. The method's first argument is an indicator of the data types to follow. The subsequent arguments are the PHP variables to which the query's placeholders are bound.

5. Update the execution of the statement to

   `$stmt->execute();`

6. Change the conditional that tests the success to

   `if ($stmt->affected_rows == 1) {`

   To confirm the success of an **INSERT** query, check the number of affected rows, here referencing the **affected_rows** property of the **MySQLi_Stmt** object.

7. Change the error reporting to use

   `echo '<p>' . $stmt->error . '</p>';`

   At this point in the script, an error would most likely be the result of something like using a duplicate value for a column that must be unique. If there was a syntactical error in the query, that would be in **$mysqli->error** after preparing the query.

8. Update how the statement is closed:

   `$stmt->close();`
   `unset($stmt);`

9. Alter how the database connection is closed:

   `$mysqli->close();`
   `unset($mysqli);`

10. Save the script, place it in your web directory, and test it in your browser **F** and **G**.

The DateTime Class

The **DateTime** class was added in PHP version 5.2. An alternative to the date- and time-related functions introduced in Chapter 11, "Web Application Development," the **DateTime** class packages together all the functionality you might need for manipulating dates and times. It's especially useful for converting and comparing dates and times.

To begin, create a new **DateTime** object:

```
$dt = new DateTime();
```

If created without providing any arguments to the constructor, the generated **DateTime** argument will represent the current date and time. To create a representation of a specific date and time, provide that as the first argument:

```
$dt = new DateTime('2018-04-20');
$dt = new DateTime('2018-04-20 11:15');
```

There are many acceptable formats for specifying the date and time, and they are detailed in the PHP manual. You can also establish the date or time after creating the object using the **setDate()** and **setTime()** methods. The **setDate()** method expects to receive, in order, the desired year, month, and day. The **setTime()** method takes the hour, minute, and optional seconds as its arguments:

```
$dt = new DateTime();
$dt->setDate(2018, 4, 20);
$dt->setTime(11, 15);
```

Outbound Parameters

As in Chapter 13, the **post_message.php** script is a demonstration of using *inbound* parameters: associating placeholders in a query with PHP variables. You can also use *outbound* parameters: binding the values returned by a query to PHP variables. To start, you prepare the query:

```
$q = 'SELECT this, that FROM tablename';
$stmt = $mysqli->prepare($q);
```

Then you bind the returned rows to variables:

```
$stmt->bind_result($this, $that);
```

Next, you call the **MySQLi_Stmt::fetch()** method, most likely as part of a **while** loop:

```
while ($stmt->fetch()) {
}
```

Within the **while** loop, **$this** and **$that** will store each record's returned columns.

Outbound parameters don't offer added security, like inbound parameters, or necessarily better performance, but if you have a query that uses prepared statements, it would make sense to use both inbound and outbound parameters. For example, take a login query:

```
SELECT user_id, first_name, pass FROM users WHERE email='?'
```

You would use inbound parameters to represent the submitted email address but use outbound parameters for the retrieved user ID, first name, and password from that same query.

The **DateTime** object will allow you to establish only valid dates and times, throwing an *exception* for invalid ones 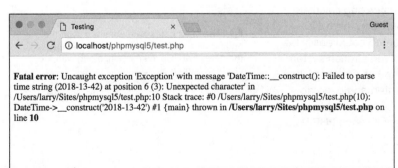:

```
$dt = new DateTime('2018-13-42');
```

Exceptions are a topic not previously introduced. Whereas procedural code may generate errors, objects *throw exceptions* (yes, it's said that they're *thrown*). When you get further along with OOP, you'll learn how to use **try...catch** blocks to "catch" and handle thrown exceptions.

The **DateTime** constructor takes an optional second argument, which is the time zone to use. If not provided, the default time zone for that PHP installation applies. You can also change the time zone after the fact by using **setTimezone()**. Note that both the **setTimezone()** method and the constructor take **DateTimeZone** objects as arguments, not strings:

```
$tz = new DateTimeZone
→ ('America/New_York');
$dt->setTimezone($tz);
```

Once you have a **DateTime** object, you can manipulate its value by adding and subtracting time periods. One way to do so is with the **modify()** method:

```
$dt->modify('+1 day');
$dt->modify('-1 month');
$dt->modify('next Thursday');
```

The values you can provide to the method are quite flexible, and correspond to those that are usable in the **strtotime()** function (which converts a string to a timestamp; see the PHP manual for details).

The **add()** method is used to add a time period to the represented date and time. It takes as its lone argument an object of type **DateInterval**:

```
$di = new DateInterval(interval);
$dt->add($di);
```

There's a specific notation used to set the interval, always starting with the letter *P*, for "period." After that, add an integer and a period designator: *Y*, for years; *M*, for months; *D*, for days; *W*, for weeks; *H*, for hours; *M*, for minutes; and *S*, for seconds. You may wonder how the letter *M* can represent both months and minutes; this is possible because hours, minutes, and seconds should also be preceded by a *T*, for time. These characters should be combined in order from largest to smallest (i.e., from years to seconds). Here are some examples:

- *P3W* represents three weeks.
- *P2Y3M* represents two years and three months.
- *P2M3DT4H18M43S* represents two months, three days, four hours, 18 minutes, and 43 seconds.

continues on next page

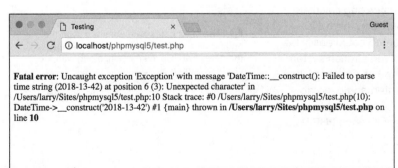

A Attempting to create a **DateTime** object with an invalid date or time results in an exception.

The **sub()** method functions just the same as **add()**, but subtracts the time period from the object:

```
$di = new DateInterval('P2W');
→ // 2 weeks
$dt->sub($di);
```

The **diff()** method returns a **DateInterval** object that reflects the amount of time between two **DateTime** objects:

```
$diff = $dt->diff($dt2);
```

The **DateInterval** class defines several properties for representing the calculated interval: **y** for years, **m** for months, **d** for days, **h** for hours, **i** for minutes, **s** for seconds, and **days**, which also represents days.

The last **DateTime** class method you should be familiar with is **format()**, which returns the represented date formatted as you want it:

```
echo $dt->format(format);
```

For the formatting, you can use the same characters as the **date()** function, covered in Chapter 11.

To demonstrate all this information, this next script will perform a task needed by many web sites: it allows the user to enter two dates to create a range . The script will make use of the new HTML5 date input type to provide a good interface to the user 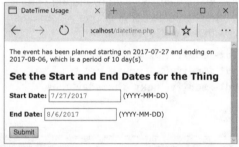.

This script will perform top-quality validation of the submitted dates and calculate the number of days between them 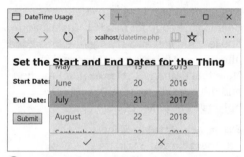. The information presented could easily be applied to, say, a hotel registration system or the like. The script will use much of the information just presented and even do a straight comparison of two **DateTime** objects, a feature possible since PHP 5.2.2.

B A simple form for entering two dates, with the format specified. Confusingly, although the value is set and passed as YYYY-MM-DD (check the HTML source to confirm), modern browsers may still format the displayed value to your regional norm (MM/DD/YYYY here).

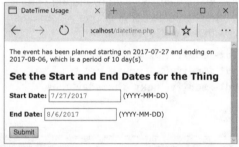

C How the Microsoft Edge browser renders the input type selector.

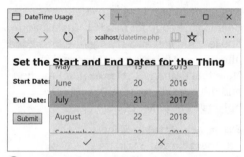

D If two valid dates are submitted, with the ending date coming after the starting date, the dates are displayed again, along with the calculated interval.

To use the DateTime class:

1. Begin a new PHP script in your text editor or IDE, to be named **datetime.php**, starting with the HTML (**Script 16.5**):

```
<!doctype html>
<html lang="en">
<head>
  <meta charset="utf-8">
  <title>DateTime Usage</title>
```

2. Add a splash of CSS:

```
<style>
body {
  font-family: Verdana, Arial,
  →Helvetica, sans-serif;
  font-size: 12px;
  margin: 10px;
}
label { font-weight: bold; }
.error { color: #F00; }
</style>
```

Only the *error* class here is significant in terms of the functionality. It will format error messages in red text.

3. Complete the head and begin the body and the PHP section:

```
</head>
<body>
<?php # Script 16.5 - datetime.php
```

4. Create two **DateTime** objects:

```
$start = new DateTime();
$end = new DateTime();
```

Whether the form has been submitted or not, two **DateTime** objects are first created, both of which will be instantiated using the current date and time. Subsequently, one or both objects will be assigned new values.

5. Add one day to the end date:

```
$end->modify('+1 day');
```

By default, when the page is first loaded, the form will be preset with today as the starting date and tomorrow as the ending date. To determine the ending date, simply modify the object's current value, adding one day.

continues on next page

Script 16.5 Emulating common date selection functionality, this script accepts and validates two dates.

```
1    <!doctype html>
2    <html lang="en">
3    <head>
4      <meta charset="utf-8">
5      <title>DateTime Usage</title>
6      <style>
7      body {
8         font-family: Verdana, Arial, Helvetica, sans-serif;
9         font-size: 12px;
10        margin: 10px;
11     }
12     label { font-weight: bold; }
13     .error { color: #F00; }
14     </style>
15   </head>
16   <body>
17   <?php # Script 16.5 - datetime.php
18
```

code continues on next page

Using the **DateInterval** object and the **DateTime::add()** method, you can do the same thing like so:

```
$day = new DateInterval('P1D');
$end->add($day);
```

6. Establish the default format for displayed dates:

```
$format = 'Y-m-d';
```

The script will use a formatted version of the date in four places. Assigning the preferred format—*YYYY-MM-DD*—to a variable makes it easier to change later, if desired.

This specific format string is used because that's what the date input type requires to preset a value.

7. Begin defining a function:

```
function validate_date($date) {
$array = explode('-', $date);
```

Both submitted dates will need to be validated in a couple of ways, and whenever you have repeating code in a script or application, defining a function to execute that code may make sense. This function takes a date string (not a **DateTime** object) as its lone argument. The string will be the user-submitted value, something like *2018/08/02*. The first thing the function does is break up the string into its three separate parts—year, month, and day—using the **explode()** function. The resulting array is assigned to the **$array** variable.

Script 16.5 *continued*

```
19   // Set the start and end date as today
     and tomorrow by default:
20   $start = new DateTime();
21   $end = new DateTime();
22   $end->modify('+1 day');
23
24   // Default format for displaying dates:
25   $format = 'Y-m-d';
26
27   // This function validates a provided
     date string.
28   // The function returns an array--month,
     day, year--if valid.
29   function validate_date($date) {
30
31       // Break up the string into its
         parts:
32       $array = explode('-', $date);
33
34       // Return FALSE if there aren't 3
         items:
35       if (count($array) != 3) return false;
36
37       // Return FALSE if it's not a valid
         date:
38       if (!checkdate($array[1], $array[2],
         $array[0])) return false;
39
40       // Return the array:
41       return $array;
42
43   } // End of validate_date() function.
44
45   // Check for a form submission:
46   if (isset($_POST['start'],
     $_POST['end'])) {
47
48       // Call the validation function on
         both dates:
49       if ( (list($sy, $sm, $sd) = validate_
         date($_POST['start'])) && (list($ey,
         $em, $ed) = validate_date($_POST
         ['end'])) ) {
50
51           // If it's okay, adjust the
             DateTime objects:
52           $start->setDate($sy, $sm, $sd);
53           $end->setDate($ey, $em, $ed);
54
```

code continues on next page

```
55          // The start date must come first:
56          if ($start < $end) {
57
58              // Determine the interval:
59              $interval = $start->
                diff($end);
60
61              // Print the results:
62              echo "<p>The event has been
                planned starting on {$start->
                format($format)} and ending on
                {$end->format($format)}, which
                is a period of $interval->days
                day(s).</p>";
63
64          } else { // End date must be
            later!
65              echo '<p class="error">The
                starting date must precede the
                ending date.</p>';
66          }
67
68      } else { // An invalid date!
69          echo '<p class="error">One or
            both of the submitted dates was
            invalid.</p>';
70      }
71
72  } // End of form submission.
73
74  // Show the form:
75  ?>
76  <h2>Set the Start and End Dates for the
    Thing</h2>
77  <form action="datetime.php"
    method="post">
78
79      <p><label for="start">Start
        Date:</label> <input type="date"
        name="start" value="<?php echo
        $start->format($format); ?>">
        (YYYY-MM-DD)</p>
80      <p><label for="end">End Date:</
        label> <input type="date" name="end"
        value="<?php echo $end->format
        ($format); ?>"> (YYYY-MM-DD)</p>
81
82      <p><input type="submit"
    value="Submit"></p>
83  </form>
84  </body>
85  </html>
```

8. If the array does not contain three elements, return **false**:

   if (count($array) != 3) return false;

   The first thing the function does is confirm that it has exactly three discrete values to work with, representing a year, month, and day. If the array does not contain three elements, the function returns the value **false** to indicate an invalid date. The **explode()** line in Step 7 and this line invalidate any submitted value that doesn't fit the pattern *X-Y-Z* (although that could still be *cat-dog-zebra*).

   Note that normally I would recommend always using brackets in conditionals, but I've made this code as short as possible by omitting them, and keeping the entire construct on a single line. Also remember that as soon as a function executes a **return** statement, the function is exited.

9. If the provided date isn't a valid date, return **false**:

   if (!checkdate($array[1], $array[2], → $array[0])) return false;

   Similar to Step 8, this code invokes PHP's **checkdate()** function to confirm that the provided date actually exists. If the date does not exist, such as *2011/13/43*, the function again returns **false**.

   Note that the incoming format is *Y-m-d* but that the **checkdate()** function takes the arguments as month, day, and year.

   continues on next page

---

10. Return the date array and complete the function:

```
   return $array;
} // End of validate_date()
→ function.
```

If the provided date is of the correct format and corresponds to an existing date, the array of date elements is returned by the function.

11. If the form has been submitted, validate the user-submitted values:

```
if (isset($_POST['start'],
→ $_POST['end'])) {
   if ( (list($sy, $sm, $sd) =
   → validate_date($_POST['start']))
   → && (list($ey, $em, $ed) =
   → validate_date($_POST['end'])) ) {
```

If the two variables are set, meaning the form has been submitted, both are run through the **validate_date()** function. If that function returns **FALSE** for either date, this conditional will be **FALSE**. If the function returns an array for both dates, assigned to corresponding month, day, and year variables, then the results can be determined and displayed.

12. Reset the dates to the user-submitted dates:

```
$start->setDate($sy, $sm, $sd);
$end->setDate($ey, $em, $ed);
```

Because the provided dates are valid at this point, both objects can be updated to represent the user-entered dates. To do so, the **setDate()** method is invoked, providing it with the individual values.

13. If the end date comes after the start date, calculate the interval between them:

```
if ($start < $end) {
   $interval = $start->diff($end);
```

Just as you can compare two numbers to see if one is greater than or less than the other, you can compare two **DateTime** objects. If the end date does come later, then the difference between the two dates is calculated by invoking the **diff()** method on one object and providing the other as its argument. The result is assigned to the **$interval** variable, which will be an object of type **DateInterval**.

14. Print the results:

```
echo "<p>The event has been
→ planned starting on {$start->
→ format($format)} and ending on
→ {$end->format($format)}, which
→ is a period of $interval->days
→ day(s).</p>";
```

Finally, the results are displayed **D**. As you can see, it's possible to invoke object methods within quotation marks, thereby printing the output of that function call, but you have to wrap the whole construct in curly brackets. Referencing attributes, such as **$interval->days**, does not require the curly brackets.

15. Complete the conditionals begun in Steps 11 and 13:

```
   } else { // End date must be
   → later!
      echo '<p class="error">The
      → starting date must precede
      → the ending date.</p>';
   }
} else { // An invalid date!
   echo '<p class="error">One or
   → both of the submitted dates
   → was invalid.</p>';
}
```

The first **else** clause applies if both dates are valid, but the end date does not follow the start date **E**. The second **else** clause applies if either of the submitted dates does not pass the **validate_date()** test. In this case, both dates will retain the default settings **F**.

16. Complete the form submission conditional, close the PHP block, and begin the HTML form:

```
} // End of form submission.
?>
<h2>Set the Start and End Dates
→ for the Thing</h2>
<form action="datetime.php"
→ method="post">
```

17. Create the two inputs for the dates:

```
<p><label for="start">Start Date:
→ </label> <input type="date"
→ name="start" value="<?php echo
→ $start->format($format); ?>">
→ (YYYY-MM-DD)</p>
<p><label for="end">End
→ Date:</label> <input type="date"
→ name="end" value="<?php echo
→ $end->format($format); ?>">
→ (YYYY-MM-DD)</p>
```

For each input, the value is preset by calling the **format()** method of the associated object. The required format that the date needs to be entered in is also indicated in parentheticals.

18. Complete the form and the HTML page:

```
<p><input type="submit"
→ value="Submit"></p>
</form>
</body>
</html>
```

19. Save the script as **datetime.php**, place it in your web directory, and test it in your browser.

If, when you run this script, you see an exception about relying upon the system's time zone setting, invoke **date_default_timezone_set()**, as explained in Chapter 11, prior to creating the **DateTime** objects.

TIP The DateTime::getTimestamp() method returns the Unix timestamp for the represented date and time.

TIP Internally, the DateTime class represents the dates and times as a 64-bit number, meaning it can represent dates from approximately 292 billion years ago to 292 billion years from now.

TIP Several constants in the DateTime class represent common date-time formats, such as DateTime::COOKIE.

TIP The DateTime methods are also represented in procedural versions.

E The result if the provided starting date actually follows the entered ending date.

F The result if either submitted date does not correspond to a valid date.

Review and Pursue

If you have any problems with the review questions or the pursue prompts, turn to the book's supporting forum (**LarryUllman.com/forums/**).

Review

- What is a *class*? What is a *method*? What are variables defined within classes called?

- What is an object? How do you create an object in PHP? How do you call an object's methods?

- What is a *constructor*?

- What is the syntax for creating a **MySQLi** object?

- How do you execute any kind of query using **MySQLi**?

- How do you make string data safe to use in a query, when using **MySQLi**? Hint: There are two answers.

- How do you check for, and display, a **MySQLi** error?

- How do you fetch the results of **SELECT** queries using the **MySQLi** (and other) objects? What is the difference between using **MySQLi_Result::fetch_array()** and **MySQLi_Result::fetch_object()**?

- How do you execute a prepared statement using the **MySQLi** and **MySQLi_Stmt** classes?

- What syntax is used to create a new **DateTime** object? What are the two ways you can set the object's date and/or time?

- What is an *exception*?

Pursue

- When you're interested in learning more about OOP, consider reading a book or tutorial on the generic subject of OOP, without respect to any given programming language.

- Check out the PHP manual's documentation on OOP in PHP (**www.php.net/oop**).

- Revisit Chapter 9 if you're unclear as to the need to apply **real_escape_string()** to string data used in queries.

- Rewrite some of the other scripts from Chapter 9 and Chapter 10, "Common Programming Techniques," using **MySQLi**.

- Read through the full documentation for the **DateTime** class in the PHP manual (**www.php.net/datetime**).

- Learn about the **strtotime()** function in the PHP manual (**www.php.net/strtotime**).

- If you want a big challenge, apply the information presented in the previous chapter, along with the jQuery UI **Datepicker** tool, to create two JavaScript date selectors for the **datetime.php** script.

Example— Message Board

The functionality of a message board (aka a forum) is rather simple: a post can either start a new topic or be in response to an existing one; posts are added to a database and then displayed on a page. That's about it. Of course, sometimes implementing simple concepts can be quite hard!

To make this example even more exciting and useful, it's going to be not just a message board but rather a *multilingual* message board. Each language will have its own forum, and the key elements—navigation, prompts, introductory text, etc.—will be language-specific.

To focus on the most important aspects of this web application, this chapter omits some others. The three glaring omissions will be user management, error handling, and administration. This shouldn't be a problem for you, though, as the next chapter goes over user management and error handling in great detail. As for the administration, you'll find some recommendations at the chapter's end.

Making the Database

The first step, naturally, is to create the database. A sample message board database **A** was developed in Chapter 6, "Database Design." Although that database is perfectly fine, a variation on it will be used here instead **B**. I'll compare the two to better explain the changes.

To start, the *forums* table is replaced with a *languages* table. Both serve the same purpose: allowing for multiple forums. In this new database, the topic—*PHP and MySQL for Dynamic Web Sites*—will be the same in every forum, but each forum will use a different language. The posts will differ in each forum (this won't be a translation

of the same forum in multiple languages). The *languages* table stores the name of a language in its own alphabet and in English, for the administrator's benefit (this assumes, of course, that English is the administrator's primary language).

The *threads* table in the new database acts like the *messages* table in the old one, with one major difference. Just as the old *messages* table relates to *forums*, *threads* relates to the *languages* and *users* tables; each message can be in only one forum and by only one user; each forum can have multiple messages; and each user can post multiple messages. However, this *threads* table will store only the subject, not the message itself.

A The model for the *forum* database developed in Chapter 6.

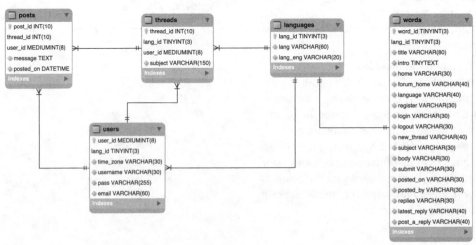

B The revised model for the forum database to be used in this chapter.

There are a couple of reasons for this change. First, having a subject repeat multiple times with each reply (replies, in my experience, almost always have the same subject anyway) is unnecessary. Second, the same goes for the *lang_id* association (it doesn't need to be in each reply if each reply is associated with a single thread). Third, I'm changing the way a thread's hierarchy will be indicated in this database (you'll see how in the next paragraph), and changing the table structures helps in that regard. Finally, the *threads* table will be used every time a user looks at the posts in a forum. Removing the message bodies from that table will improve the performance of those queries.

Moving on to the *posts* table, its sole purpose is to store the actual bodies of the messages associated with a thread. In Chapter 6's database, the *messages* table had a *parent_id* column, used to indicate the message to which a new message was a response. It was hierarchical: message 3 might be the starting post; message 18 might be a response to 3, message 20 a response to 18, and so on ⓒ. That version of the database more directly indicated the responses; this version will store only the thread that a message goes under: messages 18 and 20 both use a *thread_id* of 3. This alteration will make showing a thread much more efficient (in terms of the PHP and MySQL required), and the date/time that each message was posted can be used to order them.

Those three tables provide the bulk of the forum functionality. The database also needs a *users* table. In this version of the forum, only registered users can post messages, which I think is a really, really, really good policy (it cuts way down on spam and hack attempts). Registered users can also have their default language (from the *languages* table) and time zone recorded along with their account information, to give them a more personalized experience. A combination of their username and password would be used to log in.

The final table, *words*, is necessary to make the site multilingual. This table will store translations of common elements: navigation links, form prompts, headers, and so forth. Each language in the site will have one record in this table. It'll be a nice and surprisingly easy feature to use. Arguably, the words listed in this table could also go in the *languages* table, but then the implication would be that the words are also related to the *threads* table, which would not be the case.

That's the thinking behind this new database design. You'll learn more as you create the tables in the following steps. As with the other examples in this book, you can also download the SQL necessary for this chapter—the commands suggested in these steps, plus more—from the book's corresponding web site (`LarryUllman.com`).

message_id	parent_id
3	0
4	0
18	3
19	4
20	18

ⓒ How the relationship among messages was indicated using the older database schema.

To make the database:

1. Access your MySQL server and set the character set to be used for communicating 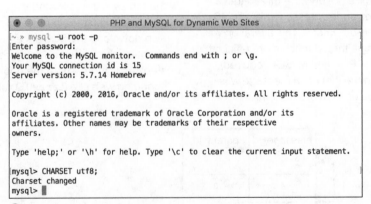:

   CHARSET utf8;

   I'll be using the mysql client in the figures, but you can use whatever interface you'd like. The first step, though, has to be changing the character set to UTF-8 for the queries to come. If you don't do this, some of the characters in the queries will be stored as gibberish in the database (see the sidebar "Strange Characters"). Note that if you're using phpMyAdmin, you'll need to establish the character set in its configuration file.

Strange Characters

If, when you're implementing this chapter's example, you see strange characters—boxes, numeric codes, or question marks instead of actual language characters—there might be several reasons why. When this happens, the underlying issue is one of *mismatching encodings* (or, in database terms, *character sets*).

A computer's ability to display a character depends on both the file's encoding and the characters (i.e., fonts) supported by the operating system. This means that every PHP or HTML page must use the proper encoding. In addition, the database in MySQL must use the proper encoding (as indicated in the steps for creating the database). Third, and this can be a common cause of problems, the communication between PHP and MySQL must also use the proper encoding. I address this issue in the **mysqli_connect.php** script. Finally, if you use the mysql client, phpMyAdmin, or another tool to populate the database, that interaction must use the proper encoding, too.

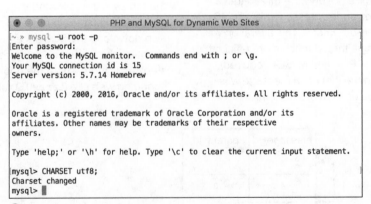

```
PHP and MySQL for Dynamic Web Sites

~ » mysql -u root -p
Enter password:
Welcome to the MySQL monitor.  Commands end with ; or \g.
Your MySQL connection id is 15
Server version: 5.7.14 Homebrew

Copyright (c) 2000, 2016, Oracle and/or its affiliates. All rights reserved.

Oracle is a registered trademark of Oracle Corporation and/or its
affiliates. Other names may be trademarks of their respective
owners.

Type 'help;' or '\h' for help. Type '\c' to clear the current input statement.

mysql> CHARSET utf8;
Charset changed
mysql>
```

D To use Unicode data in queries, you need to change the character set used to communicate with MySQL.

2. Create a new database **E**:

```
CREATE DATABASE forum2 CHARACTER
→ SET utf8;
USE forum2;
```

So as not to muddle things with the tables created in the original *forum* database (from Chapter 6), a new database will be created.

If you're using a hosted site and cannot create your own databases, use the database provided for you and select that. If your existing database has tables with these same names—*words*, *languages*, *threads*, *users*, and *posts*, rename the tables (either the existing or the new ones) and change the code in the rest of the chapter accordingly.

```
● ● ●         PHP and MySQL for Dynamic Web Sites
mysql> CREATE DATABASE forum2 CHARACTER SET utf8;
Query OK, 1 row affected (0.01 sec)

mysql> USE forum2;
Database changed
mysql> ▊
```

E Creating and selecting the database for this example. This database uses the UTF-8 character set so that it can support multiple languages.

```
● ● ●         PHP and MySQL for Dynamic Web Sites
mysql> CREATE TABLE languages (
    -> lang_id TINYINT UNSIGNED NOT NULL AUTO_INCREMENT,
    -> lang VARCHAR(60) NOT NULL,
    -> lang_eng VARCHAR(20) NOT NULL,
    -> PRIMARY KEY (lang_id),
    -> UNIQUE (lang)
    -> );
Query OK, 0 rows affected (0.12 sec)

mysql> ▊
```

F Creating the *languages* table.

Whether you create this database from scratch or use a new one, it's very important that the tables use the UTF-8 encoding to be able to support multiple languages (see Chapter 6 for more). If you are using an existing database and don't want to potentially cause problems by changing the character set for all your tables, just add the **CHARACTER SET utf8** clause to each table definition (Steps 3 through 7).

3. Create the *languages* table **F**:

```
CREATE TABLE languages (
lang_id TINYINT UNSIGNED NOT NULL
→ AUTO_INCREMENT,
lang VARCHAR(60) NOT NULL,
lang_eng VARCHAR(20) NOT NULL,
PRIMARY KEY (lang_id),
UNIQUE (lang)
);
```

This is the simplest table of the bunch. There won't be many languages represented, so the primary key (*lang_id*) can be a **TINYINT**. The *lang* column is defined a bit larger, since it'll store characters in other languages, which may require more space. This column must also be unique. Note that I don't call this column "language," because that's a reserved keyword in MySQL (actually, I *could* still call it that, and you'll see what would be required to do that in Step 7). The *lang_eng* column is the English equivalent of the language so that the administrator can easily see which languages are which.

continues on next page

4. Create the *threads* table Ⓖ

```
CREATE TABLE threads (
thread_id INT UNSIGNED NOT NULL
→ AUTO_INCREMENT,
lang_id TINYINT(3) UNSIGNED
→ NOT NULL,
user_id INT UNSIGNED NOT NULL,
subject VARCHAR(150) NOT NULL,
PRIMARY KEY (thread_id),
INDEX (lang_id),
INDEX (user_id)
);
```

The *threads* table contains four columns and relates to both the *languages* and *users* tables (through the *lang_id* and *user_id* foreign keys, respectively). The *subject* here needs to be long enough to store subjects in multiple languages (characters take up more bytes in non-Western languages).

The columns that will be used in joins and **WHERE** clauses—*lang_id* and *user_id*—are indexed, as is *thread_id* (as a primary key, it will be indexed).

5. Create the *posts* table Ⓗ

```
CREATE TABLE posts (
post_id INT UNSIGNED NOT NULL
→ AUTO_INCREMENT,
thread_id INT UNSIGNED NOT NULL,
user_id INT UNSIGNED NOT NULL,
message TEXT NOT NULL,
posted_on DATETIME NOT NULL,
PRIMARY KEY (post_id),
INDEX (thread_id),
INDEX (user_id)
);
```

The main column in this table is *message*, which stores each post's body. Two columns are foreign keys, tying into the *threads* and *users* tables. The *posted_on* column is of type **DATETIME** but will use UTC (Coordinated Universal Time; see Chapter 6). Nothing special needs to be done here for that, though.

```
●  ●  ●       PHP and MySQL for Dynamic Web Sites
mysql> CREATE TABLE threads (
    -> thread_id INT UNSIGNED NOT NULL AUTO_INCREMENT,
    -> lang_id TINYINT(3) UNSIGNED NOT NULL,
    -> user_id INT UNSIGNED NOT NULL,
    -> subject VARCHAR(150) NOT NULL,
    -> PRIMARY KEY (thread_id),
    -> INDEX (lang_id),
    -> INDEX (user_id)
    -> );
Query OK, 0 rows affected (0.02 sec)

mysql>
```

Ⓖ Creating the *threads* table. This table stores the topic subjects and associates them with a language (i.e., a forum).

```
●  ●  ●       PHP and MySQL for Dynamic Web Sites
mysql> CREATE TABLE posts (
    -> post_id INT UNSIGNED NOT NULL AUTO_INCREMENT,
    -> thread_id INT UNSIGNED NOT NULL,
    -> user_id INT UNSIGNED NOT NULL,
    -> message TEXT NOT NULL,
    -> posted_on DATETIME NOT NULL,
    -> PRIMARY KEY (post_id),
    -> INDEX (thread_id),
    -> INDEX (user_id)
    -> );
Query OK, 0 rows affected (0.03 sec)

mysql>
```

Ⓗ Creating the *posts* table, which links to both threads and users.

6. Create the *users* table **I**:

```
CREATE TABLE users (
user_id MEDIUMINT UNSIGNED NOT
→ NULL AUTO_INCREMENT,
lang_id TINYINT UNSIGNED
→ NOT NULL,
time_zone VARCHAR(30) NOT NULL,
username VARCHAR(30) NOT NULL,
pass VARCHAR(255) NOT NULL,
email VARCHAR(60) NOT NULL,
PRIMARY KEY (user_id),
UNIQUE (username),
UNIQUE (email),
INDEX login (username, pass)
);
```

For the sake of brevity, I'm omitting some of the other columns you'd put in this table, such as registration date, first name, and last name. For more on creating and using a table like this, see the next chapter.

In my thinking about this site, I expect users will select their preferred language and time zone when they register so that they can have a more personalized experience. They can also have a user-name, which will be displayed in posts (instead of their email address). Both the username and the email address must be unique, which is something you'd need to address in the registration process.

```
PHP and MySQL for Dynamic Web Sites
mysql> CREATE TABLE users (
    -> user_id MEDIUMINT UNSIGNED NOT NULL AUTO_INCREMENT,
    -> lang_id TINYINT UNSIGNED NOT NULL,
    -> time_zone VARCHAR(30) NOT NULL,
    -> username VARCHAR(30) NOT NULL,
    -> pass VARCHAR(255) NOT NULL,
    -> email VARCHAR(60) NOT NULL,
    -> PRIMARY KEY (user_id),
    -> UNIQUE (username),
    -> UNIQUE (email),
    -> INDEX login (username, pass)
    -> );
Query OK, 0 rows affected (0.02 sec)

mysql>
```

I Creating a bare-bones version of the *users* table.

7. Create the *words* table **J**:

```
CREATE TABLE words (
word_id TINYINT UNSIGNED NOT NULL
→ AUTO_INCREMENT,
lang_id TINYINT UNSIGNED NOT NULL,
title VARCHAR(80) NOT NULL,
intro TINYTEXT NOT NULL,
home VARCHAR(30) NOT NULL,
forum_home VARCHAR(40) NOT NULL,
`language` VARCHAR(40) NOT NULL,
register VARCHAR(30) NOT NULL,
login VARCHAR(30) NOT NULL,
logout VARCHAR(30) NOT NULL,
new_thread VARCHAR(40) NOT NULL,
subject VARCHAR(30) NOT NULL,
body VARCHAR(30) NOT NULL,
submit VARCHAR(30) NOT NULL,
posted_on VARCHAR(30) NOT NULL,
posted_by VARCHAR(30) NOT NULL,
replies VARCHAR(30) NOT NULL,
latest_reply VARCHAR(40) NOT NULL,
post_a_reply VARCHAR(40) NOT NULL,
PRIMARY KEY (word_id),
UNIQUE (lang_id)
);
```

continues on next page

```
PHP and MySQL for Dynamic Web Sites
mysql> CREATE TABLE words (
    -> word_id TINYINT UNSIGNED NOT NULL AUTO_INCREMENT,
    -> lang_id TINYINT UNSIGNED NOT NULL,
    -> title VARCHAR(80) NOT NULL,
    -> intro TINYTEXT NOT NULL,
    -> home VARCHAR(30) NOT NULL,
    -> forum_home VARCHAR(40) NOT NULL,
    -> `language` VARCHAR(40) NOT NULL,
    -> register VARCHAR(30) NOT NULL,
    -> login VARCHAR(30) NOT NULL,
    -> logout VARCHAR(30) NOT NULL,
    -> new_thread VARCHAR(40) NOT NULL,
    -> subject VARCHAR(30) NOT NULL,
    -> body VARCHAR(30) NOT NULL,
    -> submit VARCHAR(30) NOT NULL,
    -> posted_on VARCHAR(30) NOT NULL,
    -> posted_by VARCHAR(30) NOT NULL,
    -> replies VARCHAR(30) NOT NULL,
    -> latest_reply VARCHAR(40) NOT NULL,
    -> post_a_reply VARCHAR(40) NOT NULL,
    -> PRIMARY KEY (word_id),
    -> UNIQUE (lang_id)
    -> );
Query OK, 0 rows affected (0.01 sec)

mysql>
```

J Creating the *words* table, which stores representations of key words in different languages.

This table will store different translations of common elements used on the site. Some elements—*home*, *forum_home*, *language*, *register*, *login*, *logout*, and *new_thread*—will be the names of links. Other elements—*subject*, *body*, *submit*—are used on the page for posting messages. Another category of elements is those used on the forum's main page: *posted_on*, *posted_by*, *replies*, and *latest_reply*.

Some of these will be used multiple times in the site, and yet, this is still an incomplete list. As you implement the site yourself, you'll see other places where word definitions could be added.

Each column is of **VARCHAR** type, except for *intro*, which is a body of text to be used on the main page. Most of the columns have a limit of 30, allowing for characters in other languages that require more bytes, except for a handful of columns that might need to be bigger.

For each column, its name implies the value to be stored in that column. For one—*language*—I've used a MySQL keyword simply to demonstrate how that can be done. The fix is to surround the column's name in backticks so that MySQL doesn't confuse this column's name with the keyword "language."

8. Populate the *languages* table:

```
INSERT INTO languages (lang,
lang_eng) VALUES
('English', 'English'),
('Português', 'Portuguese'),
('Français', 'French'),
('Norsk', 'Norwegian'),
('Romanian', 'Romanian'),
('Ελληνικά', 'Greek'),
('Deutsch', 'German'),
('Srpski', 'Serbian'),
('日本語', 'Japanese'),
('Nederlands', 'Dutch');
```

This is just a handful of the languages the site will represent thanks to some assistance provided to me (see the sidebar "A Note on Translations"). For each, the native and English word for that language is stored **K**.

K The populated *languages* table, with each language written in its own alphabet.

9. Populate the *users* table **L**:

```
INSERT INTO users (lang_id,
→ time_zone, username, pass,
→ email) VALUES
(1, 'US/Eastern', 'troutster', '',
→ 'email@example.com'),
(7, 'Europe/Berlin', 'Ute', '',
→ 'email1@example.com'),
(4, 'Europe/Oslo', 'Silje', '',
→ 'email2@example.com'),
(2, 'America/Sao_Paulo', 'João', '',
→ 'email3@example.com'),
(1, 'Pacific/Auckland', 'kiwi', '',
→ 'kiwi@example.org');
```

Because the PHP scripts will show the users associated with posts, a couple of users are necessary. A language and a time zone are associated with each (see Chapter 6 for more on time zones in MySQL). Each user's password will be represented as an empty string for now—real password hashing would be done using PHP's **password_hash()** function (see Chapter 13, "Security Methods," for more).

continues on next page

A Note on Translations

Several readers around the world were kind enough to provide me with translations of key words, names, message subjects, and message bodies. For their help, I'd like to extend my sincerest thanks to (in no particular order): Angelo (Portuguese), Iris (German), Johan (Norwegian), Gabi (Romanian), Darko (Serbian), Emmanuel and Jean-François (French), Andreas and Simeon (Greek), Darius (Filipino/Tagalog), Olaf (Dutch), and Tsutomu (Japanese).

If you know one of these languages, you may see linguistic mistakes made in this text or in the corresponding images. If so, it's almost certainly my fault, having miscommunicated the words I needed translated or improperly entered the responses into the database. I apologize in advance for any such mistakes but hope you'll focus more on the database, the code, and the functionality. My thanks, again, to those who helped!

```
PHP and MySQL for Dynamic Web Sites
mysql> INSERT INTO users (lang_id, time_zone, username, pass, email) VALUES
    -> (1, 'US/Eastern', 'troutster', '', 'email@example.com'),
    -> (7, 'Europe/Berlin', 'Ute', '', 'email1@example.com'),
    -> (4, 'Europe/Oslo', 'Silje', '', 'email2@example.com'),
    -> (2, 'America/Sao_Paulo', 'João', '', 'email3@example.com'),
    -> (1, 'Pacific/Auckland', 'kiwi', '', 'kiwi@example.org');
Query OK, 5 rows affected (0.00 sec)
Records: 5  Duplicates: 0  Warnings: 0

mysql>
```

L A few users are added manually, since there is no registration process in this site (but see Chapter 18, "Example—User Registration," for that).

10. Populate the *words* table:

```
INSERT INTO words VALUES
(NULL, 1, 'PHP and MySQL for
→ Dynamic Web Sites: The Forum!',
→ '<p>Welcome to our site....
→ please use the links above...
→ blah, blah, blah.</p>\r\n<p>
→ Welcome to our site....please
→ use the links above...blah,
→ blah, blah.</p>', 'Home', 'Forum
→ Home', 'Language', 'Register',
→ 'Login', 'Logout', 'New Thread',
→ 'Subject', 'Body', 'Submit',
→ 'Posted on', 'Posted by',
→ 'Replies', 'Latest Reply', 'Post
→ a Reply'),
```

These are the words associated with each term in English. The record has a *lang_id* of 1, which matches the *lang_id* for English in the *languages* table. The SQL to insert words for other languages into this table is available from the book's supporting website.

TIP This chapter doesn't go through the steps for creating the `mysqli_connect.php` page, which connects to the database. Instead, just copy the one from Chapter 9, "Using PHP with MySQL." Then change the parameters in the script to use a valid username/password/hostname combination to connect to the forum2 database.

TIP As a reminder, the foreign key in one table should be of the exact same type and size as the matching primary key in another table.

Writing the Templates

This example, like any site containing lots of pages, will make use of a template to separate out the bulk of the presentation from the logic. Following the instructions laid out in Chapter 3, "Creating Dynamic Web Sites," a header file and a footer file will store most of the HTML code. Each PHP script will then include these files to make a complete HTML page **A**. But this example is a little more complicated.

One of the goals of this site is to serve users in many different languages. Accomplishing that involves not just letting them *post messages* in their native language but making sure they can use the *whole site* in their native language as well. This means that the page title, the navigation links, the captions, the prompts, and even the menus need to appear in their language **B**.

The instructions for making the database illustrate how this is accomplished: by storing translations of all key words in a table. The header file, therefore, needs to pull out all these key words so that they can be used as needed. This header file will also display different links based on whether the user is logged in or not. Adding just one more little twist: if the user is on the forum page, viewing all the threads in a language, the user will also be given the option to post a new thread **C**.

continues on next page

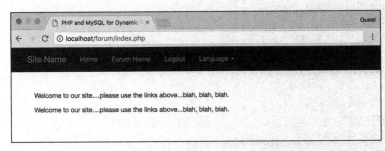

A The basic layout and appearance of the site.

B The home page viewed in Norwegian (compare with **A**).

C The added link allowing the user to start a new thread in the current forum.

The template itself uses Bootstrap (**www.getbootstrap.com**) for the formatting and layout. All the required CSS and JavaScript files are either inline or loaded via a CDN.

To make the template:

1. Begin a new document in your text editor or IDE, to be named **header.html** (Script 17.1):

```
<?php # Script 17.1 - header.html
header('Content-Type: text/html;
→ charset=UTF-8');
```

Since this script will need to do a fair amount of data validation and retrieval, it starts with a PHP block. The script also indicates to the browser its encoding—UTF-8—using the **header()** function. The idea of setting the encoding via a **header()** function call was mentioned in a tip in Chapter 11, "Web Application Development." This isn't absolutely required since you could set the encoding in the HTML instead, but because the application may work with multiple languages, this is an extra precaution.

Script 17.1 The **header.html** file begins the template. It also sets the page's encoding, starts the session, and retrieves the language-specific key words from the database.

```
1   <?php # Script 17.1 - header.html
2   /* This script...
3    * - starts the HTML template
4    * - indicates the encoding using
        header()
5    * - starts the session
6    * - gets the language-specific words
        from the database
7    * - lists the available languages
8    */
9
10  // Indicate the encoding:
11  header('Content-Type: text/html;
        charset=UTF-8');
12
13  // Start the session:
14  session_start();
15
16  // For testing purposes:
17  $_SESSION['user_id'] = 1;
18  $_SESSION['user_tz'] =
        'America/New_York';
19  // For logging out:
20  //$_SESSION = [];
21
22  // Need the database connection:
23  require('../mysqli_connect.php');
24
25  // Check for a new language ID...
26  // Then store the language ID in the
        session:
27  if (isset($_GET['lid']) &&
28      filter_var($_GET['lid'],
            FILTER_VALIDATE_INT,
            array('min_range' => 1))
29      ) {
30      $_SESSION['lid'] = $_GET['lid'];
31  } elseif (!isset($_SESSION['lid'])) {
32      $_SESSION['lid'] = 1; // Default.
33  }
34
35  // Get the words for this language:
36  $q = "SELECT * FROM words WHERE
        lang_id = {$_SESSION['lid']}";
37  $r = mysqli_query($dbc, $q);
38  if (mysqli_num_rows($r) == 0) { //
        Invalid language ID!
```

code continues on next page

```
39
40        // Use the default language:
41        $_SESSION['lid'] = 1; // Default.
42        $q = "SELECT * FROM words WHERE
          lang_id = {$_SESSION['lid']}";
43        $r = mysqli_query($dbc, $q);
44
45    }
46
47    // Fetch the results into a variable:
48    $words = mysqli_fetch_array
      ($r, MYSQLI_ASSOC);
49
50    // Free the results:
51    mysqli_free_result($r);
52    ?>
53    <!DOCTYPE html>
54    <html lang="en">
55    <head>
56        <meta charset="utf-8">
57        <meta http-equiv="X-UA-Compatible"
          content="IE=edge">
58        <meta name="viewport"
          content="width=device-width,
          initial-scale=1">
59        <title><?php echo $words['title'];
          ?></title>
60        <link rel="stylesheet"
          href="https://maxcdn.bootstrapcdn.
          com/bootstrap/3.3.7/css/bootstrap.
          min.css" integrity="sha384-BVYi
          iSIFeK1dGmJRAkycuHAHRg32OmUcww7
          on3RYdg4Va+PmSTsz/K68vbdEjh4u"
          crossorigin="anonymous">
61        <style type="text/css">
62    body {
63      padding-top: 50px;
64    }
65    .starter-template {
66      padding: 40px 15px;
67      text-align: left;
68    }
69    </style>
70    </head>
71    <body>
72    <nav class="navbar navbar-inverse
      navbar-fixed-top">
73        <div class="container">
74            <div class="navbar-header">
```

code continues on next page

2. Start a session:

```
session_start();
$_SESSION['user_id'] = 1;
$_SESSION['user_tz'] =
→ 'America/New_York';
// $_SESSION = [];
```

To track users after they log in, the site will use sessions. Since the site doesn't have registration and login functionality in this chapter, two lines can virtually log in the user. Ordinarily, both values would come from a database, but they'll be set here for testing purposes. To virtually log the user out, uncomment the third line.

3. Include the database connection:

```
require('../mysqli_connect.php');
```

As with many other examples in this book, the assumption is that the **mysqli_connect.php** script is stored in the directory above the current one, outside of the web root. If that won't be the case for you, change this code accordingly.

4. Determine the language ID:

```
if (isset($_GET['lid']) &&
    filter_var($_GET['lid'],
    → FILTER_VALIDATE_INT,
    → array('min_range' => 1))
    ) {
    $_SESSION['lid'] = $_GET['lid'];
} elseif (!isset($_SESSION['lid'])) {
    $_SESSION['lid'] = 1; // Default.
}
```

continues on page 561

```
75                  <a class="navbar-brand" href="index.php">Site Name</a>
76              </div>
77          <div id="navbar" class="collapse navbar-collapse">
78              <ul class="nav navbar-nav">
79  <?php // Display links:
80
81  // Default links:
82  echo '<li><a href="index.php">' . $words['home'] . '</a></li>
83  <li><a href="forum.php">' . $words['forum_home'] . '</a></li>';
84
85  // Display links based upon login status:
86  if (isset($_SESSION['user_id'])) {
87
88      // If this is the forum page, add a link for posting new threads:
89      if (basename($_SERVER['PHP_SELF']) == 'forum.php') {
90          echo '<li><a href="post.php">' . $words['new_thread'] . '</a></li>';
91      }
92
93      // Add the logout link:
94      echo '<li><a href="logout.php">' . $words['logout'] . '</a></li>';
95
96  } else {
97
98      // Register and login links:
99      echo '<li><a href="register.php">' . $words['register'] . '</a></li>
100     <li><a href="login.php">' . $words['login'] . '</a></li>';
101 }
102
103 // Retrieve all the languages...
104 echo '<li class="dropdown"><a href="forum.php" class="dropdown-toggle" data-toggle="dropdown"
    role="button" aria-haspopup="true" aria-expanded="false">' . $words['language'] . '
    <span class="caret"></span></a>
105 <ul class="dropdown-menu">';
106
107 $q = "SELECT lang_id, lang FROM languages ORDER BY lang_eng ASC";
108 $r = mysqli_query($dbc, $q);
109 if (mysqli_num_rows($r) > 0) {
110   while ($menu_row = mysqli_fetch_array($r, MYSQLI_NUM)) {
111     echo '<li><a href="forum.php?lid=' . $menu_row[0] . '">' . $menu_row[1] . '</a></li>';
112   }
113 }
114 mysqli_free_result($r);
115 ?>
116                  </ul></li>
117              </ul>
118          </div><!-- navbar -->
119      </div><!-- container -->
120 </nav>
121
122 <div class="container">
123     <div class="starter-template">
```

Next, the language ID value (abbreviated *lid*) needs to be established. The language ID controls what language is used for all the site elements, and it also dictates the forum to be viewed. The language ID could be found in the session, after retrieving that information upon a successful login (because the user's language ID is stored in the *users* table). Alternatively, any user can change the displayed language on the fly using the language dropdown in the navigation links (see Ⓐ). In that case, the submitted language ID needs to be validated as an integer greater than 1; this is easily accomplished by using the Filter extension (see Chapter 13).

The second clause applies if the page did not receive a language ID in the URL and the language ID has not already been established in the session. In that case, a default language is selected. This value corresponds to English in the *languages* table in the database. You can change it to any ID that matches the default language you'd like to use.

5. Get the keywords for this language:

```
$q = "SELECT * FROM words WHERE
→ lang_id = {$_SESSION['lid']} ";
$r = mysqli_query($dbc, $q);
```

The next step in the header file is to retrieve from the database all the key words for the given language.

6. If the query returned no records, get the default words:

```
if (mysqli_num_rows($r) == 0) {
  $_SESSION['lid'] = 1;
  $q = "SELECT * FROM words WHERE
  → lang_id = {$_SESSION['lid']} ";
  $r = mysqli_query($dbc, $q);
}
```

It's possible, albeit unlikely, that `$_SESSION['lid']` does not equate to a record from the *words* table. In that case, the query would return no records (but run without error). Consequently, the default language words must now be retrieved. Notice that neither this block of code, nor that in Step 5, actually fetches the returned record. That will happen, for both potential queries, in Step 7.

7. Fetch the retrieved words into an array, free the resources, and close the PHP section:

```
$words = mysqli_fetch_array
→ ($r, MYSQLI_ASSOC);
mysqli_free_result($r);
?>
```

After this point, the `$words` array represents all the navigation and common elements in the user's selected language (or the default language).

Calling `mysqli_free_result()` isn't necessary but makes for tidy programming.

8. Start the HTML page:

```
<!DOCTYPE html>
<html lang="en">
<head>
    <meta charset="utf-8">
    <meta http-equiv="X-UA-
    → Compatible" content="IE=edge">
    <meta name="viewport"
    → content="width=device-width,
    → initial-scale=1">
    <title><?php echo
    → $words['title']; ?></title>
```

Note that the encoding is also indicated in a **META** tag, even though the PHP **header()** call already identifies the encoding. This is just a matter of being thorough.

continues on next page

The header file as written uses as the title of every page a value in the $words array (i.e., the page title will always be the same for every page in a chosen language). You could easily modify this code so that the page's title is a combination of the language word and a page-specific variable, such as $page_title used in Chapter 3 and subsequent examples.

9. Add the CSS:

```
<link rel="stylesheet"
→ href="https://maxcdn.
→ bootstrapcdn.com/
→ bootstrap/3.3.7/css/
→ bootstrap.min.css"
→ integrity="sha384-BVYiiSIF
→ eK1dGmJRAkycuHAHRg320mUcww
→ 7on3RYdg4Va+PmSTsz
→ /K68vbdEjh4u"
crossorigin="anonymous">
<style type="text/css">
body {
  padding-top: 50px;
}
.starter-template {
  padding: 40px 15px;
  text-align: left;
}</style>
```

This is all taken from the Bootstrap starter template. Normally you'd put all CSS in an external file, but because there's so little of it, I'm putting the additional CSS in the document itself.

10. Complete the HTML head and begin the page:

```
</head>
<body>
<nav class="navbar navbar-inverse
→ navbar-fixed-top">
    <div class="container">
        <div class="navbar-
        → header">
            <a class="navbar-
            → brand" href="index.
            → php">Site Name</a>
        </div>
        <div id="navbar"
        → class="collapse
        → navbar-collapse">
            <ul class="nav
            → navbar-nav">
```

The only repeating content on the page is the navigation bar across the top, begun here.

11. Start displaying the links:

```
<?php // Display links:
echo '<li><a href="index.php">' .
→ $words['home'] . '</a></li>
<li><a href="forum.php">' . $words
→ ['forum_home'] . '</a></li>';
```

The first two links will always appear, whether or not the user is logged in and regardless of the page the user is currently viewing. For each link, the text of the link itself will be language specific.

12. If the user is logged in, show "new thread" and logout links:

```
if (isset($_SESSION['user_id'])) {
  if (basename($_SERVER['PHP_
  → SELF']) == 'forum.php') {
        echo '<li><a href="post.
        → php">' . $words['new_
        → thread'] . '</a></li>';
  }
  echo '<li><a href="logout.php">'
→ . $words['logout'] . '</a></li>';
```

Confirmation of the user's logged-in status is achieved by checking for the presence of a **$_SESSION['user_id']** variable. If it's set, then the logout link can be created. Before that, a check is made to see if this is the **forum.php** page. If so, then a link to start a new thread is created (users can only create new threads if they're on the forum page; you wouldn't want them to create a new thread on some of the other pages, like the home page, because it wouldn't be clear to which forum the thread should be posted). The code for checking what page it is, using the **basename()** function, was first introduced in Chapter 12, "Cookies and Sessions."

13. Display the links for users not logged in:

```
} else {
  echo '<li><a href="register.php">'
  → . $words['register'] . '</a></li>
    <li><a href="login.php">' .
    → $words['login'] . '</a></li>';
}
```

If the user isn't logged in, links are provided for registering and logging in.

Logout	Language ▾
	Nederlands
There	English	es
	Français
	Deutsch
	Ελληνικά
	日本語
	Norsk
	Português
	Romanian
	Srpski

D The language dropdown menu, with each option in its native language.

14. Start the dropdown for choosing a language:

```
echo '<li class="dropdown">
→ <a href="forum.php"
→ class="dropdown-toggle"
→ data-toggle="dropdown"
→ role="button" aria-haspopup="true"
→ aria-expanded="false">' .
→ $words['language'] . '
→ <span class="caret"></span></a>
<ul class="dropdown-menu">';
```

The user can choose a language (which is also a forum) via a dropdown navigation menu **D**. The text for the dropdown will be the word "language," in the user's default language.

15. Retrieve every language from the database, and add each to the menu:

```
$q = "SELECT lang_id, lang FROM
→ languages ORDER BY lang_eng ASC";
$r = mysqli_query($dbc, $q);
if (mysqli_num_rows($r) > 0) {
  while ($menu_row = mysqli_fetch_
  → array($r, MYSQLI_NUM)) {
    echo '<li><a href="forum.
    → php?lid=' . $menu_row[0] .
    → '">' . $menu_row[1] . '</a>
    → </li>';
  }
}
mysqli_free_result($r);
```

This query retrieves the languages and the language ID from the *languages* table. Each is added as a list item to the dropdown menu.

Each link points to **forum.php** and passes along the language ID in the URL, as a *lid* parameter. When users select their language, they'll be taken to the forum of their choice.

continues on next page

Again, calling **mysqli_free_result()** isn't required, but doing so can help limit bugs and improve performance. In particular, when you have pages that run multiple **SELECT** queries, **mysqli_free_result()** can help avoid confusion issues between PHP and MySQL.

16. Complete the PHP section and the initial content:

```
?>
            </ul></li>
        </ul>
    </div><!-- navbar -->
  </div><!-- container -->
</nav>
<div class="container">
    <div class="starter-template">
```

17. Save the file as **header.html**.

Even though it contains a fair amount of PHP, this script will still use the **.html** extension (which I prefer to use for template files). Make sure that the file is saved using UTF-8 encoding.

18. Create a new document in your text editor or IDE, to be named **footer.html** (**Script 17.2**):

```
<!-- Script 17.2 - footer.html -->
```

19. Complete the HTML page:

```
        </div><!-- starter-template -->
    </div><!-- container -->
    <script src="https://ajax.
    → googleapis.com/ajax/libs/
    → jquery/3.2.1/jquery.min.js">
    → </script>
    <script src="https://maxcdn.
    → bootstrapcdn.com/bootstrap/
    → 3.3.7/js/bootstrap.min.js"
    → integrity="sha384-Tc5IQib027
    → qvyjSMfHjOMaLkfuWVxZxUPnCJA7l2
    → mCWNIpG9mGCD8wGNIcPD7Txa"
    → crossorigin="anonymous"></script>
    </body>
    </html>
```

There's no content in the footer; it just completes the *DIV*s begun in the header and includes two JavaScript files. Again, this comes from the Bootstrap template.

20. Save the file as **footer.html**.

Again, make sure that the file is saved using UTF-8 encoding.

21. Place both files in your web directory, within a folder named *includes*.

Script 17.2 The footer file completes the HTML page.

```
1   <!-- Script 17.2 - footer.html -->
2       </div><!-- starter-template -->
3   </div><!-- container -->
4
5   <!-- Bootstrap core JavaScript
6   ================================================== -->
7   <!-- Placed at the end of the document so the pages load faster -->
8   <script src="https://ajax.googleapis.com/ajax/libs/jquery/3.2.1/jquery.min.js"></script>
9   <script src="https://maxcdn.bootstrapcdn.com/bootstrap/3.3.7/js/bootstrap.min.js"
    integrity="sha384-Tc5IQib027qvyjSMfHjOMaLkfuWVxZxUPnCJA7l2mCWNIpG9mGCD8wGNIcPD7Txa"
    crossorigin="anonymous"></script>
10  </body>
11  </html>
```

Creating the Index Page

The index page in this example won't do that much. It will provide some introductory text and the links for the user to register, log in, choose the preferred language/forum, and so forth. From a programming perspective, it will show how the template files are to be used.

Script 17.3 The home page includes the header and footer files to make a complete HTML document. It also prints some introductory text in the chosen language.

```
1   <?php # Script 17.3 - index.php
2   // This is the main page for the site.
3
4   // Include the HTML header:
5   include('includes/header.html');
6
7   // The content on this page is
    introductory text
8   // pulled from the database,
    based upon the
9   // selected language:
10  echo $words['intro'];
11
12  // Include the HTML footer file:
13  include('includes/footer.html');
14  ?>
```

To make the home page:

1. Begin a new PHP document in your text editor or IDE, to be named **index.php** (**Script 17.3**):

   `<?php # Script 17.3 - index.php`

   Because all the HTML is in the included files, this page can begin with the opening PHP tags.

2. Include the HTML header:

   `include('includes/header.html');`

   The included file uses the **header()** and **session_start()** functions, so you have to make sure that nothing is sent to the browser prior to this line. That shouldn't be a problem as long as there are no spaces before the opening PHP tag.

3. Print the language-specific content:

   `echo $words['intro'];`

   The **$words** array is defined within the header file. It can be referred to here, since the header file was just included. The value indexed at *intro* is a bit of welcoming text in the selected or default language.

4. Complete the page:

   `include('includes/footer.html');`
   `?>`

   That's it for the home page!

5. Save the file as **index.php**, place it in your web directory, and test it in your browser (see Ⓐ and Ⓑ in the previous section).

   Once again, make sure that the file is saved using UTF-8 encoding. This will be the last time I remind you!

Creating the Forum Page

The next page in the website is the forum page, which displays the threads in a forum (each language is its own forum). The page will use the language ID, passed to this page in a URL and/or stored in a session, to know what threads to display.

The basic functionality of this page—running a query, displaying the results—is simple **A**. The query this page uses is perhaps the most complex one in the book. It's complicated for three reasons:

- It performs a **JOIN** across three tables.

- It uses three aggregate functions and a **GROUP BY** clause.

- It converts the dates to the user's time zone, but only if the person viewing the page is logged in.

So, again, the query is intricate, but I'll go through it in detail in the following steps.

To write the forum page:

1. Begin a new PHP document in your text editor or IDE, to be named **forum.php** (**Script 17.4**):

```php
<?php # Script 17.4 - forum.php
include('includes/header.html');
```

2. Determine what dates and times to use:

```php
if (isset($_SESSION['user_tz'])) {
    $first = "CONVERT_TZ
    (p.posted_on, 'UTC',
    '{$_SESSION['user_tz']}')";
    $last = "CONVERT_TZ(p.posted_on,
    'UTC', '{$_SESSION['user_tz']}')";
} else {
    $first = 'p.posted_on';
    $last = 'p.posted_on';
}
```

As already stated, the query will format the date and time to the user's time zone (presumably selected during the registration process), but only if the viewer is logged in. Presumably, this information would be retrieved from the database and stored in the session upon login.

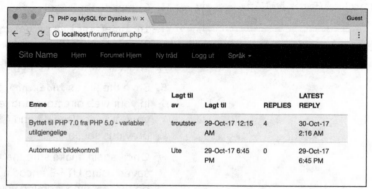

A The forum page, which lists information about the threads in a given language. The threads are linked to a page where they can be read.

To make the query dynamic, what exact date/time value should be selected will be stored in a variable to be used in the query later in the script. If the user *is not* logged in, which means that **$_SESSION['user_tz']** is not set, the two dates—when a thread was started and when the most recent reply was posted—will be unadulterated values from the table. In both cases, the table column being referenced is *posted_on* in the *posts* table (*p* will be an alias to *posts* in the query).

If the user *is* logged in, the **CONVERT_TZ()** function will be used to convert the value stored in *posted_on* from UTC to the user's chosen time zone. See Chapter 6 for more on this function. Note that using this function requires that your MySQL installation include the list of time zones (see Chapter 6 for more).

3. Define and execute the query:

```
$q = "SELECT t.thread_id, t.subject,
→ username, COUNT(post_id) - 1 AS
→ responses, MAX(DATE_FORMAT($last,
→ '%e-%b-%y %l:%i %p')) AS last,
→ MIN(DATE_FORMAT($first, '%e-%b-%y
→ %l:%i %p')) AS first FROM threads
→ AS t INNER JOIN posts AS p USING
→ (thread_id) INNER JOIN users AS
→ u ON t.user_id = u.user_id WHERE
→ t.lang_id = {$_SESSION['lid']}
→ GROUP BY (p.thread_id) ORDER BY
→ last DESC";
$r = mysqli_query($dbc, $q);
if (mysqli_num_rows($r) > 0) {
```

continues on page 569

Script 17.4 This script performs one rather complicated query to display five pieces of information—the subject, the original poster, the date the thread was started, the number of replies, and the date of the latest reply—for each thread in a forum.

```
1    <?php # Script 17.4 - forum.php
2    // This page shows the threads in a forum.
3    include('includes/header.html');
4
5    // Retrieve all the messages in this forum...
6
7    // If the user is logged in and has chosen a time zone,
8    // use that to convert the dates and times:
9    if (isset($_SESSION['user_tz'])) {
10       $first = "CONVERT_TZ(p.posted_on, 'UTC', '{$_SESSION['user_tz']}')";
11       $last = "CONVERT_TZ(p.posted_on, 'UTC', '{$_SESSION['user_tz']}')";
12   } else {
13       $first = 'p.posted_on';
14       $last = 'p.posted_on';
15   }
16
17   // The query for retrieving all the threads in this forum, along with the original user,
18   // when the thread was first posted, when it was last replied to, and how many replies
       it's had:
```

code continues on next page

```php
19   $q = "SELECT t.thread_id, t.subject, username, COUNT(post_id) - 1 AS responses,
     MAX(DATE_FORMAT($last, '%e-%b-%y %l:%i %p')) AS last, MIN(DATE_FORMAT($first,
     '%e-%b-%y %l:%i %p')) AS first FROM threads AS t INNER JOIN posts AS p USING (thread_id)
     INNER JOIN users AS u ON t.user_id = u.user_id WHERE t.lang_id = {$_SESSION['lid']} GROUP BY
     (p.thread_id) ORDER BY last DESC";
20   $r = mysqli_query($dbc, $q);
21   if (mysqli_num_rows($r) > 0) {
22
23       // Create a table:
24       echo '<table class="table table-striped">
25       <thead>
26         <tr>
27            <th>' . $words['subject'] . '</th>
28            <th>' . $words['posted_by'] . '</th>
29            <th>' . $words['posted_on'] . '</th>
30            <th>' . $words['replies'] . '</th>
31            <th>' . $words['latest_reply'] . '</th>
32         </tr>
33       </thead>
34       <tbody>';
35
36       // Fetch each thread:
37       while ($row = mysqli_fetch_array($r, MYSQLI_ASSOC)) {
38
39           echo '<tr>
40                 <td><a href="read.php?tid=' . $row['thread_id'] . '">' . $row['subject'] . '</a>
                 </td>
41                 <td>' . $row['username'] . '</td>
42                 <td>' . $row['first'] . '</td>
43                 <td>' . $row['responses'] . '</td>
44                 <td>' . $row['last'] . '</td>
45           </tr>';
46
47       }
48
49       echo '</tbody></table>'; // Complete the table.
50
51   } else {
52       echo '<p>There are currently no messages in this forum.</p>';
53   }
54
55   // Include the HTML footer file:
56   include('includes/footer.html');
57   ?>
```

The query needs to return six things: the ID of each thread, the subject of each thread (which comes from the *threads* table), the name of the user who posted the thread in the first place (from *users*), the number of replies to each thread, the date the thread was started, and the date the thread last had a reply (all from *posts*).

The overarching structure of this query is a join between *threads* and *posts* using the *thread_id* column (which is the same in both tables). This result is then joined with the *users* table using the *user_id* column.

As for the selected values, three aggregate functions are used (see Chapter 7 "Advanced SQL and MySQL"): **COUNT()**, **MIN()**, and **MAX()**. Each is applied to a column in the *posts* table, so the query has a **GROUP BY (p.thread_id)** clause. **MIN()** and **MAX()** are used to return the earliest (for the original post) and latest dates. Both will be shown on the forum page (see Ⓐ). The latest date is also used to order the results so that the most recent activity always gets returned first. The **COUNT()** function is used to count the number of posts in a given thread. Because the original post is also in the *posts* table, it will be factored into **COUNT()** as well, so 1 is subtracted from that value.

Finally, aliases are used to make the query shorter to write and to make it easier to use the results in the PHP script. If you're confused by what this query returns, execute it using the mysql client Ⓑ or phpMyAdmin.

4. Create a table for the results:

```
echo '<table class="table
table-striped">
<thead>
  <tr>
    <th>' . $words['subject'] .
    '</th>
    <th>' . $words['posted_by'] .
    '</th>
    <th>' . $words['posted_on'] .
    '</th>
    <th>' . $words['replies'] .
    '</th>
    <th>' . $words['latest_reply'] .
    '</th>
  </tr>
</thead>
<tbody>';
```

As with some items in the header file, the captions for the columns in this HTML page will use language-specific terminology.

continues on next page

```
PHP and MySQL for Dynamic Web Sites
mysql> SELECT t.thread_id, t.subject, username, COUNT(post_id) - 1 AS responses, MAX(DATE_FORMAT(CONVERT_TZ(p.posted_on, 'UTC', 'America/New_York'),
'%e-%b-%y %l:%i %p')) AS last, MIN(DATE_FORMAT(CONVERT_TZ(p.posted_on, 'UTC', 'America/New_York'), '%e-%b-%y %l:%i %p')) AS first FROM threads AS t I
NNER JOIN posts AS p USING (thread_id) INNER JOIN users AS u ON t.user_id = u.user_id WHERE t.lang_id = 4 GROUP BY (p.thread_id) ORDER BY last DESC;
+-----------+---------------------------------------------------------+-----------+-----------+-------------------+-------------------+
| thread_id | subject                                                 | username  | responses | last              | first             |
+-----------+---------------------------------------------------------+-----------+-----------+-------------------+-------------------+
|         1 | Byttet til PHP 7.0 fra PHP 5.0 - variabler utilgjengelige | troutster |         4 | 30-Oct-17 2:16 AM | 29-Oct-17 12:15 AM |
|         2 | Automatisk bildekontroll                                | Ute       |         0 | 29-Oct-17 6:45 PM | 29-Oct-17 6:45 PM |
+-----------+---------------------------------------------------------+-----------+-----------+-------------------+-------------------+
2 rows in set (0.00 sec)

mysql>
```

Ⓑ The results of running the complex query in the mysql client.

5. Fetch and print each returned record:

```php
while ($row = mysqli_fetch_array
→ ($r, MYSQLI_ASSOC)) {
  echo '<tr>
        <td><a href="read.php?tid='
        → . $row['thread_id'] . '">'
        → . $row['subject'] .
        → '</a></td>
        <td>' . $row['username'] .
        → '</td>
        <td>' . $row['first'] .
        → '</td>
        <td>' . $row['responses'] .
        → '</td>
        <td>' . $row['last'] .
        → '</td>
    </tr>';

}
```

This code is fairly simple, and there are similar examples many times over in this book. The thread's subject is linked to **read.php**, passing that page the thread ID in the URL.

6. Complete the page:

```php
    echo '</tbody></table>';
} else {
    echo '<p>There are currently no
    → messages in this forum.</p>';
}
include('includes/footer.html');
?>
```

This **else** clause applies if the query returned no results. In actuality, this message should also be in the user's chosen language. I've omitted that for the sake of brevity. To fully implement this feature, create another column in the *words* table and store for each language the translated version of this text.

7. Save the file as **forum.php**, place it in your web directory, and test it in your browser **C**.

> **TIP** If you see no values for the dates and times when you run this script, it is probably because your MySQL installation hasn't been updated with the full list of time zones.

> **TIP** As noted in the chapter's introduction, I've omitted all error handling in this example. If you have problems with the queries, apply the debugging techniques outlined in Chapter 8, "Error Handling and Debugging."

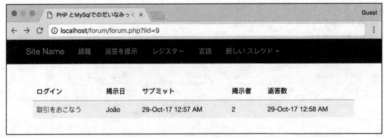

C The **forum.php** page, viewed in another language (compare with **A**).

Creating the Thread Page

Next up is the page for viewing all the messages in a thread 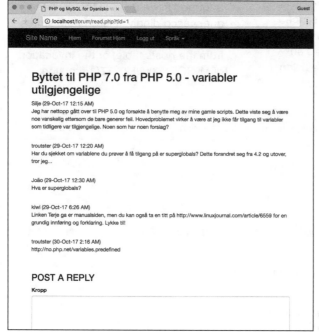. This page is accessed by clicking a link in **forum.php** 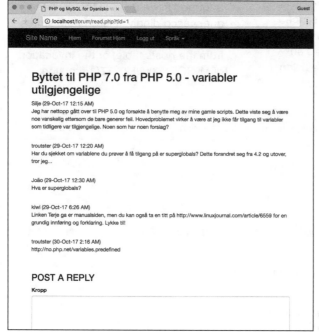. Thanks to a simplified database structure, the query used by this script is not that complicated (with the database design from Chapter 6, this page would have been much more complex). All this page has to do, then, is make sure it receives a valid thread ID, display every message, and display the form for users to add their own replies.

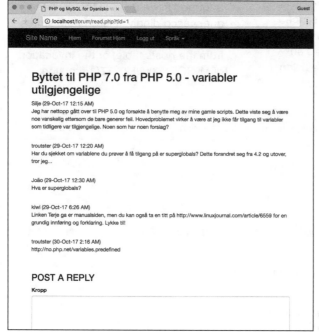

A The **read.php** page shows every message in a thread.

```
53        <tbody><tr>
54                <td><a href="read.php?tid=1">Byttet til PHP 7.0 fra PHP 5.0 - variabler
   utilgjengelige</a></td>
55                <td>troutster</td>
56                <td>29-Oct-17 12:15 AM</td>
57                <td>4</td>
58                <td>30-Oct-17 2:16 AM</td>
59        </tr><tr>
60                <td><a href="read.php?tid=2">Automatisk bildekontroll</a></td>
61                <td>Ute</td>
62                <td>29-Oct-17 6:45 PM</td>
63                <td>0</td>
64                <td>29-Oct-17 6:45 PM</td>
```

B Part of the source code from **forum.php** shows how the thread ID is passed to **read.php** in the URL.

To make read.php:

1. Begin a new PHP document in your text editor or IDE, to be named **read.php** (Script 17.5):

   ```php
   <?php # Script 17.5 - read.php
   include('includes/header.html');
   ```

2. Begin validating the thread ID:

   ```php
   $tid = FALSE;
   if (isset($_GET['tid']) &&
   → filter_var($_GET['tid'],
   → FILTER_VALIDATE_INT,
   → array('min_range' => 1)) ) {
   ```

   To start, a flag variable is defined as FALSE, a way of saying that you want to prove that the thread ID is valid, which is the most important aspect of this script. Next, a check confirms that the thread ID was passed in the URL and that it is an integer greater than 1. This is done using the Filter extension (see Chapter 13).

Finally, the value passed to the page is assigned to the **$tid** variable so that it no longer has a FALSE value.

3. Determine whether the dates and times should be adjusted:

   ```php
   if (isset($_SESSION['user_tz'])) {
     $posted = "CONVERT_TZ
   → (p.posted_on, 'UTC',
   → '{$_SESSION['user_tz']}')";
   } else {
     $posted = 'p.posted_on';
   }
   ```

   As in the **forum.php** page (Script 17.4), the query will format all the dates and times in the user's time zone if the user is logged in. To be able to adjust the query accordingly, this variable stores either the column's name (*posted_on*, from the *posts* table) or the invocation of MySQL's **CONVERT_TZ()** function.

Script 17.5 The **read.php** page shows all of the messages in a thread, in order of ascending posted date. The page also shows the thread's subject at the top and includes a form for adding a reply at the bottom.

```
1    <?php # Script 17.5 - read.php
2    // This page shows the messages in a thread.
3    include('includes/header.html');
4
5    // Check for a thread ID...
6    $tid = FALSE;
7    if (isset($_GET['tid']) && filter_var($_GET['tid'], FILTER_VALIDATE_INT,
     array('min_range' => 1)) ) {
8
9        // Create a shorthand version of the thread ID:
10       $tid = $_GET['tid'];
11
12       // Convert the date if the user is logged in:
13       if (isset($_SESSION['user_tz'])) {
14           $posted = "CONVERT_TZ(p.posted_on, 'UTC', '{$_SESSION['user_tz']}')";
15       } else {
16           $posted = 'p.posted_on';
17       }
18
```

code continues on next page

```
19      // Run the query:
20      $q = "SELECT t.subject, p.message,
        username, DATE_FORMAT($posted,
        '%e-%b-%y %l:%i %p') AS posted FROM
        threads AS t LEFT JOIN posts AS p
        USING (thread_id) INNER JOIN users
        AS u ON p.user_id = u.user_id WHERE
        t.thread_id = $tid ORDER BY
        p.posted_on ASC";
21      $r = mysqli_query($dbc, $q);
22      if (!(mysqli_num_rows($r) > 0)) {
23          $tid = FALSE; // Invalid thread
            ID!
24      }
25
26      } // End of isset($_GET['tid']) IF.
27
28      if ($tid) { // Get the messages in this
        thread...
29
30          $printed = FALSE; // Flag variable.
31
32          // Fetch each:
33          while ($messages = mysqli_fetch_
            array($r, MYSQLI_ASSOC)) {
34
35              // Only need to print the subject
                once!
36              if (!$printed) {
37                  echo "<h2>{$messages
                    ['subject']}</h2>\n";
38                  $printed = TRUE;
39              }
40
41              // Print the message:
42              echo "<p>{$messages['username']}
                ({$messages['posted']})<br>{$mess
                ages['message']}</p><br>\n";
43
44          } // End of WHILE loop.
45
46          // Show the form to post a message:
47          include('includes/post_form.php');
48
49      } else { // Invalid thread ID!
50          echo '<p class="bg-danger">This page
            has been accessed in error.</p>';
51      }
52
53      include('includes/footer.html');
54      ?>
```

4. Run the query:

```
$q = "SELECT t.subject, p.message,
→ username, DATE_FORMAT($posted,
→ '%e-%b-%y %l:%i %p') AS posted
→ FROM threads AS t LEFT JOIN
→ posts AS p USING (thread_id)
→ INNER JOIN users AS u ON p.user_
→ id = u.user_id WHERE t.thread_id
→ = $tid ORDER BY p.posted_on ASC";
$r = mysqli_query($dbc, $q);
if (!(mysqli_num_rows($r) > 0)) {
    $tid = FALSE; // Invalid
    → thread ID!
}
```

This query is like the query on the forum page, but it's been simplified in two ways. First, it doesn't use any of the aggregate functions or a **GROUP BY** clause. Second, it returns only one date and time. The query is still a **JOIN** across three tables to get the subject, message bodies, and usernames. The records are ordered by their posted dates in ascending order (i.e., from the first post to the most recent).

If the query doesn't return any rows, then the thread ID isn't valid and the flag variable is made false again.

5. Complete the **$_GET['tid']** conditional and check, again, for a valid thread ID:

```
} // End of isset($_GET['tid']) IF.
if ($tid) {
```

Before printing the messages in the thread, one last conditional is used. This conditional would be false if

▸ No **$_GET['tid']** value was passed to this page.

▸ A **$_GET['tid']** value was passed to the page, but it was not an integer greater than 0.

continues on next page

- A **$_GET['tid']** value was passed to the page and it was an integer greater than 0, but it matched no thread records in the database.

6. Print each message:

```
$printed = FALSE;
while ($messages = mysqli_fetch_
→ array($r, MYSQLI_ASSOC)) {
    if (!$printed) {
        echo "<h2>{$messages
        → ['subject']}</h2>\n";
        $printed = TRUE;
    }
    echo "<p>{$messages['username']}
    → ({$messages['posted']})<br>
    → {$messages['message']}</p>
    → <br>\n";
} // End of WHILE loop.
```

As you can see in **Ⓐ**, the thread subject needs to be printed only once.

However, the query will return the subject for each returned message **Ⓒ**. To achieve this effect, a flag variable is created. If **$printed** is FALSE, then the subject needs to be printed. This would be the case for the first row fetched from the database. Once that's been displayed, **$printed** is set to TRUE so that the subject is not printed again. Then the username, posted date, and message are displayed.

7. Include the form for posting a message:

include('includes/post_form.php');

Because users could post messages in two ways—as a reply to an existing thread and as the first post in a new thread—the form for posting messages is defined within a separate file (to be created next), stored within the *includes* directory.

```
                    PHP and MySQL for Dynamic Web Sites
mysql> SELECT t.subject, p.message, username, DATE_FORMAT(CONVERT_TZ(p.posted_on, 'UTC',
'America/New_York'), '%e-%b-%y %l:%i %p') AS posted FROM threads AS t LEFT JOIN posts AS
p USING (thread_id) INNER JOIN users AS u ON p.user_id = u.user_id WHERE t.thread_id = 1
ORDER BY p.posted_on ASC\G
*************************** 1. row ***************************
 subject: Byttet til PHP 7.0 fra PHP 5.0 - variabler utilgjengelige
 message: Jeg har nettopp gått over til PHP 5.0 og forsøkte å benytte meg av mine gamle s
cripts. Dette viste seg å være noe vanskelig ettersom de bare generer feil. Hovedprobleme
t virker å være at jeg ikke får tilgang til variabler som tidligere var tilgjengelige. No
en som har noen forslag?
username: Silje
 posted: 29-Oct-17 12:15 AM
*************************** 2. row ***************************
 subject: Byttet til PHP 7.0 fra PHP 5.0 - variabler utilgjengelige
 message: Har du sjekket om variablene du prøver å få tilgang på er superglobals? Dette f
orandret seg fra 4.2 og utover, tror jeg...
username: troutster
 posted: 29-Oct-17 12:20 AM
*************************** 3. row ***************************
 subject: Byttet til PHP 7.0 fra PHP 5.0 - variabler utilgjengelige
 message: Hva er superglobals?
username: João
 posted: 29-Oct-17 12:30 AM
*************************** 4. row ***************************
 subject: Byttet til PHP 7.0 fra PHP 5.0 - variabler utilgjengelige
 message: Linken Terje ga er manualsiden, men du kan også ta en titt på http://www.linuxj
ournal.com/article/6559 for en grundig innføring og forklaring. Lykke til!
username: kiwi
 posted: 29-Oct-17 6:26 AM
*************************** 5. row ***************************
 subject: Byttet til PHP 7.0 fra PHP 5.0 - variabler utilgjengelige
 message: http://no.php.net/variables.predefined
username: troutster
 posted: 30-Oct-17 2:16 AM
5 rows in set (0.00 sec)

mysql>
```

Ⓒ The results of the **read.php** query when run in the mysql client. This version of the query converts the dates to the logged-in user's preferred time zone.

8. Complete the page:

```
} else { // Invalid thread ID!
  echo '<p class="bg-danger">This
  → page has been accessed in
  → error.</p>';
}
include('includes/footer.html');
?>
```

Again, in a complete site, this error message would also be stored in the *words* table in each language. Then you would write

```
echo "<p class="bg-danger">{$words
→ ['access_error']}</p>";
```

9. Save the file as **read.php**, place it in your web directory, and test it in your browser **D**.

Browser window:

PHP とMySqlでのだいなみっく ×   Guest

localhost/forum/read.php?tid=5

Site Name   話題   返答を提示   言語   新しい スレッド ▾

取引をおこなう

Ute (29-Oct-17 12:57 AM)
PHP を使って　MySqlでは、取引を どのようにしたら良いかと　まよっています。良い方法が、あったらお
しえてください。

Silje (29-Oct-17 12:57 AM)
次のようにしたらどうですか?

João (29-Oct-17 12:58 AM)
反れとも、このようにも　できます。

最新の返答
ログアウト

本文

D The **read.php** page, viewed in Japanese.

Posting Messages

The final two pages in this application are the most important, because you won't have threads to read without them. Two files for posting messages are required: one will *make* the form, and the other will *handle* the form.

Creating the form

The first page required for posting messages is **post_form.php**. It has some contingencies:

- It can only be included by other files and never accessed directly.

- It should be displayed only if the user is logged in (which is to say only logged-in users can post messages).

- If it's being used to add a reply to an existing message, it only needs a message body input .

- If it's being used to create a new thread, it needs both subject and body inputs .

- It needs to be sticky 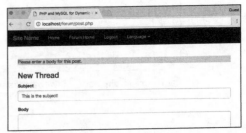.

Still, all of this can be accomplished in 60 lines of code and some smart conditionals.

To create post_form.php:

1. Begin a new PHP document in your text editor or IDE, to be named **post_form.php** (Script 17.6):

   `<?php # Script 17.6 - post_form.php`

2. Redirect the browser if this page has been accessed directly:

   ```
   if (!isset($words)) {
     header ("Location: http://www.
     → example.com/index.php");
     exit();
   }
   ```

A The form for posting a message, as shown on the thread-viewing page.

B The same form for posting a message, if being used to create a new thread.

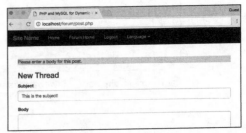

C The form will recall entered values when not completed correctly.

This script does not include the header and footer and therefore won't make a complete HTML page. Consequently, the script must be included by a script that does all that. PHP has no **been_included()** function that will indicate whether this page was included or loaded directly. Instead, since I know that the header file creates a **$words** variable, if that variable isn't set, then **header.html** hasn't been included prior to this script and the browser should be redirected.

Change the URL in the **header()** call to match your site.

3. Confirm that the user is logged in and begin the form:

```
if (isset($_SESSION['user_id'])) {
    echo '<form action="post.php"
→ method="post"
→ accept-charset="utf-8">';
```

Because only registered users can post, the script checks for the presence of **$_SESSION['user_id']** before displaying the form. The form itself will be submitted to **post.php**, to be written next. The **accept-charset** attribute is added to the form to make it clear that UTF-8 text is acceptable (although this isn't technically required, since each page uses the UTF-8 encoding already).

continues on next page

Script 17.6 This script will be included by other pages (notably, **read.php** and **post.php**). It displays a form for posting messages that is also sticky.

```
1    <?php # Script 17.6 - post_form.php
2    // This page shows the form for posting messages.
3    // It's included by other pages, never called directly.
4
5    // Redirect if this page is called directly:
6    if (!isset($words)) {
7        header ("Location: http://www.example.com/index.php");
8        exit();
9    }
10
11   // Only display this form if the user is logged in:
12   if (isset($_SESSION['user_id'])) {
13
14       // Display the form:
15       echo '<form action="post.php" method="post" accept-charset="utf-8">';
16
17       // If on read.php...
18       if (isset($tid) && $tid) {
19
20           // Print a caption:
21           echo '<h3>' . $words['post_a_reply'] . '</h3>';
22
23           // Add the thread ID as a hidden input:
24           echo '<input name="tid" type="hidden" value="' . $tid . '">';
25
```

code continues on next page

4. Check for a thread ID:

```
if (isset($tid) && $tid) {
  echo '<h3>' . $words['post_a_
  →reply'] . '</h3>';
  echo '<input name="tid"
  →type="hidden" value="' .
  →$tid . '">';
```

This is where things get a little bit tricky. As mentioned earlier, and as shown in Ⓐ and Ⓑ, the form will differ slightly depending on how it's being used. When included on **read.php**, the form will be used to provide a reply to an existing thread. To check for this scenario, the script sees if **$tid** (short for *thread ID*) is set and if it has a TRUE value. That will be the case when this page is included by **read.php**. When this script is included by **post.php**, **$tid** will be set but have a FALSE value.

If this conditional is true, the language-specific version of "Post a Reply" will be printed and the thread ID will be stored in a hidden form input.

5. Complete the conditional begun in Step 4:

```
} else { // New thread
  echo '<h3>' . $words
  →['new_thread'] . '</h3>';
  echo '<div class="form-group">
  →<label for="subject">' .
  →$words['subject'] . '</label>
  →<input name="subject"
  →type="text" class="form-control"
  →size="60" maxlength="100" ';
  if (isset($subject)) {
    echo "value=\"$subject\" ";
  }
  echo '></div>';
} // End of $tid IF.
```

If this is not a reply, then the caption should be the language-specific version

Script 17.6 *continued*

```
26    } else { // New thread
27
28        // Print a caption:
29        echo '<h3>' . $words['new_thread']
. '</h3>';
30
31        // Create subject input:
32        echo '<div class="form-group">
<label for="subject">' .
$words['subject'] . '</label>
<input name="subject" type="text"
class="form-control" size="60"
maxlength="100" ';
33
34        // Check for existing value:
35        if (isset($subject)) {
36            echo "value=\"$subject\" ";
37        }
38
39        echo '></div>';
40
41    } // End of $tid IF.
42
43    // Create the body textarea:
44    echo '<div class="form-group"><label
for="subject">' . $words['body']
. '</label> <textarea name="body"
class="form-control" rows="10"
cols="60">';
45
46    if (isset($body)) {
47        echo $body;
48    }
49
50    echo '</textarea></div>';
51
52    // Finish the form:
53    echo '<input name="submit"
type="submit" class="form-control"
value="' . $words['submit'] . '">
54        </form>';
55
56    } else {
57        echo '<p class="bg-warning">You must
be logged in to post messages.</p>';
58    }
59
60    ?>
```

of "New Thread" and a subject input should be created. That input needs to be sticky. To check for that, look for the existence of a **$subject** variable. This variable will be created in **post.php**, and that file will then include this page.

6. Create the textarea for the message body:

```
echo '<div class="form-group">
→<label for="subject">' . $words
→['body'] . '</label> <textarea
→name="body" class="form-control"
→rows="10" cols="60">';
if (isset($body)) {
  echo $body;
}
echo '</textarea></div>';
```

Nouvelle discussion

Sujet

Contenu

Soumettez

Ⅾ The form prompts and even the submit button will be in the user's chosen language (compare with the other figures in this section of the chapter).

Both uses of this page will have this textarea. Like the subject, it will be made sticky if a **$body** variable (defined in **post.php**) exists. For both inputs, the prompts will be language-specific.

7. Complete the form:

```
echo '<input name="submit"
→type="submit" class="form-control"
→value="' . $words['submit'] . '">
</form>';
```

All that's left is a language-specific submit button **Ⅾ**.

8. Complete the page:

```
} else {
  echo '<p class="bg-warning">You
  →must be logged in to post
  →messages.</p>';
}
?>
```

Once again, you could store this message in the *words* table and use the translated version here. I didn't only for the sake of simplicity.

9. Save the file as **post_form.php**, place it in the **includes** folder of your web directory, and test it in your browser by accessing **read.php** **Ⅾ**.

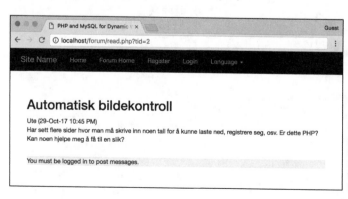

PHP and MySQL for Dynamic ... ×   Guest

← → C ⓘ localhost/forum/read.php?tid=2

Site Name   Home   Forum Home   Register   Login   Language ▾

Automatisk bildekontroll

Ute (29-Oct-17 10:45 PM)
Har sett flere sider hvor man må skrive inn noen tall for å kunne laste ned, registrere seg, osv. Er dette PHP? Kan noen hjelpe meg å få til en slik?

You must be logged in to post messages.

Ⅾ The result of the **post_form.php** page if the user is not logged in (remember that you can emulate not being logged in by using the **$_SESSION = [];** line in the header file).

Handling the form

This file, **post.php**, will primarily be used to handle the form submission from **post_form.php**. That sounds simple enough, but there's a bit more to it. This page will actually be called in three different ways:

- To handle the form for a thread reply
- To display the form for a new thread submission
- To handle the form for a new thread submission

This means that the page will be accessed using either POST (modes 1 and 3) or GET (mode 2). Also, the data that will be sent to the page, and therefore needs to be validated, will differ between modes 1 and 3 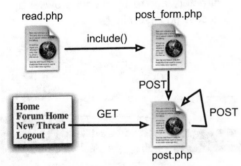.

Adding to the complications, if a new thread is being created, two queries must be run: one to add the thread to the *threads* table and a second to add the new thread body to the *posts* table. If the submission is a reply to an existing thread, then only one query is required, inserting a record into *posts*.

Of course, successfully pulling this off is just a matter of using the right conditionals, as you'll see. In terms of validation, the subject and body, as text types, will just be checked for a non-empty value. All tags will be stripped from the subject (because why should it have any?) and turned into entities in the body. This will allow for HTML, JavaScript, and PHP code to be *written* in a post but still not be *executed* when the thread is shown (because in a forum about web development, you'll need to show some code).

To create post.php:

1. Begin a new PHP document in your text editor or IDE, to be named **post.php** (Script 17.7):

```
<?php # Script 17.7 - post.php
include('includes/header.html');
```

This page will use the header and footer files, unlike **post_form.php**.

2. Check for the form submission and validate the thread ID:

```
if ($_SERVER['REQUEST_METHOD'] ==
→'POST') {
if (isset($_POST['tid']) &&
→filter_var($_POST['tid'],
→FILTER_VALIDATE_INT,
→array('min_range' => 1)) ) {
  $tid = $_POST['tid'];
} else {
  $tid = FALSE;
}
```

continues on page 582

read.php   post_form.php

include()

POST

Home
Forum Home   GET
New Thread
Logout

POST

post.php

F The various uses of the **post.php** page.

Script 17.7 The **post.php** page will process the form submissions when a message is posted. This page will be used to both create new threads and handle replies to existing threads.

```php
1    <?php # Script 17.7 - post.php
2    // This page handles the message post.
3    // It also displays the form if creating a new thread.
4    include('includes/header.html');
5
6    if ($_SERVER['REQUEST_METHOD'] == 'POST') { // Handle the form.
7
8        // Language ID is in the session.
9        // Validate thread ID ($tid), which may not be present:
10       if (isset($_POST['tid']) && filter_var($_POST['tid'], FILTER_VALIDATE_INT,
         array('min_range' => 1)) ) {
11           $tid = $_POST['tid'];
12       } else {
13           $tid = FALSE;
14       }
15
16       // If there's no thread ID, a subject must be provided:
17       if (!$tid && empty($_POST['subject'])) {
18           $subject = FALSE;
19           echo '<p class="bg-danger">Please enter a subject for this post.</p>';
20       } elseif (!$tid && !empty($_POST['subject'])) {
21           $subject = htmlspecialchars(strip_tags($_POST['subject']));
22       } else { // Thread ID, no need for subject.
23           $subject = TRUE;
24       }
25
26       // Validate the body:
27       if (!empty($_POST['body'])) {
28           $body = htmlentities($_POST['body']);
29       } else {
30           $body = FALSE;
31           echo '<p class="bg-danger">Please enter a body for this post.</p>';
32       }
33
34       if ($subject && $body) { // OK!
35
36           // Add the message to the database...
37
38           if (!$tid) { // Create a new thread.
39               $q = "INSERT INTO threads (lang_id, user_id, subject) VALUES ({$_SESSION['lid']},
               {$_SESSION['user_id']}, '" . mysqli_real_escape_string($dbc, $subject) . "')";
40               $r = mysqli_query($dbc, $q);
41               if (mysqli_affected_rows($dbc) == 1) {
42                   $tid = mysqli_insert_id($dbc);
43               } else {
44                   echo '<p class="bg-danger">Your post could not be handled due to a system error.
                   </p>';
45               }
```

code continues on next page

The thread ID will be present if the form was submitted as a reply to an existing thread (the thread ID is stored as a hidden input **G**). The validation process is fairly routine, thanks to the Filter extension.

3. Validate the message subject:

```php
if (!$tid && empty($_POST
→['subject'])) {
    $subject = FALSE;
    echo '<p class="bg-danger">
    →Please enter a subject for
    →this post.</p>';
} elseif (!$tid && !empty($_POST
→['subject'])) {
    $subject = htmlspecialchars
    →(strip_tags($_POST['subject']));
} else { // Thread ID, no need
→for subject.
    $subject = TRUE;
}
```

The tricky part about validating the subject is that three scenarios exist. First, if there's no valid thread ID, then this should be a new thread and the subject can't be empty. If the subject element *is* empty, then an error occurred and a message is printed.

Script 17.7 *continued*

```php
46          } // No $tid.
47
48          if ($tid) { // Add this to the
            replies table:
49              $q = "INSERT INTO posts
                (thread_id, user_id, message,
                posted_on) VALUES ($tid,
                {$_SESSION['user_id']},
                '" . mysqli_real_escape_
                string($dbc, $body) . "',
                UTC_TIMESTAMP())";
50              $r = mysqli_query($dbc, $q);
51              if (mysqli_affected_rows($dbc)
    == 1) {
52                  echo '<p class="bg-
success">Your post has been entered.</
p>';
53              } else {
54                  echo '<p class="bg-
danger">Your post could not be handled
due to a system error.</p>';
55              }
56          } // Valid $tid.
57
58      } else { // Include the form:
59          include('includes/post_form.php');
60      }
61
62  } else { // Display the form:
63
64      include('includes/post_form.php');
65
66  }
67
68  include('includes/footer.html');
69  ?>
```

```
43  <h2>Sample Thread</h2>
44  <p>troutster (29-Oct-17 1:12 AM)<br>This is the body of the sample thread. This is the body of the sample
    thread. This is the body of the sample thread. </p><br>
45  <p>troutster (29-Oct-17 1:44 AM)<br>I like your thread. It's simple and sweet.</p><br>
46  <form action="post.php" method="post" accept-charset="utf-8"><h3>Post a Reply</h3><input name="tid"
    type="hidden" value="7"><div class="form-group"><label for="subject">Body</label> <textarea name="body"
    class="form-control" rows="10" cols="60"></textarea></div><input name="submit" type="submit" class="form-
    control" value="Submit">
```

G The source code of **read.php** shows how the thread ID is stored in the form. This indicates to **post.php** that the submission is a reply, not a new thread.

In the second scenario, there's no valid thread ID and the subject *isn't* empty, meaning this is a new thread and the subject was entered, so it should be handled. In this case, any tags are removed, using the **strip_tags()** function, and **htmlspecialchars()** will turn any remaining quotation marks into their entity format. Calling this second function will prevent problems should the form be displayed again and the subject placed in the input to make it sticky. To be more explicit, if the submitted subject contains a double quotation mark but the body wasn't completed, the form will be shown again with the subject placed within **value=""**, and the double quotation mark in the subject will cause problems.

The third scenario is when the form has been submitted as a reply to an existing thread. In that case, **$tid** will be valid and no subject is required.

4. Validate the body:

```
if (!empty($_POST['body'])) {
    $body = htmlentities($_POST
    →['body']);
} else {
    $body = FALSE;
    echo '<p class="bg-danger">
    →Please enter a body for this
    →post.</p>';
}
```

This is a much easier validation, since the body is always required. If present, it will be run through **htmlentities()**.

5. Check whether the form was properly filled out:

```
if ($subject && $body) {
```

6. Create a new thread, when appropriate:

```
if (!$tid) { // Create a new thread.
    $q = "INSERT INTO threads
    →(lang_id, user_id, subject)
    →VALUES ({$_SESSION['lid']},
    →{$_SESSION['user_id']}, '" .
    →mysqli_real_escape_string($dbc,
    →$subject) . "')";
    $r = mysqli_query($dbc, $q);
    if (mysqli_affected_rows($dbc) ==
    →1) {
        $tid = mysqli_insert_id($dbc);
    } else {
        echo '<p class="bg-danger">Your
        →post could not be handled
        →due to a system error.</p>';
    }
} // No $tid.
```

If there's no thread ID, then this is a new thread and a query must be run on the *threads* table. That query is simple, populating the three columns. Two of these values come from the session (after the user has logged in). The other is the subject, which is run through **mysqli_real_escape_string()**. Because the subject already had **strip_tags()** and **htmlspecialchars()** applied to it, you could probably get away with not using this function, but there's no need to take that risk.

If the query worked, meaning it affected one row, then the new thread ID is retrieved.

continues on next page

7. Add the record to the *posts* table:

```
if ($tid) { // Add this to the
→ replies table:
  $q = "INSERT INTO posts
  → (thread_id, user_id, message,
  → posted_on) VALUES ($tid,
  → {$_SESSION['user_id']}, '" .
  → mysqli_real_escape_string
  → ($dbc, $body) . "',
  → UTC_TIMESTAMP())";
  $r = mysqli_query($dbc, $q);
  if (mysqli_affected_rows($dbc)
  → == 1) {
    echo '<p class="bg-success">
    → Your post has been entered.
    → </p>';
  } else {
    echo '<p class="bg-danger">
    → Your post could not be
    → handled due to a system
    → error.</p>';
  }
} // Valid $tid.
```

This query should only be run if the thread ID exists. That will be the case if this is a reply to an existing thread or if the new thread was just created in the database (Step 6). If that query failed, then this query won't be run.

The query populates four columns in the table, using the thread ID; the user ID (from the session); the message body, run through `mysqli_real_escape_string()` for security; and the posted date. For this last value, the `UTC_TIMESTAMP()` column is used so that it's not tied to any one time zone (see Chapter 6).

Note that for all the printed messages in this page, I've just used hard-coded English. To finish rounding out the examples, each of these messages should be stored in the *words* table and printed here instead.

How This Example Is Complicated

In the introduction to this chapter, I state that the example is fundamentally simple but that sometimes the simple things take some extra effort to do. So how is this example complicated, in my opinion?

First, supporting multiple languages does add a couple of issues. If the encoding isn't handled properly everywhere—when creating the pages in your text editor or IDE, in communicating with MySQL, in the browser, etc.—things can go awry. Also, you must have the proper translations for every language for every bit of text that the site might need. This includes error messages (ones the user should actually see), the bodies of emails, and so forth.

How the PHP files are organized and what they do also complicates things. In particular, some variables are created in one file but used in another. Doing this can lead to confusion at best and bugs at the worst. To overcome those problems, I recommend adding lots of comments indicating where variables come from or where else they might be used. Also, try to use unique variable names within pages so that they are less likely to conflict with variables in included files.

Finally, this example was complicated by the way only one page is used to display the posting form and only one page is used to handle it, despite the fact that messages can be posted in two different ways, with different expectations.

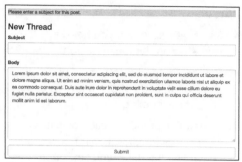

H The result if no subject was provided while attempting to post a new thread.

I The reply has been successfully added to the thread.

8. Complete the page:

```
    } else { // Include the form:
      include('includes/
        ↪ post_form.php');
    }
  } else { // Display the form:
    include('includes/
      ↪ post_form.php');
  }
  include('includes/footer.html');
  ?>
```

The first **else** clause applies if the form was submitted but not completed. In that case, the form will be included again and can be sticky, since it will have access to the **$subject** and **$body** variables created by this script. The second **else** clause applies if this page was accessed directly (by clicking a link in the navigation), thereby creating a GET request (i.e., without a form submission).

9. Save the file as **post.php**, place it in your web directory, and test it in your browser (**H** and **I**).

Administering the Forum

Much of the administration of the forum would involve user management, discussed in the next chapter. Depending on who is administering the forum, you might also create forms for managing the languages and lists of translated words.

Administrators would also likely have the authority to edit and delete posts or threads. To accomplish this, store a user level in the session as well (the next chapter shows you how). If the logged-in user is an administrator, add links to edit and delete threads on **forum.php**. Each link would pass the thread ID to a new page (like **edit_user.php** and **delete_user.php** from Chapter 10, "Common Programming Techniques"). When deleting a thread, you have to make sure you delete all the records in the *posts* table that also have that thread ID. A foreign key constraint (see Chapter 6) can help in this regard.

Finally, an administrator could edit or delete individual posts (the replies to a thread). Again, check for the user level and then add links to **read.php** (a pair of links after each message). The links would pass the post ID to edit and delete pages (different ones than are used on threads).

Review and Pursue

If you have any problems with the review questions or the pursue prompts, turn to the book's supporting forum (LarryUllman.com/forums/).

Note: Most of these questions and some of the prompts rehash information covered in earlier chapters to reinforce some of the most important points.

Review

- What impact does a database's *character set*, or a PHP or HTML page's *encoding*, have?

- Why does the encoding and character set have to be the same everywhere? What happens if there are differences?

- What is a *primary key*? What is a *foreign key*?

- What is the benefit of using *UTC* for stored dates and times?

- How do you begin a session in PHP? How do you store a value in a session? How do you retrieve a previously stored value?

- How do you create an *alias* in an SQL command? What are the benefits of using an alias?

Pursue

- Review Chapter 6 if you need a refresher on database design.

- Review Chapter 6 to remind yourself as to what kinds of columns in a table should be indexed.

- Review Chapter 6's section on time zones if your MySQL installation is not properly converting the dates and times from the UTC time zone to another (i.e., if the returned converted date value is **NULL**).

- Review Chapter 7 for a refresher on joins and the aggregating functions.

- Modify the header and other files so that each page's title uses both the default language page title and a subtitle based on the page being viewed (e.g., the name of the thread currently shown).

- Add pagination—see Chapter 10—to the **forum.php** script.

- If you want, add the necessary columns to the *words* table, and the appropriate code to the PHP scripts, so that every navigational, error, and other element is language specific. Use a web site such as Google Translate (**https://translate.google.com/**) for the translations.

- Apply the **redirect_user()** function from Chapter 12 to **post_form.php** here.

- Create a search page for this forum. If you need some help, see the **search.php** basic example available in the downloadable code.

Example— User Registration

The second example in the book—a user registration system—has already been touched on in several other chapters, because the registration, login, and logout processes make for good examples of many concepts. But this chapter will place all those ideas within the same context using a consistent programming approach.

Users will be able to register, log in, log out, and change their password. This chapter includes three features not shown elsewhere: the ability to *reset a password*, should it be forgotten; the requirement that users *activate their account* before they can log in; and support for *different user levels*, allowing you to control the available content according to the type of user logged in.

As in the preceding chapter, the focus here will be on the public side of things, but along the way you'll see recommendations as to how this application could easily be expanded or modified, including how to add administrative features.

Creating the Templates

The application in this chapter will use a new template design . This template makes extensive use of Cascading Style Sheets (CSS), creating a clean look without the need for images. The layout for this site is derived from one freely provided by BlueRobot (**www.bluerobot.com**).

Creating this chapter's example begins with two template files: **header.html** and **footer.html**. As in the Chapter 12, "Cookies and Sessions," examples, the footer file will display certain links depending on whether or not the user is logged in, determined by checking for the existence of a session variable. Taking this concept one step further, additional links will be displayed if the logged-in user is also an administrator (a session value will indicate such).

The header file will begin sessions and *output buffering*, whereas the footer file will terminate output buffering. Output buffering hasn't been formally covered in this book, but it's introduced sufficiently in the sidebar.

To make header.html:

1. Begin a new document in your text editor or IDE, to be named **header.html** (Script 18.1):

   ```php
   <?php # Script 18.1 - header.html
   ```

A The basic appearance of this web application.

Script 18.1 The header file begins the HTML, starts the session, and turns on output buffering.

```php
1   <?php # Script 18.1 - header.html
2   // This page begins the HTML header for
    the site.
3
4   // Start output buffering:
5   ob_start();
6
7   // Initialize a session:
8   session_start();
9
10  // Check for a $page_title value:
11  if (!isset($page_title)) {
12      $page_title = 'User Registration';
13  }
14  ?>
15  <!doctype html>
16  <html lang="en">
17  <head>
18      <meta charset="utf-8">
19      <title><?php echo $page_title;
        ?></title>
20      <link rel="includes/layout.css">
21  </head>
22  <body>
23  <div id="Header">User Registration</div>
24  <div id="Content">
25  <!-- End of Header -->
```

Using Output Buffering

By default, anything that a PHP script prints or any HTML outside of the PHP tags (even in included files) is immediately sent to the browser. *Output buffering* (or *output control*, as the PHP manual calls it) is a PHP feature that overrides this behavior. Instead of immediately sending HTML to the browser, that output will be placed in a buffer—temporary memory. Then, when the buffer is *flushed*, it's sent to the browser. There can be a performance improvement with output buffering, but the main benefit is that it eradicates those pesky *headers already sent* error messages. Some functions—**header()**, **setcookie()**, and **session_start()**—can only be called if nothing has been sent to the browser. With output buffering, nothing will be sent to the browser until the end of the page, so you are free to call these functions at any point in a script.

To begin output buffering, invoke the **ob_start()** function. Once you call it, the output from every **echo**, **print**, and similar function call will be sent to a memory buffer rather than the browser. Conversely, HTTP calls (like **header()** and **setcookie()**) will not be buffered and will operate as usual.

At the conclusion of the script, call the **ob_end_flush()** function to send the accumulated buffer to the browser. Or use the **ob_end_clean()** function to delete the buffered data without sending it. Both functions have the secondary effect of turning off output buffering.

2. Begin output buffering and start a session:

```
ob_start();
session_start();
```

This website will use output buffering, eliminating any error messages that could occur when using HTTP headers, redirecting the user, or sending cookies. Every page will make use of sessions as well. It's safe to place the **session_start()** call after **ob_start()**, since nothing has been sent to the browser yet.

Because every public page will use both output buffering and sessions, placing these lines in the **header.html** file saves the hassle of placing them in every single page. In addition, if you later want to change the session settings (for example), you need to edit just this one file.

3. Check for a **$page_title** variable and close the PHP section:

```
if (!isset($page_title)) {
$page_title = 'User Registration';
}
?>
```

As in the other times this book has used a template system, the page's title—which appears at the top of the browser window—will be set on a page-by-page basis. This conditional checks if the **$page_title** variable has a value and, if it doesn't, sets it to a default string. This is a nice, but optional, check to include in the header.

continues on next page

4. Create the HTML head:

```
<!doctype html>
<html lang="en">
<head>
   <meta charset="utf-8">
   <title><?php echo $page_title;
   → ?></title>
   <link rel="includes/layout.css">
</head>
```

The PHP **$page_title** variable is printed between the **title** tags here. Then, the CSS document is included. It will be called **layout.css** and stored in a folder called **includes**. You can find the CSS file in the downloadable code found at the book's supporting web site (**LarryUllman.com**).

Script 18.2 The footer file concludes the HTML, displaying links based on the user status (logged in or not, administrator or not), and flushes the output to the browser.

```
1    <!-- Start of Footer -->
2    </div><!-- Content -->
3
4    <div id="Menu">
5        <a href="index.php" title="Home Page">Home</a><br>
6        <?php # Script 18.2 - footer.html
7        // This page completes the HTML template.
8
9        // Display links based upon the login status:
10       if (isset($_SESSION['user_id'])) {
11
12           echo '<a href="logout.php" title="Logout">Logout</a><br>
13       <a href="change_password.php" title="Change Your Password">Change Password</a><br>
14       ';
15
16           // Add links if the user is an administrator:
17           if ($_SESSION['user_level'] == 1) {
18               echo '<a href="view_users.php" title="View All Users">View Users</a><br>
19           <a href="#">Some Admin Page</a><br>
20           ';
21           }
22
23       } else { //  Not logged in.
24           echo '<a href="register.php" title="Register for the Site">Register</a><br>
25       <a href="login.php" title="Login">Login</a><br>
26       <a href="forgot_password.php" title="Password Retrieval">Retrieve Password</a><br>
27       ';
28       }
29       ?>
30       <a href="#">Some Page</a><br>
31       <a href="#">Another Page</a><br>
32   </div><!-- Menu -->
33
34   </body>
35   </html>
36   <?php // Flush the buffered output.
37   ob_end_flush();
38   ?>
```

5. Begin the HTML body:

```
<body>
<div id="Header">User Registration
→ </div>
<div id="Content">
```

The body creates the banner across the top of the page and then starts the content part of the web page (up until *Welcome!* in Ⓐ).

6. Save the file as **header.html**.

To make footer.html:

1. Begin a new document in your text editor or IDE, to be named **footer.html** (**Script 18.2**):

```
</div><!-- Content -->
<div id="Menu">
  <a href="index.php" title="Home
  → Page">Home</a><br>
  <?php # Script 18.2 -
  → footer.html
```

Home
Logout
Change Password
Some Page
Another Page

Ⓑ The user will see these navigation links while logged in.

Home
Logout
Change Password
View Users
Some Admin Page
Some Page
Another Page

Ⓒ A logged-in administrator will see extra links (compare with Ⓑ).

2. If the user is logged in, show logout and change password links:

```
if (isset($_SESSION['user_id'])) {
  echo '<a href="logout.php"
  → title="Logout">Logout</a><br>
<a href="change_password.php"
→ title="Change Your Password">
→ Change Password</a><br>
';
```

If the user is logged in (which means that **$_SESSION['user_id']** is set), the user will see links to log out and to change his or her password Ⓑ.

3. If the user is also an administrator, show some other links:

```
if ($_SESSION['user_level'] == 1) {
  echo '<a href="view_users.php"
  → title="View All Users">
  → View Users</a><br>
<a href="#">Some Admin Page
→ </a><br>
';
}
```

If the logged-in user also happens to be an administrator, she or he should see some extra links Ⓒ. To test for this, check the user's access level, which will also be stored in a session. A level value of 1 will indicate that the user is an administrator (nonadministrators will have a level of 0).

continues on next page

4. Show the links for non-logged-in users and complete the PHP block:

```php
} else { //  Not logged in.
  echo '<a href="register.php"
    →title="Register for the Site">
    →Register</a><br>
<a href="login.php" title="Login">
→Login</a><br>
<a href="forgot_password.php"
→title="Password Retrieval">
→Retrieve Password</a><br>
';
}
?>
```

If the user isn't logged in, she or he will see links to register, log in, and reset a forgotten password **D**.

5. Complete the HTML:

```html
<a href="#">Some Page</a><br />
<a href="#">Another Page</a><br />
</div>
</body>
</html>
```

Two dummy links are included for other pages you could add.

6. Flush the buffer:

```php
<?php
ob_end_flush();
?>
```

The footer file will send the accumulated buffer to the browser, completing the output buffering begun in the header script (again, see the sidebar).

Home
Register
Login
Retrieve Password
Some Page
Another Page

D If not logged in, the user will see these links.

7. Save the file as **footer.html** and place it, along with **header.html** and **layout.css** (from the book's supporting web site), in your web directory, storing all three in an **includes** folder 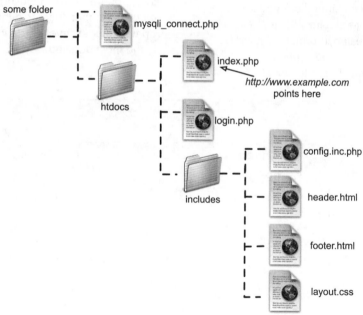.

TIP If this site has any page that does not make use of the header file but does need to work with sessions, that script must call `session_start()` on its own. If you fail to do so, that page won't be able to access the session data.

TIP In more recent versions of PHP, output buffering is enabled by default. The buffer size—the maximum number of bytes stored in memory—is 4096, but this can be changed in PHP's configuration file.

TIP The `ob_get_contents()` function will return the current buffer so that it may be assigned to a variable, should the need arise.

TIP The `ob_flush()` function will send the current contents of the buffer to the browser and then discard them, allowing a new buffer to be started. This function allows your scripts to maintain more moderate buffer sizes. Conversely, `ob_end_flush()` turns off output buffering after sending the buffer to the browser.

TIP The `ob_clean()` function deletes the current contents of the buffer without stopping the buffer process.

TIP PHP will automatically run `ob_end_flush()` at the conclusion of a script if it is not otherwise done.

some folder

mysqli_connect.php

index.php

http://www.example.com
points here

htdocs

login.php

config.inc.php

header.html

includes

footer.html

layout.css

E The directory structure of the site on the web server, assuming **htdocs** is the document root (where **www.example.com** points).

Writing the Configuration Scripts

This web site will make use of two configuration-type scripts. One, `config.inc.php`, will be the most important script in the entire application. It will

- Have comments about the site as a whole
- Define constants
- Establish site settings
- Dictate how errors are handled
- Define any necessary functions

Because it does all this, the configuration script will be included by every other page in the application.

The second configuration-type script, `mysqli_connect.php`, will store all the database-related information. It will be included only by those pages that need to interact with the database.

Making a configuration file

The configuration file is going to serve many important purposes. It'll be like a cross between the site's owner's manual and its preferences file. The first purpose of this file will be to document the site overall: who created it, when, why, for whom, and so forth. The version in the book will omit all that, but you should put this information in your script (or separately in a README file). The second role will be to define all sorts of constants and settings that the various pages will use.

Third, the configuration file will establish the error-management policy for the site. The technique involved—creating your own error-handling function—was covered in Chapter 8, "Error Handling and Debugging." As in that chapter, during the development stages, every error will be reported in the most detailed way 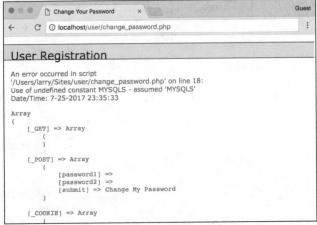.

A During the development stages of the web site, all errors should be as obvious and as informative as possible.

User Registration

A system error occurred. We apologize for the inconvenience.

B If errors occur when the site is live, the user will see only a message like this (but a detailed error message will be emailed to the administrator).

Script 18.3 This configuration script dictates how errors are handled, defines sitewide settings and constants, and could (but doesn't) declare any necessary functions.

```
1    <?php # Script 18.3 - config.inc.php
2    /* This script:
3     * - define constants and settings
4     * - dictates how errors are handled
5     * - defines useful functions
6     */
7
8    // Document who created this site, when,
     why, etc.
9
10
11   // ******************************** //
12   // *********** SETTINGS *********** //
13
14   // Flag variable for site status:
15   define('LIVE', FALSE);
16
17   // Admin contact address:
18   define('EMAIL', 'InsertRealAddressHere');
19
20   // Site URL (base for all redirections):
21   define('BASE_URL',
     'http://www.example.com/');
22
23   // Location of the MySQL connection
     script:
24   define('MYSQL',
     '/path/to/mysqli_connect.php');
25
26   // Adjust the time zone for PHP 5.1 and
     greater:
27   date_default_timezone_set
     ('America/New_York');
28
29   // *********** SETTINGS *********** //
30   // ******************************** //
31
```

code continues on next page

Along with the specific error message, all the existing variables will be shown, as will the current date and time. The error reporting will be formatted so that it fits within the site's template. During the production, or live, stage of the site, errors will be handled more gracefully **B**. At that time, the detailed error messages will not be printed in the browser but instead sent to an email address.

Finally, this script could define any functions that might be used multiple times in the site. This site won't have any, but that would be another logical use of such a file.

To write the configuration file:

1. Begin a new PHP document in your text editor or IDE, to be named **config.inc.php** (Script 18.3):

   ```
   <?php # Script 18.3 - config.inc.php
   ```

2. Establish two constants for error reporting:

   ```
   define('LIVE', FALSE);
   define('EMAIL',
   → 'InsertRealAddressHere');
   ```

   The **LIVE** constant will be used as it was in Chapter 8. If it is FALSE, detailed error messages are sent to the browser **A**. Once the site goes live, this constant should be set to TRUE so that detailed error messages are never revealed to the user **B**. The **EMAIL** constant is where the error messages will be sent when the site is live. You would obviously use your own email address for this value.

continued on page 597

```
32
33     // ***************************************** //
34     // ************ ERROR MANAGEMENT ************ //
35
36     // Create the error handler:
37     function my_error_handler($e_number, $e_message, $e_file, $e_line, $e_vars) {
38
39         // Build the error message:
40         $message = "An error occurred in script '$e_file' on line $e_line: $e_message\n";
41
42         // Add the date and time:
43         $message .= "Date/Time: " . date('n-j-Y H:i:s') . "\n";
44
45         if (!LIVE) { // Development (print the error).
46
47             // Show the error message:
48             echo '<div class="error">' . nl2br($message);
49
50             // Add the variables and a backtrace:
51             echo '<pre>' . print_r ($e_vars, 1) . "\n";
52             debug_print_backtrace();
53             echo '</pre></div>';
54
55         } else { // Don't show the error:
56
57             // Send an email to the admin:
58             $body = $message . "\n" . print_r ($e_vars, 1);
59             mail(EMAIL, 'Site Error!', $body, 'From: email@example.com');
60
61             // Only print an error message if the error isn't a notice:
62             if ($e_number != E_NOTICE) {
63                 echo '<div class="error">A system error occurred. We apologize for the
       inconvenience.</div><br>';
64             }
65         } // End of !LIVE IF.
66
67     } // End of my_error_handler() definition.
68
69     // Use my error handler:
70     set_error_handler('my_error_handler');
71
72     // ************ ERROR MANAGEMENT ************ //
73     // ***************************************** //
```

3. Establish two constants for sitewide settings:

```
define('BASE_URL',
→'http://www.example.com/');
define('MYSQL',
→'/path/to/mysqli_connect.php');
```

These two constants are defined just to make it easier to do certain things in the other scripts. The first, **BASE_URL**, refers to the root domain (*http://www.example.com/*), with an ending slash. If developing on your own computer, this might be *http://localhost/* or *http://localhost/ch18/*. When a script redirects the browser, the code can simply be something like

```
header('Location: ' . BASE_URL
→.'page.php');
```

The second constant, **MYSQL**, is an absolute path to the MySQL connection script (to be written next). Setting this as an absolute path ensures that any file can include the connection script by referring to this constant:

```
require(MYSQL);
```

Change both values to correspond to your environment. When using XAMPP on Windows, for example, the proper value for the **MYSQL** constant may be C:\\xampp\mysqli_connect.php.

If you move the site from one server or domain to another, just change these two constants and the application will still work.

4. Establish any other sitewide settings:

```
date_default_timezone_set
→('America/New_York);
```

As mentioned in Chapter 11, "Web Application Development," any use of a PHP date or time function requires that the time zone be set. Change this value to match your time zone (see the PHP manual for the list of zones).

5. Begin defining the error-handling function:

```
function my_error_handler
→($e_number, $e_message, $e_file,
→$e_line, $e_vars) {
$message = "An error occurred in
→script '$e_file' on line
→$e_line: $e_message\n";
```

The function definition will be like the one explained in Chapter 8. The function expects to receive five arguments: the error number, the error message, the script in which the error occurred, the line number on which PHP thinks the error occurred, and an array of variables that existed at the time of the error. Then the function begins defining the **$message** variable, starting with the information provided to this function.

6. Add the current date and time:

```
$message .= "Date/Time: " .
→date('n-j-Y H:i:s') . "\n";
```

To make the error reporting more useful, it will include the current date and time in the message. A newline character terminates the string to make the resulting display more legible.

continues on next page

7. If the site is not live, show the error message in detail:

```
if (!LIVE) { // Development (print
→ the error).
  echo '<div class="error">' .
  → nl2br($message);
  echo '<pre>' . print_r
  → ($e_vars, 1) . "\n";
  debug_print_backtrace();
  echo '</pre></div>';
```

As mentioned earlier, if the site *isn't* live, the entire error message is printed for any type of error. The message is placed within **<div class="error">**, which will format the message per the rules defined in the site's CSS file. The first part of the error message is the string already defined, with the added touch of converting newlines to HTML break tags. Then, within preformatted tags, all the variables that exist at the time of the error are shown, along with a *backtrace* (a history of function calls and such). See Chapter 8 for more explanation on any of this.

8. If the site is live, email the details to the administrator and print a generic message for the visitor:

```
} else { // Don't show the error:
  $body = $message . "\n" .
  → print_r ($e_vars, 1);
  mail(EMAIL, 'Site Error!', $body,
  → 'From: email@example.com');
  if ($e_number != E_NOTICE) {
    echo '<div class="error">
    → A system error occurred.
    → We apologize for the
    → inconvenience.</div><br>';
  }
} // End of !LIVE IF.
```

If the site *is* live, the detailed message should be sent in an email and the user should see only a generic message. To take this one step further, the generic message will not be printed if the error is of a specific type: **E_NOTICE**. Such errors occur for things like referring to a variable that does not exist, which may or may not be a problem. To avoid potentially inundating the user with error messages, only print the error message if **$e_number** is not equal to **E_NOTICE**, which is a constant defined in PHP (see the PHP manual).

9. Complete the function definition and tell PHP to use your error handler:

```
}
set_error_handler
→ ('my_error_handler');
```

You must use the **set_error_handler()** function to tell PHP to use your own function for errors.

10. Save the file as **config.inc.php**, and place it in your web directory within the **includes** folder.

Note that in keeping with many other examples in this book, because this script will be included by other PHP scripts it omits the terminating PHP tag.

Making the database script

The second configuration-type script will be **mysqli_connect.php**, the database connection file used multiple times in the book already. Its purpose is to connect to MySQL, select the database, and establish the character set in use. If a problem occurs, this script will make use of the error-handling tools established in **config.inc.php**. To do so, this script will call the **trigger_error()** function when appropriate. The **trigger_error()** function lets you tell PHP that an error occurred. Of course PHP will handle that error using the **my_error_handler()** function, as established in the configuration script.

To connect to the database:

1. Begin a new PHP document in your text editor or IDE, to be named **mysqli_connect.php** (Script 18.4):

```
<?php # Script 18.4 -
→ mysqli_connect.php
```

2. Set the database access information:

```
DEFINE('DB_USER', 'username');
DEFINE('DB_PASSWORD', 'password');
DEFINE('DB_HOST', 'localhost');
DEFINE('DB_NAME', 'ch18');
```

As always, change these values to those that will work for your MySQL installation.

3. Attempt to connect to MySQL and select the database:

```
$dbc = @mysqli_connect(DB_HOST,DB_
→ USER, DB_PASSWORD, DB_NAME);
```

In previous scripts, if this function didn't return the proper result, the **die()** function was called, terminating the execution of the script. Since this site will be using a custom error-handling function instead, I'll rewrite the connection process.

Any errors raised by this function call will be suppressed (thanks to the **@**) and handled using the code in the next step.

4. Handle any errors if the database connection was not made:

```
if (!$dbc) {
    trigger_error('Could not
    → connect to MySQL: ' .
    → mysqli_connect_error() );
```

continues on next page

Script 18.4 This script connects to the *ch18* database. If it can't, then the error handler will be triggered, passing it the MySQL connection error.

```
1    <?php # Script 18.4 - mysqli_connect.php
2    // This file contains the database access information.
3    // This file also establishes a connection to MySQL
4    // and selects the database.
5
6    // Set the database access information as constants:
7    define('DB_USER', 'username');
8    define('DB_PASSWORD', 'password');
9    define('DB_HOST', 'localhost');
10   define('DB_NAME', 'ch18');
11
12   // Make the connection:
13   $dbc = @mysqli_connect (DB_HOST, DB_USER, DB_PASSWORD, DB_NAME);
14
15   // If no connection could be made, trigger an error:
16   if (!$dbc) {
17       trigger_error('Could not connect to MySQL: ' . mysqli_connect_error() );
18   } else { // Otherwise, set the encoding:
19       mysqli_set_charset($dbc, 'utf8');
20   }
```

If the script could not connect to the database, the error message should be sent to the **my_error_handler()** function. By doing so, the error will be handled according to the currently set management technique (live stage versus development). Instead of calling **my_error_handler()** directly, use **trigger_error()**, whose first argument is the error message **C**.

5. Establish the encoding:

```
} else {
  mysqli_set_charset($dbc, 'utf8');
}
```

If a database connection could be made, the encoding used to communicate with the database is then established. See Chapter 9, "Using PHP with MySQL," for details.

6. Save the file as **mysqli_connect.php**, and place it in the directory above the web document root.

This script, as an includable file, also omits the terminating PHP tag. As with other examples in this book, ideally the file should not be within the web directory, but wherever you put it, make sure the value of the **MYSQL** constant (in **config.inc.php**) matches.

7. Create the database **D**.

See the sidebar "Database Schema" for a discussion of the database and the command required to make the one table. If you cannot create your own database, just add the table to whatever database you have access to. Also make sure that you edit the **mysqli_connect.php** file so that it uses the proper username/password/ hostname combination to connect to this database.

User Registration

An error occurred in script
'/Users/larry/Sites/user/mysqli_connect.php' on line 13:
mysqli_connect(): (HY000/1044): Access denied for user
'username'@'localhost' to database 'ch18'
Date/Time: 7-25-2017 23:43:34

```
Array
(
    [_GET] => Array
        (
        )

    [_POST] => Array
```

C A database connection error occurring during the development of the site.

PHP and MySQL for Dynamic Web Sites

```
mysql> CREATE DATABASE ch18;
Query OK, 1 row affected (0.00 sec)

mysql> USE ch18;
Database changed
mysql> CREATE TABLE users (
    -> user_id INT UNSIGNED NOT NULL AUTO_INCREMENT,
    -> first_name VARCHAR(20) NOT NULL,
    -> last_name VARCHAR(40) NOT NULL,
    -> email VARCHAR(60) NOT NULL,
    -> pass VARCHAR(255) NOT NULL,
    -> user_level TINYINT(1) UNSIGNED NOT NULL DEFAULT 0,
    -> active CHAR(32),
    -> registration_date DATETIME NOT NULL,
    -> PRIMARY KEY (user_id),
    -> UNIQUE KEY (email)
    -> );
Query OK, 0 rows affected (0.07 sec)

mysql>
```

D Creating the database for this chapter.

TIP On one hand, it might make sense to place the contents of both configuration files in one script for ease of reference. On the other hand, doing so would add unnecessary overhead (namely, connecting to and selecting the database) to scripts that don't require a database connection (e.g., index.php).

TIP In general, define common functions in the configuration file or a separate functions file. One exception would be any function that requires a database connection. If you know that a function will be used only on pages that also connect to MySQL, then defining that function within the mysqli_connect.php script is only logical.

Database Schema

The database being used by this application is called *ch18*. The database currently consists of only one table, *users*. To create the table, use this SQL command:

```
CREATE TABLE users (
user_id INT UNSIGNED NOT NULL AUTO_INCREMENT,
first_name VARCHAR(20) NOT NULL,
last_name VARCHAR(40) NOT NULL,
email VARCHAR(60) NOT NULL,
pass VARCHAR(255) NOT NULL,
user_level TINYINT(1) UNSIGNED NOT NULL DEFAULT 0,
active CHAR(32),
registration_date DATETIME NOT NULL,
PRIMARY KEY (user_id),
UNIQUE KEY (email)
);
```

Most of the table's structure should be familiar to you by now; it's quite similar to the *users* table in the *sitename* database, used in several examples in this book. One new addition is the *active* column, which will indicate whether or not a user has activated their account (by clicking a link in the registration email). This column will either store the 32-character-long activation code or have a **NULL** value. Because the *active* column may have a **NULL** value, it cannot be defined as **NOT NULL**. If you do define *active* as **NOT NULL**, no one will ever be able to log in (you'll see why later in the chapter). The other new addition is the *user_level* column, which will differentiate the kinds of users the site has.

Creating the Home Page

The home page for the site, called **index.php**, will be a model for the other pages on the public side. It will require the configuration file (for error management) and the header and footer files to create the HTML design. This page will also welcome the user by name, assuming the user is logged in 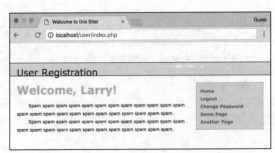.

To write index.php:

1. Begin a new PHP document in your text editor or IDE, to be named **index.php** (Script 18.5):

   ```php
   <?php # Script 18.5 - index.php
   ```

2. Include the configuration file, set the page title, and include the HTML header:

   ```php
   require('includes/config.inc.php');
   $page_title = 'Welcome to this
   → Site! ';
   include('includes/header.html');
   ```

   The script includes the configuration file first so that everything that happens afterward will be handled using the error-management processes established in this file. Then, the **header.html** file is included, which will start output buffering, begin the session, and create the initial part of the HTML layout.

Script 18.5 The script for the site's home page, which will greet a logged-in user by name.

```php
1    <?php # Script 18.5 - index.php
2    // This is the main page for the site.
3
4    // Include the configuration file:
5    require('includes/config.inc.php');
6
7    // Set the page title and include the
     HTML header:
8    $page_title = 'Welcome to this Site!';
9    include('includes/header.html');
10
11   // Welcome the user (by name if they are
     logged in):
12   echo '<h1>Welcome';
13   if (isset($_SESSION['first_name'])) {
14   echo ", {$_SESSION['first_name']}";
15   }
16   echo '!</h1>';
17   ?>
18   <p>Spam spam spam spam spam spam
19   spam spam spam spam spam spam
20   spam spam spam spam spam spam
21   spam spam spam spam spam spam.</p>
22   <p>Spam spam spam spam spam spam
23   spam spam spam spam spam spam
24   spam spam spam spam spam spam
25   spam spam spam spam spam spam.</p>
26
27   <?php include('includes/footer.html'); ?>
```

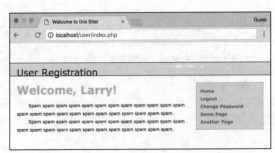

A If the user is logged in, the index page will greet them by name.

3. Greet the user and complete the PHP code:

```php
echo '<h1>Welcome';
if (isset($_SESSION['first_name'])) {
  echo ", {$_SESSION['first_name']}
  → ";
}
echo '!</h1>';
?>
```

The *Welcome* message will be printed to all users. If a **$_SESSION['first_name']** variable is set, the user's first name will also be printed. The end result will be either just *Welcome!* **B** or *Welcome, <Your Name>!* **A**.

4. Create the content for the page:

```
<p>Spam spam...</p>
```

You might want to consider putting something more useful on the home page of a real site. Just a suggestion....

5. Include the HTML footer:

```php
<?php include('includes/footer.
→ html'); ?>
```

The footer file will complete the HTML layout (primarily the menu bar on the right side of the page) and conclude the output buffering.

6. Save the file as **index.php**, place it in your web directory, and test it in a browser.

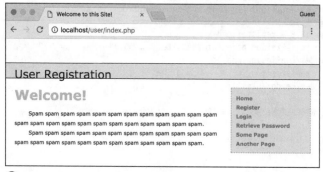

B If the user is not logged in, this is the home page that's displayed.

Registration

The registration script was first started in Chapter 9. It has since been improved on in many ways. This version of **register.php** will do the following:

- Both display and handle the form
- Validate the submitted data using regular expressions and the Filter extension
- Redisplay the form with the values remembered if a problem occurs (the form will be *sticky*)
- Process the submitted data using the **mysqli_real_escape_string()** function for security

- Ensure a unique email address
- Use PHP to securely hash the password
- Send an email containing an activation link (users will have to activate their account prior to logging in—see the "Activation Process" sidebar)

To write **register.php**:

1. Begin a new PHP document in your text editor or IDE, to be named **register.php** (Script 18.6):

   `<?php # Script 18.6 - register.php`

   continues on page 607

Script 18.6 The registration script uses regular expressions for security and a sticky form for user convenience. It sends an email to the user upon a successful registration.

```php
1   <?php # Script 18.6 - register.php
2   // This is the registration page for the site.
3   require('includes/config.inc.php');
4   $page_title = 'Register';
5   include('includes/header.html');
6
7   if ($_SERVER['REQUEST_METHOD'] == 'POST') { // Handle the form.
8
9       // Need the database connection:
10      require(MYSQL);
11
12      // Trim all the incoming data:
13      $trimmed = array_map('trim', $_POST);
14
15      // Assume invalid values:
16      $fn = $ln = $e = $p = FALSE;
17
18      // Check for a first name:
19      if (preg_match('/^[A-Z \'.-]{2,20}$/i', $trimmed['first_name'])) {
20          $fn = mysqli_real_escape_string($dbc, $trimmed['first_name']);
21      } else {
22          echo '<p class="error">Please enter your first name!</p>';
23      }
24
25      // Check for a last name:
26      if (preg_match('/^[A-Z \'.-]{2,40}$/i', $trimmed['last_name'])) {
27          $ln = mysqli_real_escape_string($dbc, $trimmed['last_name']);
28      } else {
```

code continues on next page

```
29        echo '<p class="error">Please enter your last name!</p>';
30     }
31
32     // Check for an email address:
33     if (filter_var($trimmed['email'], FILTER_VALIDATE_EMAIL)) {
34        $e = mysqli_real_escape_string($dbc, $trimmed['email']);
35     } else {
36        echo '<p class="error">Please enter a valid email address!</p>';
37     }
38
39     // Check for a password and match against the confirmed password:
40     if (strlen($trimmed['password1']) >= 10) {
41        if ($trimmed['password1'] == $trimmed['password2']) {
42           $p = password_hash($trimmed['password1'], PASSWORD_DEFAULT);
43        } else {
44           echo '<p class="error">Your password did not match the confirmed password!</p>';
45        }
46     } else {
47        echo '<p class="error">Please enter a valid password!</p>';
48     }
49
50     if ($fn && $ln && $e && $p) { // If everything's OK...
51
52        // Make sure the email address is available:
53        $q = "SELECT user_id FROM users WHERE email='$e'";
54        $r = mysqli_query($dbc, $q) or trigger_error("Query: $q\n<br>MySQL Error:
           " . mysqli_error($dbc));
55
56        if (mysqli_num_rows($r) == 0) { // Available.
57
58           // Create the activation code:
59           $a = md5(uniqid(rand(), true));
60
61           // Add the user to the database:
62           $q = "INSERT INTO users (email, pass, first_name, last_name, active,
              registration_date) VALUES ('$e', '$p', '$fn', '$ln', '$a', NOW() )";
63           $r = mysqli_query($dbc, $q) or trigger_error("Query: $q\n<br>MySQL Error:
              " . mysqli_error($dbc));
64
65           if (mysqli_affected_rows($dbc) == 1) { // If it ran OK.
66
67              // Send the email:
68              $body = "Thank you for registering at <whatever site>. To activate your account,
                 please click on this link:\n\n";
69              $body .= BASE_URL . 'activate.php?x=' . urlencode($e) . "&y=$a";
70              mail($trimmed['email'], 'Registration Confirmation', $body, 'From:
                 admin@sitename.com');
71
```

code continues on next page

```
72              // Finish the page:
73              echo '<h3>Thank you for registering! A confirmation email has been sent to
                your address. Please click on the link in that email in order to activate your
                account.</h3>';
74              include('includes/footer.html'); // Include the HTML footer.
75              exit(); // Stop the page.
76
77          } else { // If it did not run OK.
78              echo '<p class="error">You could not be registered due to a system error.
                We apologize for any inconvenience.</p>';
79          }
80
81      } else { // The email address is not available.
82          echo '<p class="error">That email address has already been registered. If you have
            forgotten your password, use the link at right to have your password sent to you.</p>';
83      }
84
85  } else { // If one of the data tests failed.
86      echo '<p class="error">Please try again.</p>';
87  }
88
89  mysqli_close($dbc);
90
91  } // End of the main Submit conditional.
92  ?>
93
94  <h1>Register</h1>
95  <form action="register.php" method="post">
96      <fieldset>
97
98      <p><strong>First Name:</strong> <input type="text" name="first_name" size="20"
        maxlength="20" value="<?php if (isset($trimmed['first_name'])) echo $trimmed['first_name'];
        ?>"></p>
99
100     <p><strong>Last Name:</strong> <input type="text" name="last_name" size="20" maxlength="40"
        value="<?php if (isset($trimmed['last_name'])) echo $trimmed['last_name']; ?>"></p>
101
102     <p><strong>Email Address:</strong> <input type="email" name="email" size="30"
        maxlength="60" value="<?php if (isset($trimmed['email'])) echo $trimmed['email']; ?>"> </p>
103
104     <p><strong>Password:</strong> <input type="password" name="password1" size="20"
        value="<?php if (isset($trimmed['password1'])) echo $trimmed['password1']; ?>">
        <small>At least 10 characters long.</small></p>
105
106     <p><strong>Confirm Password:</strong> <input type="password" name="password2" size="20"
        value="<?php if (isset($trimmed['password2'])) echo $trimmed['password2']; ?>"></p>
107     </fieldset>
108
109     <div align="center"><input type="submit" name="submit" value="Register"></div>
110
111 </form>
112
113 <?php include('includes/footer.html'); ?>
```

2. Include the configuration file and the HTML header:

```php
require('includes/config.inc.php');
$page_title = 'Register';
include('includes/header.html');
```

3. Create the conditional that checks for the form submission and then include the database connection script:

```php
if ($_SERVER['REQUEST_METHOD'] ==
→'POST') {
  require (MYSQL);
```

Because the full path to the **mysqli_connect.php** script is defined as a constant in the configuration file, the constant can be used as the argument to **require()**. The benefit to this approach is that any file stored anywhere in the site, even within a subdirectory, can use this same code to successfully include the connection script.

4. Trim the incoming data and establish some flag variables:

```php
$trimmed = array_map('trim',
→$_POST);
$fn = $ln = $e = $p = FALSE;
```

The first line runs every element in **$_POST** through the **trim()** function, assigning the returned result to the new **$trimmed** array. The explanation for this line can be found in Chapter 13, "Security Methods," when **array_map()** was used with data to be sent in an email. In short, the **trim()** function will be applied to every value in **$_POST**, saving the hassle of applying **trim()** to each individually.

The second line initializes four variables as FALSE. This one line is just a shortcut in lieu of

```php
$fn = FALSE;
$ln = FALSE;
$e = FALSE;
$p = FALSE;
```

5. Validate the first and last names:

```php
if (preg_match('/^[A-Z \'.-]
→{2,20}$/i', $trimmed['first_
→name'])) {
    $fn = mysqli_real_escape_string
    →($dbc, $trimmed['first_name']);
} else {
    echo '<p class="error">Please
    →enter your first name!</p>';
}
if (preg_match('/^[A-Z \'.-]
→{2,40}$/i', $trimmed
→['last_name'])) {
    $ln = mysqli_real_escape_string
    →($dbc, $trimmed['last_name']);
} else {
    echo '<p class="error">Please
    →enter your last name!</p>';
}
```

Much of the form will be validated using regular expressions, covered in Chapter 14, "Perl-Compatible Regular Expressions." For the first name value, the assumption is that it will contain only letters, a period (as in an initial), an apostrophe, a space, and the dash. Further, the value should be within the range of 2 to 20 characters long. To guarantee that the value contains only these characters, the caret and the dollar sign are used to match both the beginning and end of the string. While using Perl-compatible regular expressions, the entire pattern must be placed within delimiters (the forward slashes).

continues on next page

If this condition is met, the **$fn** variable is assigned the value of the **mysqli_real_escape_string()** version of the submitted value; otherwise, **$fn** will still be FALSE and an error message is printed Ⓐ.

The same process is used to validate the last name, although that regular expression allows for a longer length. Both patterns are also case-insensitive, thanks to the *i* modifier.

One thing to be aware of when using regular expressions to validate strings is cultural bias. The pattern used to validate these names works fine for most non-accented European names but fails for names with non-Latin characters. This registration script also assumes every user has two names, which is not always the case. Try to be aware of who your users are and then strike the right balance between proper validation and improper assumptions.

6. Validate the email address Ⓑ:

```
if (filter_var($trimmed['email''],
→ FILTER_VALIDATE_EMAIL)) {
  $e = mysqli_real_escape_string
  → ($dbc, $trimmed['email']);
} else {
  echo '<p class="error">Please
→ enter a valid email address!
→ </p>';
}
```

An email address can easily be validated using the Filter extension, discussed in Chapter 13

7. Validate the passwords:

```
if (strlen($trimmed['password1'])
→ >= 10) {
  if ($trimmed['password1'] ==
  → $trimmed['password2']) {
    $p = password_hash
    → ($trimmed['password1'],
    → PASSWORD_DEFAULT);
  } else {
    echo '<p class="error">Your
    → password did not match the
    → confirmed password!</p>';
  }
} else {
  echo '<p class="error">Please
  → enter a valid password!</p>';
}
```

User Registration

Please enter your first name!
Please try again.

Register

First Name: <
Last Name: Ullman
Email Address: email@example.com

Ⓐ If the first name value does not pass the regular expression test, an error message is printed.

User Registration

Please enter a valid email address!
Please try again.

Register

First Name: Larry
Last Name: Ullman
Email Address: email

Ⓑ The submitted email address must be of the proper format.

The password must be at least 10 characters **C**. This may seem too lax, but the truth when it comes to security is that requiring longer passwords—ideally longer than 10 characters, even—is the most important security factor. Further, while requiring numbers, capital letters, and symbols may help against dictionary attacks, mostly they just make it harder for users to remember their password (i.e., *themustideallydictionary* is a more secure password than *Password1B!*).

There is no maximum length limit.

Finally, the first password (*password1*) must match the confirmed password (*password2*) **D**.

C The passwords are checked for the proper length and...

D ...that the password value matches the confirmed password value.

Assuming the password passes both validations, it's run through the PHP `password_hash()` function so it's ready to be stored.

8. If every test was passed, check for a unique email address:

```
if ($fn && $ln && $e && $p) {
    $q = "SELECT user_id FROM users
→ WHERE email='$e'";
    $r = mysqli_query($dbc, $q)
→ or trigger_error("Query:
→ $q\n<br>MySQL Error: " .
→ mysqli_error($dbc));
```

If the form passed every test, this conditional will be TRUE. Then the script must search the database to see whether the submitted email address is currently being used, since that column's value must be unique across each record. As with the MySQL connection script, if a query doesn't run, call the `trigger_error()` function to invoke the self-defined error reporting function. The specific error message will include both the query being run and the MySQL error **E** so that the problem can easily be debugged.

continues on next page

E If a MySQL query error occurs, it should be easier to debug thanks to this informative error message.

9. If the email address is unused, register the user:

```
if (mysqli_num_rows($r) == 0)
→{ // Available.
  $a = md5(uniqid(rand(), true));
  $q = "INSERT INTO users (email,
  → pass, first_name, last_name,
  → active, registration_date)
  → VALUES ('$e', '$p', '$fn', '$ln',
  → '$a', NOW() )";
  $r = mysqli_query($dbc, $q)
  → or trigger_error("Query:
  → $q\n<br>MySQL Error: " .
  → mysqli_error($dbc));
```

The query itself is rather simple, but it does require the creation of a unique activation code. Generating that requires the **rand()**, **uniqid()**, and **md5()** functions. Of these, **uniqid()** is the most important; it creates a unique identifier. It's fed the **rand()** function to help generate a more random value. Finally, the returned result is *hashed* using **md5()**, which creates a string exactly 32 characters long (a hash is a mathematically calculated representation of a piece of data). You do not need to fully comprehend these three functions; just note that the result will be a unique 32-character string.

As for the query itself, it should be familiar enough to you. Most of the values come from variables in the PHP script, after applying **trim()** and **mysqli_real_escape_string()** to them. The MySQL **NOW()** function is used to set the registration date as the current moment. Because the *user_level* column has a default value of 0

(i.e., not an administrator), that column does not have to be provided a value in this query. Presumably the site's main administrator would edit a user's record to give him or her administrative power after the user has registered.

10. Send an email if the query worked:

```
if (mysqli_affected_rows($dbc) ==
→1) {
  $body = "Thank you for
  → registering at <whatever
  → site>. To activate your
  → account, please click on this
  → link:\n\n";
  $body .= BASE_URL . 'activate.
  → php?x=' . urlencode($e) .
  → "&y=$a";
  mail($trimmed['email'],
  → 'Registration Confirmation',
  → $body, 'From: admin@sitename.
  → com');
```

With this registration process, the important thing is that the confirmation mail gets sent to your users, because they will not be able to log in until after they've activated their account. This email should contain a link to the activation page, **activate.php**. The link to that page starts with **BASE_URL**, which is defined in **config.inc.php**. The link also passes two values along in the URL. The first, generically called *x*, will be the user's email address, encoded so that it's safe to have in a URL. The second, *y*, is the activation code. The URL, then, will be something like *http://www.example.com/activate. php?x=email%40example.com&y= 901e09ef25bf6e3ef95c93088450b008.*

Activation Process

New in this chapter is an activation process, where users have to click a link in an email to confirm their accounts prior to being able to log in. Using a system like this prevents bogus registrations from being usable. If an invalid email address is entered, that account can never be activated. And if someone registered another person's address, hopefully the maligned person would not activate this undesired account.

From a programming perspective, this process requires the creation of a unique activation code for each registered user, to be stored in the *users* table. The code is then sent in a confirmation email to the user (as part of a link). When the user clicks the link, she or he will be taken to a page on the site that activates the account (by removing that code from the record). The result is that no one can register and activate an account without receiving the confirmation email (i.e., without having a valid email address that the registrant controls).

User Registration

Thank you for registering! A confirmation email has been sent to your address. Please click on the link in that email in order to activate your account.

F The resulting page after a user has successfully registered.

11. Tell the user what to expect and complete the page:

```
echo '<h3>Thank you for
→ registering! A confirmation
→ email has been sent to your
→ address. Please click on the
→ link in that email in order to
→ activate your account.</h3>';
include('includes/footer.html');
exit();
```

A thank-you message is printed out upon successful registration, along with the activation instructions **F**. Then the footer is included and the page is terminated.

12. Print errors if the query failed:

```
} else { // If it did not run OK.
  echo '<p class="error">You could
  → not be registered due to a
  → system error. We apologize
  → for any inconvenience.</p>';
}
```

If the query failed for some reason, meaning that **mysqli_affected_rows()** did not return 1, an error message is printed to the browser. Because of the security methods implemented in this script, the live version of the site should never have a problem at this juncture.

continues on next page

13. Complete the conditionals and the PHP code:

```php
        } else { // The email address
→ is not available.
          echo '<p class="error">That
→ email address has
→ already been registered.
→ If you have forgotten
→ your password, use the
→ link at right to have
→ your password sent to
→ you.</p>';
        }
      } else { // If one of the data
→ tests failed.
        echo '<p class="error">Please
→ try again.</p>';
      }
      mysqli_close($dbc);
    } // End of the main Submit
→ conditional.
    ?>
```

The first **else** is executed if a person attempts to register with an email address that has already been used ⓖ. The second **else** applies when the submitted data fails one of the validation routines (see Ⓐ through Ⓓ).

User Registration

That email address has already been registered. If you have forgotten your password, use the link at right to have your password sent to you.

Register

First Name: Larry

Last Name: Ullman

Email Address: email@example.com

ⓖ If an email address has already been registered, the user is told as much.

14. Begin the HTML form Ⓗ:

```html
<h1>Register</h1>
<form action="register.php"
→ method="post">
  <fieldset>
  <p><strong>First Name:</strong>
→ <input type="text"
→ name="first_name" size="20"
→ maxlength="20" value="<?php if
→ (isset($trimmed['first_name']))
→ echo $trimmed['first_name'];
→ ?>"></p>
```

The HTML form has text inputs for all the values. Each input has a name and a maximum length that match the corresponding column definition in the *users* table. The form will be sticky, using the trimmed values.

15. Add inputs for the last name and email address:

```html
<p><strong>Last Name:</strong>
→ <input type="text"
→ name="last_name" size="20"
→ maxlength="40" value="<?php if
→ (isset($trimmed['last_name']))
→ echo $trimmed['last_name'];
→ ?>"></p>
<p><strong>Email Address:</strong>
→ <input type="email"
→ name="email" size="30"
→ maxlength="60" value="<?php if
→ (isset($trimmed['email'])) echo
→ $trimmed['email']; ?>"> </p>
```

16. Add inputs for the password and the confirmation of the password:

```
<p><strong>Password:</strong>
→ <input type="password"
→ name="password1"
→ size="20" value="<?php if
→ (isset($trimmed['password1']))
→ echo $trimmed['password1']; ?>">
→ <small>At least 10 characters
→ long.</small></p>
<p><strong>Confirm Password:
→ </strong> <input type="password"
→ name="password2" size="20"
→ value="<?php if (isset($trimmed
→ ['password2'])) echo $trimmed
→ ['password2']; ?>"></p>
```

When you are placing restrictions for the input's format, including its length, it's best to indicate those requirements to the user in the form itself. When you do so, the site won't report an error to the user for doing something the user didn't know she or he couldn't do.

17. Complete the HTML form:

```
</fieldset>
<div align="center"><input
→ type="submit" name="submit"
→ value="Register" /></div>
</form>
```

18. Include the HTML footer:

```
<?php include('includes/footer.
→ html'); ?>
```

19. Save the file as **register.php**, place it in your web directory, and test it in your browser.

> **TIP** Because every column in the *users* table cannot be NULL (except for *active*), each input must be correctly filled out. If a table has an optional field, you should still confirm that it is of the right type if submitted, but not require it.

> **TIP** Except for encrypted fields (such as the password), the maximum length of the form inputs and regular expressions should correspond to the maximum length of the column in the database.

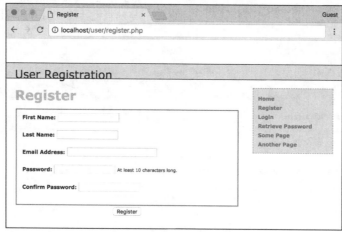

H The registration form as it looks when the user first arrives.

Activating an Account

As described in the "Activation Process" sidebar earlier in the chapter, each user will have to activate his or her account prior to being able to log in. Upon successfully registering, the user will receive an email containing a link to **activate.php** . This link also passes two values to this page: the user's registered email address and a unique activation code. To complete the registration process—to activate the account—the user will need to click that link, taking the user to the **activate.php** script on the web site.

The **activate.php** script needs to first confirm that those two values were received in the URL. Then, if the received two values match those stored in the database, the activation code will be removed from the record, indicating an active account.

To create the activation page:

1. Begin a new PHP script in your text editor or IDE, to be named **activate.php** (Script 18.7):

```php
<?php # Script 18.7 - activate.php
require('includes/config.inc.php');
$page_title = 'Activate Your
→ Account';
include('includes/header.html');
```

2. Validate the values that should be received by the page:

```php
if (isset($_GET['x'], $_GET['y'])
  && filter_var($_GET['x'],
  → FILTER_VALIDATE_EMAIL)
  && (strlen($_GET['y']) == 32 )
  ) {
```

When the user clicks the link in the registration confirmation email, two values will be passed to this page: the email address and the activation code. Both values must be present and validated before attempting to use them in a query activating the user's account.

The first step is to ensure that both values are set. Since the **isset()** function can simultaneously check for the presence of multiple variables, the first part of the validation condition is **isset($_GET['x'], $_GET['y'])**.

continues on page 616

Ⓐ The registration confirmation email.

Script 18.7 To activate an account, the user must come to this page, passing it her or his email address and activation code (all part of the link sent in an email upon registering).

```php
1   <?php # Script 18.7 - activate.php
2   // This page activates the user's account.
3   require('includes/config.inc.php');
4   $page_title = 'Activate Your Account';
5   include('includes/header.html');
6
7   // If $x and $y don't exist or aren't of the proper format, redirect the user:
8   if (isset($_GET['x'], $_GET['y'])
9       && filter_var($_GET['x'], FILTER_VALIDATE_EMAIL)
10      && (strlen($_GET['y']) == 32 )
11      ) {
12
13      // Update the database...
14      require(MYSQL);
15      $q = "UPDATE users SET active=NULL WHERE (email='" . mysqli_real_escape_string
        ($dbc, $_GET['x']) . "' AND active='" . mysqli_real_escape_string($dbc, $_GET['y']) . "')
        LIMIT 1";
16      $r = mysqli_query($dbc, $q) or trigger_error("Query: $q\n<br>MySQL Error: " .
        mysqli_error($dbc));
17
18      // Print a customized message:
19      if (mysqli_affected_rows($dbc) == 1) {
20          echo "<h3>Your account is now active. You may now log in.</h3>";
21      } else {
22          echo '<p class="error">Your account could not be activated. Please re-check the link or
            contact the system administrator.</p>';
23      }
24
25      mysqli_close($dbc);
26
27  } else { // Redirect.
28
29      $url = BASE_URL . 'index.php'; // Define the URL.
30      ob_end_clean(); // Delete the buffer.
31      header("Location: $url");
32      exit(); // Quit the script.
33
34  } // End of main IF-ELSE.
35
36  include('includes/footer.html');
37  ?>
```

Second, **$_GET['x']** must be in the format of a valid email address. The same code as in the registration script can be used for that purpose (either the Filter extension or a regular expression).

Third, for *y* (the activation code), the last clause in the conditional checks that this string's length (how many characters are in it) is exactly 32. The **md5()** function, which created the activation code, always returns a string 32 characters long.

3. Attempt to activate the user's account:

```
require (MYSQL);
$q = "UPDATE users SET active=NULL
→ WHERE (email='" . mysqli_real_
→ escape_string($dbc, $_GET['x'])
→ . "' AND active='" . mysqli_
→ real_escape_string($dbc,
→ $_GET['y']) . "') LIMIT 1";
$r = mysqli_query($dbc, $q) or
→ trigger_error("Query: $q\n<br>
→ MySQL Error: " . mysqli_error
→ ($dbc));
```

If all three conditions (in Step 2) are TRUE, an **UPDATE** query is run. This query removes the activation code from the user's record by setting the *active* column to **NULL**. Before using the values in the query, both are run through **mysqli_real_escape_string()** for extra security.

4. Report on the success of the query:

```
if (mysqli_affected_rows($dbc) ==
→ 1) {
    echo "<h3>Your account is now
    → active. You may now log in.
    → </h3>";
} else {
    echo '<p class="error">Your
    → account could not be
    → activated. Please re-check
    → the link or contact the
    → system administrator.</p>';
}
```

If one row was affected by the query, then the user's account is now active and a message says as much **B**. If no rows are affected, the user is notified of the problem **C**. This would most likely happen if someone tried to fake the *x* and *y* values or if there's a problem in following the link from the email to the browser.

5. Complete the main conditional:

```
    mysqli_close($dbc);
} else { // Redirect.
    $url = BASE_URL . 'index.php';
    ob_end_clean();
    header("Location: $url");
    exit();
} // End of main IF-ELSE.
```

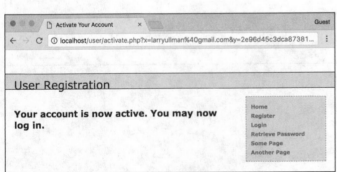

B If the database *could be* updated using the provided email address and activation code, the user is notified that the account is now active.

The **else** clause takes effect if **$_GET['x']** and **$_GET['y']** are not of the proper value and length. In such a case, the user is just redirected to the index page. The **ob_end_clean()** line here deletes the buffer (whatever was to be sent to the browser up to this point, stored in memory), since it won't be used.

6. Complete the page:

```
include('includes/footer.html');
?>
```

7. Save the file as **activate.php**, place it in your web directory, and test it by clicking the link in the registration email.

> **TIP** If you wanted to be a little more forgiving, you could have this page print an error message if the correct values are not received, rather than redirect users to the index page (as if they were attempting to hack the site).

> **TIP** I specifically use the vague *x* and *y* as the names in the URL for security purposes. Although someone may figure out that the one is an email address and the other is a code, it's sometimes best not to be explicit about such things.

Logging In and Logging Out

In Chapter 12 you created many versions of **login.php** and **logout.php** scripts, using variations on cookies and sessions. Here both scripts will be created once again, this time adhering to the same practices as the rest of this chapter's web application. The login query itself is slightly different in this example in that it must also check that the *active* column has a **NULL** value, which is the indication that the user has activated his or her account.

To write **login.php**:

1. Begin a new PHP document in your text editor or IDE, to be named **login.php** (Script 18.8):

```
<?php # Script 18.8 - login.php
require('includes/config.inc.php');
$page_title = 'Login';
include('includes/header.html');
```

2. Check whether the form has been submitted and require the database connection:

```
if ($_SERVER['REQUEST_METHOD'] ==
 'POST') {
   require (MYSQL);
```

continues on next page

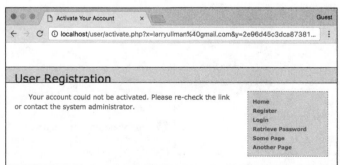

C If an account is not activated by the query, the user is told of the problem.

3. Validate the submitted data:

```
if (!empty($_POST['email'])) {
  $e = mysqli_real_escape_string
  →($dbc, $_POST['email']);
} else {
  $e = FALSE;
  echo '<p class="error">You
  →forgot to enter your email
  →address!</p>';
}
if (!empty($_POST['pass'])) {
  $p = trim($_POST['pass']);
} else {
  $p = FALSE;
  echo '<p class="error">You
  →forgot to enter your
  →password!</p>';
}
```

There are two ways of thinking about the validation. On the one hand, you could use regular expressions and the Filter extension, copying the same code from **register.php**, to validate these values. On the other hand, the true test of the values will be whether or not the login query returns a record, so you could arguably skip more stringent PHP validation. This script uses the latter thinking.

If the user does not enter any values into the form, error messages will be printed .

4. If both validation routines were passed, retrieve the user information:

```
if ($e && $p) { // If
→everything's OK.
  $q = "SELECT user_id,
  →first_name, user_level, pass
  →FROM users WHERE email='$e'
  →AND active IS NULL";
  $r = mysqli_query($dbc, $q)
  →or trigger_error("Query:
  →$q\n<br>MySQL Error: " .
  →mysqli_error($dbc));
```

The query will attempt to retrieve the user ID, first name, user level, and password for the record whose email address matches that submitted. The query has to retrieve the password since it will be validated with PHP.

The query also checks that the *active* column has a **NULL** value, meaning that the user has successfully accessed the **activate.php** page.

If you know an account has been activated but you still can't log in using the

A The login form checks only if values were entered without using regular expressions.

Script 18.8 The login page will redirect the user to the home page after registering the user ID, first name, and access level in a session.

```
1    <?php # Script 18.8 - login.php
2    // This is the login page for the site.
3    require('includes/config.inc.php');
4    $page_title = 'Login';
5    include('includes/header.html');
6
7    if ($_SERVER['REQUEST_METHOD'] ==
     'POST') {
8        require(MYSQL);
9
10       // Validate the email address:
11       if (!empty($_POST['email'])) {
12           $e = mysqli_real_escape_
             string($dbc, $_POST['email']);
13       } else {
14           $e = FALSE;
15           echo '<p class="error">You forgot
             to enter your email address!
             </p>';
16       }
17
18       // Validate the password:
19       if (!empty($_POST['pass'])) {
20           $p = trim($_POST['pass']);
21       } else {
22           $p = FALSE;
23           echo '<p class="error">You forgot
             to enter your password!</p>';
24       }
25
26       if ($e && $p) { // If everything's
         OK.
27
28           // Query the database:
29           $q = "SELECT user_id, first_name,
             user_level, pass FROM users WHERE
             email='$e' AND active IS NULL";
30           $r = mysqli_query($dbc, $q)
             or trigger_error("Query:
             $q\n<br>MySQL Error: " .
             mysqli_error($dbc));
31
32           if (@mysqli_num_rows($r) == 1) {
             // A match was made.
33
```

code continues on next page

proper values, it's likely because your *active* column was erroneously defined as **NOT NULL**.

5. If a match was made in the database, retrieve the values:

```
if (@mysqli_num_rows($r) == 1) {
  list($user_id, $first_name,
  →$user_level, $pass) = mysqli_
  →fetch_array($r, MYSQLI_NUM);
  mysqli_free_result($r);
```

The login process consists of storing the retrieved values in the session (which was already started in **header.html**) and then redirecting the user to the home page. But first the database values need to be fetched into local variables.

The **list()** function has not been formally discussed in the book, but you may have run across it. It's a shortcut function that allows you to assign array elements to other variables. Since **mysqli_fetch_array()** will always return an array, even if it's an array of just one element, using **list()** can save having to write

```
$row = mysqli_fetch_array($r,
→MYSQLI_NUM);
$user_id = $row[0];
```

6. Verify the password and redirect the user:

```
if (password_verify($p, $pass)) {
  $_SESSION['user_id'] = $user_id;
  $_SESSION['first_name'] =
  →$first_name;
  $_SESSION['user_level'] =
  →$user_level;
  mysqli_close($dbc);
  $url = BASE_URL . 'index.php';
  ob_end_clean();
  header("Location: $url");
  exit();
```

continues on page 621

```
34          // Fetch the values:
35          list($user_id, $first_name, $user_level, $pass) = mysqli_fetch_array($r, MYSQLI_NUM);
36          mysqli_free_result($r);
37
38          // Check the password:
39          if (password_verify($p, $pass)) {
40
41              // Store the info in the session:
42              $_SESSION['user_id'] = $user_id;
43              $_SESSION['first_name'] = $first_name;
44              $_SESSION['user_level'] = $user_level;
45              mysqli_close($dbc);
46
47              // Redirect the user:
48              $url = BASE_URL . 'index.php'; // Define the URL.
49              ob_end_clean(); // Delete the buffer.
50              header("Location: $url");
51              exit(); // Quit the script.
52
53          } else {
54
55              echo '<p class="error">Either the email address and password entered do not match
                those on file or you have not yet activated your account.</p>';
56          }
57
58      } else { // No match was made.
59          echo '<p class="error">Either the email address and password entered do not match
            those on file or you have not yet activated your account.</p>';
60      }
61
62  } else { // If everything wasn't OK.
63      echo '<p class="error">Please try again.</p>';
64  }
65
66  mysqli_close($dbc);
67
68  } // End of SUBMIT conditional.
69  ?>
70
71  <h1>Login</h1>
72  <p>Your browser must allow cookies in order to log in.</p>
73  <form action="login.php" method="post">
74      <fieldset>
75      <p><strong>Email Address:</strong> <input type="email" name="email" size="20"
        maxlength="60"></p>
76      <p><strong>Password:</strong> <input type="password" name="pass" size="20"></p>
77      <div align="center"><input type="submit" name="submit" value="Login"></div>
78      </fieldset>
79  </form>
80
81  <?php include('includes/footer.html'); ?>
```

The first line was explained in Chapter 13. If a match is made, the user's information is stored in the session and the user is redirected to the home page.

The **ob_end_clean()** function will delete the existing buffer (the output buffering is also begun in **header.html**), since it will not be used.

7. Complete the conditionals and close the database connection:

```php
        } else {
            echo '<p class="error">
            → Either the email
            → address and password
            → entered do not match
            → those on file or you
            → have not yet activated
            → your account.</p>';
        }
    } else { // No match was made.
```

B An error message is displayed if the login query does not return a single record.

C The login form.

```php
        echo '<p class="error">
        → Either the email address
        → and password entered do
        → not match those on
        → file or you have not yet
        → activated your account.
        → </p>';
    }
} else { // If everything
→ wasn't OK.
    echo '<p class="error">Please
    → try again.</p>';
}
mysqli_close($dbc);
} // End of SUBMIT conditional.
?>
```

The error message **B** indicates that the login process could fail for two possible reasons. One is that the submitted email address and password do not match those on file. The other reason is that the user has not yet activated the account.

8. Display the HTML login form **C**:

```html
<h1>Login</h1>
<p>Your browser must allow
→ cookies in order to log in.</p>
<form action="login.php"
→ method="post">
    <fieldset>
    <p><strong>Email Address:
    → </strong> <input type="email"
    → name="email" size="20"
    → maxlength="60"></p>
    <p><strong>Password:</strong>
    → <input type="password"
    → name="pass" size="20"></p>
    <div align="center"><input
    → type="submit" name="submit"
    → value="Login"></div>
    </fieldset>
</form>
```

continues on next page

The login form, like the registration form, will submit the data back to itself. This one is not sticky, though, but you could add that functionality.

Notice that the page includes a message informing the user that cookies must be enabled to use the site (if a user does not allow cookies, she or he will never get access to the logged-in user pages).

9. Include the HTML footer:

```php
<?php include('includes/footer.
→ html'); ?>
```

10. Save the file as **login.php**, place it in your web directory, and test it in your browser 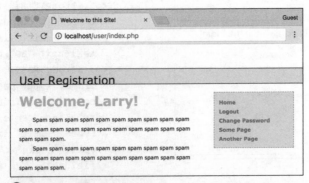.

To write logout.php:

1. Begin a new PHP document in your text editor or IDE, to be named **logout.php** (Script 18.9):

```php
<?php # Script 18.9 - logout.php
require('includes/config.inc.php');
$page_title = 'Logout';
include('includes/header.html');
```

Script 18.9 The logout page destroys all of the session information, including the cookie.

```php
1   <?php # Script 18.9 - logout.php
2   // This is the logout page for the site.
3   require('includes/config.inc.php');
4   $page_title = 'Logout';
5   include('includes/header.html');
6
7   // If no first_name session variable
    exists, redirect the user:
8   if (!isset($_SESSION['first_name'])) {
9
10      $url = BASE_URL . 'index.php'; //
        Define the URL.
11      ob_end_clean(); // Delete the buffer.
12      header("Location: $url");
13      exit(); // Quit the script.
14
15  } else { // Log out the user.
16
17      $_SESSION = []; // Destroy the
        variables.
18      session_destroy(); // Destroy the
        session itself.
19      setcookie(session_name(), '', time()-
        3600); // Destroy the cookie.
20
21  }
22
23  // Print a customized message:
24  echo '<h3>You are now logged out.</h3>';
25
26  include('includes/footer.html');
27  ?>
```

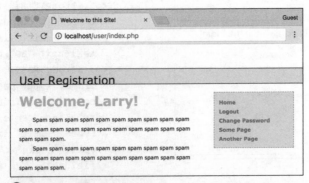

D Upon successfully logging in, the user will be redirected to the home page, where the user will be greeted by name.

2. Redirect the user if she or he is not logged in:

```php
if (!isset($_SESSION['first_name'])) {
  $url = BASE_URL . 'index.php';
  ob_end_clean();
  header("Location: $url");
  exit();
```

If the user is not currently logged in (determined by checking for a `$_SESSION['first_name']` variable), the user will be redirected to the home page (because there's no point in trying to log the user out).

3. Log out the user if she or he is currently logged in:

```php
} else { // Log out the user.
  $_SESSION = [];
  session_destroy();
  setcookie (session_name(),'',
  → time()-3600);
}
```

To log the user out, the session values will be reset, the session data will be destroyed on the server, and the session cookie will be deleted. These lines of code were first used and described in Chapter 12. The cookie name will be the value returned by the `session_name()` function. If you decide to change the session name later, this code will still be accurate.

4. Print a logged-out message and complete the PHP page:

```php
echo '<h3>You are now logged out.
→ </h3>';
include('includes/footer.html');
?>
```

5. Save the file as **logout.php**, place it in your web directory, and test it in your browser **E**.

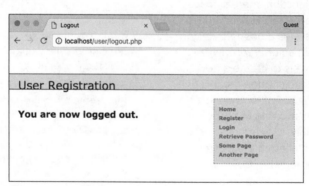

E The results of successfully logging out.

Password Management

The final aspect of the public side of this site is the management of passwords. There are two processes to consider: resetting a forgotten password and changing an existing one.

Resetting a password

It inevitably happens that people forget their login passwords for web sites, so having a contingency plan for these occasions is important. One option would be to have the user email the administrator when this occurs, but administering a site is difficult enough without that extra hassle. Instead, this site will have a script whose purpose is to reset a forgotten password.

Because the passwords stored in the database are encrypted using PHP's `password_hash()` function, there's no way to retrieve an unencrypted version (the database actually stores a *hashed* version of the password, not an *encrypted* version). The alternative is to create a new, random password and change the existing password to this value. Rather than just display the new password in the browser (that would be terribly insecure), the new password will be emailed to the address with which the user registered.

To write `forgot_password.php`:

1. Begin a new PHP document in your text editor or IDE, to be named `forgot_password.php` (Script 18.10):

   ```php
   <?php # Script 18.10 -
   → forgot_password.php
   require('includes/config.inc.php');
   $page_title = 'Forgot Your
   → Password';
   include('includes/header.html');
   ```

2. Check whether the form has been submitted, include the database connection, and create a flag variable:

   ```php
   if ($_SERVER['REQUEST_METHOD'] ==
   → 'POST') {
     require (MYSQL);
     $uid = FALSE;
   ```

An Alternative Approach

The primary negative to this password reset approach is that it allows anyone to force-change anyone else's password as long as the email address has been registered. That wouldn't deny the actual registered user access, but it is annoying.

An alternative approach that avoids this problem requires adding one more step. Instead of immediately resetting the password, send an email to the user with a link to reset the password. If it's a legitimate request from the registered user, the user will click the link, the site can reset the password, and the user can then log in. If it's not a legitimate request from the registered user, the user can just ignore the email and his or her current password is retained (add a note to the email saying such).

Script 18.10 The `forgot_password.php` script allows users to reset their password without administrative assistance.

```
1    <?php # Script 18.10 -
     forgot_password.php
2    // This page allows a user to reset
     their password, if forgotten.
3    require('includes/config.inc.php');
4    $page_title = 'Forgot Your Password';
5    include('includes/header.html');
6
7    if ($_SERVER['REQUEST_METHOD'] ==
     'POST') {
8        require(MYSQL);
9
10       // Assume nothing:
11       $uid = FALSE;
12
13       // Validate the email address...
14       if (!empty($_POST['email'])) {
15
16           // Check for the existence of
             that email address...
17           $q = 'SELECT user_id FROM
             users WHERE email="'.
             mysqli_real_escape_string
             ($dbc, $_POST['email']) . '"';
18           $r = mysqli_query($dbc, $q)
             or trigger_error("Query:
             $q\n<br>MySQL Error: " .
             mysqli_error($dbc));
19
20           if (mysqli_num_rows($r) == 1) {
             // Retrieve the user ID:
21               list($uid) = mysqli_fetch_
                 array($r, MYSQLI_NUM);
22           } else { // No database match
             made.
23               echo '<p class="error">The
                 submitted email address does
                 not match those on file!</p>';
24           }
25
26       } else { // No email!
27           echo '<p class="error">You forgot
             to enter your email address!
             </p>';
28       } // End of empty($_POST['email']) IF.
29
30       if ($uid) { // If everything's OK.
```

code continues on next page

This form will take an email address input and change the password for that record. To do that, the script first needs to retrieve the user ID value that matches the submitted email address. To begin that process, a flag variable is assigned a FALSE value as an assumption of no valid user ID.

3. Validate the submitted email address:

```
if (!empty($_POST['email'])) {
    $q = 'SELECT user_id FROM
    ⇢ users WHERE email="'.
    ⇢ mysqli_real_escape_string
    ⇢ ($dbc, $_POST['email']) . '"';
    $r = mysqli_query($dbc, $q) or
    ⇢ trigger_error("Query: $q\n<br>
    ⇢ MySQL Error: " . mysqli_error
    ⇢ ($dbc));
```

This is a simple validation for a submitted email address (without using a regular expression or the Filter extension). If the submitted value is not empty, an attempt is made to retrieve the user ID for that email address in the database. You could, of course, add more stringent validation if you'd prefer.

4. Retrieve the selected user ID:

```
if (mysqli_num_rows($r) == 1) {
    list($uid) = mysqli_fetch_array
    ⇢ ($r, MYSQLI_NUM);
} else {
    echo '<p class="error">The
    ⇢ submitted email address does
    ⇢ not match those on file!</p>';
}
```

If the query returns one row, it'll be fetched and assigned to **$uid** (short for *user ID*). This value will be needed to update the database with the new password, and it'll also be used as a flag variable.

continues on page 627

```
31
32          // Create a new, random password:
33          $p = substr(md5(uniqid(rand(), true)), 3, 15);
34          $ph = password_hash($p);
35
36          // Update the database:
37          $q = "UPDATE users SET pass='$ph' WHERE user_id=$uid LIMIT 1";
38          $r = mysqli_query($dbc, $q) or trigger_error("Query: $q\n<br>MySQL Error: " .
            mysqli_error($dbc));
39
40          if (mysqli_affected_rows($dbc) == 1) { // If it ran OK.
41
42              // Send an email:
43              $body = "Your password to log into <whatever site> has been temporarily changed to
                '$p'. Please log in using this password and this email address. Then you may change
                your password to something more familiar.";
44              mail($_POST['email'], 'Your temporary password.', $body, 'From: admin@sitename.com');
45
46              // Print a message and wrap up:
47              echo '<h3>Your password has been changed. You will receive the new, temporary
                password at the email address with which you registered. Once you have logged in with
                this password, you may change it by clicking on the "Change Password" link.</h3>';
48              mysqli_close($dbc);
49              include('includes/footer.html');
50              exit(); // Stop the script.
51
52          } else { // If it did not run OK.
53              echo '<p class="error">Your password could not be changed due to a system error. We
                apologize for any inconvenience.</p>';
54          }
55
56      } else { // Failed the validation test.
57          echo '<p class="error">Please try again.</p>';
58      }
59
60      mysqli_close($dbc);
61
62  } // End of the main Submit conditional.
63  ?>
64
65  <h1>Reset Your Password</h1>
66  <p>Enter your email address below and your password will be reset.</p>
67  <form action="forgot_password.php" method="post">
68      <fieldset>
69      <p><strong>Email Address:</strong> <input type="email" name="email" size="20"
        maxlength="60" value="<?php if (isset($_POST['email'])) echo $_POST['email']; ?>"></p>
70      </fieldset>
71      <div align="center"><input type="submit" name="submit" value="Reset My Password"></div>
72  </form>
73
74  <?php include('includes/footer.html'); ?>
```

If no matching record could be found for the submitted email address, an error message is displayed **A**. For security purposes, you could be more vague, saying something like *If the email address has been registered, a temporary password has been sent there.*

5. Report on no submitted email address:

```
} else { // No email!
    echo '<p class="error">You
    → forgot to enter your email
    → address!</p>';
} // End of empty($_POST['email']) IF.
```

If no email address was provided, that is also reported **B**.

6. Create a new, random password:

```
if ($uid) {
    $p = substr(md5(uniqid(rand(),
    → true)), 3, 15);
    $ph = password_hash($p);
```

A If the user entered an email address that is not found in the database, an error message is shown.

B Failure to provide an email address also results in an error.

Creating a new, random password will make use of four PHP functions. The first is **uniqid()**, which will return a unique identifier. It is fed the arguments **rand()** and **true**, which makes the returned string more random. This returned value is then sent through the **md5()** function, which calculates the MD5 hash of a string. At this stage, a hashed version of the unique ID is returned, which ends up being a string 32 characters long. This part of the code is similar to that used to create the activation code in **activate.php** (Script 18.7).

From this string, the password is created by pulling out fifteen characters starting with the third one, using the **substr()** function. All in all, this code will return a very random and meaningless ten-character string (containing both letters and numbers) to be used as the temporary password.

Note that the creation of a new, random password is only necessary if **$uid** has a TRUE value by this point.

Although this represents an acceptable way of creating a new password, if you're using PHP 7 or greater, you can use the more secure **random_bytes()** function instead.

7. Update the password in the database:

```
$q = "UPDATE users SET pass='$ph'
→ WHERE user_id=$uid LIMIT 1";
$r = mysqli_query($dbc, $q)
→ or trigger_error("Query:
→ $q\n<br>MySQL Error: " .
→ mysqli_error($dbc));
if (mysqli_affected_rows($dbc) ==
→ 1) {
```

continues on next page

Using the user ID (the primary key for the table) that was retrieved earlier, the password for this particular user is updated to the **password_hash()** version of **$p**, the random password.

8. Email the password to the user:

```
$body = "Your password to log
→ into <whatever site> has been
→ temporarily changed to '$p'.
→ Please log in using this
→ password and this email
→ address. Then you may change
→ your password to something more
→ familiar.";
mail($_POST['email'], 'Your
→ temporary password.', $body,
→ 'From: admin@sitename.com');
```

Next, the user needs to be emailed the new password so that she or he may log in **C**. It's safe to use **$_POST['email']** in the **mail()** code, because to get to this point, **$_POST['email']** must match an address already stored in the database. That address would have already been validated via the Filter extension (or a regular expression) in the registration script.

9. Complete the page:

```
echo '<h3>Your password has been
→ changed. You will receive the
→ new, temporary password at the
→ email address with which you
→ registered. Once you have
→ logged in with this password,
→ you may change it by clicking
→ on the "Change Password" link.
→ </h3>';
mysqli_close($dbc);
include('includes/footer.html');
exit(); // Stop the script.
```

Next, a message is printed and the page is completed so as not to show the form again **D**.

10. Complete the conditionals and the PHP code:

```
} else { // If it did not
→ run OK.
    echo '<p class="error">Your
    → password could not be
    → changed due to a system
    → error. We apologize for
    → any inconvenience.</p>';
}
} else { // Failed the
→ validation test.
    echo '<p class="error">Please
    → try again.</p>';
}
mysqli_close($dbc);
} // End of the main Submit
→ conditional.
?>
```

The first **else** clause applies only if the **UPDATE** query did not work, which hopefully shouldn't happen on a live site.

C The email message received after resetting a password.

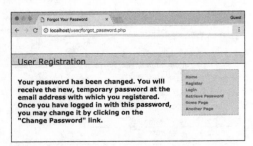

D The resulting page after successfully resetting a password.

The second **else** applies if the user didn't submit an email address or if the submitted email address didn't match any in the database.

11. Make the HTML form **E**:

```
<h1>Reset Your Password</h1>
<p>Enter your email address
→ below and your password will be
→ reset.</p>
<form action="forgot_password.
→ php" method="post">
  <fieldset>
  <p><strong>Email Address:
  → </strong> <input type="email"
  → name="email" size="20"
  → maxlength="60" value="<?php
  → if (isset($_POST['email']))
  → echo $_POST['email']; ?>"></p>
  </fieldset>
  <div align="center"><input
  → type="submit" name="submit"
  → value="Reset My Password">
  → </div>
</form>
```

The form takes only one input, the email address. If there is a problem when the form has been submitted, the submitted email address value will be shown again (i.e., the form is sticky).

12. Include the HTML footer:

```
<?php include('includes/footer.
→ html'); ?>
```

13. Save the file as **forgot_password.php**, place it in your web directory, and test it in your browser.

E The simple form for resetting a password.

14. Check your email to see the resulting message after a successful password reset **C**.

Changing a password

The **change_password.php** script was initially written in Chapter 9 (called just **password.php**), as an example of an **UDPATE** query. The one developed here will be very similar in functionality but will differ in that only users who are logged in will be able to access it. Therefore, the form will only need to accept the new password and a confirmation of it (the user's existing password and email address will have already been confirmed by the login page).

To write change_password.php:

1. Begin a new PHP document in your text editor or IDE, to be named **change_password.php** (Script 18.11):

```
<?php # Script 18.11 -
→ change_password.php
require('includes/config.inc.php');
$page_title = 'Change Your
→ Password';
include('includes/header.html');
```

2. Redirect if the user is not logged in:

```
if (!isset($_SESSION['user_id'])) {
  $url = BASE_URL . 'index.php';
  → ob_end_clean();
  header("Location: $url");
  exit();
}
```

The assumption is that this page is only to be accessed by logged-in users. To enforce this idea, the script checks for the existence of the **$_SESSION['user_id']** variable (which would be required by the **UPDATE** query). If this variable is not set, then the user will be redirected.

continues on next page

3. Check if the form has been submitted and include the MySQL connection:

```
if ($_SERVER['REQUEST_METHOD'] ==
→'POST') {
  require (MYSQL);
```

The key to understanding how this script performs is remembering that there are three possible scenarios: the user is not logged in (and therefore redirected), the user is logged in and viewing the form, and the user is logged in and has submitted the form.

The user will get to this point in the script only if she or he logged in. Otherwise, the user would have been redirected by now. At this point the script just needs to determine whether or not the form has been submitted.

4. Validate the submitted password:

```
$p = FALSE;
if (strlen($_POST['password1']) >=
→ 10) {
  if ($_POST['password1'] ==
→ $_POST['password2']) {
    $p = password_hash($_POST
→ ['password1'] , PASSWORD_
→ DEFAULT);
  } else {
    echo '<p class="error">Your
→ password did not match the
→ confirmed password!</p>';
  }
} else {
  echo '<p class="error">Please
→ enter a valid password!</p>';
}
```

continues on page 632

Script 18.11 With this page, users can change an existing password (if they are logged in).

```
1    <?php # Script 18.11 - change_password.php
2    // This page allows a logged-in user to change their password.
3    require('includes/config.inc.php');
4    $page_title = 'Change Your Password';
5    include('includes/header.html');
6
7    // If no user_id session variable exists, redirect the user:
8    if (!isset($_SESSION['user_id'])) {
9
10       $url = BASE_URL . 'index.php'; // Define the URL.
11       ob_end_clean(); // Delete the buffer.
12       header("Location: $url");
13       exit(); // Quit the script.
14
15   }
16
17   if ($_SERVER['REQUEST_METHOD'] == 'POST') {
18       require(MYSQL);
19
20       // Check for a new password and match against the confirmed password:
21       $p = FALSE;
22       if (strlen($_POST['password1']) >= 10) {
23           if ($_POST['password1'] == $_POST['password2']) {
24               $p = password_hash($_POST['password1'], PASSWORD_DEFAULT);
```

code continues on next page

```
25          } else {
26              echo '<p class="error">Your password did not match the confirmed password!</p>';
27          }
28      } else {
29          echo '<p class="error">Please enter a valid password!</p>';
30      }
31
32      if ($p) { // If everything's OK.
33
34          // Make the query:
35          $q = "UPDATE users SET pass='$p' WHERE user_id={$_SESSION['user_id']} LIMIT 1";
36          $r = mysqli_query($dbc, $q) or trigger_error("Query: $q\n<br>MySQL Error: " .
            mysqli_error($dbc));
37          if (mysqli_affected_rows($dbc) == 1) { // If it ran OK.
38
39              // Send an email, if desired.
40              echo '<h3>Your password has been changed.</h3>';
41              mysqli_close($dbc); // Close the database connection.
42              include('includes/footer.html'); // Include the HTML footer.
43              exit();
44
45          } else { // If it did not run OK.
46
47              echo '<p class="error">Your password was not changed. Make sure your new password is
                different than the current password. Contact the system administrator if you think an
                error occurred.</p>';
48
49          }
50
51      } else { // Failed the validation test.
52          echo '<p class="error">Please try again.</p>';
53      }
54
55      mysqli_close($dbc); // Close the database connection.
56
57  } // End of the main Submit conditional.
58  ?>
59
60  <h1>Change Your Password</h1>
61  <form action="change_password.php" method="post">
62      <fieldset>
63      <p><strong>New Password:</strong> <input type="password" name="password1" size="20">
        <small>At least 10 characters long.</small></p>
64      <p><strong>Confirm New Password:</strong> <input type="password" name="password2"
        size="20"></p>
65      </fieldset>
66      <div align="center"><input type="submit" name="submit" value="Change My Password"></div>
67  </form>
68
69  <?php include('includes/footer.html'); ?>
```

The new password should be validated using the same tests as those in the registration process. Error messages will be displayed if problems are found **F**.

5. Update the password in the database:

```
if ($p) { // If everything's OK.
  $q = "UPDATE users SET pass='$p'
  → WHERE user_id={$_SESSION
  → ['user_id']} LIMIT 1";
  $r = mysqli_query($dbc, $q)
  → or trigger_error("Query: $q\n
  → <br>MySQL Error: " .
  → mysqli_error($dbc));
```

Using the user's ID—stored in the session when the user logged in—the password field can be updated in the database. The **LIMIT 1** clause isn't strictly necessary but adds extra insurance.

6. If the query worked, complete the page:

```
if (mysqli_affected_rows($dbc) ==
→ 1) {
  echo '<h3>Your password has been
  → changed.</h3>';
  mysqli_close($dbc);
  include('includes/footer.html');
  exit();
```

If the update worked, a confirmation message is printed to the browser **G**.

7. Complete the conditionals and the PHP code:

```
} else { // If it did not
→ run OK.
  echo '<p class="error">
  → Your password was not
  → changed. Make sure your
  → new password is different
  → than the current password.
  → Contact the system
  → administrator if you think
  → an error occurred.</p>';
}
} else { // Failed the
→ validation test.
  echo '<p class="error">
  → Please try again.</p>';
}
mysqli_close($dbc);
} // End of the main Submit
→ conditional.
?>
```

The first **else** clause applies if the **mysqli_affected_rows()** function did not return a value of 1. This could occur for two reasons. The first is that a query or database error happened. Hopefully, that's not likely on a live site, after you've already worked out all the bugs.

Please enter a valid password!
Please try again.

Change Your Password

New Password: _____ At least 10 characters long.

Confirm New Password: _____

Change My Password

F As in the registration process, the user's new password must pass the length requirement; otherwise, the user will see error messages.

User Registration

Your password has been changed.

G The script has successfully changed the user's password.

Site Administration

For this application, how the site administration works depends on what you want it to do. One additional page you would probably want for an administrator would be a **view_users.php** script, like the one created in Chapter 9 and modified in Chapter 10, "Common Programming Techniques." It's already listed in the administrator's links. You could use such a script to link to an **edit_user.php** page, which would allow the administrator to manually activate an account, declare that a user is an administrator, or change a person's password. An administrator could also delete a user using such a page.

Although the footer file creates links to administrative pages only if the logged-in user is an administrator, every administration page should also include such a check.

Change Your Password

New Password: [   ] At least 10 characters long.

Confirm New Password: [   ]

[Change My Password]

H The Change Your Password form.

TIP Once this script has been completed, users can reset their password with the previous script and then log in using the temporary, random password. After logging in, users can change their password back to something easier to remember with this page.

TIP Because the site's authentication does not rely on the user's password from page to page (in other words, the password is not checked on each subsequent page after logging in), changing a password will not require the user to log back in.

The second reason is that the user tried to "change" the password but entered the same password again. In that case, the **UPDATE** query wouldn't affect any rows because the password column in the database wouldn't be changed. A message implying such is printed.

8. Create the HTML form **H**:

```
<h1>Change Your Password</h1>
<form action="change_password.php"
→ method="post">
  <fieldset>
  <p><strong>New Password:
  → </strong> <input
  → type="password"
  → name="password1" size="20">
  → <small>At least 10 characters
  → long.</small></p>
  <p><strong>Confirm New
  → Password:</strong> <input
  → type="password"
  → name="password2" size="20">
  → </p>
  </fieldset>
  <div align="center"><input
  → type="submit" name="submit"
  → value="Change My Password">
  → </div>
</form>
```

This form takes two inputs: the new password and a confirmation of it. A description of the proper format is given as well. Because the form is so simple it's not sticky, but that's a feature you could add.

9. Complete the HTML page:

```
<?php include('includes/footer.
→ html'); ?>
```

10. Save the file as **change_password.php**, place it in your web directory, and test it in your browser.

Review and Pursue

If you have any problems with the review questions or the pursue prompts, turn to the book's supporting forum (LarryUllman.com/forums/).

Note: Most of these questions and some of the prompts rehash information covered in earlier chapters to reinforce some of the most important points.

Review

- What is *output buffering*? What are the benefits of using it?

- Why shouldn't detailed error information be displayed on live sites?

- Why must the *active* column in the *users* table allow for **NULL** values? What is the result if *active* is defined as **NOT NULL**?

- What are the three steps in terminating a session?

- What does the `session_name()` function do?

- What are the differences between truly *encrypting* data and creating a *hash* representation of some data?

Pursue

- Check out the PHP manual's pages for output buffering (or output control).

- Check out the PHP manual's pages for the `rand()`, `uniqid()`, and `md5()` functions.

- Check out the PHP manual's page for the `trigger_error()` function.

- Apply the same validation techniques to `login.php` as used in `register.php`.

- Make the login form sticky.

- Add a *last_login* **DATETIME** field to the *users* table and update its value when a user logs in. Use this information to indicate to the user how long it has been since the last time she or he accessed the site.

- If you've added the *last_login* field, use it to print a message on the home page as to how many users have logged in in the past, say, hour or day.

- Validate the submitted email address in `forgot_password.php` using the Filter extension or a regular expression.

- Check out the PHP manual's page for the `list()` function.

- Create `view_users.php` and `edit_user.php` scripts as recommended in the final sidebar. Restrict access to these scripts to administrators (those users whose access level is 1).

Installation

There are three technical requirements for executing all this book's examples: MySQL (the database application), PHP (the scripting language), and the web server application (that PHP runs through). This appendix describes the installation of these tools on two different platforms—Windows 10 and macOS. If you are using a hosted web site, all of this will already be provided for you, but these products are all free and easy enough to install, so putting them on your own computer still makes sense.

After covering installation, the appendix discusses related issues that will be of importance to almost every user. First, I introduce how to create users in MySQL. Next, I demonstrate how to test your PHP and MySQL installation, showing techniques you'll want to use when you begin working on any server for the first time. Then, you'll learn how to configure PHP to change how it runs. Finally, I introduce how to change the Apache web server's behavior to address common needs.

Installation on Windows

Although you can certainly install a web server (such as Apache, Nginx, or IIS), PHP, and MySQL individually on a Windows computer, I strongly recommend you use an all-in-one installer instead. It's simply easier and more reliable to do so.

Several all-in-one installers are out there for Windows. The four that I see mentioned most frequently are

- XAMPP (www.apachefriends.org)
- WAMP (www.wampserver.com/en/)
- AMPPS (www.ampps.com)
- Bitnami (www.bitnami.com), which also partners with XAMPP

For this appendix, I'll use XAMPP, which runs on most modern versions of Windows.

Along with Apache, PHP, and MySQL, XAMPP also installs the following:

- phpMyAdmin, the web-based interface to a MySQL server
- OpenSSL, for secure connections
- A mail server (for sending email)
- Several useful extensions

As of this writing, XAMPP (Version 7.1.7) installs PHP 7.1.7, Apache 2.4.26, and phpMyAdmin 4.7.0. There is one catch, however!

As of XAMPP 5.5.30, the installer includes MariaDB (www.mariadb.com) instead of MySQL. MariaDB is an open source fork of MySQL that is functionally equivalent. Despite the fact that XAMPP installs MariaDB instead of MySQL, you shouldn't have any problems following all the MySQL-specific instructions or code in this book.

On Firewalls

Modern versions of Windows include a firewall, which prevents communications in many ways, the most common of which is over *ports*: an access point to a computer. You can also download and install third-party firewalls. Firewalls improve the security of your computer, but they may also interfere with your ability to run Apache, MySQL, and some of the other tools used by XAMPP because they all use ports.

When running XAMPP for the first time, or during the installation process, if you see a security prompt indicating that the firewall is blocking Apache, MySQL, or the like, choose *Unblock* or *Allow access*. Otherwise, you can configure your firewall manually through the operating system settings.

The ports that need to be open are as follows: 80 for Apache, 3306 for MySQL, and 25 for the Mercury mail server. If you have any problems starting or accessing one of these, disable your firewall and see if it works then. If so, you'll know the firewall is the problem and that it needs to be reconfigured.

Just to be clear, firewalls aren't found just on Windows, but in terms of the instructions in this appendix, the presence of a firewall will more likely trip up a Windows user than any other.

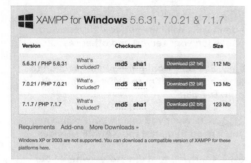

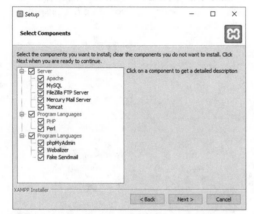

A From the Apache Friends web site, grab the latest installer for Windows.

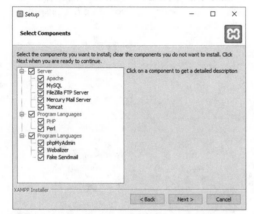

B The XAMPP components that can be installed.

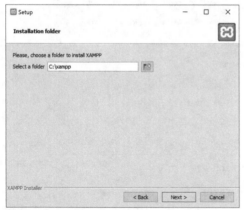

C Select where XAMPP should be installed.

I'll run through the installation process in these next steps. Note that if you have any problems, you can use the book's supporting forum (`LarryUllman.com/forums/`), but you'll probably have more luck turning to the XAMPP site (it is their product, after all). Also, the installer works well and isn't that hard to use, so rather than detail every single step in the process, I'll highlight the most important considerations.

To install XAMPP on Windows:

1. Download the latest release of XAMPP for Windows from **www.apachefriends.org** **A**.

   I suggest that you grab the latest version of PHP available, although you'll be fine with most of this book's content if you use a PHP 5 version instead.

2. On your computer, double-click the downloaded file to begin the installation process.

3. When prompted **B**, install all the components.

   Admittedly, you don't need Tomcat— a Java server—or Perl, but it's fine to install them, too.

4. When prompted **C**, install XAMPP somewhere other than in the Program Files directory.

   You shouldn't install it in the Program Files directory because of a permissions issue in Windows. I recommend installing XAMPP in your root directory (e.g., `C:\`).

   Wherever you decide to install the program, make note of that location, because you'll need to know it several other times as you work through this appendix.

continues on next page

5. After the installation process has done its thing, opt to start the XAMPP Control Panel.

6. To start, stop, and configure XAMPP, use the XAMPP Control Panel 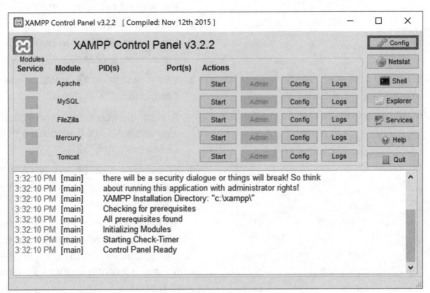.

   Apache has to be running for every chapter in this book. MySQL must be running for about half of the chapters. Mercury is the mail server that XAMPP installs. It needs to be running in order to send email using PHP (see Chapter 11, "Web Application Development").

7. Immediately set a password for the root MySQL user.

   How you do this is explained in the "Managing MySQL Users" section later in this appendix.

TIP The XAMPP Control Panel's various admin links will take you to different web pages (on your server) and other resources.

TIP See the "Configuring PHP" section to learn how to configure PHP by editing the `php.ini` file.

TIP Whenever you restart your computer, you'll need to restart the XAMPP services.

TIP Your web root directory—where your PHP scripts should be placed to test them—is the `htdocs` folder in the directory where XAMPP was installed. Following my installation instructions, this would be `C:\xampp\htdocs`.

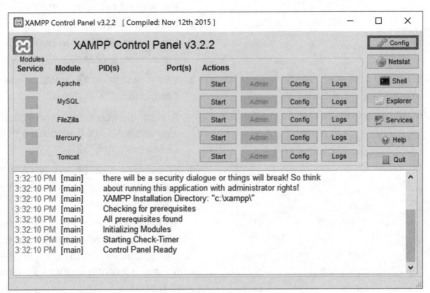

D The XAMPP Control Panel, used to manage the software.

Installation on macOS

macOS is at its heart a version of Unix, and because PHP and MySQL were originally written for Unix-like systems, numerous options are available for installing them on macOS. In fact, macOS already comes with Apache installed, saving you that step.

Seasoned developers and those at home in the Terminal will likely want to install PHP and MySQL using package installers such as **http://php-osx.liip.ch/** and Homebrew (**http://brew.sh/**). But for beginners, I recommend using an all-in-one installer such as

- XAMPP (**www.apachefriends.org**)
- AMPPS (**www.ampps.com**)
- Bitnami (**www.bitnami.com**), which also partners with XAMPP
- MAMP (**www.mamp.info**)

Not only are these installers relatively foolproof, but they also won't leave you scrambling when an operating system update overwrites your Apache configuration file. For this appendix, I'll use XAMPP, which runs on macOS 10.6 and later.

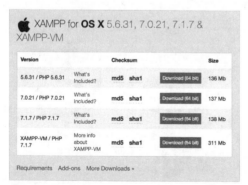

A From the Apache Friends web site, grab the latest installer for macOS.

Along with Apache, PHP, and MySQL, XAMPP also installs the following:

- phpMyAdmin, the web-based interface to a MySQL server
- OpenSSL, for secure connections
- Several useful extensions

As of this writing, XAMPP (Version 7.1.7) installs PHP 7.1.7, Apache 2.4.26, and phpMyAdmin 4.7.0. There is one catch, however!

As of XAMPP 5.5.30, the installer includes MariaDB (**www.mariadb.com**) instead of MySQL. MariaDB is an open source fork of MySQL that is functionally equivalent. Despite the fact that XAMPP installs MariaDB instead of MySQL, you shouldn't have any problems following all the MySQL-specific instructions or code in this book.

I'll run through the installation process in these next steps. Note that if you have any problems, you can use the book's supporting forum (**LarryUllman.com/forums/**), but you'll probably have more luck turning to the XAMPP site (it is their product, after all). Also, the installer works well and isn't that hard to use, so rather than detail every single step in the process, I'll highlight the most important considerations.

To install XAMPP on macOS:

1. Download the latest release of XAMPP for macOS from **www.apachefriends.org** **A**.

   I suggest that you grab the latest version of PHP available, although you'll be fine with most of this book's content if you use a PHP 5 version instead.

   continues on next page

2. On your computer, double-click the downloaded file to mount the disc image.

3. In the mounted disk image, double-click the package installer to begin the installation process.

4. When prompted **Ⓑ**, install all the components.

   You'll see only two, broad options; install both.

5. After the installation process has done its thing **Ⓒ**, opt to launch XAMPP.

6. To start, stop, and configure XAMPP, use the XAMPP Control Panel **Ⓓ**.

   Apache has to be running for every chapter in this book. MySQL must be running for about half of the chapters. You probably won't ever need the FTP application, because you can just move your files directly.

7. Immediately set a password for the root MySQL user.

   How you do this is explained in the "Managing MySQL Users" section later in this appendix.

TIP See the **"Configuring PHP" section** to learn how to configure PHP by editing the `php.ini` file.

TIP Whenever you restart your computer, you'll need to restart the XAMPP services.

TIP Your web root directory—where your PHP scripts should be placed in order to test them—is the `htdocs` folder in the directory where **XAMPP** was installed. This would be `/Applications/XAMPP/xamppfiles/htdocs`.

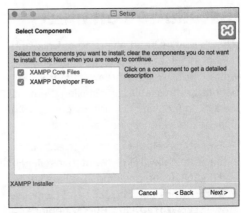

Ⓑ The XAMPP components that can be installed.

Ⓒ The installation of XAMPP is complete!

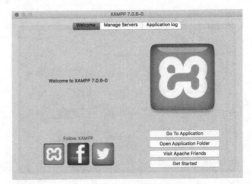

Ⓓ The XAMPP Control Panel, used to manage the software.

Managing MySQL Users

Once you've successfully installed MySQL, you can begin creating MySQL users. A MySQL user is a fundamental security concept, limiting access to, and influence over, stored data. Just to clarify, your databases can have several different users, just as your operating system might. But MySQL users are different from operating system users. While learning PHP and MySQL on your own computer, you don't necessarily need to create new users, but live production sites need to have dedicated MySQL users with appropriate permissions.

The initial MySQL installation comes with one user (named *root*) with no password set (except when using MAMP, which sets a default password of *root*). At the very least, you should create a new, secure password for the root user after installing MySQL. After that, you can create other users with more limited permissions. As a rule, you shouldn't use the root user for normal, day-to-day operations.

I'll walk you through both processes over the next couple of pages. Note that if you're using a hosted server, they'll likely create the MySQL users for you. These instructions require use of either the command-line mysql client or phpMyAdmin. If you don't know how to access either of these on your computer, quickly read the "Accessing MySQL" section of Chapter 4, "Introduction to MySQL."

Setting the root user password

When you install MySQL, no value—or no secure password—is established for the root user. This is certainly a security risk that should be remedied before you begin to use the server (since the root user has unlimited powers).

You can set any user's password using either phpMyAdmin or the mysql client, as long as the MySQL server is running. If MySQL isn't currently running, start it now using the steps outlined earlier in the appendix.

Second, you must be connected to MySQL as the root user in order to be able to change the root user's password.

To assign a password to the root user via the MySQL client:

1. Connect to the MySQL client.

   See Chapter 4 for detailed instructions, if needed.

2. Enter the following command, replacing *the password* with the password you want to use **Ⓐ**:

   ```
   SET PASSWORD FOR
   → 'root'@' localhost' =
   → PASSWORD('thepassword');
   ```

   Keep in mind that passwords in MySQL are case-sensitive, so *Kazan* and *kazan* aren't interchangeable. The term **PASSWORD** that precedes the actual quoted password tells MySQL to encrypt that string. And there cannot be a space between *PASSWORD* and the opening parenthesis.

   continues on next page

```
MariaDB [(none)]> SET PASSWORD FOR 'root'@'localhost' = PASSWORD('thepassword');
Query OK, 0 rows affected (0.00 sec)

MariaDB [(none)]>
```

Ⓐ Updating the root user's password using SQL within the MySQL client.

3. Exit the MySQL client:

```
exit
```

4. Test the new password by logging in to the MySQL client again.

Now that a password has been established, you need to add the **-p** flag to the connection command. You'll see an *Enter password:* prompt, where you enter the just-created password.

To assign a password to the root user via phpMyAdmin:

1. Open phpMyAdmin in your browser.

See the preceding set of steps for detailed instructions.

2. On the home page, click the Privileges tab.

You can always click the home icon, in the upper-left corner, to get to the home page.

3. In the list of users, click the Edit Privileges icon on the root user's row **B**.

4. Use the Change Password form **C**, found farther down the resulting page, to change the password.

5. Change the root user's password in phpMyAdmin's configuration file, if necessary.

The result of changing the root user's password will likely be that phpMyAdmin is denied access to the MySQL server. This is because phpMyAdmin, on a local server, normally connects to MySQL as the root user, with the root user's password hard-coded into a configuration file. After following Steps 1–4, find the **config.inc.php** file in the phpMyAdmin directory—likely **/Applications/MAMP/bin/phpMyAdmin** (macOS with MAMP) or **C:\xampp\phpMyAdmin** (Windows with XAMPP). Open that file in any text editor or IDE and change this next line to use the new password:

```
$cfg['Servers'][$i]['password'] =
→'the_new_password';
```

Then save the file and reload phpMyAdmin in your browser.

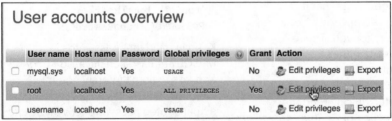

User accounts overview

	User name	Host name	Password	Global privileges	Grant	Action
☐	mysql.sys	localhost	Yes	USAGE	No	🐱 Edit privileges 🖥 Export
☐	root	localhost	Yes	ALL PRIVILEGES	Yes	🐱 Edit privileges 🖥 Export
☐	username	localhost	Yes	USAGE	No	🐱 Edit privileges 🖥 Export

B The list of MySQL users, as shown in phpMyAdmin.

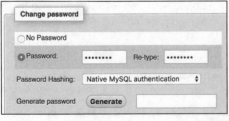

C The form for updating a MySQL user's password within phpMyAdmin.

Creating users and privileges

After you have MySQL successfully up and running, and after you've established a password for the root user, you can add other users. To improve the security of your databases, you should always create new users to access your databases rather than always using the root user.

The MySQL privileges system was designed to ensure proper authority for certain commands on specific databases. This technology is how a web host, for example, can let several users access several databases without concern. Each user in the MySQL system can have specific capabilities on specific databases from specific hosts (computers). The root user—the MySQL root user, not the system's—has the most power and is used to create

TABLE A.1 MySQL Privileges

PRIVILEGE	ALLOWS
SELECT	Read rows from tables.
INSERT	Add new rows of data to tables.
UPDATE	Alter existing data in tables.
DELETE	Remove existing data from tables.
INDEX	Create and drop indexes in tables.
ALTER	Modify the structure of a table.
CREATE	Create new tables or databases.
DROP	Delete existing tables or databases.
RELOAD	Reload the grant tables (and therefore enact user changes).
SHUTDOWN	Stop the MySQL server.
PROCESS	View and stop existing MySQL processes.
FILE	Import data into tables from text files.
GRANT	Create new users.
REVOKE	Remove users' permissions.

subusers, although subusers can be given rootlike powers (inadvisably so).

When a user attempts to do something with the MySQL server, MySQL first checks to see if the user has permission to connect to the server at all (based on the username, the user's host, the user's password, and the information in the *mysql* database's *user* table). Second, MySQL checks to see if the user has permission to run the specific SQL statement on the specific databases—for example, to select data, insert data, or create a new table. **Table A.1** lists most of the various privileges you can set on a user-by-user basis.

There are a handful of ways to set users and privileges in MySQL, but to start, you should formally create the user:

```
CREATE USER 'username'@'hostname'
IDENTIFIED BY 'password';
```

This command creates a user without any abilities. The username has a maximum length of 32 characters. When creating a username, be sure to avoid spaces (use the underscore instead), and note that usernames are case-sensitive.

The hostname is the computer from which the user is allowed to connect. This could be a domain name, such as *www.example.com*, or an IP address. Normally, *localhost* is specified as the hostname, meaning that the MySQL user must be connecting from the same computer that the MySQL database is running on. To allow for any host, use the hostname wildcard character (%):

```
CREATE USER 'username'@'%'
IDENTIFIED BY 'password';
```

But that is also not recommended. When it comes to creating users, it's best to be explicit and confining.

continues on next page

The password has no length limit but is also case-sensitive. The passwords are encrypted in the MySQL database, meaning they can't be recovered in a plaintext format. Omitting the **IDENTIFIED BY** **'password'** clause results in that user not being required to enter a password (which, once again, should be avoided).

Next the user needs to be granted permissions. The syntax goes like this:

```
GRANT privileges ON database.*
TO 'username'@'hostname'
IDENTIFIED BY 'password';
```

For the *privileges* aspect of this statement, you can list specific privileges from Table A.1, or you can allow for all of them by using **ALL** (which isn't prudent). The **database.*** part of the statement specifies which database and tables the user can work on. You can name specific tables using the **database.tablename** syntax or allow for every database with ***.*** (again, not prudent). Finally, you can specify the username, the hostname, and a password.

As an example of this process, you'll create two new users with specific privileges on a new database named *temp*. Keep in mind that you can grant permissions only to users on existing databases. This next sequence will also show how to create a database.

To create new users:

1. Log in to the MySQL client as a root user.

   Use the steps explained in Chapter 4 to do this, if you don't already know. You must be logged in as a user capable of creating databases and other users.

2. Create the *temp* database:

   ```
   CREATE DATABASE temp;
   ```

   Creating a database is quite easy, using the preceding syntax. This command will work as long as you're connected as a user with the proper privileges.

3. Create a user that has basic-level privileges on the *temp* database **D**:

   ```
   CREATE USER 'webuser'@'localhost'
   IDENTIFIED BY 'BroWs1ng';
   GRANT SELECT, INSERT, UPDATE, DELETE
   ON temp.* TO 'webuser'@'localhost';
   ```

   The generic *webuser* user can browse through records (**SELECT** from tables) and add (**INSERT**), modify (**UPDATE**), or **DELETE** them. The user can only connect from *localhost* (from the same computer) and can only access the *temp* database.

```
                PHP and MySQL for Dynamic Web Sites

mysql> CREATE DATABASE temp;
Query OK, 1 row affected (0.00 sec)

mysql> CREATE USER 'webuser'@'localhost'
    -> IDENTIFIED BY 'BroWs1ng';
Query OK, 0 rows affected (0.00 sec)

mysql> GRANT SELECT, INSERT, UPDATE, DELETE
    -> ON temp.* TO 'webuser'@'localhost';
Query OK, 0 rows affected (0.00 sec)

mysql>
```

D Creating a user that can perform basic tasks on one database.

```
     PHP and MySQL for Dynamic Web Sites
mysql> FLUSH PRIVILEGES;
Query OK, 0 rows affected (0.00 sec)

mysql>
```

E Don't forget this step before you try to access MySQL using the newly created users.

4. Apply the changes **E**:

   FLUSH PRIVILEGES;

   The changes just made won't take effect until you've told MySQL to reset the list of acceptable users and privileges, which is what this command does. Forgetting this step and then being unable to access the database using the newly created users is a common mistake.

   TIP Any database whose name begins with *test_* can be modified by any user who has permission to connect to MySQL. Therefore, be careful not to create a database named this way unless it truly is experimental.

   TIP The DROP command removes users and the REVOKE command removes permissions.

Creating Users in phpMyAdmin

To create users in phpMyAdmin, start by clicking the Privileges tab on the phpMyAdmin home page. On the Privileges page, click Add A New User. Complete the Add A New User form to define the user's name, host, password, and privileges. Then click Go. This creates the user with general privileges but no database-specific privileges.

On the resulting page, select the database to apply the user's privileges to and then click Go. On the next page, select the privileges this user should have on that database, and then click Go again. This completes the process of creating rights for that user on that database. Note that this process allows you to easily assign a user different rights on different databases.

Finally, click your way back to the Privileges tab on the home page and then click the Reload The Privileges link.

Testing Your Installation

Now that you've installed everything and created the necessary MySQL users, you should test the installation. Two quick PHP scripts can be used for this purpose. In all likelihood, if an error occurred, you would already know it by now, but these steps will allow you to perform tests on your (or any other) server before getting into complicated PHP, or PHP and MySQL, programming.

The first script being run is **phpinfo.php**. It both tests if PHP is enabled and shows a ton of information about the PHP installation. As simple as this script is, it is one of the most important scripts PHP developers ever write, in my opinion, because it provides so much valuable knowledge.

The second script will serve two purposes. It will first see if support for MySQL has been enabled. If not, you'll need to see the next section of this chapter to change that. The script will also test if the MySQL user has permission to connect to a specific MySQL database.

To test PHP:

1. Create the following PHP document in a text editor or IDE (**Script A.1**):

   ```php
   <?php
   phpinfo();
   ?>
   ```

   The **phpinfo()** function returns the configuration information for a PHP installation in a table. It's the perfect tool to test that PHP is working properly.

   You can use almost any application to create your PHP script as long as it can save the file in a plain-text format.

2. Save the file as **phpinfo.php**.

   You need to be certain that the file's extension is just **.php**. Be careful when using Notepad on Windows; it will secretly append **.txt**. Similarly, TextEdit on macOS wants to save everything as **.rtf**.

3. Place the file in the proper directory on your server.

   What the proper directory is depends on your operating system and your web server. If you are using a hosted site, check with the hosting company. For users who installed XAMPP, the directory is called **htdocs** and is within the XAMPP directory.

Script A.1 The **phpinfo.php** script tests and reports on the PHP installation.

```
1    <?php
2    phpinfo();
3    ?>
```

Script A.2 The `mysqli_test.php` script tests for MySQL support in PHP and if the proper MySQL user privileges have been set.

```
1   <?php
2   mysqli_connect('localhost', 'webuser',
    'BroWs1ng', 'temp');
3   ?>
```

4. Test the PHP script by accessing it in your browser 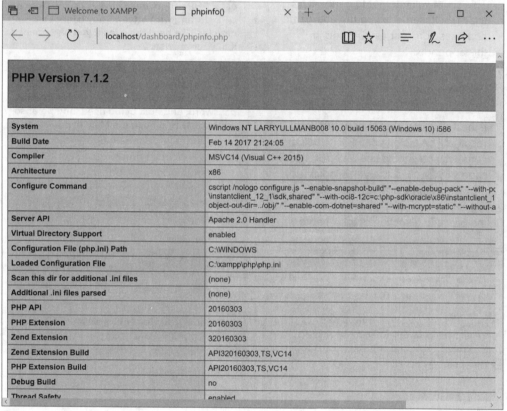.

Run this script in your browser by going to **http://*your.url.here*/phpinfo.php**. On your own computer, this may be something like **http://localhost/phpinfo.php** (XAMPP).

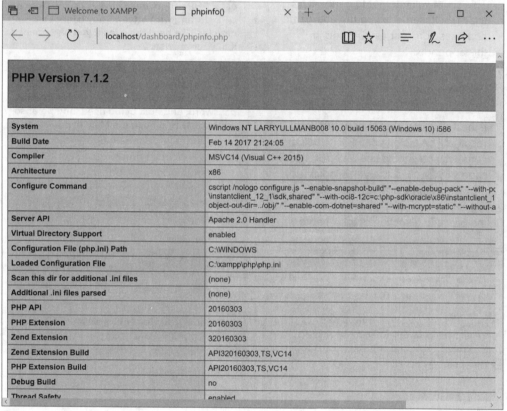

System	Windows NT LARRYULLMANB008 10.0 build 15063 (Windows 10) i586
Build Date	Feb 14 2017 21:24:05
Compiler	MSVC14 (Visual C++ 2015)
Architecture	x86
Configure Command	cscript /nologo configure.js "--enable-snapshot-build" "--enable-debug-pack" "--with-pc \instantclient_12_1\sdk,shared" "--with-oci8-12c=c:\php-sdk\oracle\x86\instantclient_1 object-out-dir=../obj/" "--enable-com-dotnet=shared" "--with-mcrypt=static" "--without-a
Server API	Apache 2.0 Handler
Virtual Directory Support	enabled
Configuration File (php.ini) Path	C:\WINDOWS
Loaded Configuration File	C:\xampp\php\php.ini
Scan this dir for additional .ini files	(none)
Additional .ini files parsed	(none)
PHP API	20160303
PHP Extension	20160303
Zend Extension	320160303
Zend Extension Build	API320160303,TS,VC14
PHP Extension Build	API20160303,TS,VC14
Debug Build	no
Thread Safety	enabled

PHP Version 7.1.2

Ⓐ The information for this server's PHP configuration.

To test PHP and MySQL:

1. Create a new PHP document in your text editor or IDE (**Script A.2**):

```php
<?php
mysqli_connect('localhost',
→ 'webuser', 'BroWsIng', 'temp');
?>
```

This script will attempt to connect to the MySQL server using the username and password just established in this appendix.

2. Save the file as **mysqli_test.php**, place it in the proper directory for your web server, and test it in your browser.

If the script was able to connect, the result will be a blank page. If it could not connect, you should see an error message like **B**. Most likely this indicates a problem with the MySQL user's privileges or the provided information (see the preceding section of this chapter).

TIP For security reasons, you should not leave the phpinfo.php script on a live server because it gives away too much information.

TIP If you run a PHP script in your browser and it attempts to download the file, then your web server is not recognizing that file extension as PHP. Check your Apache (or other web server) configuration to correct this.

TIP PHP scripts must always be run from a URL starting with http://. They cannot be run directly off a hard drive (as if you had opened it in your browser).

TIP If a PHP script cannot connect to a MySQL server, it is normally because of a permissions issue. Double-check the username, password, and host being used, and be absolutely certain to flush the MySQL privileges.

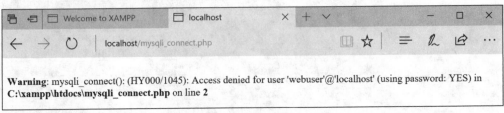

Warning: mysqli_connect(): (HY000/1045): Access denied for user 'webuser'@'localhost' (using password: YES) in **C:\xampp\htdocs\mysqli_connect.php** on line **2**

B The script was not able to connect to the MySQL server.

Enabling Extension Support

Many PHP configuration options can be altered by just editing the **php.ini** file. But enabling (or disabling) an extension—in other words, adding support for extended functionality—requires more effort. To enable support for an extension for just a single PHP page, you can use the **dl()** function. Enabling support for an extension for all PHP scripts requires a bit of work. Unfortunately, for Unix and macOS users, you'll need to rebuild PHP with support for this new extension (a process that's not for the faint of heart). Windows users have it easier:

First, edit the **php.ini** file (see the steps in this section), removing the semicolon before the extension you want to enable. For example, to enable Improved MySQL Extension support, you'll need to find the line that says

```
;extension=php_mysqli.dll
```

and remove that semicolon.

Next, find the line that sets the *extension__dir* and adjust this for your PHP installation. Assuming you installed PHP using XAMPP into **C:\xampp**, then your **php.ini** file should say

```
extension_dir = "C:/xampp/php/ext"
```

This tells PHP where to find the extension.

Next, make sure that the actual extension file, **php_mysqli.dll** in this example, exists in the extension directory.

Save the **php.ini** file and restart your web server. If the restart process indicates an error finding the extension, double-check to make sure that the extension exists in the *extension_dir* and that your pathnames are correct. If you continue to have problems, search the web or use the book's corresponding forum for assistance.

Configuring PHP

One of the benefits of installing PHP on your own computer is that you can configure it however you prefer. How PHP runs is determined by the **php.ini** configuration file, which is normally created when PHP is installed.

Changing PHP's behavior is very simple and will most likely be required at some point in time. Just a few of the things you'll want to consider adjusting are

- Whether or not *display_errors* is on
- The default level of error reporting
- Support for the Improved MySQL Extension functions
- SMTP values for sending emails

What each of these means—if you don't already know—is covered in the book's chapters and in the PHP manual. But for starters, I highly recommend that you make sure that *display_errors* is on and that you set error reporting to its highest level.

Changing PHP's configuration is simple. The short version is: edit the **php.ini** file and then restart the web server. But because many different problems can arise, I'll cover configuration in more detail. If you are looking to enable support for an extension, like the MySQL functions, the configuration is more complicated (see the sidebar).

To alter PHP's configuration:

1. In your browser, execute a script that invokes the **phpinfo()** function.

   The **phpinfo()** function, discussed in the previous section of the appendix (see **Ⓐ**), reveals oodles of information about the PHP installation.

2. In the browser's output, search for Loaded Configuration File **Ⓐ**.

   The value next to this text is the location of the active configuration file. This will be something like **C:\xampp\php\php.ini** or **/Applications/MAMP/conf/php5.3/php.ini**. Your server may have multiple **php.ini** files on it, but this is the one that counts.

   If there is no value for the Loaded Configuration File, your server has no active **php.ini** file. In that case, you'll need to download the PHP source code, from **www.php.net**, to find a sample configuration file.

3. Open the **php.ini** file in any text editor.

   If you go to the directory listed and there's no **php.ini** file there, you'll need to download this file from the PHP web site (it's part of the PHP source code).

Enabling Mail

The PHP **mail()** function works only if the computer running PHP has access to sendmail or another mail server. One way to enable the **mail()** function is to set the **smtp** value in the **php.ini** file (for Windows only). This approach works, for example, if your Internet provider has an SMTP address you can use. Unfortunately, you can't use this value if your ISP's SMTP server requires authentication.

For Windows, there are also a number of free SMTP servers, like Mercury. It's installed along with XAMPP, or you can install it yourself if you're not using XAMPP.

macOS comes with a mail server installed—postfix and/or sendmail—that needs to be enabled. Search Google for instructions on manually enabling your mail server on macOS.

Alternatively, you can search some of the PHP code libraries to learn how to use an SMTP server that requires authentication.

Server API	Apache 2.0 Handler
Virtual Directory Support	enabled
Configuration File (php.ini) Path	C:\WINDOWS
Loaded Configuration File	C:\xampp\php\php.ini
Scan this dir for additional .ini files	(none)

Ⓐ Use a **phpinfo()** script to confirm the active PHP configuration file to be edited.

4. Make any changes you want, keeping in mind the following:

- Comments are marked using a semicolon. Anything after the semicolon is ignored.

- Instructions on what most of the settings mean are included in the file.

- The top of the file lists general information with examples. Do not change these values! Change the settings where they appear later in the file.

- For safety purposes, don't change any original settings. Just comment them out (by preceding the line with a semicolon) and then add the new, modified line afterward.

- Add a comment (using the semicolon) to mark what changes you made and when. For example:

```
; display_errors = Off
; Next line added by LEU 08/28/2017
display_errors = On
```

5. Save the **php.ini** file.

6. Restart your web server.

You do not have to restart the entire computer, just the web serving application (Apache, IIS, etc.). How you do this depends on the application being used, the operating system, and the installation method. XAMPP users can use the XAMPP Control Panel.

7. Rerun the **phpinfo.php** script to make sure the changes took effect.

TIP If you edit the php.ini file and restart the web server but your changes don't take effect, make sure you're editing the proper php.ini file (you may have more than one on your computer).

Configuring Apache

Like PHP, Apache is an open source technology and has become a dominant force in web technologies. If you installed XAMPP on your computer, you now have a functional version of Apache. If you're using a hosted web site, more than likely you're being provided with Apache there as well.

Once Apache with support for PHP has successfully been installed, many PHP programmers never think twice about the web server. But as you continue to learn about web development, picking up a bit more knowledge of Apache is a logical next step.

The most common reasons you'll need to know more about Apache include being able to do the following:

- Create virtual hosts
- Add Secure Sockets Layer (SSL) support
- Protect directories
- Enable URL rewrites

These, and other changes to Apache's behavior, can be made in two ways: by editing the primary configuration file or by creating directory-specific files. The primary configuration file is **httpd.conf**, found within a **conf** directory, and it dictates how the entire Apache web server runs. An **.htaccess** (pronounced "H-T access") file is placed within the web directories and is used to affect how Apache behaves within just that folder and subfolders.

Generally speaking, it's preferred to make changes in the **httpd.conf** file, since this file needs to be read only by the web server each time the server is started. Conversely, **.htaccess** files must be read by the web server once for every request to to which an **.htaccess** file might apply. For example, if you have **www.example.com/somedir/.htaccess**, any request to **www.example.com/somedir/whatever** requires reading the **.htaccess** file, as well as reading an **.htaccess** file that might exist in **www.example.com/**. On the other hand, in shared hosting environments, individual users are not allowed to customize the entire Apache configuration, but they may be allowed to use **.htaccess** to make changes that affect only their sites.

Over the next few pages, I'll explain some of the fundamentals for working with these two types of files. In the process, you'll learn how to perform some standard Apache customizations.

> **TIP** To be safe, I recommend making a backup copy of your original Apache configuration file before pursuing any of the subsequent edits.

> **TIP** In this book, I cannot adequately explain how to enable HTTPS (HTTP over an SSL) as the key component—obtaining and installing an SSL certificate varies too much from one person and server to the next. Look online for specific details, or post a message in my support forums (LarryUllman.com/forums/), if you need assistance. If you have a hosted account wherein you want to enable SSL, speak with your hosting company.

Creating virtual hosts

When you install Apache on a computer, Apache is set up to serve one web site, such as **www.example.com**. For the web site being served, Apache associates a hostname (and/or an IP address) with a directory on the server, called the *web document root*. When a user visits **www.example.com**, Apache provides files from that site's directory **A**.

But Apache can easily be configured to serve several different sites, all hosted on the same computer, by creating *virtual hosts*. After establishing one or more virtual hosts, Apache will know

that when a user makes a request of **www.example.com**, documents from X directory should be served but requests of **www.example.net** should be pointed to the documents from Y directory **B**.

Understand that setting up virtual hosts does not, in fact, make **www.example.com** or **www.example.net** a valid domain name, accessible over the Internet. Accomplishing that requires use of DNS (Domain Name System), a much more complicated subject. You can, however, use virtual hosts to create different hosts for your own development projects on your home computer, as explained in the following sequence.

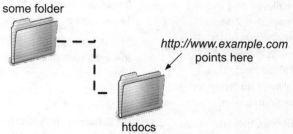

some folder

http://www.example.com
points here

htdocs

A The web server associates a URL or hostname with a directory or file on the computer.

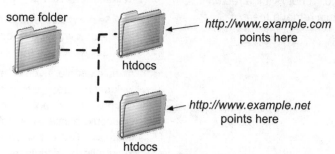

some folder

http://www.example.com
points here

htdocs

http://www.example.net
points here

htdocs

B Thanks to virtual hosts, different directories on the computer can be associated with different hostnames.

To create a virtual host:

1. Open **httpd.conf** in any text editor or IDE.

   If you're using XAMPP on Windows, the file to open is **C:\xampp\apache\ conf\httpd.conf** (assuming XAMPP is installed in the root of the C drive). If you're using XAMPP on macOS, the file to open is **/Applications/XAMPP/ xampfiles/etc/httpd.conf**.

2. At the very end of the configuration file, add

   NameVirtualHost 127.0.0.1

   Virtual hosts are conventionally defined at the end of the configuration file (or in a separate configuration file, to be included by this one). This line says that Apache should watch for *named* virtual hosts (as opposed to IP address-based virtual hosts) on the 127.0.0.1 IP address. This is a special IP address, always equating to *localhost* (i.e., this same computer).

   Depending on your server, this line may already be present in the configuration file, but prefaced by a **#**, which makes it a comment (i.e., renders it ineffectual). In that case, just remove the **#**.

3. On the next line, add

   <VirtualHost 127.0.0.1>
   </VirtualHost>

   The **VirtualHost** tags are used to create a new virtual host. For each opening tag, there needs to be a closing one. Within the opening tag, the IP address or hostname to watch for is identified here: 127.0.0.1. This value needs to match that used on the **NameVirtualHost** line.

   The rest of the virtual host definition will go between these opening and closing tags.

4. Within the virtual host tags, add

   DocumentRoot */path/to/folder*
   ServerName *servername*

   The **DocumentRoot** directive indicates the web root directory for the virtual host: in other words, where the actual files for this site can be found. On XAMPP on Windows, this value might be **C:/xampp/htdocs/***something*. On XAMPP on macOS, this value might be **/Applications/XAMPP/xamppfiles/ htdocs/***something*.

   The **ServerName** is where you put the *hostname*: what you'll enter into the browser to access this site.

   As an example, if you wanted to create a virtual host for the forums site from Chapter 17, "Example—Message Board," you could create a new folder within **htdocs**, called **forums**, and copy all the applicable scripts there. Then you would use **C:/xampp/htdocs/forums** or **/Applications/XAMPP/xamppfiles/ htdocs/forums** as the **DocumentRoot** value. For the **ServerName** value, I would use something meaningful, such as **forums.local**: a local version of a forums site.

5. Add a second virtual host for localhost
C:

```
<VirtualHost 127.0.0.1>
  DocumentRoot "C:/xampp/htdocs"
  ServerName localhost
</VirtualHost>
```

The previous set of steps created a new virtual host, but in the process, the one original web site (*localhost*, the default for your own computer) will become unusable. The fix is to create another virtual host for that site.

6. Save the configuration file.

```
512   # Enable virtual hosting:
513   NameVirtualHost 127.0.0.1
514
515   # Add a virtual host for the forums site:
516   <VirtualHost 127.0.0.1>
517       DocumentRoot "C:/xampp/htdocs/forums"
518       ServerName forums.local
519   </VirtualHost>
520
521   # Add localhost:
522   <VirtualHost 127.0.0.1>
523       DocumentRoot "C:/xampp/htdocs"
524       ServerName localhost
525   </VirtualHost>
```

C The new directives added to the end of the Apache configuration file.

7. Restart Apache.

Any changes to the configuration file will not take effect until the web server is restarted. You can restart Apache using the XAMPP control panel.

If there is an error in the configuration file, Apache will not be able to start and you'll need to check the error logs to find out why.

Note that you can't access the virtual host using your browser yet, as you still need to update your computer's list of hosts.

TIP The default Apache configuration file, httpd.conf, has comments in it indicating what each section of code does. You can browse through it to learn some things about configuring Apache.

TIP The DocumentRoot value, or any value in the httpd.conf file, must be quoted if it contains spaces.

TIP The definition of a virtual host can contain other directives, but I'm trying to introduce these fundamental Apache concepts as simply as possible.

TIP It's actually preferable to have Apache only listen for activity on a specific port, commonly 80. In that case, the virtual hosts configuration would start

```
NameVirtualHost 127.0.0.1:80
<VirtualHost 127.0.0.1:80>
```

TIP On a full-scale web server, it's preferable to create multiple configuration files, which will then be read and used by the primary configuration file. On your own personal computer, without too much customization, a single configuration file is fine.

Updating your computer's hosts

The previous sequence of steps created a virtual host in Apache, allowing you to access, in this example, the forums web site by going to **http://forums.local** in your browser. There is a catch, however: if you were to enter that URL into your browser, the browser would attempt to find **forums.local** on the Internet and would be unable to do so 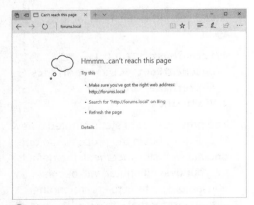. To solve this dilemma, you need to tell your browser(s) that **forums.local** can be found on your computer. This is done by modifying your operating system's **hosts** file, per these directions.

D The error that Edge displays when it can't find the local virtual host.

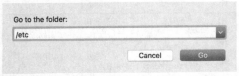

E The Finder's Go > Go To Folder option can be used to access hidden directories.

To update your computer's hosts:

1. Open your computer's **hosts** file in any text editor or IDE.

   This is the only tricky part of this process: finding and opening the **hosts** file. On macOS and Unix, the **hosts** file is **/etc/hosts** (there's no file extension), where **/** refers to the computer's root directory. On macOS, **/etc** is a *hidden* directory, making **hosts** a hidden file. There are three easy ways of finding this file:

   ▸ Use your editing application to open it directly, if the application is capable of opening hidden files.

   ▸ In the Finder, select Go > Go To Folder, and enter **/etc** in the prompt **E** to open the **/etc** directory in the Finder. Then drag the **hosts** file onto the editing application in the Dock.

   ▸ Use the Terminal to find and open the file.

F You can open Notepad in administrator mode in order to edit system files.

G The forums site, available locally through the URL `http://forums.local`.

On Windows, barring a nonstandard installation, the file in question is `C:\Windows\System32\drivers\etc\hosts`. Unfortunately, you may have permissions issues in trying to edit this file. I had good luck by opening Notepad in administrator mode (right-click on Notepad in the Start Menu to be given this option **F**), and then opening the file within Notepad.

2. At the very end of the file, add

   `127.0.0.1    forums.local`

   This associates the name *forums.local* with the IP address 127.0.0.1, which is to say the same computer.

3. Save the file.

4. Load `http://forums.local` in your browser **G**.

TIP Repeat these two sequences of steps—creating the virtual host in Apache and adding the host to your hosts file—anytime you want to create a new web site project with its own associated hostname.

Using `.htaccess` files

As already stated, all Apache configuration can be accomplished within the `httpd.conf` file. In fact, doing so is preferred. But the configuration file is not always available for you to edit, so it's worth also knowing how to use `.htaccess` files to change how a site functions.

An `.htaccess` file is just a plain-text file, with the name `.htaccess` (again, no file extension, and the initial period makes this a hidden file). When placed within a web directory, the directives defined in the `.htaccess` file will apply to that directory and its subdirectories.

continues on next page

A common hang-up when using `.htaccess` files is that permission must be granted to allow `.htaccess` to make server behavior changes. Depending on the installation and configuration, Apache, on the strictest level of security, will not allow `.htaccess` files to change Apache behavior. This is accomplished with code like the following, in **httpd.conf**:

```
<Directory />
AllowOverride None
</Directory>
```

The **Directory** directive is used within **httpd.conf** to modify Apache's behavior within a specific directory. In the previous code, the root directory (*/*) is the target, meaning that Apache will not allow overrides—changes—made within any directories on the computer at all. Prior to creating `.htaccess` files, then, the main

configuration file must be set to allow overrides in the applicable web directory (or directories).

The **AllowOverride** directive takes one or more flags indicating what, specifically, can be overridden:

- *AuthConfig*, for using authorization and authentication
- *FileInfo*, for performing redirects and URL rewriting
- *Indexes*, for listing directory contents
- *Limit*, for restricting access to the directory
- *Options*, for setting directory behavior, such as the ability to execute CGI scripts or to index folder contents
- *All*
- *None*

Setting the Default Directory Page

Commonly, browsers make requests without specifying a file, such as **www.example.com/** or **www.example.com/folder/**. In these cases, Apache must decide as to what to do. Historically, Apache provides an **index.htm** or **index.html** file, if one exists in the directory. If no index file exists, and if directory browsing is allowed by the server, Apache will instead reveal a list of files in the directory (this is not secure, but you've no doubt seen this online before).

The applicable directive to tell Apache what to do in these situations is **DirectoryIndex**. Following it, you list the file to use as the folder's index, with multiple options placed in order of preference. For example, the following will attempt to load **index.htm**, then **index.html** if **index.htm** does not exist, then **index.php** if **index.html** does not exist:

```
DirectoryIndex index.htm index.html index.php
```

Similarly, the **ErrorDocument** directive tells Apache what file to provide when a server error occurs. Its syntax is

```
ErrorDocument error_code /page.html
```

The error code value comes from the server status codes, such as 401 (Unauthorized), 403 (Forbidden), and 500 (Internal Server Error). For each code you can dictate what page should be served. Note that you'll want to provide an absolute path to the error files (i.e., start them with */*, which is the web root directory).

For example, to allow *AuthConfig* and *FileInfo* to be overridden within the forums directory (just created), the **httpd.conf** file should include

```
<Directory /path/to/forums>
AllowOverride AuthConfig FileInfo
</Directory>
```

As long as this code comes after any **AllowOverride None** block, an **.htaccess** file in the **forums** directory will be able to make some changes to Apache's behavior when serving files from that directory (and its subdirectories).

```
512   # Enable virtual hosting:
513   NameVirtualHost 127.0.0.1
514
515   # Add a virtual host for the forums site:
516   <VirtualHost 127.0.0.1>
517       DocumentRoot "C:/xampp/htdocs/forums"
518       ServerName forums.local
519
520       # Allow overrides in this site:
521       <Directory "C:/xampp/htdocs/forums">
522       AllowOverride All
523       </Directory>
524
525   </VirtualHost>
```

H The updated virtual hosts configuration, now allowing for overrides within the forums web directory.

To allow .htaccess overrides:

1. Open **httpd.conf** in any text editor or IDE.

2. Within the **VirtualHost** tag for the site in question, add

   ```
   <Directory /path/to/directory>
   </Directory>
   ```

   The **Directory** tag is how you customize Apache behavior within a specific directory or its subdirectories. Within the opening tag, provide an absolute path to the directory in question, such as **C:\xampp\htdocs\somedir** or **/Applications/MAMP/htdocs/somedir**.

3. Within the **Directory** tags, add **H**:

   AllowOverride All

   This is a heavy-handed solution, but it will do the trick. On a live, publicly available server, you'd want to be more specific about what exact settings can be overridden, but on your home computer, this won't be a problem.

4. Save the configuration file.

5. Restart Apache.

TIP The **Directory** directive does not have to go within the **VirtualHost** tag for the involved site, but it makes sense to place it there.

TIP If a directory is not allowed to override a setting, the **.htaccess** file will just be ignored.

TIP Anything accomplished within an **.htaccess** file can also be achieved using a **Directory** tag within **httpd.conf**.

Enabling URL rewriting

The final topic to be discussed in this appendix is how to perform *URL rewriting*. URL rewriting has gained attention as part of the overbearing focus on *search engine optimization* (SEO), but URL rewriting has been a useful tool for years. With a dynamically driven site, like an e-commerce store, a value will often be passed to a page in the URL to indicate what category of products to display, resulting in URLs such as **www.example.com/category.php?id=23**. The PHP script, **category.php**, would then use the value of **$_GET['id']** to know what products to pull from the database and display. (There are oodles of similar examples in this book.)

With URL rewriting applied, the URL shown in the browser, visible to the end user, and referenced in search engine results can be transformed into something more obviously meaningful, such as **www.example.com/category/23/** or, better yet, **www.example.com/category/garden+gnomes/**. Apache, via URL rewriting, takes the more user-friendly URL and parses it into something usable by the PHP scripts. This is made possible by the Apache **mod_rewrite** module. To use it, the **.htaccess** file must first check for the module and turn on the rewrite engine:

```
<IfModule mod_rewrite.c>
RewriteEngine on
</IfModule>
```

After enabling the engine, and before the closing **IfModule** tag, you add rules dictating the rewrites. The syntax is

RewriteRule *match rewrite*

For example, you could do the following (although it's not a good use of **mod_rewrite**):

RewriteRule somepage.php otherpage.php

Part of the complication with performing URL rewrites is that Perl-compatible regular expressions (PCRE) are needed to most flexibly find matches. If you're not already comfortable with regular expressions, you'll need to read Chapter 14, "Perl-Compatible Regular Expressions," to follow the rest of this material.

For example, to treat **www.example.com/category/23** as if it were **www.example.com/category.php?id=23**, you would have the following rule:

RewriteRule ^category/([0-9]+)/?$
→ category.php?id=$1

The initial caret (^) says that the expression must match the beginning of the string. After that should be the word *category*, followed by a slash. Then, any quantity of digits follows, concluding with an optional slash (allowing for both *category/23* and *category/23/*). The dollar sign closes the match, meaning that nothing can follow the optional slash. That's the pattern for the example match (and it's a simple pattern at that, really).

Changing PHP's Configuration

If PHP is running as an Apache module, you can also change how PHP runs within specific directories using an Apache **.htaccess** file. The directives to use are **php_flag** and **php_value**:

```
php_flag item value
php_value item value
```

The **php_flag** directive is for any setting that has an on or off value; **php_value** is for any other setting. For example:

```
php_flag display_errors on
php_value error_reporting 30719
```

Note that you cannot use PHP constants, such as **E_ALL** for the highest level of error reporting, since this code is within Apache configuration files, not within PHP scripts.

(You can also change how PHP runs by editing the **httpd.conf** file, but if you're going to make a global server change that requires a restart of Apache anyway, you might as well just edit the PHP configuration file instead.)

The rewrite part is what will actually be executed, unbeknownst to the browser and the end user. In this line, that's **category.php?id=$1**. The *$1* is a *backreference* to the first parenthetical grouping in the match (e.g., 23). Thus, **www.example.com/category/23** is treated by the server as if the URL were actually **www.example.com/category.php?id=23**.

This is the underlying premise with **mod_rewrite**. Unfortunately, mastering **mod_rewrite** requires mastery, or near mastery, of PCRE, which can be daunting. If you want to practice this, you can take the simple example just explained and apply it to any of the examples in the book in which a value is passed in the URL. For example, in Chapter 10, "Common Programming Techniques," a user ID is passed in the URL to **delete_user.php** and **edit_user.php**. Both could be transformed into "prettier" URLs, such as **www.example.com/delete/45/** or **www.example.com/edit/895/**.

As always, search online for more information on this subject, should you be interested, and post a question in the supporting forums (**LarryUllman.com/forums/**) if you run into problems.

Index

"big" databases, 235. *See also* databases
BIGINT[] data types, 117, 198
binary, converting to, 239
BINARY text type, 119
Bitnami installer, 636
blacklist validation, 425
blank pages, debugging, 8, 260
blank spaces, 44
body tag, placement, 4
Boolean **FULLTEXT** searches, performing, 229–231
Boolean variables, 14
Bootstrap framework, 90
bound variable types, 443. *See also* variables
boundaries, using, 471
braces ({})
    arrays, 56, 68, 62
    conditionals, 45
    using with characters, 468
    using with conditionals, 48
brackets ([]), 104, 469–471
break element, 48
browser
    sending data to, 6–9
    sending HTML code, 8, 11–12
brute-force attacks, preventing, 449
buffer size, limit, 593

C

calculator.html file
    DOM manipulation, 500–504
    jQuery, 496–497
calculator.js page, saving, 498
calculator.php script
    creating, 86–90
    default argument values, 101–104
    Filter extension, 439–441
    radio buttons, 98–100
    rewriting, 91–94
    validating data by type, 430
    values from functions, 105–109
calendar form, 60, 72
calendar.php, creating, 60–62
call to undefined function error, 260
cannot redeclare function error, 260
capitalizing characters, 22
CAPTCHA test, 424
carriage return, 29
CASCADE action, 198

CASE() function, 221
case insensitivity, 6
CEILING() function, 159
CHANGE COLUMN clause, 224
CHAR[Length] data type, 117–118
character classes, using, 469–471
character sets
    assigning, 188–190
    changing, 224
    listing, 186
characters. *See also* meta-characters
    capitalizing, 22
    escaping, 6
    escaping in patterns, 466
    mismatching encodings, 550
    representing, 2
chmod command, adjusting folder permissions, 349
cinema database, 174
class meta-characters, 464
classes, using brackets ([]) with, 469–471
client-server request model, 505
closing database connections, 281
COALESCE() function, 220
code blocks, indenting, 48
collations
    assigning, 188–190
    changing, 224
    using with character sets, 186–187
column lengths, fine tuning, 158
column names, determining, 115
column properties, choosing, 120–122
column types, choosing, 116–119
columns
    applying functions, 155
    changing definition, 452
    including in indexes, 181
    listing in SELECT statements, 141
    listing in tables, 134
    populating, 137
comments
    using with HTML forms, 42
    writing, 10–13
COMMIT, using with transactions, 236, 238
comparative operators, 45
comparison functions, 220. *See also* functions
CONCAT() function, 156–158, 219
CONCAT_WS() function, 158
concatenating strings, 21–22

validation results, 53

variables, 16

echo statement, sortable links, 335

editing records, 316–322

edit.user.php script, 316–319

else clause, 89

else conditional, 45–48

elseif conditional, 45–48

email, sending, 338–343

email addresses, validating, 470–471

email conditional, 320

email element, using with HTML forms, 42

email input, adding to HTML forms, 39

email.php script, 339–343, 420

embedding PHP code, 5

empty() function, 49, 51, 104

empty variable value error, 260

encoding. *See also* mismatching encodings

declaring, 5

displaying, 186

indicating to browser, 2

encrypting data, 137, 239–241, 350

enctype, using with form tag, 350, 355

Enter and Return, 10

ENUM data type, 116–117, 121, 148

equals (=) operator, 14, 142

ERD (entity-relationship diagram), 171, 180

error handlers, customizing, 255–259

error management, die() and exit(), 263

error reporting, adjusting, 252–254

error types, overview, 244–245

error_log() function, 259

errors. *See also* debugging; warnings

causes, 264

displaying, 33

echo, 6

INSERT, 139

NULL, 139

revealing in PHP, 250

suppressing with @, 252, 274

$errors conditional, 321

escape meta-character, 464

escape sequences, 29

escaping characters, 6

event handling, jQuery, 495–498

event listener, creating for Ajax request, 512

exclusive or operator, 45, 48

executing queries, 276–283, 526–531

exit command, 126

exit() function, 263

EXPLAIN EXTENDED command, 235

EXPLAIN keyword, 232–235

extension support, enabling, 649

extensions, 3, 269

external files. *See* files; multiple files PHP files

F

FALSE keyword, 144

fetch_object() method, 534

FILE privilege, 643

file uploads

allowing for, 344–345

configurations, 344

directory access, 348

with PHP, 350–355

preparing server, 346–349

secure folder permissions, 345

set_time_limit() function, 349

validating, 355

Fileinfo extension, 432–434

files, validating by type, 431–434. *See also*
multiple files; PHP files

$_FILES array, 350

Filter extension

vs. regular expressions, 477

using, 438–441

firewalls and installation, 636

first normal form (1NF), 171–173

first.php script

creating, 3–5

sending data to browser, 7

FLOAT[Length, Decimals] data type, 117, 119

floating-point type, 14, 25

FLOOR() function, 159

folder permissions, securing, 345

footer.html file

saving, 564

user registration, 590–593

for loops, 70–72

foreach loop, using with arrays, 59–60, 63–65

foreign key constraints

action options, 197

CASCADE action, 198

creating, 199–203

requirement, 203

home page
message board, 565
user registration, 602–603
HOUR() function, 161
.htaccess file, 345, 652, 657–659
HTML attributes, double-quoting, 94
HTML code, sending to browser, 8, 11–12
HTML document, creating, 4
HTML errors, debugging, 8, 249
.html extension, 3, 40
HTML forms, 54. *See also* hidden forms; sticky forms
  action attribute, 90
  creating, 36–40
  elements to variables, 42
  fields, 54
  GET and **POST** methods, 36
  GET request, 85
  handling, 41–44, 85–90
  input types, 44
  inputs, 39, 41
  jQuery, 492–494
  multidimensional arrays, 65
  POST method, 85
  pull-down menus, 39, 61–62
  radio buttons, 39
  select menu options, 94
  submitting back, 90
  text and email inputs, 39
  text box, 40
  textarea element, 40
  Trip Cost Calculator, 86
  validating, 50
HTML resources, 5
HTML table, using with arrays, 67
HTML templates, 78–79
HTML5 page, 2
HTML5 validation rules, 426
HTML-embedded scripted language, 2
htmlentities() function, 435–436
htmlspecialchars() function, 435–437, 583
HTTP (Hypertext Transfer Protocol), 381
http://, using with PHP code, 5, 7
HTTP headers, 364–369
httpd.conf file, 652

I

IDE (integrated development environment), 2–3
identifiers in databases, 114–115
if conditional, 45–48, 52
IF() function, 220–221, 223
if-else conditional, 52
if-elseif-else conditional, 47
IFNULL() function, 223
images.php script
  date and time functions, 371–373
  HTTP headers, 364
  JavaScript and PHP, 361–362
IN operator, 142
include() functions, 76–77, 84
increment operator, 23
indenting code blocks, 48
index page for message board, 565
INDEX privilege, 643
INDEX type, 181
indexes
  creating, 181–183
  and keys, 120
index.php file
  creating, 82–83
  creating functions, 96–97
  home page for user registration, 602–603
ini_set() function, 250–251
inner joins, 207–209, 211
InnoDB storage engine, 184
INSERT command
  errors, 139
  records, 135–139
INSERT privilege, 643
INSERT query, running, 276–279
installation
  firewalls, 636
  macOS, 639–640
  testing, 646–648
  Windows, 636–638
INT[Length] data type, 117
intdiv() function, 25
integers, 14, 25
INTO term, 139
is equal to operator, 45
IS FALSE operator, 142
is not equal to operator, 45

phpMyAdmin (*continued*)

  SELECT queries, 141

  using, 123–129

pipe (|), using with regular expressions, 465

pop-up window

  creating, 360

  resizing, 359

$_POST array, 57–58

POST method, using with HTML forms, 36, 85

post_form.php script, creating, 576–580

post_message.php

  prepared statements, 535–537

  saving, 448

posting messages, 576–585

post.php script, creating, 580–585

pound sign (#), using with comments, 10

POW() function, 159

predefined variables, 14–17

preg_match() function, 460, 472

preg_replace() function, 478, 480–481

preg_split() function, 475

prepared statements

  OOP and MySQL, 534–537

  using, 442–448

PRIMARY KEY, 120–121, 181–182

primary keys

  assigning, 169

  2NF (second normal form), 175

  foreign-key link, 180

print function. *See also* **echo** function

  debugging scripts, 261–263

  language construct, 8

  over multiple lines, 9

  using, 6–7

privileges in MySQL, 643–644

procedural vs. OOP, 520

PROCESS privilege, 643

proxy scripts, 364, 369

pull-down menus, using on HTML forms, 39, 61–62, 91

Q

quantifiers

  meta-characters, 464

  using, 467–468

queries. *See also* simple queries

  executing, 132–133, 275–283, 526–531

  explaining, 233–235

  optimizing, 232–235

  quotation marks, 136

  running, 141

query results

  fetching, 531–534

  limiting, 149–150

  paginating, 323–330

  retrieving, 284–287

  sorting, 147–148

quit command, 126

quotation marks

  vs. ` (backtick), 139

  printing, 6

  in queries, 136

  single vs. double, 29–31

  variables, 18

R

\r escape sequence, 29

radio buttons, using on HTML forms, 39, 92, 98–100

RAND() function, 159–160, 240

range() function, using with arrays, 62

ranges, MySQL operators, 142

read.php page, 571–575, 582

records. *See also* returned records

  adding to databases, 276–279

  deleting, 153–154, 203

  editing, 316–322

  inserting in phpMyAdmin, 139

  inserting in SQL, 135–139

  matching, 145–146

  updating with PHP, 296–303

REGEXP() function, 158

register.php script

  executing queries, 526–531

  modifying, 295

  mysqli_real_escape_string(), 289–291

  securing passwords, 452–454

  user registration, 604–613

registration script, creating, 275–283, 604–613

regular expressions

  character classes, 469–471

  data validation, 430

  defining patterns, 464–466

  vs. Filter extension, 477

  finding matches, 472–475

greediness, 473–474

lazy matches, 473

matching and replacing patterns, 478–481

matching patterns, 461–463

modifiers, 476–477

pipe (|), 465

preg_match() function, 460

quantifiers, 467–468

searches, 158

test script, 460–463

relationships, 170–171

relative vs. absolute paths, 76

RELOAD privilege, 643

RENAME TO clause, 224

REPLACE command, 139

REPLACE() function, 156

report_errors script, saving, 254

$_REQUEST variable, 42, 44

require() functions, 76–77, 84

resetting passwords, 624–629

resource variable type, 14

return, creating, 9–10

return statement, using with functions, 109

returned records, counting, 293–295. *See also* records

REVOKE privilege, 643

RIGHT() function, 156

right joins, 210–211

ROLLBACK, using with transactions, 236

root user password, setting, 641–642

ROUND() function, 159

round() function, 23

rsort() function, 66

RTF MIME type, 433

run-time errors, 244

S

sanitization filters, 438

savepoints, creating in transactions, 238

scalar values, using with constants, 26

scalar variables, 14

schema, 168, 171, 601

scripts. *See* PHP scripts

searches, FULLTEXT, 224–231

SECOND() function, 161

second normal form (2NF), 174–176

second.php script, saving, 7

security. *See also* SQL security

approach, 419

recommendations, 450

of sortable links, 335

SELECT command, 140. *See also* advanced selections

and joins, 206–207

listing columns, 141

SELECT privilege, 643

select_db() method, 526

selecting data, 140–141, 158

self-joins, 212–213

semicolons (;), using with queries, 132–133

sending email, 338–343

server settings, confirming, 346

server-side PHP validation, 517

$_SESSION, 408, 411

session behavior, changing, 412

session fixation, preventing, 415

session hijacking, 412–413

session security, improving, 412–415

session variables

accessing, 407–409

deleting, 409–411

setting, 404

session_start(), calling, 593

sessions

beginning, 405–406

vs. cookies, 404

garbage collection, 411

storing arrays in, 406

SET data type, 116–117

setcookie() function, 394, 396, 398

sha1() function, 413–414

SHA2() function, 137, 139, 144, 239

SHOW CHARACTER SET command, 186

SHOW COLLATION LIKE command, 187

SHOW command, 189–190

SHOW ENGINES command, 185

SHOW WARNINGS command, 139

show_image.php, 361, 367–368

SHUTDOWN privilege, 643

simple queries, 284. *See also* queries

single quotation mark ('), 29–31

site administration, 633

site structure, 78

sitename database, 132–134

slashes (/ and //), including with tags, 8, 10, 23

V

validating
  data by type, 425–430
  email addresses, 470–471
  files by type, 431–434
  form data, 49–54, 88
  passwords, 279
  server-side PHP, 517
validation, approaches, 425
values
  MySQL operators, 142
  sending to scripts, 306–309
VARBINARY text type, 119
VARCHAR[Length] data type, 117–118
variable scope, 110
variables. *See also* bound variable types
  altering output, 20
  appending to URLs, 309
  checking, 49
  vs. constants, 26
  HTML forms, 42
  and numbers, 24
  and strings, 19
  typecasting, 427–428
  undefined, 44
  using, 14–17
versions, confirming, 247
vi editor, 3
view_users.php script
  counting returned records, 293–295
  object-oriented version, 534
  paginating, 323–330
  retrieving query results, 285–286
  sending values to scripts, 306–307
  sortable links, 331–335
virtual hosts, using with Apache, 653–655

W

W3C validation tools, using, 249
WAMP installer, 636
warnings, showing, 139. *See also* errors
web server, confirming, 247–248
WHEN clauses, advanced selections, 221
WHERE conditional, using with **UPDATE**, 151–152
while loops, 70–72, 284, 287
white space, 10
whitelist validation, 425
Widget Cost Calculator, 425
Windows, XAMPP installer, 637–638
WITH QUERY EXPANSION modifier, 231

X

XAMPP installer
  accessing, 636
  Windows, 636–637
XML-style tags, 4
XOR operator, 142
xor operator, 45, 48
XSS attacks, preventing, 435–437

Y

YEAR() function, 161

Z

ZEROFILL number type, 121
zones. *See* time zones
Zulu time. *See* UTC (Coordinated Universal Time)